THE**GREEN**GUIDE
New England

View of Green Mountains, Vermont / © Christian Guy / hemis.fr / Photoshot

MICHELIN

THEGREENGUIDE **NEW ENGLAND**

Editorial Director	Cynthia Clayton Ochterbeck
Edited & Produced by	Jonathan P. Gilbert, Azalay Media
Contributing Writers	Diane Bair, Pamela Wright
Production Manager	Natasha G. George
Cartography	Peter Wrenn
Picture Research	Sean Sachon
Interior Design	Chris Bell
Layout	Michelin Travel Partner, Natasha G. George
Cover Design	Chris Bell, Christelle Le Déan
Cover Layout	Michelin Travel Partner, Natasha G. George

Contact Us	Michelin Travel and Lifestyle North America
	One Parkway South
	Greenville, SC 29615
	USA
	travel.lifestyle@us.michelin.com
	www.michelintravel.com
	Michelin Travel Partner
	Hannay House
	39 Clarendon Road
	Watford, Herts WD17 1JA
	UK
	ℰ01923 205240
	travelpubsales@uk.michelin.com
	www.ViaMichelin.com
Special Sales	For information regarding bulk sales,
	customized editions and premium sales,
	please contact us at:
	travel.lifestyle@us.michelin.com
	www.michelintravel.com

and Martha's Vineyard. To the west are the Berkshire Hills, a patchwork of rural villages laced with cultural attractions. To the east lies the Atlantic Ocean, dotted with little green islands that make up a national park.

NEW HAMPSHIRE *(pp290-323)*

If you're fond of outdoors pursuits, this is your place. The centerpiece of the aptly-named Granite State is 6,288-foot Mount Washington, towering above the 780,000-acre White Mountain National Forest. Mount Washington and the other peaks in the Presidential Range draw hikers and skiers. Peak-baggers get a special thrill: the state has 48 summits higher than 4,000 feet. Yes, there are large cities, and a short stretch of coastline, but the mountains and forests are the true marvel.

Block Island, Rhode Island
© Block Island Tourism Council

VERMONT *(pp352-385)*

If a New England vacation conjures images that include biking along rolling hills past white-steepled churches, put Vermont on your short list of destinations. Almost unbelievably picturesque, Vermont is a patchwork of farmlands and quaint villages, sprinkled with country stores and places to load up on cheddar cheese and fresh produce. Looking for something more challenging than a country drive or bike ride? Take on some of the state's famously challenging mountain biking terrain, or a hike up one of Vermont's dozens of mountains.

Springtime on Mount Washington
© NHDTTD / Kenny Salvatore

RHODE ISLAND *(pp324-351)*

The smallest state in the nation has charms all its own, from the dazzling mansions of Newport to the metropolitan vibe of Providence. Some of the less-celebrated sites in the state are also worth seeking out, like windswept Block Island, reachable by ferry and a true taste of New England's past, and sweet, small villages like Little Compton.

Cycling in the Green Mountains, Vermont
© Andre Jenny / VermontVacation.com

*Kancamagus Scenic Byway, the
White Mountains, New Hampshire*
© NHDTTD / Ellen Edersheim

Michelin Driving Tours

REGIONAL DRIVES
See the Driving Tours Map p12

NEW YORK TO MONTREAL
376 miles – 3 days

This tour starts and ends in a world-class city, with the best of bucolic Western New England in between. Much of the travel is on US Route 7, a mostly two-lane highway that runs through Connecticut and Massachusetts before its terminus in Burlington, VT. Stop for a snack in Litchfield, CT, a comely New England village with gourmet grocery shops. Heading north, you'll enter Massachusetts, where Route 7 winds through the beautiful towns of the Berkshire Hills. Stay at an inn in Williamstown before heading into Vermont. Manchester, VT, is chock-a-block with places to eat and shop; from there, the roadway reveals great views of the eastern slopes of the Green Mountains. North of Rutland, Route 7 becomes especially scenic, bypassing the northern section of the Green Mountain National Forest. Beyond the picturesque town of Middlebury, Lake Champlain shimmers in the distance. Stop in Burlington, and stroll on the lakeside path before entering Quebec.

SOUTHERN NEW ENGLAND
704 miles – 7 days

This loop tour is a whirlwind of seaside beauty spots and historic attractions. Start with the coastal route so you won't have to rush through cities like Mystic, Newport, and Provincetown. Re-fuel at iconic Pepe Pizzeria in New Haven, CT, and head on to Mystic, where you'll need a full day to tour Mystic Seaport (a top-notch living history museum). Enjoy a meal in Newport, RI, and stretch your legs with a ramble along the famous Cliff Walk. Spend at least a couple of days exploring Cape Cod, and the glorious beaches of the National Seashore (lovely in any season.) On to Boston, for museum-hopping and the must-do Freedom Trail. Your next stop: Old Sturbridge Village, a time-travel trip to rural New England (c.1790-1840), Back in the present, visit Hartford, CT (and the Modern Pastry Shop) before completing your tour.

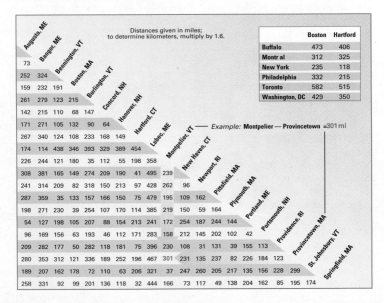

Distances given in miles; to determine kilometers, multiply by 1.6.

	Boston	Hartford
Buffalo	473	406
Montréal	312	325
New York	235	118
Philadelphia	332	215
Toronto	582	515
Washington, DC	429	350

Example: **Montpelier — Provincetown** =301 mi

	Augusta, ME	Bangor, ME	Bennington, VT	Boston, MA	Burlington, VT	Concord, NH	Hanover, NH	Hartford, CT	Lubec, ME	Montpelier, VT	New Haven, CT	Newport, RI	Pittsfield, MA	Plymouth, MA	Portland, ME	Portsmouth, NH	Providence, RI	Provincetown, MA	St. Johnsbury, VT
Bangor, ME	73																		
Bennington, VT	252	324																	
Boston, MA	159	232	191																
Burlington, VT	261	279	123	215															
Concord, NH	142	215	110	68	147														
Hanover, NH	171	271	105	132	90	64													
Hartford, CT	267	340	124	108	233	168	149												
Lubec, ME	174	114	438	346	393	329	389	454											
Montpelier, VT	226	244	121	180	35	112	55	198	358										
New Haven, CT	308	381	165	149	274	209	190	41	495	239									
Newport, RI	241	314	209	82	318	150	213	97	428	262	96								
Pittsfield, MA	287	359	35	133	157	166	150	75	479	109	162	209							
Plymouth, MA	198	271	230	39	254	107	170	114	385	219	150	59	164						
Portland, ME	54	127	198	105	207	88	154	213	241	172	254	187	244	144					
Portsmouth, NH	96	169	156	63	193	46	112	171	283	158	212	145	202	102	42				
Providence, RI	209	282	177	50	282	118	181	75	396	230	108	31	131	39	155	113			
Provincetown, MA	280	353	312	121	336	189	252	196	467	301	231	135	237	82	226	184	123		
St. Johnsbury, VT	189	207	162	178	72	110	63	206	321	37	247	260	205	217	135	156	228	299	
Springfield, MA	258	331	92	99	201	136	118	32	444	166	73	117	49	138	204	162	85	195	174

Provincetown Harbor, Massachusetts

© Tim Grafft / Massachusetts Office of Travel & Tourism

COAST NORTH OF BOSTON
522 miles – 7 days

Explore the salt-tinged resort towns of the Atlantic coast. Hit a witch-themed attraction in Salem, MA, or a Cape Ann beach to get into full vacation-mode. Plan to have dinner and an overnight in bustling Portsmouth, NH, before heading north to Maine. Gallery-rich Ogunquit is a top stop. Plan to dine at Portland's Old Port district, where revitalized warehouse buildings house excellent restaurants. Next up: Downeast Maine's storied landscape. Pine-spiked fingers of land plunge to the sea, dotted with inviting resorts and inns. This is the place to savor lobster-in-the-rough and a boat excursion. Don't miss a drive to Pemaquid Point, and allow ample time to visit Camden, and the wonders of Acadia National Park (great hiking) on Mount Desert Island.

VERMONT AND NEW HAMPSHIRE
984 miles – 8 days

This inland route features great places to explore the outdoors. Heading West from Boston on the Mohawk Trail, city sights give way to rolling hills. Follow the loop clockwise to southern Vermont, where you'll find welcoming inns and good day hikes in Green Mountain National Forest. The village of Woodstock is another great stop, with gentle walks at Billings Farm and Mt. Tom. Heading north, don't miss Burlington, home of Lake Champlain (watersports) and the Northeast Kingdom, famous for mountain biking trails. Next up: New Hampshire's White Mountains, where you can climb (or drive) lofty Mt. Washington, and enjoy the rugged beauty of the White Mountain National Forest and the outdoorsy vibe of surrounding towns.

LOCAL DRIVES
The Discovering section of the guide features even more local tours.

CONNECTICUT
♦ Connecticut Valley
♦ Litchfield Hills

MAINE
♦ Acadia National Park
♦ Cobscook Bay
♦ Maine Coast

MASSACHUSETTS
♦ Cape Cod
♦ Mohawk Trail

NEW HAMPSHIRE
♦ Mount Monadnock Region
♦ White Mountains

VERMONT
♦ Manchester
♦ Middlebury
♦ Montpelier
♦ St. Johnsbury

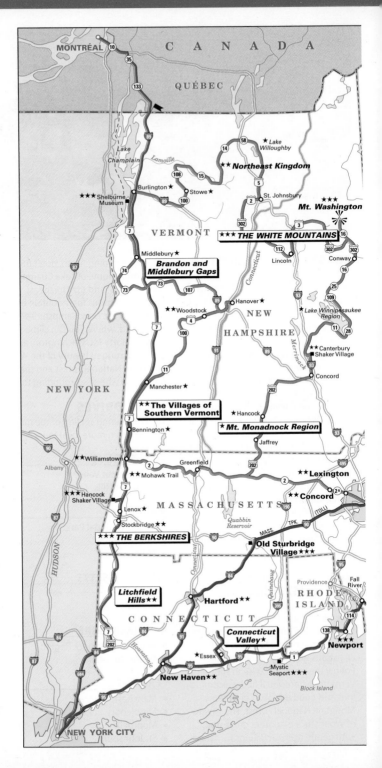

MONTRÉAL 10

35

133

QUÉBEC

CANADA

Lake
Champlain

Lamoille

58 ★ Lake
Willoughby

14

89

★★★ *Northeast Kingdom*

108

15

Burlington ★

Stowe ★

5

100

St. Johnsbury

★★★ Shelburne
Museum

2

302

Mt. Washington ★★★

3

7

VERMONT

★★★ THE WHITE MOUNTAINS

16

Middlebury ★

112

302

302

*Brandon and
Middlebury Gaps*

74

73

73

107

Lincoln

Conway

89

16

Hanover ★

25

109

★★ Woodstock

4

NEW

Lake Winnipesaukee
Region

7

100

HAMPSHIRE

11

28

91

93

Connecticut

Merrimack

★★ Canterbury
Shaker Village

11

93

Manchester ★

Concord

202

NEW YORK

7

★★ The Villages of
Southern Vermont

★ Hancock

★ Mt. Monadnock Region

Bennington ★

Jaffrey

★★ Williamstown

Albany

2

Greenfield

202

495

★★ Lexington

90

★★ Mohawk Trail

2

★★ Concord

2A

7

MASSACHUSETTS

190

★★★ Hancock
Shaker Village

Lenox ★

Quabbin
Reservoir

TPK.

90 (TOLL)

Stockbridge ★★

MASS.

87

★★★ THE BERKSHIRES

90

★★★ Old Sturbridge
Village ★★★

HUDSON

84

Connecticut

Quinebaug

95

Providence

Fall
River

*Litchfield
Hills* ★★

Hartford ★★

RHODE
ISLAND

114

7

CONNECTICUT

91

84

*Connecticut
Valley* ★

138

Newport ★★★

202

★ Essex

Housatonic

684

Mystic
Seaport ★★★

New Haven ★★

Block Island

84

95

NEW YORK CITY

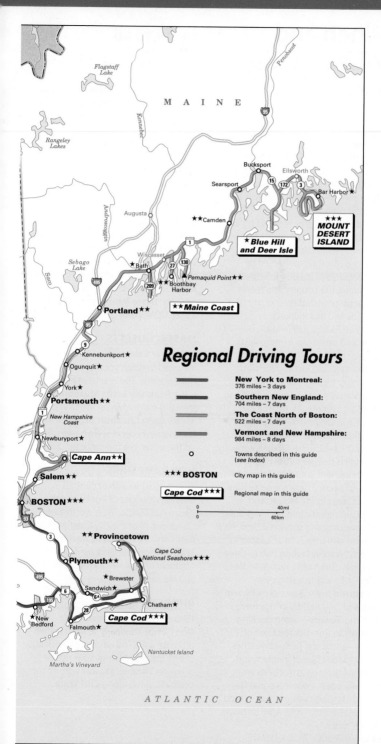

MAINE

Flagstaff Lake

Rangeley Lakes

95

Penobscot

Bucksport
Ellsworth
Searsport
15
172
3
Bar Harbor ★

Kennebec

Androscoggin

Augusta

★★ Camden

★★★ MOUNT DESERT ISLAND

★ Blue Hill and Deer Isle

Sebago Lake

1

Wiscasset

130

★ Bath

27

209

★★ Boothbay Harbor

★ Pemaquid Point ★★

★★ Maine Coast

Saco

485

Portland ★★

95

Regional Driving Tours

9

Kennebunkport ★

Ogunquit ★

York ★

Portsmouth ★★

New Hampshire Coast

1

Newburyport ★

Cape Ann ★★

Salem ★★

BOSTON ★★★

93

3

★★ Provincetown

Plymouth ★★

Cape Cod National Seashore ★★★

★ Brewster

Sandwich ★

6

6A

495

195

Chatham ★

★ New Bedford

28

Cape Cod ★★★

Falmouth ★

Nantucket Island

Martha's Vineyard

▬▬▬	**New York to Montreal:** 376 miles – 3 days
▬▬▬	**Southern New England:** 704 miles – 7 days
▬▬▬	**The Coast North of Boston:** 522 miles – 7 days
▬▬▬	**Vermont and New Hampshire:** 984 miles – 8 days
○	Towns described in this guide (*see Index*)
★★★ BOSTON	City map in this guide
Cape Cod ★★★	Regional map in this guide

0   40mi
0   60km

ATLANTIC OCEAN

13

When and Where to Go

WHEN TO GO

New England attracts vacationers to its mountains and shores in every season. **Summer** months are generally mild. Daytime temperatures along the coast and in the north average 70 to 80°F (21 to 27°C); in the central region temperatures rarely climb above 90°F (32°C)—July is the warmest month.

Considered the glory of New England, **Indian summer** (a period of warm, mild weather in late fall or early winter) is often accompanied by the spectacle of blazing fall color. In autumn, the countryside teems with activity, including country fairs, auctions and flea markets.

For Fall Foliage, see below.

Skiers and other snow enthusiasts applaud the long New England **winter**, typically lasting from late November through April. Daytime temperatures in the south and along the coast average 20° to 30°F (–7° to –1°C). In the north and at higher elevations, temperatures may stay below 0°F (–18°C) for 60 days annually. Snowfall is heavier in the higher elevations, with an annual average of 60in/154cm. There are more than 100 ski areas in the region, and opportunities abound for ice-skating, snowshoeing and snowmobiling. New England's infamous **"nor'easter"** storms, typically lasting two to three days, can dump ten or more inches (25cm) of snow in a single day.

The **spring** thaw, a mixture of warm days and cold nights, brings forth budding flowers—often peeking through an unexpected layer of snow—and is the perfect weather for the cultivation of maple syrup. Outdoor-themed attractions are typically open from Memorial Day to mid-October; some sights extend their season from mid-April through late October.

See INTRODUCTION, CLIMATE.

WHERE TO GO

CONNECTICUT

The town of **Mystic** (*see MYSTIC SEAPORT*) is perfect for a quick getaway. Stay at an inn in town (or at one of the nearby casinos, Foxwoods or Mohegan Sun) and take in **Mystic Seaport** and **Mystic Aquarium**, or perhaps the **Mashantucket Pequot Museum**. After dark, the casinos offer a full line-up of concerts and live music.

MAINE

Boothbay Harbor (*see MAINE COAST*) has a friendly, easy-going vibe, and it's fun to explore on foot. Stay downtown and visit the small shops that line the wharves, buy some fudge and sign up for a **harbor cruise** or a boat trip to **Monhegan Island** (*see MONHEGAN ISLAND*).

MASSACHUSETTS

The city of **Salem** (*see SALEM*) may well bewitch you, for all the right reasons. The real treat here is the **Peabody Essex Museum**, a treasure-trove of Asian art. Don't miss a walk along **Chestnut St.**, lined with handsome, Federal-style homes. **Finz**, on the water, is a fun place for dinner.

NEW HAMPSHIRE

Thanks to its wealth of cultural offerings, the city of **Portsmouth** (*see PORTSMOUTH*) is worth a trip. Check out 70 of the city's architectural gems on a **Portsmouth Harbour Trail** walking tour *(pick up a map at the Chamber of Commerce Visitor Center at 500 Market St.)*.

RHODE ISLAND

Who can resist **Newport** (*see NEWPORT*)? This lively seaport is the ultimate weekend getaway. Check out the historic **mansions**, soak up the scene on **Thames St.**, and admire the dramatic views along **Cliff Walk**.

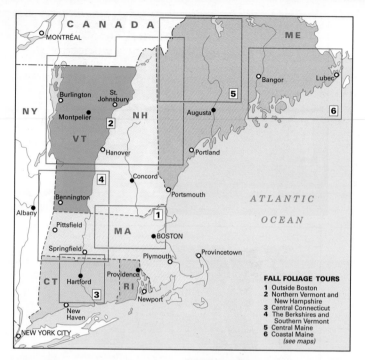

VERMONT

For a classic Vermont experience, it's hard to top the village of **Woodstock** (&see WOODSTOCK). It's home to lovely inns, a charming downtown, and nice hikes at **Mt. Tom** and **Billings Farm and Museum**.

FALL FOLIAGE TOURS

New England's grand foliage season begins in early September along the Canadian border and higher elevations, and moves southward until the end of October. Advance reservations (two to three months) are recommended during this time.
&See the Fall Foliage driving tours:

OUTSIDE BOSTON
(2 drives featured)

N. VERMONT & NEW HAMPSHIRE
(11 drives featured)

CENTRAL CONNECTICUT
(3 drives featured)

LOCAL COLOR

Call the fall foliage hotlines or access the websites below for up-to-date information on fall color (mid Sept–Oct):

- ☎800-282-6863, www.ctbound.org
- ☎888-624-6345 www.mainefoliage.com
- ☎800-227-6277 www.mass-vacation.com
- ☎800-556-2484 www.visitrhodeisland.com
- ☎800-386-4664, www.visitnh.gov
- ☎800-837-6668 www.travel-vermont.com
- www.visitnewengland.com www.yankeefoliage.com

CENTRAL MAINE
(2 drives featured)

BERKSHIRES & S. VERMONT
(5 drives featured)

COASTAL MAINE
(3 drives featured)

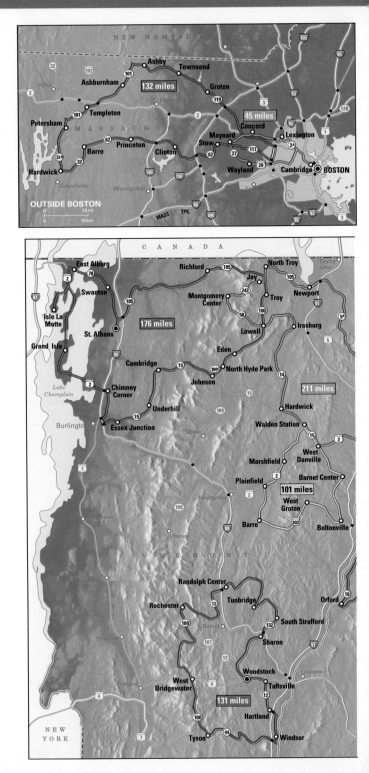

OUTSIDE BOSTON

132 miles

45 miles

176 miles

211 miles

101 miles

131 miles

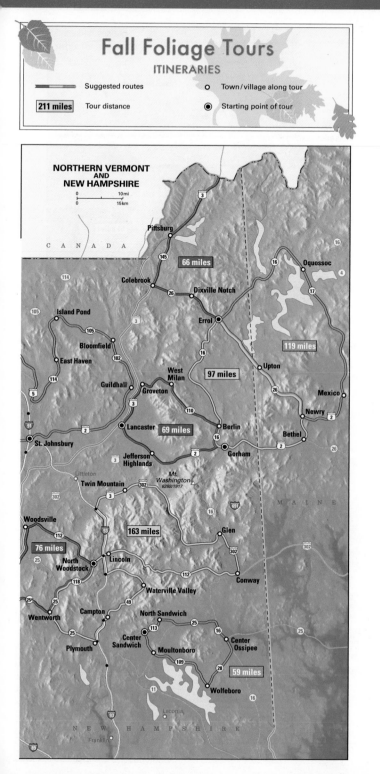

Fall Foliage Tours
ITINERARIES

Suggested routes   O   Town / village along tour

| 211 miles | Tour distance

◉   Starting point of tour

NORTHERN VERMONT
AND
NEW HAMPSHIRE

0   10mi
0   15km

C A N A D A

Pittsburg

145

66 miles

Colebrook

26   Dixville Notch

114

105   Island Pond

105

Bloomfield

East Haven   102

114

5

81

2

Guildhall

West
Milan

Groveton

3

110

Lancaster   69 miles

Berlin

16

Errol

16

Upton

97 miles

Oquossoc

16

4

17

119 miles

26

Mexico

Newry

2

Bethel

26

St. Johnsbury

Jefferson
Highlands

2   Gorham

Littleton

Mt.
Washington
6288/1917

M A I N E

Twin Mountain   302

3

302

Woodsville

112

302

16   691

163 miles

Glen

302

302

76 miles

25

North
Woodstock   Lincoln

118

112

Conway

Waterville Valley

25

25

49

North Sandwich

25

Wentworth

Campton

113   Center
Sandwich

16   Center
Ossippee

25

25

Plymouth

Moultonboro

109

28   59 miles

11

Wolfeboro

16

Laconia

N E W   H A M P S H I R E

Franklin

93

17

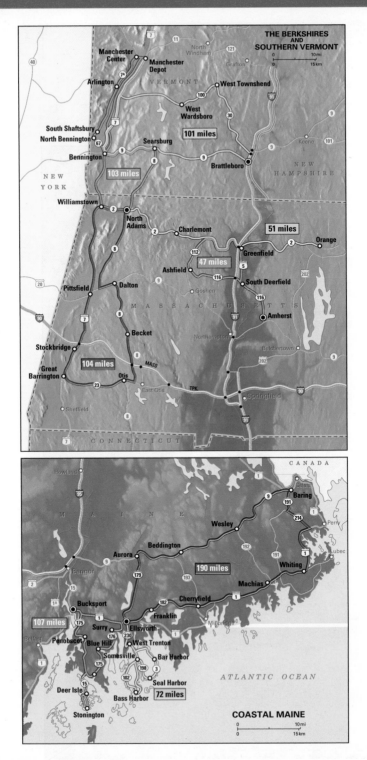

THE BERKSHIRES
AND
SOUTHERN VERMONT

0   10mi
0   15km

101 miles

103 miles

51 miles

47 miles

104 miles

190 miles

107 miles

72 miles

COASTAL MAINE

0   10mi
0   15km

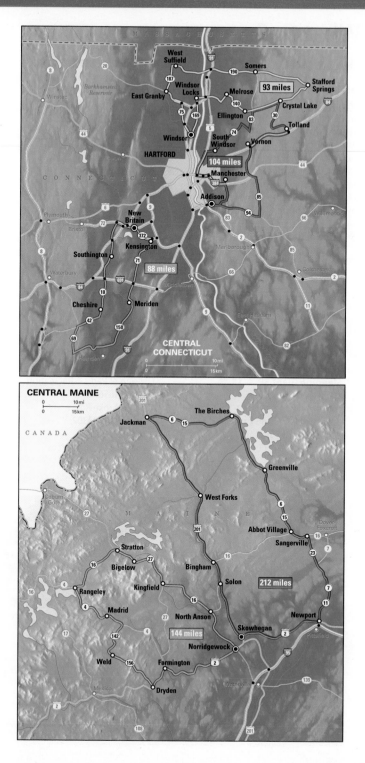

CENTRAL CONNECTICUT

MASSACHUSETTS

West Suffield

Somers

Stafford Springs

93 miles

Melrose

Windsor Locks

East Granby

Crystal Lake

Ellington

Tolland

Windsor

South Windsor

Vernon

HARTFORD

104 miles

Manchester

Addison

New Britain

Kensington

Southington

88 miles

Cheshire

Meriden

CONNECTICUT

Barkhamsted Reservoir

Winsted

Plymouth

Bristol

Waterbury

Hamden

Middletown

East Haddam

Marlborough

Colchester

Willimantic

0   10mi
0   15km

CENTRAL MAINE

0   10mi
0   15km

CANADA

The Birches

Jackman

Greenville

West Forks

Abbot Village

Sangerville

Dover-Foxcroft

Stratton

Bigelow

Bingham

Solon

212 miles

Kingfield

Rangeley

Madrid

North Anson

Newport

Skowhegan

144 miles

Norridgewock

Pittsfield

Weld

Farmington

Dryden

Mexico

Waterville

MAINE

Coburn Gore

19

What to See and Do

OUTDOOR FUN
SELECTED STATE PARKS

New England's state parks are a treasure trove of natural beauty and outdoor recreation. Hike a wooded trail to a waterfall, trek up a mountain summit for views of oceans and bays, camp on the beach, or simply relax and enjoy some of the region's loveliest landscapes.

Connecticut
State Parks Division
79 Elm St., Hartford, CT 06106;
☎ 860-424-3200
www.ct.gov/dep

- **Gillette Castle SP** 🚶
- **Housatonic Meadows SP** ⛺🚶🎣
- **Kent Falls SP** ⛺🚶🎣
- **Macedonia Brook SP** ⛺🚶🎣
- **Sleeping Giant SP** ⛺🚶🎣

Maine
Bureau of Parks and Land
22 State House Station,
Augusta, ME 04333;
☎ 207-287-3821
www.maine.gov/doc/parks

- **Baxter SP** ⛺🚶🏊🎣
- **Camden Hills SP** ⛺🚶
- **Cobscook Bay SP** ⛺🚶🎣
- **Crescent Beach SP** ⛺🚶🏊🎣
- **Grafton Notch SP** 🚶🎣
- **Mt. Blue SP** ⛺🚶🏊🎣
- **Popham Beach SP** 🚶🏊🎣
- **Quoddy Head SP** 🚶
- **Rangeley Lake SP** ⛺🚶🏊🎣
- **Sebago Lake SP** ⛺🚶🏊🎣
- **Two Lights SP** 🚶🎣
- **Wolfe's Neck Woods SP** 🚶

Massachusetts
Division of Forests and Parks
251 Causeway St., Suite 600
Boston, MA 02114;
☎ 617-626-1250
www.mass.gov/dcr

- **Halibut Point SP** 🚶🎣
- **Natural Bridge SP** 🚶🎣
- **Nickerson SP** ⛺🚶🏊🎣
- **Skinner SP** 🚶

New Hampshire
Division of Parks & Recreation
P.O. Box 1856
172 Pembroke Rd.
Concord, NH 03302;
☎ 603-271-3556
www.nhparks.state.nh.us

Cycling along the Eagle Lake, Acadia National Park, Maine

© Ray Radigan / National Park Service

- **Lake Francis SP** △ ⅃ ⤜
- **Monadnock SP** △ 🚶
- **Mt. Sunapee SP** △ ⅃ ⤜
- **Rhododendron SP** 🚶
- **Rye Harbor SP** ⤜
- **Wallis Sands SP** ⅃
- **White Lake SP** △ 🚶 ⅃ ⤜

🇷🇮 **Rhode Island**
Department of Parks and
Recreation
232 Hartford Ave.
Johnston, RI 02919;
📞401-222-2632
www.riparks.com

- **Brenton Point SP** 🚶 ⤜
- **Fort Adams SP** ⅃ ⤜

🇻🇹 **Vermont**
Department of Forests,
Parks & Recreation
103 S. Main St.
Waterbury, VT 05671;
📞802-241-3655
www.vtstateparks.com

- **Branbury SP** △ 🚶 ⅃ ⤜
- **Lake St. Catherine SP** △🚶⅃⤜
- **Silver Lake SP** △ ⅃ ⤜
- **Woodford SP** △ 🚶 ⅃

△ camping; 🚶 hiking;
⅃ swimming; ⤜ fishing

HIKING AND BIKING

Many trail systems lace the region.
State and local parks provide
opportunities for hiking and biking.
The **Long Trail** 🚶 (265mi) in Vermont
runs north to south along the Green
Mountains from the Canadian to
the Massachusetts border; in New
England, the **Appalachian Trail** 🚶
extends from Mt. Katahdin in Maine
to the Connecticut/New York border.
Acadia National Park offers 165 acres
of moderately easy hiking trails. The
175mi of wilderness trails in **Baxter
State Park** and 1,200mi of trails in
White Mountain National Forest
are more challenging. When hiking
in the backcountry, stay on marked
trails. ♿Taking shortcuts is dangerous
and causes erosion. If hiking alone,
notify someone of your destination
and proposed return time. In addition,
1,003mi of former railroad tracks
throughout New England have been
converted into paved and dirt paths
for bikers and pedestrians (*for maps
and information, contact: Rails-to-
Trails Conservancy, 1100 17th St. NW,
Washington, DC 20036; 📞202-331-
9696; www.railtrails.org*).
Bicycles are prohibited on most
unpaved trails. Riders should
stay on paved paths and roads
(on public roads, stay to the right
and ride in single file). Cyclists are
encouraged to wear helmets and
other protective gear. ♿Both hikers
and bicyclists are cautioned to be well
equipped (including detailed maps
of the areas to be explored) and alert
to weather conditions, particularly
in higher elevations. For more
information on trails and on local
mountain biking regulations, contact
local tourism offices.
Llama hikes provide a novel way to
enjoy the terrain while allowing these
gentle creatures to carry the meals
and gear. Several outfitters sponsor
llama treks: Northern Vermont Llama
Company, 766 Lapland Rd., Waterville,
VT 05492 (📞802-644-2257; www.
northernvermontllamaco.com); and
Berkshire Mountain Llama Hike, 322
Lander Rd., Lee, MA 01238 (📞413-243-
2224; www.hawkmeadowinlee.com).
The following organizations provide
information about hiking and cycling
trails in New England:
- **New England Hiking Holidays,**
  P.O. Box 1648,
  North Conway, NH 03860;
  📞800-869-0949 or 603-356-9696;
  www.nehikingholidays.com.
- **Appalachian Mountain Club,**
  5 Joy St., Boston, MA 02108;
  📞617-523-0655;
  www.outdoors.org.
- **Appalachian Trail Conference,**
  P.O. Box 807,
  Harpers Ferry, WV 25425;
  📞304-535-6331;
  www.appalachiantrail.org.

- **Back Country Excursions**,
  42 Woodward Rd.,
  Parsonsfield, ME 04047;
  ☎ 207-625-8189;
  www.bikebackcountry.com.
- **Discovery Bicycle Tours**,
  P.O. Box 207,
  Woodstock VT 05091;
  ☎ 800-257-2226 or 802-457-3553;
  www.discoverybicycletours.com.
- **Vermont Bicycle Touring**,
  614 Monkton Rd.,
  Bristol, VT 05443;
  ☎ 800-245-3868;
  www.vbt.com.
- **Vermont Department of
  Forests, Parks & Recreation**,
  103 S. Main St.,
  Waterbury, VT 05671;
  ☎ 802-241-3655;
  www.vtfpr.org.
- **Green Mountain National
  Forest**, Supervisor,
  231 N. Main St., Rutland,
  VT 05701; ☎ 802-747-6700;
  www.fs.fed.us/r9/forests/
  greenmuntain/Index/htm.
- **The Green Mountain Club**,
  4711 Waterbury-Stowe Rd.,
  Waterbury Center, VT 05677;
  ☎ 802-244-7037;
  www.greenmountainclub.org.

Fishing in the Mad River, Vermont
© VermontVacation.com

HUNTING AND FISHING

With an abundance of game and fish
(including deer, moose and trout),
New England is a hunting and angling
paradise. Licenses are required to hunt
and fish in all six states.
Nonresident fishing licenses are
available in fishing-supply stores
(some offer rental equipment).
Nonresident hunting licenses tend
to be considerably more expensive
than resident licenses. Many fish are
in season year-round, whereas most
game can only be hunted seasonally.
If being transported, a rifle or shotgun
must be unloaded (no permit
required; some states require it to be
in a secure case).
Contact the following agencies for
additional information (including
regulations on transporting game
out of state):

- **Department of Environmental
  Protection**, Wildlife Division,
  79 Elm St., Hartford, CT 06106;
  ☎ 860-424-3000;
  www.ct.gov/dep/site.
- **Department of Inland
  Fisheries and Wildlife**,
  284 State St., 41 State House
  Station, Augusta, ME 04333;
  ☎ 207-287-8000; www.maine.gov/
  ifw; the *Maine Guide to Hunting
  and Fishing* is available from the
  Maine Tourism Association.
- **Massachusetts Department
  of Fish and Game**,
  251 Causeway St. #400, Boston,
  MA 02114; ☎ 617-626-1500;
  www.mass.gov/dfwele/dfw.
- **Fish & Game Department**,
  11 Hazen Dr., Concord,
  NH 03301; ☎ 603-271-3421;
  www.wildlife.state.nh.us.
- **Division of Fish & Wildlife**,
  Department of Environmental
  Management
  235 Promenade St.
  Providence, TI 03908,
  ☎ 401-222-6800;
  www.dem.ri.gov/programs.
- **Department of Fish
  and Wildlife**,
  103 S. Main St., Building 10 South,

Waterbury, VT 05671;
☎ 802-241-3700
www.vtfishandwildlife.com.

WATER SPORTS

New England's coastal waters, lakes and rivers offer ample opportunities for canoeing, kayaking, sailing (especially in Newport, RI), and whitewater rafting. Contact the individual state tourism offices for listings of outfitters. Kayakers will want to check out the 325mi-long **Maine Island Trail**, which links 100 public and private islands between Casco Bay and the Canadian border (*for information, contact the Maine Island Trail Association in Portland, ME; ☎ 207-761-8225; www.mita. org*). For canoers, Maine's **Allagash Wilderness Waterway** traverses ponds and rivers through the North Woods. To canoe the entire 92mi length of the waterway takes from 7 to 10 days (*for information, contact the Maine Dept. of Conservation, Bureau of Parks & Lands, 22 State House Station, Augusta, ME 04333; ☎ 207-287-3821; www.maine.gov/doc*).

Whitewater rafting is popular on Maine's Kennebec, Penobscot and Dead rivers from May to mid-October. **Raft Maine** is an association of whitewater outfitters conducting raft trips on all three rivers (*www. raftmaine.com*). In New Hampshire **Saco Bound, Inc.** and the **Rapid River Rafting Co**. in Conway (*☎ 603-447-2177; www.sacobound.com*) offer paddling and kayaking classes, as well as raft trips on Maine's Androscoggin River—a popular whitewater passage best suited to experienced paddlers—and canoe treks on Maine's Saco River.

Ocean Swimming

Beaches along the coast of New England are generally clean and sandy; several are rocky, the beaches a mixture of sand with pebbles (walking barefoot may be uncomfortable). Summer water temperatures vary: Connecticut and Rhode Island waters range from 65° to 75°F (18°–24°C); in southern Massachusetts (including Cape Cod), water temperatures average 65° to 75°F (18°–24°C); northern Massachusetts, New Hampshire and Maine waters average a brisk 50° to 65°F (10°–18°C). Excellent surfing can be found along the coastlines of Rhode Island, Massachusetts, and Maine. Swimmers should be aware of the occasional riptide or undertow (strong underlying currents that pull swimmers away from the shore). Many New England communities employ lifeguards seasonally. Care should be taken when swimming at an unguarded beach. Children should be supervised at all times.

WALKING TOURS

Whether you go with a guide to get an insider's view, or put on some comfortable shoes, get a good map and do-it-yourself, New England is best explored on foot.

Connecticut

During fall foliage season, a tour of northeastern **Connecticut's "Last Green Valley"** (*see CONNECTICUT*) is a real treat. About half the size of Grand Canyon National Park, this 1,085-acre rural area sits between the Quinebaug and Shetucket rivers. Natural features include more than 80 ponds and lakes, seven state forests, 16 wildlife areas and five state parks, laced with 130 miles of trails (www. thelastgreenvalley.org).

Maine

The sea-faring town of **Bath** (*see MAINE COAST*) has a maritime history that dates back to 1607, when the first ship of the New World was launched here. Bath Iron Works still turns out frigates and destroyers. Sagadahoc Preservation Inc. offers guided walking tours for groups, and a self-guided tour map on its website: www.sagadahocpreservation.org.
Portland (*see PORTLAND*), Maine's **Old Port** area, is one of the most successful revitalized

Sampling New England's Cities and Museums

The villages and cities that developed along the coast looked out toward the sea and the rest of the world. This expansive point of view contributed to the richness of local architecture and home decoration, enhanced by treasures brought back by sailors and whalers who traveled to faraway ports. The region's most beautiful seaports include:

- **Nantucket★★★** (Massachusetts)
- **Newburyport★** (Massachusetts)
- **Newport★★★** (Rhode Island)
- **Plymouth★★** (Massachusetts)
- **Portsmouth★★** (New Hampshire)
- **Salem★★** (Massachusetts)

A growing appreciation for the strength and beauty of Colonial design, and renewed interest in renovation and restoration, have resulted in new life for old districts. Arts and crafts stalls, shops and restaurants eventually appeared, and today, visitors can enjoy a leisurely stroll or have a meal in the following colorful districts:

- **Bowen's Wharf★** (Newport)
- **Market Square District★** (Newburyport)
- **Old Port Exchange★★** (Portland)
- **Quincy Market★★** (Boston)

The museums of New England vary widely in their conception and in their collections. A listing of must-see art and marine museums follows:

- **Clark Art Institute★★★** (Williamstown)
- **Isabella Stewart Gardner Museum★★★** (Boston)
- **Museum of Art, Rhode Island School of Design★★** (Providence)
- **Museum of Fine Arts★★★** (Boston)
- **Maine Maritime Museum★★** (Bath)
- **Mystic Seaport★★★** (Mystic)
- **Peabody Essex Museum★★★** (Salem)
- **Penobscot Marine Museum★** (Searsport)
- **Wadsworth Atheneum Museum of Art★★** (Hartford)
- **Whaling Museum★★** (Nantucket)
- **Whaling Museum★★** (New Bedford)
- **Worcester Art Museum★★** (Worcester)
- **Yale University Art Gallery★★** (New Haven)

warehouse districts in the country. This working waterfront offers good shopping, entertainment and dining (featuring fresh Maine lobster.) A preservation society called Greater Portland Landmarks offers guided walking tours *(July–Oct)* and a good, self-guided tour map of the Old Port district, available online at www.portlandlandmarks.org.

Massachusetts

Boston's (*see BOSTON*) **Freedom Trail** is the ultimate self-guided walking tour. This red-brick, 2.5-mile walking path features 16 historic sites, including the Paul Revere House and Old North Church. The trail begins at the Boston Common Visitor Information Center and ends at the Bunker Hill Monument in Charlestown; pick up a map at a Visitor Information Center located in the city or visit www.

freedomtrail.org. Other walking tours in Boston include the **Black Heritage Trail** and the **Women's History Trail**. For information, and more walks, visit www.bostonusa.com and www.walkboston.org.

Visit the meeting places and watering holes of **Boston's most popular early American authors (**Nathaniel Hawthorne, Louisa May Alcott, Charles Dickens, Ralph Waldo Emerson and others) on a 90-minute Literary Landmarks tour, offered by Boston by Foot *($15; www.bostonbyfoot.com).*

New Hampshire

The city of Portsmouth is easily New Hampshire's hippest city, and it's full of architectural gems. The self-guided **Portsmouth Harbour Trail** (*see PORTSMOUTH*) features more than 70 points of scenic and historic interest, including 10 buildings listed on the National Register of Historic Buildings. The *Portsmouth Harbor Trail Map & Guide*, available for a small fee at the Portsmouth Chamber of Commerce Visitor Center *(www.portsmouth chamber.org)* on Market Street, breaks down the route into three separate walks: one route covers most of downtown; one covers Ceres St. and the North End; and the other covers the South End (Strawbery Banke, etc.). Historic houses are open seasonally.

Rhode Island

Cliff Walk is **Newport** (*see NEWPORT*), **Rhode Island**'s most famous (and spectacular) walk. This 3-mile stretch, marked with signs, follows the coastline on cliffs overlooking the ocean. It begins on Memorial Boulevard and ends at Bailey's Beach at the end of Bellevue Avenue and Ocean Drive.

While in Newport, spend some time getting to know the city with a walk around the neighborhoods of Historic Hill or The Point. Pick up a map at the Visitor Information Center on America's Cup Avenue *(www.gonewport.com).* Or, visit the exquisitely-preserved neighborhoods of Newport with a guide. Newport Historical Society offers 90-minute guided tours with themes like "Pirates and Scoundrels" and "Newport's Buried History" *($12; www.newporthistorytours.org).*

Vermont

Vermont (*see VERMONT*) offers an interesting twist on sightseeing by foot: **inn-to-inn walking tours**. On these four- or five-day trips, you'll do the walking, and arrive at a different country inn each night. The folks at Vermont Inn to Inn Walking Tours *(www.vermontinntoinnwalking. com)* make arrangements and transport your baggage. Tours are based in pastoral villages in Chester and Ludlow in southern Vermont.

WHALE-WATCHING

Because of the abundance of plankton, whales can be seen in large numbers on their migration route from the Caribbean to Greenland and Newfoundland from early spring to mid-October, primarily along the Stellwagen Bank (*27mi east of Boston*) in the Gulf of Maine.

Selected Cruise Companies
 MASSACHUSETTS:
- **Boston Harbor Cruises**
  Boston; 617-227-4321;
  www.bostonharborcruises.com;
  May–mid Oct.
- **New England Aquarium**
  Boston; 617-973-5200;
  www.neaq.org;
  Apr–Oct.
- **Cape Ann Whale Watch**
  Gloucester; 800-877-5110;
  www.caww.com;
  May–mid Oct
- **Captain Bill's Whale Watch**
  Gloucester;
  800-339-4253;
  www.captainbillandsons.com;
  May–Oct.
- **Seven Seas Whale Watching**
  Gloucester; 888-283-1776;
  www.7seaswhalewatch.com;
  May–mid Oct.

Humpback whale in Stellwagen Bank National Marine Sanctuary, Massachusetts

© Jose Gil / Bigstockphoto.com

- **Yankee Whale Watch**
  Gloucester; ✆800-942-5464;
  www.yankeefleet.com; Apr–Oct.
- **Captain John Boats**
  Plymouth; ✆800-242-2469;
  www. captjohn.com; Apr–Oct.
- **Newburyport Whale Watch**
  Newburyport; ✆800-848-1111;
  www.newburyportwhalewatch.
  com; May–Oct.
- **Hyannis Whale Watcher Cruises**
  Hyannis; ✆800-287-0374;
  www.whales.net; Apr–Oct.
- 🌐 **MAINE**
- **Bar Harbor Whale Watch Co.**
  Bar Harbor; ✆888-WHALES-4;
  www. barharborwhales.com;
  May–Oct.
- **Cap'n Fish's Boat Cruises**
  Boothbay Harbor; ✆207-633-3244
  or 800-636-3244; www.maine
  whales.com; May–Oct.

PUFFINS

Between June and early August
(*prime viewing time: July*) you can
spot puffins in their summer colonies
in the Gulf of Maine on Easter Egg
Rock, Matinicus Rock and Machias
Seal Island.
On-land viewing (*bring binoculars*)
is allowed only on Machias Seal
Island by the following companies:
Cap'n Fish's Boat Cruises, Boothbay
Harbor, ME (✆*207-633-3244; www.*

mainewhales.com); **Norton of
Jonesport**, Jonesport, ME (✆*207-497-5933; www.machiassealisland.com*).

HISTORIC TOURS

The following organizations offer
their members free admission to their
historic properties in New England:
**Society for the Preservation of
New England Antiquities**, 141
Cambridge St., Boston, MA 02114;
✆617-227-3956 www.spnea.org
(*annual charge $45*);
🌐**Antiquarian and Landmarks
Society**, 255 Main St., Hartford,
CT 06106; ✆860-247-8996
www.ctlandmarks.org
(*annual charge $40*).
The **National Trust for Historic
Preservation** maintains sights
located nationwide: 1785
Massachusetts Ave. NW, Washington,
DC 20036; ✆202-588-6000;
www.preservationnation.org
(*annual charge $20*).

ACTIVITIES FOR KIDS 👪

Throughout this guide, sights of
particular interest to children are
indicated with a 👪 symbol. Many
museums and other attractions
have special children's programs
and resources. Most attractions
throughout New England offer
discounted admission to visitors

under 18 years of age. In addition, various hotels make family discount packages available, and restaurants often have children's menus.

LIVING HISTORY MUSEUMS

For many visiting families, New England is synonymous with history. The region makes history fun for kids, thanks to a wonderful collection of living history museums. Instead of dusty old exhibits, these offer a lively trip back in time, with costumed interpreters, historic buildings, and demonstrations of Colonial skills. At **Plimoth Plantation** (www.plimoth. org), in Plymouth, MA, guests are transported to a c.1627 Pilgrim village, peopled by folks posing as real Pilgrims (and native people) to re-create life in the Plymouth Colony. Thanksgiving is a great time to visit, when you can have dinner at the place where it all began. Engage in more time-tripping at **Old Sturbridge Village** (www.osv.org), in Sturbridge, MA, a re-created rural New England town circa the 1830s. Here, a printer, blacksmith, tinsmith, and others ply their trades in authentically-restored buildings. (Many were transported to Old Sturbridge Village from throughout New England.) Activities change with the season, and might include sheep-shearing or a turkey shoot. Connecticut gets into the act with **Mystic Seaport** (www.mystic seaport.org), America's largest maritime museum. This site boasts tall ships and a re-created 19C seaport village. Sing sea chanteys, learn to tie sailor's knots, and—most fun for kids—try walking on stilts or rolling a hoop on the green. Role-players demonstrate skills like boat building and wood-carving; climb aboard an 1841 whaleship, and take a short cruise on a coal-fired steamboat. New Hampshire's **Strawbery Banke** (www.strawberybanke.org) is a restored waterfront town, with houses spanning from17C-20C. Daily workshops, best for ages 6 and up, teach 19C skills like basket-making and yarn-spinning. Rhode Island doesn't have a living history museum per se, but the Newport mansions offer a peak at the past. **The Breakers** (www. newportmansions.com), is a 70-room stunner, c.1895, of marble, mosaics, and 22-carat gilded plaster, and it's open nearly all year.

WINTER ACTIVITIES
SKIING

The primary ski areas in New England are the Green Mountains of Vermont and the White Mountains of New Hampshire; there are also excellent ski resorts in northwestern Maine, western Connecticut and the Berkshires of Massachusetts. Many ski area communities offer a variety of accommodations including major hotel chains, B&Bs and alpine lodges. Discount packages for stays of three or more days, which may include lift tickets, equipment rental, meals and transportation to the slopes, are often available.

Radio stations throughout the Northeast report local ski conditions. Most ski resorts have snow-making equipment.

Ski New England: Online Resources

- www.skimaine.com
- www.skinh.com
- www.skivermont.com

CROSS-COUNTRY SKIING

Many local parks and recreation departments maintain trail systems through recreation areas and forests. Always ask permission before skiing on private land. Some of the trail systems have warming huts, while others offer cabins with sleeping accommodations. Most backcountry trails are ungroomed.

Trail Conditions & Information
Maine
    888-624-6345 or 800-754-9263 (XC); www.visitmaine.com, www.skimaine.com.

Bromley Mountain Ski Resort in Peru, Vermont

© Dennis Curran / VermontVacation.com

New Hampshire
800-887-5454 (downhill & XC);
www.skinh.com, www.xcskinh.com.

Vermont
802-223-2439;
www.skivermont.com.

SNOWMOBILING

New England offers enthusiasts
miles of maintained trails on both
public and private lands. The
organizations listed below provide
guided tours, rental equipment and
trail information, as well as details
about regional snowmobile licensing
requirements, registration, fees and
restrictions.

**Department of State Parks
& Forests**
860-424-3200,
www.ct.gov/dep.

Snowmobile Association
413-369-8092,
www. sledmass.com.

Snowmobile Association
207-622-6983,
www. mesnow.com.

Snowmobile Association
603-273-0220,
www. nhsa.com.

Association of Snow Travelers
802-229-0005,
www. vtvast.org.

Snowmobile Vermont
802-422-2121,
www.snowmobilevermont.com.

Trails Bureau, NH State Parks
603-271-3254,
www.nhparks.state.nh.us.

DOGSLEDDING

This ancient mode of transportation
offers a unique way to view the beauty
of Maine's winter wilderness. Trips
vary from one-hour excursions to
day and overnight trips. **Mahoosuc
Guide Service** (*1513 Bear River Rd.,
Newry, ME 04261;* 207-824-2073;
www.mahoosuc.com) offers day and
overnight trips throughout Maine,
New Hampshire and Canada. **Moose
Country Safaris** (*191 North Dexter Rd.,
Sangerville, ME 04479;* 207-876-4907;
www.moosecountrysafaris.com) offers
trips in the Moosehead Lake region.

SHOPPING
WHAT TO BUY

New Englanders have unique habits
when it comes to shopping—such as
buying more ice cream and less gold
jewelry than the rest of America—but
shopping options suit all tastes. You'll
find everything from quaint general
stores to mega-outlet malls, as well as
a Boston street that rivals New York's
Fifth Avenue.
If you're seeking that **classic "country
store" experience**, visit the region's
villages and small towns. The ultimate
is the Vermont Country Store, in
Weston, VT, which stocks everything

from candy to flannel nightgowns, plus a range of hard-to-find gadgets and gizmos.

When it comes to **outdoor gear**, few stores compare to L.L. Bean. The company's flagship store in Freeport, Maine, is open all year. It is such a tourist attraction, a whole neighborhood of outlet stores has grown up around it.

New England residents tend to brag about how little, not how much, they paid for an item, so **bargain shopping** is an art form here. Sadly, Boston's famous discount shopping mecca, Filene's Basement, has closed for good. For now, shoppers in search of great deals on name-brand goods head to Marshall's, on Boylston Street. Posh Newbury Street, surprisingly enough, is home to several consignment shops, where gently-worn (by someone else) designer clothing is a major draw. One of the top stops is The Closet at 175 Newbury.

If price is no object, or you simply like the ambience of picturesque brownstone town houses chock-a-block with stores and **boutiques**, head to Boston's Newbury Street. Interspersed with shopping places are sidewalk cafes and galleries, making up an eight-block stretch that's also prime for people-watching.

New England's huge population of college students has also had an impact on the shopping scene. College towns, in particular, offer lots of shopping in the "**cheap-and-chic**" category, and lots of used book and music stores, vintage clothing stores, and places to drape your dorm room in neo-bohemian style. One example: the Garment District, "an alternative department store" in Cambridge, Massachusetts, where you can buy recycled clothing by the pound. Another fun haunt, for vintage menswear, is Bobby from Boston, at 19 Thayer St. in the South End.

Savvy shoppers also take advantage of New England's **museum shops**. Nearly every museum has a store that

😊 A Bit of Advice 😊

If you see a small storefront shop that says "Spa" but doesn't look like a place to get a facial, it's because convenience-type stores were called "spas" in the old days. And if you hear someone from Massachusetts mention "the packy" or "package store," they're referring to a liquor store (alcohol isn't sold in grocery stores in the state).

features unique gift items, books and other merchandise.

What are some "uniquely New England" things to buy? **Food** plays a big part: Vermont cheese and maple syrup, of course, and products made from Maine blueberries and Massachusetts cranberries. Rhode Island's gift shops (and some grocery stores) offer take-home mixes for local treats such as Del's Lemonade and johnnycakes and coffee syrup, so Ocean State visitors can whip up coffee milk (coffee syrup mixed with milk) once they return home. Maine and New Hampshire have a lock on the "moose" category. Local gift shops will help you decorate your entire home in a moose theme, should you desire, or you can simply pick up a pair of earrings adorned with moose droppings (true!). **Wineries** in Vermont, Rhode Island and Massachusetts offer wines made with local grapes. Meanwhile, Connecticut is home to scores of antique shops, as well as galleries specializing in nautically-themed art and artifacts.

WHERE TO SHOP

New England's shopping zones run the gamut from antique shops to outlet malls. Along the way are a few surprises, like a giant furniture store that houses an IMAX movie theater and a trapeze school (Jordan Furniture in Reading, MA), and a drive-in movie that morphs into a flea market on weekends (Wellfleet Drive-In, Wellfleet, MA).

Collecting saps from maple trees, Vermont

© Stephen Goodhue / VermontVacation.com

Antiquing

Displayed in elegant Boston shops or in simple roadside stands along rural roadways, New England antiques will delight both the seasoned and novice collector in variety and quality.

The town of Woodbury, CT, in Litchfield County, is considered one of the best antiquing towns in the state. Hallowell, Maine, two miles south of Augusta, is Maine's antiques capital. The best area for finding gracefully aged, "don't make 'em like that anymore" objects in Massachusetts is the town of Essex, home to some 30 antiques shops, where you can eat fried clams at Woodman's (where they were invented) after you browse. New Hampshire's prime zone for sleuthing out elderly treasures is Antique Alley, a stretch of Rte. 4 that encompasses the towns of Northwood, Lee, Epsom and Chichester, home to more than 500 dealers. Antiques mavens visiting Vermont should put the Antiques Mall at Quechee Gorge Village at the top of their list. This 18,000sq ft barn building houses 450 booths. Wickford Village in N. Kingston, RI, boasts a charming stretch of antique shops and vintage clothing stores on Broom Street.

Farmers' Markets and Maple Sugaring

During the New England harvest season (mid- to late June through early October), many farmers sell fresh-grown **produce** at roadside stands. Visitors can also pick their own fruits and vegetables at farms open to the public. Look in the calendar sections and weekend editions of daily newspapers for listings.

Maple syrup is harvested in the spring. Farmers collect sap from maple trees and boil down the watery substance into syrup. Visitors are welcome at a number of sugarhouses. For listings, contact the ⓦVermont Dept. of Agriculture (*www.vtmaple. org*) or the ⓦNew Hampshire Dept. of Agriculture (*www.nhfarms.com*).

Outlet Malls

Although outlet malls increasingly offer the same line-up of stores, most bargain hunters can't resist a look. Connecticut's prime destination is **Clinton Crossing Premium Outlets**, where targets include Calvin Klein and Cole Haan. Maine offers a couple of serious outlet shopping zones: **Kittery**, just over the border from New Hampshire, and **Freeport**, where L.L. Bean's flagship store anchors several blocks of outlet shops. **Wrentham Premium Village Outlets** in Wrentham, MA, are the Boston area's answer to outlet shopping. **North Conway** is New Hampshire's prime destination for budget-minded shoppers; here, you can stay at a country inn after a day of hard-core shopping. The same is true of **Manchester**, **Vermont**, where outlet stores share the neighborhood with tony inns. Rhode Island's **Blackstone Valley** is home to several manufacturers' outlets, where savvy shoppers find bargains on furniture, textiles and home goods.

High-End Shopping
Boston's Newbury Street isn't the only place to find designer names in New England: Copley Place, also in Boston's Back Bay, draws well-heeled shoppers to stores such as Neiman Marcus. Providence Place in Providence, RI, offers a mix of fashionable stores.

Local Color
One of the pleasures of visiting New England is discovering shops and galleries with a dash of local flair. Funky New Haven, CT, is loaded with boutiques and specialty shops, including the beloved Atticus Bookstore. Newport, RI, is home to more than 60 shops in a 10-mile radius, with goods that celebrate the city's character as a Colonial seaport. Bar Harbor, ME, is a fun place to shop (with special emphasis on the moose theme!), In Newburyport, MA, boutiques are housed in converted red-brick mill buildings and tanneries.

BOOKS
FICTION

A New England Tale or Sketches of New England Character and Manners. Catharine Sedgwick (1995). This collec-
tion of rare works of fiction by 18C and 19C women ranges from serious cautionary tales to amusing social satire. These stories provide a unique look at early American life.

REFERENCE

The Magnificent History in New England's Stone Walls. Robert Thorson (2002). Calling abandoned stone walls "the signatures of rural New England," author Thorson, a professor at the University of Connecticut, tells their story.

CHILDREN'S LITERATURE

Carry on, Mr. Bowditch. Jean Lee Latham (1955). The story of "Nat," a math whiz who's an indentured servant to a ship's chandler in the 18C, Salem, MA. In this Newbury Medal-winning tale, the unassuming Nat becomes a New England hero.

Johnny Tremaine. Esther Forbes (1943). This timeless story of adventure, loss, and courage focuses on a 14-year-old silversmith's apprentice in Boston, as the American Revolution simmers.

FILMS

Jaws (1975). Directed by Steven Spielberg, this film about a great white shark that terrorized beachgoers was shot on Martha's Vineyard, MA.

Mystic Pizza (1988). This story of three waitresses who pursue summer romance launched Julia Roberts' career. The movie was filmed in Mystic and Stonington, CT. The pizzeria still exists.

Carousel (1956). This classic musical, about the romance between a carnival barker and a factory worker was filmed in Boothbay Harbor and Newcastle, Maine.

Mystic River (2003). Gritty murder mystery, starring Sean Penn, which won a slew of Academy Awards. Shot in and around Boston.

Calendar of Events

Below is a selection of New England's most popular annual events; some dates may vary from year to year. For detailed information, contact local tourism offices (✆ telephone numbers are given in the **Discovering New England** section) or state tourism offices (listed in the section **Planning Your Trip**).

JANUARY
late Jan: **Stowe Winter Carnival**
www.stowewintercarnival.com
✆ 802-253-7321; Stowe (VT)
late Jan–Feb: **Chinese New Year Parade** www.bostonusa.com
✆ 888-733-2678; Boston (MA)

FEBRUARY
Dartmouth Winter Carnival
www.dartmouth.edu
✆ 603-646-3399; Hanover (NH)
late Feb: **Newport Winter Festival**
www.newportwinterfestival.com
✆ 401-847-7666; Newport (RI)
Mount Washington Valley Ice Fest: www.ime-usa.com ✆ 603-356-7064; North Conway (NH)

MARCH
mid Mar: **Restaurant Week Boston**
www.bostonusa.com/
restaurantweek ✆ 888-SEE-BOSTON; Boston (MA)
mid–late Mar: **Boston Flower & Garden Show** www.boston
flowershow.com ✆ 800-258-8912; Boston (MA)

APRIL
mid-Apr: **Boston Marathon**
www.bostonmarathon.com
✆ 617-236-1652; Boston (MA)
mid Apr–early May: **Daffodil Days**
www.blithewold.org
✆ 401-253-2707; Bristol (RI)
late Apr: **Fishermen's Festival**
www.boothbayharbor.com
✆ 207-633-2353 Boothbay Harbor (ME)

Vermont Antiquarian Spring Book & Ephemera Fair
www.VermontisBookCountry.com
✆ 802-527-7243 S; Burlington (VT)
Daffodil Festival www.nantucket
chamber.org ✆ 508-228-1700; Nantucket (MA)

MAY
late May: **Lisbon Annual Lilac Festival**
www.uncommondays.com
✆ 603-828-6336; Lisbon (NH)
May–Jun: **MooseMainea**
www.mooseheadlake.org
✆ 207-695-2702; Moosehead Lake Region (ME)
May–Oct: **Waterfire**
www.waterfire.org ✆ 401-273-1155; Providence (RI)

JUNE
early Jun: **Yale-Harvard Regatta**
www.yale.edu ✆ 203-432-4771; New London (CT)
Old Port Festival www.portland
maine.com ✆ 207-772-6828; Portland (ME)
Jun–late Aug: **Jacob's Pillow Dance Festival** www.jacobs
pillow.org ✆ 413-243-0745; Becket (MA)
mid-Jun: **Market Square Days Celebration** www.pro
portsmouth.org ✆ 603-433-4398; Portsmouth (NH)
mid-Jun: **International Festival of Arts and Ideas** www.artidea.org
✆ 203-498-1212; New Haven (CT)
mid-Jun–Aug: **Williamstown Theater Festival** www.wtfestival.org
✆ 413-597-3400
Williamstown (MA)
late Jun: **Block Island Race Week**
www.blockislandraceweek.com
✆ 203-458-3295; Block Island (RI)
late Jun–late Aug: **Berkshire Theatre Festival** www.berkshire
theatre.org ✆ 413-298-5576; Stockbridge (MA)
late Jun: **Windjammer Days**
www.boothbayharbor.com
✆ 207-633-2353
Boothbay Harbor (ME)

Harborfest drummers, Boston

© Greater Boston Convention & Visitors Bureau

late Jun: Vermont Quilt Festival
www.vqf.org ☎802-872-0034
Essex Junction (VT)

JULY

early Jul: Harborfest www.boston
harborfest.com ☎617-227-1528;
Boston (MA)
Bow Street Fair www.seacoast
rep.org ☎603-443-4793;
Portsmouth (NH)
Wickford Art Festival
www.wickfordart.org ☎401-
294-6840; Wickford (RI)
4 Jul: Bristol Fourth of July Parade
www.july4thbristolri.com
☎401-253-7000; Bristol (RI)
mid-Jul: Litchfield Open House Tour
www.litchfieldct.com ☎860-567-
4045; Litchfield (CT)
Newport Music Festival
www.newportmusic.org ☎401-
849-0700; Newport (RI)
late Jul: Lowell Folk Festival
www.lowellfolkfestival.org ☎978-
970-5000; Lowell (MA)
Great Connecticut Jazz Festival
www.greatctjazz.org ☎800-468-
3836; Guilford (CT)
Vermont Mozart Festival
www.vtmozart.org ☎802-862-
7352; Burlington (VT)
**late Jul–early Aug: Yankee
Homecoming Days** www.yankee
homecoming.com ☎978-462-
4760 Newburyport (MA)

AUGUST
early Aug: Maine Lobster Festival
www.mainelobsterfestival.com
☎207-596-0376; Rockland (ME)
**League of New Hampshire
Craftsmen's Fair**
www.nhcrafts.org
☎603-224-3375 Mt. Sunapee
Resort, Newbury (NH)
**Southern Vermont Art
and Craft Festival** www.craft
producers.com ☎802-425-3399;
Manchester (VT)
Boat Builders Festival
www.bbrit.org ☎207-633-4818;
E. Boothbay (ME)
**2nd weekend in Aug: Newport JVC
Jazz Festival** www.newport
jazzfest.net ☎410-848-5055;
Newport (RI)
**mid-Aug: Fall River Celebrates
America** www.fallrivercelebrates.
com ☎508-676-8226;
Fall River (MA)
**Portland Chamber Music
Festival** www.pcmf.org ☎800-
320-0257; Portland (ME)
**Mt. Washington Hillclimb
(bicycle race)** www.
mtwashingtonbicycle
hillclimb.org ☎603-466-3988;
Gorham (NH)
**late Aug–early Sept: Champlain
Valley Fair** www.cvexpo.org
☎802-878-5545; Essex Junc. (VT)

Block Island Race Week

© Block Island Tourism Council

SEPTEMBER

early Sept: **Vermont State Fair**
www.vermontstatefair.net
☎802-775-5200; Rutland (VT)
Norwalk Oyster Festival
www.seaport.org ☎203-838-9444; Norwalk (CT)
mid-Sept: **Eastern States Exposition**
www.thebige.com ☎413-737-2443
West Springfield (MA)
NH Highland Games
www.nhscot.org ☎603-229-1975;
Lincoln (NH)
late Sept–early Oct:
**Northeast Kingdom Fall Foliage
Festival** www.nekchamber.com
☎802-748-3678; Northeast
Kingdom (VT)
Fall Foliage Festival
www.fallfoliageparade.com
☎413-499-4000; North Adams (MA)

OCTOBER

early Oct: **Pumpkin Festival**
www.pumpkinfestival.org
☎603-358-5344; Keene (NH)
Oct: **Haunted Happenings**
www.hauntedhappenings.org
☎978-744-3663; Salem (MA)

NOVEMBER

early Nov: **Maine Brewer's Festival**
www.mainebrew.com
Portland (ME)
Thanksgiving Day: **Plimoth
Plantation: Thanksgiving
Celebration;** www.plimoth.org
☎508-746-1622; Plymouth (MA)
late Nov–Dec: **Nantucket Noel**
www.nantucketchamber.org
☎508-228-1700; Nantucket (MA)
Nov–Dec: **Berkshire Museum
Festival of Trees** www.berkshire
museum.org ☎413-443-7171;
Pittsfield (MA)

DECEMBER

early Dec: **Woodstock
Wassail Celebration**
www.woodstockvt.com
☎888-496-6378; Woodstock (VT)
Festival of Trees & Traditions
www.wadsworthantheneum.org
☎860-278-2670; Hartford (CT)
31 Dec: **First Night Boston**
www.firstnight.org ☎617-542-1399; Boston (MA)

Know Before You Go

USEFUL WEBSITES

www.bostonusa.com
Greater Boston Convention & Visitors Bureau site offers a comprehensive guide to attractions, accommodations, restaurants and events.

www.yankeemagazine.com
Regional guide to fall foliage tours, New England travel and other highlights from the magazine.

www.vermontmagazine.com
Good for arts calendar listings, including theater, music, craft events and festivals.

www.boston.com
Features up-to-date museum and gallery exhibits, music, theater and dance listings, restaurant reviews, local weather and traffic reports.

www.explorenewengland.com
A travel site compiled by the *Boston Globe* and Boston.com.

www.newenglandtimes.com
This site features getaways, vacations, events, real estate, history, folklore, news, and lifestyles.

www.bostonmagazine.com
News, lifestyles stories and trends, covering Boston and beyond. Especially good for sleuthing out their annual "Best of Boston" award winners (restaurants, nightlife, hair salons and more). For content culled from *Boston Magazine*'s annual travel publication, *New England Travel & Life*, see also www.bostonmagazine.com/travel.

www.downeast.com
Online version of the "magazine of Maine" is a great source for up-to-date events listings.

TOURIST OFFICES

State tourism offices provide information and brochures on points of interest, seasonal events and accommodations, as well as road and city maps.
In this guide, contact information for local tourism offices (if available) is indicated by the 🄸 symbol. On maps, information centers are indicated by the 🄸 symbol.

CT COMMISSION ON CULTURE & TOURISM
One Constitution Plaza, 2nd Fl.
Hartford, CT 06103
℘860-256-2800, 888-288-4748
www.ctvisit.com

MAINE OFFICE OF TOURISM
59 State House Station
Augusta, ME 04333
℘888-624-6345
www.visitmaine.com

OFFICE OF TRAVEL & TOURISM
10 Park Plaza, Suite 4510
Boston, MA 02116
℘617-973-8500, 800-227-6277
www.massvacation.com

OFFICE OF TRAVEL & TOURISM DEVELOPMENT
172 Pembroke Road, P.O. Box 1856
Concord, NH 03302-1856
℘603-271-2665, 800-386-4664
www.visitnh.gov

STATE TOURISM DIVISION
315 Iron Horse Way, Suite 101
Providence, RI 02908
℘401-278-9100, 800-250-7384
www.visitrhodeisland.com

DEPARTMENT OF TOURISM & MARKETING
National Life Building, 6th Floor
Montpelier, VT 05620
℘802-828-3237, 800-837-6668
www.travel-vermont.com

INTERNATIONAL VISITORS
NEW ENGLAND EMBASSIES AND CONSULATES ABROAD

♿Visitors from outside the US can obtain information from the tourism agencies (listed under Tourist Offices), from the nearest US embassy or consulate, or from the US Department of State (♿*see www.usembassy.gov for complete listings*).

♦ **Australia**
Moonah Place
Yarralumla ACT 2600
℘(02) 6-214-5600
http://usembassy-australia.state.gov

♦ **Canada**
490 Sussex Drive
Ottawa ON K1N 1G8
℘613-688-5335
http://canada.usembassy.gov

♦ **France**
2, avenue Gabriel, 75008 Paris
℘(33) 1-43-12-22-22
http://france.usembassy.gov

♦ **Germany**
Clayallee 170
14191 Berlin
℘(49) 030-8305-0
http://germany.usembassy.gov

♦ **Italy**
Via V. Veneto 121-00187 Rome
℘(39) 06-46741
http://rome.usembassy.gov

♦ **Japan**
1-10-5, Akasaka, Minato-ku
Tokyo 107-8420
℘(81) 3-3224-5000
http://tokyo.usembassy.gov

♦ **Mexico**
Paseo de la Reforma 305
Colonia Cuauhtemoc, 06500
℘(52) 55-5080-2000
http://mexico.usembassy.govv

♦ **Spain**
Calle Serrano 75, 28006 Madrid
℘(34) 91-587-2200
http://madrid.usembassy.gov

♦ **United Kingdom**
24 Grosvenor Square
London W1A 1AE
℘(44) 0-20-7499-9000
http://london.embassy.gov

ENTRY REQUIREMENTS

Citizens of countries participating in the Visa Waiver Pilot Program (VWPP) are not required to obtain a visa to enter the US for visits of fewer than 90 days if they have a machine-readable passport. Citizens of non-participating countries must have a visitor's visa. Upon entry, non resident foreign visitors must present a valid passport and round-trip transportation ticket. Canadian citizens now need a government-issued photo I.D., such as a driver's license, plus proof of citizenship (such as a birth certificate) to enter the US. Naturalized Canadian citizens should carry their citizenship papers. Inoculations are generally not required, but check with the US embassy or consulate before departing. For details, see www.travel.state.gov.

CUSTOMS REGULATIONS

All articles brought into the US must be declared at the time of entry. The following items are **exempt** from customs regulations: personal effects; one liter of alcoholic beverage (providing visitor is at least 21 years old); either 200 cigarettes, 50 cigars or 2 kilograms of smoking tobacco; and gifts (to persons in the US) that do not exceed $100 in value.

Prohibited items include plant material, firearms and ammunition (if not intended for sporting purposes), and meat and poultry products. For further information regarding US customs (*www.customs.gov*), contact the US embassy or consulate before you depart. Foreign visitors should

Marsh-Billings-Rockefeller National Historical Park

© E. Sharon / Marsh-Billings-Rockefeller National Historical Park

contact the customs service in their country of residence to determine re-entry regulations.

HEALTH

The US does not have a national health program that covers foreign nationals. Before departing, visitors from abroad should check with their health-care insurance agency to determine if it covers doctor's visits, medication and hospitalization in the US. Prescription drugs need to be properly identified and accompanied by a copy of the prescription.

ACCESSIBILITY

Federal law requires that businesses (including hotels and restaurants) provide access for the disabled, devices for the hearing impaired, and designated parking spaces. Many public buses are equipped with wheelchair lifts; numerous hotels have rooms designed for visitors with special needs. For further information, contact the state access offices:
🆑 ☎860-297-4380 🆒 ☎800-452-1948 🆓 ☎800-322-2020 🆔 ☎800-834-1721 🆕 ☎401-462-0100 🆖 ☎802-229-1355.

NATIONAL PARKS

All national parks have restrooms and other facilities for the disabled (such as wheelchair-accessible nature trails or tour buses). Disabled persons are eligible for the "America the Beautiful Pass" (*free*), which entitles the bearer to free admission to all national parks and a 50 percent discount on user fees (campsites, boat launches). For information, contact the National Park Service: ☎888-ASK-USGS; www.nps.gov.

STATE PARKS

Some state parks offer permanently disabled persons a discount on campsites and day-use fees. Carry proof of identification and disability.

TRANSPORTATION

Train travel: Amtrak passengers needing assistance should give 24hr-advance notice (☎*800-872-7245 or 800-523-6590/TDD www.amtrak. com*). **Bus travel**: Notify **Greyhound** 48hrs in advance for special needs (☎*800-752-4841* (*US only*); *www.greyhound.com*). For general information contact the Society for Accessible Travel & Hospitality, ☎212-447-7284; www.sath.org.

Getting There and Getting Around

BY PLANE

Most flights to New England stop at La Guardia or John F. Kennedy international airports in New York, or Logan International Airport in Boston before making connecting flights to the principal New England airports.

LOGAN INTERNATIONAL AIRPORT (BOS)

3mi northeast of downtown Boston, MA, ℰ800-235-6426 www.massport.com

JOHN F. KENNEDY INTERNATIONAL AIRPORT (JFK)

15mi southeast of Midtown Manhattan, NY. ℰ718-244-4444 www.jfkinternationalairport.org

LA GUARDIA AIRPORT (LGA)

8mi northeast of Midtown Manhattan, NY ℰ718-533-3400 www.panynj.gov/airports/laguardia

BANGOR INTERNATIONAL AIRPORT (BGR)

2mi north of Bangor, ME ℰ207-992-4600 www.flybangor.com

BRADLEY INTERNATIONAL AIRPORT (BDL)

12mi north of Hartford, CT ℰ860-292-2000 www.bradleyairport.com

BURLINGTON INTERNATIONAL AIRPORT (BTV)

3mi east of Burlington, VT ℰ802-863-1889 www.burlingtonintlairport.com

MANCHESTER AIRPORT (MHT)

4mi south of Manchester, NH ℰ603-624-6556 www.flymanchester.com

PORTLAND INTERNATIONAL JETPORT (PWM)

3mi south of Portland, ME. ℰ207-874-8877 www.portlandjetport.org

T.F. GREEN AIRPORT (PVD) WARWICK, RI

10mi south of Providence, RI ℰ401-691-2471 www.pvdairport.com

BY SHIP

Nearly every New England seaport offers opportunities to get out on the water. Options include lobster boat trips (where a captain shares lobster lore and demonstrates how to set and bait traps), cruises to see seals and seabirds, moose-watching cruises, whale watch trips, and a variety of deep-sea and charter fishing trips. Out of Rockland, Maine, windjammer schooner trips are a classic way to tour the coastline. Guests can take a turn at the helm, help hoist the sails, or simply enjoy the views.

The Maine Windjammer Association (www.sailmainecoast.com) runs trips from spring through fall that last 3–6 days. Several cruise companies also ply the New England coastline. American Cruise Lines (www.americancruiselines. com) operates small-ship cruises departing from Providence, RI, and Portland, ME.

Ports of call from Providence include New Bedford, Nantucket and Martha's Vineyard, MA; the Maine coast cruise includes stops in Boothbay, Bar Harbor and Camden, ME. Some of the major cruise lines sail out of Boston, with itineraries that take advantage of New England's fabled fall foliage season. Holland America Line (www.holland america.com) offers 7-14-day cruises of coastal New England and Canada from May through September. Ports of call include Bar Harbor, Halifax, Quebec City and Montreal. Norwegian Cruise Lines (www.ncl.com) sails in late September and October, with a seven-day cruise from Boston to Quebec City that includes the Bay of Fundy, Halifax, Sydney, and Bar Harbor. Royal Caribbean (www.royalcaribbean.com)

offers seven-night cruises out of Boston sailing in September and October; ports include Portland, St. John and Halifax.

BY TRAIN

With access to over 50 communities in New England, the **Amtrak** rail network offers a relaxing alternative for the traveler with time to spare. Advance reservations are recommended. First class, coach and sleeping accommodations are available; fares are comparable to air travel. The high-speed rail travels daily from New York City to Boston in just over five hours.

For schedules and routes, call ✆800-872-7245 (*toll-free in North America only*) or visit www.discoverypass.com.

BY COACH/BUS

Greyhound, the largest bus company in the US, offers access to most communities in New England at a leisurely pace. Overall, fares are lower than other forms of public transportation. The **Discovery Pass** allows unlimited travel for anywhere from 7 to 60 days. Advance reservations are suggested. For fares, schedules and routes, call ✆800-231-2222 or visit www.greyhound.com.

BY CAR

New England has an extensive system of well-maintained major roads. In remote areas, minor roads tend to be unmarked, and many small rural routes are unpaved.

DOCUMENTS

Visitors bearing valid driver's licenses issued by their country of residence are not required to obtain an International Driver's License to drive in the US. Drivers must carry vehicle registration and/or rental contract and proof of automobile insurance at all times.

CAR RENTAL

Most large rental-car agencies have offices at major airports and in the larger cities in New England. A major

RENTAL COMPANY	✆Reservations
Alamo	800-462-5266 www.alamo.com
Enterprise	800-736-8222 www.enterprise.com
Avis	800-230-4898 www.avis.com
Hertz	800-654-3131 www.hertz.com
Budget	800-527-0700 www.budget.com
National	800-227-7368 www.nationalcar.com
Dollar	800-800-3665 www.dollar.com
Thrifty	800-847-4389 www.thrifty.com

Toll-free numbers may not be accessible outside North America

credit card and valid driver's license are required for rental (some agencies also require proof of insurance). Drop-off charges may apply if a vehicle is returned to a location other than where it was rented.

GASOLINE (PETROL)

Gasoline is sold by the gallon (*1 US gallon = 3.8 liters*). Many self-service gas stations do not offer car repair, although many do sell standard maintenance items. Some also sell maps and snacks.

ROAD REGULATIONS

Road regulations in the US require that vehicles be driven on the right side of the road. Distances are posted in miles (*1 mile = 1.6 kilometers*). Travelers are advised to obey posted speed limit signs. The maximum speed limit on major freeways is 65mph (105km/h) in rural areas and 55mph (90km/h) in and around cities (in Rhode Island, maximum speed limits are 55mph). Speed limits range from 30 to 40mph (45-65km/h) within cities, and average 25mph (30km/h) in residential areas. Use of **seat belts** is mandatory for all persons in the car in all states except

New Hampshire (required only for passengers under 18 years of age) and Connecticut. In Connecticut, seat-belt use is mandatory for all persons age seven and over who are riding in the front seat. In Rhode Island children aged four to five years must ride in the back seat with a seat belt fastened. Child safety seats are required in Vermont, Connecticut and Massachusetts for children under five years of age; they are required in Connecticut, Maine, Rhode Island and New Hampshire for children under four years old (or 40lbs and below). **School bus** law in effect for the six-state area requires motorists to bring vehicles to a full stop when red lights on a school bus are activated. Unless otherwise posted, it is permissible to turn right at a red traffic light after coming to a complete stop. Parking spaces identified with &. are reserved for disabled persons only.

Anyone parking in these spaces without proper identification is subject to a ticket with a hefty fine attached. Connecticut has banned the use of all hand-heldcell phones while driving; Maine has passed a law against driving while distracted. Most of the states in the U.S. have banned text messaging while driving, including all of the New England states. Best practice is to limit cell phone use to times when the vehicle is parked and off the roadway.

In Case of Accident

If you are involved in an accident resulting in personal or property damage, you must notify the local police and remain at the scene until dismissed. If blocking traffic, vehicles should be moved if possible.

Where to Stay

Hotel and restaurant recommen dations are located in the Address Books throughout the **Discovering New England** section of this guide. For coin ranges and for a description of the symbols used in the Address Books, refer to the Legend on the cover flap. Luxury **hotels** are generally found in major cities, **motels** in clusters on the edge of town, or where two or more highways intersect. **Bed and breakfasts** (B&Bs) are normally located in residential areas of cities and villages.

Local tourist offices (telephone numbers are listed under entry headings in the **Discovering New England** section) provide detailed information about accommodations. In season and during weekends, advance reservations are recommended. Always advise reservations clerk of late arrival; rooms, even though reserved, might not always be held after 6pm

otherwise. Off-season and weekday rates are usually lower than seasonal and weekend rates, although many city hotels offer weekend discounts.

HOTELS/MOTELS

Accommodations range from luxury hotels to budget motels. Rates vary with season and location; rates tend to be higher in cities and in coastal and vacation areas. Many hotels offer packages (including meals and sightseeing passes) and weekend specials. Amenities may include a swimming pool, and smoking/non-smoking rooms. More elegant hotels also offer in-room dining and valet service. Opposite right is a list of major hotel chains with locations throughout New England.

BED AND BREAKFASTS/ COUNTRY INNS

Many B&Bs are privately owned and located in historic homes. Breakfast, and in some cases, afternoon tea, is included in the rates; private baths are not always available. Smoking indoors may not be allowed. Some inns have been in operation since colonial times. Inns often include a restaurant on premises; meals are available on an à la carte basis. ⓖ Maine: for a free copy of the *Lodging and Dining Guide,* contact the Maine Innkeepers Assn: 304 US Rte. 1, Freeport, ME 04032; ☎207-865-6100; www.maineinns.com.

Reservations Services

ⓖ **Nutmeg B&B Agency**, 1204 Main St, Woodbury, CT 06798; ☎203-263-4479 or 800-727-7592; www.nutmegbb.com.

ⓖ **Bed Breakfast Agency of Boston**; ☎617-720-3540 or 800-248-9262; www.boston-bnbagency.com.

ⓖ **Newport Inns and Bed and Breakfasts Association**, Rhode Island, P.O. Box 1063, Newport, RI 02840; www.newportinns.com.

HOSTELS

A simple, low-cost alternative to hotels and inns, hostels average $15–$35 per night; amenities may include community living room, showers, laundry facilities, full-service kitchen and dining room, and dormitory-style rooms (blankets and pillows are provided, but guests are required to bring their own linens). Membership cards are recommended. **Hosteling International USA**, 8401 Coleville Rd., Suite 600, Silver Spring, MD 20910; ☎301-495-1240; www.hiusa.org.

CAMPING

Campsites are located in national and state parks, national forests and in private campgrounds. Amenities range from full RV hook-ups to rustic backcountry sites. Most camping areas provide recreational amenities. Advance reservations are recommended from mid-May through mid-October. **Wilderness camping** is available on most public lands; check with state tourism offices.

HOTEL/MOTEL	☎/ Website
Best Western	800-780-7234 www.bestwestern.com
Hyatt	800-233-1234 www.hyatt.com
Comfort Inn	877-424-6423 www.comfortinn.com
Marriott	888-236-2427 www.marriott.com
Days Inn	800-329-7466 www.daysinn.com
Radisson	888-201-1718 www.radisson.com
Hilton	800-774-1500 www.hilton.com
Ramada	800-272-6232 www.ramada.com
Holiday Inn	800-465-4329 www.holiday-inn.com
Ritz-Carlton	800-241-3333 www.ritzcarlton.com
Westin	800-228-3000 www.westin.com

Toll-free numbers may not be accessible outside of North America

FARM VACATIONS

Host farms allow paying visitors the opportunity to participate in the daily activities of a working farm. Rates vary from $75 to $150 per night. For more information, contact the following organizations:

ⓖ **Maine Farm Vacation B&B Assn.**; www.mainefarmvacation.com.

ⓖ **Dept. of Agricultural Resources**, 251 Causeway St., Boston, MA 02114; ☎617-626-1720; www.mass.gov/agr/,massgrown/bed_and_breakfast_farms.

ⓖ **NH Office of Travel & Tourism**, P.O. Box 1856, 172 Pembroke Rd., Concord, NH 03302; ☎603-271-2655; www.nhfarms.com.

ⓖ **Vermont Farms**, P.O. Box 828, Montpelier, VT 05601; ☎866-348-FARM; www.vtfarms.org.

Where to Eat

From meatloaf and mashed potatoes to Malaysian cuisine, dining in New England is an adventure in itself. Fresh seafood plays a starring role on local menus, especially along the coast. The **clam shack** is quintessentially "New England," with a certain rustic charm. If the place uses the phrase "eat in the rough," expect picnic tables, paper plates and plastic lobster bibs. Decor, such as it is, runs to old lobster traps and giant plastic crustaceans. Dine on boiled lobster and fried clams, served with huge piles of French fries and onion rings, and a side of slaw—a grand, greasy indulgence that often comes with an ocean view. The **diner** is another classic New England eating spot. The first "night lunch wagon'" appeared in Providence, Rhode Island in 1858, serving late-shift workers at the *Providence Journal*. Those handsome dining cars still dot the New England landscape . The diner experience hasn't changed a bit, and the pie is just as good as ever.

New England's big cities offer the full spectrum of fine-dining options, as well as an exotic array of ethnic eateries. But here's a secret: some of the region's finest dining happens in **country inns**. Innkeepers entice visitors off the beaten path with creative cookery and award-winning wine lists.

Wherever you go, keep in mind that many New Englanders are "early to bed" Yankees, so you probably won't be seated for a meal after 9pm.

Basic Information

BUSINESS HOURS

Retail stores are typically open Monday through Saturday from 10am–6pm, with extended hours during the holiday season (late Nov. through Dec.) Shopping malls stay open until 9 or 10pm Monday through Saturday, and open from 11am or noon until 5 or 6pm on Sundays. Some pharmacy chains (CVS, RiteAid) open as early as 7am; some are open 24 hours a day. Banks are usually open on weekdays from 9am–4 or 5pm, and Saturdays from 9am to noon. Opening hours of museums and attractions vary; many are closed on Mondays.

COMMUNICATIONS

To place an **international call**, dial **011**+country code+number. US phone numbers use a three-digit area code and a seven-digit local number. Within most calling areas in New England, you must dial the entire ten-digit number. To call another area-code region, dial 1 first, and then dial the ten-digit number. The cost for a local call from a pay phone is typically 25-50¢. Most hotels add a costly surcharge for local and long-distance calls. Telephone numbers that start with **1-800**, **1-866**, **1-877** or **1-888** are toll-free (*no charge*) and may not be accessible outside North America. Due to the popularity of cell phones, pay phones are rare. The US is linked with several GSM (global) networks, so multiband phones from most countries will work in New England. Check with your phone company before you leave home. Another option is to purchase a pay-as-you-go cell phone from a company like Tracfone (*www.tracfone.com*) or Virgin Mobile (*www.virginmobileusa.com*); you purchase the phone without a rental agreement, and pay for service as you use it.

ELECTRICITY

Electrical current in the US is 110 volts AC, 60 Hz. Plugs have two flat, parallel blades.

HOLIDAY	STATES OBSERVING	DATE
New Year's Day		1 January
Martin Luther King's Birthday*		3rd Monday in January
Presidents' Day*		3rd Monday in February
Town Meeting Day*		1st Tuesday in March
Patriots' Day*		3rd Monday in April
Memorial Day		Last Monday in May or 30 May
Independence Day		4 July
Victory Day*		2nd Monday in August
Bennington Battle Day*		16 August
Labor Day		1st Monday in September
Columbus Day*		2nd Monday in October
Veterans Day*		11 November
Thanksgiving Day		4th Thursday in November
Christmas Day		25 December

Foreign-made appliances may need voltage transformers and North American flat-blade adapter plugs (available at specialty travel and electronics stores).

EMERGENCIES
Contact the police, an ambulance or the fire department by dialing 911. Emergencies may also be reported by dialing 0 for the operator.

LIQUOR LAWS
The legal age for the purchase and consumption of alcoholic beverages is 21 throughout New England; proof of age may be required.

MAIL/POST
First-class postage rates within the US: letter 46¢ (1 oz), postcard 33¢. Overseas: letter 1.10¢ (1 oz), postcard 1.05¢ (see the Yellow Pages phone directory under "Mailing Services" or "Post Offices"; www.usps.gov). Most post offices are open Monday–Friday 9am–5pm; some are open Saturday 9am–noon.

MONEY
CURRENCY
The American **dollar** is divided into 100 cents. One **penny** = 1 cent; one **nickel** = 5 cents; one **dime** = 10 cents; one **quarter** = 25 cents.

BANKS
Most banks are members of the network of ATMs, allowing visitors from around the world to withdraw cash using bank cards and major credit cards. ATMs can be found in most banks, airports and grocery stores. To inquire about ATM service locations and transaction fees, contact your local bank; Cirrus (800-424-7787); or Plus (www.visa.com).
You can send money, have money wired to you, or send a **telegram** via **Western Union** (800-325-6000; www.westernunion.com).

CREDIT CARDS AND TRAVELER'S CHECKS
Most banks will cash traveler's checks and process cash advances on major credit cards with proper identification. Traveler's checks are accepted at most stores, restaurants and hotels.

To report a lost or stolen **credit card**, call the issuing bank or credit card company: American Express (℘800-668-2639; www.americanexpress.com); Diners Club (℘800-234-6377; www.dinersclub.com); MasterCard (℘800-627-8372; www.mastercard.com); Visa (℘800-336-3386; www.visa.com).

CURRENCY EXCHANGE

Most main offices—and some branch offices—of national banks will exchange foreign currency for a small fee. Boston's Logan International Airport has several currency-exchange offices (*Travelex World Wide Money; ℘800-228-9792; www.travelex.com*). **Thomas Cook Currency Services** (www.thomascook.com) and **American Express Travel Services** (www.amextravelresources.com) operate exchange offices in large cities.

PUBLIC HOLIDAYS

Most banks and government offices in the New England states are closed on the legal holidays shown in the chart on p43 (*many retail stores and restaurants remain open on days indicated by an asterisk**).

REDUCED RATES

Children get a reduced rate on admissions at most attractions, museums and historic sites, and lower fares on subways and trains. College students get reduced admission to many attractions if they show a student I.D. **Senior discounts** are typically offered to guests age 62 and up. Some museums offer free or reduced-admissions evenings; check websites for details.

SMOKING REGULATIONS

Many cities throughout New England have ordinances that prohibit smoking in public places.

TIME ZONE

New England is on Eastern Standard Time (EST), 1hr ahead of Chicago (CST), 3hrs ahead of Los Angeles (PST) and 5hrs behind London (Greenwich Mean Time). Daylight Saving Time (*clocks advanced 1hr*) is in effect from the second Sunday in March through the first Sunday in November.

TAXES AND TIPPING

Prices displayed or quoted in the US do not generally include the **sales tax**. Sales tax is added at the time of purchase and is not reimbursable as in other countries. State taxes vary from state to state (⊙*see chart*). New Hampshire has no sales tax. In the US it is customary to give a **tip** for services received from restaurant servers, porters, hotel maids and taxi drivers. It is customary in restaurants to tip the server 15–20 percent of the bill (unless the menu specifies that the gratuity is included). At hotels, porters should be tipped $1 per suitcase, and hotel maids $1 per night of stay. Taxi drivers are usually tipped 15 percent of the fare.

STATE SALES TAX				
State	General Sales Tax	Room Tax	Restaurant Tax	Exemptions
⊙	6%	12%	6%	Clothing purchases under $50, grocery items
⊙	5%	7%	7%	Grocery items
⊙	6.25%	5.7-12.4%	6.25%	Articles of clothing under $175, grocery items
⊙	none	8%	8%	None
⊙	7%	7%	7%	Clothing and grocery items
⊙	6%	9%	9%	Articles of clothing under $110, grocery items

CONVERSION TABLES

Weights and Measures

1 kilogram (kg) 6.35 kilograms 0.45 kilograms	2.2 pounds (lb) 14 pounds 16 ounces (oz)	2.2 pounds 1 stone (st) 16 ounces	*To convert* *kilograms* *to pounds,*
1 metric ton (tn)	1.1 tons	1.1 tons	*multiply by 2.2*
1 litre (l) 3.79 litres 4.55 litres	2.11 pints (pt) 1 gallon (gal) 1.20 gallon	1.76 pints 0.83 gallon 1 gallon	*To convert litres* *to gallons, multiply* *by 0.26 (US)* *or 0.22 (UK)*
1 hectare (ha) 1 sq kilometre (km²)	2.47 acres 0.38 sq. miles (sq mi)	2.47 acres 0.38 sq. miles	*To convert* *hectares to* *acres, multiply* *by 2.4*
1 centimetre (cm) 1 metre (m)	0.39 inches (in) 3.28 feet (ft) or 39.37 inches or 1.09 yards (yd)	0.39 inches	*To convert metres* *to feet, multiply* *by 3.28; for* *kilometres to miles,*
1 kilometre (km)	0.62 miles (mi)	0.62 miles	*multiply by 0.6*

Clothing

Women					Men			
	35	4	2½			40	7½	7
	36	5	3½			41	8½	8
	37	6	4½			42	9½	9
Shoes	38	7	5½		Shoes	43	10½	10
	39	8	6½			44	11½	11
	40	9	7½			45	12½	12
	41	10	8½			46	13½	13
	36	6	8			46	36	36
	38	8	10			48	38	38
Dresses	40	10	12		Suits	50	40	40
& suits	42	12	14			52	42	42
	44	14	16			54	44	44
	46	16	18			56	46	48
	36	6	30			37	14½	14½
	38	8	32			38	15	15
Blouses &	40	10	34		Shirts	39	15½	15½
sweaters	42	12	36			40	15¾	15¾
	44	14	38			41	16	16
	46	16	40			42	16½	16½

Sizes often vary depending on the designer. These equivalents are given for guidance only.

Speed

KPH	10	30	50	70	80	90	100	110	120	130
MPH	6	19	31	43	50	56	62	68	75	81

Temperature

Celsius (°C)	0°	5°	10°	15°	20°	25°	30°	40°	60°	80°	100°
Fahrenheit (°F)	32°	41°	50°	59°	68°	77°	86°	104°	140°	176°	212°

To convert Celsius into Fahrenheit, multiply °C by 9, divide by 5, and add 32.
To convert Fahrenheit into Celsius, subtract 32 from °F, multiply by 5, and divide by 9.
NB: Conversion factors on this page are approximate.

Eight man sculls on the Charles River in front of Harvard University, Cambridge, Massachusetts

The Region Today

The economic evolution of New England paralleled that of the area's mother country. A period of intense agricultural activity was followed by maritime prosperity and then by industrialization, which formed the backbone of the economy through the 19C and into the 20C. After World War II the region fell into an economic slump, due to the movement of many of its factories to the South. As a result New England turned to new, diversified, high-value industries, such as electronics, as its principal sources of revenue. Tourism remains a strong draw in the region, due to New England's attractive blend of historic sites, picturesque villages and natural beauty.

21ST CENTURY NEW ENGLAND
POPULATION

New England's population of 14 million inhabitants is unevenly distributed; the majority live in the southern half of the region, where the largest cities (Boston, Worcester, Providence, Springfield, Hartford and New Haven) are found. The large waves of immigrants who arrived in the 19C brought with them a diversity of cultures that is still reflected in the ethnic character of the population today.

The **Indians** of the Algonquian Nation were the first to inhabit the region. They were woodland Indians who farmed, hunted, fished and camped along the coast. The largest group, the **Narragansett** tribe of Rhode Island, was virtually wiped out by the English colonists in the **Great Swamp Fight** during **King Philip's War**. Similarly the **Pequot** tribe of Connecticut was decimated by colonists and enemy tribes in the Pequot War of 1637. Today the Mashantucket Pequot Indians operate a number of successful enterprises near Mystic. Present-day descendants of the **Passamaquoddy**

and **Penobscot** tribes live on reservations at Pleasant Point and Old Town in Maine. Members of the **Wampanoag** tribe make their home on Cape Cod and Martha's Vineyard.

Descendants of the 17C and 18C Puritan settlers dominated New England's population until the mid-19C. Hard work, frugality and "Yankee ingenuity"—the talent for making the best of any situation—characterized these early New Englanders, some of whom amassed great fortunes in trade and shipping, and later in industry and finance.

The population remained basically homogeneous until the 1840s, when the potato famine in Ireland caused thousands of **Irish** to emigrate to New England, where they found work in the mills. The **Italians** followed in the 1870s, and at the end of the 19C **French Canadians**, attracted by jobs in the region's factories, began to settle here. Communities of **Portuguese** fishermen from the Azores developed in coastal ports such as Gloucester, Provincetown, and Quincy, while successive waves of immigrants brought **Swedes**, **Russians** and other **Eastern Europeans** to the cities and factory towns. As Boston's **African-American** community vacated the North End for Beacon Hill, the Irish, followed by the Jews and eventually the Italians made the North End their home. Each ethnic group formed its own cohesive neighborhood, where the unity of language, culture and religion drew them together. Irish, Italians, and Jews tended to settle in or near the large cities, while the Portuguese continue to reside in the coastal areas. French names are common in northern New England, where French Canadians form a significant part of the population. The majority of the region's black and **Hispanic** populations reside in southern New England.

Religion

Religious freedom and diversity have been the foundation of New England society since the first immigrants settled in the region in the 1600s. The Pilgrims left England so they could believe and

Faneuil Hall Marketplace, Boston

© Jorge Salcedo / Fotolia.com

worship as they wished. The Puritans, who demanded a strict reading of the Bible, followed. It wasn't long, however, before the colonists were disagreeing among themselves. Fortunately, the New World had plenty of space, so when two theologians couldn't agree, one of them just left town and set up a new church and congregation in another area. That's what Roger Williams did when he founded Providence, Rhode Island. A strong believer in tolerance of all religious beliefs, Williams welcomed many different congregations.

The 19th century transcendental movement was started in New England, by Ralph Waldo Emerson, Henry David Thoreau and others, who believed that God existed within everyone and true happiness and harmony could only be achieved by understanding and communing with nature. This was the catalyst for Thoreau's life in the woods, as described in *Walden Pond*. Today, visitors can learn more about the movement and its philosophers by visiting Concord, Massachusetts, to tour Walden Pond and visit the homes of noted authors like Emerson, Nathanial Hawthorne, and Louisa May Alcott.

The Shakers were also present in New England, organizing into small, closed communities, devoted to celibacy, hard work and pious living. The Shakers separated themselves from the rest of society so they could live and worship in peace without outside influences. They worked diligently, believing that hard work was a holy act. Shaker designs, including baskets, furniture and more, are still sought after and admired. To learn more about the Shaker religion, community and lifestyle, visit Hancock Shaker Village in western Massachusetts, Canterbury Shaker Village near Concord, New Hampshire, and the Shaker Village at Sabbathday Lake in Maine. Today, there are only a few people still devoted to the Shaker life and religion, living at the Sabbathday Lake Shaker Village.

One of the better known New England religions is Christian Science. Founder Mary Baker Eddy believed in spiritual, prayer-based Christian healing, available and accessible to everyone. Considered one of the country's most interesting and powerful women, she founded The First Church of Christ, Scientist, the Massachusetts Metaphysical College, and the prize-winning *Christian Science Monitor* newspaper. Today, Christian Science is headquartered in Boston, with branch churches in more than 65 countries.

Perhaps one of the most interesting religions flourishing in New England is witchcraft. The seaside town of Salem, Massachusetts, tormented by its fear of witchcraft in the 17C, has become a center for followers of the ancient religion of Wicca.

It started in 1692 when several young girls whose imaginations had been stirred by tales of voodoo told to them by the West Indian slave Tituba, began to have visions and convulsive fits. A local doctor claimed that they were victims of "the evil hand." The frightened youngsters accused Tituba and two other women of having bewitched them, and the women were put into prison. Fear and panic began to spread through Salem and more than 200 persons were accused of witchcraft, 150 of whom were imprisoned and 19 found guilty and hanged.

Today, Salem makes much of its witchy past, drawing visitors to its Witch Museums and sites. Each year at Halloween, the city hosts Haunted Happenings, a month-long festival that recalls the city's past. A number of local shops devoted to the occult offer tarot and psychic readings and sell witchcraft items.

Currently, there are several thousand witches living in the area, quietly practising Wicca (a belief system based on goddesses and nature), and attempting to dispel long-held negative opinions concerning witchcraft.

GOVERNMENT

The New England town is the base for local government in all six states. Only about 5 percent of the region's municipalities are cities. Towns are legally incorporated and have similar power of cities in other states. Nearly all land in New England falls under the jurisdiction of a town, and many towns date back to early colonial times. Characteristic of the strong independent streak of New Englanders, towns have a lot of autonomy, giving residents a strong voice in local affairs. Town meetings, based on earlier meetings held by local church elders, are still the basis of government in many towns. Citizens are invited to the meetings to discuss and vote on issues, where a show of hands may still be the method of voting. But in recent times, many towns have adopted other forms of government, too.

Eight presidents of the United States have been born in New England: John Adams (Massachusetts), John Quincy Adams (Massachusetts), Franklin Pierce (New Hampshire), Chester A. Arthur (Vermont), Calvin Coolidge (Vermont), John F. Kennedy (Massachusetts), George H. W. Bush (Massachusetts) and George W. Bush (Connecticut).

Today, the Democratic Party is the dominant party in New England and the region is known for its liberal tendencies. Vermont was the first state in the nation to allow civil unions between same sex couples. Massachusetts was the first to allow same sex marriages. Some form of same-sex unions exist in all New England states except Rhode Island.

New Hampshire boasts the largest state legislature (400) in the country and is one of only two states that limit its governor to a two-year term. The Live Free or Die state is also known for its first in the nation presidential primary. Since 1920, New Hampshire has hosted the first primary, according to the tenets set out in its state Constitution. Tiny Dixville Notch in northern New Hampshire, with a population of 75, has gained international recognition for being the first in the nation to vote in the Presidential primaries and general elections. Eligible voters gather at midnight on election day to cast their ballots.

ECONOMY
INDUSTRY

In the 19C profits from trade, shipping and whaling, together with the influx of immigrants from Europe and Canada—which provided the large labor force needed for industrialization—fostered New England's transformation into one of the world's leading manufacturing centers.

The Mill Towns

The region's many waterways compensated for the lack of raw materials and fuel by providing the power necessary to operate factory machinery. Mill towns, supporting factories that specialized in a single product, sprung up on the banks of rivers and streams. Textiles and leather goods were made in Massachusetts and New Hampshire, precision products such as clocks and firearms were manufactured in Connecticut, and machine tools were produced in Vermont. The large manufacturing centers in the Merrimack Valley—**Lowell**, Lawrence and **Manchester**—developed into world leaders in textile production. Strings of brick factories, dwellings and stores still dominate these cities.

During the 20C most of these industries moved south to the Sun Belt, but the region remained a leader in the manufacture of woolen cloth. The production of machine tools and fabricated metals has now replaced textiles, and the shoe industry is important in New Hampshire and Maine.

Lobster traps

© Comstock Images

The New Industries

The rebirth of New England after World War II was linked to the development of its research-oriented industries, which could draw on the region's excellent educational institutions and highly trained personnel. These new industries, located essentially in the Boston area (on Rte. 128), in southern New Hampshire and in Hartford, contributed to advances made in space and computer technology and electronics. Their existence gave rise to the production of high-value goods, such as information systems, precision instruments and electronic components, and provided an increasing number of jobs. **Boston**, known for its medical research firms, is also home to producers of medical instruments and artificial organs.

AGRICULTURE

Despite the poor soil and rocky, hilly terrain, subsistence farming was an important activity until the mid 19C. In the spring settlers cleared land to ready it for planting. The mounds of rock they removed from the soil were used to build the low stone walls that appear to ramble aimlessly through the woods. Farming reached a peak in New England between 1830 and 1880 with 60 percent of the region under cultivation. After 1880 the opening of the fertile plains south of the Great Lakes drew farmers

westward. They abandoned their farms, and the forests gradually reclaimed the land. Today only 6 percent of the surface of New England continues to be devoted to agriculture, while 70 percent of the region's land (90 percent in Maine and 80 percent in New Hampshire) remains covered with woodlands. Despite this fact, certain areas have been successful in cultivating single-crop specialties.

Dairy and Poultry Farming

The major portion of income from agriculture is provided by dairy and poultry farming. The region's dairy farms supply milk products to the sprawling urban areas of southern New England. Dairy farms, well suited to the terrain, predominate in Vermont, where large red barns with their shiny aluminum silos dominate the landscape.

Poultry farming is practised throughout the region. Connecticut and Rhode Island focus on raising chickens. In fact, Rhode Island is famous for raising a breed of chicken called the Rhode Island Red.

Specialty Crops

Shade-grown **tobacco** is raised in the fertile Connecticut River Valley. Firm and broad-leafed, this tobacco, grown beneath a layer of netting and hung in large sheds to dry, is used as the outer wrapping of cigars. Fruit is cultivated in many areas: apple, peach, and pear orchards extend along the banks of Lake Champlain and abound on the sunny slopes of New Hampshire, in the Connecticut and Nashua valleys and in Rhode Island. Maine leads all other states in production of lowbush **blueberries**, and the sandy bogs on Cape Cod and in nearby areas yield the nation's largest crop of **cranberries**, the small, red berries traditionally made in to the sauce served as part of the Thanksgiving Day feast each November. Maine's other specialty crop is potatoes, grown in the fertile soil of Aroostook County. The state's potato industry ranks in the nation's top ten.

Forests

Despite the enormous area that they cover, New England's deciduous and coniferous forests are not significant as sources of income because of large-scale deforestation of the region throughout the 19C. Today, vast tracts of land are under federal and state protection. Only the commercial timberlands owned by the large paper companies in northern Maine and New Hampshire constitute important sources of revenue. A major portion of the timber harvested is processed into wood pulp for the mills in Maine and New Hampshire, with Maine's factories ranking among the world's leading paper producers. Other plants and mills transform timber into a variety of wood products, including lumber, veneer, furniture and boxes. The production of **maple syrup** is a traditional springtime activity in Vermont, New Hampshire and Maine.

FISHING

As early as the 15C, European fishermen were drawn to the rich fishing grounds off the coast of New England. These shallow, sandy banks (such as George's Bank), extending 1,500mi east-to-west off Cape Cod, teemed with fish. The fishing industry was so vital to New England that fishermen were exempt from military service, and **Massachusetts Bay Colony** adopted the cod as its symbol. Commercial fishing has been especially important to the ports of Gloucester,

New Bedford and Boston. Modern techniques of filleting, freezing and packaging fish, and larger, more efficient vessels have made New England a leader in the packaged and frozen seafood industry. However, the region's fishing industry has seen dramatic curtailment over the past three decades, stemming from over fishing (particularly of cod, flounder, tuna and haddock), pollution and insufficient conservation. More recently, stringent federal regulations have been proposed to reduce stock depletion.

Lobstering ranks as an activity approaching an art in Maine, where it is practised by thousands of Down East lobstermen, who can often be observed in a variety of craft, checking their traps in the offshore waters. Maine lobster is a delicacy that is shipped to markets across the nation.

INSURANCE

Insurance has been an important business in New England since the 18C, when investors offered to underwrite the risks involved in international shipping. With the decline of sea trade, the insurance industry expanded to include losses due to fire, and the center of the industry shifted inland. Hartford, Connecticut, a national insurance center, is the seat of a substantial number of insurance companies. The modern office towers built in Boston to serve as headquarters of the John Hancock and Prudential insurance companies are the tallest structures in New England, symbolizing the importance of this industry to the economy.

EDUCATION

Traditionally renowned as a national center of culture and learning, New England is home to four prestigious Ivy League universities (Harvard, Yale, Brown and Dartmouth) and two choice preparatory schools (Phillips Exeter Academy in Exeter, New Hampshire, and Phillips Academy in Andover, Massachusetts). The concentration of schools, academies and some 258 institutions of higher learning in the six-state area makes education a significant contributor to the economy. Small businesses in cities (Worcester, New Haven, Providence) and towns (Middlebury, Hanover, Brunswick, Amherst) depend on the revenue generated by the schools within their borders. In Massachusetts, the state's 80 private colleges alone have generated $10 billion in revenue.

TOURISM

Tourism ranks with manufacturing as one of New England's major industries. Mountain and seaside resorts in New England have been welcoming visitors for over a century, and with the growing popularity of winter sports since the 1940s, the region has developed into a year-round vacation area. Fine handicrafts, fashioned by artisans working in New Hampshire, Vermont and along the coast, abound throughout New England. Their sale depends to a great extent on tourists.

TRADITIONS AND FOLKLORE

Like most regions, New England's traditions center around holidays, seasons and special events. Come winter, in seaside towns up and down the coast, historic lighthouses are decked in twinkling holiday lights and Santa Claus arrives by boat. In Maine, lobster boats are strung with lights as they bob in the harbors, and single candles are lit in the windows of sea captain homes. In Boston, Christmas caroling in posh Louisburg Square on Beacon Hill is a long-held holiday tradition.

Many major towns across the region host First Night events on New Year's Eve. New England's biggest First Night is held in Boston, where the concept originated more than 30 years ago. The alcohol-free event features more than 250 exhibitions and performances by local and internationally recognized artists, and attracts more than 1 million people annually.

New Englanders know spring has arrived when the Swan Boats open in the Boston Public Garden. First launched in the 1870s, the beloved swan boats ply the tranquil waters of an artificial pond traversed by a whimsical suspension bridge and bordered by weeping willows. After the boat ride, families visit The Make Way For Ducklings statue grouping in the northeast section of the garden, which re-creates the title of the characters of Robert McCloskey's classical children's book.

New England has two additional harbingers of spring: The Boston Marathon and opening day at Fenway Park. The Boston Marathon, held each year on Patriot's Days (a holiday in New England) is the world's oldest annual marathon. The first race was held on 19 April 1897 with a starting field of 15 runners. Thousands of spectators line the streets to cheer on the runners and to witness what is widely regarded as one of the world's most prestigious road races.

A party-like atmosphere and excited anticipation surrounds opening day at Fenway Park. The Red Sox Nation is alive and well throughout New England and opening day is a treasured event. There's no escaping the chatter and predictions from faithful fans, and you can count on TVs and radios throughout the region to be tuned in. Even if you can't snag tickets to the game, you can visit Boston's beloved ballpark. Opened in 1912, the Fenway is the smallest park in the major league. Tours are offered seven days a week, year-round; if there's a home game, the last tour starts three hours before game time.

Festivals are held throughout New England in the summer. One of the biggest events is the Fourth of July celebration in Boston, featuring the annual Boston Pops concert and fireworks. The celebration is free and takes place outdoors on the Esplanade, along the Charles River. Thousands of visitors line the riverfront and boaters clog the waters to see the event. The festival ends with the Pops' now-classic Independence Day rendition of Tchaikovsky's "1812 Overture," featuring cannons and church bells, and ending with a massive fireworks display.

Come fall, visitors from around the world come to New England for its spectacular foliage. Foliage hotlines are set up in all six New England states to help fall leaf peepers track down the best foliage spots throughout the season. The Sunday drive (or weekend getaway) along some of New England's most scenic byways is a popular fall tradition. Some well-traveled routes include the Kancamagus Highway in New Hampshire, the Mohawk Trail (Rte. 2) in Massachusetts, and driving loops through the Litchfield Hills of Connecticut and Vermont's Northeast Kingdom. Other fall traditions include a visit to Salem, Massachusetts, during its legendary, month-long Haunted Happenings event. Site of the infamous Salem witch trials, this city, with an official witch of its own, really knows how to celebrate Halloween! In neighboring state New Hampshire, the city of Keene hosts its annual pumpkin festival, featuring one of the world's largest collections of jack-o-lanterns. Nearly 30,000 pumpkins, in all shapes, sizes and faces, line town streets and decorate the parks.

Superstitions abound in New England: two-toed cats bring good luck to mariners, and thousands of visitors rub the foot of the John Harvard Statue in Harvard Yard for good luck. If lobstermen find a lumpfish in their trap, they kiss it and toss it over their left shoulder for good luck. Superstitious lobstermen never put the hatch cover on upside down or say the word "pig" on the boat; both are bad luck.

New England is chock-full of ghosts and haunted houses. Most notable haunted places in the region include the 1881 Sise Inn in Portsmouth, New Hampshire, the Old Stagecoach Inn in Waterbury, Vermont, the Captain Lord Mansion and Fairfield Inn in Kennebunk, Maine, Longfellow's Wayside Inn in Sudbury, Massachusetts, and Old Yarmouth Inn on Cape Cod.

FOOD AND DRINK

New England has a well-deserved reputation for simple, hearty fare. In addition to seafood, the region boasts regional specialties ranging from maple syrup and Vermont cheddar cheese to Boston cream pie. Country inns and taverns serve traditional Yankee fare, while waterfront clam shacks and dockside lobster pounds offer the best in seafood dining experiences. In Boston, you'll find a big-city array of fine restaurants and ethnic food.

NATIVE AMERICAN TRADITIONS

Many local dishes trace their roots to the New England Indians, who were the first to make maple sugar, **cranberry sauce**, **Johnnycakes** (fried cornmeal patties) and **Indian pudding**. Slow-cooked **Boston baked beans** flavored with molasses and salt pork also derive from a native recipe, as does their traditional accompaniment, **brown bread**.

LOBSTER IN THE ROUGH

New England's popular crustacean takes center stage, especially in the summer, when it's best served from steaming kettles, on outdoor decks and picnic areas—preferably in view of the water! The traditional New England **clambake** (&see below) can be a day-long event. Another Indian custom, meal preparation begins with digging a pit on the beach, lining it with stones, and then lighting a large wood fire. Once the stones are hot, the cook throws in clams, mussels, unhusked corn-on-the-cob, potatoes, onions, chicken and lobsters, and covers it all with seaweed and a wet tarp until it's steamed to perfection.

Fish and Shellfish

Brook trout is a popular freshwater fish, while swordfish and tuna, **bluefish** and **striped bass** are saltwater favorites. **Blue mussels** grow in clusters around shoreline rocks; try them steamed in wine and herbs. Equally popular are **clams**, harvested by rake from the sandy bottoms of warm-water bays and salt ponds. Fall and winter are the seasons for tiny, delicate **bay scallops** and **oysters**.

CHOWDERS AND STEWS

Thought to have originated with settlers from the Channel Islands, **chowders** are thick, slow-simmered soups traditionally made with milk and vegetables.

Fresh produce, Plymouth Farmers Market

© Tim Grafft / Massachusetts Office of Travel & Tourism

Corn chowder is a regional specialty. Fish chowder usually features cod or haddock; steamers (soft-shell clams) or quahogs (round or hard-shelled clams), potatoes and onions—never tomatoes—are key ingredients of **clam chowder**.

FRESH PRODUCE

Seasonal favorites include wild fiddlehead ferns (spring), and strawberries (early summer). Maine is famous for its wild lowbush blueberries. Late summer produces vine-ripened tomatoes, corn on the cob and pumpkins. In autumn, stop at a pick-your-own orchard for cider and some of the best apples grown in the US.

MAPLE SYRUP

Come early spring, maple trees are tapped for sap, which is cooked down into a sweet syrup used for baking and as a topping for pancakes, waffles, and ice cream. 1.5 inch holes are drilled into the bark of maple trees, into a which a tap is inserted. The sap runs, aided by gravity, through plastic tubing to collection points. The amount of syrup harvested tends to vary day-by-day with the weather conditions. The syrup is then passed through an evaporator. Vermont and New Hampshire lead New England in maple syrup production. A quarter of Vermont's trees are sugar maples, with approximately 2,000 "sugarhouses" throughout the state producing close to 1 million gallons of syrup a year. The best quality is Grade A light amber, followed by Grade A medium and dark ambers.

DRINKS

Massachusetts is the leading grower of cranberries; more than 14,000 acres of cranberry bogs are spread across the southeastern section of the state. You'll find cranberry juice in a host of creative concoctions, including the popular Cosmopolitan cocktail.

Micro breweries are scattered throughout New England, including the widely-popular and award-winning Samuel Adams, brewed by the Boston Beer Company since its founding in 1984. Other popular New England brands include Harpoon, New England's largest craft brewery; Shipyard Brewery out of Portland, Maine; Smuttynose Brewery out of Portsmouth, New Hampshire, and Long Trail Brewery, based in Bridgewater Corners, Vermont.

Finally, at ice cream shops, be sure to order a frappe, if you want a milkshake. If you order a "milkshake," you'll get cold milk mixed with a little syrup, containing no ice cream at all.

History

FIRST AMERICANS

The Pilgrims, seeking religious freedom, were the first English colonists to permanently settle in New England. In November 1620, after 65 days at sea, they anchored off the tip of Cape Cod, in an area that is now known as Massachusetts. They had no legal right to settle in the region, so they drew up the Mayflower Compact, creating their own government. The Pilgrims explored the area on land and foot, and in December 1620 settled in a location near Plymouth Harbor.

The new settlers were met by New England's earliest inhabitants, Algonquian-speaking Native Americans including the Abenaki, the Penobscot, and the Wampanoag. Prior to the arrival of Europeans, the Western Abenakis occupied New Hampshire and Vermont, and parts of Québec and western Maine. The Penobscot settled along the Penobscot River in Maine, and the Wampanoag settled in southeastern Massachusetts, Rhode Island, and the islands of Martha's Vineyard and Nantucket.

Though there was much co-operation and peace among the new settlers and Native Americans, there were also skirmishes and major battles. One of the bloodiest battles occurred in 1637 when the colonists and local tribes mounted a devastating attack on the Pequots. In 1675, the peace that had existed between the colonists and the local native tribes ended in a bloody war known as King Phillip's War.

In 1623, two groups of English settlers arrived in what is now called New Hampshire and established a fishing village near the mouth of the Piscataqua River. In 1628 the Puritans came to Massachusetts and settled Naumkeag (later called Salem). John Winthrop, carrying the Massachusetts Bay Charter, arrived in 1630 and founded Boston. In 1635 Roger Williams was driven from Salem, Massachusetts, for promoting religious and political freedom. He bought land from the Narragansett Indians and settled in what is now called Providence, Rhode Island. The same year, the Connecticut Colony established its own government. New Hampshire and Maine were governed by Massachusetts, and Vermont was still unsettled.

EXPLORATION

1497	**John Cabot** explores the coast of North America.
1602	The English explorer **Bartholomew Gosnold**, sailing south along the New England coast, names Cape Cod, the Elizabeth Islands and Martha's Vineyard.
1604	The Frenchmen **Samuel de Champlain** and **Pierre de Gua**, **Sieur de Monts**, explore the Maine coast.

Landing of the Pilgrims, after a painting by H. Sargent

Library of Congress

1607	Virginia Colony, the first permanent English settlement in North America, is established at Jamestown.
1613	The Jesuits establish a mission on Mt. Desert Island, Maine.
1614	**Captain John Smith** returns to England with a cargo of fish and furs. The term "New England" is used for the first time in his account of the voyage.

COLONIZATION

1620	The Pilgrims arrive on the **Mayflower** and establish Plymouth Colony.
1630	**Boston** is founded by Puritans led by **John Winthrop**.
1635	**Thomas Hooker** leads a group of settlers from Massachusetts Bay Colony to the Connecticut Valley and founds Hartford Colony.
1636	**Harvard College** established. **Roger Williams** flees the intolerance of Massachusetts Bay Colony and establishes Providence, Rhode Island.
1638	**Anne Hutchinson** settles on an island near present-day Portsmouth, Rhode Island.
1639	The **Fundamental Orders of Connecticut**, the governing document drawn up by members of Hartford Colony, is regarded as the New World's first constitution.
1701	Yale University is founded.
1763	The **Treaty of Paris** ends the French and Indian War (1756-63). France cedes Canada and territories east of the Mississippi to Britain.

AMERICAN REVOLUTION

Tensions between the colonists and the Crown escalated during the 1760s. Britain's decision to maintain troops in the colonies after the end of the French and Indian War (1754-63) infuriated many settlers. A further alienating factor was the British Parliament's decision in 1763 to forbid settlement beyond the Appalachian Mountains. The final straw was the passage of a series of taxes—including a tax on tea—levied on the colonists, who lacked directly elected representation in Parliament. In late 1773 a group of Patriots boarded cargo ships in Boston Harbor and tossed cases of tea overboard. The incident, today known as the Boston Tea Party, prompted the English to clamp down even harder on the rebellious citizens. Sixteen months later, in April 1775, colonists clashed with English soldiers at Lexington, Massachusetts in the first battle of the American Revolution.

Couriers riding horses spread the news of the battle, telling stories of savage British soldiers attacking innocent farmers. It prompted more colonists to join the fight, and militia from the other New England colonies poured in to join the Massachusetts men.

During the first months of the war, the English held the advantage, winning most of the battles and laying siege to Boston. Still, the colonists persevered, meeting in Philadelphia in July 1776 to adopt the **Declaration of Independence**, formally severing ties with England.

In December of 1776, the war's tide turned when Gen. George Washington repelled British general William Howe at Trenton, New Jersey. Although Howe returned to take Philadelphia the following summer, Washington's triumph galvanized the colonists. Their cause was further bolstered in 1778 when Britain's old enemy France came to the aid of the Colonial army.

In 1781 Revolutionary and French forces managed to trap Gen. Charles Cornwallis on the narrow peninsula at Yorktown, Virginia. Cut off from the British Navy, Cornwallis surrendered.

The 1783 **Peace of Paris** granted the young nation independence from Britain.

1765	The **Stamp Act**, a direct tax levied by Britain on the American colonies, is passed.
1766	The Stamp Act is repealed.
1767	Parliament passes the **Townshend Acts**.
1770	The majority of the Townshend Acts are repealed, but the tax on tea remains.
1773	Colonists stage the Boston Tea Party at Boston Harbor.
1774	Parliament passes the four **Coercive Acts**—called the **Intolerable Acts** by the colonists. Colonists who oppose Britain's policies hold the **First Continental Congress**.
1775	Outbreak of the **American Revolution**: **18 April** – Ride of Paul Revere. **19 April** – Battles of Lexington and Concord. **10 May** – Siege of Fort Ticonderoga by Ethan Allen and the Green Mountain Boys, along with Benedict Arnold and his men. **17 June** – Battle of Bunker Hill.
1776	British troops evacuate Boston on 17 March. The **Declaration of Independence** is adopted on 4 July.
1777	Vermont declares its independence and adopts its own state constitution.
1781	Colonists defeat British troops led by General Cornwallis at Yorktown, Virginia.
1783	End of the American Revolution.
1788	The US Constitution is ratified. Connecticut, Massachusetts, and New Hampshire are admitted to the Union as the fifth, sixth and ninth states, respectively.
1789	**George Washington** is chosen as the first president of the US.
1790	Rhode Island becomes the 13th state.
1791	Vermont, the last New England colony to join the Union, is admitted as the 14th state in the US.
1812	Britain declares war on the US.
1814	The Treaty of Ghent ends the War of 1812 on Christmas Eve.
1820	Maine enters the Union as the 23rd state.

CIVIL WAR

America expanded westward; the booming industrial age brought massive strides in technology and transportation, and the population increased. But by the mid-1800s, the North and South, roughly equal in population, were two separate and radically different societies. The North was dominated by trade and manufacturing, the South by agriculture. By 1861, the separate regions became separate nations. On April 12, the Civil War began when Confederates fired on Fort Sumter, in Charleston, South Carolina's harbor. The New England states joined the ranks of the North and sent volunteer regiments into conflict.

Many famous authors and orators, who spoke out against slavery, were from New England, including **Harriet Beecher Stowe**. Stowe, who lived in Maine, was the author of *Uncle Tom's Cabin* (1852), a famous anti-slavery novel that is often linked to the Civil War.

Boston, which had the largest area of pre-Civil War black-owned structures in the US, became a center for the abolitionist movement. Abolitionists such as **Maria Stewart**, **Wendell Phillips**, **Frederick Douglass** and others spoke out against slavery at the African Meeting House and the Charles Street Meeting House in Boston.

The war lasted four long years and claimed more than 600,000 lives, in what remains the highest casualty rate for any war ever fought by Americans. Although Lincoln's **Emancipation Proclamation** had technically granted slaves their freedom in 1863, the passage of the **13th** and **14th Amendments** furthered their cause by banning slavery (1865) and guaranteeing civil rights (1868).

19C AND 20C

After the Civil War, **industrialization** spread rapidly and oil, coal, copper and steel production soared. New England led the way from an agrarian to an industrial economy. It became the hub of the textile industry, boasting some of the largest mills in the country. Lowell, Massachusetts, the first planned industrial city in the nation, became the world's leading producer of textiles. The exodus of the textile factories to the South after World War II, led to an emphasis on diversified manufacturing, including the manufacturing of electronics, machine tools and electrical equipment.

New England remained a hotbed of ideas and political clout throughout the 20C. In 1961, at the age of 43, **John F. Kennedy** from Massachusetts, became the youngest man ever to be elected U.S. president.

In 1966, Massachusetts Attorney General Edward Brooke became the first African American elected to the US Senate since Reconstruction.

Education continued to play an important role in New England. The region was home to some of the oldest and best educational institutions in the country, including Harvard in Massachusetts, Yale University in Connecticut, Brown University in Rhode Island, and Dartmouth College in New Hampshire. New England is also home to the Massachusetts Institute of Technology (MIT).

1861-65	**Civil War**
1905	The Treaty of Portsmouth, ending the Russo-Japanese War, is signed at the Portsmouth Naval Base in Kittery, Maine.
1914-18	**World War I**
1929	Stock market crash signals the start of the Great Depression.
1939-45	**World War II**
1944	Bretton Woods Conference is held in New Hampshire.
1954	World's first nuclear-powered submarine is constructed in Groton, Connecticut.
1961	At age 43, John F. Kennedy from Massachusetts becomes the youngest man ever to be elected US president.
1963	On 22 November, President Kennedy is assassinated in Dallas, Texas.
1966	Massachusetts attorney general Edward W. Brooke is the first African American elected to the US Senate since Reconstruction.
1976	The Liberian tanker **Argo Merchant** runs aground near Nantucket Island and spills 7.5 million gallons of crude oil into the North Atlantic.
1980	Boston celebrates its 350th anniversary.
1985	Vermont voters elect the nation's first foreign-born woman governor, Madeleine M. Kunin.
1988	Democratic candidate, Michael Dukakis, former governor of Massachusetts, loses the US presidential election to George H. W. Bush (took office 1989).
1990	Twelve works of art, valued at $100 million, are stolen from the Isabella Stewart Gardner Museum in Boston.
1992	Mashantucket Pequot Indians open Foxwoods, a resort casino in Connecticut.
1993	The Norman Rockwell Museum at Stockbridge opens in Massachusetts.
1994	**Harvard University**, the most generously endowed of private universities

($6 billion), launches largest fund-raising drive in the history of higher education.

1995 **Boston Garden**, one of the oldest sports arenas in the nation, is torn down and replaced by a new sports and entertainment complex.

Part of the largest public works project in the US (the "Big Dig"), Boston's new Ted Williams Tunnel opens, connecting the city to Logan Airport.

1997 From its Charlestown berth, the *USS Constitution*, America's oldest commissioned warship afloat, sails under its own power for the first time in 116 years.

1998 The worst ice storm of the century hits the Northeast, killing trees and causing power outages in Maine, New Hampshire and Vermont.

1999 The **Massachusetts Museum of Contemporary Art** (MASS MoCA) opens in a renovated factory in North Adams.

The second major milestone of the Big Dig project—the Leverett Circle Connector Bridge—opens, connecting downtown Boston to I-93 in Charlestown.

THE NEW MILLENNIUM

New England is ethnically more and more diverse, welcoming immigrants from Ireland, Asia, Italy, South America, Portugal, and beyond. Yet it maintains its regional character and reverence for its historic places and past.

The region is also economically diverse, with a thriving service industry, including tourism, education, financial and insurance services, plus architectural, building and construction services. It boasts one of the lowest unemployment rates in the country. Boston remains the region's cultural and economic hub; it's also home to about 700 research and development firms. Its universities are training grounds for scientists and research specialists.

New England continues to attract visitors, new business and residents, drawn to the region for its strong economy, renowned educational systems, historic charm, beautiful landscapes and quality of life.

2000 The first US census of the new century is conducted, revealing the growth patterns of the towns and cities of New England as well as the nation.

Nearly 5,000 workers are employed in the $14 billion Big Dig project.

2001 On September 11, two Boeing 767s departing from Boston's Logan Airport are hijacked by terrorists and crashed into the World Trade Center in New York City. George W. Bush took office as president of US, January 2001.

2002 **New England Patriots** win the Super Bowl.

Leonard P. Zakim Bunker Hill Bridge, part of the Big Dig project, is completed.

2003 New Hampshire's **Old Man in the Mountain** rock formation collapses.

100 people killed in Rhode Island night club fire.

Anglicans elect first openly gay bishop in New Hampshire.

2004 **New England Patriots** win the Super Bowl.

Massachusetts is first in the nation to recognize gay marriages.

Massachusetts senator John Kerry accepts the Democratic presidential candidate nomination.

Boston Red Sox win the World Series, the team's first title in 86 years.
George W. Bush defeats Kerry in presidential election.

2005 **New England Patriots** win the Super Bowl.

2006 A ceiling panel in Boston's Ted Williams Connector Tunnel collapses, killing one woman and forcing Logan airport traffic to be rerouted until repairs on this section of the Big Dig are completed.
Democrat Deval L. Patrick won a landslide victory to become the first African-American elected governor of Massachusetts.

2007 New Hampshire sets 9 January 2008 state primary date, the earliest it's ever been held, preserving its status as "First in the Nation."
Boston Red Sox win the World Series.

2008 The Rose Fitzgerald Kennedy Greenway opens in Boston, on urban land reclaimed from the Big Dig project.
Barack Obama, a 47-year-old first-term senator from Illinois, shatters more than 200 years of history on 4 November by winning election as the first African-American president of the United States.
The National Bureau of Economic Research declares that the U.S. is officially mired in a recession.

2009 Senator Edward Kennedy of Massachusetts dies of brain cancer at the age of 77.

2010 In a major upset, Republican Scott Brown captures Sen. Kennedy's vacant US Senate seat.

NEW ENGLAND AND THE SEA

New England has been closely related to the sea ever since the colonists turned from the rocky soil to the off-shore waters for their food. At first the colonists erected weirs, similar to those used to this day by the Indians in Maine to snare fish near the shore. Not until the mid 17C did Yankee vessels sail in large numbers to the Grand Banks, the fishing grounds off the southern coast of Newfoundland, which teemed with cod, haddock and pollock. The Sacred Cod, hanging in the Massachusetts State House in Boston, symbolizes the important role played by the cod fisheries in the history of Massachusetts. New England's fisheries became the backbone of the region's trade with Europe, and boat yards sprang up along the coast from Connecticut to Maine to construct fishing and cargo vessels.

Fisheries, trade and shipbuilding prospered, reaching their zenith in the mid 19C. The south (Connecticut, Rhode Island and southeastern Massachusetts) was home to the Yankee whaling fleet; ports along the northern coast of Massachusetts and New Hampshire led the trade with the Orient (the China trade) and the shipbuilding industry. With its protected inlets and thick forests, the Maine coast focused on wooden shipbuilding. From 1830–60, a third of new boats in the US were built in Maine.

Small coastal villages grew into sophisticated urban centers, as merchants, ship masters and sea captains accumulated great wealth and built the handsome Federal and Greek Revival homes that still stand in Salem, Nantucket, Portsmouth, Newburyport, New Bedford, Providence, and other seaport cities.

Several museums preserve New England's seafaring past. Mystic Seaport and the whaling museums in New Bedford and Nantucket recall the Yankee whaling tradition. In Salem the Peabody Essex Museum focuses on New England's trade with the Orient, while museums in Bath and Searsport recall the history of Maine shipbuilding.

WHALING

During the 19C whale oil was used to light homes and streets across America and Europe. New Bedford and Nantucket, leading whaling centers, were busy day and night with vessels arriving, departing or preparing for whaling voyages. Herman Melville's novel, *Moby Dick* (1851) vividly re-creates New England's whaling days.

A Prized Catch

The sperm whale, averaging 63 tons, was hunted in large numbers; it was the species on which New England's whaling industry depended for candles, fuel and perfumes.

A Meteoric Industry

Indians were hunting whales long before the first settlements were established. The colonists learned how to hunt inshore whales by observing the Indians. They built tall watchtowers and set up large black cauldrons, called try-pots, in which the whale fat was melted down, on the beaches. In the 18C the discovery of sperm whales in deep ocean waters led to the construction of larger vessels that were outfitted for long ocean voyages. By 1730 Yankee whalemen had moved the tryworks from the beaches to the decks of whaling vessels so they could process whales at sea.

Did you know?

A blue whale's eye is the size of a teacup. Its ear is the size of a pencil tip. But the tongue weighs more than a small car. This is just some of the information visitors can learn at the New Bedford Whaling Museum in New Bedford, Massachusetts *(t508-997-0046; www.whalingmuseum.org)*, the largest museum in America devoted to the history of the American whaling industry. Exhibits include the skeleton of a rare blue whale (one of only 500 or so in the north Atlantic), and a 45-ton sperm whale.

In the late 18C Nantucket boasted a fleet of 150 whaling vessels; in its heyday, New Bedford was the home port of nearly 400. New London, Provincetown, Fairhaven, Mystic, Stonington and Edgartown also launched fleets. Shipyards turned out sturdier ocean-going vessels, factories manufactured spermaceti candles, tons of baleen were dried in the fields and thousands of barrels of whale oil were stored along the wharves. Whaling ships built, owned and commandeered in New England sailed the oceans from Greenland to the North Pacific, from the Azores to Brazil, and from Polynesia to Japan. The decline of the whaling industry in New England was precipitated by the discovery of petroleum in Pennsylvania in 1859 and the loss of nearly half of New England's whaling fleet during the Civil War years. After the war New England sent out fewer and fewer whalers. In 1971, whale hunting was finally outlawed in the US.

MARITIME COMMERCE

New England's maritime commerce with Africa, Europe and the West Indies brought prosperity to many of its coastal ports in the early 18C. After the Revolution, when Americans were free to trade with the Orient, Boston, Providence, Portsmouth, and Salem developed into rich centers of the China trade.

China Trade

Boats sailing to the Far East rounded Cape Horn, and then generally made detours to ports along the way to obtain returns—goods that could be traded in China for silk, porcelain, and tea. Furs were acquired along the northwest Pacific coast, sandalwood from the Sandwich Islands, and the delicacy *bêche-de-mer* (sea grub) from the Polynesian Islands. Later, when opium replaced furs, boats called at ports in India and Turkey to barter for the illicit drug before continuing to China.

Other exotic products obtained along the route included pepper purchased in Sumatra, sugar and coffee from Java, cotton from Bombay and Madras, ivory from

Zanzibar, and spices from Indonesia. New England's museums and historical houses display countless examples of Chinese decorative arts and furnishings brought back to America from the Orient during this time.

Ice: A New England Industry

The ice trade developed in the 19C when ice was harvested north of Boston and in Maine, and shipped to the southern states, the West Indies and as far away as Calcutta to be used for refrigeration. Ice was harvested from frozen rivers, lakes and ponds. Snow was cleared with the aid of oxen or horses. The ice field, marked off into squares, was cut into blocks weighing up to 200lbs each and transported by boat. The ice business prospered until the introduction of mechanical refrigeration in the late 19C.

SHIPBUILDING

The wooden sailing vessel has been the basis of New England's shipbuilding tradition since 1607, when the pinnace, *Virginia,* was built on the banks of the Kennebec River in Maine.

Early Days

As the colonists established their first settlements, shipyards began to dot the coast. At first they built small, one-masted ketches and fishing sloops, followed in the early 18C by two- and three-masted schooners capable of crossing the Atlantic. The schooner enjoyed a long and glamorous career in the waters off the New England coast. When English dominance of American trade led to widespread smuggling by the colonists, it was the schooner, with its ability to evade British revenue ships, that carried prohibited cargo safely into port. During the American Revolution, armed, privately owned schooners (privateers) were authorized by the Continental Congress to capture enemy vessels. The schooner remained in service as a cargo carrier until the end of World War I.

Age of the Clipper Ship

With the opening of Chinese ports in the 1840s, Americans clamored for Chinese goods. Knowing that American customers would pay high prices for the freshest teas from the Orient, shrewd shippers demanded faster vessels to transport this perishable commodity in the shortest possible time. The clipper was designed to meet their needs. Between the mid 1840s and the mid 1850s, these three-masted vessels, with their lean hulls, narrow bows and acres of canvas sails, became famous for the great speeds they could attain. The major boat yards working to turn out these ships were located in New York, Boston, and Bath, Maine, and the master designer was **Donald McKay** of East Boston. The first ship to round the Cape to San Francisco in under 90 days, the McKay-built *Flying Cloud* set a record of 89 days on her maiden voyage in 185.

Last Sailing Ships

From the 1850s to the early 1900s, the ports of Maine specialized in the production of commercial wooden sailing vessels: the **down-easter** and the **great schooner**. The down-easter, a three-masted square-rigger, had the long, clean lines of a clipper, and could attain comparable speeds, with increased cargo space.

The down-easters and two- and three-masted schooners were used in shipping until the 1880s, when boat builders discovered that four-masted schooners, though larger, cost little more to operate. The construction of the great schooners—four-, five- and six-masted vessels—followed. These ships hauled large bulk cargoes (coal, lumber, granite, grain) from the East Coast, around Cape Horn and up to the West Coast. Striving to compete with the steamboat, Maine shipyards stepped up the production of the great schooners. The profitable days of sailing were numbered, however: the efficient, regularly scheduled steamer triumphed.

Architecture

Best known for its Colonial architecture, New England nevertheless retains a rich heritage of building traditions from all periods, ranging from practical Indian dwellings to the magnificent seaside estates of the Gilded Age and the high rises of post-Modernism. A plethora of art museums, artist galleries and studios, gardens, historic homes, antique shops, and more showcase New England's rich artistic heritage and thriving arts community.

NATIVE AMERICAN

The traditional Algonquin dwelling was not the familiar tepee of the Great Plains but the **wigwam**, a domed or conical hut made of bent saplings covered with reed mats or bark. Quick and easy to build, these snug shelters were adopted as temporary housing by the first Massachusetts colonists until they could construct timber-framed homes. Wigwams built in the traditional manner may be seen at Salem's Pioneer Village and at the Institute for American Indian Studies in Litchfield Hills.

EARLY COLONIAL

The prevailing early Colonial dwelling was the two-story post-and-beam house, characterized by a steeply pitched roof originally designed to support thatch. Several examples dating from about 1660 to 1720 still exist in Connecticut (Buttolph-Williams House in Wethersfield) and in the early Massachusetts Bay town of Ipswich (Parson Capen House) and at Plimoth Plantation in Plymouth. Settlers, finding an unlim-

Early Colonial

© R. Corbel / MICHELIN

ited timber supply in the new country, continued a building technique that was already familiar. The typical house plan comprised two large, multipurpose rooms with exposed beams and a massive center chimney hugged by a narrow stairway leading to chambers above. Clad in shingles or clapboard siding, the exterior featured small casement windows with diamond-shaped glass panes imported from England. When the steep roof extends almost to the ground over a rear kitchen lean-to, the house is known as a **saltbox**. Built low to brace against shoreline winds, the smaller, one-and-a-half-story **Cape Cod cottage** features a pitched or bowed roof.

By court decree all 17C New England villages were laid out according to a similar plan, with the houses set around a park-like central **green**, or common, to provide protection against Indians and assure close proximity to the **meetinghouse**, the largest building in a settlement.

GEORGIAN

This term generally refers to an English architectural style developed by such noted architects as Christopher Wren and James Gibbs and popularized in America from about 1720 until the Revolution (during the reigns of Kings George II and III) largely through pattern books and British-trained builders. Based primarily on the design principles of ancient Rome, this style incorporated the Classical orders, especially Doric, Ionic and Corinthian.

Dignified and formal, the high-style Georgian house proved ideally suited to the tastes of a growing mercantile class. Mansions in wood, stone or brick soon appeared in every major port city. Crowned by a pitched, hipped or gambrel roof, the Georgian house featured a symmetrical facade accentuated with even rows of double-hung windows. Often a central projecting pavilion front with a Palladian window and a pedimented portico graced the entryway. Heavy quoins (stone or wood blocks) typically marked the corners, and the elaborate front door was topped by a round-arched fanlight and a sculptural pediment.

A central-hall plan with end chimneys accommodated larger rooms (now with specific uses such as dining and music), robust wood carving and plaster decoration, and colorful paint treatments. In rural farm towns the Georgian house frequently retained the old center-chimney plan but boasted ornate exterior features, such as the heavy swan's-neck door pediments used in the Connecticut River Valley (Deerfield). Several Georgian public buildings were designed by **Peter Harrison** (1716-75), perhaps America's most important colonial architect. Harrison's Redwood Library in Newport is based on a Roman temple. His Touro Synagogue, also in Newport, and King's Chapel in Boston are notable for their interior paneling. During this period many New England churches gained their familiar front towers and steeples, often adapted from the published designs of Wren (Trinity Church) or Gibbs (First Baptist Church in America).

FEDERAL

Popular from about 1780 to 1820, this British Neoclassical style, sometimes called Adam style, was first adopted in America by an affluent merchant class, primarily Federalists who retained close trade ties to England even after the Revolution. Bostonian **Charles Bulfinch** (1763-1844) was New England's best-known Federal-period architect, responsible for Beacon Hill's Massachusetts State House, while **Samuel McIntire** (1757-1811) designed Fçederal-style structures for the city of Salem.

Like its Georgian counterpart, the high-style Federal mansion, often with bowed or rounded walls, was symmetrical, and its central door was topped by a Palladian window (Harrison Gray Otis House in Boston). But the overall appearance was far lighter and more conservative, with proportions elongated, exterior decoration reduced and fanlights flattened from half-rounds into ellipses. The style is most notable for its refined interior decor, influenced by the work of

Georgian

© R. Corbel / MICHELIN

British architect **Robert Adam**. Oval and round rooms were introduced, along with graceful freestanding staircases and exquisitely decorated fireplace mantels and surrounds. Extremely popular, Federal-style design eventually spread to even the most modest of farm- and village houses and churches throughout New England (look for the telltale elliptical front-door fanlight).

GREEK REVIVAL

The Greek Revival style was popular from about 1820 to 1845. While the Georgian and Federal styles were based on Roman prototypes, the new architectural mode adhered to ancient Greek orders and design principles, notable for squarer proportions, a more monumental scale and less surface ornament. Imitative of Greek temples, buildings in the style were almost always white and usually featured the so-called "temple front." This two-story portico with Doric, Ionic or Corinthian columns supported an unbroken triangular pediment at the roof line.

Among the educated elite the Greek Revival style represented a symbolic link between the republic of ancient Greece and the new American nation. It was adopted for many impressive

Federal

© R. Corbel / MICHELIN

Greek Revival

© R. Corbel / MICHELIN

public buildings, including marble or granite courthouses, banks, libraries (Providence's Athenaeum), churches (United First Parish Church), and temples of trade (Providence's Arcade), as well as for domestic architecture. Elegant Greek Revival-styled mansions appeared in affluent towns and seaports (Whale Oil Row in New London).

Among the major designers of the period were **Alexander Parris** (Quincy Market in Boston) and **Robert Mills** (Custom House). **Asher Benjamin**, who wrote some of the most influential builder's handbooks in America, designed many New England churches (Boston's Old West Church) and fine Bostonian homes (Nos. 54-55 Beacon Street).

19C VERNACULAR

A distinctive feature of rural New England is the **covered bridge** (West Cornwall and Windsor). In 1820 noted New Haven architect Ithiel Town (Center and Trinity Churches in New Haven) patented the **lattice truss**, the interwoven framework visible on the inside of the bridge. The roof, of pine or spruce, was designed to protect the structural elements from harsh weather. The **connected farm**, a complex of attached houses, barns and animal sheds prevalent in northern New England in the mid 19C, developed as old outbuildings were moved from farm property and added to the main residence.

Along the coast, 19C **lighthouses** mark harbor entrances and dangerous shoals. These structures originally included a tower and beacon, first lit with oil lamps and parabolic reflectors, as well as housing for the keeper, who was often a US customs agent. Many lights can be visited by the public (Sheffield Island in Norwalk; Owl's Head in Rockland).

Still visible in many industrial towns are 19C **textile mills**, originally powered by water turbine (steam power became common in the 1850s). Manned largely by cheap immigrant labor, mills were designed as self-contained complexes and typically included railroads, parks, canals, churches and employee housing. Punctuated by rhythmic rows of windows and an occasional clock tower or smokestack, these granite- or brick-walled buildings, usually five or more stories, can stretch for miles along a riverfront. Some complexes now contain museums (the National Historic Park in Lowell); others have been converted to house small business and retail outlets (Lowell's Amoskeag Manufacturing Complex).

VICTORIAN ECLECTICISM

During the Victorian era (1837-1901), classical design was abandoned in favor of a broad range of styles, many inspired by the dark, romantic architecture of medieval Europe. Pointed-arch windows, steeply pointed gables, and gingerbread cornice boards are hallmarks of the picturesque **Gothic Revival** style (Kingscote) that is also seen in board-and-batten **Carpenter's Gothic** villas and cottages. Other Victorian-era styles include **Italianate** (square towers, flat or low-pitched roof and broad porch; Victoria Mansion); **Second Empire** (mansard roof, ornate cornice and round dormers; Boston's Old City Hall); and **Queen Anne** (turrets, spindlework, asymmetrical porches, bay windows and gingerbread trim; Oak Bluffs, Martha's Vineyard). In the early 1870s Boston architect **Henry Hobson Richardson** developed Romanesque Revival (also known as Richardsonian Romanesque), a distinctly American style rooted in the Medieval architecture of France and Spain. His masterpiece, Trinity Church in Boston, incorporates the characteristic squat columns, round arches and heavy, rough-cut stone. Favored for seaside resorts were the **Shingle** style (dark wood shingles, towers and piazzas, steeply pitched roofline and asymmetrical facade; Newport's Hammersmith Farm and Casino) and **Stick** style (gabled roof, rustic woodwork with diagonal bands, contrasting paint colors, decoratively shaped shingles; Newport's Art Museum and Mark Twain House in Hartford).

TURN OF THE 20C

Late in the 19C architects trained in the academic principles of the prestigious École des Beaux-Arts in Paris rejected the eccentric Victorian styles. Typical of the highly decorative **Beaux-Arts** style are great estates such as The Breakers and Marble House (both in Newport) by the fashionable society designer **Richard Morris Hunt**, and grandiose public buildings (Boston Public Library).

Developing at the same time was the **Colonial Revival** style, which drew on America's own Colonial architecture, reinterpreted on a larger scale. A Palladian window, classical columns, swan's-neck pediments, and a large entry portico are typical features. Promoted by such prestigious architectural firms as **McKim**, **Mead and White** (Rhode Island State House), the style was used primarily for Georgian Revival town houses and country estates from about 1900 through 1920 (North and South Streets in Litchfield).

CONTEMPORARY ARCHITECTURE

New England attracted many of the European architects who brought the **International Style** to America in the 1930s, including **Walter Gropius** (1883-1969), founder of the German design school known as the **Bauhaus**.

Representative of **early Modernism**, which rejected ornament and historical references and embraced machine-age technology and materials, is the 1938 Gropius House, a streamlined cubic design incorporating the then-new materials of glass block, acoustical plaster, and chrome. Among other innovative modernist works is **Eero Saarinen**'s 1955 M.I.T. Chapel in Cam-

Italianate

© R. Corbel / MICHELIN

bridge. The heir of early Modernism was the so-called **glass box** design, ubiquitous in the 1960s in the construction of multistoried urban apartments and public buildings. An unusual example is the 1963 Beinecke Library at Yale University by **Gordon Bunshaft** of **Skidmore, Owings and Merrill**, designed with self-supporting walls of translucent marble.

Many glass boxes appeared in New Haven, Boston and other New England cities during periods of widespread urban redevelopment that resulted in the demolition of older buildings. In concert with the growing preservation movement of the last two decades, innovative design programs have, however, helped save endangered structures .

From the early 1970s innovators such as Robert Venturi, Robert Stern, **Philip Johnson** and others developed **post-Modernism**, a movement promoting a deliberate return to ornament.

Familiar historical motifs such as the classical pediment are often playfully exaggerated. The Palladian window is simplified, even caricatured, or the classical column is reduced to a plain shaft, topped by a ball rather than a traditional capital. Unexpected exterior color combinations are another feature. In recent years New England campuses and city skylines, notably Boston (222 Berkeley Street and 500 Boylston Street), Providence and Hartford, have become national showcases for buildings in the style, which emphasizes scale, compatible materials and the relationship of a building to its neighbors.

Visual and Decorative Arts

PAINTING

From the beginning of the colonial period to the late 17C, painting was appreciated primarily for its practical uses for trade signs and portraiture.

18TH-CENTURY DEVELOPMENT

The arrival of Scottish painter **John Smibert** (1688-1751) in America in 1729 initiated the era of professional painting. His works, such as *Bishop Berkeley and his Entourage* (1731, Yale University Art Gallery, New Haven), served as models for the Americans who studied with him, including **John Singleton Copley** (1738-1815), America's first important portraitist. Copley painted the well-known persons of his day (*Paul Revere*, 1768, Museum of Fine Arts, Boston), rendering his subjects amazingly lifelike. Rhode Islander **Gilbert Stuart** (1755-1828) was the most important American painter of the period.

Although he is best remembered for his portraits of George Washington, Stuart in fact painted only three portraits of the president from life, using these as models for his later works. The most well-known of these, *George Washington* (*The Athenaeum Portrait*), was begun in 1796 and never finished. It now hangs in the Smithsonian's National Portrait Gallery in Washington, D.C.

19C

Following the American Revolution, the opening of the West led to an increased awareness of the vast scale and beauty of the nation, and the American scene became a popular theme for artists. Painters of the **Hudson River school** in the 1820s followed the lead of **Thomas Cole** and **Albert Bierstadt** by setting up their easels outdoors and painting directly from nature. Their favorite New England subjects were the White Mountains and the Connecticut Valley. The sea was a source of inspiration for other artists. **Fitz Henry Lane** (1804-65), living in Gloucester, MA, illustrated in soft, glowing tones the serene beauty of the sea and the offshore islands. New Bedford, MA, artist **William Bradford** (1823-92), fascinated by maritime themes and the northern lights, depicted the rising and setting of the arctic sun, and whalers sailing among icebergs (New Bedford Whaling Museum).

Beginning in the 1860s, Americans began to live and study abroad for longer periods of time. Italian-born **John Singer Sargent** (1856-1925) traveled extensively in Europe and won acclaim as the portraitist of the international social set. The career of the self-taught watercolorist and master of the naturalist movement, **Winslow Homer** (1836-1910), began during the Civil War, when Homer served as an illustrator for *Harper's Weekly*. He is known for large canvases of the sea that he painted during summers at Prout's Neck, Maine.

20C

Several painters have been identified with New England. **Grandma Moses** (1860-1961) illustrated themes associated with rural New England (*Sleigh Ride*, 1844; *Sugaring-Off*, 1943).

Norman Rockwell (1894-1978), for many years an illustrator for the *Saturday Evening Post*, painted a chronicle of American life. His principal works can be viewed in Stockbridge. **Andrew Wyeth** (1917-2009) spent several summers in Maine. The Wyeth Family Center at the Farnsworth Art Museum in Rockland exhibits many of his works.

SCULPTURE

Until the 19C, sculpture consisted predominantly of folk art—shop and trade signs, weather vanes, figureheads. New Hampshire-born **Daniel Chester French** (1850-1931) and **Augustus Saint-Gaudens** (1848-1907), who lived his latter years in New Hampshire, trained abroad and exerted a strong influence on American sculpture from the period following the Civil War until the early 20C. French became known for his statue *The Minute Man* (1874, Concord, MA), while the monumental seated *Lincoln* (1920, Lincoln Memorial in Washington, DC) is recognized as his most impressive achievement. Saint-Gaudens executed delicate, bas-relief portrait plaques and monumental sculptures, such as the Shaw Memorial in Boston, for which he is best remembered (1884-87).

In more recent times, award-winning sculptor **Louise Nevelson** (1900-1988), who was born in Russia, grew up in Rockland, Maine. By the mid-1950s, she had developed the style for which she is best known: open boxes of monochromatically painted wood stacked to form a freestanding wall. Her work may be seen at the Farnsworth Art Museum in Rockland. Among other New England locations, sculptural works (particularly contemporary sculpture) are on view at the DeCordova Sculpture Park in Lincoln, Massachusetts and the sculpture garden at the Aldrich Museum of Contemporary Art in Ridgefield, Connecticut, as well as on the campuses of Yale University and Massachusetts Institute of Technology.

FURNITURE

American furnishings were influenced during the period from colonialism to the 19C by European—particularly English—designs.

PILGRIM

Furniture made between 1620 and 1690—tables, chairs, Bible boxes and chests—reflect the Medieval influences of the English Tudor and Jacobean styles. Oak is the principal wood used. The Connecticut-made Hadley, Guilford, and Sunflower chests, ornamented with carved and painted floral designs or geometric motifs are characteristic of this period.

WILLIAM AND MARY

This style was in vogue from 1689 through 1702 during the reign of William of Orange and his wife, Mary. The Flemish influence and contact with the Orient introduced such techniques as japanning (floral or scenic designs on lacquered wood surfaces) and turning (wooden pieces shaped on a lathe). Japanned highboys, chests with bold turnings, and chairs with caned or leather backs were popular.

QUEEN ANNE

Curved lines, such as the gracefully shaped cabriole leg, are a stylistic feature of furniture made between 1720 and 1750. Maple, walnut, and cherry are the woods typically used.

The **Windsor chair**, unrelated to the Queen Anne style, was imported from England in the early 18C and remains popular in America.

CHIPPENDALE

English cabinetmaker, Thomas Chippendale, borrowed elements of French Rococo and Chinese art in creating the wide range of furniture forms illustrated in his design manuals. Pieces from 1750 through 1785 are generally fashioned of mahogany, with curved legs (ending in the ball-and-claw foot) and chair backs pierced with lacy fretwork.

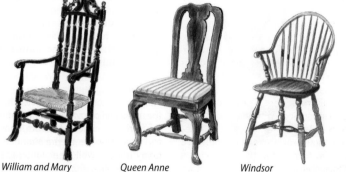

William and Mary   *Queen Anne*   *Windsor*

© R. Corbel / MICHELIN

Chippendale

© R. Corbel / MICHELIN

The **Goddard and Townsend** families of Newport, Rhode Island, were among the most celebrated cabinetmakers working in this style.

FEDERAL

Inspired by British architect **Robert Adam** and English cabinetmakers **George Hepplewhite** and **Thomas Sheraton**, the style that won favor from 1785 through 1815 is defined by light, straight lines and refined decoration: Veneers, inlay and marquetry in contrasting woods. The square, tapered leg—fluted, reeded or ending in a spade foot—is common. Cabinetmakers working in the Federal style included John and Thomas Seymour and John and Simeon Skillin of Boston.

EMPIRE

Imported from Europe, this heavy, massive style, popular from 1815 through 1840, was inspired by Greek and Egyptian antiquity. Bronze, gilt, winged and caryatid supports, lion's-paw feet, roll-back chairs, and sofas with upswept ends distinguish this style.

VICTORIAN

Furniture of the period between 1840 and the late 19C, inspired by a variety of styles including Gothic, Elizabethan, Renaissance and French Rococo, is heavy and ornate. Upholstered chairs and sofas are overstuffed, and velvet coverings are typical. Balloon-back and fiddleback chairs, and tables with marble tops were popular.

SHAKER FURNITURE

Produced primarily from 1800 until the middle of the 19C, Shaker chairs, tables and cupboards, simple and functional, are admired for their clean, pure lines and superb craftsmanship. Shaker chairs are recognized by their ladder backs, and seats made of rush, cane, splint or woven webbing.

FOLK ART

In rural New England, necessities for daily living were handmade by the farmers or by tradesmen who received a modest fee for their services. The tools, household utensils, cloth, weather vanes and furniture they produced revealed the tastes, flair and loving attention to detail of their creators. Today these items are admired for their charm, and for the picture of early rural American life they present.

QUILTS

Quilted bed coverings were essential during the long, cold New England winter. Often finished in a geometric or floral motif, the quilt became one of a rural household's few decorative accessories. Quilting had a pleasant social aspect as well: The **quilting bee**.

STENCILS

This early decorative technique, which uses paint and precut patterns to embellish furniture, implements, cloth, floors, and walls, brightened the interiors of many homes. Wall stenciling added color to the otherwise plain white plaster

Hepplewhite

© R. Corbel / MICHELIN

or wooden plank surfaces, and in the 19C it was a low-cost alternative to expensive imported wallpapers.

WEATHER VANES

When most New Englanders farmed or went to sea, weather vanes were important as indicators. The simple profile of a weather vane topped most buildings of any significant height. A weather vane made to crown a church spire might be in the shape of a cockerel or fish, the symbols of early Christianity. In rural areas the silhouette of a cow, horse or sheep rose above farm buildings, while along the coast, the whale, clipper ship and mermaid were popular. New England's famous grasshopper weather vane, atop the cupola of Boston's Faneuil Hall, has been the symbol of the port of Boston since the 18C.

FIGUREHEADS, TRADE SIGNS AND SHOP FIGURES

During the age of sailing, carvers sculpted figureheads, sternboards and other accessories for new vessels. Excellent examples of figureheads can be found in the maritime museums in Mystic, CT; New Bedford, andNantucket, MA, Penobscot, ME; and Shelburne, VT. Ship carvers also produced trade signs and shop figures. The streets of the Old Port Exchange in Portland are lined with such eye-catching signs.

GLASS

Until the mid-19C most glass manufactured in New England was for windows and glass containers. Handmade glassware was a luxury only a few could afford. However, Deming Jarves and his workmen at **Sandwich** made available, for the first time, attractive glassware at affordable prices. The factory at Sandwich became famous for pressed glass with lace patterns. Despite large-scale production of pressed glass, the art of glassblowing continued to thrive. Items varied from tableware to decorative art glass and may be seen at the Glass Museum in Sandwich, and at the Bennington Museum in Vermont.

SCRIMSHAW

Perfected by New England sailors in the 19C, scrimshaw, the art of etching the surface of the teeth or jawbone of a whale, or the tusks of a walrus, is considered by some the only art form indigenous to America. The tooth or tusk was allowed to dry, then the surface was polished with shark skin, and the picture or design to be etched was incised onto the bone with a jackknife or sail needles. Ink, soot or tobacco juice was applied for color. Exceptional scrimshaw collections can be found at the whaling museums in New Bedford and Nantucket, MA.

DECOYS

Wooden decoys sculpted and painted to resemble geese, ducks, shorebirds and waterfowl have been used since colonial times to lure birds within range of the hunter. By the 19C decoy-making had developed into an art form.

Craftsmen portrayed birds with increasing realism, taking into consideration the natural conditions where the decoys would be used. Craftsmen along the coast from Cape Cod to Maine still engage in producing these lures. The Shelburne Museum in Vermont owns a fine collection of over 1,000 decoys.

GRAVESTONES

The Puritans have left outstanding examples of the skill of their early stonecutters in the gravestones that stand in New England's old burial grounds. The designs were initially symbolic and plain. In the 17C the hourglass, sun, scythe, winged skull, hearts and cherubim (symbols for life, death and resurrection) were typical motifs. Throughout the 18C, realistic portraits and detailed scenes of the death of the deceased became popular. The romantic tendencies of the 19C were represented by extensive use of the weeping willow and the urn, classical symbols for death. The old cemeteries in Boston, Lexington, Newburyport and Salem (MA), and in New London (CT) and Newport (RI) contain splendid examples of gravestone art.

Literature

New England has been home to some of America's greatest writers, many of whom are laid to rest on Authors' Ridge at the Sleepy Hollow Cemetery in Concord, Massachusetts. The literature produced in the colonies in the 17C and 18C consisted primarily of histories and religious writings. The *History of Plimoth Plantation* by William Bradford, governor of Plimoth Plantation between 1621 and 1657, remains one of the principal records of this period.

COMING OF AGE

In the 19C a distinctly American literature emerged in New England. The transcendentalist movement gained popularity under the leadership of **Ralph Waldo Emerson** (1803-82). **Henry David Thoreau** (1817-62) recounts his life in the woods in *Walden* (1854). **Louisa May Alcott** (1832-88) became famous for her novel *Little Women*. Other writers included **Nathaniel Hawthorne** (1806-64), author of *The Scarlet Letter* (1850) and *The House of the Seven Gables*, and **Herman Melville** (1819-91), who wrote *Moby Dick* in 1851 while living in the Berkshires. Hartford resident **Mark Twain** (1835-1910) was a master of the new regional literature. His most popular works, *The Adventures of Tom Sawyer* (1876) and *Adventures of Huckleberry Finn* (1885), portrayed life on the Mississippi River. In 1828 **Noah Webster** (1758-1843), a native of New Haven, published the first *American Dictionary of the English Language*.

20C–21C

In the 20C the American theater won international acclaim through the works of playwright **Eugene O'Neill** (1888-1953). New England was the setting for his *Desire Under the Elms, Mourning Becomes Electra* and the Pulitzer Prize-winning *Beyond the Horizon*. Other New England authors include native-born John P. Marquand, Kenneth Roberts, William Dean Howells and Jack Kerouac as well as writers who adopted New England as their second home, including Edith Wharton, Pearl Buck, Norman Mailer and Alexander Solzhenitsyn. Harvard graduate **John Updike** (1932-2009), perhaps best known for his novels *Rabbit Run* and Pulitzer Prize-winning *Rabbit is Rich* (1981) and *Rabbit at Rest* (1990), moved to Ipswich in the 1960s. He used New England as the setting for much of his later fiction, including *The Witches of Eastwick* (1984). Best-selling author **Stephen King**, a master of the horror genre, was born in Portland. The prolific writer has used New England, and in particular Maine, as the background for many of his short stories and novels, such as *Salem's Lot*. Former New Hampshire resident Bill Bryson has attracted more attention to the popular Appalachian Trail with his humorous best-seller *A Walk in the Woods* (1998). Best-selling author Jodi Picoult (b. 1966) of Hanover, New Hampshire, specializes in emotionally-charged, topically-themed novels.

Several of her books are set in New England, including *Second Glance* (2003), *Salem Falls* (2001), and *Nineteen Minutes* (2007). The dark, gritty side of life in working-class Boston is explored by award-winning Boston-based author Dennis Lehane, (b. 1965). Lehane's crime thrillers are often made into movies, including *Mystic River* and *Shutter Island*.

POETRY

Henry Wadsworth Longfellow (1807-82), born in Portland, was one of the most widely read poets of his day. **Emily Dickinson** (1830-86), an Amherst resident, wrote verses rich in lyricism and sensitivity. Known for his poems about nature, **Robert Frost** (1874-1963) lived on a farm in New Hampshire from 1901 to 1909, and later spent his summers in Vermont.

The poetry of **ee Cummings** (1894-1962), a native of Cambridge, is distinguished by his unconventional use of typography and punctuation. Another New England-born poet whose work has made an impact on modern poetry is **Robert Lowell** (1917-77).

Nature

Framed by the White Mountains to the north and the Green Mountains to the west, New England's gently rolling hills and valleys taper off to an irregular rockbound coastline edged with sandy beaches to the south. Vast woodlands coupled with an extensive river and stream system complete the picture.

The region's major mountain ranges are remnants of higher peaks that were formed 300 million to 500 million years ago. Much younger in geologic age, the numerous ponds, lakes, U-shaped valleys and winding ridges owe their existence to the Laurentide ice sheet and associated glaciers that covered this portion of the North American continent until about 10,000 years ago.

GEOGRAPHIC FEATURES

APPALACHIAN MOUNTAINS

The Appalachians, extending about 1,600mi from Canada's St. Lawrence Valley to Alabama, form the spine of New England. Several parallel ranges with a primarily north-south orientation make up the northeastern Appalachian system.

THE WHITE MOUNTAINS

These once heavily glaciated mountains, characterized by rocky, cone-shaped summits and U-shaped valleys, claim the highest peak in the northeastern US: Mt. Washington (6,288ft).

THE GREEN MOUNTAINS

The most prominent peaks in Vermont form a north-south ridge through the center of the state. Composed of ancient metamorphic rocks, including Vermont's rich marble deposits, this mountain chain extends into Massachusetts, where it is known as the Berkshires.

THE TACONIC RANGE

Extending along the common border of New York and Massachusetts, and into southern Vermont, this range, comprised primarily of schist, includes Mt. Equinox in Vermont and Mt. Greylock in Massachusetts.

THE MONADNOCKS

Several isolated mountains, called monadnocks, the remnants of ancient crystalline rock more resistant to erosion than the surrounding rock strata, dominate the countryside. Mt. Monadnock in New Hampshire exemplifies this type of relief; its name has been adopted by geographers to describe similar formations found elsewhere. Other monadnocks include mounts Katahdin and Blue in Maine, mounts Cardigan and Kearsage in New Hampshire, and Mount Wachusetts in Massachusetts.

THE CONNECTICUT VALLEY

New England is bisected by this 400mi-long, north-south incision carved by the Connecticut River. The valley follows a fault that is punctuated by several craggy basalt ridges (mounts Sugarloaf and Holyoke) rising above the valley floor in Massachusetts and north of New Haven, Connecticut.

THE COAST

In the north the coast is jagged and indented, with countless peninsulas and bays and hundreds of offshore islands. Melting glacier waters, together with a rising sea level, inundated this land, hiding most of the glacial landforms

West Quoddy Head Lighthouse, Lubec, Maine

© Maine Office of Tourism

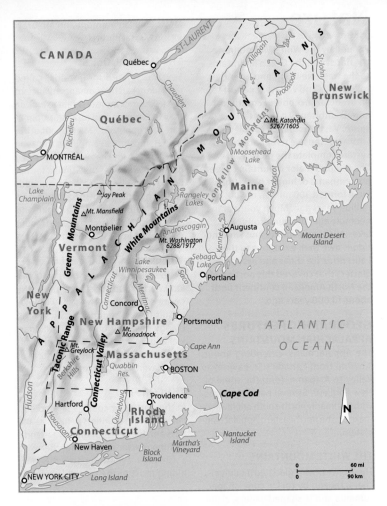

and creating a coastline of elongated bays and hundreds of offshore islands. South of Portland, Maine, the broad, flat coastal plain gives way to sandy beaches. The estuaries and lagoons of quiet water protected by barrier beaches have given rise to vast salt marshes that provide food and resting grounds for birds and waterfowl in the Atlantic Flyway. Farther south, enormous accumulations of sand cover the glacial moraines of Cape Cod and the islands, creating the landscape that typifies the Cape.

CLIMATE

Mark Twain once observed that "there is a sumptuous variety about the New England weather, that compels admiration—and regret... In the spring I have counted 136 different kinds of weather inside of 24 hours." This varied climate results from the fact that the region lies in a zone where cool, dry air from Canada meets warm, humid air from the southeast. Annual precipitation averages 42in, and the seasons are sharply defined.

Winter is cold, particularly in the north, where temperatures can range from −10°F to 10°F (−23°C to −12°C).

A pattern of hazy or foggy days alternating with showers and followed by clear weather characterizes the humid **summer**. Daytime temperatures peak at 90°F

(32°C); evenings are cool along the coast, in the mountains and near the lakes.

Autumn, with its sunny days and cool nights, is the season when "leaf lookers" inundate New England to view the spectacular fall foliage. A cool spell in late September is often followed by **Indian summer**, a milder period when the leaves take on their most brilliant color. Northeasters, coastal storms accompanied by high tides, heavy rain (or snow in winter) and gale-force winds, can occur at any time of year, especially off the coast of Maine.

VEGETATION

With more than 70 percent of the region's surface covered by woodlands, New England's landscape is appealing in the summer for its thick cover of green, and even more so in the fall for its blazing leaf colors. The forests consist of a combination of deciduous trees and evergreens. The most common deciduous trees are beech, birch, hickory, oak, and sugar or rock maple. Among the conifers, the white pine is found while hemlock, balsam fir and spruce forests abound in the north.

FALL FOLIAGE

Dramatic and unforgettable, the colorful New England foliage transforms the countryside into a palette of vivid golds (birches, poplars, gingkos), oranges (maples, hickories, mountain ash) and scarlets (red maples, red oaks, sassafras and dogwoods), framed by the dark points of spruce and fir trees. What makes the scene especially impressive are the flaming crimsons of the maple trees that cover New England. The Indian summer climate, with its crisp, clear sunny days followed by increasingly longer and colder nights, catalyzes the chemical reaction that halts the production of chlorophyll in the leaves, and causes the previously concealed pigments—yellowish carotene, brown tannin, and red anthocyanin—to appear.

Leaves begin to change color in the northern states in mid-September and continue to change until mid-October, and until late October farther south. However, the first two weeks in October remain the most glorious period, when bright color blankets the New England landscape. In all six states, information centers provide foliage reports by telephone. ⓘ*See MICHELIN DRIVING TOURS.*

SUGAR MAPLES

Capable of adapting to a cold climate and rocky soil, the sugar or rock maple is found throughout Vermont and New Hampshire. In early spring, when the sap begins to rise in the maple trees, farmers insert a tube, from which a bucket is suspended, into the trunk. The sap

Fall foliage near Mount Mansfield, Stowe, Vermont

© Andre Jenny / VermontVacation.com

Jack-in-the-Pulpit   *Aster*   *Wild Lupine*   *Lady's Slipper Orchid*

© R. Corbel/MICHELIN

that collects in the bucket is transferred to an evaporator in a nearby wooden shed called a sugarhouse, where it is boiled down into syrup. It takes about 40 gallons of sap to produce one gallon of syrup. Modern technology has simplified this process; now, plastic tubes lead directly from the tree to the sugarhouse. *Visitors can watch this process; see WHAT TO SEE AND DO/SHOPPING.*

MARSHES AND BOGS

Because of its glacial origin, the soil in New England is often swampy. Vast marshlands, distinguished by tall grasses and reedy plants, line the region's coast. Bogs are wetlands characterized by the high acid content of the soil. They support plants such as sedges, heaths, orchids, Labrador tea, sphagnum moss and, in low-lying sandy areas, cranberries. Dead matter that accumulates in the bog is prevented from decaying because of the acidic environment, and over a period of time this material is transformed into peat. Gradually the surface of the bog may be covered with a thick, soggy mat of sphagnum moss. Peat deposits will support trees and shrubs, and eventually vegetation will fill in the bog, converting it into dry, forested land.

WILDFLOWERS

By late spring the mantle of snow has almost disappeared and the flowers in the woods, along the roadside and in the fields and mountains burst into bloom. The magnificent **rhododendron** and **laurel** bushes lend pink accents to the dark green woods. During the summer the roadsides are alternately tinted with the orange of the flowering **Turk's-cap lily**, the yellow of the tall-stemmed **goldenrod**, the pale blue of the multitude of tiny **asters** and the purplish hue of broad, swaying patches of **lupine**. Maine's mountains and woods are filled with wild blueberries. Hundreds of species of more familiar wildflowers, including buttercups, daisies, sunflowers, Queen Anne's lace, and lily-of-the-valley, adorn the fields and grassy meadows. In moist, marshy areas, look for the delicate **lady's slipper**, a small pink or white member of the orchid family, and the greenish **Jack-in-the-pulpit**, so named because of the curved flap that gives the flower its appearance of a preacher in a pulpit.

WILDLIFE

There are virtually no forms of wildlife unique to New England, yet several species are typical of the region's fauna.

Rhododendron   *Turk's-Cap Lily*   *Mountain Laurel*   *Goldenrod*

© R. Corbel/MICHELIN

Forest near the Connecticut river, Cheshire County, New Hampshire

© NHDTTD / Jeffrey Newcomer

THE FORESTS

The **white-tailed deer**, characterized by its white, bushy tail, inhabits the northern spruce and fir forests together with **black bears** and **moose**. The region's largest mammal and the state animal of Maine, moose may be encountered in the middle of forest roads, along marsh lands and boggy areas. Outfitters in northern New Hampshire and Maine offer a variety of moose-watching excursions, including guided kayak, canoe, pontoon, seaplane, and bus trips. Greenville, Maine, near Moosehead Lake, hosts MooseMainea, a popular festival held each fall.

In ponds and streams, colonies of **beavers** toil, felling trees with their teeth to build dams. Their structures often create deep ponds or cause flooding in low-lying areas.

Among the other forest inhabitants are the masked **raccoon**, the **porcupine** with its protective bristly quills, the black-and-white-striped **skunk**, and the **red squirrel**. The **chipmunk**, a member of the squirrel family, is a small mammal that frequents settled areas as well as woodlands.

THE COAST

Seagulls and **terns** are ever-present along the coast, always searching for food on boats, on the beaches, in inlets and marshes and on the piers that line the waterfront. The **great cormorants** are larger in size and live principally on the rocky sea cliffs that they share with several species of seals.

Coastal marshes serve as the feeding and resting grounds for hundreds of species of birds. Located along the Atlantic Flyway, broad stretches of salt marshes, such as those west of Barnstable Harbor on Cape Cod, are frequented by large numbers of bird-watchers during the spring and fall migrations. Flocks of Canada geese, their graceful V-formation a familiar sight in the New England sky during migratory seasons, rest in these tranquil areas. Puffins have nesting and feeding grounds on northern Maine islands and bald eagles and hawks can be seen along the coastline. New England waters are home to a variety of species of **whale, dolphin** and **porpoises**. Whales migrate here to their feeding grounds at Stellwagen Bank, a 19-by-5-mile underwater plateau between Gloucester and Provincetown, Massachusetts, that is the centerpiece of the Stellwagen Bank National Marine Sanctuary. The region has been called one of the best places in the world to see whales in the wild. Several whale watching cruises sail from major towns along the coast, including Boston, Gloucester, Provincetown, Plymouth, Newburyport and Hyannis, Massachusetts; Portsmouth and Rye, New Hampshire; and Boothbay, Portland, and Bar Harbor, Maine.

Barn and horse in Vermont's Northeast Kingdom
© Dennis & Ellen Curran / VermontVacation.com

This rectangle—extending about 90mi east to west and 55mi north to south—bears the name of the river that divides it almost in half: the Connecticut, an Indian word meaning "beside the long tidal river." Small colonial villages scattered throughout the state offer a pleasing contrast to the densely populated, industrialized centers in the Hartford region and to the cities of Stamford, Bridgeport, Stratford, and New Haven on the south shore. The affluent communities in southwestern Connecticut's Fairfield County (Greenwich, Ridgefield, New Canaan) are, in essence, suburbs of New York City.

Highlights

1 Soaring through space on a flight simulator at the **New England Air Museum** (p92)

2 Browsing the nearly 50 antique shops in **historic Woodbury** (p94)

3 Following the **Art Trail** to 15 top museums and historic sites (p97)

4 Rafting Class-IV whitewater on the **Housatonic River** (p98)

5 Taking a carriage ride through the 19C village at **Mystic Seaport** (p99)

▶ **Population:** 3,518,288.

Info: ☎888-288-4748, www.ctvisit.com.
Area: 5,018sq mi.
Capital: Hartford.
Official Designation: The Constitution State.
Nickname: The Nutmeg State.
State Flower: Mountain laurel.

The Constitution State

Connecticut has multiple personalities. Travel from one end to the other and you'll pass a diverse collection of bustling cities and wealthy suburbs, tiny, time-forgotten villages and seaside towns. Much of the state remains rural; two-thirds of its woodlands are included in the state park and forest system. To the south, on the shores of Long Island Sound, sandy beaches separate the former whaling ports of New London, Mystic and Stonington. The idyllic Litchfield Hills, rising in the northern part of the state, are an extension of the Green Mountains and the Berkshire Hills. The area's first permanent settlers were staunch Puritans who found the atmos-

Mystic Seaport

© PhotoDisc, Inc

phere in Boston too liberal. They arrived from Massachusetts in 1633 by the Connecticut River and within two years had founded the towns of Hartford, Windsor, and Wethersfield. In 1638 these towns joined to form Hartford Colony, later to become Connecticut Colony. The **Fundamental Orders of Connecticut**, statutes drawn up and adopted on 14 January 1639, was the first constitution drafted in the New World—thus the state's nickname, the Constitution State.

Economy

Benefiting from the wide range of products developed by the state's inventors, Connecticut has traditionally been a prosperous manufacturing center. Connecticut clockmakers created one of the state's earliest industries and put a clock in almost every home in America. In the 19C the production of firearms became an important business. The Colt-45 revolver, developed by **Samuel Colt**, and the Winchester rifle were made in Connecticut. During the same period, **Eli Whitney** manufactured his revolutionary cotton gin in New Haven and introduced the use of standardized parts at his firearms factory nearby. Danbury became known for its hats, Torrington and Waterbury for brass items, and Meriden for its fine silverware.

Connecticut continues to obtain a great part of its income from manufacturing. The Electric Boat Division of General Dynamics at Groton builds submarines for the nation's fleet. A number of corporations (General Electric, Union Carbide, Xerox) and more than 100 insurance companies maintain headquarters in the state.

Locally marketed dairy products, poultry, and fruits and vegetables are major sources of agricultural income. Broadleaf tobacco, used for cigar wrapping, is shade-grown in the Connecticut and Farmington valleys.

Sports and Recreation

Connecticut has 137 state parks and forests, 800 miles of hiking trails, and 230 lakes and ponds. Hiking and nature walks are popular throughout the state.

Bear Mountain in Salisbury, that state's highest peak, is one of the most popular hiking destinations. Climb to the 2,136-foot summit for sweeping views of Connecticut's rolling mountains and picturesque lakes.

Top-notch hiking can be found in the expansive 24,000-acre Pachaug State Forest, Connecticut's largest state forest. Trails crisscross the woods, near waterfalls, cascades, river banks, ponds, and scenic lakes. The famed Appalachian Trail travels for 52 miles through Connecticut, much of it through the Litchfield Hills region.

Anglers will find plenty to like about Connecticut's well-stocked rivers and streams, including the Housatonic, considered one of the top fishing rivers in the Northeast. In spring, the Housatonic is also popular for exhilarating whitewater rafting. Local guides and outfitters are plentiful. Along the coast, you'll find a slew of boating, sailing and kayaking excursions.

Cultural Hubs

New Haven, home to prestigious Yale University, is the cultural hub of Connecticut. It boasts a cluster of top-notch museums, including the Yale University Art Gallery, Yale Center of British Art and the Yale Repertory Theater.

New Haven's Shubert Performing Arts Center hosts Broadway-bound productions, road shows and concerts. The New Haven Symphony Orchestra is considered one of the finest in the nation. Seaside Norwalk is the site of the annual SoNo Arts Celebration and home to the Aldrich Museum of Contemporary Art.

Lighthouses

The Connecticut coastline and Long Island Sound are dotted with historic lighthouses that offer a peek into the state's seafaring past. There are 17 lighthouses in Connecticut, including Sheffield Island Lighthouse in Norwalk, the Stamford Harbor Light, Mystic Lighthouse and Saybrook Breakwater. Lighthouses are best seen by boat; several narrated excursions are offered from towns along the coast.

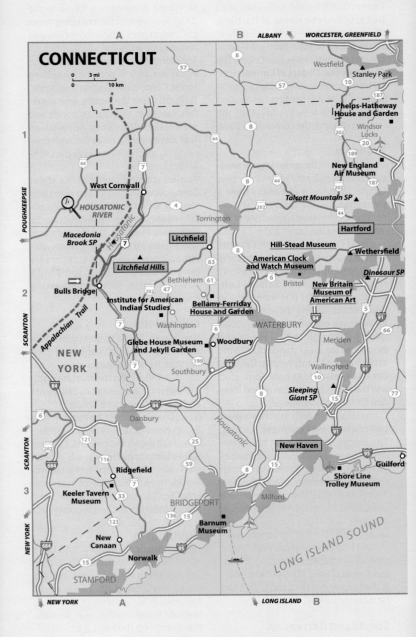

CONNECTICUT

ALBANY WORCESTER, GREENFIELD

Westfield

Stanley Park

Phelps-Hatheway House and Garden

Windsor Locks

New England Air Museum

Talcott Mountain SP

Torrington

Hartford

West Cornwall

HOUSATONIC RIVER

Macedonia Brook SP

Litchfield

Hill-Stead Museum

Wethersfield

Litchfield Hills

American Clock and Watch Museum

Dinosaur SP

Bethlehem

Bristol

New Britain Museum of American Art

Bulls Bridge

Institute for American Indian Studies

Bellamy-Ferriday House and Garden

Washington

WATERBURY

Meriden

Glebe House Museum and Jekyll Garden

Woodbury

Southbury

Wallingford

APPALACHIAN TRAIL

NEW YORK

Sleeping Giant SP

Danbury

Housatonic

New Haven

Ridgefield

Guilford

Shore Line Trolley Museum

Keeler Tavern Museum

BRIDGEPORT

Milford

Barnum Museum

New Canaan

Norwalk

STAMFORD

LONG ISLAND SOUND

NEW YORK

LONG ISLAND

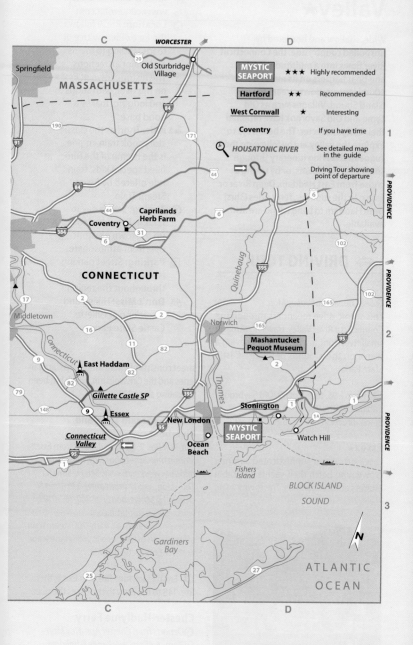

Springfield

MASSACHUSETTS

Old Sturbridge Village

MYSTIC SEAPORT ★★★ Highly recommended

Hartford ★★ Recommended

West Cornwall ★ Interesting

Coventry If you have time

HOUSATONIC RIVER See detailed map in the guide

Driving Tour showing point of departure

Caprilands Herb Farm

Coventry

CONNECTICUT

Middletown

Norwich

Mashantucket Pequot Museum

East Haddam

Gillette Castle SP

Essex

Stonington

New London

Connecticut Valley

MYSTIC SEAPORT

Ocean Beach

Watch Hill

Fishers Island

BLOCK ISLAND SOUND

Gardiners Bay

N

ATLANTIC OCEAN

PROVIDENCE

PROVIDENCE

PROVIDENCE

Connecticut Valley★

Wide, shallow and bordered by unspoiled countryside, the Connecticut River flows into a multitude of coves and boat harbors on its more than 400mi journey downstream to Long Island Sound. Villages such as Old Lyme and Old Saybrook have retained their early character. The best ways to explore the valley are by following the suggested driving itinerary through small riverside towns, or by taking a cruise from East Haddam, Deep River or Essex. In the summer, ferry rides (3hrs) from Haddam to Long Island are also available.

🚗 DRIVING TOUR

26mi.

See Connecticut Valley Map.
This scenic drive meanders through the Connecticut River Valley, traveling through small riverfront towns. Consider having a picnic on the grounds of Gilletre Castle State Park.

▶ From I-95, take Exit 69 (Old Saybrook), and follow Rte. 9 to Exit 3 in the direction of Essex.

Essex★

Essex attracts a sophisticated summer crowd who berth their yachts and cabin cruisers at local marinas. The town's main

Gillette Castle State Park
© Gwen Cannon / MICHELIN

- **Info:** 📞860-787-9640; www.centerofct.com.
- **Location:** Rte. 9 follows the Essex River with exit roads leading to towns and major attractions. The historic town of Essex on the river, with shops and lodging, makes a good base.
- **Kids:** Thomas the classic storybook train engine is the theme of the fun-filled special kids' train ride offered by Essex Steam Train.
- **Timing:** Save a day to relax in Essex and soak up the town's historic, riverfront atmosphere.
- **Parking:** Street parking is available in towns throughout the region.
- **Don't Miss:** Hiking and picnicking at Gillette Castle State Park.

street consists of interesting shops, art galleries and the Griswold Inn, which has been operating since 1776.

👫 Essex Steam Train and Riverboat

Exit 3 off Rte. 9. 🕐 *Train departs from Essex Station mid-Jun–Labor Day, daily May–mid-Jun, weekends only, Sep Fri-Sun Oct Thu–Mon.* 💲*$17 (train only), $26 (train & cruise).* 🅿️🍴*(riverboat).* 📞*860-767-0103; www.essexsteamtrain.com.*
Rides on the railroad's early-20C steam train afford views of the bucolic valley landscape and the Connecticut River.

▶ From Essex take Rte. 9 to Exit 6, then Rte. 148 to the ferry that crosses the river.

Chester-Hadlyme Ferry

🕐*Departs from Chester Apr–Nov Mon–Fri 7am–6.45pm, weekends & holidays 10.30am–5pm.* 🕐*Closed Thanksgiving Day. One-way 5min.* 💲*$3 (car & driver).* 📞*860-443-3856. www.ct.gov/dot.*

Goodspeed Opera House

© Robert Benson / Goodspeed Musicals

During the crossing there is a good view of Gillette Castle, perched high on a hilltop above the east bank.

▶ Take Rte. 148, then turn left, following signs for Gillette.

Gillette Castle State Park★

🕒 *Park open daily year-round 8am–dusk. Castle open Memorial Day–Columbus Day daily 10am–4.30pm.*
✕ 🎟 *$6. ☎860-526-2336. www.ct.gov/dep.*
The castles of the Rhine Valley inspired the design of this bizarre stone castle built in 1919 by actor **William Gillette**, who drew up the plans for the castle and decorated each of the 24 rooms himself.
Furniture that slides on metal tracks and other devices were developed by Gillette, who had a fascination for gadgetry.
The 190-acre estate offers splendid **vistas★** of the Connecticut River and the valley below. On the grounds you'll find picnic areas and hiking trails.

▶ Take Rte. 82 to East Haddam.

East Haddam

This small town with beautiful old homes is proud of its little red **schoolhouse** where Nathan Hale once taught, and of being the site

of the **Goodspeed Opera House**, a Victorian opera house dating from the era when New York-to-Connecticut steamers called at East Haddam. ☎*860-873-8668; www.goodspeed.org.*

▶ Follow Rte. 149, which offers good views of the river before turning northeast.

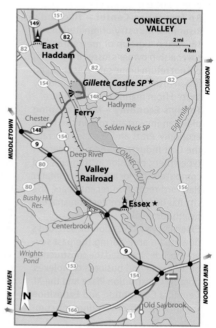

Hartford★★

Rising beside the Connecticut River, the state capital also bears the nickname "Insurance Capital of the Nation." The headquarters of several major insurance companies are located here. The downtown holds a tight cluster of skyscrapers, a sprawling convention center, an indoor shopping mall, several landmark buildings and some striking examples of 1980s architecture such as the One Corporate Center.

A BIT OF HISTORY

From Good Hope to Connecticut Colony – Hartford's location on a waterway navigable to the sea led the Dutch to establish a trading post, named Fort Good Hope, on this site in the early 17C. In the 1630s, the region's abundant supply of furs and timber attracted Puritans from the Massachusetts Bay Colony. Their village grew quickly, and in 1638 it joined with Wethersfield and Windsor to form **Hartford Colony**. In 1662 Hartford Colony joined New Haven Colony to become the Colony of Connecticut.

An Insurance Center – Hartford's insurance industry originated in the 18C when a group of men agreed to cover a ship owner's losses if his vessel did not return home safely. As shipping began to decline in the 19C, the industry shifted from marine to fire insurance.

Today's Economy – Manufacturing plays an important role in the city's economy. Pratt and Whitney Aircraft, the Colt Industries and producers of typewriters, precision instruments and computers are located in the Greater Hartford region. In recent years, the city has become a center for managed-health companies.

Extensive revitalization of Hartford's downtown area during the past several decades included the construction of shopping and business complexes, notably Constitution Plaza and the XL Center, a Convention and Exposition Center, and an entertainment complex, with shops and restaurants situated along the banks of the Connecticut River.

▶ **Population:** 124,512.
& **Map:** p87 and p88
▯ **Info:** ✆888-288-4748; www.ctvisit.com.
◗ **Location:** Bisected by east-west I-84/US6, the central core of the city lies off the west bank of the Connecticut River.
👥 **Kids:** Children will love the hands-on exhibits at the Connecticut Science Museum, as well as making plaster casts of dinosaur tracks at Dinosaur State Park.
🕐 **Timing:** After stopping in the Old State House (be sure to see the museum of curiosities), walk to the Wadsworth Atheneum and allow at least an hour to view the exhibits. An hour minimum is needed for the Mark Twain House.
🅿 **Parking:** Parking is available off Market St. opposite Constitution Plaza and behind it, off Columbus Blvd.
⊙ **Don't Miss:** Wadsworth Atheneum Museum of Art (especially the Wallace Nutting furniture collection) and the Mark Twain House.

DOWNTOWN

& *See Hartford Map.*

⊙ *A staffed visitor center is located a half-block south of the XL Center (31 Pratt St.). Downtown visitors can also obtain directions and information from the cadre of Hartford guides, recognizable by their red coats.*

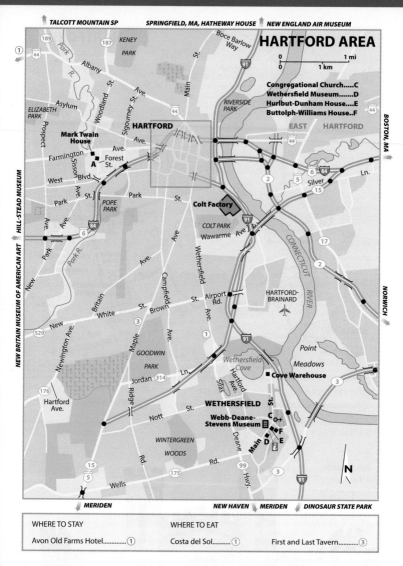

HARTFORD AREA

0   1 mi
0   1 km

Congregational Church.....C
Wethersfield Museum.......D
Hurlbut-Dunham House.....E
Buttolph-Williams House..F

WHERE TO STAY		WHERE TO EAT	
Avon Old Farms Hotel..............①		Costa del Sol...........①	First and Last Tavern.............③

XL Center

One Civic Center Plaza. ℘860-249-6333. www.xlcenter.com.

Completed in 1975, this concrete-and-glass structure is one of Hartford's premier entertainment venues. A pedestrian walkway links the center to City Place, designed by Skidmore, Owings and Merrill; exhibits and concerts are offered year-round in the atrium. Diagonally across from the XL Center, on Church Street, is the award-winning

Hartford Stage Company (℘860-527-5151; www.hartfordstage.org).

Old State House★

800 Main St. ♿ ⊙Mon–Fri 10am–5pm Jul–mid–Oct Tue–Sat 10am–5pm. ➧$6 ℘860-522-6766. www.ctoldstatehouse.org.

This elegant Federal-style building (1792) with its graceful staircases, arches, balustrades and classical pediments was designed by Charles Bulfinch, the archi-

87

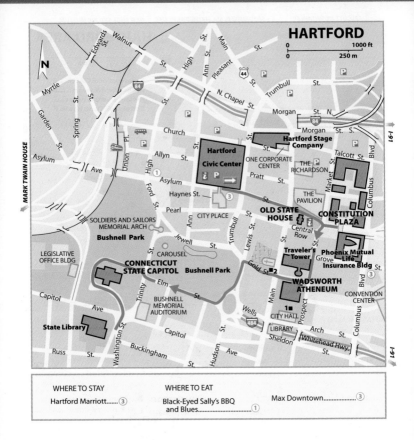

HARTFORD

0 — 1000 ft
0 — 250 m

WHERE TO STAY
Hartford Marriott....... ③

WHERE TO EAT
Black-Eyed Sally's BBQ
and Blues................................ ①

Max Downtown.................. ③

Wadsworth Atheneum Museum of Art

© Allen Phillips / Wadsworth Atheneum

The Charter Oak

The independence of the Hartford Colony was guaranteed by the Royal Charter of 1662. In 1687, however, the royal governor, Edmond Andros, demanded the return of the charter. According to legend, during a meeting that took place one evening to discuss the matter, someone fled with the document. The charter was hidden in an oak tree where it remained until Sir Edmond returned to England a few years later. The tree, which became known as the "Charter Oak", fell during a storm in the 19C. The original charter remains intact and is on display with the Fundamental Orders at the State Library (*231 Capitol Ave.*).

tect of the state houses of Maine and Massachusetts. Second-floor legislative chambers contain original furnishings; the Amistad trial began in the Senate chamber here. Don't miss the small Steward's Museum of Curiosities containing such oddities as a two-headed calf, also on the second floor.

Constitution Plaza★

Across from Old State House, bordered by Market St. and Columbus Blvd.
The modern 12-acre plaza completed in the 1960s provided Hartford with new office buildings, shops and an open mall, and added a striking landmark to the city's skyline: the **Phoenix Mutual Life Insurance Building**.
This elliptical, glass-sheathed tower is referred to as "the Boat" because of its shape. The plaza is the site of the **Hartford Festival of Light**, an annual lighting display held every evening from late November to the first of January.

Connecticut Science Center

250 Columbus Blvd. ✕♿🅿 ⏰Open daily Jul–Aug, 10am-5pm. Rest of the year Tue–Sun 10am–5pm . ⬒$19. ✆860 -724-3623. www.ctsciencecenter.org.
There are more than 150 exhibits that encourage visitors to touch, feel and think. You can test your own prototypes, build an invention, travel with polar bears to the ends of the earth and actually feel sound and hear light! The hands-on, interactive museum, which opened in June 2009, also has a state-of-the-art 3-D theater and a slew of daily programs and activities.

Wadsworth Atheneum Museum of Art★★

600 Main St. ✕♿⏰ Open Wed–Fri 11am–5pm, weekends 10am–5pm, and until 8pm the first Thu of each month. ⏰Closed Mon & Tue and major holidays. ⬒$10. ✆860-278-2670. www.thewadsworth.org.
Founded in 1842, this formidable museum, whose initial collection consisted of landscapes by such artists as John Trumbull, Frederic Church and Thomas Cole, now houses some 50,000 works spanning more than 5,000 years. In addition to paintings by the Hudson River school, highlights include European porcelain, 19C European paintings and the comprehensive Nutting collection of 17C American furniture.
Outside the museum stands the giant **Stegosaurus (1)** by **Alexander Calder**. Across from the Atheneum, note Carl Andre's controversial sculpture **Stone Field (2)**, a group of 36 boulders arranged in a geometrical pattern.

Connecticut State Capitol★

210 Capitol Ave. ✕♿🅿 ⏰Tours offered year-round, Mon–Fri 9.15am– 1.15pm, Sat (Apr–Oct) 10.15am–2.15pm ⏰Closed major holidays. ✆860-240- 0222. www.cga.ct.gov/capitoltours.
This array of turrets, finials, gables, porches and towers, designed by Richard Upjohn, was the talk of the town when it was built in 1879. Rising above heavily sculpted walls, the capitol's golden dome overlooks **Bushnell Park**, originally designed by Frederick Law Olmsted. The elaborate stenciling, painted columns, courtyards, stained-

glass windows, marble floors and balconies of the interior are stunning.

State Library

231 Capitol Ave. &🕐*Open year-round Tue–Fri 9am–5pm, Sat 9am–2pm.* 🕐*Closed major holidays.* ✆*860-757-6500. www.cslib.org.*
This building, across from the capitol, houses the State Library (*east wing*), the state's Supreme Court (*west wing*) and the State Museum (*center;* 🕐*open Mon–Fri 9am–4pm; Sat 9am–2pm*). Museum exhibits include Colt firearms, revolving displays of Connecticut history and the original **Fundamental Orders of Connecticut**.

ADDITIONAL SIGHTS
&*See Hartford Area Map.*

Mark Twain House★★

351 Farmington Ave. From downtown Hartford, take I-84 west to Exit 46. Turn right on Sisson Ave., then right on Farmington. ☛*Visit by guided tour (1hr) only.* P🕐*Open Mon–Sat 9.30am–5.30pm, Sun noon–5.30pm;* 🕐*Closed major holidays and Tue Jan–Mar.* ☞*$16.* ✆*860-247-0998. www.marktwainhouse.org.*
This Stick-style house, commissioned by Twain in 1874, was one of the Victorian dwellings that stood on **Nook Farm**, a "nook" of woodlands beside the north branch of the Park River. In the 19C a community of writers lived in this pastoral setting, including Twain and Harriet Beecher Stowe. Outside, open porches, balconies, towers and steeply pitched roofs give the structure an irregular shape. Silver stenciling, carved woodwork and elaborate wall coverings adorn the inside. During his residency in this house (1874–91), Twain wrote seven of his most successful works, including *The Adventures of Tom Sawyer* (1876) and *The Adventures of Huckleberry Finn* (1884).

Harriet Beecher Stowe Center (A)

77 Forest St. House tours (☞$8) P 🕐*Open Wed–Fri 9.30am–4.30pm, Sat 9.30am–5.30pm, Sun noon–5.30pm House tours (☞$10)* 🕐*Closed Mon–Tue & major holidays.* ✆*860-522-9258. www.harrietbeecherstowecenter.org.*
This simple 1871 Victorian cottage was home to writer **Harriet Beecher Stowe** (1811–96) from 1873 until her death. Stowe, whose 1852 book *Uncle Tom's Cabin* served to solidify Northern feelings against slavery, also wrote several novels about New England. The airy interior contains Stowe family furnishings and memorabilia. Next door is the handsome Katharine Seymour Day House (also featured on the tour), which contains the Nook Farm research library and changing exhibits. Day was Stowe's grandniece and a prime force in preserving the farm's structures. The site also includes a Visitor Center with the museum store, historic gardens and Stowe's Nook Farm neighborhood.

EXCURSIONS
Wethersfield★
▷*5mi south of Hartford via I-91.*
&*See WETHERSFIELD.*

Mark Twain

Among America's best-loved authors and humorists, Mark Twain (1835–1910) gave voice through his writings to the burgeoning culture of America's heartland. Born Samuel Langhorne Clemens in Florida, Missouri, Twain moved with his family to the Mississippi River town of Hannibal, Missouri when he was four years old. Here the young Twain was bewitched by the river life, which he brought to life so artfully in his most famous works, *The Adventures of Tom Sawyer* (1876) and *The Adventures of Huckleberry Finn* (1884). As an adult, the high-spirited and good-natured individualist smoked 20 cigars a day, slept backward in his bed in order to face its carved headboard, and did most of his best writing in the Billiard Room of his Hartford home.

Mark Twain House

© John Groo / The Mark Twain House & Museum

👥 Dinosaur State Park★

▶10mi south of Hartford, in Rocky Hill. 400 West St. Take I-91 North to Exit 23; turn left onto West St. at the light. ♿🅿️🕐Park open year-round daily 9am–4.30pm. Exhibits open Tue–Sun 9am–4.30pm. 🕐Closed major holidays. 💰$6. 📞860-529-8423. www.dinosaurstatepark.org.

The park offers a good opportunity to observe, intact and at their original site, more than 500 dinosaur tracks. A full-scale model of Dilophosaurus, the dinosaur considered the best match for these tracks, and a model of Coelophysis, some skeletal remains of which have been found in the Connecticut Valley, are part of the exhibit. A geodesic dome protects the excavated site and accompanying displays. In the casting area, visitors may make plaster casts of actual tracks (🕐open May–Oct daily 9am–3.30pm; visitors must provide their own materials; call for information).

Hill-Stead Museum★

▶35 Mountain Rd., in Farmington. 🅿️🕐Open Tue–Sun 10am–4pm. 🕐Closed Mon & major holidays. 💰$12. 📞860-677-4787. www.hillstead.org.

In 1900 Theodate Pope, one of America's early female architects, helped design this Colonial Revival country house for her father, Cleveland iron industrialist Alfred Atmore Pope. Pope's passion for Impressionist art led him to purchase a large number of the works displayed here, notably fine paintings by Monet, Manet, Degas and several canvases by Whistler and Mary Cassatt. The centerpiece of the 152-acre grounds is the sunken garden, designed c.1920 by Beatrix Jones Farrand.

New Britain Museum of American Art★

▶15mi southwest of Hartford, in New Britain. 56 Lexington St. ♿🕐Open year-round Tue–Fri 11am–5pm (Thu until 8pm), Sat 10am–5pm, Sun noon–5pm. 🕐Closed Mon & major holidays. 💰$12. 📞860-229-0257. www.nbmaa.org.

The holdings of this small museum illustrate trends in American art from the colonial period to the present.

The 18C portraitists (Trumbull, Stuart, Smibert), the Hudson River school, the eight artists of the Ashcan school (including Sloan, Henri, Luks), and such renowned 19C and 20C masters as Homer, Whistler, Wyeth and Cassatt dominate the collection.

Talcott Mountain State Park

▶8mi northwest of Hartford. Leave Hartford on Rte. 189, then follow Rte. 185 to park entrance. 🅿️🕐Grounds open year-round daily 8am–dusk. Tower open mid-May–Aug Thu–Sun 10am–5pm. 📞860-242-1158. www.ct.gov/dep.

The park is noted for a trail (1.5mi) that leads up to the 165ft-high Heublein

Nathan Hale Homestead

© Connecticut Landmarks

Nathan Hale

The small town of **Coventry** in rural northeastern Connecticut was the birthplace of the American patriot **Nathan Hale** (1755–76). During the Revolutionary War, he volunteered for the perilous mission of gathering intelligence about the British troops on Long Island. Young Hale was discovered by the British and hanged as a spy on 22 September, 1776. The last words he spoke on the scaffold, "I only regret that I have but one life to lose for my country," are among the most memorable in American history.

Today the **Nathan Hale Homestead** (*23mi east of Hartford in Coventry; 2299 South St.;* 🅿 🕑*open May–mid-Oct Wed–Sun 1pm–4pm;* 🕑*Closed major holidays;* 🎟*$7;* 📞*860-742-6917; www.ctlandmarks.org*) stands on the site of the home where Hale was born. A variety of tours are offered.

Tower. From the top of the tower there are sweeping **views★** across the Farmington Valley to Hartford and south to Long Island Sound.

👥 New England Air Museum

▶ *14mi northeast of Hartford, in Windsor Locks. On the grounds of Bradley International Airport. Take I-91 North to Exit 40 (Rte. 20 West), then right on Rte. 75 North for 3mi.* ♿🕑*Open year-round daily 10am–5pm.* 🕑*Closed major holidays.*🎟*$12.* 📞*860-623-3305. www.neam.org.*

Located in two spacious hangars on the west side of Bradley airport, the museum displays some 70 aircraft that trace the history of aviation, including a 1909 Bieriot XI, one of the first to be produced on a broad scale.

Kids will enjoy hopping inside the cockpit of an airplane and riding the Dreamseeker—the Museum's full-motion simulator.

Phelps-Hatheway House & Garden

▶ *18mi north of Hartford, in Suffield. Take I-91 North to Rte. 20 West, then Rte. 75 North. 55 S. Main St.* 🚶*Visit by guided tour (1hr) only,* 🕑*May–Oct Sat–Sun 1pm–4pm.* 🕑*Closed major holidays.* 🎟*$7.* 📞*860-668-0055. www.ctlandmarks.org.*

The house, actually three structures in one, owes its present size to Oliver Phelps, a merchant and land speculator who acquired the property in 1788. Phelps enlarged the main section of the house ((c.1760) by adding a single-story structure to the south end. About 1795 Phelps had the Federal-style north wing built. The central section is simple and functional, furnished with William and Mary and Queen Anne pieces. In contrast, the Federal wing is elegant, decorated with Adamesque ornamentation and fine Hepplewhite, Sheraton and Chippendale furnishings.

ADDRESSES

🏨 STAY

$$$ Avon Old Farms Hotel – *279 Avon Mountain Rd., Avon. ☎860-677-1651. www.avonoldfarmshotel.com. 160 rooms.* **Restaurant.** Down the road from the Hill-Stead Museum, this attractive hotel features rooms ranging from motor-inn basic to country-inn luxury. Setting the tone are 400 local artists' watercolors depicting the Farmington River Valley, a three-story staircase worthy of Scarlett O'Hara, and an enchanting restaurant-in-the-round overlooking a mountain stream. An English-style pub, health club, pool and 20 acres of woods, trails and gardens round out the facilities.

$$$ Hartford Marriott – *200 Columbus Rd. (next to Convention Center), Hartford. ☎860-249-8000 or 866-373-9806. www.marriott.com/hotels/travel/bdldt-hartford-marriott-downtown. 401 rooms & 8 suites.* This contemporary hotel, connected to the Convention Center, draws plenty of business travellers, but its spacious rooms and central Connecticut location are also convenient for families and leisure travelers. Plain Jane rooms are super quiet (lots of soundproofing!) with neutral palettes, a work area, flat screen TVs, CD players, and Wi-Fi. Marble, modern bathrooms are a plus, as is the on-site fitness center and full-service spa, on the 22nd floor; the perfect place to wind down and relax after a day of sightseeing. The lobby lounge and **Crush**, the hotel bar, are popular hangouts, too.

🍽 EAT

$$$ Max Downtown – *185 Asylum St., Hartford. ☎860-522-2530. www.max restaurantgroup.com. Reservations recommended.* **Continental.** The flagship of Hartford-area restaurant impresario Rich Rosenthal, Max Downtown is the place for chophouse classics, creative New American fare (sourdough-crusted cod, rosemary-braised lamb shank and roasted chicken with gorgonzola mac-and-cheese), The restaurant is also known for its top-quality steaks. With city-sleek decor, streetside windows and a stunning three-wall mural, there's ample food for the eye as well.

$$$ Costa del Sol – *901 Wethersfield Ave., Hartford. Closed Mon. ☎860-296-1714. www.costadelsolrestaurant.com.* **Spanish.** This long-standing and beloved eatery has brought the taste of Spain to downtown Hartford for more than 20 years. The family-owned restaurant features traditional and updated Spanish cuisine. Start with the Mediterranean fish and mussel soup or traditional tapas, like the grilled squid, Galician style octopus or the Iberica plate with chorizo, serrano ham and manchego cheese. Signature dishes include the paella for two (including a vegetarian offering) and the house-cured codfish.

$$ Black-eyed Sally's Bar-B-Que & Blues – *350 Asylum St., Hartford. ☎860-278-7427. www.blackeyedsallys.com.* **Southern.** Hartford's take on a Memphis juke joint, Sally's offers an authentic Southern dining experience, complete with colorful Southern folk art on the walls, a velvet Elvis above the bar, and live jazz and blues that keep the joint jumpin' into the wee hours most nights. Fare is down-home delicious, from the signature fallin'-off-the-bone ribs to fried okra and pickle chips to jambalaya and cornmeal-crusted catfish, accompanied by corn bread and collard greens. For dessert, what else but bourbon pecan pie and Mississippi mud pie?

$ First and Last Tavern – *939 Maple Ave., Hartford. ☎860-956-6000. www.first andlasttavern.com.* **Italian.** Think *Cheers*, add Italian comfort food and you'll have a sense of this beloved more than 70-year-old tavern in Hartford's Little Italy, with its warm family atmosphere and friendly staff. Unpretentious fare ranges from superior brick-oven breads and pizza to the original house special spaghetti with meatball, sausage and salad (all served on the same plate). Save room for the homemade cannoli bread pudding or, for true pizza aficionados, apple or cherry pie pizza.

Litchfield Hills★★

The area known as the Litchfield Hills, situated in Connecticut's northwest territory just south of Massachusetts' Berkshire Hills, covers some 1,000sq mi of countryside and woodland—much of it preserved as state parks and wildlife sanctuaries. Some 30-odd towns, such as Litchfield, Norfolk, Woodbury and Washington, distinguished by pristinely preserved main streets and 18C homes, dot the region. Comely country inns and B&Bs, antique shops, art galleries and craft stores greet visitors to this tranquil corner of New England. The broad Housatonic River quietly traverses the thickly wooded and hilly extreme northwest section of Connecticut, between the foothills of the Taconic Mountains and the Berkshire Hills. The beauty of Housatonic Valley and its proximity to New York have made Litchfield Hills a favorite destination for artists, writers and tourists.

Michelin Map: 581 H, I 9, 10

Info: ℰ800-663-1273; www.litchfieldhills.com.

Location: Rte. 7 is the major access road running north-south through the region. Base yourself in one of the popular, scenic towns, like Woodbury, or Litchfield, for easy day trips.

Kids: Kayak or canoe the Housatonic River.

Timing: Allow a day to poke around Woodbury and browse shops, and another day to explore Litchfield.

Parking: Street parking is available in towns throughout the region, and near state parks and nature centers.

Don't Miss: The beautiful White Memorial Foundation Wildlife Sanctuary.

Also See: CONNECTICUT RIVER VALLEY.

LITCHFIELD★★

A photographer's paradise in Indian summer when the trees flame with color, Litchfield is a small, reserved New England village with broad streets and stately 18C clapboard dwellings.

In the 19C, both the railroad and industrial development bypassed the center of town, a fact that accounts for Litchfield having one of the loveliest and best-preserved ensembles of early-American architecture in Connecticut.

The Green

North, South, East and West Streets meet at the green, which is dominated by Litchfield's **First Congregational Church**. Nearby, the **Litchfield History Museum★** organizes exhibits related to early life in the town (*7 South St.;* ⟨Ġ⟩ *open mid-Apr–Nov Tue–Sat 11am–5pm, Sun 1pm–5pm;* ⟨⟩*$5;* ℰ*860-567-4501; www.litchfieldhistoricalsociety.org*). Many handsome dwellings can be

Antiquing in Woodbury

Settled in 1673, Woodbury ranks as an antiquarian treasure. But antiquers prize it most for the more than 45 18C and 19C houses lining Main Street *(Rte. 6)*, which double as quality antiques emporia. Among the most highly regarded dealers are **Charles Haver Antiques**, for country furniture and period lighting; **Thomas Schwenke**, for Federal pieces; **G. Sergeant**, for English and Continental antiques; **Woodbury Antiques & Fine Arts**, for 18C and19C American and British furniture; **Joel Einhorn**, for American clocks, maps, toys and ship paintings; and **Monique Shay**, for French-Canadian painted pieces.

found along **North Street** and **South Street**; most are privately owned and are accessible to the public only during the historic homes tour in mid-July.

White Memorial Foundation Wildlife Sanctuary★

80 Whitehall Rd., 2.5mi west of Litchfield center via Rte. 202 West. 🅿 🕐*Grounds open daily year-round.* ℘*860-567-0857. www.whitememorialcc.org.*

This 4,000-acre preserve is owned and operated by the White Memorial Foundation. A map of the hiking trails and historic buildings may be purchased on the grounds at the museum (🕐*open year-round Mon–Sat 9am–5pm, Sun noon–5pm;* 🕐*closed major holidays;* ⊗*$6) or at the Foundation office.*

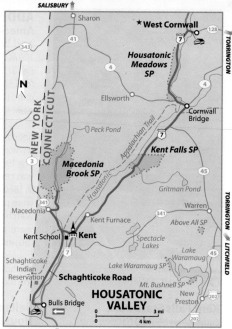

🚗 DRIVING TOUR

24mi.

This itinerary along the river follows Rte. 7, once a major route linking Montreal and New York City, from Bulls Bridge along the Housatonic River north to West Cornwall. Three state parks are included as well as Kent and West Cornwall.

▶ Begin at Bulls Bridge, 3mi north of Gaylordsville on US-7. Turn left onto Bulls Bridge Rd., which crosses a covered bridge and the Housatonic River. After crossing a second bridge, turn right onto Schaghticoke Rd.

Schaghticoke Road

🚶*The first mile of this narrow road is largely unpaved.*

The road follows the river as it winds through wooded terrain that is offset by patches of gnarled ledges and rock formations bordering the riverbed. After

1mi, the road arrives at the **Schaghticoke Indian Reservation** and passes an old Indian burial ground. The road also passes the buildings of **Kent School**, a prestigious private secondary school.

▶ Turn left onto Rte. 341; go north (1mi) to Macedonia; then right and follow signs to Macedonia Brook State Park.

Macedonia Brook State Park

Off Rte. 341, 4mi north of Kent in Macedonia. ⛺ 🅿 *(seasonal)* 🕐*Open year-round daily 8am–dusk.* ℘*860-927-3238. www.ct.gov/dep.*

With its rocky gorge, streams and web of trails, this state park offers recreation galore in the form of camping, fishing and hiking.

▶ Take Rte. 341 South back to Kent.

Kent

Nestled among the hills bordering the Housatonic River, Kent is the home of artists and craftspeople whose works are often displayed in shops in the village center.

Covered bridge in West Cornwall

▶ Follow US-7 North.

Kent Falls State Park
Entrance on US-7. 🅿🕐*Open year-round daily 8am–dusk.* ☜*$15/car on weekends & holidays.* ✆*860-927-3238. www.ct.gov/dep.*
To view the falls from above, climb the steps to the right of the falls. From this vantage point, you can cross the bridge and descend to the parking lot by following a path through the woods. North of Kent Falls, Rte. 7 passes through the hamlet of **Cornwall Bridge**, where the local general store is a welcome sight to hikers on the Appalachian Trail.

Housatonic Meadows State Park
Entrance on US-7, 1mi north of Cornwall Bridge. 🅿🕐*Open year-round daily 8am–dusk.* ✆*860-927-3238. www.ct.gov/dep.*
The Pine Knob Loop Trail ☜ (round-trip 2hrs from the parking lot on the west side of US-7) leads to the summit of Pine Knob (1,160ft) where there are views across the Housatonic Valley.

▶ Head N on US-7 to West Cornwall.

West Cornwall★
This tiny village is known for its pictur-esque covered bridge, built in 1864.

ADDITIONAL SIGHTS
American Clock and Watch Museum★
100 Maple St., Bristol. Take I-84 East to Exit 31. Follow Rte. 229 North to the right for 5.5mi. Turn left on Woodland St. and follow signs. 🅿🕐*Open Apr–Nov daily 10am–5pm. Winter by chance or appointment.*🕐*Closed major holidays.*☜*$6.* ✆*860-583-6070. www.clockandwatchmuseum.org.*
The 19C America's clockmaking industry was centered in the Bristol area, where in 1860 alone, more than 200,000 clocks were produced. Most of the clocks and watches in the museum's collection were produced in Connecticut. The museum and its research library are housed in the 1801 home of Miles Lewis, the historic Ebenezer Barnes wing and the modern Edward Ingraham wing.

Bellamy-Ferriday House and Garden★
9 Main St. North, Bethlehem (at the intersection of Rtes. 61 & 132). ☜*Visit by guided tour (45min) only,* 🅿🕐*Open mid May–mid Oct Wed, Fri & weekends 11am–4pm.* 🕐*Closed major holidays.* ☜*$7.* ✆*203-266-7596. www.ctlandmarks.org.*

Bellamy-Ferriday House and Garden

Connecticut Impressionist Art Trail

Follow the Art Trail (*www.arttrail.org*) to sites showcasing American painters.

Bruce Museum – *One Museum Dr., Greenwich.* ✆*203-869-0376. www.brucemuseum.org.* Represents several artists who painted in Cos Cob and Greenwich, an area particularly important to the development of the American Impressionist movement.

Bush-Holley House Museum – *39 Strickland Rd., Cos Cob.* ✆*203-869-6899. www.hstg.org.* Takes visitors back to the 19C, when this Colonial saltbox was a gathering place for Hassam, Twachtman and others.

Weir Farm National Historic Site – *735 Nod Hill Rd., Wilton.* ✆*203-834-1896. www.nps.gov/wefa.* Preserves the bucolic landscapes that inspired American Impressionist J. Alden Weir.

Yale University Art Gallery & **Yale Center for British Art** – *1111 Chapel St., New Haven.* ✆*203-432-0600.* ◔*See NEW HAVEN.*

Aldrich Contemporary Art Museum – *258 Main St., Ridgefield.* ✆*203-438-4519. www.aldrichart.org.* The innovative museum is known for presenting the works of emerging artists.

Florence Griswold Museum – *96 Lyme St., Old Lyme.* ✆*860-434-5542. www.florencegriswoldmuseum.org.* Presents the studio of William Chadwick and a collection of works by artists belonging to the famous 19C Lyme art colony.

Lyman Allyn Art Museum – *625 Williams St., New London.* ✆*860-443-2545.* ◔*See NEW LONDON.*

William Benton Museum of Art – *University of Connecticut at Storrs.* ✆*860-486-4520.* Showcases works by Emil Carlsen, Mary Cassatt, J. Alden Weir and more.

Wadsworth Atheneum of Art – *600 Main St., Hartford.* ✆*860-278-2670.* ◔*See HARTFORD.*

Hill-Stead Museum – *35 Mountain Rd., Farmington.* ✆*860-677-4787.* ◔*See HARTFORD/Excursions.*

New Britain Museum of American Art – *56 Lexington St., New Britain.* ✆*860-229-0257.* ◔*See HARTFORD/Excursions.*

Mattatuck Museum – *144 W Main St., Waterbury.* ✆*203-753-0381.* The state's only museum devoted exclusively to Connecticut history and artists.

Located on the village green, this two-story Georgian-style clapboard house, graced with a Palladian portico, was built c.1745 and enlarged and embellished over the next 200 years. Dotted with white barns and orchards, the grounds feature a 1912 garden where lilacs, peonies, magnolias and roses bloom in season.

Institute for American Indian Studies

38 Curtis Rd., Washington Depot. Take Rte. 199 South 2mi to Curtis Rd. and follow signs to the institute. ◔*Open year-round Mon–Sat 10am–5pm, Sun noon–5pm.* ◔*Closed major holidays.* ☞*$5.* ✆*860-868-0518. www.iaismuseum.org.*

This small museum in a peaceful woodland setting honors the culture and history of Connecticut Indians. Exhibits include archaeological artifacts, handcrafted splint baskets and a longhouse room. Outside, a short nature trail leads to a re-created Algonquin encampment, complete with a longhouse and several **wigwams**.

Glebe House Museum and Jekyll Garden

149 Hollow Rd. off Rte. 6, Woodbury. 🅿
🕐*Open May–Oct Wed–Sun 1pm–4pm. Nov weekends 1pm–4pm.* 🎟*$5.* 📞*203-263-2855. www.theglebehouse.org.*
In 1783 a group of Anglican clergy met here and elected Samuel Seabury (1729–96) the first bishop in the colonies. Considered the birthplace of the Episcopal Church in this country, the restored c.1750 gambrel-roof dwelling built on a **glebe** (land set aside for the parish priest) reflects the Revolutionary period.

ADDRESSES

🛏STAY

$$$$$ The Mayflower Inn – *118 Woodbury Rd. (Rte. 47), Washington Depot.* 📞*860-868-9466. www.mayflowerinn.com. 30 rooms.* **Restaurant.** This New England inn has been dramatically reinvented as a grand English-style country house, and has been accepted into the prestigious Relais & Châteaux group. Inside, you'll be surrounded by fine art and antiques; outside, you'll find a Shakespearean garden, bocce court and pool, all on 58 wooded acres. There's also a well-regarded, full-service spa on-site.

$$ Heritage Hotel – *522 Heritage Rd., Southbury.* 📞*203-264-8200 or 800-932-3466. www.heritagesouthbury.com. 183 rooms.* **Restaurant.** In a beautifully landscaped setting overlooking the Pomperaug River, this contemporary country resort has a health club, indoor and outdoor pools, tennis and racquetball courts, a nine-hole golf course and cross-country ski trails. Spacious rooms with river or golf course views sport country decor.

🍽EAT

$$$ Carole Peck's Good News Café – *694 Main St. S. (Rte. 6), Woodbury. Closed Tue.* 📞*203-266-4663. www.good-news-cafe.com.* **American.** The atmosphere is funky and fun (art exhibits vie for space with Peck's antique radios); the menu is creative. Combining fresh, local (often organic) ingredients in original ways, Peck is known for her crispy onion bundles, pecan-crusted oysters, and inspired desserts.

$$$ West Street Grill – *43 West Street, on the green, Litchfield.* 📞*860-567-3885. www.weststreetgrill.com.* **American.** Not only the place to see and be seen, this stylish restaurant is also the place for excellent, often ahead-of-the-curve New American cuisine. Best of show are the spicy, crab-stuffed avocado, homemade ravioli and fresh seafood dishes.

$$ Village Restaurant – *43 West St., Litchfield. Closed Mon.* 📞*860-567-8307. www.village-litchfield.com.* **American.** This intimate neighborhood eatery is a favorite among visitors and locals alike. The menu features a handful of daily specials, like sautéed red snapper, burgundy marinated lamb and handmade lobster ravioli. Classic desserts such as bannoffee pie, key lime pie and apple crisp are an indulgent way to finish your meal.

STOPS EN-ROUTE

White Flower Farm – *Rte. 63, 3mi south of Litchfield.* 📞*800-503-9624. www.whiteflowerfarm.com.* Exploring this quintessential Connecticut landscape of tree-shaded lanes, meadows and perennial gardens is more like visiting a botanical park than a working nursery. Highlights of the self-guided walking tour are the rose arbor, a spring cottage garden, and a greenhouse display of lush tuberous begonias.

Hickory Stick Bookshop – *At the junction of Rtes. 47 & 109, in Washington.* 📞*860-868-0525. www.hickorystick bookshop.com.* Although one of the many nationally known authors living in Litchfield Hills—which have included Philip Roth and Arthur Miller—might be on hand for a signing, the real draw at this bookstore is the vast selection of current books.

RECREATION

April is the time to shoot the rapids on the Housatonic River. Just when the waters are wildest, trained guides from **Clarke Outdoors** (*163 US-7, West Cornwall;* 📞*860-672-6365; www.clarkeoutdoors. com*) offer class IV-V whitewater rafting trips through the Bulls Bridge Gorge *(call for reservations)*. For a calmer paddle in summer or fall, rent a canoe or kayak and travel a 6mi stretch of flat water.

Mystic★★★

The village of Mystic, on the Mystic River, has been a shipbuilding center since the 17C. Today Mystic (population 4,000) is known primarily as the site of Mystic Seaport, an interpretive museum that re-creates the atmosphere of America's maritime past. This living replica of a 19C waterfront community features tall ships, a village center and a working shipyard, all of which add to the authenticity of the setting. Museum buildings house extensive collections of marine art and artifacts, providing visitors with insight into America's seagoing past.

- **Michelin Map:** 581 L 11
- **Info:** ℘860-536-8822; www.mystic.org.
- **Location:** Mystic sits on the Connecticut waterfront, easily accessed by north-south I-95 and east-west I-91.
- **Kids:** Youngsters will enjoy the many attractions of **Mystic Seaport**, with child-size fishing boats and a large aquarium.
- **Timing:** Allow at least a day to tour the Mystic Seaport museum and another to explore the surrounding area.
- **Parking:** There is metered parking on the street and ample parking is available at the Mystic Seaport.
- **Don't Miss:** The waterfront area at Mystic Seaport museum, filled with 19C shops.
- **Also See:** NEW LONDON.

MYSTIC SEAPORT

From I-95 Exit 90, follow Rte. 27 south.
✕ P ◷ *Open daily 9am–5pm.* ◷*Closed Jan 2–Mar.* ⊜$24 good for two day if used within 7 days of validation. ℘860-572-5302 or 888-973-2767. www.mysticseaport.org.

The museum has grown from a collection of nautical memorabilia displayed in a renovated mill to a complex of some 60 buildings covering 17 acres, formerly the site of timber ponds and shipbuilding yards. In 1978 the name Mystic Seaport was adopted and today the popular attraction is maintained as a private, nonprofit educational facility.

The **waterfront** is lined with wharves and adjacent streets where shops and businesses commonly found in a 19C seaport abound. Three such tall ships and a vintage steamboat are moored at the waterfront. In addition, Mystic

Mystic Seaport 19C village

© Mystic Seaport

The Nutmeg State

In the 1830s a series of essays satirizing the proverbially dishonest Connecticut peddler by Canadian writer Thomas Haliburton included the apparently false accusation that crafty Yankee salesmen were passing off wooden nutmegs. Cheap and plentiful, nutmegs were imported from the West Indies into the country through Connecticut ports, and it is doubtful that anyone would bother to carve wooden imitations when the real thing was so easily accessible. Nevertheless, the story stuck. One entrepreneur did sell wooden nutmegs as Connecticut souvenirs at the 1876 Philadelphia Centennial Exhibition—claiming they were made from Hartford's famed Charter Oak. For their own part, Connecticut residents took characteristically perverse pleasure in the sobriquet **Nutmeg State** and adopted the nickname as their own.

Seaport preserves nearly 500 small craft and more than 1 million maritime photographs—the largest two collections of their kinds in the world.

The Charles W. Morgan

This 133ft-long whaleboat, sole survivor of America's 19C whaling fleet, has been declared a National Historic Site. Fully rigged, the Morgan can carry 13,000sq ft of sail. Visitors may board the 1841 ship to examine the crew's quarters and gigantic try-pots, the cauldrons used to boil the oil out of whale fat.

The Joseph Conrad

This Danish-built training vessel, built as the Georg Stage in 1882 and designed to accommodate a crew of 80, has sailed under the Danish, British and American flags. Renamed in 1934 and now the property of Mystic Seaport, the 117ft-long schooner serves its original function as a training ship.

The L.A. Dunton

This graceful 124ft schooner, built in 1921, typifies the round-bow fishing vessels that sailed from New England to Newfoundland in the 19C and early 20C.

Sabino

Built in 1908, the steamboat *Sabino* is the last wood-hulled, coal-fired passenger-carrying steam vessel operating in the US today. Visitors can board the *Sabino* for 30min waterfront tours from the river (*depart from the*

Sabino dock near the main entrance to Mystic Seaport mid-May–mid-Oct daily 10.30am–3.30pm, every hour on the hour; $5.50).

Henry B. du Pont Preservation Shipyard

All kinds of boats from the museum's vast collection are restored here. Visitors may observe craftsmen at work from a platform on the second level.

Mallory Building

Here a collection of ships' models, half-models and portraits traces the growth of America's maritime industry through the life of one prominent shipping family.

Mystic River Scale Model

The Mystic River area appears in small scale here as it did in the 1870s. At more than 50ft long, the model features some 250 detailed structures.

Wendell Building

The first exhibit building at Mystic Seaport, the Wendell Building houses the seaport's rich collection of wooden **figureheads** and **ships' carvings**.
Also on-site is the **Schaefer Building**, which contains special exhibitions from the museum's collection of maritime art and artifacts; and the **Planetarium**, with programs that focus on sailors' dependence on celestial navigation.

Guest in the water with a beluga whale, Mystic Aquarium

ADDITIONAL SIGHTS
🏊 Mystic Aquarium and Institute for Exploration★★
55 Coogan Blvd. in Mystic. ✕🅿️♿
🕐*Open Apr–Oct daily 9am–5pm, Dec–Feb daily 10am–4pm. Mar & Nov 9am–4pm.* 🕐*Closed major holidays.*
👓*$29.95.* 📞*860-572-5955.*
www.mysticaquarium.org.

More than 6,000 sea creatures, including four-eyed fish and Australian mudskippers, make their home here. It's one of the largest and most ecologically minded aquariums in the nation.

Living specimens of marine animals and plants are grouped into some 45 major exhibits demonstrating aquatic communities, habitat and adaptation. In the Ocean **Planet Pavilion**, bonnethead sharks prowl a 30,000-gallon tank along with 500 exotic fish, while the **Sunlit Seas** exhibits feature species that thrive in ecosystems such as estuaries and coral reefs. Atlantic bottlenose dolphins, known for their sunny dispositions, play in the World of the Dolphin tank (*daily demonstrations are held in the theater*). Another favorite is the Hidden Amazon with electric eels, poison dart frogs, and more. Outside, view the underwater world of northern fur seals and graceful beluga whales at the **Alaskan Coast**; and watch African black-footed penguins frolic above and below the water in the **Roger Tory Peterson Penguin Exhibit**.

EXCURSIONS
🏊 Mashantucket Pequot Museum★★
▶ *7mi northeast of Mystic. From I-95, take Exit 92, then Rte. 2 West and follow signs to museum.* ✕🅿️♿🕐*Open Wed-Sat 9am–5pm.* 🕐*Closed Sun–Tue & major holidays.* 👓*$15.* 📞*860-396-6800 or 800-411-9671.*
www.pequotmuseum.org.

This tribally owned and operated museum—the largest Native American museum in the country—is devoted to the native and natural history of southern New England, including the history and culture of the Mashantucket Pequot Indians. Located on the original reservation, the glass and concrete facility pays homage to nature by embracing woodland views and integrating stone and gurgling streams into the modern structure. Inside the museum, dioramas, interactive videos, films, campfire aromas and recorded bird songs create a multisensory experience that focuses on the Pequots' day-to-day life from prehistoric times to the present. The highlight of the museum is the indoor 16C **Pequot Village**, a 22,000sq ft re-creation of a native dwelling site.

Scene from the Pequot Village exhibit, Mashantucket Pequot Museum

Stonington★
▶ *4mi east of Mystic on Rte. 1, then Rte. 1A.*
Overlooking a tranquil harbor studded with boats, Stonington is justly known

as one of the prettiest coastal villages in Connecticut. The early character of this former shipbuilding center is preserved in the lovely 18C and 19C homes lining the tree-shaded streets of Stonington borough. Spend some time browsing through the antique shops and boutiques clustered on Main Street.

Captain Palmer House★

40 Palmer St. ☞☜*Visit by guided tour (45min) only May–Oct Thu–Sun 1pm–5pm.* ☞*$9 (includes Lighthouse Museum).* ☎*860-535-8445. www. stoningtonhistory.org/palmer.htm.*
Perched on the highest hill in Stonington, this Greek Revival manse is crowned with an octagonal cupola that commands water views in all directions.

Old Lighthouse Museum

7 Water St. ☉*Open May–Oct Thu–Mon 10am–5pm, Apr Sat–Sun 1–5pm.* ☞*$9 (including Captain Palmer House).* ☎*860-535-1440. www.stonington history.org/light.htm.*
Seasonal exhibits in the 1840 stone lighthouse serve as nostalgic reminders of Stonington's past as a shipbuilding center. The lighthouse was once the beacon for vessels approaching Stonington's harbor from Long Island Sound. The original 30-foot stone tower held a lantern consisting of ten oil lamps and parabolic reflectors.

ADDRESSES

☚ STAY

$$$$ Steamboat Inn – *73 Steamboat Wharf, Mystic.* ☎*860-536-8300. www.steamboatinnmystic.com. 11 rooms.*
Originally a ship's store, today it's a luxury B&B on the Mystic River in downtown Mystic. Each room is unique in configuration and decor; all are designer-decorated and equipped with whirlpool baths (some with baths for two), and most have fireplaces and river views (the Mystic Suite has views on two sides). The pretty common room is open for serve-yourself "continental-plus" breakfast, afternoon tea and evening sherry.

$$$ Inn at Stonington – *60 Water St., Stonington.* ☎*860-535-2000. www.theinn atstonington.com. 18 rooms.* It's rare that a "new" country inn is built on a prime waterfront site in an old seafaring town, but here is one and it's a gem. Luxurious antiques-appointed guest rooms with fireplaces and harbor views await visitors here. Facilities include a common room with a bar (for breakfast and evening wine and cheese), an exercise room, bikes at the ready, and kayaks to launch from the inn's own deep-water dock. Restaurants, shops, historic houses and secret gardens lie within an easy walk or bike ride away.

$$$$ The Old Mystic Inn – *52 Main St., Old Mystic.* ☎*860-572-9422. www.old mysticinn.com. 8 rooms.* Two miles down the road from bustling Mystic Seaport, the charming Old Mystic Inn is a red 1784 Colonial surrounded by gardens. Guest rooms in the house, and in the 1988 carriage house, boast canopy beds and fireplaces, wide-plank or inlaid floors, stenciling and wainscoting. The owner, a graduate of the Culinary Institute of America, turns out lavish breakfasts like scrambled eggs in puff pastry with steamed asparagus and Mornay sauce, and strawberry-stuffed French toast with maple-pecan syrup. No children under 15 years allowed.

$$ Brigadoon Bed & Breakfast – *180 Cow Hill Rd., Mystic.* ☎*860-536-3033. www.brigadoonofmystic.com. 8 rooms.* You'll find a touch of Scotland a mile from downtown Mystic at this rambling 250-year-old farmhouse-turned-B&B located on a quiet side street. Hosted by Scottish-born Kay and her husband Ted, their labor of love offers charming light-filled rooms in pretty pastels, with king- or queen-sized beds and often oversized private baths. The honeymoon suite features a brass-and-iron bed, cathedral ceiling and a separate entrance. Complimentary breakfast is served in the dining room overlooking the garden or, in season, under a tree outside.

♀/EAT

$$$ Restaurant Bravo Bravo – *20 E. Main St., Mystic. Closed Mon.* ☎*860-536-3228. www.bravobravoct.com.* **Italian.** The name may seem a bit self-congratulatory, but in this case it is warranted. This 50-seat restaurant overlooking Mystic's Main Street sidewalk scene wins steady applause for its contemporary takes on pasta and seafood, often creatively combined. Typical are the roasted goat cheese salad, champagne risotto with lobster and asparagus, crab cakes, or stuffed veal medallions with garlic spinach cheese. In summer there may be a wait, but it's worth it.

$$$ Latitude 41º – *105 Greenmanville Ave. (Rte. 27), Mystic.* ☎*860-572-5303. www.mysticseaport.org.* (*click through to where to dine*) **American.** A formal restaurant and more casual pub overlooking the Mystic River that turns out classic New England fare—creamy clam chowder, fresh fish, prime rib, chocolate bread pudding—in a series rooms, most with fireplaces and many decorated with photographs from the Rosenfeld Collection (the maritime photography archive owned by the Mystic Seaport Museum).

$$ Abbott's Lobster In The Rough – *117 Pearl St., Noank* (*2.5mi southwest of Mystic via Rte. 215*). ☎*860-536-7719. www. abbotts-lobster.com. Open daily Memorial Day–Labor Day, noon–9pm. Fri–Sun in May and Sep–mid Oct.* **Seafood.** The large parking lot is a clue that Abbott's is indeed a popular place to eat. This rambling lobster shack right on the waters of Fishers Island Sound boasts great views, especially while you're consuming some of the best—and biggest lobsters around. Bring your own alcoholic beverages; they'll provide ice.

$$ Captain Daniel Packer Inne – *32 Water St., Mystic.* ☎*860-536-3555. www.danielpacker.com.* **American.** Across from the marina, this 1756 National Historic Register inn still caters to travelers, but today they're more likely to come by car than by boat or stagecoach. It remains a step back in time, with oversized hearths, stone interior walls and wide-plank floors. A cozy spot for

updated New England fare creatively interpreted, like the lobster ravioli, grilled wild salmon, and seafood stew. The menu also includes standard favorites like filet mignon, lamb chops and several pasta dishes.

$ Kitchen Little – *135 Greenmanville Ave., Mystic.* ☎*860-536-2122. www. kitchenlittle.org.* **American.** Located near Mystic Seaport, this tiny, waterside eatery is well known for its huge and inventive breakfasts (*6.30am–2pm; breakfast only on weekends*), featuring such egg dishes as the Mystic Melt, the Portuguese Fisherman or the Kitchen Sink. If indoor seating is not available, share a picnic table outside at the rear with the seagulls.

$ Mystic Pizza – *56 W. Main St., Mystic.* ☎*860-536-3700. www.mysticpizza.com.* **Italian.** Yes, there really is a Mystic Pizza and, yes, it starred in the popular 1988 movie of the same name that launched Julia Roberts. The place that boasts of "the pizza that made the movie famous" still features the secret-recipe pie that the Zelepos family opened with in 1973. Beyond pizza, there's a full menu from fried calamari to burgers, salads to chicken-Parmesan. There's a Mystic Pizza II in nearby North Stonington, too.

TAKING A BREAK

Clyde's Cider Mill – *129 N Stonington Rd., Mystic. Open Sept–Dec.* ☎*860-536-3354. www.bfclydescidermill.com.* Making fresh apple cider is an autumn tradition throughout New England, but perhaps nowhere more than at Clyde's, where six generations of the Clyde family have steadfastly upheld the practice of cider-pressing that their grandfather started in 1881. It's the oldest steam-powered cider mill in the US. Designated a National Historical Mechanical and Engineering Landmark, the mill still employs its all-steel screw cider press.

Beside sweet cider and a wide variety of apple wines, Clyde's sells seasonal goodies: apples, pumpkins, gourds, homemade apple butter and johnnycake meal ground on the premises.

New Haven★★

Seen from I-95, New Haven's skyline is pierced by tall office structures, such as the 23-story, glass-faced Knights of Columbus Building (L), set off by four 320ft brown tile towers. On closer look, however, quaint commercial districts (College and Chapel Streets), serene residential streets (Whitney Avenue, Hillhouse Avenue and Prospect Street), a historic green and the ivy-covered buildings of prestigious Yale University characterize Connecticut's third-largest city.

A BIT OF HISTORY

The first planned city in America was founded as an "independent kingdom of Christ" in 1638 by a group of Puritans. In the late 18C and early 19C, New Haven became an important seaport. The War of 1812 brought an end to this prosperous period in New Haven, as it did in other ports throughout New England. The face of the town changed forever with the arrival of the railroad in the 19C. Industry and manufacturing developed, and immigrants came by the thousands to work in Connecticut's clock, firearms and carriage factories. One of the many innovative men in New Haven was Eli Whitney, who is recognized as the father of mass production. Whitney introduced the use of standardized parts as the basis of the assembly line in his arms factory outside the city. In New Haven today you'll find a mix of traditional and contemporary architectural styles.

YALE UNIVERSITY★★★

This Ivy League school is one of the oldest and most distinguished institutions of higher learning in the US. The university was founded in 1701 by a group of Puritan clergymen who wished to provide Connecticut with an institution where young men could be trained to serve the church and state.
Yale gained university status in 1887, long after its Medical School (1810) and Law School (1824) were established. The nation's first Ph.D.

▶ **Population:** 123,669.
ⓒ **Michelin Map:** 581 J 11
🆔 **Info:** ℘203-787-6735; www.newhaven chambercom.
◗ **Location:** Situated on New Haven Harbor on the northern coast of Long Island Sound, New Haven is halfway between the New York City and New England metro areas. The city is easily accessible off north-south I-95 and I-91. Rte. US34 travels east-west.
👫 **Kids:** Take a hike on the 1.6-mile Tower Path in nearby Sleeping Giant State Park.
🕐 **Timing:** Begin your visit at **INFO New Haven** (*1000 Chapel St.*) where you can pick up information and maps, purchase tickets for local events, make restaurant and theater reservations and access an interactive web station. The tour of Yale will take half a day; save an hour or two to visit the University Art Museum.
🅿 **Parking:** Metered parking is available along Elm, Orange and Court Streets. Lots can also be found on Elm Street (between Orange and State Streets) and Orange Street (between Elm and Wall Streets). Yale University opens its lots to the public free of charge on weekends.
👁 **Don't Miss:** A walking tour of the prestigious Yale University.

degrees were awarded by Yale in 1861.
Architecture—The architectural diversity that characterizes the Yale campus is dominated by the Gothic style, with its Medieval turrets, spires, massive towers,

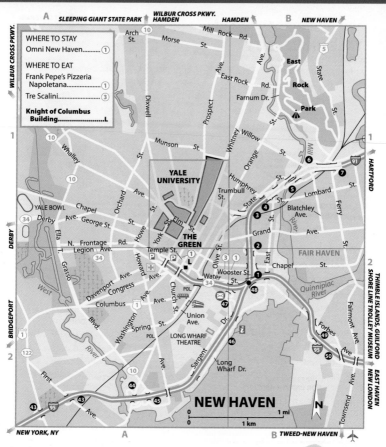

WHERE TO STAY
Omni New Haven..........(1)

WHERE TO EAT
Frank Pepe's Pizzeria
 Napoletana....................(1)
Tre Scalini.....................(3)

**Knight of Columbus
 Building.......................L**

leaded stain glass, and cathedral-like buildings. The Georgian influence is also significant, although the facades of most of these handsome structures are visible only from their courtyards. In the 1920s and 30s, James Gamble Rogers designed Harkness Tower (1921), Sterling Memorial Library (1930), Pierson and Davenport Colleges (1932), and several other campus structures and spaces while serving as Yale's consulting architect. Because of his considerable impact on Yale's design, he has been called "the architect of Yale University." Since the 1950s, Yale has commissioned leading architects of the day to design the university's most recent modern structures, including Louis Kahn (the Yale Art Gallery and the Yale Center for British Art), Paul Rudolph (School of Art and Architecture) and Philip Johnson (Kline Biology Tower).

WALKING TOUR

This self-guided tour of Yale University leads to the major sites on campus, showcasing its impressive art and architecture.

▶ Begin at the visitor center on Elm St. See University map.

Visitor Center

149 Elm St. Open year-round Mon–Fri 9am–4.30pm, weekends 11am–4pm. Closed Thanksgiving Day and 23 Dec–1 Jan. Guided tours (1hr 15min) of the campus available Mon–Fri 10.30am & 2pm, weekends 1.30pm. 203-432-2300. www.yale.edu/visitor. Historically known as the Pierpont House, this two-story Georgian Colonial white frame structure (1767) is the oldest surviving house in New Haven.

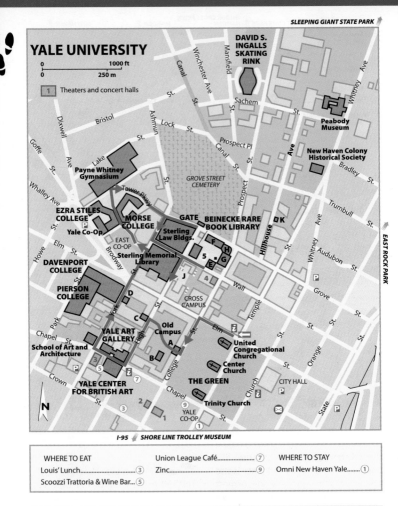

YALE UNIVERSITY

SLEEPING GIANT STATE PARK

0 — 1000 ft
0 — 250 m

1 Theaters and concert halls

DAVID S. INGALLS SKATING RINK

Peabody Museum

New Haven Colony Historical Society

GROVE STREET CEMETERY

Payne Whitney Gymnasium

EZRA STILES COLLEGE

Yale Co-op

MORSE COLLEGE

GATE

BEINECKE RARE BOOK LIBRARY

Sterling Law Bldgs.

EAST CO-OP

Sterling Memorial Library

DAVENPORT COLLEGE

PIERSON COLLEGE

CROSS CAMPUS

Old Campus

YALE ART GALLERY

School of Art and Architecture

YALE CENTER FOR BRITISH ART

THE GREEN

United Congregational Church

Center Church

CITY HALL

Trinity Church

YALE CO-OP

EAST ROCK PARK

I-95 SHORE LINE TROLLEY MUSEUM

WHERE TO EAT		
Louis' Lunch	3	
Scoozzi Trattoria & Wine Bar	5	
Union League Café	7	
Zinc	9	

WHERE TO STAY	
Omni New Haven Yale	1

Cultural New Haven

The presence of Yale University has made New Haven a prominent cultural center. New Haven's theaters, once a proving ground for Broadway productions, have become well known in their own right. Numbers and letters in parentheses refer to the New Haven map.

Long Wharf Theater – 222 Sargent Dr. ℘203-787-4282. www.longwharf.org. Located in a former warehouse, this theater received a regional Tony award.

Shubert Performing Arts Center (1) – 247 College St. ℘203-562-5666. www.shubert.com. The Shubert's varied program of performances includes Broadway-bound productions, Broadway road shows and concerts.

Yale Repertory Theater (3) – 1120 Chapel St. ℘203-432-1234. www.yalerep.org. The "Rep" focuses on plays written by young playwrights and on modern interpretations of the classics.

New Haven Symphony Orchestra – 105 Court St. ℘203-865-0831. www.newhavensymphony.org. One of the oldest and finest in the nation, the city's resident symphony orchestra performs at **Woolsey Hall (G)** on campus.

Here visitors can obtain a fact booklet and other brochures about the university. Yale College undergraduates lead guided tours from the visitor center.

▶ Proceed to Phelps Gate (A) on College St. and enter the Old Campus.

Old Campus

This is the site of Yale's earliest college buildings, including **Connecticut Hall (B)**, the university's oldest structure. A statue of Nathan Hale, a Yale alumnus, stands in front of this simple Georgian hall where Hale lived as a student.

▶ Cross the Old Campus and exit onto High St.

Across High Street is the landmark **Harkness Tower (C)** (1920), a 221ft Gothic Revival bell tower heavily ornamented with carved figures of famous Yale alumni, among them Noah Webster and Eli Whitney.

▶ Turn left on High St., pass under an arch, then turn right onto Chapel St.

The **Yale University Art Gallery**, Louis Kahn's first major work, stands facing his last creation, the **Yale Center for British Art.** Both buildings present interesting conceptions of museum architecture from the point of view of building materials, light and the use of space. ♿ *See descriptions of the collections, under Museums on following pages.*

▶ Continue to York St.

The former Gothic Revival-style church is now the **Yale Repertory Theater (3)**, home of the Yale Repertory Company, a professional acting troupe in residence at the university. Diagonally opposite stands Paul Rudolph's high-rise **School of Art and Architecture**. Seemingly seven stories tall, the building actually has 36 levels that are visible only from the interior.

Harkness Tower

© Michael Marsland / Yale University

▶ Turn right onto York St. and continue halfway down the street.

Pierson and Davenport Colleges★

These elegant Georgian buildings hidden beyond the colleges' Medieval-style, street-side facades may be seen from the courtyards. On the opposite side of the street stands **Wrexham Tower (D)**, designed after the church in Wales where Elihu Yale is buried.

▶ Cross Elm St. and continue on York St. At no. 306 York St., walk through the narrow passageway on the left.

Morse and Ezra Stiles Colleges★

Eero Saarinen's design for this ensemble of contemporary buildings was inspired by an Italian hill town. A continuous play of light and shadows is created throughout the day by the maze of stone passages with their vertical planes, geometric forms and sharp angular turns. Nearby is another of Saarinen's works, the **Yale Co-op** (now known as the West Co-op, since an adjacent building, the East Co-op, has been constructed).

On Tower Parkway, across the street from Morse and Ezra Stiles Colleges, is the **Payne Whitney Gymnasium**, one of Yale's cathedral-like structures.

▶ Continue along Tower Pkwy., which becomes Grove St., to High St.

Note the massive Egyptian Revival-style **gate★** at the entrance to Grove Street Cemetery. Its architect, **Henry Austin**, was responsible for several of the 19C houses on Hillhouse Avenue.

▶ Return via Grove St. to York St. Turn left onto York St., then left onto Wall St.

Sterling Law Buildings

Law students live in this group of buildings, which are similar in design to the English Inns of Court where students studied law from the 16C to the 18C. Portraits of police and robbers have been carved in stone above the windows.

▶ Cross High St.

Beinecke Rare Book and Manuscript Library★

121 Wall St.
The exterior walls of this library (1961, Gordon Bunshaft) are composed of a granite framework fitted with translucent marble panels. Enter the library and observe the unusual effect produced by the sunlight streaming through the marble slabs. A **Gutenberg Bible** and changing exhibits are displayed on the mezzanine.

Isamu Noguchi's **sculptures (5)** of geometric shapes anchor the sunken courtyard that fronts the library.

Facing the library are several buildings erected to celebrate Yale's bicentennial: **Woodbridge Hall (E)** offices, the **University Dining Hall (F)** and **Woolsey Hall (G)** auditorium.

The rotunda, **Memorial Hall (H)**, contains a large group of commemorative plaques. On the plaza, near Woodbridge Hall, note Alexander Calder's red stabile *Gallows and Lollipops* (1960).

▶ Return to the corner of Wall and High St. and turn left onto High St. A number of small statues ornament the rooftops of buildings along this street.

Sterling Memorial Library

120 High St.
At first glance, Yale's main library, with its stained-glass windows, frescoes and archways, resembles a cathedral.
The **Cross Campus Library (J)**, located beneath Cross Campus (*to the left*), was built underground to allow the green to remain intact.

MUSEUMS
Yale University Art Gallery★★

1111 Chapel St. ♿🕐*Open year-round Tue–Fri 10am–5pm, Sat–Sun 11am–5pm, Thu 10am–8pm. (Sept–Jun).* 🕐*Closed Mon & major holidays.* ✆*203-432-0600. www.artgallery. yale.edu.* ♿*Detailed floor plans are available at the information desk.*
This gallery was founded in 1832 with a gift of some 100 works of art by the patriot artist **John Trumbull**. Today selections from an 80,000-piece collection ranging from early Egyptian times to the present are displayed in two interconnected units: a 1928 Gothic-style building and a 1953 addition designed by Louis Kahn. Particularly strong are the holdings of American decorative arts, which focus on the colonial and federal eras, and American painting and sculpture.

Ground Floor

The collection of **ancient Mediterranean art** featured here comprises more than 12,000 objects and spans 5,000 years.
Artifacts include a Mithraic shrine (*Temple to the Sun God*) with elaborate paintings and reliefs from **Dura-Europos**, an ancient Roman town in Syria; and *Leda and the Swan* (370 BC), a Roman copy of a Greek sculpture attributed to Timotheos. Equally noteworthy are the stone, clay, and jade artifacts in the growing **pre-Columbian** collection.

First Floor (special exhibits and contemporary art)

Noteworthy in the Sculpture Hall is Richard Serra's site-specific *Stacks* (1990), two steel monoliths placed 60ft apart. The Albers Corridor features a rotating selection of the gallery's 74 paintings and 110 prints by the German-born artist Joseph Albers, who chaired Yale's art department for 10 years (1950–60).

Second Floor (11C to 19C European painting and sculpture; African sculpture)

In addition to Impressionist paintings, the 19C collection includes works by Manet (*Young Woman Reclining in Spanish Costume, 1862*), Courbet (*Le Grand Pont, 1864*), Van Gogh (*Night Café, 1888*), Millet, Corot, Degas and Matisse.

In the section devoted to early modern art, the visitor will find works by Marcel Duchamp (*Tu'm, 1918*), Stella (*Brooklyn Bridge, c1919*), Magritte (*Pandora's Box, 1951*) and Dalí (*The Phantom Cart, 1933*) and canvases by Tanguy, Ernst, Klee and Kandinsky. The collection of **African art** highlights masks and ceremonial and royal objects.

Third Floor (late-19C European and Contemporary art; American art)

The **Jarves Collection** of early Italian painting (13–16C) includes such jewels as da Fabriano's *Madonna and Child* (c.1423) and Ghirlandaio's *Portrait of a Lady with a Rabbit* (c.1505). The adjacent galleries, devoted to European art, contain the Medieval collection. Among the European paintings are portraits by Holbein and Hals, an oil sketch by Rubens, Correggio's *Assumption of the Virgin* (1530), and the *Allegory of Intemperance* (c.1495) attributed to Hieronymus Bosch.

The **Garven Collection** of colonial and early-19C Americana is arranged didactically for the university's teaching purposes. Furniture, silver, pewter and ironware are used to illustrate the development of American art forms and their relationship to the society that produced them.

The Yankee Peddler

No figure of Connecticut lore better personifies the New Englander's reputation for driving a hard bargain than the **Yankee peddler**. By 1800 the word was used as a verb specifically meaning "to cheat." As the western frontier opened up in the 19C, Yankee became synonymous with the peripatetic Connecticut salesmen who set out for remote rural areas with wagons and wicker baskets full of locally made goods—and the occasional broken watch, stagnant barometer and magic nostrum said to cure everything from bunions to head colds.

On view in the gallery of American paintings and sculpture from the 19C and 20C are masterpieces by, among others, Eakins, Homer, Church, Cole, Remington, Hopper, and O'Keeffe. One section of the gallery displays works of John Trumbull, including the original paintings *The Battle of Bunker Hill* (1786) and *Signing of the Declaration of Independence* (1795), used as models for copies later produced by Trumbull for the Capitol in Washington, DC. Hiram Powers' sculpture *The Greek Slave* (1844) is also on display.

Fourth Floor (Asian art; prints and drawings)

Japanese sculpture and Chinese bronzes, ceramics and paintings span the period from the 12C BC to the present. You can trace the history of the graphic arts by way of 25,000 prints, 6,000 drawings and 3,000 photographs that date from the 15C to the 20C.

Yale Center for British Art★★

1080 Chapel St. &.◐*Open year-round Tue–Sat 10am–5pm, Sun noon–5pm.* ◐*Closed Mon & major holidays.* ℘*203-432-2800. www.britishart.yale.edu.* Established by a gift from philanthropist Paul Mellon in 1966, the Yale Center for

The *Amistad* Affair, 1839–1841

For more than two years, New Haven was the focal point of the *Amistad* Affair, a major milestone in the long struggle to end slavery in the US. In August 1839, the officers of the US brig *Washington* discovered a Spanish ship anchored off the coast of Long Island. On board were 53 native Africans who had been kidnapped from their home in West Africa by Spaniards and sold into slavery in Cuba. En route from Havana to Puerto Principe, Cuba, aboard the schooner *Amistad*, the captives—under the leadership of a slave who came to be known as "Cinque"—overcame their captors and attempted to sail home with the help of two Spanish passengers whose lives they spared. The Spaniards, however, surreptitiously guided the ship northward and westward by night in hopes that the *Amistad* would be intercepted. After being recaptured by the Americans, the slaves were taken to New Haven, where they were charged with piracy and murder.

Yale professor Josiah Willard Gibbs gave the Africans a voice to defend themselves. Gibbs searched the wharves of New York City until he found an African sailor who could serve as an interpreter for the captives. Antislavery leaders aroused the public to raise funds to return them to their homeland, and promote the abolitionist cause. The Africans were finally granted their freedom by courts in the Connecticut co-capitals of Hartford and New Haven; soon after, the decision was upheld by the Supreme Court, thanks to the persuasive arguments of former president John Quincy Adams.

Today a 14ft bronze sculpture in front of New Haven City Hall *(165 Church St.)* pays tribute to the 53 Africans aboard the *Amistad*. The **Amistad Memorial** marks the former site of the New Haven Jail, where the Africans were incarcerated while awaiting trial.

British Art possesses the most comprehensive collection of British art outside Great Britain.

The Collection

Based on Mellon's original donation of more than 60,000 works—including 1,300 paintings, 10,000 drawings, 20,000 prints and 20,000 rare books—the collection illustrates British life and culture from the 16C to today. The museum also organizes large, often provocative temporary shows of British art (both contemporary and historical), as well as related lectures and film screenings. On the fourth floor, paintings and sculptures are installed chronologically to provide a survey of British art from the late 16C through the early 19C. Several rooms on this floor are reserved for the works of **Gainsborough**, **Reynolds**, **Stubbs**, **Turner** and **Constable**. A selection of 19C and 20C paintings and sculptures fill the second floor.

👥 Peabody Museum of Natural History

170 Whitney Ave. ♿ 🅿 🕐*Open year-round Mon–Sat 10am–5pm, Sun noon–5pm.* 🕐*Closed major holidays.* 💶*$9.* ☎*203-432-5050. www.peabody.yale.edu.*

Endowed in 1866 by financier George Peabody, Yale's Natural History Museum showcases more than 11 million specimens. In the first-floor **Great Hall**, you'll find the Peabody's famous collection of **dinosaurs**, featuring the first *Stegosaurus* ever mounted, the ever-popular *Apatosaurus* (67ft long, 35 tons), and the 10ft *Archelon* (75 million years old), a giant sea turtle. Spanning the Great Hall is Rudolph Zallinger's mural *The Age of Reptiles* (1947), which vividly summarizes over 300 million years of animal and plant evolution.

The first floor also houses a collection of mammals, primates and artifacts representing the cultures of Mesoamerica, the

Plains Indians and New Guinea. Rocks and minerals, the Hall of Connecticut Birds and dioramas of North American flora and fauna can be found on the third floor. The second floor is reserved for special exhibits.

Yale Collection of Musical Instruments (K)

15 Hillhouse Ave. ○*Open Sept–Jul Tue– Fri 1pm–4pm. Sun 1pm–5pm.* ○*Closed Jul & Aug, major holidays and during academic holidays.* ◉*$2 contribution requested.* ☏*203-432-0822. www.yale.edu/musicalinstruments.* Established in 1900, this rare collection assembles more than 1,000 fine and decorative musical instruments documenting the European music tradition from 1550 through 1900. Here you'll find violins by Jakob Stainer (1661) and Stradivari (1736) and an outstanding array of keyboard instruments dating back to 1569.
A series of concerts is held annually featuring restored instruments from the collection (for information, call ☏203- 432-4158).

ADDITIONAL SIGHTS
◐*See New Haven map.*

The Green★
When New Haven was a Puritan colony, the town was laid out as a large square subdivided into nine smaller squares. Now a National Historic Landmark, the center square, or green, was reserved for the use of the entire community as pastureland, parade ground and burial ground, and has served as the heart of the downtown district since 1638. The upper green is characterized by its three early-19C churches: 1752 **Trinity Church** (*129 Church St.;* ☏*203-624- 3101; www.trinitynewhaven.org*), the first Gothic-Revival church built in the US; the Georgian **The First Church of Christ**, or **Center Church** (*311 Temple St.;* ☏*203-787-0121; www.newhavencenterchurch.org*), whose present structure dates to 1812 and lies over part of the old burial ground; and the Federal-style **United Congregational Church**, or

no. 46 Hillhouse Avenue
© Michael Marsland / Yale University

North Church (*323 Temple St.;* ☏*203- 787-4195; www.unitedchurchonthegreen. org*), whose steeple has been replicated in churches across the country.

Hillhouse Avenue
Most of the beautiful mansions on this street were built in the 19C by wealthy industrialists and merchants and are now owned by Yale University. Architectural styles represented include Greek Revival (no. 46), High Victorian Gothic (no. 43), Beaux-Arts Revival (no. 38) and Italianate (no. 24).

David S. Ingalls Skating Rink★
Corner of Sachem and Prospect Sts.
One of the most distinguished collegiate hockey facilities in the country, this lantern-shaped rink (1958) was designed for Yale by the Finnish-born architect Eero Saarinen. Its 300ft-long curved, arched roof accounts for its nickname, the Yale Whale.

New Haven Colony Historical Society
114 Whitney Ave. ♿🅿○*Open year- round Tue–Fri 10am–5pm, Sat noon– 5pm.* ◉*$4.* ☏*203-562-4183. www.newhavenmuseum.org.*
Recounting 300 years of New Haven's history, exhibits in 11 galleries here display antique pewter, china and toys dating from the period of the New Haven Colony, among other items. The

The Thimble Islands

Legend has it that Captain Kidd buried treasure on one of the 365 Thimble Islands that lie off the coast of Stony Creek (*12mi east of New Haven*). The miniature islands range in size from a few boulders to several acres of farmland. Twenty-five of the Thimbles are inhabited and many are privately owned. Narrated boat tours of the islands on the **Sea Mist** (*45 min; $10; schedules: 203-488-8905; www.thimbleislandcruise.com*) and the **Volsunga IV** (*45min; $10; schedules: 203-481-3345; www.thimbleislands.com*) leave from the Stony Creek town dock from May through Columbus Day.

society also preserves notable artifacts, including an original model of Eli Whitney's cotton gin and one of Samuel F.B. Morse's first code receivers.

East Rock Park

Follow Orange St.; cross Mill River and turn left, then bear right. The road leads to the summit parking lot. P *Open year-round daily 8am–dusk. Summit drive open Apr–Oct 8am–dusk; Nov–Mar weekends 8am–4pm. 203-946-6086. wwwcityofnewhaven.com/parks.*
New Haven's oldest park features walking trails, a road to the summit of East Rock, and the Giant Steps up the cliff, as well as a rose garden and athletic fields. From the summit of this basalt ridge stretches a **view★★** of the New Haven area with Long Island Sound in the distance.

EXCURSIONS
👥 Shore Line Trolley Museum

▶ *5mi east of New Haven. 17 River St., in East Haven. Take I-95 North to Exit 51; turn right onto Hemingway Ave., then left onto River St.* ♿P *Open Memorial Day–Labor Day daily 10am–5pm; May, Sep & Oct weekends only 10am–5pm. $10. 203-467-6927. www.shorelinetrolley.com.*
Primarily the work of volunteer trolley buffs who have restored one-third of the nearly 100 vintage street, subway and elevated railway cars on the grounds, the museum features a collection of trolley cars from 1878–1962. Visitors can ride restored cars on a 3mi trolley excursion along the Connecticut shore.

Sleeping Giant State Park

▶ *6mi north of New Haven, in Hamden. Take Whitney Ave. to Hamden and turn right on Mt. Carmel Ave.* P *Open year-round daily 8am–dusk. Trail maps and information available at ranger headquarters. $15/car Memorial Day–Labor Day weekends & holidays. 203-789-7498. www.ct.gov/dep.*
Carved by glaciers more than 15,000 years ago, the rocky sandstone and trap rock ridge known as the Sleeping Giant resembles a colossal man lying on his back. The park is threaded by 30mi of trails, including the popular **Tower Path** (*1.6mi round-trip*), which leads to Mt. Carmel, the highest point in the park. From a stone observation tower here stretch **views★★** of New Haven, Long Island Sound and the Connecticut hills.

Guilford

▶ *13mi east of New Haven. Take I-95 North to Exit 58 and follow Rte. 146 South to Guilford.*
In 1639 Minister Henry Whitfield arrived here with 25 families and bought the land that became Guilford from the Menunketuck Indians. Today his 1639 home—the oldest stone dwelling in New England—has been restored to its 17C appearance as the **Henry Whitfield State Museum** (*248 Old Whitfield St.;* P *Open May–mid-Dec Wed–Sun 10am–4.30pm, rest of the year by appointment; $8 203-453-2457; www.cultureand tourism.org/cct.*
Guilford's early prosperity is reflected in its lovely green and its 18C and 19C homes. Noteworthy among them are two

typical saltbox structures, the late-17C **Hyland House** (*84 Boston St.;* ⚐*visit by 45min guided tour only,* ⏱*Open Jun–Labor Day Tue–Fri & Sun noon–4.30pm Sat 11am–4.30pm. Mid-Sep–early-Oct, Sat 11am–4.30pm Sun noon–4.30pm.* ☎ *203-453-9477; www.hylandhouse. com*), and the beautifully restored **Thomas Griswold House** (*171 Boston St.;* ⚐*visit by 45min guided tour only.* 🅿 ⏱*Open Jun–Sept Tue–Sun 11am–4pm Oct weekends 11am–4pm;* 👝*$3;* ☎ *203-453-3176; www.guilfordkeeping society.com*).

ADDRESSES

🛏 STAY

$$$ Omni New Haven Hotel at Yale – *155 Temple St.* ☎*203-772-6664 or 800-THE-OMNI. www.omnihotels.com. 306 rooms. Restaurant.* Just a block from the Yale campus, the New Haven Green, the Schubert Theater and New Haven's museums and shops, it can't be beat for convenience. Parents and children alike will appreciate the Omni Sensational Kids program, with amenities and a menu especially designed for young travelers, as well as a list of top local family attractions in the surrounding area. You also get the guest-friendly amenities such as a fully stocked refreshment center in your room, a well-equipped fitness center, and a fine-dining rooftop (19th floor) restaurant, **John Davenport's**, with dramatic views of the city skyline and harbor.

🍴 EAT

New Haven claims to be the home of America's primo pizza—thin-crusted Neapolitan style, with brick-oven flavor. Competing for top honors on Wooster Street, the city's Little Italy, are Pepe's, (established 1925) and Sally's (established 1938). Pepe's partisans claim Pepe's white-clam-with-garlic is top pie; Sally's supporters swear by Sally's white-broccoli-rabe pie (seasonal). **Frank Pepe's Pizzeria Napoletana** (*157 Wooster St.;* ☎*203-865-5762, www. pepespizzeria.com*); **Sally's Apizza** (*237 Wooster St.; Dinner only; closed Mon & Tue;* ☎*203-624-5271; www.sallysapizza.com*).

$$$$ Union League Café – *1032 Chapel St. Closed Sun.* ☎*203-562-4299. www.unionleaguecafe.com.* **French.** This French brasserie located just off the Green is housed in the graciously restored Sherman Building, incorporating the former home of Roger Sherman, a signer of the Declaration of Independence. Inside, the restaurant offers an elegant setting. Start with a selection from the raw bar or the duck foie gras followed by dishes like the pepper-crusted duck breast or slow braised veal cheeks.

$$$ Tre Scalini – *100 Wooster St.* ☎*203-777-3373. www.trescalinirestaurant.com.* **Italian.** This upscale trattoria is a top choice in a city rich with Italian restaurants. You'll find classic Italian fare here, but the real allure runs to the more inventive dishes—grilled lamb chops with figs and pignoli nuts, and fresh schrod with littleneck clams in a pomodoro sauce.

$$$ Zinc – *964 Chapel St.* ☎*203-624-0507. www.zincfood.com.* **American.** This city-sleek restaurant has won a following among diners with a taste for New American fare with Asian accents. The menu offers a nice assortment of small plates, like smoked duck nachos and steamed pork and ginger dumplings. The menu changes frequently but includes entrées like the grilled lamb and rosemary sausages, and tamari-cured tuna.

$ Louis' Lunch – *261-263 Crown St.* ☎*203-562-5507. www.louislunch.com. Closed Sun, Mon , first two weeks in Jan & month of August. No credit cards.* **American**. One of New Haven's main claims to fame—after Yale—is this tiny eatery, with a menu that redefines "limited." Louis' is considered the birthplace of the hamburger and is on the National Register of Historic Places. The burger is served here today as it was 100 years ago: straight up, on toast, with cheese, tomatoes, onions, chips, even potato salad if you like, but no fries or—perish the thought—ketchup.

$$ Scoozzi Trattoria & Wine Bar – *1104 Chapel St.* ☎*203-776-8268. www.scoozzi.com.* **Italian.** This popular and elegant trattoria and wine bar features freshly-made pasta and risotto dishes, like the sweet potato and walnut ravioli, and lobster meat and squash risotto.

New London

Located on a harbor at the mouth of the Thames River, New London has always depended on the sea for its livelihood. Home to the US Coast Guard Academy, the city retains its ties with the ocean today. The shipping industry and the US Naval Submarine Base located across the Thames River in Groton are major contributors to the local economy.

A BIT OF HISTORY

New London's deep-water port was a haven for privateers during the Revolution, a fact that led to the British attack on New London and Groton in 1781. During this assault, led by Benedict Arnold, **Fort Trumbull** (*90 Walbach St. Open late May–mid-Oct Wed–Sun 9am–4pm; 860-444-7591; www.ct.gov/dep*) and **Fort Griswold** (*57 Fort St., Groton; Open Memorial Day–Labor Day, daily 10am–5pm. Labor Day–Memorial Day weekends only 10am–5pm. 860-449-6877, www.ct.gov/dep*) fell to the enemy, and nearly all of New London was destroyed by fire. In the mid-19C the city was a principal whaling port. Elegant homes built from the profits of whaling, such as the Greek Revival mansions in **Whale Oil Row** (*nos. 105–119 Huntington St.*), still stand in neighborhoods that have remained residential, despite surrounding development. Revitalization of the downtown area has included the renovation of several 19C Greek Revival houses on **Starr Street** and the 19C Union Railroad Station.

SIGHTS
Hempsted Houses★

11 Hempsted St. Visit by guided tour (45min) only, Open May–Jun Sat–Sun 1pm–4pm Jul–Aug Thu–Sun 1pm–4pm Sep–Oct Sat–Sun 1pm–4pm. $7. 860-443-7949. www.ctlandmarks.org.
Built in 1678, the timber-framed Joshua Hempsted House provides a splendid example of 17C American architecture. Inside, the low-ceilinged rooms contain fine, primitive American furnishings. The

- **Population:** 25,891.
- **Michelin Map:** 581 K 11
- **Info:** 860-444-7264; www.ci.new-london.ct.us.
- **Location:** The city is easily accessible off I-95 and Highway 32.
- **Kids:** Ocean Beach Park has swimming, nature trails, amusement rides and more.
- **Timing:** Begin your visit at New London Visitor Information Center at the Trolley Waiting Station, housed in the restored 1893 Trolley Waiting Station building. You can pick up maps and guides here. Allow a day to explore the waterfront and visit beaches and parks.
- **Parking:** The Water Street Parking Garage and the Shaw's Cove lot are near the city's waterfront parks and historic district.
- **Don't Miss:** A self-guided walking tour of the waterfront historic district.
- **Also See:** MYSTIC SEAPORT.

granite Nathaniel Hempsted House was built by Joshua's grandson in 1759.

Lyman Allyn Art Museum★

625 Williams St. Open year-round Tue–Sat 10am–5pm, Sun 1pm–5pm. Closed major holidays. $10. 860-443-2545. www.lymanallyn.org.
This small museum, established by a bequest of the Allyn family, specializes in paintings by Connecticut artists and in the decorative arts of the state. Attractively arranged furnishings, paintings, sculpture and decorative arts, dating from classical civilizations to the present, complement the **American collection** (*1680–1920*), housed in the first-floor Palmer Galleries.
Housed in a handsome Neoclassical building designed by Charles A. Platt,

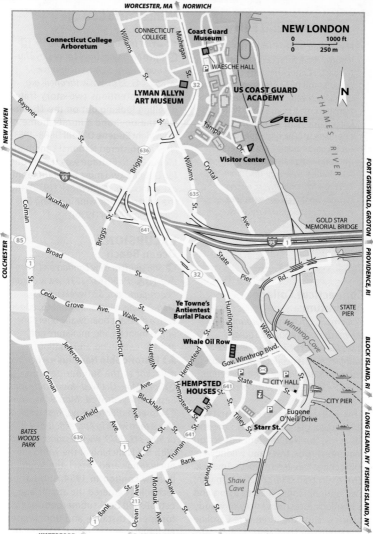

NEW LONDON

WORCESTER, MA / NORWICH

Connecticut College Arboretum

CONNECTICUT COLLEGE

Coast Guard Museum

WAESCHE HALL

LYMAN ALLYN ART MUSEUM

US COAST GUARD ACADEMY

EAGLE

Visitor Center

THAMES RIVER

NEW HAVEN

GOLD STAR MEMORIAL BRIDGE

COLCHESTER

FORT GRISWOLD, GROTON

PROVIDENCE, RI

STATE PIER

Winthrop Cove

Ye Towne's Antientest Burial Place

Whale Oil Row

Gov. Winthrop Blvd.

CITY HALL

BLOCK ISLAND, RI

HEMPSTED HOUSES

CITY PIER

Eugene O'Neill Drive

Starr St.

BATES WOODS PARK

LONG ISLAND, NY / FISHERS ISLAND, NY

Shaw Cave

WATERFORD

E. O'NEILL THEATER CENTER
OCEAN BEACH

MONTE CRISTO COTTAGE, FORT TRUMBULL

the permanent collection includes over 10,000 paintings, drawings, prints, sculptures, furniture, and decorative arts.

👥 United States Coast Guard Academy

15 Mohegan Ave. ♿🕐*Open year-round daily 9am–4.30pm.* 🚶*Self-guided walking maps from the Museum and Admissions. Tours offered Mon & Fri 1pm.* 📞*800-883-8724. www.uscga.edu.*

A four-year military college that trains officers for the Coast Guard, the academy began in 1876 when the schooner *Dobbin* was chosen to serve as a floating training school to prepare cadets for the Revenue Marine (which later evolved into the Coast Guard). In 1932 the academy moved to its present site beside the Thames. The small Coast Guard Museum, in Waesche Hall, features exhibits recounting the history of the Coast Guard.

Cross Sound Ferry

For a scenic alternative to the lengthy drive from Long Island to coastal Connecticut, try the Cross Sound ferry. The company offers both vehicle and passenger transportation from Orient Point, Long Island to New London, Connecticut. The high-speed Sea Jet I accommodates passengers only and makes the crossing in 40 minutes. *One-way 1hr 30min.* $53.91 *(car and driver); reserve for vehicles;* ✕ 🅿 . *For schedules, contact Cross Sound Ferry Services, Inc. (* 860-443-5281 *in New England or* 631-323-2525 *on Long Island; www.longislandferry.com).*

Connecticut College Arboretum

Williams St. 🕐 *Open year-round daily dawn–dusk.* 🔊 *Sun free guided tours May–Oct at 2pm. A self-guided tour brochure is available at the main entrance to the Native Plant Collection.* 860-439-5020. www.arboretum. conncoll.edu.

This 750-acre preserve consists of three major plant collections. Covering 20 acres, the Native Plant Collection features shrubs, trees and wildflowers indigenous to eastern North America. The main trail (*2mi*) circles a marsh; two optional loops lead to a bog and a hemlock forest. A variety of woody plants occupy the three-acre Caroline Black Garden. The Campus Landscape comprises 120 acres with over 200 trees from different parts of the world.

Ye Towne's Antientest Burial Place

Huntington St. Entrance Hempstead St. In this old burial ground you'll find many early New England slate tombstones carved with winged angels, skulls and crossbones, geometric patterns and other designs.

Monte Cristo Cottage

325 Pequot Ave., off Howard St. 🔊 *Visit by guided tour (1hr) only.* 🅿 🕐 *Open Memorial Day–Labor Day Thu–Sat noon–4pm, Sun 1pm–3pm.* $7. 860-443-5378. www.theoneill.org. The unpretentious two-story frame dwelling looking out on the Thames was the boyhood summer home of playwright **Eugene O'Neill** (1888–1953). Now a Registered National Landmark, Monte Cristo Cottage was the setting for O'Neill's two most autobiographical works: *Ah, Wilderness!* (1932) and the Pulitzer Prize-winning *Long Day's Journey into Night* (1956).

EXCURSIONS
Ocean Beach

⬖ *5mi south of New London on Ocean Ave.* 🅿 ♿ 860-447-3031. www.ocean-beach-park.com. $20 weekend $15 Mon-Fri. This wide, sandy beach, edged with a pleasant boardwalk, offers an amusement arcade, miniature golf, archery, swimming, and boating.

👥 **Historic Ship Nautilus★** – *Berthed adjacent to the Submarine Base.* 🅿 🕐 *Open May–Oct Wed–Mon 9am–5pm. Rest of the year Wed–Mon 9am–4pm.* 🕐 *Closed major holidays, first week of Nov & third week in Apr.* 860-694-3174 or 800-343-0079. www.ussnautilus.org. With the launching of the world's first nuclear-powered vessel, the *Nautilus,* in New London in 1954, submarine technology entered the atomic age. It established new submerged records for speed, distance and underwater endurance, and in 1958 it became the first submarine to reach the North Pole. Decommissioned in 1980, the 320ft ship is now the principal attraction at the USS Nautilus/Submarine Force Library and Museum complex. The torpedo room, control room and other sections of the vessel may be viewed. Changing exhibits in the **Submarine Force Museum** draw from the museum's collection of more than 18,000 artifacts, 20,000 documents and 30,000 photographs. Explore the story of underwater navigation, the construction of the *Nautilus* and life aboard a submarine.

Norwalk

Long famed for its oyster industry, this once lively 19C seaport has revived its spirit in SoNo (an acronym for South Norwalk) along the Norwalk River. Here, restored Victorian buildings lining Washington Street between Main and Water Streets house attractive restaurants, shops, clubs and galleries. This area is also the site of the annual SoNo Arts Celebration (*early Aug; www.sonoarts.org*).

Along the riverfront, Heritage State Park incorporates museums, an amphitheater, a visitor center, fishing piers, and playgrounds.

SIGHTS
★★ Maritime Aquarium★

10 N. Water St. ✕ ♿ 🅿 🕐*Open daily 10am–5pm. Jul–Aug 10am–6pm.* 🕐*Closed Thanksgiving Day & 25 Dec.* ☞*Aquarium $13.95, aquarium & IMAX theater $20.95.* ✆*203-852-0700. www.maritimeaquarium.org.*

A renovated 19C brick warehouse on the river houses this three-story complex, which features an aquarium devoted to Long Island Sound habitats, a new environmental education center and an IMAX theater. Aquarium exhibits highlight life in the Long Island Sound, from tidal shellfish to sharks and rays, housed in the 110,000gal **Open Ocean** tank. Harbor seals, river otters and a ray touch-pool round out the attractions here.

Lockwood-Mathews Mansion Museum

295 West Ave. 🚶*Visit by guided tour only (1hr),* 🕐*Open Apr–Jan Wed–Sun noon–3pm. Jan & Feb open by appointment only.* 🕐*Closed major holidays.* ☞*$10.* ✆*203-838-9799. www.lockwoodmathewsmansion.com.*

The three-story, turreted Victorian summer "cottage" of investment banker LeGrand Lockwood was completed in 1869 in granite with a mansard roof. The 62-room interior, including an art gallery, children's theater and Moor-

- ⚲ **Michelin Map:** 581 I 12
- 🛈 **Info:** ✆860-567-4506 or 800-663-1273; www.visit fairfieldcountyct.com.
- ▷ **Location:** Norwalk sits on the Connecticut coastline on the northern reaches of Long Island Sound. North-south I-95 and US-7 provide easy access.
- 👪 **Kids:** The Maritime Aquarium is top-notch; its exhibits, touch tanks and IMAX theater will fascinate children.
- 🕐 **Timing:** Start at the Maritime Aquarium (allow an hour or two), hop aboard the ferry to Sheffield Island Lighthouse, and when you return explore the docks, piers and boardwalks that lace through Heritage State Park.
- 🅿 **Parking:** There are several parking lots scattered throughout downtown, including the Main St. lot (on Main St. near the Wall St. intersection), Maritime Parking Garage (on Water St.) and the North Water lot (at junction of Liberty and Washington Streets), which gives easy access to the aquarium.
- 🏵 **Don't Miss:** A stroll through bustling Heritage State Park.
- ⚲ **Also See:** NEW HAVEN.

ish sitting room, boasts marble floors and mahogany and walnut woodwork crafted by Italian artisans. The grand staircase alone, with 266 balusters, reportedly cost $50,000.

EXCURSIONS
New Canaan

▷ *10mi north of Norwalk, via Rte. 123.* This choice suburb in Connecticut's Fairfield County has been an arts center

Safely touch live sharks, the Maritime Aquarium at Norwalk

© The Maritime Aquarium at Norwalk

since 1922, when the **Silvermine Guild of Artists** was founded here. The guild—which currently has 300 members—maintains a complex of studios, galleries and a year-round art school on a five-acre wooded site (*1037 Silvermine Rd., east of Rte. 123; ℘203-966-9700; www.silvermineart.org*). Highlighting its program of events is the annual spring exhibition **Art of the Northeast**.

Ridgefield

▶ *15mi northwest of Norwalk. Take US-7 North to Branchville and pick up Rte. 102 West to Rte. 35 North.*
Although Ridgefield lies just an hour's drive from the hustle and bustle of

---

An Impression of Connecticut

"The very warm heart of 'New England at its best,' such a vast abounding Arcadia of mountains and broad vales and great rivers and large lakes and white villages embowered in prodigious elms and maples. It is extraordinarily beautiful and graceful and idyllic—for America."

Henry James, May 1911.

Manhattan, this charming town, with its tree-shaded avenues, shops and mansions, retains a distinctly New England character.

Keeler Tavern Museum

▶ *132 Main St., at the intersection of Rtes. 33 & 35.* 👣*Museum open Wed, Sat & Sun 1pm-4pm. Guided tours (45min) Feb–Dec Wed, Sat & Sun 1pm–4pm.* ◷*Closed major holidays.* ⌘*$5.* ℘*203-438-5485. www.keelertavern museum.org.*
The Keeler Tavern operated as an inn from colonial days to the early 20C. During the Battle of Ridgefield, 27 April 1777, a cannonball lodged in the wall post, where it remains to this day. This fact accounts for the tavern's nickname, the Cannonball House.

Aldrich Museum of Contemporary Art

▶ *258 Main St.* ◷*Open year-round Tue–Sun noon–5pm.* ◷*Closed major holidays.* ⌘*$10.* 🅿 ℘*203-438-4519. www.aldrichart.org*
Changing exhibits by both established and upcoming contemporary artists are presented in this handsome Colonial dwelling. The **sculpture garden** displays changing works (◷*open year-round daily dawn to dusk*).

ADDRESSES

🏨 STAY

$$$ West Lane Inn – *22 West Lane (Rte. 35), Ridgefield.* 📞*203-438-7323. www.westlaneinn.com. 18 rooms.* Passers-by often stop to admire this gracious mansion, an 1849 Colonial surrounded by towering maples. All rooms have queen-sized four-poster beds, air conditioning and private baths, and some have fireplaces (a favorite is the semicircular front room—no fireplace, but three windows in a bay). Continental breakfast, available in the breakfast room in winter, is served on the expansive front porch in summer.

🍴 EAT

$$$ Bassos – *124 New Canaan Ave., Norwalk.* 📞*203-354-6566. www.basso bistrocafe.com.* **Mediterranean.** A local favorite, this lively bistro, headed up by chef Renato Donzelli, features artfully-prepared dishes influenced by Italian and Latin American cuisine. The casual and contemporary cafe offers a wide selection of appetizers and small plates, like the warm goat cheese and mushroom tart, or tuna and mango sashimi salad, and entrées including spicy pork tenderloin, veal stuffed with pecorino and asparagus and seafood linguine.

$$$ Bernard's Inn at Ridgefield – *20 West Lane, Ridgefield.* 📞*203-438-8282. www.bernardsridgefield.com. Closed Mon.* **French.** Located in a lovely clapboard house, this establishment boast stellar dishes, courtesy of Bernard, who has cooked at Le Cirque. The foie-gras, crispy sweetbreads, portobello crusted halibut, and roasted duck breast with figs are all outstanding. Sarah's Wine Bar upstairs has a more affordable menu, and more than 1,300 wines on the wine list.

TAKING A BREAK

A feast for the eyes as well as the palate, **Balducci's** (*1385 Post Road East, Westport. 203-254-5200; www.balduccis.com*) offers an impressive selection of fresh fruit and vegetables, along with meat, seafood, breads, cheeses, confections, condiments and gifts. If you're overwhelmed by the selection and artful displays, take a restorative espresso break in the cafe, where a rack of daily newspapers is on hand.

To satisfy your sweet cravings, head to **Chocopologie** (*12 S Main St., Norwalk.* 📞*203-854-4754; www.chocopologie.com*)**,** a cafe and retail store chockfull of handmade chocolates, along with fruit and chocolate-inspired drinks, soups, sandwiches and main dishes. The menu is a two- or three-course offering and might include white hot chocolate with lavender foam, pomegranate seed salad, wild mushroom blinis and chocolate braised beef ribs. Of course, desserts are a must; signature endings include the chocolate mousse and chocolate lava cake. Grab a box of chocolates to take home with you on your way out.

Cinnamon truffles, Chocopologie

© Simone Caprifogli / Chocopologie

Wethersfield ★

Unspoiled by industry throughout the 20C, Wethersfield (population 26,271) remains a pleasant suburb of Hartford. Approximately 200 dwellings in the town's picturesque historic district, Old Wethersfield, date from the 17C and 18C. A number of these houses, built by wealthy merchants and shipowners, have been restored. Established in 1634 along a natural harbor in the Connecticut River, Wethersfield was an important center of trade until the 18C, when floods changed the course of the river, leaving only a cove at the original harbor site. This change drastically affected the town's commercial activity, which decreased rapidly until, by the late 18C, farming had replaced trade as the economic mainstay.

- **Michelin Map:** 581 J 10
- **Info:** ℘860-721-2939; www.historicwethersfield.org.
- **Location:** The town is just south of Hartford, accessible off I-91.
- **Timing:** Allow a full day to visit the Wethersfield Museum, homes and stroll the Historic District.
- **Parking:** Visitor parking is behind the Wethersfield Museum on Main St.
- **Don't Miss:** A walk through the largest Historic District in Connecticut where you'll find 50 houses built before the Revolutionary War and more than 200 built around the Civil War.
- **Also See:** LITCHFIELD HILLS.

OLD WETHERSFIELD ★★
Main Street

This wide street is lined with attractively restored 18C houses, many of which have monumental double doors with carved swan's neck pediments distinctive to the Connecticut River Valley. The 1764 brick **Congregational Meetinghouse (C)** adjoins an early burial ground with tombstones dating from the 17C.

Webb-Deane-Stevens Museum ★★

211 Main St. ↝Visit by guided tour only (1hr). ▣◷ *May–Oct Mon & Wed–Sat 10am–4pm. Sun 1pm-4pm. Apr & Nov Sat 10am–4pm Sun 1pm–4pm. Special holiday tours are offered in Dec.* ⊗$10. ℘860-529-0612. *www.webb-deane-stevens.org.*
Owned by the National Society of the Colonial Dames of America, these three houses allow a study in architectural styles and decorative arts from 1752 to 1840, and a comparison of the lifestyles of a wealthy merchant, a politician and a modest craftsman.
Webb House –This elegant Georgian residence (1752), built by the prosperous merchant Joseph Webb Sr., was the scene of a four-day conference in May 1781 between Gen. George Washington and the French Count Rochambeau. Plans for the Yorktown campaign, which ultimately led to the defeat of the British in the American Revolution, were discussed by the two military leaders during this time.

The house contains a fine collection of period furnishings and decorative arts. Highlights include the south parlor where Washington and Rochambeau met—note the Colonial Revival mural (c.1916) that depicts Revolutionary events—and the bedchamber used by General Washington, who lodged at the Webb House during his stay in Wethersfield. The bedroom features the original flocked wool wallpaper, which Washington admired and noted in his diary.
Deane House – This house was built in 1766 for Silas Deane, an American diplomat who traveled to France during the Revolution to negotiate arms and equipment for the Continental Army. While abroad, Deane became involved in business deals that aroused suspicions about his loyalty, and he was accused of

Yorktown Parlor in the Joseph Webb House

© Charles Lyle / Webb-Deane-Stevens Museum

treason. He returned home and spent the rest of his life attempting, unsuccessfully, to clear his name. The entry hall is notable for the splendid side stairway with its carved cherrywood balusters, stained to imitate more expensive mahogany. The off-center stairway is unusual for a house of its period.

Stevens House – Isaac Stevens was a leather worker who built this house in 1788 for his bride. The dwelling passed by marriage to the Francis family, many of whose possessions are on view. Among the typical mid-19C furnishings are the Hitchcock chairs. The modest interiors make an interesting contrast to those of the more richly embellished Webb and Deane houses.

Wethersfield Museum (D)

200 Main St. ♿ 🅿 🕐 *Open year-round Tue–Sat 10am–4pm, Sun 1pm–4pm.* 🕐 *Closed major holidays.* 💲*$5.* 📞*860-529-7656. www.wethhist.org.* A former schoolhouse, this Victorian-era brick building (1893) serves as a visitor center and features a thematic exhibit that brings Wethersfield's history alive with interactive displays and artifacts ranging from a tiny arrowhead to a massive Connecticut Valley doorway. Two galleries have changing exhibits.

Hurlbut-Dunham House★ (E)

212 Main St. 🐾 *Visit by guided tour only (45min).* 🅿 🕐 *Open mid-May–mid-Oct Sat 11am–2pm, Sun 1pm–4pm.* 🕐 *Closed major holidays.* 💲*$5.* 📞*860-529-7656. www.wethhist.org.* During the early 1900s Jane and Howard Dunham, a prominent Wethersfield couple, traveled the world to collect furnishings for the gracious brick house that had been in their family since 1875. The Georgian-style house, which passed to the Wethersfield Historical Society with the Dunham belongings intact, has been restored to reflect the period of 1907–1935. Rococo Revival wallpapers, trompe l'œil cornices and crystal chandeliers are among the featured appointments.

Buttolph-Williams House★ (F)

249 Broad St. 🐾 *Visit by guided tour only (45min).* 🕐 *Open May–Oct Mon & Wed–Sat 10am–4pm. Sun 1pm–4pm.* 🕐 *Closed Tue & major holidays.* 💲*$5.* 📞*860-529-0612. www.ctlandmarks.org.* This center-chimney house (c. 1720), distinguished by oak clapboards, casement windows and a hewn overhang, is considered to be one of the most faithful restorations of an early Colonial dwelling

AMERICAN COOKE

OR THE ART OF DRESSING

VIANDS, FISH, POULTRY and VEGETABLES,

AND THE BEST MODES OF MAKING

PASTES, PUFFS, PIES, TARTS, PUDDINGS,
CUSTARDS AND PRESERVES,

AND ALL KINDS OF

C A K E S,

FROM THE IMPERIAL PLUMB TO PLAIN CAKE.

ADAPTED TO THIS COUNTRY,

AND ALL GRADES OF LIFE.

By Amelia Simmons,

AN AMERICAN ORPHAN.

PUBLISHED ACCORDING TO ACT OF CONGRESS.

HARTFORD:

PRINTED BY HUDSON & GOODWIN,

FOR THE AUTHOR.

1796.

Library of Congress

Cover of American Cookery by Amelia Simmons published in Hartford in 1796

Connecticut Firsts

The State of Connecticut distinguishes itself by claiming many firsts in US history. Among them are:

1639 – America's first Constitution, the Fundamental Orders of Connecticut, established a representative government.

1764 – The *Connecticut Courant* is the first newspaper published in America. The paper, still published today, is now called the *Hartford Courant*.

1794 – First cotton gin is patented by Eli Whitney and produced in New Haven.

1796 – Amelia Simmons of Hartford publishes the first cookbook in America, *American Cookery*.

1806 – Hartford native Noah Webster publishes his first dictionary.

1810 – The country's first insurance company, ITT Hartford Group, Inc. is established.

1836 – Samuel Colt, another Hartford native, patents the first revolver.

1860 – The corkscrew is patented by Philios Blake of New Haven.

1861 – Yale University awards the country's first Doctor of Philosophy degree.

1865 – Howe Machine Company is founded in Bridgeport to manufacture sewing machines, the first of which was patented by Elias Howe in 1846.

1868 – Alvin Fellows of New Haven is granted a patent for the first tape measure.

1908 – The first lollipop is made in New Haven by the Bradley and Smith Company.

1919 – Hartford's Traveler's Insurance Company becomes the first to issue aircraft liability insurance.

1939 – Russian-born engineer and US émigré Igor Sikorsky designs the first successful helicopter in the Western Hemisphere. It is produced by the United Aircraft Corporation in Bridgeport.

1949 – The prototype for the heart-lung machine is developed at Yale New Haven Hospital.

1954 – First nuclear submarine, the USS *Nautilus*, is launched in New London.

1975 – Ella T. Grasso becomes the first woman in America to be elected governor in her own right. She serves two terms as Governor of Connecticut.

1982 – Stamford native Dr. Robert K. Jarvik invents the world's first artificial heart.

1988 – The first heart-lung transplant is performed at Yale New Haven Hospital.

Buttolph-Williams House

© Nick Lacy / Connecticut Landmarks

in Connecticut. Particularly evocative of the Pilgrim era, the house served as the inspiration for the popular children's book *The Witch of Blackbird Pond* (1958) by Elizabeth George Speare.

Cove Warehouse
At Cove Park, north end of Main St. 🅿
🕐 *Open mid-May–mid-Oct Sat 10am–4pm, Sun 1pm–4pm.* 👓$2. ✆*860-529-7656. www.wethhist.org.*
Goods that arrived by sea in the 17C were stored in Wethersfield's seven warehouses before they were transported inland. About 1700, floods demolished six of the warehouses, leaving only Cove Warehouse intact. The structure houses an exhibit on the town's maritime trade between 1650 and 1830.

ADDRESSES

🍴/EAT

$$ Puket Cafe Thai Cuisine – *1030 Silas Deane Hwy., Wethersfield.* ✆*860-529-6590. www.puketcafe.com.* Don't let the non-descript, shopping strip facade of this unassuming cafe fool you. Inside, you'll find sophisticated decor and authentic, creatively-prepared and elegantly-presented Thai cuisine. The dining room is bright, with yellow walls and mint green-colored booths. Start with appetizers like the chicken satay, crispy calamari with Thai sauce, fish and shrimp cakes, or dumplings. There's a variety of specialty noodle and curry dishes, along with signature items, like the crispy-fried fish in chili sauce, shrimp mango, tamarind duck and grilled ribs with lemongrass and herbs.

$$ Village Pizza – *233 Main St., Old Wethersfield.* ✆*860-563-1513. www.villagepizzau.com.* This come-as-you-are pizza joint has been a downtown Wethersfield mainstay since it opened in 1983. If you're looking for a quick bite to eat, order one of the specialty grinders, wraps or club sandwiches. But most folks come for the wide selection of homemade pizza pies. The menu includes more than 20 choices, like the artichoke with fresh garlic and mozzarella, the spicy buffalo chicken, the clams casino, or the seafood with shrimp, clams and crabmeat. The menu also has a selection of salads and pasta dishes.

$ Main Street Creamery – *271 Main St., Old Wethersfield.* ✆*860-529-0509. www.mainstreetcreamery.com.* Few can pass up this friendly Main Street eatery, known for its creamy, homemade ice cream. Locals and visitors alike mingle outside, while deciding which flavor to choose. At last count, there were more than 50 hard and soft ice cream, sherbert and sorbet flavors. Even dogs get in on the act; order the special pooch vanilla soft serve cone, accompanied with a milk bone.

MAINE

Equal in surface area to the combined size of the other five New England states, Maine is a vast, thickly forested region fringed with a 3,500mi coastline. The origin of the name Maine is attributed by some historians to the Maine region in western France; others believe it derives from "the main," a term used by fishermen to distinguish the mainland from the hundreds of offshore islands. Maine is also referred to as Down East because of the winds that carry sailing vessels eastward along this section of the coast. Pine trees grow on the islands, along the shore and across the interior to the north, giving the state its nickname.

Highlights

1 Seeing the sun rise from the top of **Cadillac Mountain** (p131)
2 Shopping for bargains in **Freeport** (p143)
3 Sailing on a **tall-masted windjammer schooner** (p146)
4 Enjoying **lobster-in-the-rough** at a seaside restaurant (p148)
5 Joining a **moose safari in Greenville** (p158)

▶ **Population:** 1,318,301.
Info: ☎888-624-6345, www.visitmaine.com.
Area: 33,215sq mi.
Capital: Augusta,
Nickname: The Pine Tree State.
State Flower: White pine cone and tassel.

A Succession of Owners

The Maine coast was explored by the Vikings in the 11C and several centuries later by European fishermen. In 1605 Pierre de Gua, Sieur de Monts and **Samuel de Champlain** founded the Acadian territory. An English settlement, the **Popham Colony**, was established at the mouth of the Kennebec River in 1607; then in 1635 the English monarch Charles I gave the region of Maine to **Sir Ferdinando Gorges**, appointing him "Lord of New England." From hereon, the coast was the scene of constant battles between the French and the English. In 1677 the Massachusetts Colony bought Maine Sir Gorges' descendants, and the region remained under the jurisdiction of Massachusetts until 1820, when Maine was granted statehood.

In the early days the state's wealth depended on its forests. Timber was harvested to supply masts for the Royal Navy during the colonial period, when all pine trees 24 inches or greater in diameter belonged to the Crown. In the 19C, wooden **shipbuilding** in Maine peaked at Wiscasset, Bath and Searsport, where boatyards turned out four-, five- and six-masted vessels. With nearly 89 percent of the state covered with forests, Maine claims some of the country's largest **paper** and **pulp mills**. Fishing, especially **lobstering**, is a major industry. The state leads the US in the sardine-packing industry.

Maine's potato crop ranks within the country's top ten, and the state produces 98 percent of the country's lowbush blueberries.

Lobster Hut near Ogunquit

© Scott Schopieray / Stock.XCHNG

Maine Today

The state is an interesting mix of bustling tourist areas, especially along the coastline, rural areas, and small-town America. Urban areas are the exception in the Pine Tree State, and include Portland and Augusta. Portland has evolved into a tourism destination and cultural hub, with its own international airport, major hotels, eclectic dining possibilities, and institutions like the Portland Museum of Art and the Museum of African Culture. The revitalized Old Port area is a lively destination, where visitors can order fresh lobster and go out on boat tours from the working fishing wharves. The capitol city of Augusta is a hub of state government and commerce.

Much of Maine is still undeveloped, and large tracts of the state's piney interior are owned by logging companies, who often allow access for hiking, paddling, and moose-watching.

The coastal cities along Rte. 1 are the biggest draw in summertime, when windjammer cruises, beaches, and lobster shacks draw crowds. Those looking for art galleries, quaint inns and fine dining head to picturesque seaport towns like Ogunquit and Camden.

Most visitors put Maine's spectacular **Acadia National Park**, on Mt. Desert Island, on their must-see list. Hikers and campers enjoy miles of trails, with views of mountains, ocean, lakes and ponds. Old carriage roads draw bicyclists.

This region of "Downeast" Maine is where you'll discover those postcard views of rocky shoreline-meets-frothy surf that the state is famous for. Coastal Maine gets heavy visitation during the short summer season, so it's not always a peaceful escape, unless you head out on the water or set out on one of Acadia National Park's less-used hiking trails.

Maine's tawny sand beaches are somewhat pebbly, and the ocean water never really gets warm, but they are luxuriously wide and inviting. Favorites include Old Orchard Beach in southern Maine, Popham Beach State Park in mid-coast Maine on the Phippsburg peninsula, and Crescent Beach State Park, just south of Portland on the Cape Elizabeth Shore.

Maine's **Western Lakes and Mountains** region is best-known for ski resorts, including Sunday River and Sugarloaf, but there's lots of ungroomed outdoor territory to explore, This inland area encompasses the Sebago and Long Lakes area, the beautiful Grafton and Evans notch regions of the White Mountain National Forest, and, farther north, the outdoor-recreation-rich Rangeley Lake and Carrabassett River Valley. Sebago Lake, the second largest in Maine, offers swimming, boating, fishing, float-plane rides, and lakeside camping at Sebago Lake State Park.

Heading north, you'll find the classic New England town of Bethel, home of restaurants, country inns, and the Sunday River ski resort. Surrounded by the Mahoosuc Mountain range and Grafton State Park, the region has also become popular with summer hikers. The **Rangeley Lake** area has long been a favorite of vacationers, with a wide range of shopping, dining and accommodations, and Rangeley Lake State Park, a woodsy escape with swimming, picnicking and camping. Maine's other major ski resort, Sugarloaf USA, is located nearby in the Carrabassett River Valley. The resort becomes a paradise for mountain bikers in summer, with more than 50 miles of trails.

For a rugged outdoors escape, Maine's premier destination is the northwoods region, home of **Moosehead Lake and Baxter State Park**. Considered one of the greatest areas in the US for hunting, fishing and paddling, this region is also prime territory for moose watching. Base yourself in Greenville, on the southern tip of 40-mile-long Moosehead Lake, and take a moosewatching cruise, or explore some of the old logging roads around the lake.

Baxter State Park stands in the shadows of the magnificent Mount Katahdin, the state's highest peak, surrounded by 46 peaks and ridges. Hiking trails lead to waterfalls and awe-inspiring summit views.

MAINE

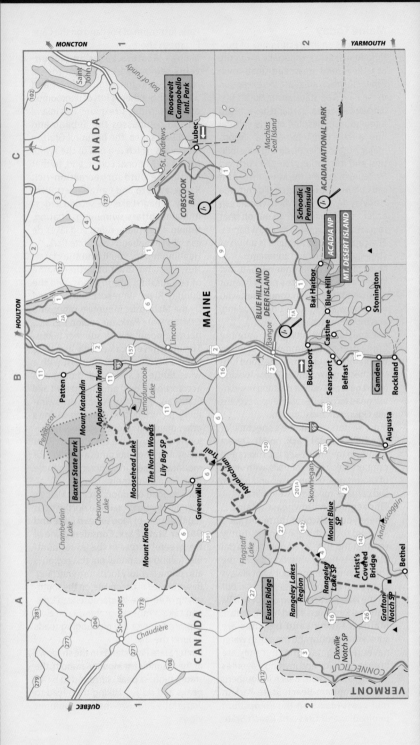

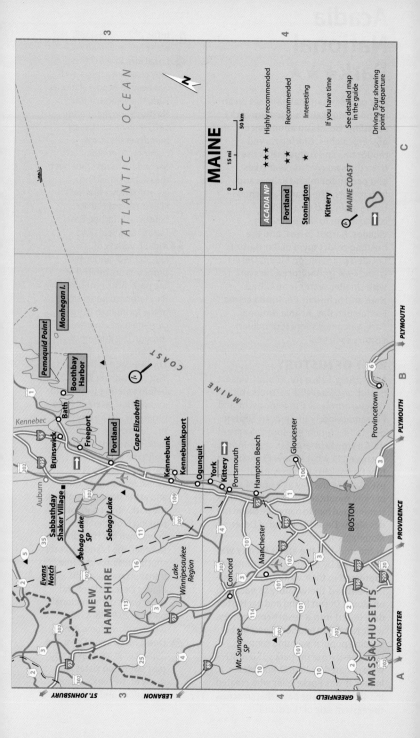

MAINE

0 15 mi
0 50 km

★★★ Highly recommended
★★ Recommended
★ Interesting

ACADIA NP

Portland

Stonington

Kittery

MAINE COAST

See detailed map in the guide

Driving Tour showing point of departure

ATLANTIC OCEAN

MAINE COAST

Pemaquid Point

Monhegan I.

Boothbay Harbor

Bath

Kennebec

Freeport

Brunswick

Portland

Cape Elizabeth

Kennebunk

Kennebunkport

Ogunquit

York

Kittery

Portsmouth

Hampton Beach

Gloucester

Auburn

Sabbathday Shaker Village

Sebago Lake SP

Sebago Lake

Evans Notch

NEW HAMPSHIRE

Lake Winnipesaukee Region

Concord

Manchester

Mt. Sunapee SP

BOSTON

MASSACHUSETTS

Provincetown

WORCESTER

PROVIDENCE

PLYMOUTH

PLYMOUTH

GREENFIELD

ST. JOHNSBURY

LEBANON

127

Acadia National Park★★★

This popular national park, set on an island along Maine's northern rocky coastline, boasts an abundance of scenic riches. Glacier-carved mountains and rugged cliffs rise from the sea; crystal-clear lakes and ponds dot inland valleys and lush forests. The island, attached to the mainland by a bridge, is also home to sleepy fishing villages, harbor towns, and the bustling resort town of Bar Harbor. Located primarily on Mount Desert Island★★★ (pronounced "dessert"), with smaller sections on Isle au Haut and Schoodic Peninsula across Frenchman Bay, Acadia National Park welcomes some four million visitors each year.

A BIT OF HISTORY

Measuring 108sq mi, Mount Desert Island once served as the summer campgrounds of the Penobscot and Passamaquoddy Indians. In September 1604 French explorers **Samuel de Champlain** and Sieur de Monts anchored in what is now **Frenchman Bay**. Champlain's impression of the largest island in the bay as a line of seven or eight mountains with rocky, treeless summits led him to name the island Isle des Monts Deserts ("Island of Deserted Mountains").

In the mid-19C the area's beauty was discovered by artists. The enthusiasm expressed in their writings and paintings enticed the wealthy to vacation on Mount Desert Island and Bar Harbor developed into a resort community, while Northeast and Southwest harbors became popular yachting centers.

Over one-third of the park's 35,000 acres were donated by John D. Rockefeller, Jr. In fact, it was Rockefeller who created the 45mi of carriage paths that crisscross the eastern side of the island.

Info: ☎207-288-3338; www.nps.gov/acad.

Location: Rte. 3 is the only road onto the island. Gateway to Acadia National Park, the village of **Bar Harbor★** (*on Rte. 3 south of US-1 on Mount Desert Island*) serves as the commercial center. Secondary roads spiderweb the island, providing access to other towns, like Northeast Harbor, Southwest Harbor, Bass Harbor and Seal Cove.

Kids: A variety of kid-focused ranger-led programs are offered at the park. Also, rent bikes in Bar Harbor to pedal some of the more than 45mi of carriage roads that weave through the interior of the park.

Timing: Stop at the Hull's Visitor Center on Rte. 3 before entering the park for information on events and programs. Plan a day for the loop drive, through the park, with stops at sights along the way.

Parking: Parking is available at major sights and attractions throughout the park. Street and lot parking is offered in downtown Bar Harbor. In summer, the Island Explorer shuttle bus provides free transportation around Mount Desert Island and other parts of the national park (☎207-288-4573, *www.exploreacadia.com*).

Don't Miss: Loop Drive; the 29mi scenic road takes you past sweeping vistas and many of the park's major attractions and sights.

© James Richey / iStockphoto.com

View of Frenchman Bay from Cadillac Mountain at sunset

🚗 DRIVING TOUR

PARK LOOP ROAD★★★
29mi. 🕐 See Acadia National Park map.

The many scenic outlooks, turnoffs and parking areas along the park's coastal road afford vistas ranging from sweeping seascapes to panoramas of pink granite mountains and island-studded waters. 😊 *Road may be fogbound during morning hours.*

▶ Begin at the Hulls Cove Visitor Center on Rte. 3. Then follow signs for the Loop Road .6mi to Frenchman Bay Overlook.

Frenchman Bay Overlook★
From the overlook here you have an unobstructed **view** to Schoodic Peninsula and across Frenchman Bay.

▶ The Loop Road is one-way from the Spur Rd. entrance to just south of Jordan Pond. After 3mi turn right for Sieur de Monts Spring.

Sieur de Monts Spring
Named after Sieur de Monts, leader of the 1604 expedition to North America, the spring and surrounding area constituted one of the first parcels of land set aside as part of the nature preserve that became Acadia National Park. The

PRACTICAL INFORMATION

Visitor Information – Acadia National Park Visitor Center
provides information about the park (*3mi north of Bar Harbor at Hulls Cove entrance;* 🕐 *open mid Apr–Jun & Oct daily 8am–4.30pm; Jul–Aug daily 8am–6pm; Sept daily 8am-5pm,* 📞*207-288-3338; www.nps.gov/acad*). In off-season, information is available at park headquarters at Eagle Lake (*Rte. 233, 3mi west of Bar Harbor;* 🕐 *open Nov–mid Apr daily 8am–4.30pm; mid Apr–Oct Mon–Fri 8am–4:30pm*). Acadia National Park is open daily year-round. The park

Loop Road is closed Dec–mid-Apr, but the Ocean Drive section is open year-round (🎫*entrance fee $20/vehicle for 7 days, $10/vehicle off-season*).
Local chambers of commerce have additional information: **Bar Harbor** (*2 Cottage St., Bar Harbor, ME 04609;* 📞*207-288-5103; www.barharborinfo. com*); **Mount Desert** (*18 Harbor Dr., Mount Desert, ME 04660;* 📞*207-276-5040; www.mountdesertchamber.org*); and **Southwest Harbor/Tremont** (329 Main St., Southwest Harbor, ME 04679; 📞*207-244-9264; www.acadiachamber.com*).

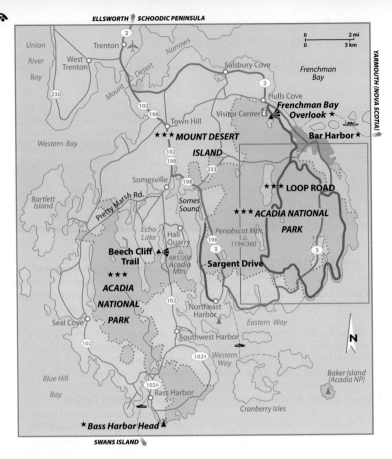

nearby **Nature Center** contains displays related to the park and its preservation (🕐*open mid-June–late-Sep daily 9am–5pm; mid-May–mid-Jun&mid-Sep–mid-Oct weeekends only*). In the **Wild Gardens of Acadia**, regional trees, flowers and shrubs are arranged according to their natural habitat: Marsh, bog, beach or mountain.

Abbe Museum [M]

&♿ 🅿 🕐*Open mid May–early-Nov daily 10am–6pm; winter Thu-Sat 10-4. Closed Jan ☞$6. ✆207-288-3519. www.abbemuseum.org.*

Dioramas and prehistoric artifacts (Stone Age tools, pottery) in this small pavilion evoke the life of Maine's earliest inhabitants, who occupied the Frenchman Bay and Blue Hill Bay areas prior to European colonization.

◗ Return to the Loop Road.

To the left stand the buildings of **Jackson Laboratory**, internationally known for its role in cancer research. The cliffs of Champlain Mountain loom on the right. Along the road you'll see scenes typical of Acadia: pink granite peaks, tall evergreens and natural roadside rock gardens.

◗ Follow signs to Sand Beach.

Sand Beach★

Composed of ground seashells, the only saltwater beach in the park provides a pleasant swimming spot for those who don't mind the bracing water temperature (50–60°F in summer). To see some spectacular scenery, walk Shore Path (*1.8mi*) from the upper parking level along the rocky coast past Thunder Hole (*below*) to the end of Otter Point.

▶ Continue south on Loop Rd.

Thunder Hole★
🅿️*Parking on the right.*
Over the years the ocean has burrowed into the rock here. At high tide the surf crashes through this narrow chasm, creating a thunderous roar.

▶ Continue .3 mi on Loop Rd.

Otter Cliffs★★
The next stop takes in the sheer cliffs just north of Otter Point, which rise 110ft above the ocean. Here, on the highest Atlantic headlands north of Rio de Janeiro, dramatic **views★★** encompass the splintered coast and the vast sea beyond.
Loop Road winds around Otter Point and Otter Cove, intersects with the road to Seal Harbor, then follows the shore of **Jordan Pond**, which lies below the cliffs of Penobscot Mountain. At the northern

end of the pond, note the large boulder balanced precariously atop one of the two rounded hills known as **The Bubbles**. For a closer look, stop at The Bubbles parking area.

▶ Continue on the Loop Road 1.4mi past The Bubbles parking area and turn right at the sign for Cadillac Mountain.

Cadillac Mountain★★★
The 3.5mi drive to the top of Cadillac Mountain (1,530ft) affords views of Eagle Lake—the largest body of freshwater in the park—Bar Harbor and the islands below. Cadillac Mountain ranks as the highest point on the Atlantic Coast. Easy **Summit Trail**, which winds for less than a mile around the barren mountaintop, offers breathtaking 360-degree **views★★★** of Frenchman Bay and the park.

▶ Return to the Loop Road, then turn right to complete the circle.

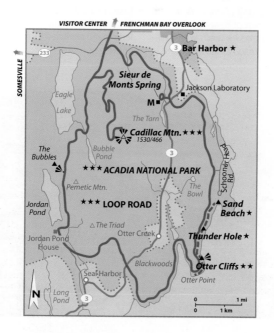

Bass Harbor Head Lighthouse, Acadia National Park

©National Park Service

OTHER AREAS OF THE PARK★★
Beech Cliff Trail

From Somesville take Rte. 102 South, turn right, then left onto Beech Cliff Rd. and continue to the end of the road.

This easy trail (*30min round-trip*) leads to the crest of Beech Cliff, where magnificent **views**★★ reach from freshwater Echo Lake to Acadia Mountain.

Bass Harbor Head★

At the end of Rte. 102A, 4mi south of Southwest Harbor.

Towering above the rocky shore of a remote headland, the **Bass Harbor Head Lighthouse** (1858) makes a delightful sight, especially at sunset.

Sargent Drive

Runs between Northeast Harbor and Rte. 3/198. Passenger cars only.

For views of the East Coast's only true fjord—a deep glacial valley now flooded by the ocean—take Sargent Drive as it traces the eastern shore of Somes Sound.

Schoodic Peninsula★★

From Mount Desert Island, take Rte. 3 North to US-1. Follow US-1 North to West Gouldsboro and turn right on Rte. 186. Just past Winter Harbor, look for signs to Acadia National Park and turn right. Road becomes one-way at park entrance.

Two thousand acres of Acadia National Park occupy the southern tip of this peninsula, which juts out from the mainland east across the bay from Mount Desert Island. Scenery along the park road takes in a kaleidoscope of tall stands of fir trees rimmed by pink granite ledges and encircled by the blue waters of the bay.

Isle au Haut, Acadia National Park

© National Park Service

Isle au Haut★

🚢Boats depart from Stonington (on Rte. 15) to Isle au Haut Harbor. One-way 45min. 🚢$18.50. Isle au Haut Boat Services. 🅿Call for seasonal schedules: ℘207-367-5193; www.isleauhaut.com.

Located south of Stonington on Deer Isle, tiny Isle au Haut measures just 6mi long and 3mi wide. The island is private, except for the 2,800 acres of woodlands that belong to Acadia National Park. To best sample its beauty, spend some time hiking or biking the web of trails that traverse the park.

ADDRESSES

🛏STAY

There are two **campgrounds** in Acadia National Park: Blackwoods (*Rte. 3, 5mi south of Bar Harbor; open year-round; $20/ day May–Oct $10 Apr & Nov; reservations: ℘800-365-2267*) and Seawall (*Rte. 102A, 4mi south of Southwest Harbor; open late May–Sept; 🚢$14–$20/day*). For a list of private campgrounds in the area, contact the area chambers of commerce.

$$$$ Chiltern Inn – *11 Cromwell Harbor Rd., Bar Harbor. ℘207-288-3371 or 800-709-0114. www.chilterninnbarharbor.com. 4 suites.* This four-suite property is a pampering oasis within walking distance to Compass Harbor in Acadia National Park and downtown Bar Harbor. The spacious rooms feature fireplaces, window seats with ocean and garden views, and oversized marble baths. Public areas include an indoor pool and spa, art gallery and gardens.

$$$$ The Claremont – *On Rte. 102 in Southwest Harbor. Closed mid-Oct–mid-May. ℘207-244-5036 or 800-244-5036. www.theclaremonthotel.com. 44 rooms and cottages.* Set on the shoreline of Mt. Desert Island, the Claremont seems unchanged since it first opened in 1884. The four-story wooden hotel with its wide veranda overlooks lovely Somes Sound and its surrounding mountains. Two facts speak volumes about the genteel attitude here: croquet is the sport of choice, and men are requested to wear jackets and ties at dinner. Rooms are simply furnished.

$$ Acadia Hotel – *20 Mount Desert St., Bar Harbor. Closed Nov–mid-Apr. ℘207-288-5721 or 888-876-2463. www.acadia hotel.com. 11 rooms.* If you're looking for value, you can't beat this prime downtown Bar Harbor property overlooking the village green. Bar Harbor shops, restaurants and waterfront are within easy walking distance from the front door. Rooms are decorated in comfortable, low-key style, with tasteful floral and print wallpapers, quality linens and furnishings. Added bonuses include free parking and Wi-Fi.

🍴EAT

$$$ Havana – *318 Main St., Bar Harbor. ℘207-288-2822. www.havanamaine.com. Dinner only.* **Cuban.** A zesty alternative to boiled lobster, Havana takes New American concepts and deftly overlays them with Latino influences. The oft-changing menu is filled with creative selections, like the local mussels sautéed with chorizo sausage or duck empanadas, and entrées like paella with Maine lobster, and short ribs braised in apple cider.

$$$ West Street Cafe – *76 West St., Bar Harbor. ℘207-288-5242. www.west streetcafe.com.* **American.** Fresh quality and a casual, friendly atmosphere have made this a favorite with locals and visitors alike for more than a quarter-century. Emphasis is on seafood and traditional New England fare, like clam chowder, lobster every which way (the shore dinner comes with mussels and a slice of blueberry pie), crab cakes, and shrimp. There is also a wide selection of sandwiches, beef, pasta and poultry dishes.

$$ Jordan Pond House – *Park Loop Rd, Acadia National Park (north of Seal Harbor). ℘207-276-3316. www.thejordanpond house.com.* **American.** Popovers and tea on the lawn of the Jordan Pond House is one of the great Acadia National Park traditions. Buttery popovers are served in the afternoons at rustic wooden tables with a view up the pond to a pair of perfectly rounded mountains. But don't overlook the rest of the menu; the lobster rolls and lobster stew are filled with succulent chunks of Maine's favorite crustacean, and are among the best on the island. In the evening and on rainy days, indoor seating is offered.

Augusta

Situated on the banks of the Kennebec River, Maine's capital is a bustling industrial and residential city. The river and its adjacent woodlands have been a source of wealth to Augusta ever since the 17C, when the Pilgrims established a trading post on its east bank. In the 18C and 19C the Kennebec River served as an important avenue for boat traffic, as well as a source of ice in winter. Wood cut from the forests bordering the river also contributed to the region's prosperity.

SIGHTS
State House

State and Capitol Sts. ⏰*Open year-round.* ☛*Free guided tours Mon–Fri 9am–12pm.* ⏰*Closed major holidays.* ℘*207-287-2301. www.maine.gov/legis.*
The domed capitol building is best viewed from the riverside park across from the front entrance of the State House. Constructed between 1829 and 1832 according to the design of eminent Boston architect Charles Bulfinch, the major portion of the State House was later remodeled and enlarged. Despite this change, the columned facade and other characteristic Bulfinch elements were preserved. The House, Senate and Executive chambers are all located in the State House. Twenty acres of garden and green space decorated the front.

Maine State Museum

83 State House Station, just south of the State House. ♿⏰*Open year-round Tue–Fri 9am–5pm, Sat 10am–4pm, Sun 1pm–4pm.* ⏰*Closed major holidays.* ☞*$5.* ℘*207-287-2301. www.mainestatemuseum.org.*
This modern building houses the State Library and Archives as well as the State Museum. Exhibits on the history, life and environment of Maine and its residents are on view in the museum's three levels. Dioramas, period rooms, artifacts and equipment tell the story of state industries, past and present, such as agriculture, lumbering and shipbuild-

▶ **Population:** 18,560.
♿ **Michelin Map:** 581 O 2
🛈 **Info:** ℘207-623-4559; www.augustamaine.com.
◖ **Location:** I-95 provides quick access to Augusta. The capitol district, located in the State Street area on the west bank of the Kennebec River, includes the State House, the State Museum and other attractions.
👪 **Kids:** Whitewater rafting on the Kennebec River is a popular adventure for older children. Get a list of professional outfitters from Raft Maine (*www.raftmaine.com*).
⏰ **Timing:** Allow half a day to see the sights in the capitol district, then plan a day or so to explore outlying areas and to be outdoors.
🅿 **Parking:** Free parking is available in lots west and north of the State Capitol and Maine State Museum. A parking garage is located at the corner of Capitol and Sewall streets.
☺ **Don't Miss:** A free tour of the Bullfinch-designed State Capitol and a visit to the Maine State Museum. If you feel like looking farther, the nearby town of Hallowell, two miles south of the State Capitol on Rte. 201, has been dubbed the state's "antique capitol." Browse shops and galleries on Water St.

ing. **Made in Maine** includes mill and factory machinery plus more than 1,000 samples of products manufactured in the state. Archaeological artifacts document the life of the area's first inhabitants and an interactive display traces early exploration routes.

Bethel

Bethel's distinguished inn and prep school are enhanced by the town's magnificent setting in the White Mountains. Here opportunities abound for hiking, biking, hunting, fishing, golfing, rock-hounding in the abandoned mines in the area, and excursions into the surrounding White Mountains.

A BIT OF HISTORY

Permanent settlement in the area dates from 1774, when a sawmill and then a gristmill were established on a brook flowing into the Androscoggin River. In 1796 the town was incorporated and named Bethel, a Biblical term meaning "house of God." With the arrival of the railroad in 1851 connecting the community to Portland and then to Montreal, the timber industry began to dominate Bethel's economy. Lumber, dairy products and tourism are major sources of the area's income today.

Today a National Historic District, the village of Bethel is a quiet residential hamlet, attracting visitors to the recreational facilities of the Bethel Inn and Country Club, and co-ed students to **Gould Academy**.

The surrounding mountains and forests are magnets for outdoor enthusiasts, and skiers are drawn to the slopes of the nearby **Sunday River Resort**.

SIGHTS
Dr. Moses Mason House

On the Green. ⟶ *Visit by 30min guided tour only.* P ⟳ *Open Jul–Aug Tue–Sat 1pm–4pm.* ⟨$3. ⟩ 207-824-2908. *www.bethelhistorical.org/museum.*
This is one of the carefully preserved houses fringing the village green. Built in 1813 for a prominent physician, the house features period furnishings and colorful folk-art murals (c.1835) adorning the central staircase.

▶ **Population:** 2,659.
🚗 **Michelin Map:** 581 M 2
📘 **Info:** ℘207-824-2282; www.bethelmaine.com.
▶ **Location:** The small, historic village, dominated by the commons and the Bethel Inn and Country Club, is located at the intersection of Rte. 26 and Rte. 2 in western Maine, just east of the New Hampshire border. Sunday River Ski Resort is located about five miles east of the village.
👪 **Kids:** Sunday River Resort offers kid-pleasing activities, including tubing, skiing, nature hikes, biking and more. Also, kids can hike the easy Androscoggin River Trail.
🕐 **Timing:** Spend your time on outdoor adventures; hiking, skiing, fishing and nature walks abound. Grafton Notch State Park, with waterfalls and hiking trails, can take the better part of a day.
🅿 **Parking:** On-street parking is available in the village. The *Mountain Explorer* offers free shuttle service between Bethel Village and Sunday River Resort, November to early April.
😎 **Don't Miss:** A visit to scenic Grafton Notch State Park. The drive along east-west Rte. 26, through mountain notches and alongside waterfalls, is especially beautiful in fall. Also walk around Bethel Commons, with historic buildings, shops and galleries. A walking-tour brochure is available from the Bethel Historical Society (℘207-824-2908; www.bethelhistorical.org).

Legendary Logger

The state of Maine is largely forested land: logging has long been a big part of the economy. Popularized by professional writers and lumber-industry publicists, the legend of **Paul Bunyan** tells how he and Babe the Blue Ox felled trees an acre at a time. Paul was known for his gigantic size and feats of strength as well as his lumbering prowess. No lumberman claimed as voracious an appetite as Paul; when he was a boy, he would eat 40 bowls of porridge. As a man, Paul ate so many pancakes that his cook required 50 men with slabs of bacon tied to their feet just to grease the humongous griddle.

Artist's Covered Bridge

Sunday River Rd., Newry 4mi northwest of North Bethel. 🅿 *☎207-624-3400. http://www.maine.gov/mdot/historic-bridges/index.htm.*

It's said that no covered bridge in Maine is more photographed, sketched or painted than this 1872 gem, featuring an arched entrance and latticework sides.

EXCURSIONS
Grafton Notch State Park★

▶ *25mi northwest of Bethel via Rte. 26 West.* ◐*Open mid-May–mid-Oct daily dawn–dusk.* ☜*$3. ☎207-824-2912 or 207-624-6080 (off season). www.state.me.us/doc/parks.*

Rte. 26 heads through the Bear River Valley and into Grafton Notch State Park, an unspoiled area in the White Mountains. An auto tour through the park offers views of the notch dominated by **Old Speck Mountain** (4,180ft) to the west and **Baldpate Mountain** to the east. Take time to visit lovely **Screw Auger Falls** and **Mother Walker Falls** (*1mi north of Screw Auger Falls*).

Evans Notch★

▶ *18mi southwest of Bethel. Follow Rte. 2 West for 10mi, then turn left onto Rte. 113.* Fine **views** of the Cold River Valley abound on the drive from Gilead to North Chatham through this notch in White Mountain National Forest (🕮 *see THE WHITE MOUNTAINS in New Hampshire*).

Canoeing and Kayaking – The Androscoggin and Ellis Rivers offer 60 miles of swift but fairly gentle water, perfect for exploring Bethel's natural beauty. Local outfitters offer canoe and kayak rentals, shuttles, guided trips, and even inn-to-inn paddling excursions.

Rockhounding – The Bethel area offers a unique activity for visitors who don't mind getting their hands dirty. Thanks to its unique pegmatite formations, Oxford County has some of the oldest and most famous mineral mines in the Northeast.

Dig for minerals excavated from the mines (and keep what you find) on an excursion with **Maine Mineralogy Expeditions** (◐*Open May–Sep;* ☜*$25; ☎207-824-4224 or 800-533-3607; www.rocksme.biz*). You might find specimens of quartz, beryl, rose quartz, feldspar, smoky quartz, or mica, left behind when the area was mined. Guides may also take you inside Bumpus Mine, where the world's largest beryl crystal was found. To see samples of the region's most sought-after stone, the watermelon tourmaline, and 300 rock specimens, visit **Mt. Mann Jewelers** on 57 Main St., *☎207-824-3030, www.mtmann.com.*

ADDRESSES

🍴EAT

$$$$ Bethel Inn & Country Club – *Broad St. ☎207-824-2175, or 800-654-0125. www.bethelinn.com.* The historic, rambling inn fronts the village green and welcomes the public at breakfast, lunch and dinner. The main dining room provides the setting for dinner specialties and traditional New England dishes, such as fresh Maine lobster, rack of lamb or seafood stuffed sole. Family fare (sandwiches, ribs, burgers) is served in the casual **$$ Millbrook Tavern**. Have lunch on the screened-in terrace, overlooking the 18-hole golf course.

Cobscook Bay

Emptying into Passamaquoddy Bay, Cobscook Bay is a natural basin that is almost entirely landlocked. The coastal fishing towns of Eastport and Lubec, separated by less than 3mi of water but nearly 40mi apart by land, stand sentinel over the channels linking the two bay areas. The exceptionally high tides (18–24ft) for which this bay and its neighboring shores are known so impressed the local Indians that they named it **Cobscook**, meaning "boiling waters."

Michelin Map: 583 V 4
Info: ℘203-871-3714; www.cobscookbay.com.
Location: Located two hours north of Bar Harbor, the bay is ringed by rural communities within Washington County.
Don't Miss: Roosevelt Campobello International Park displays some of the most stunning scenery in New England. This region is known for birding; check out the Downeast Birding Festival, held here annually on Memorial Day weekend.

🚗 DRIVING TOUR

LUBEC TO EASTPORT
60mi.

This seaside ramble offers spectacular views of island-studded Cobscook Bay and Passamaquoddy Bay.

Along the way, stop at two pretty state parks and the Roosevelt Campobello International Park.

Lubec

During the 17C and 18C, this small fishing port was a center for goods smuggled into the US from Canada. Ships authorized to sail to Europe set out from Lubec and returned several days later with cargoes of rum, sugar and other staples.

The record-breaking time of these highly profitable round-trip "transatlantic voyages"—in fact only short trips to Canada where goods were available at low prices—was never questioned. By the late 1800s, 20 sardine-packing factories had been established in Lubec, forming the basis of the town's economy.

▶ From Lubec, cross the Franklin Delano Roosevelt International Bridge to Campobello Island and follow the signs to Roosevelt Campobello International Park.

Roosevelt Campobello International Park★★

Campobello Island is part of the Canadian province of New Brunswick. US citizens must present a passport at the border. 🅿️♿🕐*Park grounds open daily year-round dawn–dusk. Buildings open late May–Columbus Day daily 9am–5pm. Columbus Day–Oct daily 9am–4pm (Atlantic time). ℘506-752-2922. www.fdr.net.*

An agreement by Canada and the US established this international park dedicated to Franklin Delano Roosevelt. Roosevelt, a four-terms US president, spent his early summers at Campobello. The vast 2,800-acre international park is a magnificent landscape of forests, bogs, cliffs, lakes and beaches. From **Friars Head** (*south of the visitor center turn right at the sign marked Picnic Area*) there is a view west of the Maine coast. A sweeping vista along the shore of **Herring Cove** to **Herring Cove Head** is visible from **Con Robinson's Point** (*follow Glensevern Rd. east to the end*). The 34-room **Roosevelt Cottage★** displays personal mementos of the Roosevelt family.

▶ Return to Lubec and follow Rte. 189 some 4mi to the gas station. Turn left at the park sign.

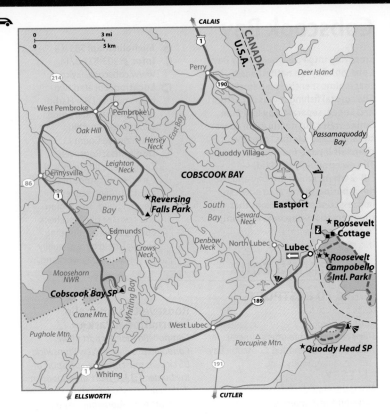

Quoddy Head State Park★

6mi south of Lubec. 🅿 🕐*Open late May–mid Oct daily 10am–4pm.* 🎫*$3.* 📞*207-733-0911. www.state.me.us/ doc/parks.*

Red-and-white-striped **Quoddy Head Lighthouse** marks the easternmost point of the US, with views of the island of Grand Manan in New Brunswick. A coastal **footpath** (🥾*round-trip 1hr 15min*) beginning at the parking lot affords a superb **view** of the sea and the granite ledges.

▶ Return to Rte. 189 and head west. The road climbs to a point that offers a view of Passamaquoddy Bay and the harbor. At Whiting take US-1 North.

Cobscook Bay State Park

⛺ 🅿 🕐*Open mid May–mid Oct daily 9am–dusk.* 🎫*$4.50.* 📞*207-726-4412. www.state.me.us/doc/parks.*

Set on the shores of Cobscook Bay, this park features tall stands of evergreens, arising from crevices in coastal ledges.

▶ Continue on US-1. In West Pembroke take the unmarked road on the right (opposite Rte. 214) and follow signs for Reversing Falls Park.

Reversing Falls Park★

From here, admire Cobscook Bay's pine-covered islands and secluded coves. Twice daily, with the changing of the tides, the current is so strong in one area that the rushing waters form a .5mi-long falls.

▶ Return to US-1. Continue through Perry, then take Rte. 190 south.

Eastport

Tiny Eastport, the easternmost city in the US, is located on Moose Island.

Maine Coast★★

Tumbling down glacier-sculpted cliffs of jagged rocks to meet the Atlantic Ocean, the coast of Maine defines the eastern edge of the state, stretching more than 3,500mi from Kittery north to the border of New Brunswick, Canada. This is a wind-whipped landscape, where fierce storms called "nor'easters" batter the shore in winter, and summer visitors are hard-pressed to find sandy beaches. Driving this rugged coast along US-1, with its tranquil harbors and lonely lighthouses, is its own reward.

Maine Coast Sights have been organized south to north beginning at the southern border of Maine in Kittery. Mileages given are for travel on US-1 unless otherwise specified.

KITTERY

📞 *207-363-4422.*
www.gatewaytomaine.org.
Shipbuilding, fishing and tourism are the mainstays of this village located just north of the New Hampshire line. Private boatyards turn out pleasure craft, adding to the town's role as a shipbuilding center. A drive along tree-shaded Rte. 103 leading to the 18C settlement of Kittery Point affords glimpses of the river and some of the area's original Colonial homes.

VISITOR INFORMATION

The **Maine Office of Tourism** (*59 State House Station, Augusta, ME 04330;* 📞*877-624-6345; www.visitmaine.com*) and the **Maine Tourism Association** (*327 Water St., Hallowell, ME 04347;* 📞*800-767-8709; www.mainetourism.com*) both provide a wealth of information to visitors. An official **Maine State Visitor Information Center** is located in Kittery at I-95 and US-1 (📞*207-439-1319*).

Michelin Map: 581 N-P 3-6

Info: 📞877-624-6345; www.mainetourism.com.

Location: Scenic US-1 traces the entire length of the Maine coastline, beginning just north of Portsmouth, NH. For quicker travel, I-95 cuts inland and travels north from Kittery to Bangor. A series of secondary roads access jutting peninsulas and small coastal towns.

Kids: Hop on a lobster boat excursion offered by outfitters along the coast; walk the boardwalk and swim in the calm waters at Old Orchard Beach.

Timing: Driving from one town to another can be time-consuming with traffic and slow-moving secondary roads. Try to spend at least two to three days each exploring the southern, mid-, and downeast coastal regions. Then reserve a day to relax on the beach overlooking the spectacular rocky Maine coastline.

Parking: On-street parking and designated lots are located in top resort towns along the coast, but, in general, parking can be tough to find. In the busiest towns: follow the parking signs, make a few passes, and hope for the best.

Don't Miss: The sandy beaches of York and Ogunquit; the bustling, hip seaside city of Portland; picturesque Boothbay Harbor, Rockland and Camden; pristine Blue Hill —and lobster-in-the-rough anywhere along the way.

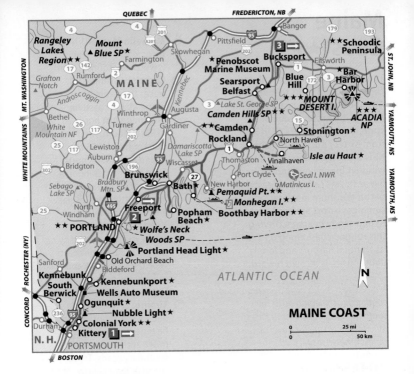

MAINE COAST

Fort McClary State Historic Site

On Rte. 103 east of Kittery in Kittery Point. P ⊙*Open Memorial Day–late Sept daily 10am–8pm.* ⊛*$3.* ℘*207-384-5160. www.maine.gov/doc/parks.*
A hexagonal-shaped 1846 blockhouse in an oceanfront park setting is all that remains of the stockade first christened

Fort William in the early 18C. During the Revolutionary War, the fort was renamed after Major Andrew McClary, who was killed at the Battle of Bunker Hill.

YORK★

▷ *9mi north of Kittery.* ℘*207-363-4422. www.gatewaytomaine.org.*
York is splintered into so many separate villages that Mark Twain once wryly observed, "It is difficult to throw a brick...any one direction without disabling a postmaster." Today the area known to locals as "the Yorks" include Colonial **York Village**; **York Harbor**, a low-key resort at the mouth of York River; **York Beach**, with its boardwalk amusement park; and the sheltered beach of **Cape Neddick**.

Colonial York★★

Along Rte. 1A in York Village, just off US-1. ⊙*Open Jun–Columbus Day Mon–Sat 9.30am–4pm.* ⊛*$6 for one building $12 all buildings (tickets available at Jefferds Tavern, which serves as the visitor center).* ℘*207-363-1756. www.oldyork.org.*

Kittery's Outlet Malls

From I-95, take Exit 3 to US-1. ℘*888-KITTERY. www.thekittery outlets.com.*
More than 120 outlet stores cluster along a 1.5mi stretch of Rte. 1 in Kittery. Offering a wide range of items including clothing, shoes, crystal, silver, housewares and furnishings, Kittery's outlets constitute a shopper's delight. Such designers as Anne Klein, Liz Claiborne, Ralph Lauren and Tommy Hilfiger are represented.

Sarah Orne Jewett

The second of three daughters born to a country doctor and his wife, Theodora Sarah Orne Jewett began life in 1849 in South Berwick, Maine. She grew up in the Georgian house (1774) that her grandfather—a wealthy sea captain and merchant—had purchased in 1819. As a young girl Jewett began writing sketches of the life she observed around her. Her first story, "Jenny Garrow's Lovers," was published in 1868, and the following year Jewett's stories began appearing in *The Atlantic* magazine. In 1877 a collection of her stories was published as the book *Deephaven*. Perhaps her best-known work, *The Country of the Pointed Firs*, an expression of her admiration for Maine and its people, came out in 1896.

Today admirers of this Victorian author can visit the house where Jewett was born and died. Furnishings and 18C antiques in the **Sarah Orne Jewett House** (*5 Portland St. in S. Berwick, 10mi north of Kittery on Rte. 236;* 🔊*visit by 45min guided tour only;* ⏰*Jun–mid Oct Fri–Sun 11am–5pm;* 💲*$5;* 📞*207-384-2454; www. historicnewengland.org*) are arranged as they were when the author lived here.

Nearby, on a site overlooking the Salmon Falls River, the stately Georgian **Hamilton House★** (*40 Vaughan's Lane in S. Berwick, 9mi west of Kittery via Rte. 236;* ⏰*Jun–mid-Oct Wed–Sun 11am–5pm;* 💲*$8;* 📞*207-384-2454; www. historicnewengland.org*) and its formal riverside gardens provided the setting for much of Sarah Orne Jewett's historical romance *The Tory Lover* (1901), set in Berwick during the Revolution.

A group of early structures flanks the village green, giving visitors a glimpse of colonial times. On the north side of Rte. 1A stands the 18C **First Parish Church**, with its cock weathervane, and the **Town Hall**, which served for a time as the York County courthouse. Across Rte. 1A flanking the **Old Burying Ground** you'll find the **Jefferds Tavern** and schoolhouse, the **Emerson-Wilcox House**, and rising from the top of a small hill, the **Old Gaol**. Nearby are the George Marshall Store (a craft shop) and fishermen's sheds covered with lobster buoys. The inviting red Colonial dwelling (c.1730) beside the river was the home of **Elizabeth Perkins** (1879-1952), one of York's most prominent residents.

The **John Hancock Warehouse** (*on Lindsay Rd.*) is one of several coastal warehouses owned by John Hancock, Revolutionary War patriot, signer of the Declaration of Independence and prosperous merchant.

York Harbor

Follow Rte. 1A South from York Village. This landlocked boating center is a haven for small craft. Beautiful homes grace the harbor's tree-covered shores. The **Sayward-Wheeler House** contains family heirlooms accumulated by prosperous trader Jonathan Sayward and his descendants (*9 Barrell Lane Ext.;* 🔊*visit by 45min guided tour only,* ⏰*Jun–mid Oct second and fourth Sat of the month 11am–5pm;* 💲*$5;* 📞*207-384-2454; www. historicnewengland.org*).

Nubble Light

© Maine Office of Tourism

◗ Rte. 1A leads past Long Sands Beach, which stretches 2mi from York Harbor to Cape Neddick and is bordered by summer cottages.

Nubble Light★

Leave Rte. 1A and turn right on Nubble Rd.; continue to the tip of Cape Neddick.
From the shore here you'll get a good view of the 1879 Nubble Lighthouse on its offshore island; the Isles of Shoals lie in the distance.

OGUNQUIT★

◗ *8mi north of York.* ℰ*207-646-2939. www.ogunquit.org.*
In the Algonquin language, *ogunquit* means "beautiful place by the sea." The artists who discovered this little beach town undoubtedly agreed with the description, for by the turn of the century many painters and writers had come to live and work close to Ogunquit's rocky shores.

Today, Ogunquit attracts hordes of summer crowds who come for the 3.5mi-long sugar white beach, upscale restaurants and resorts, and shops and galleries. Works by members of the town's present-day artists' colony are exhibited in galleries scattered throughout the village, including the **Fran Scully Gallery** (*locations on Main St. and Perkins Cove*) and the rustic **Barn Gallery** (*Bourne's Lane at Shore Rd.*). Overlooking the sea, the small, modern **Ogunquit Museum of American Art** (*on Shore Rd. just south of Perkins Cove;* ℰ*207-646-4909; www.ogunquit museum.org*) showcases the work of 20C American artists. During the summer a different play is presented every week at the **Ogunquit Playhouse** (ℰ*207-646-5511; www.ogunquitplayhouse.org*).

Perkins Cove★

From Rte 1, take Shore Rd. and follow signs to cove. ℗*Parking is limited.*
This charming man-made anchorage harbors dozens of shops and several seafood restaurants along its shores. A footbridge across the entrance to the cove can be raised to accommodate local traffic. Perkins Cove is also the departure point for a variety of excursions and fishing boats.

Marginal Way★

℗*Parking available at Perkins Cove and at Israel's Head lighthouse.*
Beginning at Perkins Cove, this scenic coastal footpath leads around the wind-swept promontory called Israel's Head and ends near the center of Ogunquit. Originally a cattle path for a local farmer, Marginal Way now provides visitors with striking **views★** of the rocky coast and Perkins Cove.

EXCURSION
♣♣ Wells Auto Museum

◗ *5mi north of Ogunquit. 1811 US-1.* ♿℗◷*Memorial Day–Sep daily 10am–5pm.* ☞*$7.* ℰ*207-646-9064. www.wellsautomuseum.com.*
Car buffs will find more than 80 vintage cars here dating from 1900 to 1963. And kids will enjoy the collection of antique toys and bicycles.

THE KENNEBUNKS★

◗ *Kennebunk is 12mi north of Ogunquit.* ℰ*207-967-0857 or www.visitthekennebunks.com.*
Popular with artists and writers, the resort villages of the Kennebunk region include **Kennebunk**, **Kennebunkport, Cape Porpoise** and their associated beaches. This area owes its early prosperity to the shipbuilding industry. In later years, from the late 19C through the early 20C, this stretch of Maine coast reigned as a fashionable resort area, with grand hotels and summer mansions.

Kennebunkport★

Take Rte. 9 East off US-1.
The town's narrow streets swell with tourists in the summer months; its most famous summer resident is George Bush, 41st president of the US, whose family estate on Walker Point is visible from Ocean Drive. When you tire of sunbathing on **Kennebunk Beach**, Kennebunkport's commercial center, **Dock Square**, harbors a variety of charming shops set along the tidal Kennebunk River.

🚹🚺 Seashore Trolley Museum

On Log Cabin Rd., about 2mi southeast of US-1. ♿🕐*Memorial Day–mid-Oct daily 10am–5pm. Also open weekends in May & Oct* ⬛*$10.* ☎*207-967-2712. www.trolleymuseum.org.*

Take a 3.5mi ride back in time here on a restored antique electric trolley car. After the tour, stroll through the car barns to see additional trolleys, and watch artisans involved in the painstaking process of restoration in the workshop.

PORTLAND★★

◐ *23mi north of Kennebunk.*
♿*See PORTLAND.*

FREEPORT

◐ *15mi north of Portland.*
ℹ*Tourist Information:* ☎*207-865-1212, 800-865-1994 or www.freeportusa.com.*

A favored shopping spot, the comely town of Freeport is the home of L.L. Bean, the famous sporting goods mail-order enterprise, as well as the more than 85 brand-name factory outlets that have sprung up along Main Street (Rte. 1) and side streets. All in all, the town is home to more than 170 outlet stores, shops, and cafes.

During Freeport's early days, the logs for ships' masts and spars were harvested from the surrounding forests and shipped to England from the town's open harbor, or "free port." In 1820 Freeport earned its sobriquet, "Birthplace of Maine," when the treaty agreeing to separate Maine from Massachusetts—and subsequently granting Maine statehood—was signed in a local tavern here.

Wolfe's Neck Woods State Park★

5mi from the center of Freeport. From Main St., turn right onto Bow St. (across from L.L. Bean); take the third right on Flying Point Rd. and veer right on Wolfe's Neck Rd. ♿🅿🕐*Open Apr–Oct daily 9am–dusk.* ⬛*$4.50.* ☎*207-865-4465. www.state.me.us/doc/parks.*

The beauty and calm of the park's wooded picnic sites and trails over-

---

Cruising the Bay and Islands

Boothbay Harbor serves as the departure point for a number of different cruises around the Boothbays and day trips to Monhegan Island. Cruises leave from several piers in the center of Boothbay Harbor (*along Commercial St.*).

For information, contact the **Boothbay Harbor Chamber of Commerce** (☎*207-633-2353; www.boothbayharbor.com*) *or one of the following companies:* Cap'n Fish's Boat Trips (*Pier 1;* ☎*207-633-6605; www.boothbayboattrips. com;*) *or* Balmy Days Cruises (*Pier 8;* ☎*207-633-2284 or 800-298-2284; www.balmydayscruises.com*).

---

looking Casco Bay offer a pleasant diversion from the shop-lined streets of Freeport village. The Casco Bay Trail (*.5mi*), which provides close-up views of Googins Island, is especially scenic. Look for ospreys nesting on Googins Island (they fly to South America in winter) and take a guided nature walk (in season; check website for schedule).

BRUNSWICK

◐ *9mi north of Freeport.*
☎*207-725-8797, 877-725-8797; www.midcoastmaine.com.*

This attractive community, with its wide avenues, is the home of Bowdoin College. Shade trees and handsome mansions line Federal Street and other streets nearby. Small manufacturing plants and the US Naval Air Station are the chief contributors to the local economy, which supports a population of some 14,800 people.

The Bowdoin campus, in the heart of Brunswick, radiates outward from the town's pleasant green, which was laid out by citizens in the early 18C.

Bowdoin College

The main campus is bounded by Maine St., Bath Rd. & College St. Information and tours available at the Moulton Union on College St. ℘207-725-3000. www.bowdoin.edu.

Established in 1794, this well-regarded small liberal arts college spreads across 110 acres and enrolls some 1,600 students. Bowdoin counts among its alumni authors Nathaniel Hawthorne and Henry Wadsworth Longfellow, explorers Robert Peary and Donald MacMillan, and the nation's 14th president, Franklin Pierce. Harriet Beecher Stowe penned *Uncle Tom's Cabin* (1852)while she and her husband, a professor at Bowdoin, lived in Brunswick.

Peary-MacMillan Arctic Museum

Hubbard Hall. ♿ 🅿 🕐Open year-round Tue–Sat 10am–5pm, Sun 2pm–5pm. 🕐Closed major holidays. ℘207-725-3416. www.bowdoin.edu/arctic-museum.

This museum, dedicated to admirals **Robert Peary** (1856-1920) and **Donald MacMillan** (1874-1970), presents the history of polar exploration from the early 1800s through the Arctic expeditions made by Peary, who is credited with being the first man to reach the North Pole (1909), and his assistant, MacMillan.

BATH★

▶ *8mi north of Brunswick. ℘877-725-8797; www.midcoastmaine.com.*

Named after its sister city in England, Bath has been a shipbuilding center since the 18C, when its coveted location on a channel to the sea provided the town with advantages over other regional boatbuilding centers. Boatyards along the Kennebec River turned out square-riggers, down-easters, and some of the largest schooners ever constructed. The buildings of the Maine Maritime Museum and the graceful old homes on Washington Street date from this time.

👤👤 Maine Maritime Museum★★

243 Washington St. ✕🅿🕐Open year-round daily 9.30am–5pm. 🕐Closed major holidays. 🎫$15. ℘207-443-1316. www.mainemaritimemuseum.org. ⛴Boat rides (additional fee) on the Kennebec River are offered late Apr–Oct.

Devoted to preserving Maine's maritime heritage, this museum maintains a historic shipbuilding complex and a boatbuilding shop where visitors can watch wooden boats being restored and built. Large wooden schooners were the specialty of the Percy and Small Shipyard, which operated on this site from 1897 to 1920.

Boothbay Harbor

© Maine Office of Tourism

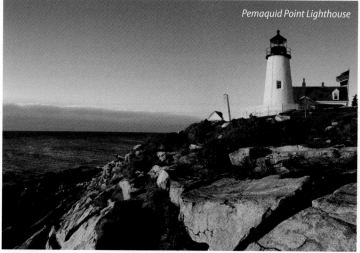

Pemaquid Point Lighthouse

© Paul Lemke / iStockphoto.com

Popham Beach★

16mi south of Bath on Rte. 209.

Situated at the tip of a finger-like peninsula reaching into the ocean, this resort village lies between the Kennebec River and the sea. At the northern tip of Popham Beach, **Fort Popham**, the granite and brick fortress overlooking the point where the Kennebec River meets the Atlantic Ocean, was built during the Civil War.

Nearby, at **Popham Beach State Park**, a broad sandy beach—rare for this section of the coast—lies on the ocean side of the point (○*open mid Apr–Oct daily 9am–5pm;* ○*$6;* ℰ*207-389-1335; www. state.me.us/doc/parks*).

BOOTHBAY HARBOR★★

○ *14mi east of Wiscasset via Rte. 27. ℰ207-633-2353. www.boothbay harbor.com.*

Boothbay Harbor lies at the tip of one of the craggy peninsulas that extend into the sea from the deeply indented, midcoast section of Maine. Protected headlands sheltering deep natural anchorages make the region a major boating center and a popular summer resort.

Small shops line the streets leading down to the wharves, and motels, hotels and inns nestle in the snug coves and along the rugged stretches of shore leading down to **Ocean Point★** (*5mi east of Boothbay Harbor via Rte. 96*) and Southeast Island, connected to the mainland by a short bridge.

PEMAQUID POINT★★

○ *20mi northeast of Wiscasset via US-1 North to Rtes. 129 & 130 South. www.pemaquidpoint.org.*

Carved by glaciers centuries ago, the gnarled ledges at Pemaquid Point are especially spectacular for their pegmatite formations—long, narrow bands of black and white rock that jut into the sea. The point is renowned for its lighthouse, which rises on the bluff above, standing guard over this dramatic section of coastline.

Pemaquid Point Lighthouse Park★★

At the end of Rte. 130 South in Bristol. ♿🅿○*Open Mother's Day–Columbus Day daily 9am–5pm.* ○*$2.* ℰ*207-677-2492. www.bristolparks.org/light house.htm.*

Commissioned by President John Quincy Adams in 1827, Pemaquid Point Lighthouse (*interior closed to the public*) helped sailors—as it still does today—avoid the jagged rocks which divide the opening between Muscongus and John's bays. From this site stretches a photographer's dream **view★★★**.

Farnsworth Art Museum Neighbors

Across the street from the Farnsworth, stop in for press-pot coffee and a pre-owned paperback at **Rock City Books & Coffee** (*328 Main St.; 207-594-4123; www.rockcitycoffee.com*). This cafe/bookstore encourages eaters to read and readers to eat. Used books at reduced prices fill the ceiling-high shelves and specialty coffees are the highlight of the menu.

Just around the corner is **Café Miranda** (*15 Oak St.; lunch & dinner daily; 207-594-2034; www.cafemiranda.com*). This quirky spot refuses to take itself too seriously but does wonders with its wide-ranging menu inspired by cuisine from around the globe. Look for selections such as crab stuffed poblano pepper, Thai calamari, fire-roasted curry squash, grilled lamb, and home-made ricotta and potato dumplings. There's a wide selection of pizza and burgers, too.

ROCKLAND

▶ *34mi north of Wiscasset via US-1. 207-236-4404. www.mainedreamvacation.com.*

Commercial center for the mid-coast, Rockland bustles as a modern seaport and one of the leading exporters of lobsters in the world today. Rockland is also home port to Maine's largest fleet of **windjammers**. During the summer months, visitors can cruise Penobscot Bay on one of these tall-masted schooners (*Maine Windjammer Association in Blue Hill: 800-807-9463; www.sailmainecoast.com.*)

Maine Lobster Festival

Held in Harbor Park in early August. 800-562-2529. www.mainelobsterfestival.com. For more than 50 years, this five-day festival has been held each year in Rockland. There are seafood-cooking contests, music, exhibits, arts and crafts, and plenty of lobster—nearly eight tons—as well as other seafood to enjoy. Hardy souls can attempt to run the **Lobster Crate Race** atop 50 bobbing crates partially submerged in the cold harbor waters. The winner is the contestant who crosses the most crates without falling into the bay. There's a lobster diaper derby and cod-fish carry for the kids, among other games.

Farnsworth Art Museum★★

16 Museum St. 🅿 ♿ 🕐 Open Jun–Oct daily 10am–5pm (Wed until 8pm) Apr–May and Nov–Dec Tue–Sun 10am–5pm, Jan–Mar Wed–Sun 10am–5pm. 🕐 Closed major holidays. ⊛ $12 (includes admission to Wyeth Center & Farnsworth Homestead). 207-596-6457. www.farnsworthmuseum.org.

Recent renovations and additions have catapulted the Farnsworth from its status as a modest gallery for Maine art to a nationally acclaimed center for the study of Maine artists, particularly the three generations of Wyeth painters—**Newell Convers** (1882–1945), **Andrew** (b. 1917) and **Jamie** (b. 1946)—who have derived inspiration from the state's rugged land- and seascapes. The museum houses the nation's second-largest collection of works by acclaimed 20C sculptor Louise Nevelson. Four new galleries showcase contemporary art.

Wyeth Center★★

The former Methodist church chosen in 1997 to house hundreds of canvases by all three Wyeth painters is itself a work of art. Its stark, white clapboard exterior has, in fact, been painted by Jamie Wyeth.

The stunning interior has been renovated to accommodate 3,500sq ft of naturally lit exhibition space, where scores of Wyeth paintings from Andrew and Betsy Wyeth's personal collection allow visitors to compare and contrast the styles, subjects and visions of these three tremendously talented artists.

Vinalhaven and North Haven Island Ferries

Depart from the foot of Main St. in Rockland and run to Vinalhaven and North Haven. Ferry takes both passengers and vehicles ⚿. For seasonal schedules and rates, call the Maine State Ferry Service (℘207-596-5400 ; www.maine.gov/mdot/msfs/).

Ferries cruise among the serene tree-clad Fox Islands in Penobscot Bay. Largest of these islands at 14mi long, quaint **Vinalhaven** was incorporated in 1789. Here lobster boats anchor in peaceful inlets, and fishing sheds furnished with stacks of lobster traps and brightly painted buoys dot the island. Several of Vinalhaven's abandoned granite quarries provide a place to swim and fish in summer. From the northern end you can spot **North Haven**, a quiet island that swells with summer residents.

Owls Head Transportation Museum

2mi south of Rockland via Rte. 73, on grounds adjacent to Knox County airport. P ⚿ ⊙Open year-round daily 10am–5pm. ⊙Closed major holidays. ☜$10. ✕(summer only) ℘207-594-4418. www.ohtm.org.

The museum's core collection of pre-1930 aircraft is complemented by antique aircraft, automobiles, bicycles, motorcycles and engines dating from the early 20C. Demonstrations of automobiles and airplanes from the collection are held at special summer events on the museum grounds (*call for events schedule*).

Nearby on the coast, the Owl's Head Lighthouse (*follow signs to Owl's Head State Park from Rte. 73 South*) perches atop a 100ft cliff overlooking West Penobscot Bay.

CAMDEN★★

▶ *8mi north of Rockland. ℘207-236-4404. www.mainedreamvacation.com.*
Snuggled at the foot of the Camden Hills, surveying the island-speckled waters of Penobscot Bay, Camden ranks as one of the loveliest towns on the New England coast. It is easy to while away

View of Camden in fall

© PhotoDisc., Inc.

a day here, exploring the shops and galleries in the attractive village center and dining leisurely in waterfront restaurants. Mansions that wealthy summer residents built still line the streets around the center of town. In the harbor, sleek yachts are anchored amid the tall two-masted windjammers, which offer a variety of pleasure cruises in season (*for information & schedules, contact the Maine Windjammer Association, ℘800-807-9463; www.sailmainecoast.com*).

Camden Hills State Park★★

2mi north of Camden off US-1.
⛺ P ⊙*Open mid May–mid Oct daily 9am–dusk. ☜$4.50. ℘207-236-3109. www.maine.gov/doc/parks.*
A narrow road snakes up 1mi to the top of Mt. Battie (800ft), where a spectacular **view**★★★ of Camden harbor, Penobscot Bay and the bay islands unfolds below. The park also includes a 30mi network of trails and a camping area.

BELFAST

▶ *21mi north of Camden. ℘207-338-5900. www.belfastmaine.org.*
Overlooking Penobscot Bay, this histo community is a popular tourist stop. Handsome brick buildings, many over a century old, and quaint street lamps line Main Street. Here you'll find antique stores, art galleries, gift shops, cafes, coffeehouses and other businesses.

Lobster Pounds

As you drive the coast of Maine, you'll see thousands of small, colorful, torpedo-shaped buoys bobbing in Maine's coves and off rocky headlands. These are lobster buoys, and each is attached to a lobster trap—or a line of traps—that sits on the seabed and is designed to capture the state's most popular crustacean.

Large and succulent, lobsters love the brisk waters of Maine, which produces more lobsters than any other state in the nation.

Much of the catch makes its way to Maine's shorefront lobster restaurants, where the lobsters are served up simply: boiled, with butter for dipping, corn on the cob, and maybe a baked potato or steamed clams. If you're on the go, the best option is a **lobster roll**. Available from myriad waterside shacks, lobster rolls consist of chunks of fresh lobster meat usually served on a simple hot dog roll. Sometimes the lobster is tossed in mayonnaise and embellished by bits of celery; sometimes the meat is just tossed in melted butter.

Maine's dozens of lobster restaurants range from the very simple—a shack with a couple of picnic tables and a vat of boiling water over an open fire—to more fancy waterfront establishments. *The following restaurants operate seasonally; call first to ensure they're open if you're traveling in the spring or after Columbus Day. (Venues are listed in geographical order, from south to north).*

Chauncey Creek Lobster Pier – *16 Chauncey Creek Rd., Kittery Point.* ☎*207-439-1030. www.chaunceycreek.com.* Just a short hop from the factory outlets of Kittery, Chauncey Creek lies a world apart from modern America. Place your order, then stake out one of the colorful picnic tables on the pier overlooking a quiet ocean inlet. Bring your own beverages and sides, if you like.

Two Lights Lobster Shack – *225 Two Lights Rd., Cape Elizabeth.* ☎*207-799-1677. www.lobstershacktwolights.com.* This shack occupies a rocky point with a view of two lighthouses made famous by the painter Edward Hopper. It's about a 15-minute drive from Portland; dining is offered both indoors and out.

Five Islands Lobster Co. – *Rte. 127, Georgetown.* ☎*207-371-2990. www.fiveislandslobster.com.* At the very end of a scenic, winding drive south of Woolwich (*follow Rte. 127 to the water*) you'll find Five Islands Lobster Co. Ask for your lobster at the pier; while it's cooking, order onion rings and drinks at the adjacent snack bar.

Thurston's Lobster Pound – *Steamboat Wharf Rd., Bernard.* ☎*207-244-7600. www.thurstonslobster.com.* Across from Bass Harbor on Mt. Desert Island, Thurston's is a stunning spot at sunset, when lobster boats at their moorings are touched with a burnished glow. Diners eat under a canary yellow awning atop a tall pier.

SEARSPORT

▶ *3mi northeast of Belfast.* ☎*207-338-5900. www.belfastmaine.org*

Located near the head of Penobscot Bay, this seafaring town was a boatbuilding center and home to more than 10 percent of the nation's merchant marine captains in the late 19C. The beautiful dwellings built for these seamen still adorn the streets near the waterfront. Second-busiest harbor in the state today, Searsport serves as an export center for manufacturing and agricultural products, notably the potato crop raised to the north in Aroostook County.

Penobscot Marine Museum★

Church St., just off US-1. 🅿️🕐*Open late-May–late Oct Mon–Sat 10am–5pm, Sun noon–5pm. Late-Oct–late-Feb Thu–Sun 11am–4pm, late-Feb–late-May Thu–Sat 11am–4pm.* 🎫*$8.* ☎*207-548-2529. www.penobscotmarinemuseum.org.*

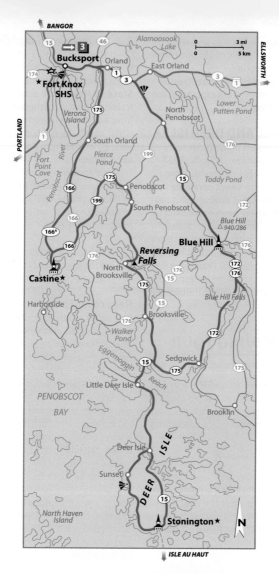

A complex of eight buildings onsite includes several restored sea captains' homes, the former Town Hall, the Phillips Memorial Library and the adjoining Douglas and Margaret Carver Memorial Gallery.

Arranged throughout the buildings, the museum's rich collection of marine paintings, models and artifacts illustrates the era of sail and trade.

EXCURSION
Fort Knox State Historic Site★

▶ 10.5mi north of Searsport on Rte. 174, Prospect. ⏱Open May–Oct daily 9am–dusk. 🎫$4.50 Fort Knox, $7 Fort Knox & Observatory. ℘207-469-7719. www.maine.gov/doc/parks.

Named after General Henry Knox, chief of artillery under General Washington during the Revolution, the fort—never completed—served as a military training ground during the Civil War. The enormous granite fortress, with its archways, buttresses and winding staircases, is a model of 19C American military architecture.

From the top of the ramparts there is a **view** of the town of Bucksport and the Penobscot River.

BLUE HILL AND DEER ISLE★

◯ *Blue Hill is 31mi northeast of Searsport via US-1 and Rte. 15 South. ℘207-374-3242. www.bluehillpeninsula.org.*

The quiet, breeze-swept peninsula that reaches from Rte. 3 down to Stonington seems to have been overlooked by modern civilization. Small, secluded villages and cozy inlets harboring lobster boats nestle in woodlands that hug the water's edge. Views of Penobscot Bay and Mount Desert Island are especially striking on a clear day, when the blue sky frames the dark green spruces.

🚗 DRIVING TOUR

96mi circuit from Bucksport.

This scenic drive around the Blue Hill peninsula will take you through historic towns and sleepy, seaside villages, with stunning ocean and harbor views along the way.

Bucksport

This small town lies on the east bank of the Penobscot River at the point where Verona Island divides the river. Bucksport's main street, lined with shops and the historic **Jed Prouty Tavern**, runs parallel to the river.

◯ From Bucksport take Rte. 1/3 North, then turn right onto Rte. 175 South. Continue straight on Rte. 166, then Rte. 166A to Castine.

Castine

℘207-374-3242.
www.bluehillpeninsula.org.

Pristine tree-lined streets and stately 18C and 19C Georgian and Federal homes delight visitors to Castine. Some of Castine's earliest architecture, including the 1790 Unitarian Church and the 1840 Ives house, later home to poet Robert Lowell,

lines the charming **village green** (*on Court St. just off Main St.*). The large brick buildings along Pleasant Street belong to the Maine Maritime Academy. The T/S **State of Maine**, the academy's 499ft training vessel is berthed at the waterfront and can be toured when the ship is in port (*☞ visit by 30min guided tour only;* 🕐 *mid Jul–late-Aug daily 10am–noon & 1pm–3pm; mid Sept–mid Dec & Feb–mid Apr weekends only 10am–noon & 1pm–3pm;* 🚫*Closed academic & major holidays; ℘800-464-6565 in Maine, ℘800-227-8465 out-of-state; www.mainemaritime.edu*).

◯ Take Rte. 166 and Rte. 199 North around the east side of the peninsula. At Penobscot, take Rte. 175 South.

Reversing Falls

Five miles south of South Penobscot there is a picnic area where an unusual phenomenon can be seen: a reversing falls. At this point, the waterway is very narrow. When the tide changes, the narrow passage creates a bottleneck, causing the water to rush in (or out, depending on whether the tide is rising or falling) with such great force that a series of falls is formed. The best view is from the bridge on Rte. 175.

◯ Continue south on Rte. 175 to Rte. 176/15. At the junction of Rtes. 175 and 15, cross the bridge to Little Deer Isle, then continue to Deer Isle. Rte. 15 passes through the village of Deer Isle and follows the eastern shore to Stonington.

Stonington★

℘207-348-6124.
www.deerislemaine.com.

This tranquil fishing village at the tip of the peninsula typifies the picturesque towns along the coast. Lobstering is the mainstay of the economy, though there is also a burgeoning arts scene, centered around Haystack Mountain School of Crafts. Boats to **Isle au Haut★**, part of which lies in Acadia National Park, leave from Stonington. Continue along the western shore of the island, where a beautiful **view** unfolds as you approach the town of Sunset.

◑ After Sunset head east and take Rte. 15 North. Cross the bridge to Little Deer Isle and pick up Rte. 175 East in Sargentville. In Sedgwick turn left onto Rte. 172. At the town of Blue Hill Falls turn right onto Rte. 175. Cross two bridges to Blue Hill Falls, another reversing falls. Return to Rte. 172 and follow it northeast to Blue Hill.

Blue Hill

Named after the hill that dominates the town and yields a hearty annual blueberry harvest, this pretty village (settled in 1762) is home to many craftsmen—including a well-known cache of potters—a fine library, chamber music at Kneisel Hall and a down-to-earth country fair held on Labor Day. A trail (*from the village drive north on Rte. 172 and turn left across from the fairgrounds; continue .8mi to trail marker*) leads to the top of Blue Hill (940ft), where you can look out across Blue Hill Bay to Mount Desert Island.

◑ Take Rte. 15 North.

The road climbs, passes along the base of Blue Hill, then gradually descends toward Rte. 1/3 offering beautiful views as it leads north.

ADDRESSES

🛏 STAY

BELFAST

$$ Alden House – *63 Church St. ☎207-338-2151. www.thealdenhouse.com. 6 rooms.* Inside this stately Greek Revival house, high ceilings, twin parlors and marble fireplaces grace the public spaces, while lace bed covers and antique furnishings decorate each pleasant bedroom (all but two have private baths).

CAMDEN

$$$ Whitehall Inn – *52 High St. Closed late Oct–late May. ☎207-236-3391 or 800-789-6565. www.whitehall-inn.com. 45 rooms. Restaurant.* A Steinway piano in the lobby sets a perfect tone for this longtime Camden institution. Choose from homey rooms in the main building (1834) or in a Victorian shingle-style cottage across the street. The restaurant serves local seafood. Rooms with shared baths are available at a reduced rate.

EAST BOOTHBAY

$$$ Five Gables Inn – *107 Murray Hill Rd. Children under 12 not welcome. ☎207-633-4551 or 800-451-5048. www.fivegables inn.com. 16 rooms. Closed late-Oct–mid-May.* Sitting a few miles drive from Boothbay Harbor, this century-old Victorian has been attractively updated. Some first-floor rooms lack privacy, but all guest rooms are appointed with country charm, such as spindle beds and wingback chairs, and boast views of Linekin Bay.

FREEPORT

$$$$ Harraseeket Inn – *162 Main St. ☎207-865-9377 or 800-342-6423. www.harraseeketinn.com. 93 rooms. Restaurant.* This venerable 1798 inn offers early-American ambience, enhanced by 23 fireplaces. Bedrooms with modern amenities feature traditional dark-wood furnishings. Enjoy regional cuisine in the inn's formal dining room or Downeast specialties in the tavern. This inn is also pet-friendly (a surcharge applies).

KENNEBUNKPORT

$$$$$ Captain Lord Mansion – *Green St. (at 6 Pleasant St.), Kennebunkport. ☎207-967-3141 or 800-522-3141. www. captainlord.com. 16 rooms.* This regal, three-story Federal-style house holds a mix of historic opulence with modern comforts. Filled with period antiques, the romantic guest rooms—even the smallest ones—have charm and amenities to spare, including heated bathroom floors, whirlpool tubs, marble baths, gas fireplaces and free Wi-Fi.

$$ The Lodge at Turbat's Creek – *7 Turbat's Creek Rd. ✉Closed Dec–Apr. ☎207-967-8700 or 877-594-5634. www.lodgeatturbatscreek.com. 26 rooms.* This two-story motel tucked away in a quiet neighborhood is a pleasant surprise. With rates lower than many Kennebunkport inns, Turbat's Creek offers simple rooms painted a sherbet yellow, and a continental breakfast. Amenities include a heated outdoor pool, free use of bicycles, in-room mini-refrigerators, and complimentary Wi-Fi. The location at the north end of Ocean Avenue makes it a good base for exploring.

OGUNQUIT

$$$ The Beachmere Inn – *62 Beachmere Place.* ℘*207-646-2021 or 800-336-3983. www.beachmereinn.com. 7 rooms.* This sprawling complex is set on the shores of the Atlantic Ocean, within walking distance to Perkins Cove. This family-owned property has been a popular lodging choice along the southern Maine coast for more than 70 years. There's a wide choice of room styles from motel units to luxury oceanfront suites. All are nicely-appointed. Guests have direct access to the scenic Marginal Way footpath and the inn's private beach. There are also restaurants, a full-service spa, a fitness center and swimming pools on-site.

PROUTS NECK

$$$$ Black Point Inn – *510 Black Point Rd.* ℘*207-883-2500. www.black pointinn.com. 25 rooms. Restaurant.* A classic Maine seaside resort, the c.1873 Inn recently got a major face-lift. New owners dramatically downsized the number of guest rooms and re-vamped the inn's restaurant. New menu items feature local produce and Maine products. Some of the best things about the property haven't changed: the big, wrap-around sun porch, proximity to the beach and golf course, the heated indoor pool, and the surrounding coastal area. Guest rooms are spacious and decorated in a simple shore-house style, with crisp linens and a pale palette. Most offer sweeping views of the ocean or bay.

♀/EAT

CAMDEN

Camden's colorful waterfront is the big draw for residents and tourists alike, especially when it comes to eating. At the marina-side **$$$$ Waterfront** restaurant (*Bayview St. at Camden Harbor;* ℘*207-236-3747; www.waterfrontcamden. com*), popular seafood dishes—such as Maine clam chowder, haddock fish and chips and fried clams—are served on the harborside deck. Also at the water's edge is **$$ Atlantica** (*Bayview St.;* ℘*207-236-6011; www.atlanticarestaurant.com*),

which offers creative regional cuisine with an international twist (the seasonal menu may include ginger lobster bisque, salmon in flaky pastry and herb crusted lamb loin) in a bistro-style setting.

$$$ Peter Ott's (*Bayview St.;* ℘*207-236-4032; www.peterottscamden.com*) may have a no-frills, ale-house interior, but it consistently impresses diners with its fare, which ranges from charbroiled black Angus steaks to fresh lobster and scallop pasta.

$$$ Lobster Pound (*US-1, 5mi north of Camden in Lincolnville Beach; Closed Nov-Apr.* ℘*207-789-5550; www.lobster poundmaine.com*) is a sprawling, family-style place situated on the beach. Creativity takes a back seat to "classic" here, but that's the way the regulars like it. Family-owned for three generations, the complex has a separate picnic area (*open in summer*) for more casual dining and take-out. You can also get a steak here, or roast turkey, but seafood takes center stage: Maine shrimp, clams, haddock, Atlantic scallops, swordfish and halibut are served blackened, broiled or grilled. And you can't go wrong with your basic lobster dinner.

KENNEBUNKPORT

$$$$ White Barn Inn – *37 Beach Ave. Dinner only. Jackets required.* ℘*207-967-2321. www.whitebarninn.com.* **Contemporary.** Housed in a handsome old barn, the AAA five-star rated restaurant is appointed with country antiques and richly upholstered chairs. The prix-fixe menu changes weekly to reflect availability of local produce and meats; choices might include an appetizer of local oyster salad and pan-seared New England quail breast with foie gras, followed by lamb loin with savoy cabbage or seared beef tenderloin in a horseradish crust.

KITTERY

$ Bob's Clam Hut – *Rte. 1* ℘*207-439-4233; www.bobsclamhut.com.* **Seafood.** A local favorite since 1956, Bob's retained its take-out vibe even after adding indoor seating. Fried foods are a revelation here, light and crispy, and Bob's ice cream menu features exclusive flavors (tartar sauce, anyone?).

OGUNQUIT

$ Amore Breakfast – *309 Shore Rd. Breakfast only. Seasonal. ☎207-646-6661. www.amorebreakfast.com.* **American**. Located near the entrance to Perkins Cove, Amore is *the* place for a delightfully decadent breakfast. Diners don't mind waiting in line for plates filled with lobster Benedict, real corned beef hash, lemon pound cake, and "black or blue" French toast topped with blackberries or blueberries.

SEARSPORT

$$ Anglers Restaurant – *Rte. 1 ☎207-548-2405. www.anglersseafoodrestaurant.com.* **Seafood.** This friendly family dining spot is a perennial favorite with the locals. Tasty food, generous portions and reasonable prices are the attractions. Lobster, haddock, scallops, salmon, clam, shrimp or trout—baked, broiled or fried—come with all the trimmings.

SOUTH HARPSWELL

$ Dolphin Marina – *515 Basin Point Rd. Seasonal. ☎207-833-6000. www.dolphin marinaandrestaurant.com.* **Seafood.** It may not be the easiest place to find but it's worth the hunt for the splendidly uncomplicated food served up with a sweeping view of Casco Bay. Diners eat at plain wooden tables or a tiny counter. Especially popular, the chowders are rich and tasty, and most meals come with homemade blueberry muffins.

STONINGTON

$$ Fisherman's Friend – *5 Atlantic Ave. Seasonal. ☎207-367-2442. www.fishermans friendrestaurant.com.* **Seafood.** Lobster lovers trek to this down-home spot for one reason—the velvety rich lobster stew. (If that doesn't tempt you, they serve lobster 30 other ways.) While the place won't win any awards for decor, and the service is harried, this is the real thing. Leave room for a traditional New England dessert, like blueberry pie and grapenut pudding.

WISCASSET

Whether you're just passing through or lingering in Wiscasset, two informal spots downtown along US-1 are worth a stop. **$$ Red's Eats** (*41 Water St. near the bridge; ☎207-882-6128*) is a tiny but bright roadside stand that specializes in lobster rolls—they're overflowing with lobster meat, served with just a dab of mayo on the side.

Across the street is **$$ Sarah's** (*42 Water St; ☎207-882-7504; www.sarahscafe.com*) where you can be sure of fresh-caught lobster (Sarah's father and brother are both lobstermen), or select from other finger-friendly fare like burritos or overfilled sandwiches on pita or croissants. Most food is fresh and homemade.

FREEPORT SHOPPING

L.L. Bean – *On Main St. at Bow St. ☎800-441-5713. www.llbean.com.* Outdoorsman and inventor Leon Leonwood Bean (1872-1967) began his merchandising empire in 1912 making and selling hunting boots. His success led him to expand his enterprise into a mail-order business specializing in outdoor clothing and equipment. The modest factory showroom blossomed over time into the firm's flagship 119,000sq ft store, where five levels—including an indoor trout pond, hiking ramps and a cafe—display equipment for nearly every outdoor sport imaginable. It is not unusual to see the parking lot filled at 3am; the store is open 24 hours a day year-round, as it has been since 1951, when its founder decided to extend the opening hours, tired of customers knocking on the door of his residence before dawn.

Master craftsmen are hard at work at **Brown Goldsmiths** (*11 Mechanic St.; ☎207-865-4126 or 800-753-4465; www.browngoldsmiths.com*), turning out customized baubles and restoring heirlooms for clients as far away as Manhattan, Boston and even the West Coast. The upscale firm, owned and managed by certified gemologists Stephen and Judith Brown, opens its studio and gem lab for a fascinating behind-the-scenes tour (15min, upon request).

An offshoot of Jackson Hole's namesake emporium, the **Mangy Moose** (*112 Main St.; ☎207-865-6414 or 800-606-6517; www. themangymoose.com*) offers all things mooselike: lampshades, pillows, furniture, frames, dishware, blankets, doormats and bed linens, as well as toys, antiques, jewelry and clothing—all emblazoned with images of, or shaped like, Maine's beloved state animal.

Monhegan Island★★

Edged by steep, rocky cliffs, Monhegan Island appears, from the mainland 12mi away, as the dark, curved back of a huge whale. Of the more than 4,600 islands off the Maine coast, Monhegan is one of only 14 that boasts a year-round island community. The resident population swells from 75 hardy souls in winter to some 200 people in summer. The island's beauty attracts artists, writers, naturalists, photographers and hikers.

A BIT OF HISTORY

Ledge markings discovered on Manana, the islet across the harbor from Monhegan, are considered by some as evidence that the Vikings landed here in the 11C. Several centuries later Monhegan served as a fishing station.

Most of the island's small year-round population earns its living from fishing and lobstering. A law prohibiting fishermen from trapping lobsters in Monhegan waters between June 25 and January 1 allows Monhegan lobsters to grow bigger and thus bring a better price. In the summer the island is a haven for daytrippers and artists.

SIGHTS
Burnt Head

Follow Trail 4 to Burnt Head for a **view★★** of the White Head cliffs.

▶ **Population:** 75.

🛈 **Info:** No cars or public transportation is available on the island (there are no paved roads); bicycles are prohibited on trails. For more information, contact the Maine Office of Tourism *(59 State House Station, Augusta, ME 04333-0059; ☎888-624-6345; www.visitmaine.com)*.

◐ **Location:** The shuttle ferries land at the town dock where you'll find the unpaved main street dissecting the tiny village. Trails lead around the island and across its interior.

🕑 **Timing:** Monhegan is best explored on foot. Trails are numbered and can be identified by tiny wooden blocks placed on tree trunks where two or more trails meet. Three of these trails are described below to give you an overview.

✦ **Also See:** MAINE COAST, ACADIA NATIONAL PARK.

White Head★★

From Burnt Head follow Trail 1, which straddles the cliff ledges alongside an evergreen forest. White Head's 150ft cliffs are generally blanketed with seagulls.

GETTING THERE

Make reservations 2 to 3 months in advance. **Monhegan Boat Line** – ☎207-372-8848. www.monheganboat.com. Departs from **Port Clyde** year-round. 1hr, $35 (roundtrip). **Hardy Boat Cruises** – ☎207-677-2026 or 800-278-3346. www.hardyboat.com. Departs from **New Harbor** mid-Jun–Sept daily; mid-May–early Jun & early Oct–mid-Oct. Wed & weekends only. Duration: 1hr, $33 (roundtrip). **Balmy Days Cruises** – ☎207-633-2284 or 800-298-2284. www.monhegandaytrip.com. Departs from **Boothbay Harbor** mid-Jun–Sept, twice daily; Memorial Day weekend, first week of Jun & first 2 weeks of Oct, weekends only. Duration: 1hr 30min, $34 (roundtrip).

Cathedral Woods

Trail 12 runs along Long Swamp to Cathedral Woods, an inland forest of evergreens towering above a lush undergrowth of fern and moss.

Monhegan Lighthouse★

Overlooking the village from the top of Lighthouse Hill, the Monhegan Light was originally built in 1824, then rebuilt in 1850 and automated in 1959. From this vantage point, you can enjoy a **panorama** of Monhegan, the harbor and the deserted islet of Manana. The lighthouse keeper's house has been transformed into a **museum** that displays photographs, artifacts and prints related to animal, plant and human life on the island (𝒫207-596-7003; www.monhegan museum.org; 🕐 open Jul–Aug daily 11.30am–3.30pm; last week of Jun & Sept 1.30pm–3.30pm).

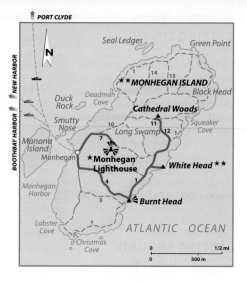

The North Woods★

A vast forested wilderness laced by miles of waterways, Maine's North Woods is a recreational paradise. Canoeing, kayaking, whitewater rafting, hunting, fishing, hiking, skiing, and snowmobiling are just a sampling of the activities that visitors to this region can enjoy. Moose, deer and black bears abound in the forests, and wild brook trout, bass and landlocked salmon run in the rivers, lakes and streams. Here you will find Maine's largest lake (Moosehead Lake) and tallest peak (Mt. Katahdin), along with more than 200,000 acres of parkland. So tread lightly, and revel in one of the last real pockets of wilderness along the East Coast. Much of the woods is currently owned by timber corporations (always give logging trucks right of way).

- 🖊 **Michelin Map:** 583 U 4
- 🗎 **Info:** 𝒫888-624-6345; www.visitmaine.com.
- ▶ **Location:** The vast area encompasses more than 3.5 million acres of commercial forest, surrounding the Allagash Wilderness Waterway. Major towns include Rockwood and Greenville on Moosehead Lake and Millinocket near Baxter State Park.
- 👥 **Kids:** A whitewater rafting trip on the Penobscot is wild fun for all.
- 🕐 **Timing:** Base yourself in the town of Greenville, where you'll find lodging, food and services.
- 👁 **Don't Miss:** A moose-watching safari and a hike to the top of Mt. Kineo.

GETTING THERE

Millinocket is the gateway to the Mt. Katahdin region; the Moosehead Lake area is accessible from Greenville. From **Bangor** to **Millinocket** (*71mi*), take I-95 North to Exit 56 and follow Rte. 11 South. From **Quebec City** to **Millinocket** (*329mi*), take I-73 South to Rte. 173 South; at the US border, take US-201 South to Rte. 16 East to Rte. 11 North. From **Bangor** to **Greenville** (*72mi*), take Rte. 15 North. From **Quebec City** to **Greenville** (*219mi*), take I-73 South to Rte. 173 South to Rte. 6/15.

GETTING AROUND

Public roads in northern Maine are scarce. Many areas are accessible only by seaplane or canoe. Lumber companies maintain private roads; many of which are unpaved; four-wheel-drive vehicles are recommended.

Scenic flights in the Moosehead Lake area are provided by Currier's Flying Service (*P.O. Box 351, Greenville Junction, ME 04442; ☎207-695-2778; www.curriersflyingservice.com*). Fly-in camping and fly-fishing trips to the Katahdin region are offered by Katahdin Air Service Inc. (*P.O. Box 171, Millinocket, ME 04462; ☎207-723-8378 or 866-359-6246; www.katahdinair. com*). *Listed services are offered May–Oct only.*

VISITOR INFORMATION

North Maine Woods provides information about access to wilderness areas, camping and guide services, as well as detailed topographic maps (*P.O. Box 425, 92 Main St. Ashland, ME 04732; ☎435-6213; www.northmainewoods.org*).

Moosehead Lake Area – The following organizations provide information about area attractions, accommodations and recreational opportunities: **Moosehead Lake Region Chamber of Commerce** (*visitor center on Rte. 15; P.O. Box 581, Greenville, ME 04441; ☎207-695-2702 or 888-876-2778; www.moosehead lake.org*); and **Moosehead Vacation & Sportsmen's Association** (*P.O. Box CM, Rockwood, ME 04478; www. rockwoodonmoosehead.org*).

Katahdin Region – **Katahdin Area Chamber of Commerce** visitor information kiosk operates seasonally on Rte. 11 (*1029 Central St., P.O. Box 426, Millinocket, ME 04462; ☎207-723-4443; www.katahdinmaine.com*).

Mount Katahdin

A giant granite monolith, Katahdin (an Indian name meaning "the greatest mountain") has long figured in local Indian mythology. One Abnaki legend tells of Pamola, a deity with the wings and claws of an eagle, the arms and torso of a man, and the enormous head of a moose, who lived on the peak of Mt. Katahdin. Whenever he was angry, Pamola cast violent rainstorms onto the lands below.

The mountain has claimed 19 lives since 1963, mostly from falls from the Knife Edge and exposure in bad weather. Be alert to weather conditions, stay on marked trails, and notfy someone of your destination before you depart.

Baxter Peak is the highest of Katahdin's four summits. Observed from the east, the **Great Basin**, a glacier-shaped formation scoured out of the mountain, is Katahdin's most distinguishable feature. Seen from the west, the **Knife Edge**—a narrow, serrated, 4,000ft-high granite ridge that joins Pamola and South Peaks—cuts a jagged profile across the sky.

Baxter State Park

BAXTER STATE PARK★★

20mi north of Millinocket, ME; follow signs from Rte. 11/157. ⌖*The main entrances to the park lead to narrow, unpaved Park Road, the only route through Baxter. The park's interior is accessible only by hiking trails.* ⌚*Open mid-May–mid-Oct daily 6am–10pm. Rest of the year call for hours.* ⌗*$14 nonresident vehicle fee.* ⌂*Park headquarters: 64 Balsam Dr., Millinocket.* ☏*207-723-5140. www.baxterstateparkauthority.com.*

Dominated by the state's highest peak, **Mount Katahdin** (5,267ft), Baxter State Park is a densely forested rectangular tract of land (204,733 acres) in the heart of the Maine wilderness. The park is named after **Percival Proctor Baxter** (1876–1969), who devoted much of his life and fortune to acquiring this land, which he deeded to the people of Maine under the condition that the park be preserved "forever in its natural wild state."

Accordingly, the park has remained primarily a wildlife sanctuary for deer, moose and bear. Here, roads are narrow and unpaved (*speed limit 15–20mph*), camping facilities are primitive, and there are no motels, shops or restaurants within the park boundaries.

The Park has over 200 miles of simple hiking trails, some of which are over 100 years old.

Hiking Trails

Before starting out, hikers should register with a ranger and check on area weather and trail conditions. Trail maps are available at the 10 park campgrounds, the visitor center at Togue Pond (south entrance), and at the park headquarters in Millinocket. Most trails are located in the south section of the park. Baxter's trails are blazed blue; white blazes mark the Appalachian Trail.

While very few scenic attractions can be observed from the park road, Baxter's 175mi of trails, which include the northern end of the **Appalachian Trail** (*which cuts through the southwest section of the park*) leads to points that afford spectacular views of this remote region. For those who wish to scale Mt. Katahdin, the challenging **Hunt Trail** (*5.2mi; begin at Katahdin Stream Campground and follow the white blazes*) rewards the experienced and well-conditioned hiker with panoramic **views**★★ of the surrounding region.

Two easier hikes to other points in the park both begin at Roaring Brook Campground: **Sandy Stream Pond Trail** (*1.5mi*) and **Chimney Pond Trail** (*ascent 3.3mi*). Lovely Chimney Pond, located on the floor of the Great Basin, is the site of one of the park's many campgrounds. A pleasant 1mi hike on the Hunt Trail leads to **Katahdin Stream Falls**.

DISCOVERING MAINE

Wildlife Spotting

- Learn about the animals you are hoping to see. Visiting the right habitat increases your chances of sightings.
- Look early in the morning and in the evening, when most animals are active.
- Walk slowly and quietly. The slightest sound can alert an animal to your presence.
- Be alert to the smallest movements; animals are well camouflaged in the dense brush.
- Look up to spot birds or small mammals on tree limbs.
- Stay on trails and watch for paths through the brush cut by animals.
- Keep a safe distance from all wildlife. If an animal signals fear by means of its vocalizations or body language, move away immediately.

Patten

8mi east of Baxter State Park via Rte. 159.

This small agricultural community straddles the border between the rich potato fields of Aroostook County and the forests of northern Maine. High-powered diesel trucks hauling wood pulp and logs are a familiar sight on local roads. Lumbering is an important business in Patten, even though the era of lumber camps and river drives has long since ended.

At the **Lumbermen's Museum** (*.5mi west of Patten on Rte. 159; ☎207-528-2650; www.lumbermensmuseum.org*), exhibits ranging from crooked knives to steam log-haulers, a sawmill and reconstructed lumber camps tell the story of the lumberjack's life. The 1820 bunkhouse replicates the type shared by as many as a dozen woodsmen during the lumbering season (🅿️🕐*open Jul–mid Oct Tue–Sun 10am–4pm; late May–Jun Fri–Sun 10am–4pm; ⊚ $8; ☎207-528-2650; www.lumbermensmuseum.org*).

MOOSEHEAD LAKE REGION★

☎207-695-2702 or 888-876-2778; www.mooseheadlake.org.

Centered on remote inland **Moosehead Lake★**, this region has been a paradise for sportsmen since the 19C. Easy-to-reach ponds and lakes, as well as isolated lakeshore sporting camps (*accessible only by plane*), attract fishermen and

hunters. Canoe and raft trips, including those on the magnificent 98mi-long stretch of white water known as the **Allagash Wilderness Waterway**, begin on the shores of Moosehead Lake.

New England's largest lake (117sq mi), Moosehead is dotted with hundreds of islands and surrounded by timberlands that reach as far as the Canadian border. Numerous bays and coves indent the lake's 350mi shoreline.

Henry David Thoreau explored the region with Indian guides in the mid-1800s. In the 19C, fashionable visitors arrived by train to summer at the grand hotels on the shores of the lake's blue waters. Logging also flourished in the mid-19C, when the rivers were jammed with logs being driven downstream.

Greenville

Situated at the southern end of Moosehead Lake, Greenville is a resort center and a major outfitting center for sportsmen heading into the north country.

A short distance to the northeast, **Lily Bay State Park** (*on Lily Bay Rd.; ☎207-695-2700; www.maine.gov/doc/parks; ⊚$4.50*) has a lakefront beach and facilities for camping and boating.

Mount Kineo

Rising abruptly from the waters of Moosehead Lake, Mt. Kineo reaches an altitude of 1,806ft offering sweeping lake views. Visitors can take a shuttle boat to the island and hike to the top.

158

ADDRESSES

🏨 STAY

Area accommodations are concentrated in Greenville and Millinocket. **Sporting camps** are located in Greenville, Rockwood and Millinocket. **Camping** is available at Lily Bay State Park (*207-695-2700; www.maine.gov/doc/parks*) and Baxter State Park (*reservations in person or by mail only; 64 Balsam Dr., Millinocket, ME 04462; 207-723-5140; www.baxter stateparkauthority.com*). Camping information is available from the **Maine Forest Service** (*22 State House Station, Augusta, ME 04333; 207- 287-2791; www.maine.gov/doc/mfs*).

GREENVILLE

$$$$ Blair Hill Inn – *351 Lily Bay Rd. 207-695-0224. www.blairhill.com. 8 rooms.* Set high on a hillside overlooking Moosehead Lake, the Blair Hill Inn is an oasis of sophistication amid the rustic North Woods. This 1891 Queen-Anne-style manor house has been lovingly restored with an eye to comfort, but neither the gracious living room nor the well-appointed guest rooms can begin to compete with the sweeping view of lake and rolling mountains.

$ Little Lyford Pond Camps – *17mi east of Greenville via unpaved logging roads. 603-466-2727. www.outdoors.org. 8 cabins.* Originally an 1870s logging camp, Little Lyford is now operated by the Appalachian Mountain Club and offers guests the chance to stay in woodsy-rustic cabins, while getting a full immersion in backwoods living. Cabins are simply decorated, and each has cold running water, a woodstove and a private outhouse. (There's also a communal shower and sauna.) Meals are served family-style in the log lodge, and during the day guests can canoe nearby ponds, or hike along the Appalachian Trail to a river gorge for an afternoon of swimming. Access to the camp is via a logging road.

WEST OF ASHLAND

$$$$ Bradford Camps – *40mi west of Ashland via logging roads off Rte. 11. Closed Dec–May. 207-746-7777; www. bradfordcamps.com. 8 cabins.* This is a destination for the truly adventurous.

Although the camp is accessible by car from Ashland, guests usually arrive via chartered floatplane from Millinocket. All eight log cabins lie steps from pristine Munsungan Lake, and all have private baths. Spend your days here canoeing or kayaking on the lake, fly-fishing, hiking, spotting bears and deer, or on a photo safari in search of moose. Meals are served in the main lodge.

🍴 EAT

$$$ Greenville Inn at Moosehead – *Norris St., Greenville. Dinner only. 207-695-2206 or 888-695-6000. www.greenvilleinn.com.* **Continental.** In 1895 a local lumber baron spared little expense building a Victorian mansion in Greenville, complete with interior cherry and mahogany woodwork fashioned by local ships' carpenters. Today this is the appealing Greenville Inn, which claims one of the region's best dining rooms. The chef often lends a regional twist to dishes like braised beef ribs and lobster agnolotti.

RECREATION

Opportunities for **fishing** and **hunting** abound throughout the region. Contact **Maine Fisheries and Wildlife** for seasons and information (*41 State House Station., Augusta, ME 04333; 207-287-8000; www.maine.gov/ifw*). The Kennebec, Penobscot and Dead rivers provide challenging **whitewater rafting**, and guided raft trips are offered Apr–Oct. **Raft Maine** (*www.raftmaine.com*) is an association of whitewater outfitters conducting raft trips on all three rivers. In addition, the **New England Outdoor Center** (*P.O. Box 669, 1221 Medway Rd., Millinocket, ME 04462; 207-723-5438 or 800-634-7238; www.neoc.com*) organizes kayaking and whitewater-rafting trips in Maine, as well as wildlife watching, fishing and hiking excursions.

Cross-country ski rentals, trail maps and sporting supplies are available in both Greenville and Millinocket.
Snowmobilers can use Maine's Interconnection Trail System (ITS).

Portland★★

The largest city in Maine, Portland is located on Casco Bay, known for its picturesque Calendar Islands. The city is an important oil and fishing port, and the financial, cultural and commercial center of northern New England's major metropolitan area.

A BIT OF HISTORY

True to its motto, *Resurgam* ("I shall rise again"), Portland has risen like a phoenix from its ashes after being almost entirely destroyed on three different occasions. During the early 17C, the English established a trading post here, which by 1658 developed into the village of Falmouth. Abandoned in the 1670s after Indian raids caused the inhabitants to flee, the village was resettled in 1716 and supported itself by its mast trade with England. Falmouth's strong anti-Loyalist sentiments led the British to bombard the town in October 1775, as an example to the other colonies. Following the war, the few hundred colonists who remained in Falmouth gradually rebuilt the city, and in 1786, 10 years after the birth of the nation, they renamed it Portland. The city served as the capital of Maine between 1820 and 1832. After the railroad linked Portland to Montreal in the mid-19C, the former capital grew into a prosperous shipping center. A fire swept through the downtown area on 4 July 1866, leveling most of the buildings in the business district; from these ashes rose the city's rich group of Victorian structures.

In the 1970s and 80s, Portland experienced a major economic and cultural rebirth. Today the city ships petroleum products to Canada via the Portland pipeline, while renewal of the Old Port Exchange and new construction projects continue to attract new businesses and visitors to the area.

The metropolitan area, cutting into Casco Bay, is rimmed with pleasant parks and strolling paths. The Eastern and Western promenades, both designed by the nation's preeminent

▶ **Population:** 64,300.

Michelin Map: 581 O 4, also see Maine Coast map.

Info: ☎207-772-4994; www.visitportland.com.

Location: Maine's largest city is nestled on the southern coastline, bisected north-south by I-95 and I-295. The waterfront, boasting a busy, working port and a cluster of fishing piers, is along Commercial St. From here, walk west, up the hill, to Old Port.

Kids: Children's Museum of Portland is a hit with young children; boat tours in Casco Bay and amphibious duck boat tours are also popular.

Timing: Start with an Old Port Walking Tour (*offered mid-Jun–Labor Day, Mon–Sat, 10.30am; 90-minute tours leave from the Visitor Center*). Spend the remainder of the day browsing the galleries and craft shops the of historic downtown and visiting the Portland Museum of Art (allow one to two hours at the museum).

Parking: Metered on-street parking and public lots are located throughout the city.

Don't Miss: An historical, architectural or foodie's tour offered by Greater Portland Landmarks (☎207-774-5561; www.portlandlandmarks.org); the views from atop the Portland Observatory, the last remaining maritime signal tower in the US.

Also See: MAINE COAST.

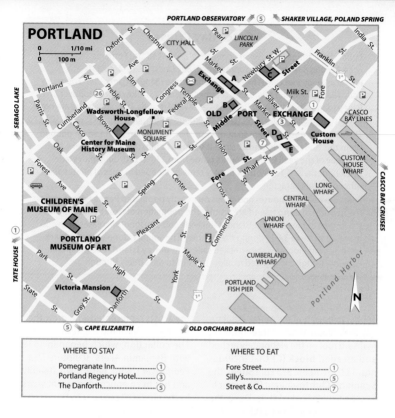

PORTLAND

0   1/10 mi
0   100 m

PORTLAND OBSERVATORY   5   SHAKER VILLAGE, POLAND SPRING

CITY HALL

LINCOLN PARK

SEBAGO LAKE

Wadsworth-Longfellow House

MONUMENT SQUARE

Center for Maine History Museum

OLD PORT

EXCHANGE

Custom House

CASCO BAY LINES

CUSTOM HOUSE WHARF

CASCO BAY CRUISES

CHILDREN'S MUSEUM OF MAINE

PORTLAND MUSEUM OF ART

LONG WHARF

CENTRAL WHARF

UNION WHARF

CUMBERLAND WHARF

TATE HOUSE

Victoria Mansion

PORTLAND FISH PIER

Portland Harbor

N

5   CAPE ELIZABETH   OLD ORCHARD BEACH

WHERE TO STAY		WHERE TO EAT	
Pomegranate Inn	1	Fore Street	1
Portland Regency Hotel	3	Silly's	5
The Danforth	5	Street & Co.	7

landscape architect, Frederick Law Olmsted, offer panoramic views of the bay and the surrounding region. Portland's skyline is best viewed from the walking path around Back Cove.

SIGHTS
Old Port Exchange★★

The warehouses, offices and shops in this old waterfront district were run-down and deteriorating rapidly when, in the early 1970s, several people decided to open a few small restaurants and shops in the area. Their immediate success encouraged other merchants to move into the district and renovate neighboring buildings into attractive specialty shops, professional offices and living spaces.

Stroll along **Exchange, Middle and Fore Streets** and admire the window displays, art galleries and craft shops, and try some of the dozens of restaurants in this area. The 19C architecture here highlights diverse styles and decorative brickwork.

The **block (A)** encompassing nos. 103-107 of Exchange Street is inspired by the Italianate style. Note the **building (B)** on the corner of Middle and Exchange Streets, which has a trompe l'œil mural; several of the windows, though they

---

GETTING AROUND

The **Convention and Visitors Bureau of Greater Portland** offers maps and information regarding attractions, accommodations and recreational opportunities. They maintain a visitor center downtown (*14 Ocean Gateway Pier; open Jun–Oct Mon–Fri 9am–5pm, Sat–Sun 9am–4pm, Nov–Mar Mon–Fri 9am–3pm, Sat 10am–3pm Apr–Jun Mon–Sat 9.30am–4,30pm; ℘207-828-0149; www.visit portland.com*).

Casco Bay Cruises

Depart from Maine State Pier at Commercial & Franklin Sts., Portland. For schedules & reservations, contact Casco Bay Lines: ✆*207-774-7871; www.cascobaylines.com.* The Bailey Island Cruise (✖♿🅿⏰*mid-Jun–Labor Day daily 10am; 5hr 45min round-trip; commentary;* ⊘*$25*) allows for a stopover at Bailey Island. The Mail Boat Run stops at several islands, but passengers are not permitted to disembark (✖♿🅿⏰*year-round daily; round-trip 3hrs;* ⊘*$15.50.*)

The islands in Casco Bay are so numerous that 17C explorer John Smith dubbed them the **"Calendar Islands,"** since it seemed to him that there was one for each day of the year. Current counts range from 130 to 220, but Smith's label stuck nonetheless. Today, their history remains steeped in tales of pirates and other colorful characters.

From the boat, the houses and shops on heavily populated **Peaks Island** and the beaches of **Long Island** are visible. The population of **Great Chebeague**, the largest of the Calendar Islands (3mi wide and 5mi long), increases from 400 in winter to some 3,000 during the summer. The solitary stone tower on **Mark Island** commemorates shipwrecked sailors. At **Bailey Island** note the granite cribwork bridge constructed to allow the surf to pass freely through the openings.

appear to be part of the mural, are actually real. Along Middle Street note the mansard roof on the elaborately arched and arcaded **block (C)** that includes nos. 133-141. At no. 373 Fore Street, the **Seaman's Club** restaurant **(D)**, exemplifies the Gothic Revival style. Down the street, **Mariner's Church (E)** (*no. 368*), with its tall windows and triangular pediment, illustrates the Greek Revival style. The Second Empire-style **Custom House** (*no. 312*) reflects the maritime wealth of 19C Portland.

Portland Museum of Art★

7 Congress Sq. ✖♿⏰*Open Memorial Day–Columbus Day daily 10am–5pm (Fri til 9pm); rest of the year Tue–Sun 10am–5pm (Fri til 9pm).* ⏰*Closed major holidays.* ⊘*$12.* ✆*207-775-6148. www.portlandmuseum.org.*

Founded in 1882, Portland's art museum is the largest and oldest public museum in Maine. Noted for its 19C and 20C American art, the museum showcases the **Elizabeth B. Noyce Collection** of works by American artists who painted in Maine. Winslow Homer (*Weather-beaten, 1894*), Andrew Wyeth (*Maine Room, 1991*), Fitz Hugh Lane (*Castine Harbor, 1851*) and Frederick Childe Hassam (*Isles of Shoals, 1913*) number among

the artists represented who drew their inspiration from the Maine landscape. The collection, which began in 1888 with Benjamin Akers' sculpture *Dead Pearl Diver* (1858), has grown steadily and has been enriched in recent years by the gifts of 17 canvases by Homer and more than 50 works by early-20C artists associated with the Ogunquit art colony. Several galleries contain sections devoted to American glass (*lower level*), American and English ceramics and the decorative arts (*4th floor*). Highlighting the displays are cases of Portland glass, and the Pepperrell collection of silver presented to Maine-born Sir William Pepperrell—leader of the successful siege in 1745 of the French fortress of Louisbourg. A regular schedule of changing exhibits of American and international art supplements the permanent collection.

👥👤 Children's Museum & Theatre of Maine★

142 Free St. ⏰*Open Mon–Sat 10am–5pm, Sun noon–5pm.*⊘*$9.* ✆*207-828-1234. www.kitetails.org.*

Children of all ages will find something to amuse them in this 17,250sq ft museum located next to the Museum of Art. On the first level, in Our Town, kids can experience the daily routines at a car repair shop, supermarket, farm, animal hospital, and on a lobster boat. The second level is devoted to hands-on science exhibits ranging from a model space shuttle to a ranger station. Highlight of the third level, the **Camera Obscura★** projects a panoramic view of Portland.

Maine Historical Society Museum

489 Congress St. ⏰*Mon–Sat 10am–5pm, Sun noon–5pm.* 🎟*$8.* 📞*207-774-1822. www.mainehistory.org.*
Exhibit galleries in the Center for Maine History Museum chronicle the history of Portland and the surrounding region. The collection of more than 15,000 artefacts includes clothing and textiles, toys, glass and ceramics, and political memorabilia.

Victoria Mansion (Morse-Libby House)

109 Danforth St. 🚶*Visit by guided tour only (45min).* ⏰ *Open May–Oct Mon–Sat 10am–4pm, Sun 1pm–5pm. Day after Thanksgiving–early Jan daily 11am–5pm.* ⏰*Closed major holidays.* 🎟*$15.* 📞*207-772-4841. www.victoriamansion.org.*
Designed by architect Henry Austin for wealthy local hotelier Ruggles Morse, this brownstone mansion (c.1860) reflects the sumptuous design and decor characteristic of the Italianate style. Inside, the lavish decoration, which includes trompe l'œil murals, elaborately carved woodwork and stained glass, suggests that of a luxury hotel.

Wadsworth-Longfellow House

489 Congress St. 🚶*Visit by guided tour (45min).* ⏰*Open May–Oct Mon–Sat 10.30am–4pm, Sun noon–4pm.* 🎟*$12.* 📞*207-774-1822. www.mainehistory.org.*
This 1785 brick dwelling—the first built in Portland—was the childhood home of poet **Henry Wadsworth Longfellow** (1807-82). Longfellow's simple narrative poems, recounting legends from America's past, won him fame across the nation and abroad. After

his death, he was the first American to be memorialized in the Poet's Corner in Westminster Abbey in London, England. Recently restored, the house displays furnishings and memorabilia relating to the poet and his family.

Tate House★

1267 Westbrook St. Drive west on Congress St., turn right on St. John St., then left on Park Ave. At I-295 overpass, continue on Congress St. to Westbrook St. 🚶*Visit by guided tour only (45min),* ⏰ *Open early Jun–mid Oct Wed–Sat 10am–4pm, Sun 1pm–4pm.* ⏰*Closed major holidays.* 🎟*$8.* 🅿📞*207-774-6177. www.tatehouse.org.*
Located in Stroudwater beside the Fore River, this unusual gambrel-roofed dwelling (1755), was the home of George Tate, the king's mast agent. Tate's duties included making shipping arrangements for trees selected as masts for Royal Navy ships.
All trees higher than 74ft and at least 24in at the base were marked as royal property, not to be felled by colonists. The trees were transported by oxen and then by ships custom-built to ferry the masts to England. The attractively furnished interior contains fine paneling, cornices, doorways and furniture that recall those in an 18C London town house.

Portland Observatory

138 Congress St., northeast of downtown on Munjoy Hill. ⏰*Open Memorial Day–Columbus Day daily 10am–5pm.* ⏰*Closed major holidays* 🎟*$8.* 📞*207-774-5561. www.portland landmarks.org.*
The last surviving 19C signal tower on the Atlantic Coast, this octagonal shingled observatory dates back to 1807. Prior to the days of the telephone and telegraph, shipowners would use this vantage point to signal (with flags) to Portlanders that ships were entering the harbor. Climb the 102 steps to the upper deck for a beautiful **view** of Portland and Casco Bay.

Poland Spring

29mi north of Portland via Rte. 26. This mountain and lake hamlet became famous in the 19C after a man who had been seriously ill drank from the spring and quickly regained his health. A small factory was established to bottle the water, and a lavish hotel complex developed near the spring. The resort, which burned down in 1975, catered to dignitaries who came "to take the waters." Poland Spring water is still bottled at a factory and sold in stores and supermarkets around the world.

EXCURSIONS
Cape Elizabeth★

10mi south of Portland. Take Rte. 77 to South Portland. At the library turn right onto Cottage Rd., which becomes Shore Rd.

A drive around Cape Elizabeth's wild and rocky shoreline provides a scenic excursion from Portland. On the northeast end of the cape sits **Portland Head Light★** (*located in Fort Williams Park on Shore Rd.*), the first lighthouse constructed on the East Coast after the Revolution (1791).

Climb up to the lighthouse deck for a panoramic **view★** of Casco Bay. Housed in the former lightkeeper's quarters, the **Museum at Portland Head Light** (*open daily Memorial Day–mid Oct daily 10am–4pm, mid Oct–late Dec weekends only; $2; 207-799-2661, www.portlandheadlight.com*) details the history of the lighthouse and of adjacent Fort Williams.

On the southeastern section of the cape stand the Cape Elizabeth Light and its inactive twin at **Two Lights State Park**, surrounded by 40 acres of shoreline for picnicking and fishing (*access via Rte. 77 South to Two Lights Rd.;* P *open year-round 9am–dusk; $4.50; 207-799-5871; www.maine.gov/doc/parks*). Boasting one of the best sand beaches in Maine, 243-acre **Crescent Beach State Park** lies just .5mi west of Two Lights (*access via Rte. 77/Bowery Beach Rd.;* *open Memorial Day–Columbus Day 9am–dusk; $6.50; 207-799-5871; www.maine.gov/doc/parks*).

Just south of Cape Elizabeth, **Old Orchard Beach** (*access via Rte. 1 South and Rte. 9 East*) has attracted Americans and Canadians to its sandy shore for more than 100 years. Motels, cottages, trailer parks and restaurants front the broad, 7mi-long saltwater beach, and carnival rides animate the pier in summer.

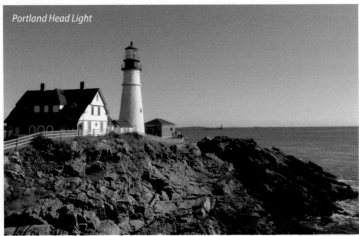

Portland Head Light

© Maine Office of Tourism

Sabbathday Lake Shaker Village and Museum★

▶ *25mi north of Portland in New Gloucester. Take I-95 North to Exit 11, then follow Rte. 26 8mi north.* **P** 🕐*Open Memorial Day–Columbus Day Mon–Sat 10am–4.30pm.* ✎*Guided tours $7.* ✆*207-926-4597. www.shaker.lib.me.us.*

This hilly lakeside property is the site of the Sabbathday Lake Shaker Village, the last active Shaker community in America.

The Shakers occupy a number of the 18 buildings on-site, only six of which are open to the public. With its granite trim and delicate wooden porch, the **Brick Dwelling House** appears elegant when contrasted with the simple white clapboard structures found throughout the village. Inside, simple furnishings and examples of clothing illustrate the Shakers' uncomplicated way of life.

Shaker industries and inventions are depicted in the **Meeting House**, the first building (1794) erected in the village.

Sebago Lake

▶ *20mi north of Portland via US-302.* Portlanders who enjoy swimming, boating and fishing favor Sebago Lake, the second-largest inland body of water (45sq mi) in Maine after Moosehead Lake. Bordering the lake, Sebago Lake State Park (*off US-302 between South Casco and Naples*), offers picnic areas, campsites and a sandy beach (△🕐*open May–mid-Oct 9am–dusk;* 🚗*$6.50;* ✆*207-693-6613; www.maine.gov/doc/parks*).

ADDRESSES

🏨STAY

$$$$ Portland Regency Hotel – *20 Milk St.* ✆*207-774-4200 or 800-727-3436. www.theregency.com. 95 rooms.* What began as an 1895 armory has morphed into an attractive and comfortable full-service hotel situated in the heart of Portland's historic Old Port district. Guest quarters are done in Colonial style—four-poster beds, cherry wood, flowered fabrics—and feature high-speed Internet access, nightly turn-down service and complimentary newspaper and coffee with your wake-up call. Just outside you'll find the numerous restaurants and shops of the Old Port (the neighborhood bar scene can be rowdy on weekends). There's a fitness club and full-service spa on-site, too.

$$$$ The Danforth – *163 Danforth St.* ✆*207-879-8755 or 800-991-6557. www.danforthmaine.com. 7 rooms.* Among Portland's wealth of regal 19C homes, The Danforth ranks as one of the most handsome. Dating to 1821, this Federal-style brick residence capped with a cupola has been meticulously restored and filled with pastel colors, understated furnishings and amenities like Wi-Fi and plush, deluxe linens. Among the inviting touches are the working fireplaces in every guest room but one, and a wood-paneled billiards room in the basement. The inn is a short walk (about 10min) from Portland's Old Port.

$$$ Pomegranate Inn – *49 Neal St.* ✆*207-772-1006 or 800-356-0408. www.pomegranateinn.com. 8 rooms.* The staid facade of this handsome 1884 Italianate house in Portland's Western Promenade Historic District gives no hint of what you will find inside. Guest rooms and common rooms are chock-full of wildly whimsical art and Classical antiques boldly painted by a local artist—some with faux vines, others with cartoonish Roman capitals—rooms are decorated in a boisterous mix of patterns and colors. Five rooms have fireplaces and all have private baths.

🍴EAT

$$$ Fore Street – *288 Fore St. Dinner only.* ✆*207-775-2717. www.forestreet.biz.* **Contemporary**. Noted chef Sam Hayward has been hailed in both *Saveur* and *Gourmet* magazines for the extraordinary food he serves at this inviting Portland eatery. Housed in a loft-like industrial space, the restaurant centers on an open kitchen with a wood grill and wood-fired oven. Fore Street specializes in grilled fish and meats, purchased from local purveyors when available.

$$$ Street & Co. – *33 Wharf St. Dinner only.* ✆*207-775-0887. www.streetand company.net.* **Seafood**. This intimate bistro occupies a warren of low-ceilinged rooms off a cobblestone alley in the Old Port. Seafood is the draw here—it's prepared grilled, sautéed, or however else you'd like. The evening specials offer the freshest catches, and rarely fail to impress. During the summer, you can dine outside in the alley.

$ Silly's – *40 Washington St.* ℘*207-772-0360. www.sillys.com.* **American.** Wraps, salads, vegan dishes, burgers and a host of unique sandwiches are some of the items you'll find in this funky hole-in-the-wall in a part of town tourists don't often frequent. This is a neighborhood joint which serves up some of the town's zestiest meals at a good price. Almost everything is homemade, from the hand-cut french fries to the thick milkshakes. Eat in, or pack a lunch and head up and over nearby Munjoy Hill for a picnic on the grassy Eastern Promenade.

RECREATION

Shops abound at the Old Port Exchange and on Congress Street. You can download maps of four self-guided walking tours of the city's historic areas from **Greater Portland Landmarks** (*165 State St.;* ℘*207-774-5561; www.portlandlandmarks.org*). You can walk along the Eastern and Western promenades, overlooking Casco Bay and the Fore River respectively, or hike the **Back Cove Trail**, which traces Portland's coastline from Maine State Pier (*Commercial & Franklin Sts.*) around Casco Bay and Back Cove. Biking trails run along the Eastern Promenade. Crescent Beach State Park on nearby Cape Elizabeth offers a sandy Atlantic beach.

Rangeley Lakes Region★

Nestled in the wooded mountains of western Maine, this region is characterized by its 111 lakes and ponds, the largest being the lakes of the Rangeley chain. Long before the area saw its first settlers, Abnaki Indians set up hunting and fishing camps on the lakeshores.
Today, visitors escape to this year-round recreational haven to go skiing, snowshoeing and snowmobiling on 150mi of trails in winter; to hunt deer, pheasant and bear in autumn amid a spectacular display of blazing foliage; and to go swimming, boating, canoeing and mountain climbing in summer. Anglers come in spring for the world-class brook trout and salmon fishing.

- ⏱ **Michelin Map:** 581 M 1.
- 🗎 **Info:** ℘207-864-5364; www.rangeleymaine.com.
- ▶ **Location:** East-west Rte. 16 and north-south Rte. 17 access the lakes region. Rangeley is the largest town and a good base for exploring the area.
- 👫 **Kids:** Take a hike, catch a trout; this area is all about the outdoors.
- 🕐 **Timing:** Base yourself in the town of Rangeley for day trips in the region.
- 👁 **Don't Miss:** Rent a kayak or canoe from local outfitters to explore the lakes. Nearby Sugarloaf USA is a year-round resort with guided nature programs, hiking, biking and golf.

SCENERY

Scenic turnoffs on Rte. 17, south of tiny Oquossoc, afford great **views★★★** of the area's largest lakes. And rewarding vistas abound along Rte. 4 South between Oquossoc and the sleepy village of **Rangeley** (population: 1,200 permanent residents), which claims no traffic lights to disrupt traffic along its Main Street. Moose can often be seen at dawn or dusk along Rte. 16, heading out of Rangeley. For those who prefer the solitude of the woods, abundant trails lead to quiet brooks and awe-inspiring mountaintops.

SIGHTS
Rangeley Lake State Park

From Rte. 4 or Rte. 17, take Southshore Dr. and follow signs to park in Rangeley. ⚠🕐*Open mid-May–Sept daily 9am–dusk.* 🚫*$4.50.* ☎*207-864-3858. www. maine.gov/doc/parks.*

Set on 869 remote acres on the south shore of Rangeley Lake, this park includes a beach area with boat ramps, docks and secluded campsites. The lake is renowned among anglers for its landlocked salmon and trout fishing.

© Brigitta L. House / MICHELIN

Rangeley Lake

Eustis Ridge★★

26mi north of Rangeley by Rte. 16. Turn left onto Rte. 27. After 3mi turn left onto the unmarked road.

From this vantage point there is a **view** of the region. Rte. 27 continues north to the Canadian border (*30mi*) through unspoiled countryside.

Mt. Blue State Park★

31mi southeast of Rangeley in Weld. Take Rte. 4 East, then Rte. 142 South. ⚠🕐*Open mid-May–Sep daily 9am–dusk; rest of the year call for hours.*

🚫*$6.* ☎*207-585-2347 or 207-585-2261 (off season). www.maine.gov/doc/parks.*

A mountain panorama rings Mt. Blue State Park, with its 5,021 acres on the shores of **Lake Webb★**.

Recreational opportunities here include hiking, horseback riding, winter sports such as snowshoeing and snowmobiling, boating, swimming, and sunbathing on the sandy beach.

Enjoy mountain and lake vistas from **State Park Beach Road**.

Skiers: Take Note

Maine's second-highest peak (4,237ft), **Sugarloaf Mountain** is located east of Rangeley in the Carrabassett Valley. Boasting 134 trails, Sugarloaf/USA (☎*207-237-2000 or 800-843-5623; www.sugarloaf.com*) offers the only above-treeline skiing with lift service in the East. In summer, there's hiking, biking, guided outdoor excursions and golf.

At 4,116ft, nearby **Saddleback Mountain** (☎*207-864-5671 or 866-918-2225; www.saddlebackmaine.com*) features more than 65 alpine trails across 220 skiable acres.

MASSACHUSETTS

Extending from the Atlantic Ocean to the border of New York state, Massachusetts reflects the region's varied topography. The tree-covered Berkshire Hills in the west gradually slope down to the fertile meadows of the Connecticut Valley in the center of the state. Miles of sandy beach lie south of Boston, while to the north the coast is irregular and rocky. The state is rectangular in shape, except for the southeast section that juts into the ocean, adding hundreds of miles to the Massachusetts coastline.

Highlights

1 Viewing fall color in **The Berkshires** (p172)
2 Getting to know the Very Hungry Caterpillar at **Eric Carle Museum of Picture Book Art** (p183)
3 Sailing in Boston's **Swan Boats** (p209)
4 Browsing bookstores in historic **Cambridge** (p225)
5 Discovering quaint fishing villages on a **Cape Ann** driving tour (p228)

▶ **Population:** 6,587,536.
Info: www.massvacation.com.
Area: 7,838sq mi.
Capital: Boston.
Nickname: The Bay State.
State Flower: Mayflower.

Birthplace of American Independence

New England's earliest permanent settlements were in Massachusetts. In search of religious freedom, the Pilgrims established Plymouth Colony in 1620, followed within 10 years by the Puritans, who founded Boston. As the population expanded and prospered, taxation by the British placed an increasing burden on the colonists.

Angered by England's policy of "taxation without representation," and inspired by the oratory of **Samuel Adams**, **James Otis** and **John Hancock**, the colonists reacted by staging the **Boston Tea Party**, which, along with the **Boston Massacre** in 1770, were the prelude to the conflicts at Lexington and Concord, and the ensuing battle for American independence.

Highland Light, Cape Cod National Seashore

Back Bay, Boston

© Armin Sepp / Fotolia.com

Economy

For two centuries Massachusetts earned its living from the sea by fishing, whaling and trade. Great fortunes were made in the China trade, and when maritime commerce declined in the 19C, this wealth helped the capital shift to industrialization.

Thanks to abundant waterpower and the increasing waves of immigration that provided a large labor force, the Berkshires, the southern coast and the Merrimack Valley were soon dotted with small industrial centers. The state developed into a prominent manufacturer of textiles and leather goods. By 1850 **Lowell**, the first planned industrial city in the nation, was the world's leading producer of textiles. In the 20C these industries migrated to the South and were supplanted by the manufacture of electronics, machine tools and electrical equipment. Today Massachusetts' most important source of revenue is its **"brain power,"** represented by the state's educational institutions, medical research, and technological and financial services industries.

Massachusetts continues to lead the New England states in commercial fishing, with Gloucester and New Bedford ranking among the nation's major ports. The Bay State's **cranberry crop**, cultivated in the regions of Cape Cod and Plymouth, is the nation's largest.

Massachusetts today

Many visitors are instantly charmed by the city of **Boston** – as long as they don't attempt to drive the labyrinth of downtown streets, or try to find a parking space. Happily, Boston is compact, and exploring by foot is the best way to

Pawtucket Canal, Lowell National Historical Park

© Jonathan Parker / National Park Service

MASSACHUSETTS

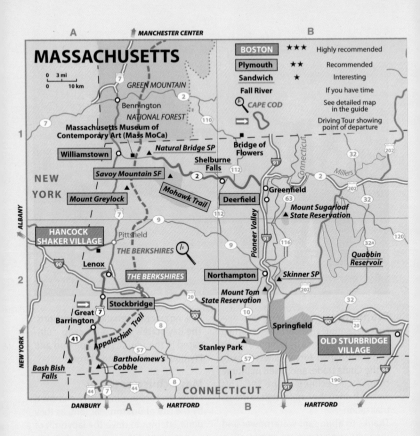

MASSACHUSETTS

BOSTON	★★★ Highly recommended
Plymouth	★★ Recommended
Sandwich	★ Interesting
Fall River	If you have time
🔍 *CAPE COD*	See detailed map in the guide
	Driving Tour showing point of departure

MANCHESTER CENTER

0 3 mi
0 10 km

GREEN MOUNTAIN

Bennington
NATIONAL FOREST

Massachusetts Museum of Contemporary Art (Mass MoCA)

Williamstown
Natural Bridge SP

Bridge of Flowers

Shelburne Falls

Savoy Mountain SF

Mohawk Trail
Deerfield
Greenfield

Mount Greylock
Pioneer Valley
Mount Sugarloaf State Reservation

NEW YORK

HANCOCK SHAKER VILLAGE
Pittsfield

THE BERKSHIRES

Lenox

THE BERKSHIRES
Northampton
Skinner SP

Quabbin Reservoir

Mount Tom State Reservation

Stockbridge

Great Barrington

Appalachian Trail

Springfield

OLD STURBRIDGE VILLAGE

Stanley Park

Bartholomew's Cobble

Bash Bish Falls

CONNECTICUT

DANBURY   HARTFORD   HARTFORD

---

enjoy the city's splendid architecture, parks and gardens, and outdoor cafes. The yearly influx of college students to nearby Harvard, MIT, and dozens of other schools lends a hip, youthful flair to the city. Hotels and B&Bs are clustered in some of the most desirable parts of the city, so visitors can walk to shops, museums and attractions.

The Bay State is small enough to explore, and it's worth venturing beyond Boston. The **North Shore** is home to Salem, home of the famous witch trials, and a series of lovely seaport towns, including Ipswich, known for its fried clams and the state's best stretch of sand, Crane Beach. To the south, **Plymouth** attracts visitors with Plimoth Plantation and the famous rock that marks where the *May-*

flower passengers landed. Farther south, **Cape Cod** lures vacationers with the promise of dune-backed beaches and classic New England charm. While some of the Cape has become suburbanized in recent years, it's still possible to find Old Cape Cod, especially in towns like Chatham and Wellfleet.

At the western edge of the state lies the **Berkshires** region, named after the Berkshire Hills. Here, small villages and old mill towns are home to a host of cultural attractions. Sprinkled across **central Massachusetts** are tourist attractions like Naismith Basketball Hall of Fame and Old Sturbridge Village. The **Mohawk Trail** (Rte. 2), running across the northern border of the state, is the quintessential fall foliage route.

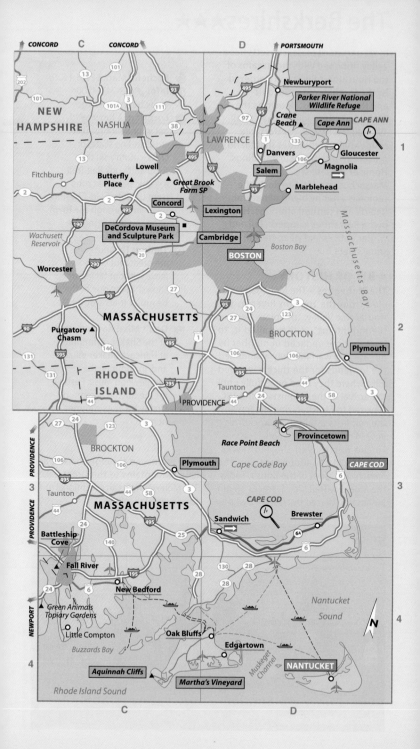

NEW HAMPSHIRE

NASHUA

Newburyport

Parker River National Wildlife Refuge

Crane Beach   **Cape Ann**   CAPE ANN

LAWRENCE

Danvers   133   Gloucester

Lowell   Magnolia

Fitchburg   Butterfly Place   **Great Brook Farm SP**   **Salem**   106

Concord   Marblehead

DeCordova Museum and Sculpture Park   **Lexington**

Wachusett Reservoir   **Cambridge**

Boston Bay

BOSTON

Worcester

MASSACHUSETTS

Massachusetts Bay

Purgatory Chasm

BROCKTON   **Plymouth**

RHODE ISLAND

Taunton

PROVIDENCE

PROVIDENCE   24   123

BROCKTON

Race Point Beach   **Provincetown**

Plymouth   Cape Code Bay   **CAPE COD**

Taunton   **CAPE COD**

MASSACHUSETTS   **Sandwich**   **Brewster**

Battleship Cove

Fall River

New Bedford   Nantucket Sound

Green Animals Topiary Gardens   N

NEWPORT   Little Compton   **Oak Bluffs**

Buzzards Bay   **Edgartown**   **NANTUCKET**

Aquinnah Cliffs   Muskeget Channel

Martha's Vineyard

Rhode Island Sound

The Berkshires★★★

In westernmost Massachusetts lies a valley ribboned with the streams of the Housatonic River and bordered by the foothills of the Taconic and Hoosac ranges. Known as the Berkshires, this region mixes small 19C mill towns with comfortable residential communities that blend gracefully with their surroundings. Home of the tallest peak in Massachusetts, Mt. Greylock, the region is a happy blend of natural beauty and cultural offerings. Hiking in the Berkshires is superb; fall and winter entices leaf-peepers and snow skiers.

- ♿ **Michelin Map:** 581 H, I 8, 9.
- 🏢 **Info:** ☎413-743-4500; www.berkshires.org.
- ▶ **Location:** A fun way to get your bearings: Bike, stroll, in-line skate, or cross-country ski the Ashuwillticook Rail Trail, a scenic path that runs from the Pittsfield-Cheshire town line through the town of Adams and along the Cheshire Lakes.
- 🕐 **Timing:** The museums are great, but don't leave without hiking or snowshoeing one of the beautiful trails around Mt. Greylock.
- 😊 **Don't Miss:** An inside look at the Shaker community at Hancock Shaker Village and, in summer, the Tanglewood Music Festival for the Boston Symphony Orchestra at its summer home.

A BIT OF HISTORY

The Mohegans – The Mohegans traveled from the Hudson River to the Housatonic Valley, "the place beyond the mountains" as they called it, to hunt. In time, reduced in number by disease and warfare, they abandoned the lowlands for the thickly wooded hills, where they lived peacefully until the arrival of the colonists in the 18C. Devoted to Christianizing the Indians, the colonists established Stockbridge in 1734 as an Indian mission.

To the north lived the **Mohawks**, enemies of the Mohegans and the French, and allies of the British. Today, the Mohawk Trail (*Rte. 2*) traces an old Indian trail blazed by the Mohawks as they journeyed through the Appalachian Mountains to the Great Lakes. The Mohawk Trail is an exceptional route for viewing fall foliage.

Hancock Shaker Village

© Hancock Shaker Village, Pittsfield, MA

GETTING THERE

From the east, take I-90 (Mass Turnpike) West to Rte. 102 West (*Boston to Stockbridge 154mi*). From the south, take I-684 East to US-7 North (*NYC to Stockbridge 130mi*). From the west, take I-90 West to Rte. 102 South to US-7 North (*Albany to Stockbridge, 57mi*). From the north, take US-7 South (*Burlington, VT to Stockbridge, 162mi*). International and domestic flights service **Bradley International Airport** (**BDL**) in Windsor Locks, CT (*℘860-292-2000; www.bradleyairport.com*) and **Albany International Airport** (ALB) in Albany, NY (*℘518-242-2200; www.albanyairport.com*).

If you're driving from Bradley airport, take I-91 North to I-90 West (*Hartford, CT, to Stockbridge, 88mi*). Major rental-car agencies are located at the airports. **Amtrak** (*℘800-872-7245; www.amtrak.com*) provides **train** service between Boston and Pittsfield. **Greyhound** (*℘800-231-2222; www.greyhound.com*) **buses** run from both Boston and Albany, NY, to Lenox and Pittsfield, MA.

VISITOR INFORMATION

The **Berkshires Visitor's Bureau** in Pittsfield provides maps and information about area attractions, accommodations, dining, recreation, and annual festivals (*℘413-743-4500; www.berkshires.org*).

GREAT BARRINGTON REGION★★
Great Barrington

Located at the junction of US-7 and Rte. 23, Great Barrington serves as the commercial center for the many vacation homes on the outskirts of this pleasant town. The Great Barrington Rapids, once the site of Mohegan camps, were the major power source for local mills in the 18C. On 20 March 1886, Great Barrington became one of the first cities in the world to have its streets and houses lit by electricity.

Bartholomew's Cobble

11mi south of Great Barrington. Take US-7 South to Sheffield Center and continue south 1.6mi. Turn right on Rte. 7A and continue .5mi; take a right on Rannapo Rd. and go 1.5mi; then right on Weatogue Rd. ◐*Open year-round daily sunrise–sunset. Visitor center open daily 9am–4.30pm (closed Sun and Mon, Dec–Mar).* ◉*$5.* ℘*413-229-8600. www.thetrustees.org.*

This natural rock garden, covered with a variety of trees, wildflowers and ferns, rises above the Housatonic River. The **Ledges Trail** (*round-trip 45min*) passes through the cobble and follows the river. At station 17, cross the road and continue on Hulburt's Hill Trail to an open pasture on Miles Mountain (1,050ft) with a view of the Housatonic Valley.

Bash Bish Falls★

16mi southwest of Great Barrington. Follow Rte. 23 West to South Egremont, then Rte. 415 at the pond, then immediate right onto Mt. Washington Rd., East St., West St. and Bash Bish Falls Rd. ◐*Open year-round daily dawn–dusk.* ◉*Can be dangerous when icy.* ℘*413-528-0330.*

From the parking area, a steep trail marked with blue triangles and white blazes leads to the falls. Down the road 1mi there is another parking area; from there, a longer, but easier, path leads to the falls. Bash Bish Brook flows over a 275ft gorge, creating a 50ft waterfall and natural pool in a forested setting.

Monument Mountain★

4.5mi north of Great Barrington on US-7. From the parking area on the west side of US-7, two trails lead to the summit. Off **Indian Monument Trail**, look for a cairn about 100yds off the trail that marks the grave of the Indian maiden for whom Squaw Peak is named (she leaped to her death from this point). Turn right and continue, always selecting the right spur. The second, more difficult trail (*ascent 45min*) begins at the right of the parking area and is blazed with round white markers. From the rocky summit of Squaw Peak you will behold a sweeping view of the Berkshires.

🚗 DRIVING TOUR

STOCKBRIDGE TO LENOX★★★

Stockbridge★★
Located at the junction of US-7 and Rte. 102. &See STOCKBRIDGE.

▷ In Stockbridge, take Pine St. opposite the Red Lion Inn. Turn left onto Prospect St. (Mahkeenac Rd.) and drive along the lakeshore of Stockbridge Bowl; continue on Hawthorne Rd. At the junction of Hawthorne Rd. and Rte. 183 there is a good view of the lake.

Tanglewood★
Tanglewood is the summer home of the Boston Symphony Orchestra and the site of one of the nation's most famous musical events, the **Tanglewood Music Festival** (*for schedules, visit www.bso. org*). More than 300,000 music lovers attend every year. The festival was inaugurated in 1934 with concerts by the New York Philharmonic Symphony Orchestra. In 1936 the New York Philharmonic was replaced by the Boston Symphony Orchestra, which has presented the summer series of concerts ever since. Tanglewood, formerly the residence of the Tappan family, was given to the Berkshire Festival Society in 1937 to serve as the festival's permanent home. Buildings on the 500 acres include the main house; the 5,000-seat Koussevitzky

Music Shed, designed by Eliel Saarinen; and the 1,180-seat Seiji Ozawa Hall, opened in 1994.

From the gardens there is a **view** of the **Stockbridge Bowl** and **Hawthorne Cottage** (*not open to the public*), a replica of the dwelling where Nathaniel Hawthorne lived for 18 months while writing *The House of the Seven Gables* (1851) (&*see SALEM*).

▷ Take Rte. 183 North to Lenox.

Lenox★
Surrounded by estates that have been transformed into schools and resorts, Lenox, with its inviting inns and restaurants, is a delightful place to stay.

▷ Take US-7 North and turn left opposite the Quality Inn onto W. Dugway Rd.; then bear left at the fork on W. Mountain Rd.

Pleasant Valley Wildlife Sanctuary
3mi north of Lenox at 472 W. Mountain Rd. 🅿🕐*Open late June–mid Oct daily dawn–dusk, open mid Oct–late Jun, Tues–Sun and Mon holidays.* ✎*$5 Trail map available online.* ☎*413-637-0320. www.massaudubon.org.*
This refuge boasts 7mi of trails that lead through forest, wetlands and meadows, and along the slopes of Mt Lenox. A beaver colony occupies the string of ponds in the valley; look for lodges along Yokun Brook. Canoe trips on the Housatonic River are offered from mid-May to Columbus Day. Come winter, the sanctuary is a favorite spot for snowshoers and cross-country skiers.

The Grand Estates

Glowing descriptions of the Berkshires written by Nathaniel Hawthorne and others attracted wealthy families to summer here in the mid 19C, building the handsome residences that still grace the countryside outside Great Barrington, Lee and Stockbridge. At the beginning of the 20C, Lenox alone could count 75 of these magnificent properties, including the estate of Andrew Carnegie.

Spiraling costs and the Great Depression brought an end to the luxuries of the era, and most of the estates were abandoned or sold. Several have found new life as year-round inns.

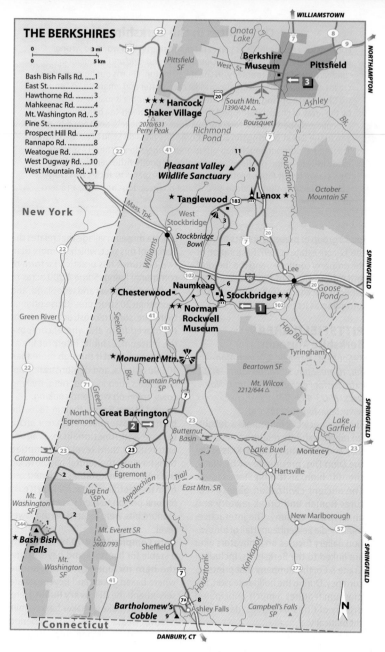

THE BERKSHIRES

0	3 mi
0	5 km

WILLIAMSTOWN

NORTHAMPTON

Onota Lake

Berkshire Museum

Pittsfield 3

Pittsfield SF

★★★ Hancock Shaker Village

South Mtn. 1390/424 △

Ashley

Bousquet

2070/631 Perry Peak

Richmond Pond

New York

Pleasant Valley Wildlife Sanctuary

★ Tanglewood

West Stockbridge

Stockbridge Bowl

★ Lenox ★

October Mountain SF

Williams

Mass. Tpk.

Lee

Goose Pond

SPRINGFIELD

★ Chesterwood

Naumkeag

Stockbridge ★★

Norman Rockwell Museum

Seekonk

★ Monument Mtn.

Fountain Pond SP

Beartown SF

Mt. Wilcox 2212/644 △

Tyringham

Green River

Lake Garfield

SPRINGFIELD

North Egremont

Great Barrington 2

Butternut Basin

Lake Buel

Monterey

Catamount

South Egremont

Hartsville

Mt. Washington SF

Jug End SP

Appalachian Trail

East Mtn. SR

New Marlborough

SPRINGFIELD

Mt. Everett SR 2602/793 △

Sheffield

★ Bash Bish Falls

Mt. Washington SF

Bartholomew's Cobble

Ashley Falls

Campbell's Falls SP

Connecticut

DANBURY, CT

Ventford Hall Mansion and Gilded Age Museum

104 Walker St. P ⊙ *Open Mon–Fri, 10am–5pm, Sat and Sun 10am–3pm.* ⊛*$16.* ℘*413-637-3206.* *www.gildedage.org.*

Glimpse into the lifestyles of Lenox's fabulously wealthy "cottage class" at Ventford Hall, built in 1893 as the summer home of Sarah Morgan, financier J.P. Morgan's sister. Located in downtown Lenox, the building was in shambles

Quick Bites in the Berkshires

Looking for a tasty nibble as you explore the sights? You won't go wrong with one of these local favorites. Open year-round *(and until midnight in summertime)*, **Soco Creamery**, in Great Barrington, churns out homemade ice cream and gelato in enticing flavors like cake batter and amaretto. In Lenox, try **Chocolate Springs Cafe**, where the dizzying aroma is matched only by the array of chocolate-dipped treats, including green-tea bon bons and chocolate-dipped prunes. New Yorkers know good bagels, and they'd steer you to the **Great Barrington Bagel Company** on Main St. in Great Barrington. This indoor-outdoor bagel shop offers great bagel sandwiches, 17 spreads made in-house, and the flagel, a super-thin, topped-with-everything bagel. Don't leave North Adams without paying your respects to **Jack's Hot Dog Stand**, a local institution since 1917. Count on great dogs and fries, and zero atmosphere!

until a group of preservationists bought the 12-acre estate in 1997. Restoration of the property continues, and the "before" and "after" views of the house as it is brought back to its former glory are as intriguing as its history.

PITTSFIELD AREA
Berkshire Museum

39 South St., Pittsfield. ◷*Open Mon–Sat, 10 am–5pm, Sun noon–5pm.* ◎*$13; extra fee for Festival of Trees (mid-Nov–Dec).* ☏*413-443-7171. www.berkshiremuseum.org.*

This small, eclectic museum is a delightful mix of exhibits relating to art, history and the natural world. Kids enjoy the Dino Dig, presided over by Wally, the 10ft-high, 26 ft-long Stegosaurus. The ancient civilization gallery features Roman and Greek jewelry and an Egyptian mummy. The interactive, multimedia Feigenbaum Hall of Innovation gallery focuses on innovators who are linked to the Berkshires, including Crane & Co, the company that prints US currency. During the holiday season, the museum features a much-anticipated display of Christmas trees, decorated thematically.

Hancock Shaker Village★★★

3mi west of Pittsfield via US-20. P◷*Open Jul–Oct daily 10am–5pm, mid-April–June open daily 10am–4pm.* ◎*$17. www.hancockshakervillage.org.*

Hancock Shaker Village, an active Shaker community between 1790 and 1960, is today a museum village that relates the history of this sect, which for more than two centuries has practiced a form of communal living. Some 1,200 acres of farmland, meadow and woodland, and more than 20 structures (those original to the site, some reconstructed and others moved from elsewhere) compose the museum. Exhibits interpret life as the Shakers lived it through more than 10,000 objects, and demonstrations of daily tasks such as gardening, milking cows, spinning wool and cooking.

Round Stone Barn – Built in 1826, the barn is a masterpiece of Shaker architecture and functionalism. Wagons entered the third level and emptied their hay into the central haymow. On the middle level, stables radiated out from the central manger, making it easy for one person to feed the entire herd. Manure pits were located on the lower level.

Barn Complex (1910-1939) – Formerly a stable for livestock and hay storage, the barn includes the Good Room, where baked goods and beverages are served, and the **Discovery Room**. Here, visitors can make a Shaker basket, milk a "cow," weave a scarf, and don period Shaker clothing, among other hands-on activities.

Meetinghouse – The Shakers met here every Sunday for their religious services. The meeting room, a large open hall on the first floor, provided ample space for dancing. Singing (a cappella) was customarily part of the worship too.

ADDRESSES

🛏 STAY

LENOX

$$$$$ The Blantyre – *16 Blantyre Rd., Lenox. Open May–early Nov. ☎413-637-3556. www.blantyre.com. 25 rooms.*
A Scottish castle in the Berkshires may be unexpected, but somehow the Blantyre looks right at home, set on 100 acres of woodlands. The hotel's amenities—pool, tennis courts, hot tub, sauna, croquet lawn, and hiking trails—are suitable for royalty. Built in 1901, the house was modeled after a castle in Lanarkshire, Scotland, complete with towers, turrets and gargoyles. The Fitzpatrick family bought the manor in 1980, restoring it to its Gilded Age grandeur. Rooms in the main house sport lavish touches such as hand-carved beds, parquet floors, oriental rugs, marble sinks and walk-in steam showers. The Paterson Suite offers the best views, but the mid-priced Corner Room is charming.

$$$$ Cranwell Resort, Spa & Golf Club – *55 Lee Rd., Lenox. ☎413-637-1364 or 800-272-6935. www.cranwell.com. 113 rooms.* Set on nearly 400 acres, this sprawling resort is a destination onto itself, and great for families with kids. Amenities include a golf school, tennis, bike rentals, and a 35,000sq ft spa area with a family-friendly indoor swimming pool. Much of this is open to the public, along with four **restaurants**. The fanciest rooms in the complex are in the century-old Tudor mansion, but families might be happier—and have more privacy—in one of two smaller buildings or in one of the cottages with its own kitchen.

$$$$ Gateways Inn – *51 Walker St., Lenox. ☎413-637-2532. www.gatewaysinn.com. 12 rooms.* Built in 1912 as the summer cottage of Harley Procter of Procter & Gamble, this Federal-style structure is warm and welcoming, thanks to innkeepers Michele and Eiran Gazit. Some rooms reflect the names of famous guests: Norman Rockwell used to show up for lunch and the staff would fight over his sketched-upon napkins; the late Boston Pops conductor Arthur Fiedler favored the suite now named after him, which is outfitted with an extra-long bathtub that suited his tall stature. Rooms are decorated with canopied four-poster beds, brass beds or sleigh beds, and gas fireplaces. The recently-added Piano Bar offers live music and an extensive wine list.

LEE

$$ Devonfield Inn – *85 Stockbridge Road, Lee. ☎413-243-3298. www.devonfield.com. 9 rooms, 1 cottage. No kids under 12 in summer.* This impeccably maintained, yellow-and-cream Federal-style inn is set on 32 acres of rolling Berkshires hillside. Inside, it's every bit as lovely. Rooms are decked out in Colonial style furnishings, with canopied four-poster beds, Oriental rugs, and (in some) working fireplaces. There's WiFi throughout. A separate cottage (pet-friendly) with a pitched cathedral ceiling has its own kitchen and deck; there's also a huge penthouse suite. For breakfast, count on tasty fare like vanilla-cinnamon crème brûlée or orange-yogurt pancakes; work it off with a swim in the pool or a ride on one of the inn's bicycles.

🍴 EAT

GREAT BARRINGTON

$$$ Bizen – *17 Railroad St., Great Barrington. Open for dinner nightly. ☎413-528-9696.* **Japanese.** Master sushi chef Michael Marcus hand-fires his restaurant's ceramic dinnerware in an on-site kiln. That same attention to detail extends to the kitchen, where magical things happen with sashimi, sushi, hand rolls, and a selection of grilled and cooked dishes. You'll remove your shoes and sit on cushions at low tables, Japanese-style, before enjoying the best sushi in the Berkshires.

LENOX

$$ Nudel Restaurant – *35 Church St., Lennox Open for lunch Thu–Sat; dinner Tue–Sun. ☎413-551-7183; www.nudelrestaurant.com.* **American.** Just when you think dining in the Berkshires has become way too pricey and predictable, along comes Nudel. Much of the meat and produce comes from organic farms and purveyors. Bold pairings, like octopus with boiled egg, or spicy bluefish and fluke tacos with a side of grits change with the seasons; a summer menu might include steamed cobia (fish) with chilled strawberry gazpacho, crispy rice and cucumbers.

PITTSFIELD

$$$ Dakota – *1035 South St. (US-7), in Pittsfield. Dinner and Sunday brunch.* ℘*413 -499-7900. www.dakotarestaurant.com.* **American.** Enjoy seafood, steaks or Maine lobster in this authentic, recreated hunting lodge, with its fieldstone fireplaces and walls decked with moose heads and Plains Indian pottery. Wood-grilled chicken and Atlantic salmon are available from the menu as well as prime rib and aged, hand-cut steaks. Selections from a sizable farm-fresh salad bar complete your dinner, along with home-baked whole-grain bread. Try to save space for Dakota's signature mud pie!

SOUTH EGREMONT

$$$$ John Andrew's Restaurant – *Rte. 23 in South Egremont. Open for dinner daily; reservations advised.* ℘*413-528-3469. www.jarestaurant.com.* **Contemporary.** This somewhat isolated house is worth the drive for elegant, understated decor and delectable cuisine. Superbly prepared and presented entrées, low-key jazz and a peaceful country setting greet diners here. Try the lobster ravioli to start, followed by pan-roasted cod, clams, chorizo and saffron rice, or perhaps try the risotto of duck confit with leeks and parmigiano reggiano. For dessert, sample the caramelized bananas with chestnut ice cream and caramel sauce.

STOCKBRIDGE

$$$ Red Lion Inn – *30 Main St., Stockbridge. Open for breakfast, lunch, and dinner daily. No shorts, jeans or sneakers in the dining room.* ℘*413-298-5545. www.redlioninn.com.* **American.** Looking at this c.1773 inn, you might expect a dinner menu that leaned toward Yankee pot roast and Indian pudding. You'd be wrong. Local ingredients go contemporary here; think lobster and scallop cakes in a saffron cream, roasted tomato and basil foam, for example. Even the ubiquitous Caesar salad gets a twist, with manchego cheese and white anchovies. The Red Lion's apple pie is a true classic, served warm with a dollop of ice cream, but adventurous palates should opt for the tangy blood orange bisque. The **$$Widow Bingham's Tavern** serves more casual fare, like fish and chips.

ENTERTAINMENT / RECREATION

Among Massachusett's most well-known events are the **Tanglewood Music Festival** (℘*413-637-1600 ; www.bso.org*) and the **South Mountain Concert Festival** (℘*413-442-2106*). The **Jacob's Pillow Dance Festival** (*Jun–Aug;* ℘*413-243-0745; www.jacobs pillow.org*) brings together international performers of ballet, modern dance and mime. Summer theater is offered at the **Berkshire Playhouse** in Stockbridge and at the **Williamstown Theater** in Williamstown (see *WILLIAMSTOWN*).

In winter, you can **ski** at: **Ski Butternut** in Great Barrington (℘*413-528-2000; www.skibutternut.com*) and **Jiminy Peak** in Hancock, the region's largest ski/snowboard resort (℘*413-738-5500; www.jiminypeak.com*). The wildest ride at Jiminy Peak is the mountain coaster, a self-controlled, twisting track sled ride that reaches speeds up to 25mph. Trek with a woolly companion on a **llama hike** in the October Mountain State Forest (*Berkshire Mountain Llama Hike, 322 Lander Rd., Lee, MA;* ℘*413-243-2224; www.hawkmeadowinlee.com*).

One-Day Itinerary – If you only have one day in the Berkshires, begin in **Stockbridge** and take US-7 North to Lenox. Continue north and visit **Hancock Shaker Village** outside Pittsfield, and the **Clark Art Institute** in Williamstown.

The map in this section covers only the southern part of the Berkshires. For attractions in the northern part of the region, see MOHAWK TRAIL and WILLIAMSTOWN.

Boston★★★

A bright, chaotic melding of old and new, modern Boston bears little resemblance to the spindly peninsula the Indians called Shawmut prior to the 17C. The city that was once the hotbed of American independence is today a renowned center of learning and culture, as well as being the administrative and financial nexus of New England. As "the hub" of the culturally diverse Greater Boston Metropolitan Area, Boston claims several universities— Harvard, Massachusetts Institute of Technology, University of Massachusetts and Boston University—along with a host of world-class museums.

Some 4.5 million people representing diverse ethnic backgrounds reside in the Boston metropolitan area; more than half a million of them live within the 46sq mi of the city proper. While offering all the advantages of a modern metropolis, Boston retains its history, which is preserved in the city's museums, villages, and architecturally significant neighborhoods such as Beacon Hill, the Back Bay and the North End.

A BIT OF HISTORY

European Settlement – In 1630 about 1,000 Puritans led by **John Winthrop** arrived on the coast of Massachusetts to establish a settlement for the Massachusetts Bay Company. Disenchanted with the living conditions in Salem and Charlestown, they set their sights on the peninsula the Indians named Shawmut, then inhabited by an eccentric Anglican clergyman, **Rev. William Blackstone**. The Englishman welcomed the Puritans, who proceeded to establish a permanent settlement on the small peninsula. When the Puritans tried to make Blackstone a member of their church, he sold them his remaining 50 acres and left for the more peaceful atmosphere of Rhode Island.

▶ **Population:** 625,087.
⌚ **Michelin Map:** 581 M 8.
ℹ **Info:** ☎617-536-4100; www.bostonusa.com.
▶ **Location:** Boston's financial district, unofficially "downtown," is framed by Chinatown, the Theater District, South Station to the south, Faneuil Hall to the north, the Boston Common and Tremont St. to the west, and the waterfront to the east.
👪 **Kids:** If you're visiting in summertime, treat the little ones to a ride on Boston's famous swan boats, plying the lagoon in the Public Garden. Anytime, the Children's Museum—one of the best in the US—is a wonderland of hands-on exhibits. The Museum of Science is always a huge hit with kids of any age.
🕐 **Timing:** This city is best explored by foot. Spend a day wandering through the Public Garden and Boston Common, and then stop at the State House. Resume your tour on the brick sidewalks of Beacon Hill to admire the stately brownstones. From there, jog across the Common to take in the sights along Freedom Trail (Faneuil Hall and Quincy Market are located along the way), or turn right to stroll Newbury Street, the city's most upscale shopping district.
🅿 **Parking:** For good rates and a handy location, try the Boston Common Garage (*enter on Charles St.*). Other big parking lots are located at Government Center/Quincy Market and Post Office Square.

The new colony, known as Trimountain because of its hilly topography, was soon renamed Boston after the town in Lincolnshire from which many of the Puritans hailed. Under the firm guidance of Governor Winthrop, the settlement developed as a theocratic society where church and state were one. A rigid moral code was enforced and a pillory was built on the common to punish offenders, among them the carpenter whose price for constructing the pillory was deemed too high. Because of its maritime commerce and shipbuilding, Boston rapidly became the largest town in the British colonies—a distinction it held until the mid-18C.

Cradle of Independence – In an attempt to replenish the Crown's coffers in the wake of the costly French and Indian War, the British parliament voted to enforce high taxes and harsh trade regulations against the American colonies. This policy enraged the colonists, who, as British citizens, claimed that their rights to representation were being denied. The **Stamp Act** (1765), a tax on publications and official documents in Massachusetts, caused public outrage that lead to violence. Mobs roamed the streets, the governor's mansion was burned and a boycott was organized. Although parliament repealed the Stamp Act the following year, renewed demonstrations erupted in 1767 with the passage of the

Statue of Paul Revere on the mall named after him

© Julia Freeman-Woolpert / iStockphoto.com

Townshend Acts, which regulated customs duties. England responded immediately by sending troops to enforce British law. The colonists, especially those who were forced to lodge and feed soldiers, grew increasingly hostile. Steadily mounting tensions eventually exploded into clashes between Bostonians and the British.

The **Boston Massacre** was the first of these clashes. On 5 March 1770, a group of Bostonians gathered at the State House to protest recent events. When a British officer answered the insults of a member of the crowd with the butt of his musket, the crowd became abusive and the guard was called out. Several Redcoats, provoked by the civilians, loaded their weapons and fired, killing five men. Political activist **Samuel Adams** seized on this incident to rally the citizens to his cause.

Three years later the **Boston Tea Party** further aggravated the situation. By 1773 parliament had repealed all the Townshend Acts except the tax on tea, which gave the East India Company a monopoly to sell tea in the colonies. This tax so angered colonists that in November 1773 Bostonians refused to allow the captains of three of the company's tea-laden ships to unload their cargo. At a well-attended meeting held on 16 December 1773, in the Old South Meeting House, an attempt was made to resolve the issue. When British compromise was not forthcoming, Samuel Adams concluded with his famed cue: "This meeting can do nothing more to save the country." Thereupon 90 Bostonians disguised as Indians fled the building with a war cry, trailed by a large crowd, and proceeded to board the ships and dump the tea into the harbor. In retaliation England closed the Port of Boston in 1774 and invoked punitive measures—known to colonists as the **Intolerable Acts**—that served only to further unite the colonists against the British.

Ride of Paul Revere – In April 1775 Gen. Thomas Gage dispatched 800 British soldiers to the outlying towns of Concord and Lexington to seize the colonists' stash of arms and arrest patriot leaders **John Hancock** and Samuel Adams. The patriots, forewarned by their network of spies, were prepared. According to a pre-arranged plan, on the night the British began to move toward Concord, the sexton of Old North Church hung two lanterns in the steeples to signal the Redcoats' departure by boat. In the meantime Paul Revere safely crossed the river to Charlestown and set out to Lexington on horseback to warn Hancock and Adams.

Land reclaimed from the sea since the early 19C

Thanks to the legendary ride by Revere, William Dawes and Dr. Samuel Prescott, the militia was ready when the British arrived at Lexington, and later at Concord.

Siege of Boston and the Battle of Bunker Hill – Following events at Lexington and Concord, the British retreated to Boston, where they were surrounded by rebel forces. While the British eyed the strategic heights around Boston, colonial leaders, informed of the British plan to fortify Bunker Hill in Charlestown, hastened to occupy nearby Breed's Hill before the arrival of the British. On 17 June 1775, when the British awoke and discovered an American redoubt had been built on Breed's Hill during the night, a force of 5,000 soldiers was sent out to capture the site. Although the colonists' position was defended by only 1,500 militiamen, the British failed in their first two attempts to secure the fort. They then set fire to Charlestown and launched the third and final attack against the rebels. Colonial leader William Prescott, aware that his men were low on ammunition, gave his famous order: "Don't fire until you see the whites of their eyes!"

The British succeeded in capturing the fort, but in doing so, they lost over 10 percent of all the British officers killed during the Revolution. Although it took place on Breed's Hill, this struggle is known by the misnomer the Battle of Bunker Hill.

British Evacuation – During the early months of 1776, the supplies captured by the colonists at Fort Ticonderoga were hauled across New England to Boston. American artillery began to bombard Boston on 2 March. By 5 March the colonists had fortified Dorchester Heights to the south with the cannons from the fort and the British were forced to accept a compromise. The colonial troops peacefully reclaimed Boston, and British General Howe and his men were permitted to evacuate the city unharmed. Soon after, General Washington made a triumphant entry into Boston, which saw little subsequent war activity as the theater of operations shifted to New York, Pennsylvania and the southern colonies.

"Cutting Down the Hills to Fill the Bays" – Modern Boston is the product of transformations wrought by two centuries of prodigious landfill projects. Familiar place names such as Back Bay, the South End and Dock Square recall features of the area's original 783-acre landmass, which has increased almost fourfold through landfill alone since the early 19C.

The Puritans who settled Shawmut found an irregularly shaped peninsula

Sailboats in Charles River Basin

© Greater Boston Convention & Visitors Bureau

joined to the mainland by a natural causeway (the "neck") stretching along a section of present-day Washington Street. On the western side rose a three-peaked ridge (Trimountain) dominated by Beacon Hill. Extending south of Beacon Hill, the tract purchased from Reverend Blackstone was set aside as "Common Field," and remains parkland to this day as the Boston Common. The eastern shore facing the harbor was indented by Town or East Cove, which divided the residential North End from commercial and public sectors that burgeoned in the vicinity of the harbor, the original South End.

Over the course of the 19C, Boston's population increased dramatically, rising from 18,000 in 1790 to 54,000 in 1825. By the turn of the century, it totaled over half a million. The pressing need for more living space prompted a flurry of landfill projects that forever transformed the city's topography. These ambitious programs, characterized by historian Walter Muir Whitehill as "cutting down the hills to fill the bays," involved hauling colossal quantities of earth into the waters around the city, thus transforming the spindly peninsula into an extension of the mainland. The filling in of the waters on either side of the narrow neck was crucial to the city's growth, for it enabled a network of railroad lines to penetrate the downtown area. Boston's great 19C transformation began with the development of the Beacon Hill district in the early 19C. In

the following decades the areas on the peninsula's east and south sides were filled in, leading to the expansion of the waterfront area and the creation of the residential district now called the South End.

The century's most spectacular landfill project took place in the Back Bay on the neck's north side. This 40-year project increased the city's area by 450 acres and resulted in one of the nation's finest planned residential districts. After the Great Fire of 1872 leveled 776 buildings downtown, many residents and churches resettled in the fashionable Back Bay, precipitating the development of the downtown as a commercial district. Landfill projects continued to increase the city's area throughout the 19C and into the present century, particularly around Charlestown and East Boston, site of Logan International Airport.

The city's system of public parks, parkways and tree-shaded malls, designed in the 19C by the nation's premier landscape architect, **Frederick Law Olmsted**, encircles the city with a nearly continuous swath of greenery.

The so-called **Emerald Necklace** begins at Boston Common and stretches southwest along the Public Garden, Commonwealth Avenue, the Fenway, Jamaica Park, the Arborway, Arnold Arboretum, and Franklin Park.

The New Boston – By the mid-20C Boston was deteriorating. Rising property taxes, the exodus of businesses to the suburbs or out of state and the general population decline had taken their toll. Faced with problems associated with urban blight, the city reacted by establishing the **Boston Redevelopment Authority (BRA)** in 1957.

Under the leadership of **Edward Logue**, BRA inaugurated a program aimed at "revitalizing" one-fourth of the city. The plan generated much controversy since it mandated the bulldozing of entire neighborhoods, including Scollay Square and the adjacent Jewish and Italian enclave known as the West End. Architect **I.M. Pei**, who had trained at the Massachusetts Institute of Technology, was among the experts called upon in the 1960s to draw up designs for the new **Government Center** on the site of Scollay Square, Boston's bawdy entertainment district.

This $260 million project called for an enormous brick-paved expanse showcasing the award-winning City Hall building alongside several contemporary structures of varying architectural merit and a 19C commercial building.

In the following decades Pei contributed to reshaping Boston's built environment by executing such important commissions as the John Hancock Tower, the Kennedy Library, and the West Wing of the Museum of Fine Arts.

A major renewal project of the 1960s, the mixed-use Prudential Center created controversy, largely because it failed to create a human scale compatible with surrounding Back Bay neighborhoods. More successful was the 1970s renovation of the Faneuil Hall Marketplace, which dramatically revived the ambience of downtown Boston by injecting new vitality into the city's historic heart. In the 1980s the **Financial District**, long established in the vicinity of Federal and Congress Streets, began expanding in the direction of the rejuvenated harbor district. The waterfront's redevelopment, which was boosted by the rehabilitation of the adjacent Faneuil Hall area, has re-established Boston's historic link to the sea. This area is being further enhanced with the dismantling of the unsightly, traffic-clogged Central Artery that has long severed the waterfront and the North End from the downtown proper. Begun in the early 1990s, the **Central Artery/Tunnel Project**, aka. the Big Dig, created a multilane underground expressway beneath the site of the former Central Artery. The goal of this ambitious, multi-billion-dollar

Unique Museums

Looking for something different? Massachusetts is home to a medley of intriguing museums. The **Fuller Craft Museum** (*450 Oak St., Brockton; ℰ508-588-6000; www.fullercraft.org*) is New England's home for collecting, exhibiting, and experiencing contemporary craft. Forget the macramé plant holders and potholders; items shown here are often avant-garde, eye-popping creations like baskets made of measuring tapes, pine needles or pencil stubs. This one is definitely worth a stop, especially if you're a crafter looking for inspiration. If you have children, you've probably read *The Very Hungry Caterpillar* (1969) by Eric Carle, with its bold, colorful illustrations. Carle, a resident of Northampton, MA, is part founder of the **Eric Carle Museum of Picture Book Art** (*124 West Bay Rd., Amherst; ℰ413-658-11100; www.carlemuseum.org*). This engaging museum showcases the work of Carle (author and illustrator of more than 70 children's books) and other illustrators. Part of the fun is seeing the artist's sketches, and watching how they evolved into the finished product. In the town of Harvard, **Fruitlands** (*102 Prospect Hill Rd.; ℰ978-456-3924; www.fruitlands.org*) is a 218-acre farm that hosted one of America's first Utopian communities, founded by Bronson Alcott in 1843. The community's goal was to "live off the fruit of the land." Most members had little experience in farming, and the venture lasted only seven months. The farmhouse is now a museum of transcendentalism.

public-works program was to alleviate Boston's infamous traffic snarls and create over 150 acres of new parkland.

Since the Big Dig relocated some previously elevated roadways underground, the city reclaimed 15 acres of prime urban land and converted it into landscaped green space that connects several Boston neighborhoods. This mile-long ribbon of land, called the Rose Kennedy Greenway, is now a public park.

BOSTON TODAY

Bostonians – Today the city is a product of the twin poles of the Boston psyche: Puritan preservationism and Patriot progressivism. The "proper Bostonian," or **Brahmin**, descends from New England's early Puritan settlers who shared a common language and culture, and whose close-knit society set Boston apart by the 19C as the city where "the Lowells talk only to the Cabots, and the Cabots talk only to God." Stereotyped as refined, conservative and Harvard-educated, the proper Bostonian today represents an ever-decreasing percentage of the city's population.

Boston's large **Irish** population began arriving by the thousands in the wake of the 1840s potato famine. Penniless yet hardworking, the Irish integrated into mainstream American life, and many succeeded in rising to positions in local and federal government. One of Boston's most famous Irish Americans was former US president John Fitzgerald Kennedy.

Toward the end of the century, many **Italian** immigrants, particularly from southern Italy, settled in Boston. The Italians eventually replaced the Irish and Jewish populations in the North End and the now-destroyed West End.

The **African-American** community, once concentrated on Beacon Hill, represents a large presence in Roxbury and the adjacent neighborhoods of Dorchester and Mattapan. Boston is home to one of the oldest black communities in the US. The first blacks were brought to colonial Boston as slaves from the West Indies in 1638, just eight years after the colony's establishment. A growing number of freed blacks settled in the North End. Many of them worked as barbers, sailors, laborers and coachmen and many—including **Crispus Attucks**, an assassinated hero of the Boston Massacre—served in the Revolution. In the 1780s the slave trade was legally abolished in Massachusetts—a reflection of the state's staunch abolitionist position. In the 19C, with the dedication of the African Meeting House on Beacon Hill, the black community moved to the north slope of the Hill in search of improved living conditions. Better housing, job opportunities and schools led blacks to move gradually out to Cambridge, the Back Bay, and the South End. Boston's rapidly growing **Hispanic** population has settled in pockets such as the South End, Jamaica Plain and East Boston. It is estimated that these and other minority groups, such as Asians, now make up about one-third of the city's population. In the 1970s and 80s, Boston became a national testing ground for controversial busing policies. In an attempt to provide quality education for students of all socioeconomic classes (and particularly blacks), the federal government attempted with limited success to integrate the city's public schools. Each year the area's colleges and universities draw a new influx of students and professors from across the country and abroad. The large **student population**, estimated in recent years at over 200,000, lends great diversity to the area's social and cultural fabric. Students reside on and around the numerous urban and suburban campuses scattered throughout the area, and they constitute a strong presence in large sections of Cambridge, Brookline and Allston-Brighton.

Economy – Since the days of the Bay Colony, shipping and trade have been the mainstays of Boston's economy. Following a period of decline in the early 20C, modernization of the port's services and the 25mi of docking space in the 1950s and 60s increased the amount of cargo the port could handle. Today, however, Boston is not among the 20 top-ranking ports in the country.

A similar surge of growth was experienced in the business sector, particularly in the insurance industry. Insurance giants Prudential and John Hancock have established a towering presence in the Back Bay through the construction of the area's two tallest skyscrapers. Boston financiers, guardians of the Yankee fortunes made in shipping and industry, continue to generate a large share of New England's economic activity from their offices in the Financial District.

Industrially, a new era was born in the 1950s with the construction of Rte. 128, a circumferential highway outside the downtown area, and the emergence along this highway of about 700 research and development firms. Boston is a recognized world leader in this field; its universities are training grounds for scientists and research specialists, especially in electronics and computer technology. Boston is also a world leader in health care; the city's medical facilities, notably **Massachusetts General Hospital**, are internationally recognized centers of research and treatment. The nationwide recession of the 1980s dealt a serious blow to Boston's economy as evidenced by skyrocketing unemployment and a sagging real-estate market. Signs of recovery were apparent in the 1990s however, and by the end of the decade Boston's financial and high-tech industries were booming.

The city positioned itself to take on major convention business with the opening of a 1,700,000sq ft convention center in 2004. The **Boston Convention and Exhibition Center** (BCEC) is located in the Seaport District, near the South Boston waterfront and Boston's World Trade Center. The city recently experienced a hotel boom. The Westin Waterfront Hotel opened in mid-2006, followed by the InterContinental Boston Hotel in the Financial District, and the Liberty Hotel, located at the former site of the Charles Street Jail. Other new properties followed, including the Mandarin Oriental, the Ames Hotel, the Fairmont Battery Wharf and the W Hotel Boston. Demand for hotel rooms softened during the recession of 2008 through 2012, but the city rebounded, and new projects were launched, including the development of the old Filene's site in Downtown Crossing.

A Cultural Hub – 🕭 *For the locations of theaters and concert halls, see the main Boston map.*

By the 19C Boston had become a gathering place for intellectuals and writers, earning the sobriquet "the Athens of America." Well-heeled and cultivated Bostonians traveled extensively, returning home with treasures that initiated the collections of the Museum of Fine Arts, the Isabella Stewart Gardner Museum and the museums of Harvard University. In 1881 philanthropist Henry Lee Higginson founded the **Boston Symphony Orchestra** (BSO). Today the BSO and the **Boston Pops**, with its repertoire of lighter music, perform seasonally at the Symphony Hall. In the summer the Pops presents free concerts on the Charles River Esplanade. The heart of the **Theater District** lies in the area near Tremont and Stuart Streets. Boston is a testing ground for Broadway productions. The Citi Emerson Colonial Theater, the Citi Performing Arts Center and the Wilbur Theatre present musicals and comedies. Dramas are staged at the Charles Playhouse and at numerous university theaters, such as Boston University's Huntington Theater and the American Repertory Theater in Harvard Square. Performances by the **Boston Ballet Company** occur seasonally at the Boston Opera House.

Education – A principal concern of the Puritans was the establishment of a sound educational system. Ever since the founding of Boston Public Latin School (c.1630), the first public school in America, and Harvard College (1636), the first college in the colonies, Boston has remained a leader in the field of education. The metropolitan area's roster of some 68 colleges and universities includes Harvard, Massachusetts Institute of Technology, Boston University, New England Conservatory of Music, Boston College, Brandeis University, Tufts University and Wellesley College.

See also the detailed maps of Beacon Hill, Back Bay, Freedom Trail, and Waterfront for hotels and restaurants in these neighborhoods.

WHERE TO STAY	
Eliot Hotel	③
Gryphon House	⑦
Hotel Commonwealth	⑪

WHERE TO EAT	
Myers + Chang	③
O Ya	⑤
Radius	⑨

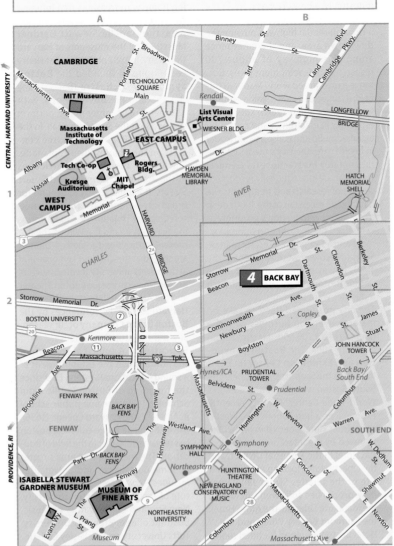

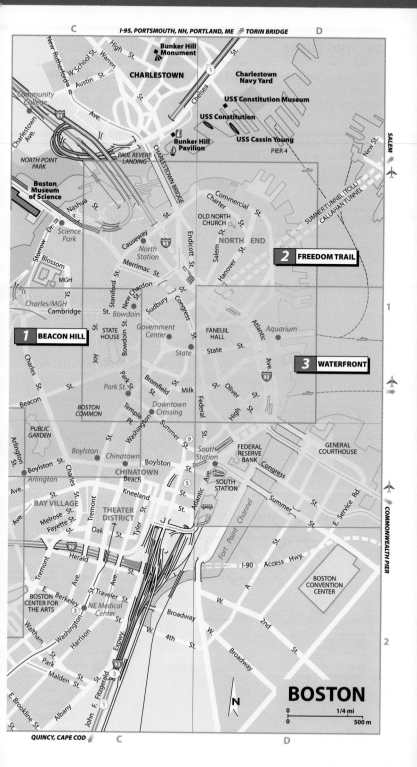

I-95, PORTSMOUTH, NH, PORTLAND, ME   TORIN BRIDGE

C   D

Bunker Hill Monument

CHARLESTOWN

New Rutherford
W. School St.   Warren
Austin   St.   High   St.   Chelsea   St.

Community
College

Charlestown Ave.

Charlestown Navy Yard

Charlestown Navy Yard

USS Constitution Museum

USS Constitution

SALEM

PAUL REVERE LANDING

Bunker Hill Pavilion

USS Cassin Young

PIER 4

NORTH POINT PARK

Boston Museum of Science

Nashua   St.

Storrow   Dr.   *Science Park*

Blossom

MGH

Commercial   St.

OLD NORTH CHURCH   Charter   St.

NORTH END

SUMNER TUNNEL (TOLL)
CALLAHAN TUNNEL

New St.

Charles/MGH
Cambridge

Causeway   St.   North Station

Merrimac St.

Endicott   St.

Salem   St.

Hanover

2 FREEDOM TRAIL

Charles   St.

1 BEACON HILL

Stanford   New Chardon   St.

Sudbury   St.

Congress   St.

Bowdoin
Bowdoin

STATE HOUSE

Government Center

FANEUIL HALL

Atlantic   *Aquarium*

1

Joy   St.

State

State   St.

St.

Oliver   St.

Ave.

3 WATERFRONT

Beacon

Park   St.   Park St.

Bromfield   St.

Milk   St.

Federal   St.

High   St.

Temple   Pl.

BOSTON COMMON

Downtown Crossing

Washington   St.

Summer   St.

PUBLIC GARDEN

Arlington   St.

Boylston

Chinatown

St.

9

FEDERAL RESERVE BANK

Congress   St.

GENERAL COURTHOUSE

Arlington

Boylston   St.   Charles   St.

Boylston

CHINATOWN

Beach   St.

South Station

SOUTH STATION

Summer   St.

E. Service Rd.

COMMONWEALTH PIER

Ave.

St.

Kneeland   St.

5

Atlantic   Ave.

BAY VILLAGE

Melrose   St.   Tremont   St.

Fayette   St.

Oak   St.

THEATER DISTRICT

Tyler   St.

Fort Point Channel

A   St.

Herald   St.

90

I-90   Access Hwy.

BOSTON CONVENTION CENTER

Tremont   Ave.

E. Berkeley   St.   Traveler   St.

BOSTON CENTER FOR THE ARTS

NE Medical Center

St.

Broadway

W.   2nd   St.

2

Waltham

3

Washington   Harrison   St.

W.   4th   St.

W.   Broadway

Park   St.

Malden   St.

John   F.   Fitzgerald   Expwy.

3

Albany

E. Brookline St.

1

N

BOSTON

0   1/4 mi
0   500 m

GETTING THERE

BY AIR – International and domestic flights service **Logan International Airport (BOS)** (*2mi northeast of downtown;* ☏*617-561-1800 or 800-235-6426; www.massport.com*). From the airport, you can get downtown via taxi. The **Massachusetts Bay Transportation Authority (MBTA)** subway's Blue Line services Logan Airport. The MBTA's Silver Line, a rapid-transit bus, runs from downtown to Logan Airport. Free shuttle buses run between the terminal and the airport station. The **Rowes Wharf Water Taxi** (*Mon–Sat 7am–10pm, Sun 7am–8pm, rest of year, Mon–Fri, 7am–7pm; $10 one-way;* ☏*617-406-8584; www.rowes wharfwatertaxitransport.com*) makes the short trip between Logan dock and Rowes Wharf (*Atlantic Ave., downtown*). Service operates on an on-call basis; look for call boxes on the dock at Rowe's Wharf and at Logan Airport or call ☏617-406-8584. Boats travel from Logan Airport to the South Shore and downtown (*year-round daily; $16 one-way to airport; for schedules contact* **MBTA**, ☏*617-722-3200; www.mbta.com*). The **Salem Ferry** (☏*617-227-4321; www.bostonharborcruises.com*) connects the city of Salem to downtown Boston (New England Aquarium dock). The high-speed catamaran operates from late May through Oct; the trip takes 45min (*$15 one way*). Major rental-car agencies are located in the baggage-claim area at all terminals.

BY BUS AND TRAIN – Amtrak **trains** leave from South Station (*Atlantic Ave. & Summer St.;* ☏*800-872-7245; www.amtrak.com*). Suburban MBTA trains depart from North Station (*150 Causeway St.*) and South Station (*for schedules and fares, call* ☏*617-222-3200; www.mbta.com.*) **Bus** service is provided by Greyhound from South Station (☏*800-231-2222; www.greyhound.com*) and Peter Pan Bus Line (*700 Atlantic Ave.;* ☏*800-343-9999; www.peterpanbus.com*).

GETTING AROUND

BY PUBLIC TRANSPORTATION - Commuter **ferry** service is available between Long Wharf and Charlestown Navy Yard (*year-round daily, except major holidays; Mon–Fri 6.30am–8pm, weekends 10am–6pm; $3 one-way; for schedules contact Boston Harbor Cruises: ☎617-227-4321; www.bostonharborcruises.com*).

Subway and Buses – The MBTA operates underground and surface transportation in greater Boston. The Red, Blue, Orange and Green subway lines radiate out from the four central downtown stations: Downtown Crossing, Park Street, State, and Government Center. Subway stations are indicated by the Ⓣ symbol at street level. Most MBTA lines operate Mon–Sat 5am–12.45am, Sun 6am–12.45am. Timetables are posted at the Park Street Station. In-city **subway** fare is $2.50; local **bus** fare is $2. Fares are discounted if you purchase a plastic, re-loadable CharlieCard, available for $5 and up. MBTA Day/Week Link Passes are good for one (*$11*) or seven (*$18*) consecutive days of unlimited travel on all MBTA subway and local bus lines, the inner-harbor ferry and commuter rail zone 1-A. Purchase passes online at www.mbta.com, at subway stations, at Logan Airport, and the information kiosks at Boston Common and Quincy Market. Free MBTA public-transport maps are available at North and South stations, at area hotels and at the MBTA's Park Street Station information stand. *For MBTA route, schedule and fare information, call ☎617-722-3200; www.mbta.com.*

BY CAR – Use of public transportation or walking is strongly encouraged within the city as roads are often congested and street parking may be difficult. Parking garages range from $6-$10/hr–$42/day. Garages at Boston Common and Prudential Center are open 24hrs daily.

BY TAXI – Boston Cab Association ☎617-536-3200; **Independent Taxi Operators Association**, ☎617-825-4000; **City Cab**, ☎617-536-5100; **Top Cab** ☎617-266-4800.

VISITOR INFORMATION

Greater Boston Convention and Visitors Bureau, Inc. offers maps and the *Boston Travel Planner* (*free*), with information regarding area attractions, accommodations, dining, festivals, and recreation (*2 Copley Pl., Suite 105, Boston, MA 02116; ☎617-536-4100 or 888-SEE BOSTON; www.boston usa.com*). Several additional visitor centers are located throughout the city: **Boston Common Visitor Information Center** (*open Mon–Sat 8.30am–5pm, Sun 9am–5pm*); **Prudential Center Visitor Information Center** (*800 Boylston St.; open Mon–Sat 8.30am–5pm, Sun 10am–6pm*); and the **National Park Service Visitor Center** (*15 State St.; open year-round daily 9am–5pm; closed 1 Jan, Thanksgiving Day & 25 Dec; ☎617-242-5642; www.nps.gov/bost*).

LOCAL PRESS

Daily news: *Boston Globe* (morning). Thursday entertainment section: *Boston Herald* (morning). Weekly entertainment: *Boston Phoenix*.

FOREIGN EXCHANGE OFFICES

Travelex World Wide Money (*☎617-567-2153*) operates currency-exchange offices in Logan International Airport: Terminal B (*open daily 6.30am–9pm*), Terminal C (*open daily 6am–8pm*) and Terminal E (*open daily 7am–10.30pm*). **American Express Travel Services** (*☎800-297-3429*) has exchange offices downtown (*432 Stuart St.; open Mon–Fri 8.30am–5.30pm; ☎617-236-1331*).

USEFUL NUMBERS

Police/Ambulance/Fire ☎911. **Police** (non-emergency) ☎617-343-4240. **Dental Emergency** (*24hrs*) ☎800-917-6453.

Medical Emergency Inn-House Doctor (*24hrs*) ℘617-859-1776
Massachusetts General Hospital ℘617-726-2000
CVS Pharmacy ℘617-437-8414 (*587 Boylston St.; open 24hrs*)
Weather ℘617-936-1234

SIGHTSEEING

CityPassBoston (*valid for 1 year; $46*) available at visitor information centers, participating attractions and major hotels, covers reduced admission to five attractions. **Old Towne Trolley Tours** offers 1hr 30min narrated tours of the city (*daily year-round; starting at 9am; $39*; ℘617-269-7150; *www. historictours.com*); visitors can board at major attractions along the route. Boston Harbor Cruises runs inner harbor sightseeing **cruises** departing from Long Wharf (*daily; $23*) and **high-speed ferry service** to Provincetown, Cape Cod (*daily May–Oct; 90min one-way; $83 round-trip; for schedules contact Boston Harbor Cruises:* ℘617-227-4321; *www.bostonharborcruises. com*). **Whale-watching cruises** – ℘*see PLANNING YOUR TRIP.*

ENTERTAINMENT

Consult the arts and entertainment sections of local newspapers for schedules of cultural events and addresses of principal theaters.
BosTix Ticket Booths (*locations at Faneuil Hall Marketplace and Copley Square*) offer half-price tickets for selected local events on the day of the performance, as well as full-price advance tickets (*open Mon–Sat 10am–6pm, Sun 11am–4pm; purchases must be made in person;* ℘617-462-8632; *www.bostix.org*).
MUSIC, DANCE AND THEATER
Boston Center for the Arts (BCA) – 539 Tremont St., ℘617-426-5000, www.bcaonline.org.
Boston Ballet – 539 Washington St., ℘617-695-6955, www.bostonballet.org.
Boston Lyric Opera – 265 Tremont St., ℘617-542-6772, www.blo.org.

Charles Playhouse, Blue Man Group Boston – 74 Warrenton St., ℘617-426-6912, www.blueman.com or www.Broadwayinboston.com.
Citi Emerson Colonial Theater – 106 Boylston St., ℘617-482-9393, www.Broadwayacrossamerica.com.
Cutler Majestic Theater – 219 Tremont St., ℘617-824-8000, www.aestages.org.
Hatch Memorial Shell – Charles River Esplanade, ℘617-626-4970.
Huntington Theater – 264 Huntington Ave., ℘617-266-0800, www.huntingtontheatre.org.
New England Conservatory of Music – Jordan Hall, 290 Huntington Ave., ℘617-585-1100 www.necmusic.edu.
Citi Performing Arts Center – 270 Tremont St., ℘617-482-9393, www.citicenter.org.
Symphony Hall – 301 Massachusetts Ave., ℘617-266-1492, www.bso.org.
Wilbur Theatre – 246 Tremont St., ℘617-248-9700, www.thewilbur theatrecom.

SPORTS

Tickets for major sporting events can be purchased at the venue, or online. The 26mi **Boston Marathon**, run every year from Hopkinton to the Back Bay, takes place on Patriots' Day (*3rd Mon in Apr*).
⊕ **Major League Baseball**.
Team: Red Sox (AL), ℘877-REDSOX-9, *www.redsox.com,* Season: Apr–Oct, Venue: Fenway Park
⬤ **Professional Football**.
Team: New England Patriots (NFL), ℘508-543-8200; www.patriots.com, Season: Sept–Dec, Venue: Gillette Stadium
⬤ **Professional Basketball**.
Team: Celtics (NBA), ℘866-4-CELTIX, www.celtics.com. Season: Oct–Apr, Venue: TD Garden
⬤ **Professional Hockey**.
Team: Bruins (NHA), ℘617-624-2327, www.bostonbruins.com, Season: Sept–Apr, Venue: TD Garden

WALKING TOURS

Ⓣ *Park St.*

Exercise caution in inclement weather as brick sidewalks can be slippery when wet.

1 BEACON HILL★★

See Beacon Hill map p192

Historically the home of Boston Brahmins and the city's early black community, the "Hill" preserves an Old World ambience undisturbed by the bustle of the surrounding metropolis.

A Remarkable Transformation

Today's Beacon Hill is the only remnant of the three peaks comprising the Trimountain ridge. Its name derives from the primitive beacon that the Puritans raised on its summit in 1634 to warn of invasion. From 1795 to 1798 preeminent architect Charles Bulfinch oversaw the erection of his golden-domed State House on the Hill's southern slope. Construction of this grand building spurred Bulfinch, Harrison Gray Otis and their business associates to create an elegant residential district on a nearby tract purchased from painter **John Singleton Copley**. From 1799 until the mid-19C, these developers transformed the entire face of the Trimountain area: Beacon Hill's summit was lowered 60ft and the two neighboring peaks were leveled, creating abundant landfill for the surrounding marshlands; the present street system was laid out; and the charming enclave of English-style brick residences that we know as Beacon Hill came into being.

The sunny south slope, between Pinckney Street and the Common, became the bastion of Boston's affluent society and the center of its respected intellectual and artistic community, whose members included Daniel Webster, Julia Ward Howe and the Alcotts. The more modest north slope, spilling into Cambridge Street, became the center of Boston's black community in the 19C, many of whose members worked for the well-to-do on the Hill.

Today Beacon Hill reigns as one of Boston's most desirable addresses. A stroll along its serene streets lined with gas lamps and brick facades transports the visitor to a bygone era.

An Architectural Showcase

Created almost entirely in the first half of the 19C, Beacon Hill constitutes a living museum of the period's architectural heritage, showcasing the works of the city's leading 19C architects. The work of Charles Bulfinch is well represented by the State House and some 15 Federal-style town houses found primarily on the fashionable south slope.

The Hill's streetscape is noteworthy for its extraordinary visual unity, resulting from the predominant use of brick, a uniform three- to four-story building height, and harmonious blending of flat and bowed facades. Quaint service lanes are lined with former stables and servants' quarters, while intimate culs-de-sac evoke a sense of mystery. The Hill's designation as a historic district in 1955 and the determination of residents to safeguard its precious architectural heritage have been instrumental in the preservation of this urban jewel.

Beacon Hill's private gardens are revealed to the public in May by special tour. 🗓 *For information, call the Beacon Hill Garden Club:* ✆*617-227-4392.*

▶ Begin at the corner of Park and Tremont Sts. and walk up the hill on Park St.

Gently sloping Park Street provides a pleasant approach to the gold-domed State House crowning **Beacon Street★**. Writer Oliver Wendell Holmes dubbed Beacon "the sunny street that holds the sifted few." The Hill's southern facade offers coveted views of Boston Common. Beyond the Common, this fashionable thoroughfare stretches west into the Back Bay and points beyond.

▶ Turn right on Beacon St.

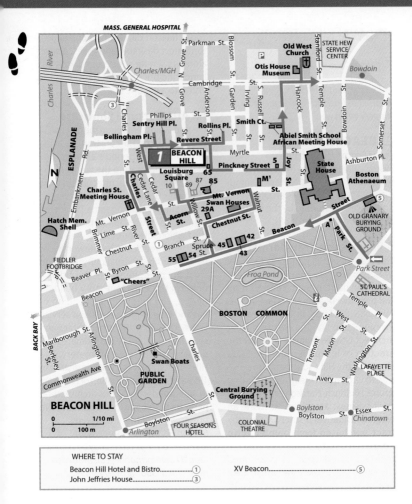

WHERE TO STAY

Beacon Hill Hotel and Bistro...................① 　　　XV Beacon...⑤
John Jeffries House......................................③

Boston Athenaeum★

10 1/2 Beacon St. &. Open year-round Mon–Wed 9am–8pm, Thu–Fri 9am-5.30pm, Sat 9am–4pm. ☎617-227-0270. www.bostonathenaeum.org.

This venerable Boston institution was established in 1807 as one of the nation's first private lending libraries. Later in the century numerous important works from the Athenaeum's art trove formed the core of the Museum of Fine Arts' world-class collection.

The library's present home on Beacon Hill was built in the 1840s to accommodate its growing holdings, which today total some 600,000 volumes and works of art. Walking through the hallowed

reading rooms packed with leather-bound volumes and fine sculptures, paintings and prints, visitors are ushered into a rarefied atmosphere. Works by Gilbert Stuart, Thomas Sully and Jean-Antoine Houdon highlight the collection. The art gallery (*1st floor*) features changing exhibits from the collection. Several rooms and terraces provide lovely **views** of the Old Granary Burying Ground.

State House★★

24 Beacon St. at the corner of Park St. ✕&. Open year-round Mon–Fri 10am–4pm. Closed 1 Jan, Thanksgiving Day & 25 Dec. ☎617-727-3676. www.cityofboston.gov.

The golden dome of Massachusetts' capitol building dominates Beacon Hill, enduring as a cherished Boston landmark for more than two centuries. Completed in 1798 by Charles Bulfinch, the original brick building, fronted by a projecting portico, was extended in 1895 and 1916 by large additions to its sides and rear. Statues on the front lawn depict Anne Hutchinson, banished from the 17C colony for her theological views; Mary Dyer, hanged for her Quaker beliefs; orator Daniel Webster; and Horace Mann, a pioneer in American education.

The main entrance of the State House leads into **Doric Hall**, named for its rows of Doric columns. The 19C addition **Nurses Hall**, with its marble walls and floors, displays paintings immortalizing Paul Revere's ride, James Otis' oratory against the Writs of Assistance, and the Boston Tea Party. Paintings in the **Hall of Flags**, which was built to house a collection of Civil War battle flags, portray the Pilgrims on the *Mayflower*, John Eliot preaching to the Indians, and the scene at Concord Bridge on 19 April 1775.

The main staircase leads to the **Third Floor Hall**, dominated by Daniel Chester French's statue of Roger Wolcott, governor of Massachusetts during the Spanish-American War. The Senate Chamber, Senate Reception Room, Governor's Office and House Chamber occupy this floor. Before leaving the domed House Chamber, note the **Sacred Cod**, a gilded, carved-wood symbol of the fish that supported Massachusetts' early fishing industry.

Upon exiting the State House, cross Beacon Street to admire the **Shaw Civil War Monument★ (A)**, a bronze relief by Augustus Saint-Gaudens that honors Col. Robert Gould Shaw and the 54th Massachusetts Colored Infantry, the Union's first regiment of free black volunteers. Shaw was killed in 1863 during the Union assault on Fort Wagner in South Carolina.

▷ Continue walking down Beacon St.

Black Heritage Trail

The Black Heritage Trail is a 1.6mi walking tour that identifies 14 significant African-American historic sites. Highlights include the African Meeting House, the oldest standing African-American church in the US. Several sites along the trail are included in the walking tour here; for more details, contact the Boston African-American National Historic Site *(14 Beacon St., Suite 401; ☎617-742-5415; www. nps.gov/boaf)*. The National Park Service conducts free tours of the Black Heritage Trail *(Memorial Day–Labor Day daily)*.

Among the street's noteworthy buildings are the exclusive Somerset Club at **nos. 42–43**, a double-bowed granite structure whose right half is attributed to Alexander Parris (1819); and **no. 45** (1808), the last of three houses that Bulfinch designed and built for Harrison Gray Otis on Beacon Hill.

▷ Cross Spruce St.

The handsome pair of bowfront Greek Revival houses at **nos. 54–55** are attributed to Asher Benjamin, architect of the Charles Street Meeting House and the Old West Church (*both described later on the tour*). The state chapter of the National Society of Colonial Dames occupies no. 55.

▷ Return to the corner of Beacon and Spruce Sts., turn up Spruce St. and take a right on Chestnut St.

As you pass narrow Branch Street on the left, note the modest buildings that once housed servants.

Chestnut Street★

This picturesque street presents a fine assortment of houses reflecting architectural styles dating from 1800 to 1830. At **no. 29A** (1800, Charles Bulfinch), note the distinctive purple glass in the

Acorn Street, Beacon Hill

© Liz Leyden / iStockphoto

house's bowfront. Other examples of the Hill's famed 18C purple window panes—resulting from the glass' manganese dioxide content—may still be seen in a few other dwellings on the Hill (including 63–64 Beacon St.). The graceful trio at nos. 13–17, known as the **Swan Houses** (c.1805), further illustrates Bulfinch's preference for a restrained Federal style.

▶ Continue one block up Chestnut St., turn left on Walnut St. and continue one block to Mount Vernon St.

Mount Vernon Street★★

Qualified by writer Henry James as "the only respectable street in America," this gracious thoroughfare boasts some of the Hill's finest residences. At no. 55 stands the **Nichols House Museum★ (M1)**, the Hill's only residence open to the public (↳visit by 30min guided tour only; ⏱open Apr–Oct Tue–Sat 11am–4pm; rest of the year Thu–Sat 11am–4pm; ⏱closed major holidays; $8; ☎617-227-6993; www.nicholshousemuseum.org). Designed by Bulfinch in 1804, the house preserves the possessions and spirit of a colorful Beacon Hill lady, Miss Rose Standish Nichols. The spacious interior contains late-19C and early-20C furniture carved by Nichols herself, as well as Flemish tap-

estries, needlepoint, ancestral paintings and sculptures she collected on trips abroad.

On your way down the hill, pause to admire the freestanding building at **no. 85** (1802) set back some 30ft from the street line. Faced with slender pilasters and topped by a wooden balustrade and an octagonal tower, this handsome residence was the second of three mansions Bulfinch designed for businessman, lawyer and politician Harrison Gray Otis. Bulfinch also conceived the neighboring mansions at nos. 87 and 89.

Louisburg Square★★

On Mount Vernon St. at Willow St.
Named in honor of the victorious siege of the French fortress at Louisbourg (Nova Scotia, Canada) led by the Massachusetts militia in 1745, this enclave epitomizes Beacon Hill's refined lifestyle. The appearance of the elegant Greek Revival bowfront row houses and the small private park have changed little since their creation in the 1830s and 40s. Writer Louisa May Alcott lived in no. 10 from 1880 until her death eight years later. Christmas Eve caroling on the square is a cherished Bostonian tradition.

▶ Leave the square via Willow St. and turn right onto Acorn St.

Acorn Street★

This romantic cobblestone passage is the most photographed street on the Hill.

▶ At the end of Acorn St., turn right on West Cedar St., then left on Mount Vernon St. to Charles St.

Charles Street★

Antique shops, art galleries and coffee shops line the Hill's bustling commercial thoroughfare. At the corner of Mount Vernon Street stands the **Charles Street Meeting House** (c.1807). This popular forum for 19C abolitionists William Lloyd Garrison, Frederick Douglass, and Sojourner Truth was converted into offices in the 1980s.

▶ Continue one block on Charles St. and turn right on Pinckney St.

Pinckney Street

This lovely, sloping street was the dividing line between the affluent neighborhood on the sunny south slope and the more modest community to the north.

▶ Turn left on West Cedar St. After one block, go right on Revere St.

Revere Street

The street's left side is interrupted by a series of intimate private courts: **Bellingham Place**, **Sentry Hill Place** and **Rollins Place**. At Rollins Place the white "house" at the end of the court is not a house at all, but rather a decorative wall at the head of a drop.

▶ Walk back to Anderson St. and turn left.

The imposing brick building (1824) crowning the corner of Pinckney and Anderson Streets **(no. 65)** formerly housed the Phillips Grammar School (1844–61), the city's first racially mixed school.

▶ Continue uphill on Pinckney St.

The small clapboard house at **no. 5**, built for two black men in the 1790s, is one of the Hill's oldest surviving structures.

▶ Turn left onto Joy St.

Joy Street

This long street descends the north slope of the Hill, the center of Boston's historic black community from the late 18C to the 19C.

Smith Court

About halfway down Joy St. past Myrtle St.

This small cul-de-sac was the heart of the black community following the Revolution. Many of its residents worked for wealthy families who lived on the elite south slope. At no. 46 Joy Street stands the 1834 **Abiel Smith School★** (&

open Mon–Sat 10am–4pm; closed 1 Jan, Thanksgiving Day & 25 Dec; ℰ617-742-5415; www.nps.gov/boaf), an elegant pedimented structure that housed the city's first black school, the first publicly funded school for black children in the country. The building today contains a restored schoolroom and exhibits on African-American history.

Behind the school stands the nation's oldest remaining black church, the **African Meeting House★** (8 Smith Ct.; same hours as Abiel Smith School; $5. ℰ617-725-0022.) Built in 1806 by black Baptists disenchanted with the discrimination encountered in the white churches, this handsome brick building provided a forum for supporters of the anti-slavery movement.

For most of the 20C, the meetinghouse served as a synagogue. Today it is preserved as a privately owned historic site managed by the National Park Service. The lower floor houses the **Museum of Afro-American History**, a showplace for exhibits on themes relating to New England's black community. The meetinghouse proper occupies the upper floor.

▶ At the foot of Joy St., cross busy Cambridge St.

Otis House Museum★

141 Cambridge St. Visit by guided tour only (45min). Open year-round Wed–Sun 11am–5pm. Closed major holidays. $8. ℰ617-994-5920. www.spnea.org.

The house (1796) was the creation of two men who permanently influenced Boston's urban landscape: architect Charles Bulfinch and Harrison Gray Otis, lawyer, speculator and politician. The first of three houses Bulfinch designed for Otis on Beacon Hill, this Federal-style dwelling reflects the refined taste of the upper classes during the early years of the Republic.

A second-story Palladian window softens the facade. Exquisite period furniture, ornate moldings, hand-blocked borders and a freestanding staircase adorn the interior.

The house serves both as a museum and as the headquarters of the Society for the Preservation of New England Antiquities. Founded in 1910, the society administers 36 house museums in five states.

Old West Church
Next door to Harrison Gray Otis House.
Complementing its Federal-style neighbor, the Otis House, this handsome structure with its strong vertical lines was designed by **Asher Benjamin** in 1806. In 1775 British troops razed the original meetinghouse that stood on this site when they suspected the patriots of using its steeple to signal American troops.

2 FREEDOM TRAIL★★★
For information about the Freedom Trail, call ☎617-242-5642 or visit www.nps. gov/bost or www.thefreedomtrail.org. See Freedom Trail Map. Park St.
The following walk includes most of the historical monuments along the Boston section of the Freedom Trail, a popular itinerary linking major Revolutionary and other sites of the **Boston National Historical Park**. The route is indicated on the pavement by red brick or a painted red line. *See CHARLESTOWN for additional Freedom Trail sights. Begin at the visitor center on Boston Common (147 Tremont St., at West St.; open year-round daily 8.30am–5pm; closed Thanksgiving Day & 25 Dec ☎617-536-4100).*

DOWNTOWN
Boston Common★
This 50-acre park in the heart of the city has belonged to the people of Boston since the 1630s, when Reverend Blackstone sold the tract to the Puritans. Designated by these early Bostonians as "Common Field" forever reserved for public use, this Boston landmark has served over the centuries as pastureland, military training ground, public execution site, rallying ground, and concert venue.
The park's hilly terrain is crisscrossed by tree-lined paths linking downtown to

Beacon Hill and the Back Bay. The **Central Burying Ground** (1756), fronting Boylston Street, contains the unmarked grave of the preeminent early American portraitist Gilbert Stuart (1755–1828).

Proceed to the corner of Tremont and Park Sts. and follow the Freedom Trail red line for the rest of the tour.

Old Granary Burying Ground★
This burial ground was named after the 17C granary that once stood nearby. Here you'll find the tombstones of the great Revolutionary War orators James Otis and **Samuel Adams**, as well as Paul Revere and John Hancock. An obelisk in the center of the cemetery honors Benjamin Franklin's parents.

King's Chapel★
Corner of Tremont and School Sts. Open Mon and Thu–Sat 10am–3pm, Sun 1.30–3pm; Tue and Wed, 10–11am and 1–3pm. Closed during religious services. Contribution requested. ☎617-227-2155. www.kings-chapel.org.
New England's first Anglican church, this granite structure (1754, **Peter Harrison**) replaced the original wooden chapel built on the site in the 1680s. Only nine years after the British evacuation of Boston, the structure was reborn as the first Unitarian church in America. Enter the church to admire its outstanding Georgian **interior**. The adjoining **King's Chapel Burying Ground★**, Boston's oldest (1630), is the final resting place of John Winthrop (the colony's first governor) and John Alden (son of Priscilla and John).

Old City Hall (B)
45 School St.
Constructed on the site of America's first public school (c.1630), this stately granite building (1865) is Boston's finest example of the Second Empire style. Its architect, Arthur Gilman, is also credited with planning the Back Bay. The structure was converted to commercial use in the late 1960s following completion of the present City Hall. A statue of Benjamin Franklin, who was born nearby, graces the left side of the forecourt.

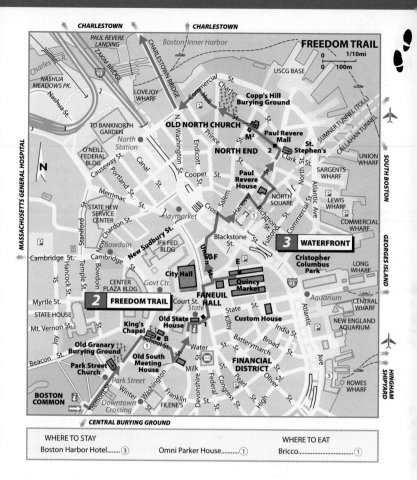

FREEDOM TRAIL

CHARLESTOWN · CHARLESTOWN

PAUL REVERE LANDING

Boston Inner Harbor

USCG BASE

Charles R.

NASHUA MEADOWS PK.

Nashua St.

ZAKIM BRIDGE

CHARLESTOWN BRIDGE

LOVEJOY WHARF

Commercial St.

Charter St.

Copp's Hill Burying Ground

SUMNER TUNNEL (TOLL)

CALLAHAN TUNNEL

TD BANKNORTH GARDEN

North Station

O'NEILL FEDERAL BLDG

North Washington St.

Endicott St.

Prince St.

OLD NORTH CHURCH

M²

Paul Revere Mall

2 **St. Stephen's**

UNION WHARF

SARGENTS WHARF

MASSACHUSETTS GENERAL HOSPITAL

N

Causeway St.

Canal St.

Cooper St.

Salem St.

NORTH END

Paul Revere House

NORTH SQUARE

Clark St.

North St.

Atlantic Ave.

LEWIS WHARF

COMMERCIAL WHARF

Merrimac St.

Portland St.

STATE HEW SERVICE CENTER

New Chardon St.

Haymarket

Cross St.

Hanover St.

Richmond St.

Commercial St.

WATERFRONT

Stanford St.

Bowdoin St.

New Sudbury St.

JFK FED. BLDG

Blackstone St.

Union St.

3 **WATERFRONT**

Cambridge St.

Cambridge St.

Hancock St.

Temple St.

Bowdoin St.

CENTER PLAZA BLDG

Govt Ctr.

City Hall

F

E

Cristopher Columbus Park

LONG WHARF

Myrtle St.

2 **FREEDOM TRAIL**

FANEUIL HALL

Quincy Market

Aquarium

CENTRAL WHARF

STATE HOUSE

Mt. Vernon St.

Joy St.

Court St.

State St.

State St.

Kilby St.

Custom House

India St.

Atlantic Ave.

NEW ENGLAND AQUARIUM

King's Chapel

B

Old State House 1 i

Beacon St.

Old Granary Burying Ground

School St.

Water St.

Broad St.

Batterymarch St.

Old South Meeting House

FINANCIAL DISTRICT

Milk St.

Pearl St.

Oliver St.

3

ROWES WHARF

Park Street Church

Park Street

Washington St.

Devonshire St.

Federal St.

Congress St.

BOSTON COMMON

i

Winter St.

Downtown Crossing

Tremont St.

Franklin St.

FILENE'S

HINGHAM SHIPYARD

SOUTH BOSTON · GEORGES ISLAND

CENTRAL BURYING GROUND

0 1/10mi
0 100m

WHERE TO STAY		WHERE TO EAT	
Boston Harbor Hotel........ ③	Omni Parker House........... ①	Bricco................................. ①

Old South Meeting House★★

310 Washington St., at Milk St. ♿
🕐*Open Apr–Oct daily 9.30am–5pm.
Nov-Mar daily 10am–4pm.* 🕐*Closed
major holidays.* ⊜*$6.* ☎*617-482-6439.
www.oldsouthmeetinghouse.org.*
Noted orators Samuel Adams and James
Otis led many of the protest meetings
held at Old South prior to the Revolution. The momentous rally that took
place on the evening of 16 December
1773, gave rise to the Boston Tea Party.
Sporting a plain brick facade and a tower
surmounted by a wooden steeple, the
edifice was inspired by the designs of
Christopher Wren. Its expansive interior was transformed by the British
into a riding stable during the siege
of Boston.

Old State House★★

206 Washington St., at State St.
🕐*Open year-round daily 9am–5pm,
Jan 9am–4pm, Jul–Aug 9am–6pm.*
🕐*Closed 1 Jan, Thanksgiving Day,
25 Dec and first week in Feb.* ⊜*$7.50.*
☎*617-720-1713.*
www.bostonhistory.org.
Boston's oldest public building (1713)
was the British government headquarters in the colonies until the Revolution
and was the site of several crucial events.
In 1770 the Boston Massacre erupted
on this site. On 4 July 1776, the colonies
declared their independence in Philadelphia. Two weeks later the Declaration
of Independence was read from the balcony here, inciting the crowds to topple
and burn the lion and unicorn—symbols

Old State House

© Greater Boston CVB / FAYFOTO, Inc.

City Hall★★

Congress & State Sts., across from Faneuil Hall. ♿🕐*Open year-round Mon–Fri 8.30am–5.30pm.* 🕐*Closed major holidays.* ✆*617-635-4000. www.cityofboston.gov.*

Rising from its brick base, this top-heavy concrete pile has remained one of Boston's controversial architectural statements since its completion in 1968. Designed by Kallman, McKinnell and Knowles, the structure recalls the works of the influential Modernist Le Corbusier and helped to bring the so-called Brutalist style to prominence in the US.

Faneuil Hall★★★

Dock Sq., main entrance facing Quincy Market. ♿🕐*Open year-round daily 9am–5pm, except during city-sponsored events.* 🕐*Closed Jan 1, Thanksgiving Day & 25 Dec.* ✆*617-242-5642. www.nps.gov/ bost/historyculture.*

Presented to Boston in 1742 by wealthy merchant Peter Faneuil, this revered landmark served as the town meeting hall throughout the Revolutionary period. Among the noted American leaders who have addressed groups here over the years are Samuel Adams, Wendell Phillips, Susan B. Anthony and John F. Kennedy. Damaged by fire in 1762, the building was reconstructed according to the original plans. In 1806 a major renovation supervised by Charles Bulfinch doubled the building's size.

Faneuil Hall's cupola is crowned with the grasshopper weather vane commissioned by Peter Faneuil in 1742. Modeled after the gilded bronze weather vanes that top the Royal Exchange in London, the grasshopper has symbolized the Port of Boston since the 18C. A statue of Samuel Adams stands in front of the building.

A staircase leads up to the large meeting hall on the second floor, where George P.A. Healy's painting *Daniel Webster's Second Reply to Hayne* (1846-50) covers the front wall. The **Ancient and Honorable Artillery Company**, America's oldest military organization,

of the British Crown—perched on the building's gables (reproductions now adorn the building). The Massachusetts government met in this building until the new State House was completed in 1798; the Old State House was later converted into shops and subsequently housed the city government. In 1881 the Bostonian Society was founded to maintain the site as a museum devoted to Boston's history.

Inside, two floors accessed by a spiral staircase feature excellent exhibits on the city, past and present. The historic balcony can be seen from the Council Chamber. To the rear of the State House, note the circle of cobblestones embedded in the traffic island in the busy intersection of Congress and State Streets, marking the actual **Boston Massacre site (1)**. Farther down State Street rises the tower of another enduring Boston landmark, the **Custom House★** (base: c.1840, A.B. Young; tower: c.1910, Peabody and Stearns).

After negotiating the intersection of Congress and State Streets, turn around to admire the east facade of the Old State House against the dramatic backdrop of a looming black metal tower (One Boston Place).

maintains a museum of historical arms, uniforms, flags and paintings on the third floor.

Quincy Market★★

Behind Faneuil Hall. &. ⊙*Open year-round Mon–Sat 10am–9pm, Sun noon–6pm. Extended hours for restaurants and pubs.* ⊙*Closed Thanksgiving Day & 25 Dec.* ☏*617-523-1300. www.faneuilhallmarketplace.com.*
The lively Faneuil Hall Marketplace complex, known as Quincy Market, exemplifies the successful revitalization of a formerly blighted urban area. Run-down market buildings and warehouses have been restored, and the renewed commercial complex has become one of the most popular sections of the city. Day and night, tourists flock to its numerous restaurants, outdoor cafes and specialty shops. The heart of the development consists of three granite buildings constructed in 1825 by Alexander Parris. The centerpiece, Quincy Market proper, is a long arcade in the Greek Revival style. Glass enclosures from the 1970s restoration flank its sides and contain dozens of small shops and eateries. The North and South Street buildings adjoining Quincy Market house upscale specialty stores. North Market is home to the family-style restaurant (known for its communal tables and jokingly grouchy waitstaff) **Durgin Park** (**E**).

Union Street

During the late 18C this street was lined with taverns and pubs. The Duke of Orleans, later King Louis-Philippe of France, lived for several months on the second floor of the venerable institution **Ye Olde Union Oyster House** (**F**) (still in operation as a restaurant), where he gave French lessons to earn his keep. Daniel Webster was also a frequent patron here.

⊙ Cross Blackstone St. to Haymarket, site of a colorful farmers' market on weekends, and continue through the pedestrian tunnel and into the North End.

NORTH END★

This colorful district has been continuously inhabited since 1630. Throughout the 17C and 18C, the North End reigned as Boston's principal residential district and included a community of free blacks. Irish and Jewish immigrants settled here in the 19C.
Eventually they moved on, replaced by Southern Italian immigrants, who have maintained a strong presence here, although this quaint neighborhood has been discovered by young urbanites in recent years. Rooftop gardens; shops bulging with fresh meats, poultry and vegetables; and restaurants and cafes that serve home-cooked pasta, pizza, pastries and espresso crowd **Hanover★** and **Salem Streets**, the main thoroughfares. The local community continues to celebrate numerous saint's days throughout the year (*schedules of feasts are posted in storefronts and churches*). These lively events feature religious processions, outdoor entertainment and an abundance of food sold by street vendors.

Paul Revere House★

19 North Sq. ⊙*Open mid Apr–Oct daily 9.30am–5.15pm. Nov–mid-Apr daily 9.30am–4.15pm.* ⊙*Closed Mon, Jan–Mar. Also closed Jan 1, Thanksgiving Day & 25 Dec.* ⊗*$3.50.* ☏*617-523-2338. www.paulreverehouse.org.*
This two-and-a-half-story wooden clapboard house is the only extant 17C structure in downtown Boston. The dwelling was already 90 years old when silversmith **Paul Revere** bought it in 1770. The house was the starting point of Revere's historic ride to Lexington on 18 April 1775. Furnishings include items owned by the Revere family.

St. Stephen's Church★

Hanover and Clark Sts. ⊙*Open year-round daily 7am–dusk.*
Of the five churches designed by Charles Bulfinch in Boston, St. Stephens (1806) is the only one still standing. The well-preserved stark interior is flanked with a delicate colonnade that supports the balcony.

Old North Church

© National Park Service

Paul Revere Mall★

This intimate brick pedestrian mall links St. Stephen's and the Old North Church. Beyond Cyrus Dallin's equestrian **statue (2)** of Paul Revere looms the spire of Old North Church. A series of bronze plaques set into the brick walls that enclose the mall traces the role of the North End's residents in Boston's history.

Old North Church★★★
(Christ Church)

193 Salem St. ♿◷Open Jan–Feb, Tue–Sun 10am–4pm, Mar–May daily 9am–5pm, June–Oct daily 9am–6pm, Nov–Dec daily 10am–5pm. ◷Closed Thanksgiving Day & 25 Dec (except for services). ◌$3 contribution requested. ℘617-523-6676. www.oldnorth.com.
It was here, on the evening of 18 April 1775, that the sexton displayed two lanterns in the steeple to signal the departure of the British from Boston by boat, on their way to Lexington and Concord. A century later this church was immortalized by Longfellow in his poem *Paul Revere's Ride* (1861). Built in 1723, Old North was surmounted by a spire that was destroyed and replaced twice following violent storms. The present spire dates from 1954.
Inside, the box pews, the large windows and the pulpit, from which President

Gerald Ford initiated the celebration of the nation's bicentennial, are characteristic features of New England's colonial churches. The four wooden cherubim near the organ were among the bounty captured from a French vessel. Replicas of the famous lantern are for sale in the combination gift shop and **museum (M2)** adjacent to the church.

Copp's Hill Burying Ground★

Next to Old North Church, bordered by Hull and Charter Sts. ◷Open year-round daily dawn–dusk. ℘617-536-4100.
This cemetery contains the graves of noted Bostonians, including three generations of the prominent Mather family: Increase Mather (1639–1723), minister and Harvard president; Cotton Mather (1663–1728), clergyman and writer; and his son, Rev. Samuel Mather (1706–85).
The Mather plots are located in the northeast corner near the Charter Street gate.
Also interred here are the remains of hundreds of black Bostonians who settled in the North End in the 18C.

▷ Return to Hanover St. to sample some Italian specialties or simply to enjoy the ambience. Note that the Freedom Trail continues to Charlestown.

3 THE WATERFRONT★

This waterfront tour features parks, museums and excellent views of Boston's working harbor. Head south on Atlantic Ave. ♿See map p202. ⊤Aquarium.

Commercial Wharf and Lewis Wharf

Built in the 1830s, these granite warehouses were transformed into luxury apartments and offices in the 1960s.

Long Wharf

This c.1710 pier, linking the Custom House Tower and the port, was used as dockage for the largest vessels coming into Boston Harbor. Over time, Long

Wharf fell into disrepair and its shops and warehouses were shuttered. In 1982, the Marriott Long Wharf Hotel was built, designed to integrate harmoniously with the architecture of the existing port. The former Bureau of Customs building has found new life as a mix of residential and commercial space. Long Wharf pier is the launching point for boat tours of Boston Harbor and the harbor islands, and the water shuttle between Boston and Charlestown.

◐ Proceed south to Central Wharf.

♞♙ New England Aquarium★★
On Central Wharf. ♿🕐*Open Jul–Labor Day Mon–Fri 9am–6pm (Wed & Thu til 8pm), weekends 9am–7pm. Rest of the year Mon–Fri 9am–5pm, weekends 9am–6pm.* 🕐*Closed Thanksgiving Day & 25 Dec.* ▨*$22.95* ☎*617-973-5200. www.neaq.org.*

This large aquarium, the first of its kind in the nation, is undergoing a major expansion. Interpretive panels, demonstrations and special exhibits help foster understanding of the 600 species of fish, invertebrates, mammals, birds, reptiles, and amphibians found around the world. Dominating the center of the aquarium is a four-story, cylindrical **ocean tank** containing a re-creation of a Caribbean coral reef. As visitors descend the ramp encircling the 200,000 gallon tank, they can watch sharks, sea turtles, moray eels, and the many species of fish that inhabit this glass-enclosed world as well as some 3,000 corals and sponges. In the Edge of the Sea tide pool, youngsters are invited to handle crabs, sea stars and urchins. The penguin pool, on level one, is home to African, rockhopper and little blue penguins. A glass-enclosed lab permits observation of routine and emergency care of sea creatures. The Marine Mammal Center offers great views of Atlantic harbor seals and Northern fur seals, and the chance to sign up to become a "trainer for a morning. A shark and ray touch tank and the large-format IMAX® theater are big draws.

New England Aquarium

© S. Cheng / New England Aquarium

Rowes Wharf
This immense brick structure (1987, Skidmore, Owings and Merrill) houses the luxurious Boston Harbor Hotel (see p218) as well as residences and office space. The monumental arch offers beautiful views of the harbor. The water taxi to Logan International Airport departs from the dock behind the hotel.

◐ Head left onto the Northern Avenue Bridge, proceeding to the left around the courthouse building. Follow the boardwalk that traces the waterfront.

Institute of Contemporary Art
100 Northern Ave. 🕐*Tue and Wed 10am–5pm, Thu and Fri 10am–9pm, Sat and Sun 10am–5pm.* ▨*$15, free Thu 5–9pm, free for families last Sat of every month except Dec.* Ⓣ*Courthouse.* ☎*617-478-3100.www.icaboston.org.*

This impressive 65,000sq ft site features a facade of translucent and transparent glass, wood and metal, and a dramatic folding ribbon shape. A cantilever extends to the water's edge, creating a sheltered but open space for visitors to enjoy views of Boston Harbor. The museum is building a permanent collection, with an emphasis on innovative paintings, installations and multimedia shows; current artists include Louise

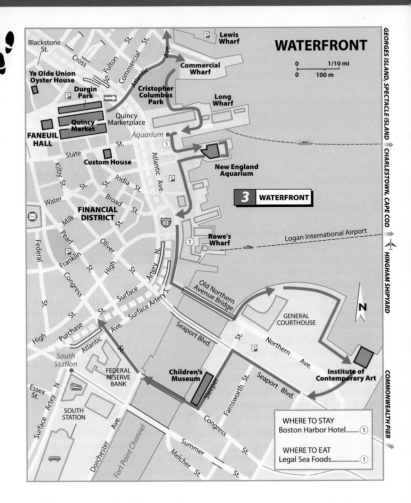

Blackstone St.

Ye Olde Union Oyster House

Durgin Park

Quincy Market

FANEUIL HALL

State St.

Kilby St.

Custom House

Water St.

FINANCIAL DISTRICT

Milk St.

Broad St.

India St.

Federal St.

Pearl St.

Franklin St.

Congress St.

Oliver St.

High St.

Surface Artery N.

High St.

Purchase St.

Atlantic Ave.

Surface Artery

South Station

FEDERAL RESERVE BANK

Essex St.

Surface Artery N.

SOUTH STATION

Dorchester Ave.

Cross St.

Fulton St.

Commercial St.

Atlantic Ave.

Commercial Wharf

Cristopher Columbus Park

Quincy Marketplace

Aquarium

Atlantic Ave.

New England Aquarium

Lewis Wharf

Long Wharf

WATERFRONT

0   1/10 mi
0   100 m

GEORGES ISLAND, SPECTACLE ISLAND   CHARLESTOWN, CAPE COD   HINGHAM SHIPYARD   COMMONWEALTH PIER

3   WATERFRONT

Rowe's Wharf

Logan International Airport

Old Northern Avenue Bridge

Seaport Blvd.

GENERAL COURTHOUSE

Northern Ave.

N

Children's Museum

Sleeper St.

Farnsworth St.

Seaport Blvd.

Congress St.

Summer St.

Melcher St.

Institute of Contemporary Art

Fort Point Channel

WHERE TO STAY
Boston Harbor Hotel........①

WHERE TO EAT
Legal Sea Foods................①

Bourgeois, Tara Donovan, Jenny Holzer, Shepard Fairey, Nan Goldin and Philip-Lorca di Corcia. The complex includes a performing arts theater and an eatery, the Water Cafe.

▶ Cross Northern Ave to Seaport Blvd. Take a right on Seaport Blvd and a left onto Sleeper St.

👥 Children's Museum★★
ᵔSee Boston map (**D2**). 300 Congress St. at Museum Wharf. Ⓣ South Station. ✕ᵕ Open year-round daily 10am–5pm (Fri til 9pm). Ⓢ Closed Thanksgiving Day & Dec 25. ⓢ$14 (for adults and kids age 1–15; $1 Fri after 5pm). ✆617-426-6500. www.bostonkids.org.

Conceived exclusively for children (but a delight to adults as well), the museum is a wonderland of learning and play. Many exhibits have a multicultural twist, such as the **Japanese House**, where visitors can kick off their shoes and visit a Kyoto silk merchant's car, and **Boston Black**, a look at ethnicity in the community, where kids play in a beauty salon and visit a Cape Verdean restaurant. The **New Balance Climb** is an irresistible three-story structure, described by the museum as a "3-D, full-body puzzle". Other favorite exhibits include the **Common**, where kids can unleash energy in a giant maze, or play with huge chess pieces, the bubble-making apparatus, and **Boats Afloat**, where kids can float wooden objects down a 28ft model of Fort Point Channel, or strap on gear to board the *Minnow*, a little lobster boat, and take a virtual ride around Boston Harbor. There's even a recycle shop, where you can buy bags of foam, paper goods, decorative materials and other reusable items for kids to make their own creations.

Cruises

Sightseeing cruises and excursion boats that depart from the waterfront are a wonderful way to see the harbor and view the Boston skyline.

Boston Harbor Islands★

High-speed ferries depart from Long Wharf to Georges and Spectacle islands in season. Free water taxis access other islands. Round-trip 40min. Commentary. $15 Boston's Best Cruises 617-770-0040. www.bostonsbestcruises. com. For information on islands, visit www.bostonislands.org, or www.nps.gov/boha.

Boston Harbor is dotted with 34 islands comprising **Boston Harbor Islands National Park Area**. Basically undeveloped, the islands offer walking trails, remnants of history, and spectacular views of the city. Some offer primitive camping in season.

Ferries depart from Long Wharf to **Georges Island** and **Spectacle Island**. Free inter-island water shuttles transport visitors to four other islands within the park. Twenty-eight-acre **Georges Island**, inhabited during colonial times and later fortified due to its strategic location, is a public recreation site with picnic areas at the water's edge.

Dominating the island is well-preserved Fort Warren, used during the Civil War to incarcerate some 2,000 Confederate military prisoners. The fort never saw battle. Park rangers tell the story of the island's ghost, the "lady in black."

The fort's observation tower offers **views** of the Boston skyline and the many islands and islets composing the Boston Harbor Islands National Park. *Free water taxis run from Georges Island to several nearby islands during the summer season.*

Spectacle Island—so named because its two drumlins look like a pair of spectacles—has a storied past. In 1717, the 105-acre island served as a quarantine

Waterfront Transformation

During Boston's long period of maritime prosperity, sailing ships brimming with exotic cargoes frequented the busy harbor. To accommodate the port's burgeoning shipping industry, the original harborfront was dramatically transformed in the first half of the 19C via a landfill project that added more than 100 acres. After 1900 Boston's shipping activities sharply declined, and the waterfront area deteriorated. The construction of two traffic arteries (Atlantic Avenue in the 1860s and the elevated Central Artery in the 1950s) severed the area from the rest of the city.

Long-awaited rehabilitation of this historic area did not begin in earnest until the 1960s. Renovation of several wharf buildings injected new commercial and residential activity, and in the 1970s the Quincy Market restoration created a crucial link between downtown and **Christopher Columbus Park** (1976), a harborside promenade extending from Commercial Wharf to Long Wharf. A flurry of new residential and hotel complexes in the 1970s and 80s significantly enhanced the waterfront's cachet while giving new texture to Boston's skyline. In 1998 the $112 million World Trade Center East Office Tower added its 16 stories to the landscape. From the harbor there is a commanding view of the new 10-story **federal courthouse** (1998). The addition of a new convention center in 2004, the Institute of Contemporary Art (2006) and several new hotels, brought increased vitality to this area, now known as the Seaport District.

Mansions

The Back Bay was once an expanse of mud flats submerged at high tide by the Charles River estuary. In the early 19C, construction of a 1.5mi tidal mill dam along present-day Beacon Street disrupted the area's natural drainage, creating acres of foul swampland. By mid-century this threat to public health and the need for additional housing provided the impetus for the most ambitious of Boston's landfill projects. From 1857 to the 1890s, more than 450 acres—contained within the present-day boundaries of the Charles River, the Public Garden, Huntington and Massachusetts Avenues—were reclaimed. For over 30 years, 3,500 carloads of earth a day were dumped into the swamp. Eventually, stately rows of four- and five-story mansions and town houses would be built on the former swamplands of Back Bay.

station for smallpox victims; in the 1840s, two summer resorts operated on Spectacle, until local authorities closed them down for gambling and other illicit activities. Later, a horse-rendering plant was built on the island.

Starting in 1920, the city of Boston began using Spectacle Island as a dump, and, by 1959, dumping had added more than 30 acres to the island. Fast-forward to the 1990s, when Spectacle Island became the repository of more then 3 million cubic yards of dirt, gravel and clay, courtesy of the Big Dig. The island was capped, and nearly five feet of top-soil laid down, to allow the growth of trees and shrubs. This wonder of recycling is now home to a marina, visitor center, snack bar, swimming beach, and five miles of walking trails.

Other islands to see include **Peddocks**, home to the remains of an old fort, and **Lovells**, a favorite destination for camping. Peddocks, Lovells, **Grape** and **Bumpkin** islands allow camping with a permit from June through Labor Day.

④ BACK BAY★★

See green route on map p205. Allow a half-day for this tour. ⊤*Prudential.*
Hailed by architectural critic Lewis Mumford as "the outstanding achievement in American urban planning for the 19C," Boston's Back Bay is a stunningly attractive, well-preserved historic district of 19C town houses, lined with flowering dogwood trees. Architectural styles run the gamut, including Gothic, Italian Renaissance and Georgian. At its east end, Back Bay meets the Public Garden;

to the north, the riverfront Esplanade is Boston's premier park and outdoor concert site.

▷ At the Prudential T stop, follow Huntington Ave. south.

South of the fast-paced Boylston Street corridor, the Back Bay takes on a dramatically different appearance. Monumental redevelopment schemes of varying quality, such as the Prudential Center, Copley Place and the Christian Science Center, create a decidedly 20C scale and flavor. Here, buildings of cement and steel offer a striking counterpoint to the low-scale brick universe of the 19C residential streets.

Christian Science Center★★

175 Huntington Ave. ✕&🅿🕐*Open year-round. Free tours of the church Thu–Sat noon–5pm (on the hour), Sun 11am–3pm, Tue noon–4pm, Wed 1–4pm.* 🕐*No tours Mon or major holidays.* ✆*617-450-2775. www. christianscience.com. Mary Baker Eddy Library/Mapparium open Tue–Sun 10am–4pm.* ⊛*$6. www.marybaker eddylibrary.org.*
This stunning ensemble houses the world headquarters of the Christian Science Church. The Christian Science religion was founded in 1866 by New Hampshire native Mary Baker Eddy following a serious injury from which she quickly recovered after meditating on a Gospel account of one of Jesus' healings. After extensive study of the Bible, she felt she had discovered a science,

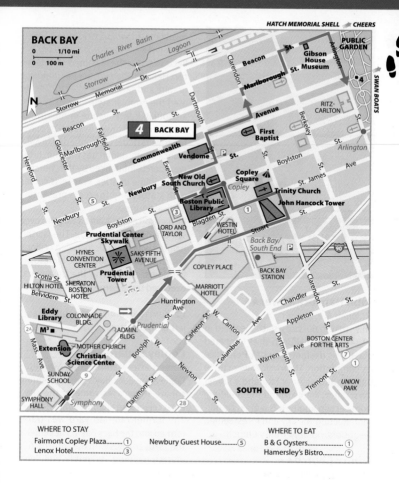

BACK BAY

0   1/10 mi
0   100 m

HATCH MEMORIAL SHELL ⎯ CHEERS

PUBLIC GARDEN

Charles River Basin
Lagoon
Storrow Memorial Dr.

Gibson House Museum

Beacon St.

Marlborough St.

Avenue

RITZ-CARLTON

SWAN BOATS

Storrow St.

Beacon St.

Fairfield

Marlborough

Gloucester

4 **BACK BAY**

Commonwealth

Vendome

First Baptist

Dartmouth

Clarendon

Berkeley

Arlington

Commonwealth St.

Boylston

St. James

Ave

Newbury

New Old South Church

Copley Square

Copley

Trinity Church

John Hancock Tower

Hereford

St.

Boston Public Library

Exeter

Blagden St.

WESTIN HOTEL

Stuart

Newbury

Boylston St.

LORD AND TAYLOR

Back Bay/ South End

Prudential Center Skywalk

HYNES CONVENTION CENTER

SAKS FIFTH AVENUE

COPLEY PLACE

BACK BAY STATION

90

Scotia St.
HILTON HOTEL
Belvidere St.

SHERATON BOSTON HOTEL

Prudential Tower

MARRIOTT HOTEL

Clarendon

Chandler St.

Eddy Library

COLONNADE BLDG.

Huntington Ave

Appleton

2A M³ ■

ADMIN. BLDG.

Prudential

Botolph St.

Carleton St. W.

Canton St. W.

Columbus Ave

Dartmouth

BOSTON CENTER FOR THE ARTS

Extension

MOTHER CHURCH

Christian Science Center

Warren St.

Tremont St.

UNION PARK

SUNDAY SCHOOL   9

Newton

SYMPHONY HALL

Symphony

Claremont St.

28

SOUTH END

WHERE TO STAY	WHERE TO EAT
Fairmont Copley Plaza..........①	Newbury Guest House..........⑤	B & G Oysters....................①
Lenox Hotel..............................③		Hamersley's Bistro.............⑦

or provable laws, behind Jesus' healing works, which can still be practiced today. She named her discovery Christian Science and wrote about this system of divine healing in her best-selling book *Science and Health with Key to the Scriptures* (c.1875).

Facing Massachusetts Avenue, the grandiose **Mother Church Extension** (1906) features Renaissance-inspired elements such as the expansive entrance portico and a central dome rising 224ft. It holds one of the 10 largest organs in the country, with over 13,000 pipes. The Romanesque-style original church (1894), with its rough granite facade and bell tower, is connected to the rear of the extension. The interior is adorned with mosaics and stenciled frescoes.

The complex was expanded in the 1970s by a group of architects led by **I.M. Pei**. Three bold concrete structures—the 26-story Administration Building the porticoed Colonnade Building, and the fan-shaped Sunday School—stand like abstract sculptures around an enormous **reflecting pool** (670ft by 100ft). Step inside the **Mary Baker Eddy Library** to experience the **Mapparium** (**M3**), a 30ft walk-through glass-paneled globe that represents the worldwide scope of the church's publishing activities.

▶ Follow Huntington Ave. north and turn right onto Stuart St., then left onto Clarendon St.

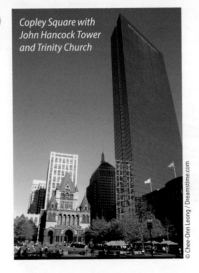

Copley Square with John Hancock Tower and Trinity Church

© Chee-Onn Leong / Dreamstime.com

John Hancock Tower★★

St. James Ave.
This striking 60-story slab, sheathed in 10,344 units of half-inch-thick tempered glass, was designed by **I.M.Pei**. Since its completion, Hancock Tower (1975) has reigned as New England's tallest skyscraper. Walk around the building; from certain angles it is a gigantic mirror reflecting the sky and its esteemed neighbors, notably Trinity Church.

Trinity Church★★

Copley Sq. ◷*Open year-round for self-guided tours, Mon–Fri 10am–3.30pm, Sat 9am–4pm, Sun 1pm–5pm.* ◎*$7.* ◉*Free guided tours every Sun*

following 11.15am service. ☏617-536-0944. www.trinitychurchboston.org.
Recognized as the masterpiece of architect Henry H. Richardson, this imposing granite and sandstone pile (1877) initiated the popular style known as Richardsonian Romanesque in America. A massive central tower, inspired by one of the towers of the Old Cathedral in Salamanca, Spain, dominates the church; the west porch, influenced by the church of St. Trophime in Arles, France, is carved with statues and friezes representing Biblical figures.
Richardson chose John La Farge to oversee the decoration inside. The lavishly painted walls, murals, paneled ceilings, and small lunettes above the high, tower windows, are among the best works executed by La Farge.

▷ Turn right onto Dartmouth St. and left onto Boylston St.

Copley Square★★

Named after painter John Singleton Copley, the Back Bay's principal public square showcases some of the city's most celebrated architectural treasures. The former railroad yard was transformed into the Back Bay's civic center in the 1870s and 80s with the construction of Boston's finest 19C public buildings. Today the square's east end is dominated by the contrasting silhouettes of massive Trinity Church and soaring John Hancock Tower. To the south rises the limestone facade of posh Copley Plaza Hotel (1912), designed in the Renaissance Revival style by Henry J. Hardenbergh, architect of New York's Plaza Hotel. The handsome 19C facade of the Boston Public Library graces the west side, while the New Old South Church, in the northwest corner, adds an exotic note to the ensemble.

Boston Public Library★★

700 Boylston St. on Copley Sq. ✕ &
◷*Open year-round Mon–Thu 9am–9pm, Fri & Sat 9am–5pm. Oct–May Sun 1–5pm, Labor Day to Memorial Day.* ◷*Closed major holidays.* ☏617-536-5400. www.bpl.org.

Finale

One Columbus Ave. ☏617-423-3184.
If you have a serious sweet tooth, make tracks to this swank dessert cafe, where the Theater District meets the Back Bay. There are sandwiches and light meals available, but the real reason to stop here is for the decadent, if pricey, desserts. Molten chocolate cake is a real crowd-pleaser, but for a true chocoholic, only the Chocolate Obsession, an orgy of a tasting plate, for two, will do.

This handsome Renaissance Revival style building (1895, McKim, Mead and White) influenced countless public buildings in the US for over half a century.

The granite facade sports elaborate wrought-iron lanterns, relief panels by Augustus Saint-Gaudens, and an elegant row of second-story arched windows. Daniel Chester French, sculptor of the seated Lincoln on the Mall in Washington, DC, crafted the bronze doors dominating the vestibule. Wander through the cavernous rooms on the upper floors to admire murals executed by Edwin Abbey (*Quest of the Holy Grail, 1891-95; delivery room, 2nd floor*) and John Singer Sargent (*Judaism and Christianity, 1895-1916; 3rd-floor corridor*) and the library's Joan of Arc collection (*Cheverus Room, 3rd floor*).

Fronting Boylston Street, the stark granite addition to the library was designed by renowned architect Philip Johnson as a contemporary complement. Across Boylston Street rises the picturesque **New Old South Church** (1874, Cummings and Sears), with its lofty bell tower, Venetian-style cupola and a profusion of Italian Gothic detailing. The Boston Marathon ends here.

▶ Continue along Boylston St.

Prudential Center Skywalk

800 Boylston St. Purchase tickets at the kiosk at Prudential Arcade; if kiosk is closed, buy tickets at the Skywalk entrance. ♿🅿⏱*Open mid-Mar–Oct daily 10am–10pm; open rest of the year 10am–8pm.* ⏱*Closed Thanksgiving Day & 25 Dec.* 💲$14. ✆*617-859-0648. www.prudentialcenter.com/shop.*

An observation deck on the 50th floor of the 52-story Prudential Tower offers sweeping 360-degree **views** of the Greater Boston, including Fenway Park, the Charles River, distant suburbs, and Cape Cod (on a clear day). An audio tour provides commentary on landmarks and local history.

▶ Turn right on Exeter St. and right on Newbury St.

Go Sox

To the Fenway Faithful, Boston's ballpark is hallowed ground. Opened in 1912, Fenway, the home of the Boston **Red Sox**, is the smallest park in the major league. Tours are offered Mon through Sun year-round, from 9am–4pm. (If there's a home game, the last tour starts three hours before game time.) Highlights include a walk around the playing field (except during inclement weather), sitting in the dugout, and posing for a photo in front of the Green Monster. The walk-up ticket sales office near Gate A sells **Fenway Park** tour tickets. With two recent World Series wins, the Sox are red-hot, but it is sometimes possible to score tickets. Opening Day is like a holiday here. www.redsox.com.

Newbury Street★

www.newbury-st.com.

Originally a quiet residential street, Newbury now reigns as the city's most exclusive shopping district. Converted town houses sport glass storefronts showcasing the city's finest boutiques, specialty stores, and cafes.

The block between Exeter and Dartmouth Streets boasts a cluster of art galleries and a lively street scene, making it one of the Back Bay's most pleasant pockets.

▶ Turn left on Dartmouth St. and continue to Commonwealth Ave.

Commonwealth Avenue★★

Inspired by the grand boulevards laid out in late-19C Paris under Napoleon III, this 200ft-wide thoroughfare was reputedly the address of choice for Boston's nouveau riche. "Comm Ave" still connotes elegant living.

On the southwest corner (*no. 160*) extends the sprawling **Vendome** (1871, W.G. Preston), once the Back Bay's most luxurious hotel and temporary home to such celebrities as Wilde, Twain, Bernhardt and Ulysses S. Grant.

Swan Boats, Boston Public Garden

© Greater Boston CVB / FAYFOTO, Inc.

▷ Cross to the planted mall and continue east one block.

Commonwealth Avenue's pleasant **mall**, lined with elm trees and punctuated by commemorative statues, offers a good vantage point to view a characteristic sampling of Back Bay houses on either side of the wide avenue.

Just before reaching the next corner, glance to the right for a view of **First Baptist Church★** (1872), a pivotal work by H.H. Richardson. The **frieze** adorning the upper portion of the bell tower is attributed to Frédéric-Auguste Bartholdi, designer of the Statue of Liberty.

▷ Turn left on Clarendon St. and right on Marlborough St.

Marlborough Street

This generously shaded residential street lined with brick sidewalks and gas lamps exudes a romantic 19C ambience.

▷ Turn left on Berkeley St. and right on Beacon St.

Beacon Street★

Favored by Boston's old-money families in the 19C, this distinguished thoroughfare is flanked by grand town houses, many converted to colleges and cultural institutions. North-side residences are prized for their views of the Charles River. The **Gibson House Museum★** (*no. 137*), built in 1859, has retained its Victorian flavor and offers a rare glimpse into the lifestyle of an affluent Back Bay family (*visit by 45min guided tour only;* ◷ *open year-round Wed–Sun 1pm–3pm;* ◷ *closed major holidays;* ◉ *$9;* ℘ *617-267-6338; www.thegibson house.org*).

Elaborate woodwork, 15ft ceilings, imported carpets, faux-leather wallpaper, and scores of curios attest to the family's tastes and financial means.

▷ Continue to the corner of Beacon and Arlington Sts.

At this point TV fans will enjoy making a detour to the nearby Bull and Finch Pub (*84 Beacon St.*) to glimpse the familiar stone and brick facade popularized by the 1980s television series **"Cheers."**

Near the corner of Beacon and Arlington Sts., the Fiedler footbridge leads to the Charles River **Esplanade**. Landscaped in the early 1930s, this waterfront park extending over 10mi attracts joggers, in-line skaters, cyclists, picnickers and sailing enthusiasts. Outdoor performances given at the **Hatch Memorial Shell** are popular in summertime.

▷ Return to the corner of Beacon and Arlington Sts. Continue on Arlington St.

Public Garden★★

Entering from the Arlington St gate, your eye is drawn to the equestrian **statue** (**4**) of George Washington (1878, Thomas Ball), facing Commonwealth Ave. This 24-acre rectangular park, bounded by a handsome cast-iron fence, was reclaimed from the swampy Back Bay in the 1830s to create a botanical garden. First launched in the 1870s, the beloved **swan boats** ply the tranquil waters of an artificial pond traversed by a whimsical suspension bridge and bordered with weeping willows. The *Make Way for Ducklings* (1987) statue in the northeast section re-creates the title characters of Robert McCloskey's classic children's book.

THE MUSEUMS
Museum of Fine Arts★★★

*See Boston map (**AZ**). 465 Huntington Ave. Museum. Open year-round Mon–Tue 10am–4.45pm, Wed–Fri 10am–9.45pm, weekends 10am–4.45pm. Closed major holidays. $25. Free Wed 4–9.45pm; voluntary donations welcome; special exhibitions require separate ticket; concert and film information: 617-369-3300 617-267-9300. www.mfa.org.*

One of the country's leading museums, the Museum of Fine Arts (MFA) houses a comprehensive collection, organized into eight departments, including Art of the Americas; Art of the Ancient World; and Prints, Drawings and Photographs. The 1909 Neoclassical building and a 1981 addition designed by I.M. Pei and Partners includes exhibition space, dining facilities, the MFA bookstore and shop, and the Remis Auditorium. Items in the permanent collections are rotated throughout the year, and are complimented by an ongoing schedule of special exhibitions.

In 2010, the museum unveiled a major new addition, the Art of Americas Wing. Incorporating a modern aesthetic into the museum's 1909 Beaux Arts building, the 121,307sq ft addition allows for more than 5,000 works from the museum's Art of the Americas collection to be on view. The collection now represents all of the Americas, presented together in a wide range of media, spanning the Pre-Columbian era to the 20th century. The new wing contains 53 galleries on four flours, allowing visitors to travel forward in time as they ascend each floor.

The museum's three enchanting **gardens** are the setting for outdoor concerts and alfresco dining, and provide a tranquil landscape for reflection.

Dining facilities at MFA range from the informal Courtyard Café (lower level, West Wing); the Galleria Café; and Bravo, whose varying, eclectic menu is often tailored to complement special exhibitions. Bravo features a rotating collection of the MFA's masterpieces.

Art of the Americas
American Paintings★★

Now broadened to include works from North, Central, and South America in an expanded space, this department has doubled in size.

The collection of American paintings is particularly strong, featuring prominent 18C portraitists including Gilbert Stuart, whose paintings of George and Martha Washington (*Athenaeum Portraits*, 1796-1828) are exhibited alternatively at the National Portrait Gallery in Washington, DC, and at the MFA; and John Singleton Copley, who painted noted Bostonians of his day (*Samuel Adams*, 1772 and *Paul Revere*, 1770).

In the 19C painters turned their attention to nature, and in particular to the sea. The adventure and beauty of the sea were portrayed on canvas by Fitz Henry Lane (*Boston Harbor; Owl's Head Penobscot Bay, Maine*) Albert Pinkham Ryder and Winslow Homer (*Fog Warning: Lookout—All's Well*).

Art of Europe
European Paintings★★

Principal European schools from the Middle Ages to the present are represented. A Catalonian chapel with a 12C apse fresco and the 15C panel painting of *St. Luke Drawing the Virgin* by Rogier van der Weyden are noteworthy early works. The lovely **Koch**

Parakeets and Gold Fish Bowl, about 1893, designed by Louis Comfort Tiffany (American, 1848–1933)

© Museum of Fine Arts, Boston

Gallery holds double-hung, gilt-framed works of the 16C and 17C, including the Rosso's renowned *Dead Christ with Angels* (1525-26); El Greco's *Fray Hortensio Felix Paravicino* (c.1605); *Don Baltasar Carlos with a Dwarf* (1632) by Velazquez; and two significant history paintings by Poussin.

The Dutch gallery boasts five Rembrandts as well as Tiepolo's majestic allegory of *Time Unveiling Truth* (c.1745). Among the 19thC French masters represented are Renoir (*Bal à Bougival*, 1883), Monet (*La Japonaise*, 1876; *Haystacks*, 1890-91; *Rouen Cathedral*, 1892-94), Degas (*Carriage at the Races*, 1869), Manet (*Execution of Maximillian*, c.1867; *The Street Singer*, c.1862), and Van Gogh (*Postman Joseph Roulin*, 1888).

Art of Asia, Oceania and Africa★★★

For over a century, the MFA's collection of Arts of Asia, Oceania and Africa has been described as "the finest collection of oriental art under one roof in the world." **Indian Art** holdings include sculpture (2C BC–5C AD), miniature paintings from the courts of North India (16C–19C), and works of various metals, jade and ivory.

The MFA also houses one of the finest collections of **Japanese Art** in the world. Highlights include Buddhist and Shinto paintings and sculpture, scroll and screen paintings, ceramics, lacquerware, swords, metalwork, inro (medicine boxes), and netsuke (toggle weights), as well as woodblock prints by ukiyo-e masters, ranging from 17C works by Moronobu to those of contemporary artists. Most recently, the collection has been expanded to represent the art of Africa and Oceania.

The MFA boasts one of the few important museum collections of **Korean Art** in the Western world, comprised of high-quality stoneware and lacquerware of the Koryo and Yi dynasties, Buddhist paintings and sculptures, and Bronze Age funerary objects.

Art of the Ancient World
Ancient Egyptian, Nubian, and Near Eastern Art★★

The bulk of the MFA's superb collection of Egyptian art, spanning 4,000 years of civilization, came to the museum as a result of a 40-year MFA/Harvard expedition to Egypt and the Sudan beginning in 1905. Excavations conducted at Giza yielded **Old Kingdom** treasures (2778–2360 BC) rivaled only by the Egyptian Museum in Cairo. Among the many pieces of sculpture excavated from the tombs and temples of Dynasty IV is **King Mycerinus** and his queen, one of the oldest extant statues portraying a couple, dating from the same period is the realistic portrait bust of **Prince Ankh-haf**.

The expedition's digs at El Bersheh and in the Sudan produced treasures from the more recent Dynasty XII: the well-preserved paintings on the coffins of **Prince Djehutynekht** and his wife, the black granite statue of **Lady Sennuwy**, and painted wooden servant models which served the dead in eternity.

Treasures from ancient Nubia (the region that today comprises southern Egypt and northern Sudan) include boldly

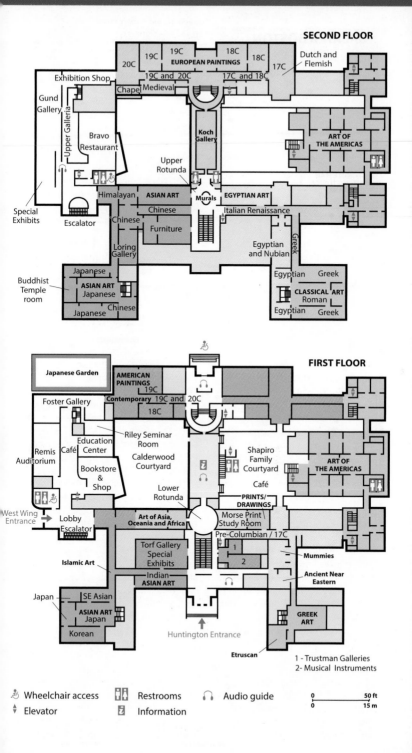

SECOND FLOOR

European Paintings: 20C, 19C, 19C, 18C, 18C, EUROPEAN PAINTINGS
19C and 20C, 17C and 18C, 17C, Dutch and Flemish
Exhibition Shop
Gund Gallery
Chapel, Medieval
Bravo Restaurant
Koch Gallery
Upper Galleria
ART OF THE AMERICAS
Special Exhibits
Upper Rotunda
Himalayan, ASIAN ART, Murals, EGYPTIAN ART
Escalator
Chinese
Chinese, Furniture, Italian Renaissance
Loring Gallery
Egyptian and Nubian
Greek
Buddhist Temple room
Japanese
ASIAN ART Japanese
Egyptian, Greek
Japanese, Chinese
CLASSICAL ART Roman
Egyptian, Greek

FIRST FLOOR

Japanese Garden
AMERICAN PAINTINGS, 19C
Foster Gallery
Contemporary, 19C and 20C, 18C
Remis Auditorium
Café
Education Center
Riley Seminar Room
Calderwood Courtyard
Shapiro Family Courtyard
Café
ART OF THE AMERICAS
Bookstore & Shop
Lower Rotunda
PRINTS/DRAWINGS
West Wing Entrance
Lobby Escalator
Art of Asia, Oceania and Africa
Morse Print Study Room
Pre-Columbian / 17C
Islamic Art
Torf Gallery Special Exhibits
1
2
Mummies
Indian ASIAN ART
Ancient Near Eastern
Japan
SE Asian
ASIAN ART Japan
Korean
GREEK ART
Huntington Entrance
Etruscan

1 - Trustman Galleries
2 - Musical Instruments

♿ Wheelchair access   🚻 Restrooms   🎧 Audio guide

↕ Elevator   ℹ Information

0 ___ 50 ft
0 ___ 15 m

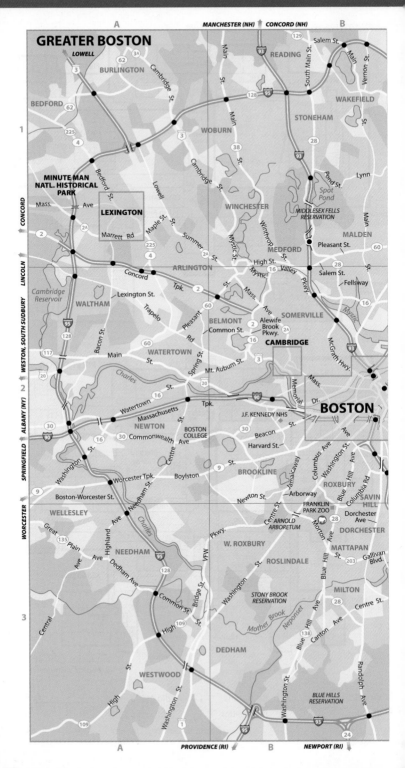

GREATER BOSTON

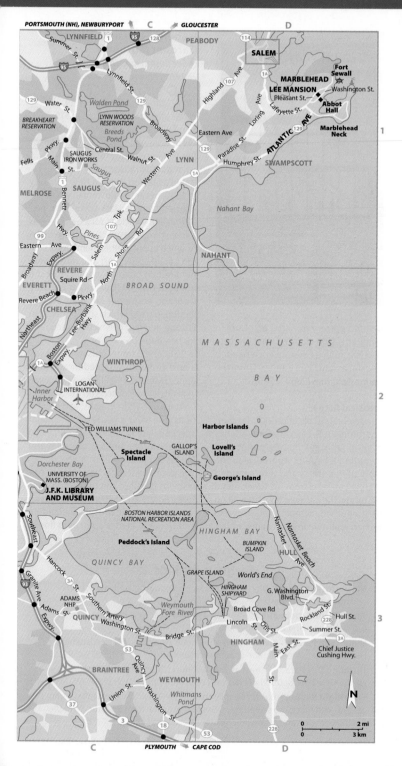

LYNNFIELD

PEABODY

SALEM

Summer St.

114

MARBLEHEAD

Fort
Sewall

LEE MANSION

Washington St.

Pleasant St.

Abbot
Hall

Lynnfield St.

Highland Ave

107

Loring Ave

Lafayette St.

Marblehead
Neck

Water St.

Walden Pond

129

ATLANTIC AVE

129

BREAKHEART
RESERVATION

LYNN WOODS
RESERVATION

Broadway

Eastern Ave

Breeds
Pond

Paradise St.

SWAMPSCOTT

Pkwy.

Central St.

Walnut St.

Western Ave

LYNN

Humphrey St.

SAUGUS
IRON WORKS

Main St.

Fells

Saugus

1A

MELROSE

SAUGUS

Bennett St.

NAHANT

Nahant Bay

Hwy.

Pines

107

Salem Tpk.

North Shore Rd.

Eastern Ave

99

Broadway

Expwy.

1A

REVERE

BROAD SOUND

MASSACHUSETTS

EVERETT

Squire Rd

BAY

Revere Beach

Pkwy.

CHELSEA

Northeast

Lee-Burbank Hwy.

Boston Expwy.

WINTHROP

1A

LOGAN
INTERNATIONAL

Inner
Harbor

TED WILLIAMS TUNNEL

Harbor Islands

GALLOP'S
ISLAND

Lovell's
Island

Spectacle
Island

Dorchester Bay

George's Island

UNIVERSITY OF
MASS. (BOSTON)

J.F.K. LIBRARY
AND MUSEUM

BOSTON HARBOR ISLANDS
NATIONAL RECREATION AREA

HINGHAM BAY

Nantasket Beach

Southeast

Peddock's Island

BUMPKIN
ISLAND

HULL

Hancock St.

QUINCY BAY

GRAPE ISLAND

World's End

Nantasket Ave

93

3A

Granite Ave

ADAMS
NHP

Adams St.

Southern Artery

Weymouth
Fore River

HINGHAM
SHIPYARD

G. Washington
Blvd.

Expwy.

QUINCY

Washington St.

Broad Cove Rd

Rockland St.

Hull St.

228

Bridge St.

Lincoln

Otis St.

Summer St.

3A

HINGHAM

Main St.

East St.

Chief Justice
Cushing Hwy.

53

BRAINTREE

Quincy Ave

WEYMOUTH

37

Union St.

Washington St.

Whitmans
Pond

N

3

18

53

228

0   2 mi
0   3 km

New wing of the Isabella Stewart Gardner Museum

© Nic Lehoux / Isabella Stewart Gardner Museum

Isabella Stewart Gardner Museum★★★

♿ *See Boston map (***AZ***).*
280 The Fenway. Ⓣ*Museum.*
✕♿Ⓒ*Open year-round Wed–Mon 11am–5pm.* Ⓒ*Closed 4 Jul, Thanksgiving Day & 25 Dec.* ⊛*$15. $2 off with same-day MFA admission. (All persons named Isabella are granted free lifetime entry).* ℰ*617-566-1401. www.gardnermuseum.org.*

Isabella Stewart, born in New York City in 1840, became a Bostonian when she married financier Jack Lowell Gardner. Daring and vivacious, Mrs. Gardner was a free spirit whose actions were often frowned upon by other members of Boston's staid society. Art and music were her lifelong delights, and in 1899 she initiated the construction of **Fenway Court** to house her fabulous art collection, part of which she gathered in Europe, and part of which was acquired for her in the US.

In 2012, the Gardner Museum unveiled a new addition, designed by architect Renzo Piano. The 70,000 sq ft wing provides space for concerts (in the 300-seat Calderwood Hall), classes, and exhibitions. The wing is home to three major special exhibitions each year, enhanced by views of the historic museum and Monks Garden.

The permanent collection features furnishings, textiles, paintings and sculpture (more than 2,500 pieces) including work from Rembrandt, Michelangelo and Degas. Galleries open onto flower

painted pottery from the first Nubian Kingdom (3100–2800 BC) and intricate jewelry, such as blue faience beaded necklaces and ivory inlay, from the Kerma Kingdom (2000–150 BC).

Classical Art★★

This celebrated collection includes cameos, bronzes, Greek vases and a series of original Greek marble sculptures, including a head of Aphrodite in the style of Praxiteles and a three-sided marble bas-relief from the Greek island of Thasos. The museum has also built up its strength in mythological vases and Roman sculpture in silver and marble.

Festivals for Kids

Harborfest Children's Day – Balloons, face painting, educational activities and more as part of Harborfest (*City Hall Plaza; early July;* ℰ*617-227-1528*).

Jimmy Fund Scooper Bowl – The nation's largest all-you-can-eat ice cream festival. (*City Hall Plaza, mid-Jun;* ℰ*800-52-JIMMY*).

Halloween Parade – Join the boys and ghouls who parade their costumes by the Common (*starts at Boston Common Playground; 27 Oct;* ℰ*617-635-4505*).

Duckling Day Parade – Dress as your favorite character from the children's classic *Make Way for Ducklings* (*Boston Common; Mother's Day;* ℰ*617-426-1885*).

First Night Boston – Boston's family-friendly New Year's Eve festival, starting at 1pm, with music, ice sculptures, a Grand Procession from Boylston St. to the Boston Common and a fireworks display (*www.firstnight.org*).

gardens in the courtyard, creating an impression of continual summer.

On the ground floor, in the **Spanish Cloister**, ceramic tiles from a 17C Mexican church cover the walls, enhancing John Singer Sargent's dramatic painting *El Jaleo*.

The **courtyard**, with its refreshing gardens, Venetian window frames and balconies brimming with fresh flowers, provides a graceful haven in the city. Classical sculptures surround an ancient Roman mosaic pavement (2C AD) from the town of Livia. In the **small galleries** off the courtyard is an exhibit of 19C and 20C French and American paintings, including portraits by Degas and Manet, and landscapes by Whistler, Matisse and Sargent. The Yellow Room houses *The Terrace of St. Tropez* (1904), the first canvas by Henri Matisse ever to enter an American museum.

On the **second floor**, the room of **early Italian paintings** contains Simone Martini's altarpiece *Madonna and Child with Four Saints,* two allegorical panels by Pesellino, Fra Angelico's *The Dormition and Assumption of the Virgin* and Constanzo da Ferrara's delicately executed *Turkish Artist*. The fresco of Hercules is the only fresco by Piero della Francesca outside of Italy.

The **Raphael Room** exhibits two of the Italian painter's works: a portrait of Count Tommaso Inghirami and a *pietà*. The *Annunciation* exemplifies the technique of linear perspective developed in the 15C. Other works in the room include Botticelli's *Tragedy of Lucretia* (1500-01) and Giovanni Bellini's *Madonna and Child* (c.1468).

Continue through the Little Salon, decorated with 18C Venetian paneling and 17C tapestries, to the **Tapestry Room**. On an easel sits *Santa Engracia* by Bermejo (15C Spain). There are also lovely 16C tapestries from France and Belgium. Rubens' masterful portrayal of Thomas Howard, Earl of Arundel, and works by Hans Holbein and Anthony Van Dyck (*Lady with a Rose*) grace the **Dutch Room**.

On the **third floor**, from the **Veronese Room**, with its Spanish and Venetian tooled and painted leather wall coverings, enter the **Titian Room**, which contains one of Titian's masterpieces, the sensual *Rape of Europa* (1562), painted for Philip II of Spain. In the **Long Gallery** the life-size terra-cotta statue *Virgin Adoring the Child* (1467-69) attributed to Matteo Civitale, provides a beautiful example of Renaissance sculpture. On the wall above a large sideboard hangs Botticelli's *Madonna and Child of the Eucharist* (c.1470s, the "Chigi Madonna"). The **Gothic Room** contains a full-length portrait (1888) of Mrs. Gardner painted by her friend John Singer Sargent.

Boston Museum of Science★★

See Boston map (**CY**). *Rte. 28. Science Park.* ✖ ♿ **P** 🕒 *Open daily 9am–5pm (Fri til 9pm); extended summer hours (Jul to Sep),* 9am–7pm. 🕒 *Closed Thanksgiving Day & 25 Dec.* ✉ *$22.* ☎ *617-723-2500. www.mos.org.*

Located alongside the Charles River, the museum explores the world of science and technology through cutting-edge, hands-on exhibits. Though the museum traces its roots to the 1830 founding of the Boston Society of Natural History, it now embraces all areas of science, including computer technology, under one huge roof.

More than 600 interactive exhibits, a planetarium and observatory, and a theater with a five-story screen greet visitors to the museum. The kaleidoscopic array of push-button displays and life-size models allows visitors to participate in activities ranging from playing with lightning produced by a Van de Graaff generator to pretending to fly through the cosmos in models of American spacecraft. Exhibits include a full-scale model of a *Tyrannosaurus rex*, musical stairs and a **mathematics lab** that melds classical thought with modern-day applications. A current exhibit, Butterfly Garden, re-creates a tropical setting in a warm conservatory filled with exotic plants and a swirl of living butterflies from New England and around the world. In the first-floor atrium, the **Charles Hayden**

Warren Tavern

2 Pleasant St., Charlestown. ℘617-241-8142. www.warrentavern.com. With its low timbered ceilings, snug fireplace and long mahogany bar, this tavern may resemble an English pub, but in fact it's just as American as they come—Patriot, that is. Constructed c.1780, the structure was one of the first to be rebuilt after the British torched Charlestown in 1775. Doubling as a Masonic hall, the alehouse was a favorite of Paul Revere. George Washington was known to quaff a few here, too. Today Warren Tavern remains a cozy place for a beer and sandwich or shepherd's pie (a house specialty), and a cup of cocoa after a long day on the Freedom Trail.

Planetarium presents programs that explore the world of stars, galaxies, pulsars, clusters, quasars, and other phenomena of outer space. There are usually two or more programs daily, in addition to IMAX movies at the domed Mugar Omni Theater (*$10; discounted combined admission available*).

John F. Kennedy Library and Museum★

Columbia Point in Dorchester, near the University of Massachusetts. Ⓣ JFK/UMass, .5mi from the museum; free shuttle bus available. ✕&🅿Ⓞ*Open year-round daily 9am–5pm.* Ⓞ*Closed 1 Jan, Thanksgiving Day & 25 Dec.* *$12. ℘866-JFK-1960. www.jfklibrary.org.*
This sleek, white concrete and glass structure, a monument to the late President John F. Kennedy, was designed by architect I.M. Pei.
About one-third of the library building is reserved for the **contemplation pavilion**, a nine-story gray glass pavilion that contains simply an American flag, a bench, and quotations from President Kennedy on the wall. The visit begins with a film on the early life of JFK. In a series of 25 exhibit bays, personal memorabilia and historic videos trace the life and accomplishments of John F. Kennedy. Included here are rare film and television footage, historic presidential documents and personal Kennedy family keepsakes. The archives on the upper floors house thousands of photos, tapes and taped interviews.

CHARLESTOWN★

Ferries depart from Boston's Long Wharf to Pier 4 in the Charlestown Navy Yard. &Ⓞ*Open year-round Mon–Fri 6.30am–8pm, weekends 10am–6pm. No service 1 Jan & 25 Dec.* *$3 (one-way). Boston Harbor Cruises. ℘877-733-9425. www.bostonharborcruises.com.*
The Freedom Trail continues across Boston Harbor in Charlestown, easily recognized by its prominent stone obelisk, the Bunker Hill Monument. During the Battle of Bunker Hill in 1775, Charlestown's colonial dwellings were destroyed by the British and replaced following the Revolution by the rows of Federal-style houses that line Main and Warren Streets. The opening of the Navy Yard in 1800 made Charlestown a renowned shipbuilding center.

Bunker Hill Monument

Adjacent to the Navy Yard on Constitution Rd. Ⓞ*Monument museum open year-round daily 9am–5pm, Jul–Aug, 9am-6pm. Monument open to climb daily, Sept–Jun, 9am–4.30pm; Jul–Aug, 9am–5.30pm. ℘617-242-5641. www.thefreedomtrail.org.*
This 221ft Quincy granite obelisk (1842), designed by Solomon Willard, marks the site of the American redoubt during the 1775 Battle of Bunker Hill. The observatory, reached by a 294-step winding stairway, offers a **view** of Charlestown, Boston and the harbor. Exhibits and a scale model of the historic battle are contained in a meetinghouse made of Carrera marble.

Charlestown Navy Yard

Visitor center, 55 Constitution Rd.
♿🅿 ⏰*Open daily 9am–5pm; July and Aug, 9am–6pm.* ⏰*Closed 1 Jan, Thanksgiving Day & 25 Dec.* ☎*617-242-5641. www.nps.gov/bost.*

Park rangers conduct free tours of the Navy Yard (*check website for schedule*). More than 200 warships were built—and thousands more maintained—here from the Navy Yard's establishment in 1800 to its closing in 1974, after which 30 of the former US Naval Shipyard's 130 acres were designated part of Boston National Historical Park.

Today the USS *Constitution* sits in its permanent berth, recalling the Navy Yard's glory days.

👥 The USS *Constitution*★★

🚶*Visit by guided tour only (30min).* ⏰*Open April–Sept Tue–Sun 10am–6pm; Oct 1–31, Thu–Sun 10am–4pm; rest of the year Thu–Sun 10am–3.30pm.* ☎*617-242-5641. www.nps.gov/bost.*

The USS *Constitution,* the pride of the American fleet, is the oldest commissioned warship afloat. Authorized by Congress in 1794, this 44-gun frigate won her greatest victories during the War of 1812 against the British: capturing the HMS *Guerrière* and the *Java* in 1812, and simultaneously seizing the *Cyane* and the *Levante* three years later. It was during the battle with the *Guerrière*, when enemy fire seemed to bounce off her planking without causing damage, that the *Constitution* was given her nickname "Old Ironsides."

By 1830, after having survived 40 military engagements, the *Constitution* was declared unseaworthy and destined for the scrap heap. Oliver Wendell Holmes' poem "Old Ironsides" aroused such strong popular sentiment in favor of the ship that funds were appropriated to rebuild it. Reconstructed in 1905, 1913 and 1973, the ship got a $12 million overhaul in 1997, to honor its 200th birthday. This was the ship's first sailing under its own power since 1881.

USS Constitution and Bunker Hill Monument

© Greater Boston Convention & Visitors Bureau..

Sailing Vessels

Sailing vessels are distinguished by the type of sail and number of masts they carry. A **sloop** is a one-masted, fore-and-aft-rigged vessel. A **schooner** carries two or more masts; all its sails are fore-and-aft rigged.

Berthed a short distance from the USS *Constitution* is the **USS *Cassin Young***, a World War II destroyer similar to the type built here in the 1930s and 40s.

👥 USS Constitution Museum

Pier 1. ♿🅿⏰*Open April–Oct daily 9am–6pm. Rest of the year daily 10am–5pm.* ⏰*Closed 1 Jan, Thanksgiving Day & 25 Dec.* ☎*617-426-1812. www.ussconstitutionmuseum.org.*
Exhibits in the granite building trace the history of Old Ironsides from 1794 to the present. The collection of some 3,000 artifacts here includes ship's logs, charts, decorative arts and paintings. Kids will enjoy hands-on activities such as hoisting a sail, steering a ship, and fighting the British in a computerized battle.

ADDRESSES

🛏 STAY

Accommodations downtown range from pricey elegant hotels to less expensive chain hotels and a youth hostel. Rates vary depending on the season and the day of the week; many downtown hotels offer discounted rates on weekends. Most bed-and-breakfast inns are located in residential areas of the city *(many B&Bs require a two-night minimum stay)*. A 12.45 percent room tax is added to the room rate in Boston.

Reservation services – Boston Reservations Inc., *℘781-547-5427; www.bostonreservations.com.* Reservation service handles hotels, inns, B&Bs, and private homes: **Host Homes of Boston**, *℘617-244-1308 or 800-600-1308; www. hosthomesofboston.com;* **Greater Boston Hospitality Bed & Breakfast Service**, *℘888-486-6018; www.bostonbedand breakfast. com.*

Hostelling International has opened a state-of-the-art (green) youth hostel in Boston; the hostel has 480 beds and is located in the heart of the city, bordering the Theater District and Chinatown. *(19 Stuart St.; open year-round; ⊖$29–$55 (private rooms, ⊖$99–$159); ℘617-536-9455); Reservations are suggested (www.bostonhostel.org).*

$$$$$ Boston Harbor Hotel – *70 Rowes Wharf. ℘617-439-7000 or 800-752-7077. www.bhh.com. 230 rooms.* Perched dramatically overlooking Boston Harbor, this grand hotel—marked by an 80-foot archway—boasts some of the city's best water views. The ambiance is classically elegant, with chandeliers, marble floors and plush upholstered furnishings. Guest rooms are comfortably posh, outfitted in luxurious sheets and featherbeds, with marble counter tops in the bathroom. **Meritage Restaurant**, with windows facing the water, showcases contemporary New England cuisine, presented as small plates paired with fine wines. During the summer months, the hotel hosts jazz concerts al fresco, outdoor movies, and other events.

$$$$ Eliot Hotel – *370 Commonwealth Ave. ℘617-267-1607 or 800-443-5468. www. eliothotel.com. 95 rooms.* In this regal 1925 building overlooking tree-lined Commonwealth Avenue in the Back Bay, most guest accommodations are two-room suites, with French doors separating the sitting rooms and bedrooms. Rooms are furnished in muted silks, with marble bathrooms; in the lobby, marble floors and chandeliers are enlivened by a zebra-print rug. The hotel's top-rated **Clio Restaurant** serves imaginative contemporary French fare.

$$$$$ Fairmont Copley Plaza – *138 St. James Ave. ℘617-267-5300 or 800-257-7544. www.fairmont.com. 383 rooms.* Back Bay's palatial property has been the home base for visiting US presidents and foreign dignitaries since 1912. A look at the lobby's gilded coffered ceilings, crystal chandeliers, and ornate French Renaissance-style furnishings may explain why Elizabeth Taylor and Richard Burton spent their second honeymoon here. Sedate plaid or floral fabrics and Louis XIV reproductions adorn the large guest rooms. The gold-level (concierge) floor offers perks like a dedicated staff, dining room, and a book and DVD library. The recently-renovated **Oak Long Bar + Kitchen** serves farm-to-table cuisine—including local cheeses and charcuterie platters, small plates, and grilled meats and fish—that draws a hip crowd of locals and hotel guests alike.

$$$$$ XV Beacon – *15 Beacon St. ℘617-670-1500 or 877-982-3226. www.xvbeacon.com. 63 rooms.* This Beacon Hill hotel offers unsurpassed luxury. Past the intimate lobby's "living room" alcove, the Beaux-Arts building's original cage elevator (1903) takes guests up to oversized rooms, studios and suites, all of which are outfitted with canopy beds, gas fireplaces and mahogany paneling. No two guest rooms are alike. Amenities include fresh flowers, 300-thread-count sheets, and surround-sound stereo. Guests have free access to a nearby health club. The hotel's signature restaurant, **Moo**, offers a modern take on traditional steakhouse fare under the helm of noted chef Jamie Mammano.

$$$-$$$$ Beacon Hill Hotel and Bistro – *25 Charles St. ℘617-723-7575 or 888-959-2442. www.beaconhillhotel.com. 13 rooms.* If the weather is mild, slip up to the roof terrace at this swanky small hotel on Beacon Hill's main street to sip a glass of wine and watch the world go by. The property blends seamlessly with neighboring antique shops and boutiques along Charles Street. Like the terrace, the property feels like a stylish urban oasis. Rooms are sleek, almost spare, sporting fluffy duvets and flat-screen TVs. Rates include a full breakfast in the Parisian-style bistro, which also serves French-inspired cuisine at lunch and dinner.

$$$$ Hotel Commonwealth – *500 Commonwealth Ave. ☎617-933-5000 or 866-784-4000. www.hotelcommon wealth.com. 150 rooms.* Choose a room with a view of busy Commonwealth Avenue or Fenway Park; either way, you'll feel cosseted here amidst the pillow-piled beds dressed in Italian linens. Floor-to-ceiling windows add to the sense that you're part of the cityscape in this sophisticated, graciously appointed property.

$$$$ Lenox Hotel – *61 Exeter St. ☎617-536-5300 or 800-225-7676. www.lenoxhotel.com. 214 rooms.* Built in the 1901, and a favorite of female business travelers, this historic property is close to Boston's prime shopping zones (Newbury Street and Copley Place) and the T (subway). Family-owned, the charming Lenox has won awards for the restoration of its handsome facade. Several rooms boast working wood-burning fireplaces. The hotel's **City Bar** and **Sólás** pub are popular with locals as well as hotel guests.

$$$ Gryphon House – *9 Bay State Rd. ☎617-375-9003. www.gryphonhouse boston.com. 8 suites.* Each suite in this four-story, 19C brownstone is decorated with its own theme. The house evokes a quieter era, and it's easy to picture ladies wearing gloves ascending the staircase, but this inn doesn't stint on modern amenities, like Wi-Fi, CD player and oversize tubs. Adding to the charm is the vintage wallpaper mural and trompe-l'œil paintings in common areas.

$$ John Jeffries House – *14 David G. Mugar Way, at Charles Circle. ☎617-367-1866. www.johnjeffrieshouse.com. 46 rooms.* At the foot of Beacon Hill, this solid-looking four-story redbrick building, built in the early 1900s, sits opposite a bustling traffic circle and the Charles Street T station. Well-maintained rooms are furnished with period reproductions; most have kitchen facilities. Though the guest rooms are not large, many have

separate sitting and sleeping areas. Enjoy a continental breakfast in the sizable parlor, which is stocked with oversize chairs and offers views of the Charles River. Another plus: Charles St.'s inviting cafes, boutiques and antique shops are right outside the door.

$$$ Newbury Guest House – *261 Newbury St. ☎617-437-7666. www.newburyguesthouse.com. 32 rooms.* You can't beat the location on Boston's prime shopping street, so savvy travelers book this one months in advance. And, on a street filled with names like Valentino, here's a surprise: Newbury Guest House is excellent value. The property comprises three attached 1880s brownstones, boasting the original (decorative) fireplaces and medallion ceilings. Guest rooms, some with bay windows, are attractively furnished with contemporary decor and a soothing pallette. A full breakfast is included in the room rate, and room service is available from the creperie next door.

$$$$ Omni Parker House – *60 School St. ☎617-227-8600 or 800-843-6664. www.omniparkerhouse.com. 572 rooms.* John F. Kennedy proposed to Jackie at table 40 at Parker's Restaurant, and Charles Dickens gave his first reading of "A Christmas Carol" here—how's that for star power? (If you want rock stars, stay at the Four Seasons) Quintessentially Boston, the Omni Parker House is the oldest continuously operating hotel in the US. You'll be transported back in time when you enter the lobby, with its gleaming wood and ornately-carved ceilings. But they've added lots of contemporary luxuries here, like feather duvets and Wi-Fi. Yes, Boston cream pie was invented here, and it is in such high demand, guests can even order it for breakfast.

♖/ EAT

$$$$ B & G Oysters – *550 Tremont St.* ♿ *☎617-423-0550. www.bandgoysters.com.* **Seafood.** At this sleek, subterranean restaurant, staff describe briny bivalves with the same reverence sommeliers have for wine. Nobody cares if you ultimately order the lobster roll instead! Chef Barbara Lynch of No. 9 Park, brings her magic touch to fresh seafood here, where the room is as sparkling as the food. It's all white marble, black stools, and silvery candlelight that evokes the inside of an oyster shell.

$$$$ Hamersley's Bistro – *553 Tremont St. Dinner only. ☎617-423-2700. www.hamersleysbistro.com.* **French.** Hamersley's helped establish the South End as a prime dining destination, and this petite bistro, where patrons turn up in everything from sweaters to suits, is still going strong. The menu stresses creative comfort food with a French flair, from the wholesome cassoulet to the signature garlicky roast chicken. Although it is cheery with its yellow walls, the dining room is a bit tight for a private tête-à-tête. Stop by in summer for a bite outside on the patio.

$$-$$$ Myers + Chang – *1145 Washington St. ☎617-542-5200. www. myersandchang.com.* **Asian.** Hotshot culinary couple Christopher Myers (Via Matta, Radius) and Joanne Chang (Flour Bakery) serve tasty, share-able eats at this funky-but-upscale dim sum diner. Inspired by Taiwanese soul food and Southeast Asian street food, the menu is as fresh and bright as the red calligraphy that adorns the restaurant's windows– think wok-roasted lemongrass mussels, tamarind-glazed local cod, and chicken with ginger-sesame waffles. The braised pork belly buns are not to be missed. There's even a dim sum menu suitable for kids, featuring nibbles like not-too-spicy wings and spring rolls.

$$$$ O Ya – *9 East St. Dinner only. ☎617-654-9900.* **Japanese.** Tucked away on a side street near South Station, O Ya is devilishly hard to find, but that hasn't stopped local foodies from discovering it—and raving about the swoon-worthy sushi and other small plates ($8–$35). Chef/co-owner Tim Cushman served as an apprentice to Nobu Matsuhisa of Nobu fame, and it shows. Little tastes of wagyu beef, sea urchin and spot prawn are artfully presented and wildly tasty. Cushman's wife, Nancy, serves as sake sommelier in this small (10 tables) restaurant. Those small plates make your tab grow quickly, but most diners agree that the food is worth it.

$$$$ Radius – *8 High St. Closed Sun. No lunch Sat. ☎617-426-1234.* **French.** Perennially one of Boston's top tables, this sleek Financial District dining room exudes a mix of efficiency and Zen-like composure, from the staff's Nehru-style jackets to the artfully prepared contemporary French fare. Business types share space with foodies here, but the opulent experience comes at a price. The menu brims with luxury ingredients: seared foie gras with tropical fruits, Maine diver scallops with heirloom squash and black trumpet mushrooms, or Colorado lamb paired with barley risotto. And who could pass up such tempting finales as warm palm-sugar cakes with chilled pineapple soup or Tahitian vanilla crème brûlée?

$$ Bricco – *241 Hanover St. ☎617-248-6800.* **Italian.** Coolly sophisticated but unpretentious, this North End trattoria is a big step up from the typical red sauce-and-Chianti joint. No wonder it's the go-to restaurant in a neighborhood chock-a-block with eateries. Italian goes nouveau here, with handmade pastas and melt-in-your -mouth dishes like veal Fiorentina and rabbit loin wrapped in pancetta. Don't miss the heavenly butternut squash bisque.

$$ Legal Sea Foods – *26 Park Sq. ☎617-426-4444; Copley Place, 100 Huntington Ave. ☎617-266-7775; Prudential Center, 800 Boylston St. ☎617-266-6800; 255 State St. ☎617-227-3115. www.legalseafoods.com.* **Seafood.** This Boston classic stays on the map thanks to its fresh, straightforward seafood. The extensive menu includes everything from Thai-grilled mahi mahi and swordfish with red onion jam to classics like whole-bellied fried clams and fish and chips. The clam chowder is a New England favorite, and you can try new items at Legal's Test Kitchen.

SHOPPING

DOWNTOWN

Downtown Crossing (*Washington & Summer Sts.*) is an outdoor walking mall anchored by Macy's department store. Across Congress Street from City Hall, **Faneuil Hall Marketplace** (*Dock Sq.; www.faneuilhallmarketplace. com*) comprises a lively cluster of more than 50 specialty shops, 14 full-service restaurants, food stalls, bars, and a comedy club in three restored 19C buildings. The nearby **Haymarket** (*Blackstone St. between Hanover & North Sts.; open Fri & Sat only*) is a popular outdoor farmers' market featuring local produce and fresh fish.

Faneuil Hall Marketplace and Custom House at dusk

© Greater Boston CVB

BACK BAY

Copley Place (*Huntington Ave. & Dartmouth St., located between and connected to the Westin and Boston Marriott hotels in Copley Place; www.shopcopleyplace.com*) boasts two levels of upscale shops and restaurants, among them such well-recognized names as Neiman-Marcus, Tiffany, Gucci and Barney's. An enclosed walkway links the Copley Place shops to **Prudential Center** (*800 Boylston St. between Gloucester & Exeter Sts.; www.prudentialcenter.com*), with its own host of retailers and restaurants featuring Lord & Taylor, Saks Fifth Avenue and Legal Sea Foods.

Boston's answer to Rodeo Drive, tony **Newbury Street** (*www.newburyst.com*) is lined with art galleries, designer boutiques and some of the city's best restaurants. As you stroll the seven blocks of Newbury Street from the Public Garden to Hereford Street, be sure to notice the lovely 19C architecture. At no. 175, the **Society of Arts and Crafts** (*℘617-266-1810; www.societyofcrafts.org*) operates a gallery where artisans sell their handmade furniture, textiles, glass and jewelry.

BEACON HILL

Antiques lovers can browse to their heart's content on **Charles Street**, which claims more antique shops than any other part of the city. Don't expect to find too many bargains in this upscale Beacon Hill neighborhood.

CAMBRIDGE

The original site of the town of Cambridge (c.1630), **Harvard Square** (*Massachusetts Ave. & John F. Kennedy St.; www.harvardsquare.com*) today teems with trendy shops, bookstores, eateries, and clubs. Dominating the square is the **Harvard Coop** (*www.thecoop.com*), where you can buy a plethora of gifts and apparel bearing the Harvard or MIT logo. Nearby you'll find the venerable **Club Passim** (*47 Palmer St.; www.clubpassim.org*), which, since 1958, has hosted such folk-music luminaries as Joan Baez and Bob Dylan.

Cambridge allegedly has more bookstores per capita than any other American city. Fueled by the 200,000 college students in the area, many of these shops stay open late (by Boston's Puritan standards), sponsor lectures and readings, and encourage browsing. Founded in 1927, **Grolier Poetry Book Shop** (*6 Plympton St.; www.grolierpoetrybookshop.com*) is one of only two stores in the US devoted to poetry. **Schoenhof's Foreign Books** (*76-A Mt. Auburn St.; www.schoenhofs.com*)—a linguist's mainstay since 1856—has titles representing more than 700 languages and dialects.

If malls are more your style, the three-level **CambridgeSide Galleria** (*100 CambridgeSide Pl., at Memorial Dr. & Edwin Land Blvd.; www.shopcambridgeside.com*) houses more than 100 apparel and specialty stores.

Cambridge★★

Located on the Charles River across from Boston, Cambridge is the home of Harvard University and the Massachusetts Institute of Technology (MIT). Massachusetts Avenue, the state's longest thoroughfare, extends the length of Cambridge from Harvard Bridge, past MIT and through the city's center, Harvard Square, with its lively coffeehouses, restaurants and theaters. Memorial Drive borders the Charles River, with great views of downtown Boston and Back Bay.

A BIT OF HISTORY

From New Towne to Cambridge – In 1630 New Towne, the small settlement across the river from Boston, was chosen as the capital of the Bay Colony. Fortifications were built to protect the town, and six years later, when the Puritans voted to establish a college to train young men for the ministry, New Towne was selected as the site. Leaders of the Bay Colony agreed to give the college a sum of money equal to the total colony tax. In 1638, recognizing the close bond between the college and the colony, they changed the name of New Towne to Cambridge, after the English university town. The school was called Harvard, in honor of the Charlestown pastor **John Harvard**, who died later that year, leaving half his estate and library to the college.

HARVARD UNIVERSITY★★★

See map p224. Ⓣ*Harvard. Campus borders the Charles River off Memorial Dr. (west of MIT).* ℘*617-495-1000. www.harvard.edu.*

Harvard College

Established in 1636, America's first college is one of the world's leading institutions of higher learning. Harvard developed as a modern university in the 19C, as professional schools were added to the original college: Medicine (1782), Divinity (1816), Law (1817), School of Dental Medicine (1867), and Arts and

▶ **Population:** 101,365.
Ⓖ **Michelin Map:** 581 M 8.
▯ **Info:** ℘617-441-2884; www.cambridge-usa.org.
▶ **Location:** The key to getting around Cambridge is knowing which "Square" (neighborhood) you're looking for: Central Square, Harvard Square, Inman Square, Kendall Square, or Porter Square.
🕐 **Timing:** You could easily spend a few hours in Harvard Square, browsing the bookstores, the Harvard Coop, and second-hand shops like the Garment District. Have lunch at Bartley's Burger Cottage and take in one of Harvard's museums.
🅿 **Parking:** Plan to pay a daily rate of about $25; hourly rates for the Harvard Square area are around $10. The Central Square parking lot, at 438 Green St., is a bargain at $5 an hour.
🅐 **Don't Miss:** Mt. Auburn Cemetery is a wonderful place to walk. This beautifully landscaped garden cemetery (the first of its kind in the US) is the final resting place of Henry Wadsworth Longfellow and Winslow Homer.

Sciences (1872). Harvard's $25.9 billion endowment is the largest of any university in the world.

Women were first admitted to the Harvard community in 1879, when Radcliffe College was founded to provide women with equal access to a Harvard education. Today, Harvard's undergraduate program is completely co-educational. Students live in one of 13 Harvard Houses, many of them lovely Georgian-style buildings that surround courtyards.

Harvard Museum of Natural History

© Adam Blanchette / www.hmnh.harvard.edu

THE CAMPUS

Harvard is a city within a city, with some 500 buildings. These reflect a variety of architectural styles, from Colonial residences to public buildings by prominent 20C figures such as Gropius—Harkness Commons and the Graduate Center, 1950; (**G**)—and Le Corbusier—Carpenter Center of Visual Arts. Begin at Harvard Information Center at 1350 Massachusetts Ave.

Harvard Yard★★

Bounded by Massachusetts Ave., Quincy St. and Cambridge St.
Harvard Yard is the oldest part of the university. Administration buildings, dormitories and the Holden Chapel, Harvard's first official chapel, are located here. To the left is **Massachusetts Hall (A)** (1720), the oldest Harvard building still standing; across from it sits **Harvard Hall (B)** (1766). Beyond Harvard Hall is **Holden Chapel (C)**. **University Hall (D)** (1815), a granite building designed by Charles Bulfinch, occupies the other side of the Yard. Daniel Chester French's **statue of John Harvard (1)** stands in front of University Hall. Because of the plaque on the statue that reads "John Harvard, founder 1638," the statue is known as the "statue of the three lies": the college was founded in 1636, John Harvard was the school's benefactor, not its founder, and the figure portrays a

student who attended Harvard in 1882. To the rear of University Hall stands **Memorial Church (E)**, dedicated to Harvard men killed in the world wars. Opposite rises the **Widener Memorial Library (F)**, with its imposing stairway. Named after Harry Widener, a former Harvard student who lost his life in the Titanic tragedy, Widener Memorial is the largest university library in the world.

THE MUSEUMS
👥 Harvard Museum of Natural History★★

26 Oxford St. ♿🅿🕐Open year-round daily 9am–5pm. 🕐Closed 1 Jan, 4 Jul, Thanksgiving Day & 25 Dec. 💲$12. Current Harvard students and one guest admitted free. ☏617-495-3045. www.hmnh.harvard.edu.
Grouped under one roof, these four museums serve as the repository for the 21 million specimens and artifacts that make up Harvard's research collections. Many of the galleries, dimly lit and packed with simple glass-and-wood display cases, have retained the old-fashioned charm of a 19C exhibition hall. Don't be put off by the no-frills presentation; the collections merit a look.

Peabody Museum of Archaeology and Ethnology★

Founded in 1866 by George Peabody, this large museum displays objects

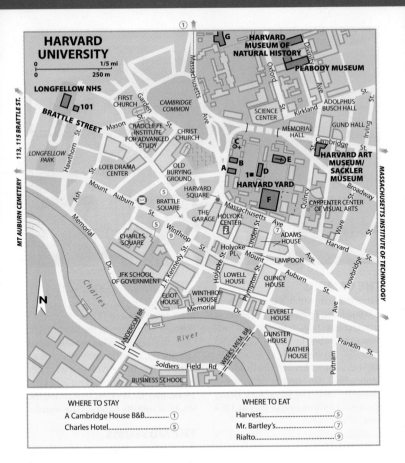

HARVARD UNIVERSITY

0 — 1/5 mi
0 — 250 m

LONGFELLOW NHS
101
BRATTLE STREET

113, 115 BRATTLE ST.

MT AUBURN CEMETERY

FIRST CHURCH
CAMBRIDGE COMMON
RADCLIFFE INSTITUTE FOR ADVANCED STUDY
CHRIST CHURCH

LONGFELLOW PARK

LOEB DRAMA CENTER

OLD BURYING GROUND

HARVARD SQUARE

BRATTLE SQUARE

THE GARAGE
HOLYOKE CENTER

CHARLES SQUARE

JFK SCHOOL OF GOVERNMENT

ELIOT HOUSE
WINTHROP HOUSE

Charles River

BUSINESS SCHOOL

ANDERSON BR

WEEKS MEM BR

Soldiers Field Rd.

G
HARVARD MUSEUM OF NATURAL HISTORY
PEABODY MUSEUM

SCIENCE CENTER
ADOLPHUS BUSCH HALL
MEMORIAL HALL
GUND HALL

C
B
A
E
D
HARVARD YARD
F

HARVARD ART MUSEUM/ SACKLER MUSEUM

CARPENTER CENTER OF VISUAL ARTS

ADAMS HOUSE
LAMPOON
LOWELL HOUSE
QUINCY HOUSE
LEVERETT HOUSE
DUNSTER HOUSE
MATHER HOUSE

MASSACHUSETTS INSTITUTE OF TECHNOLOGY

N

WHERE TO STAY		WHERE TO EAT	
A Cambridge House B&B	①	Harvest	⑤
Charles Hotel	⑤	Mr. Bartley's	⑦
		Rialto	⑨

and works of art brought back from the early-20C Harvard-sponsored exhibitions. The ground floor contains a delightful museum shop and an exhibit that explores the evolution of North American cultures to the present day. The Victorian-style **Oceania** exhibit (*4th floor*) reveals a variety of exquisitely crafted artifacts from the Pacific Rim. *The other museums are accessible from the third-floor gallery.*

Among the numerous minerals, gemstones and meteorites featured in the three galleries of the **Mineralogical and Geological Museum**, do not miss the eye-catching giant gypsum crystals from Mexico.

The world-renowned collection of **Blashka Glass Flowers** occupies the **Botanical Museum's** two galleries. Crafted in Germany by Leopold and Rudolph Blashka between 1886 and 1936, the nearly 3,000 hand-blown glass models accurately represent some 830 species of flowering plants and are prized for their scientific and aesthetic value.

Some of the rare finds on view in the fossil collections of the **Museum of Comparative Zoology** are the 25,000-year-old Harvard mastodon, unearthed in New Jersey; a *Paleosaurus*, one of the oldest fossil dinosaurs (180 million years old); and a *Kronosaurus* (120 million years old), perhaps the largest marine reptile to have ever lived.

In the adjacent galleries, scores of large glass cases enclose specimens of animals from around the globe. Note the impressive North American bird collection of 650 species.

Literary Cambridge

Cambridge developed as a publishing center in the 17C, when the first printing press in the colonies was established here. A Bible in an Indian language, an almanac and the *Bay Psalm Book* were among the first works printed. As the seat of Harvard College, Cambridge became the home of many leading educators and scholars. By the mid-19C the city had developed into a center of progressive thought, attracting a circle of prominent writers, reformers and intellectuals. Among the more famous figures associated with Cambridge are **Henry Wadsworth Longfellow**, Oliver Wendell Holmes, Margaret Fuller and Dorothea Dix.

Cambridge claims more bookstores per capita (nearly 30, in a 6sq mi radius) than any other US city. **Harvard Book Store** (*1265 Massachusetts Ave.; 617-661-1515*) is considered the best of the big independents. Homey **Lorem Ipsum Books** (*1299 Cambridge St.; 617-497-7669*) deals mostly in used books. . **MIT Coop** (*3 Cambridge Center, Main St.; 617-499-3200*), heavy on scientific tomes, stocks more than 125,000 textbooks, while the **Globe Corner Bookstore** (*90 Mt. Auburn St.; 617-497-6277*) specializes in travel literature.

Art Museum/ Sackler Museum★

485 Broadway. ♿☉Open Tue–Sat 10am–5pm. ☉Closed all national holidays. ☞$9 (Harvard students free with one guest). 617-495-9400. www.artmuseums.harvard.edu.

The Quincy Street building that formerly housed Harvard's Fogg Art Museum and Busch-Reisinger Museum is closed for a major renovation (in collaboration with Renzo Piano).

During this period, the Sackler has been re-installed with the finest works representing all three museums. This dramatic post-Modern building, designed by James Stirling (1985) is currently exhibiting work that spans the Middle Ages to the present, including Italian Renaissance paintings, works by the Expressionists, and Ancient, Near Eastern and Far Eastern Art.

HISTORIC CAMBRIDGE★
Brattle Street★

Loyalists to the British Crown, wealthy Tories built homes here in the 18C, thus the street's former name, Tory Row. The stately residences now lining Brattle Street date primarily from the 19C. Note **no. 101** (Hastings House) and **nos. 113 and 115** (these two structures belonged to Longfellow's daughters).

Longfellow National Historic Site★

105 Brattle St. ☞Visit by guided tour only (1hr). ☉Open Jun–Oct Wed–Sun 9.30am–4.30pm. ☉Closed major holidays. ☞Free. 617-876-4491. www.nps.gov/long.

This Georgian dwelling, built in 1759 by the Loyalist John Vassall, served as the headquarters of General Washington during the siege of Boston.

In the 19C **Henry Wadsworth Longfellow** lived in the house between 1837 and 1882, the period during which he wrote *Evangeline* (1847) and *The Song of Hiawatha* (1855).

Today the house contains many of the Longfellows' original furnishings, including 10,000 books, artworks by such noted painters as Gilbert Stuart and Albert Bierstadt, and in the poet's study, a chair crafted from the wood of the "spreading chestnut tree," made famous by Longfellow's *The Village Blacksmith* (1841). A small garden graces the rear of the house.

MASSACHUSETTS INSTITUTE OF TECHNOLOGY★

Ⓣ Kendall Center/MIT. Campus borders the Charles River along Memorial Dr. and Massachusetts Ave. 617-253-1000. www.mit.edu.

One of the nation's premier science and research universities, Massachusetts Institute of Technology (MIT), overlooks the Charles River. Inviting green spaces, broad concrete plazas and vast recreational fields interweave with a variety of architecturally styled buildings, from Neoclassical to post-Modern.

The school was established as the Massachusetts Institute of Technology in 1861 by **William Barton Rogers**, a natural scientist who stressed the practical application of knowledge as the institute's principal goal. Guided through its early years by Rogers, MIT continued to pursue its original objective in the 20C and is today a leader in modern research and development, with schools of Engineering, Science, Architecture and Planning, Management, and Humanities and Social Science. The international character of the institute is reflected in its enrollment of some 10,000 students from 50 states and 100 foreign countries.

East Campus
To the right of Massachusetts Ave., arriving from Harvard Bridge.
A low dome tops the **Rogers Building** (*77 Massachusetts Ave.*), where a visitor center stocks free maps of the campus. Next door at the **Hart Nautical Gallery**, part of the MIT Museum, you can view more than 40 ship models dating from the late 19C through the 20C (*55 Massachusetts Ave.; &open year-round daily 10am–5pm; 617-253-5942; www.mit. edu/museum*).

Contemporary art is displayed in the **List Visual Arts Center** on the main floor of the Wiesner Building, a Postmodern structure by MIT graduate I.M. Pei. The three galleries hold temporary exhibits curated with an eye toward aesthetic experimentation and political engagement (*20 Ames St.; &open Sept–Jun Tue, Wed, Fri, Sat, and Sun noon–6pm, Thu until 8pm; closed major holidays; $5 contribution suggested; 617-253-4680; www.listart.mit.edu*).

Between the Hayden Memorial Library and the Earth Sciences Center looms Alexander Calder's stabile *LaGrande Voile (The Big Sail)* (1965). Nearby stands *Transparent Horizon* (1975), a black steel sculpture by Louise Nevelson.

Farther north on Massachusetts Avenue (*no. 265*), the **MIT Museum** is a funhouse of eye-catching, mind-boggling art (&open year-round daily 10am–5pm; Jul–Aug, Thu 10am–7pm. closed major holidays; $8.50; 617-253-5927; www.mit.edu/museum). Defying the truism that art and science don't mix, permanent exhibits include an array of stop-motion photographs, mobiles based on geometric principles, kinetic sculptures and **holograms.**

West Campus
To the left of Massachusetts Ave., arriving from Harvard Bridge.
The modern Student Center houses the **Tech Co-op**, the student union and restaurants. **Kresge Auditorium★** and the **MIT Chapel★** were designed by **Eero Saarinen** in 1956. The interfaith chapel, a cylindrical brick structure, is topped with an aluminum sculpture by Theodore Roszak.

EXCURSIONS
Mount Auburn Cemetery★
580 Mt. Auburn St. Open May–Sept daily 8am-7pm; Oct–Apr daily 8am–5pm. 617-547-7105. www.mountauburn.org.
The nation's first garden cemetery (1831), Mt. Auburn is the final resting place of Amy Lowell, Mary Baker Eddy and Henry Wadsworth Longfellow. Many of the tombstones are lavish and sculptural; others are heart-breakingly simple, like the headstone that reads simply 'Baby." The landscaped grounds are especially lovely in spring and fall. A variety of maps and information is available at the entrance gate, where you can also rent or buy walking and driving audio tours (*additional charge*).

Lexington★★
9.5mi northwest of Cambridge.

Concord★★
15mi northwest of Cambridge.

&*See CONCORD AND LEXINGTON.*

ADDRESSES

🛏️ STAY

$$$$$ Charles Hotel – *One Bennett St.* 📞*617-864-1200 or 800-882-1818.* *www.charleshotel.com. 294 rooms.* Shaker-style furnishings and quilts blend with modern blond-wood fixtures and mirror TVs at this contemporary luxury hotel, an understated oasis in hopping Harvard Square. Amenities include one of the area's best spas and the **Regattabar Jazz Club**, a venue for top local and national jazz acts.

$$$$ Le Meridien Cambridge – *20 Sidney St.* 📞*617-577-0200.* *www.starwoodhotels.com. 210 rooms.* Art on loan from the MIT collection adds edgy style to rooms done up in earthy tones of copper, moss and maize. Earth-friendly touch: guests have the option of foregoing daily room cleaning in exchange for a $5 voucher each day. Located at the edge of the MIT campus, the hotel is a T stop away from Harvard Square and a quick cab ride to Boston. Location and value make this one a top choice for techie business travelers and weekend vacationers.

$$$ A Cambridge House Inn at Porter – *2218 Massachusetts Ave.* 📞*617-491-6300 or 800-232-9989. www.acambridgehouse.com. 15 rooms.* Small touches, like bowls of M&Ms and homemade cookies win over guests at this gracious 1892 Greek Revival inn and adjacent carriage house. This child-friendly B&B is lushly turned out with cherry paneling, Victorian antiques, oriental rugs and canopy beds. Carriage house rooms are smaller, but each has a fireplace.

$$$ A Friendly Inn at Harvard *1673 Cambridge Street, Cambridge, MA.* 📞*617-547-7851. www.afinow.com.* Within minutes of Harvard University and Harvard Square, this good value red-brick house offers free wireless Internet and a discount of 5 percent discount if you settle your bill in cash or by cheque.

🍽️ EAT

$$$$ Rialto – *One Bennett St., in the Charles Hotel. Dinner only.* 📞*617-661-5050. www.rialto-restaurant.com.* **Italian.** Consistently ranked among the Boston area's top restaurants, Rialto serves up epicurean elegance in a snazzy setting. Chef Jody Adams' food derives its inspiration from southern Europe, updated with Boston gourmet panache: Expect savory seafood dishes, pastas, and game prepared with seasonal vegetables and plated with artful precision. Leave room for the luscious coconut semifreddo with roasted pineapple and lime-rum syrup.

$$$ Hungry Mother – *233 Cardinal Medeiros Ave. Dinner only, Tues-Sun.* 📞*617-499-0090. www.hungrymother cambridge.com.* **American.** The most celebrated dish here is shrimp and grits, which reveals chef Barry Maiden's MO: re-inventing Southern dishes with local ingredients and a dollop of creative flare. Cornmeal catfish with dirty rice is another standout. White-washed brick walls add a laid-back vibe. Early bird special alert: dine before 6pm and get discounted movie tickets for shows at Kendall Square Cinema across the street.

$$ Harvest – *44 Brattle St.* 📞*617-868-2255. www.harvestcambridge.com.* **American.** At this beloved Harvard Square landmark, the menu reflects Northeastern bounty, served with a twist. Dinner entrées might include miso-glazed salmon with fermented black bean beurre blanc or roasted halibut in a salt-cured olive sauce. The rack of pork is a perennial favorite, and who can resist sharing a plate of chili-spiced fries with lime-chipotle aioli? Chocolate espresso torte makes a great finale.

GOOD EATS FOR SMALL FRY

Wondering where to take the kids for a quick bite? For an "indoor clambake" vibe, try the **Summer Shack** in Boston's Back Bay. **Stephanie's on Newbury** *(Newbury St. in Boston)* has cozy booths and updated comfort food In Cambridge, the top choice for kids is **Mr. and Mrs. Bartley's Burger Cottage**. You can't go wrong with burgers (or veggie patties), sweet potato fries and cartoon-covered walls.

Cape Ann★★

Salty sea air pervades the fishing villages, coastal estates, and harbors of this rocky peninsula north of Boston. A 32mi road (Rtes. 127 and 127A) rings the periphery of Cape Ann and offers stunning views of the beaches, cliffs and towns that make this area a summertime vacation classic.

A BIT OF HISTORY

The cape was explored in 1604 by Samuel de Champlain, then in 1614 by Capt. John Smith, who mapped and named the area in honor of Queen Anne, wife of James I of England. A small colony was established in 1623 at Gloucester by a group of Englishmen who had come "to praise God and catch fish." Their descendants were the generations of cape-born sailors who have made the region a major fishing center. **Whale-watching cruises** (*see PLANNING YOUR TRIP*) take visitors to the whales' summer feeding grounds.

🚗 DRIVING TOUR

CAPE ANN★★

This 32mi itinerary follows Rtes. 127 and 127A around Cape Ann, passing through quaint fishing villages and offering views of the coast and the ocean. Begin on the southern shore of the cape in Magnolia.

Magnolia

This former fishing village developed into a summer resort in the 19C. Shore Road follows the coastline.

▶ From Magnolia Center, take Hesperus Ave. 1mi east toward Gloucester and follow signs to Hammond Castle.

🧑‍🧑 Hammond Castle Museum

80 Hesperus Ave. 🅿 🕐*Open May–late Jun, Sat and Sun, 10am–4pm; late Jun–Labor Day, daily 10am–4pm.* 🕐*Closed major holidays.* 🎫*$10.*

- 🚹 **Michelin Map:** 581 N 7.
- ℹ **Info:** ℘978-465-6555; www.northofboston.org.
- ▶ **Location:** The towns of Manchester-by-the-Sea, Magnolia, Gloucester and Rockport are located on Cape Ann.
- 🧑‍🧑 **Kids:** Good Harbor Beach is great for kids, and parking is free after 4pm.
- 🕐 **Timing:** A driving tour of Rtes. 127 and 127A offer a great overview of Cape Ann, with plenty of opportunities to stop for a clam roll, an ice cream cone or a cup of chowder. Plan to overnight at one of the local inns, such as Emerson Inn by the Sea (*www.emersoninnbythesea.com;* ℘*800-964-5550*).
- 🅿 **Parking:** Parking isn't a big issue in these seaside communities—unless you're looking for a spot at the beach in summertime. Arrive early to beat the crowds (most beach lots close after they reach capacity). You don't need a car to get to Singing Beach, in Manchester-by-the-Sea; the commuter rail from Boston (*MBTA; www.mbta.com*) has train service to the town; from there, it's a 1mi walk to Singing Beach.
- 🐾 **Don't Miss:** A stroll around Rockport's Bearskin Neck, where old fishing sheds have been converted to shops, galleries and restaurants. For a woodsy walk, try Gloucester's Ravenswood Park, on Rte. 127, which has gentle hiking trails (good for snowshoeing and cross-country skiing in winter.)

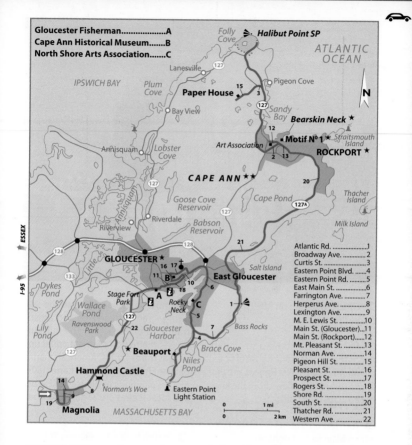

Gloucester Fisherman.................A
Cape Ann Historical Museum.......B
North Shore Arts Association.......C

Atlantic Rd. 1
Broadway Ave. 2
Curtis St. 3
Eastern Point Blvd. 4
Eastern Point Rd. 5
East Main St. 6
Farrington Ave. 7
Herperus Ave. 8
Lexington Ave. 9
M. E. Lewis St. 10
Main St. (Gloucester)...11
Main St. (Rockport).......12
Mt. Pleasant St. 13
Norman Ave. 14
Pigeon Hill St. 15
Pleasant St. 16
Prospect St. 17
Rogers St. 18
Shore Rd. 19
South St. 20
Thatcher Rd. 21
Western Ave. 22

978-283-7673. www.hammond castle.org.

Inspired by castles built in the Middle Ages, this stone castle was completed in 1929 by inventor John Hays Hammond, Jr. Twin towers rise 80ft above terraced gardens, a drawbridge and an enclosed exercise yard that Hammond built for his 18 cats.

Below the opposite towers lie the treacherous rocks of Norman's Woe, the setting for Longfellow's poem *"The Wreck of the Hesperus"* (1842). The interior contains Hammond's collection of Medieval art and furnishings. The **Great Hall★** houses an 8,200-pipe organ that Hammond constructed over a period of 20 years.

◗ Return to Hesperus Ave.; follow it northeast to Rte. 127 (Western Ave.) and turn right toward Gloucester.

Before Gloucester, you'll pass **Stage Fort Park**, site of the settlement established in 1623. Cross the drawbridge that links the cape to the mainland.

To the right is Leonard Craske's statue the **Gloucester Fisherman★ (A)**, a tribute to the thousands who have died at sea, and the Fishermen's Wives Memorial (1999).

Gloucester★

The oldest seaport in the nation, Gloucester is one of the world's leading fishing ports. Its fleet of schooners was immortalized by **Rudyard Kipling** in his novel *Captains Courageous* (1897). Gloucester's fishermen, many of whom are of Portuguese or Italian descent, remain devoted to their traditions, and especially to the annual **Blessing of the Fleet**, which takes place during the last weekend in June on the feast of St. Peter.

Fishing shack, Motif Number 1 in Rockport

© Christian Delbert / Fotolia.com

▶ Enter Gloucester on Rte. 127 (Rogers St.).

Crowning a knoll above a small park stands the austere stone house of noted 19C maritime artist Fitz Henry Lane (*not open to the public*). Views from the knoll sweep across the harbor.

▶ Turn left on Manuel E. Lewis St., left on Main St. and right on Pleasant St.

Cape Ann Historical Museum (B)★
27 Pleasant St. ♿☾*Open year-round except Feb, Tue–Sat 10am–5pm; Sun, 1–4.* ◉$10. ✆*978-283-0455.*
www.capeannhistoricalmuseum.org.

The museum is dedicated to the seafaring, granite quarrying and artistic traditions of Cape Ann. The museum boasts the nation's largest collection of **seascapes** by 19C American marine painter **Fitz Henry (Hugh) Lane** (1804-65). His paintings of Gloucester Harbor and local scenes are admired for their luminous colors.

▶ Return to Rte. 127 (Rogers St.) by Prospect St. You will pass the Portuguese-inspired Our Lady of Good Voyage Church, which is surmounted by two blue cupolas.

▶ Follow Rte. 127 North to E. Main St. and bear right.

North Shore Best Bets

Here's what North Shore insiders (Cape Ann and the coastal communities north of Boston are considered the North Shore) recommend to visitors:

♦ **Singing Beach in Manchester-by-the-Sea**: Take the commuter rail, then take a pleasant 1mi walk to the beach (squeaky sand makes it "sing"). Stop for an ice cream at Cap'n Dusty's.
♦ **Le Grand David and His Own Spectacular Magic Company**: Old-fashioned vaudevillian-style magic show at an historic theater in Beverly.
♦ **Myopia Polo**: Sunday afternoon polo matches are a tradition in Hamilton. From late May–mid-Oct. Bring a picnic.
♦ **Wenham Museum**: This charming little museum will delight small fry.

East Gloucester

Among East Main Street's restaurants and art galleries is the **North Shore Arts Association (C)**, open seasonally (*11 Pirate's Lane*). Nearby, jutting out into the water, **Rocky Neck** has harbored an artists' colony since the 19C.

▶ Follow Eastern Point Rd. to Eastern Point (private). Visitors to Beauport are permitted access via the private road.

Beauport★

75 Eastern Point Blvd. ◆ *Visit by guided tour only (1hr).* ◑ *Open Jun–mid Oct Tue–Sat 10am–5pm (last tour 4pm).* ◑ *Closed major holidays.* ⊛ *$10.* ✆ *978-283-0800. www.historicnewengland.org.* Overlooking Gloucester Harbor, this 40-room summer residence of architect-decorator Henry Davis Sleeper (1878-1934) contains an imaginative mix of period styles and decors.

▶ Return along Eastern Point Blvd. to the entrance of the private road, then turn right onto Farrington Ave. and left onto Atlantic Rd.

The drive east along Atlantic Road offers a good **view** of the coast and, across the water, of Thatcher Island's twin lights.

▶ Follow Atlantic Rd. to Rte. 127A (Thatcher Rd.), which skirts beaches, salt marshes and rocky, wooded areas. Thatcher Rd. becomes South St. as you approach Rockport town.

Rockport★

This tranquil fishing village, which developed as an artists' colony in the 1920s, enjoyed its industrial heyday in the 19C, when granite quarried from its shores was shipped to ports as far away as South America.

Rockport's art galleries, shops (*in the vicinity of Main St.*) and its seaside charm attracts many visitors. Look for the red fishing shed **Motif No. 1★**, named after the many paintings it has inspired. The shed is accessible from **Bearskin Neck★**, a small promontory where old fishing sheds have been converted into shops. On Main Street (*no. 12*), the **Rockport Art Association** exhibits the works of regional artists.

A public pathway passes through private lawns and leads to beaches.

▶ Leave Rockport on Mt. Pleasant St., which turns into Main St. and leads back to Rte. 127 (Railroad Ave.). Just before Pigeon Cove, turn left onto Curtis St., then left onto Pigeon Hill St. Stop for a look at no. 52, the Paper House, a house made almost entirely of newspapers (furnishings, too). Return to Rte. 127; continue north for almost 1mi and turn right on Gott Ave.

Halibut Point State Park

♿ 🅿 ◑ *Open May–Labor Day daily 8am–8pm. Rest of the year daily dawn–dusk.* ⊛ *$2/vehicle.* ✆ *978-546-2997. www.mass.gov/dcr/parks.*
From the parking lots, numerous self-guided trails wind through the woods and past granite quarries to the northern tip of Pigeon Cove.
Vantage points on the rocky shore provide extensive **views★** across Ipswich Bay to the south, and as far as Maine to the north. The visitor center is set in a World War II fire tower.

ADDRESSES

♀/ EAT

$ Woodman's – *121 Main St., Essex; about 6mi northwest of Gloucester via Rte. 133.* ✆ *978-768-6057. www.woodmans.com.* Woodman's doesn't merely serve up fried clams—Lawrence "Chubby" Woodman claims to have *invented* them back in 1914. Today this sprawling clam shack (where you can also order a boiled lobster) is a North Shore fixture. Lines of eager diners snake out the door on a summer weekend (it's a post-beach/post-antiquing favorite). Once inside at the counter, you have your choice of all things clam: friend clams, fried clam strips, award-winning clam chowder, clam cakes and other items, including whole boiled lobster, scallops, corn on the cob and onion rings.

Cape Cod★★★

Shaped like a muscular arm curled in a flex, celebrated Cape Cod is fringed with 300mi of sandy beaches, whitewashed fishing villages, towering dunes, salt marshes, and windswept sea grasses. The product of a fascinating geological and human past, the Cape has been a favorite resort since the development of the automobile.

A BIT OF HISTORY

Cape Cod was named by explorer **Bartholomew Gosnold**, who landed here in 1602 and was impressed by the cod-filled waters surrounding the peninsula. Eighteen years later, the *Mayflower*, en route to its original destination in Virginia, anchored at the present site of Provincetown, and the Pilgrims spent five weeks exploring the region before continuing on to Plymouth.

The earliest permanent settlements were established around 1630 with fishing and farming as the mainstays. In the 18C whaling grew into a principal industry, as vessels sailed out of Barnstable, Truro, Wellfleet and Provincetown for the open sea. The rocky, treacherous shoals, a challenge to even the most expert seamen, posed a great danger to all shipping in these waters. Traces of several of the hundreds of vessels that sank off the Cape before the construction of the Cape Cod Canal are occasionally revealed on the beach during low tide; as the tide rushes in, they are buried by shifting sands.

The Cape Today – In the summer, traffic along the Cape's two main thoroughfares—US-6 and Rte. 28—can slow to a crawl and the strip malls that flank the roads provide little diversion. Despite the encroachment of motels, fast-food outlets, souvenir shops and condominiums, the Cape has managed to preserve pockets of its natural beauty and seafaring charm. Small colonial towns and fishing villages dot the bay side; to the east, miles of windswept dunes are protected in the Cape Cod National Seashore (CCNS). Acres of low-lying

Michelin Map:
581 N-P 9, 10.

Info: 508-362-3225; www.capecodchamber.org.

Location: Rte. 6A, a National Scenic Byway, runs nearly 35mi from Bourne to Orleans: the Upper Cape, the section that's closest to the Sagamore Bridge (and the rest of MA); the Mid-Cape is the part in the middle (Hyannis, Barnstable, Yarmouth, Dennis); the Lower Cape (Harwich, Brewster, Chatham, Orleans); and the Outer Cape (Eastham, Wellfleet, Truro and Provincetown).

Kids: Whale-watching trips out of Provincetown are a good choice for kids, since the trip to see them is only 6mi out to sea (vs. much longer trips from other MA locales). The whales' main feeding grounds are close to P'town.

Timing: Don't try to squeeze in all of the Cape's highlights in one visit. Choose an area, and get to know it well; Cape Cod is best when savored.

Parking: Parking isn't the issue; driving is. The Cape's roadways get crowded in summertime. Ride your bike when you can, or, if you're visiting the Upper Cape, take the Whoosh Trolley, running from Falmouth to Woods Hole.

Don't Miss: A walk along Cape Cod National Seashore, in the steps of Henry David Thoreau. The Wampanoag Powwow is held during the first weekend of July at the Tribal Grounds in Mashpee.

VISITOR INFORMATION

Cape Cod Chamber of Commerce Visitor Center offers additional information on attractions, lodging, dining, shopping and recreation (*Junction, Rtes. 6 & 132, Centerville MA; 508-362-3225 or 888-33-CAPECOD; www.capecodchamber.org*). They also operate a visitor center on Rte. 3 in Plymouth.

GETTING THERE

From **Boston** to **Sagamore Bridge** (*72mi*), take I-93 South to Rte. 3 South, continue east on US-6. From **Providence** to **Sagamore Bridge** (*66mi*), take I-195 South to Rte. 25 East and follow US-6 East across the Sagamore Bridge. International and domestic flights service **Logan International Airport (BOS)** in Boston (617-561-1800 or 800-235-6426; www.massport.com) and **T.F. Green Airport (PVD)** in Warwick, RI, near Providence (401-737-8222; www.pvdairport.com). Major rental-car agencies are located at the airports. Year-round **shuttle** service between Logan Airport, Plymouth and Provincetown is provided by Plymouth & Brockton Street Railway Co. (508-746-0378; www.p-b.com).

The closest Amtrak **train** station is in Boston (800-872-7245; www.amtrak.com). Peter Pan Bus Lines (800-343-9999; www.peterpanbus.com) offers **bus** service from Boston to points on the Cape. **Ferry** service between Boston (Commonwealth Pier, World Trade Center) and Provincetown is provided by the Bay State Cruise Company via excursion boat (*Provincetown II, Jul, Sat only, 3hrs, $46 round trip*) and high-speed ferry, (*Provincetown III, mid-May–mid-Oct daily, 1hr 30min, $85 round-trip*). *Reservations recommended 877-783-3779; www.baystatecruisecompany.com*).

GETTING AROUND

Cape Cod is easily navigated by car or bicycle. Bicycle rentals are available in most Cape towns; cars can be rented in Hyannis.

cranberry bogs and salt marshes, pine and scrub oak forests, and dozens of lakes, ponds and small, gray-shingled "Cape Cod" cottages add to the allure of the sandy landscape.

A large number of craftspeople live on Cape Cod. Local shops feature their handmade creations including glassware, leather goods, candles and pottery. For details, pick up a copy of *Arts & Artisans Trails of Cape Cod* (*www.CapeAndIslandsArtsGuide.com*).

The Islands – The Cape islands, **Martha's Vineyard**, **Nantucket** and the **Elizabeth Islands** lie to the south. Purchased by Englishman Thomas Mayhew in 1642, the islands developed into whaling centers in the 18C and 19C, and remained unspoiled by industry into the 20C. Bordered by magnificent beaches bathed by the warm Gulf Stream waters, the islands today are primarily devoted to tourism.

🚗 DRIVING TOUR

ALONG THE BAY★★
30mi. See Cape Cod map.

Rte. 6A follows the north shore (known as the **Bay Side** because it fronts Cape Cod Bay), passing through tiny villages that were prosperous 19C ports.

▶ Begin at the intersection of US-6 and Rte. 6A; take Rte. 6A east for .5mi.

Pairpoint Glass Works
851 Sandwich Rd. (Rte. 6A), in Sagamore. Glassblowing demonstrations *Mon–Fri 9am–4pm. 800-899-0953. www.pairpoint.com.*

At America's oldest glassworks, visitors may observe skilled glassblowers as they produce and decorate pieces of Pairpoint crystal using traditional 19C methods.

Cycling the Cape

Shining Sea Bikeway (*10.7mi, Skating Ln. in Falmouth to Locust St., Woods Hole*) is Cape Cod's only seashore bike path. Meandering through and along woodlands, marshes, salt ponds and seashore, it's a scenic ride from Falmouth to the ferry dock at Wood's Hole. For informatioin, contact Falmouth Chamber of Commerce (*℘508-548-7611; www.falmouthmass.us*).

Cape Cod Rail Trail (*22mi, Rte. 134 in South Dennis to Le Count Hollow Rd. in South Wellfleet*) follows a paved, former rail bed through the towns of Dennis, Harwich, Brewster, Orleans, Eastham, and Wellfleet. Scenery includes forests and ocean, with occasional views of cranberry bogs. For information, contact Nickerson State Park (*℘508-896-3491; www.mass.gov/dcr/parks/southeast/ccrt*).

Nauset Trail (*1.6mi, Salt Pond Visitor Center to Coast Guard Beach*) winds through the forests and marshlands of Cape Cod National Seashore (CCNS) to the beach. CCNS Headquarters can provide details (*℘508-771-2144; www. nps.gov/caco*). Bicycle trail maps are available at visitor centers in Eastham and Provincetown.

Bike Rentals: Holiday Cycles (*465 Grand Ave., Falmouth Heights; ℘508-540-3549*) offers free parking for the Shining Sea Bikeway with rental. **Little Capistrano Bike Shop** (*30 Salt Pond Rd., US-6, Eastham; ℘508-255-6515; www. capecodbike.com*) rents helmets, car racks and bikes equipped with baby seats as well as the usual array of bicycles. This one's close to the Cape Cod Rail Trail.

▶ From Rte. 6A bear right onto Rte. 130 (Main St.).

Sandwich★

The first settlement on Cape Cod—founded in 1637—Sandwich has long been famous for the manufacture of glass. Today the town is known for its glass museum and picturesque spots such as Shawme Pond, created by the early settlers to power their mills. Clustered around the willow-shaded pond are several 17C sites that evoke the colonial charm of Sandwich; these include the **Hoxie House** and **Dexter Mill**.

In 1825 Boston entrepreneur Deming Jarves chose the village as the site of his Boston and Sandwich Glass Company because the region's vast forests provided the wood needed to fuel the furnaces in which he fired glass. With the help of skilled craftsmen from Europe, Jarves reintroduced the use of the three-part mold that had been used centuries before by the Romans, and developed a process to mass-produce clear, cut glass in a variety of shapes, forms and patterns. The delicate lacy pattern of the glass Jarves made became known

as **Sandwich glass** and brought fame to the town. By 1850, 500 workers were employed at the factory, but labor disputes in 1888 eventually forced the company to shut its doors permanently.

Sandwich Glass Museum★

129 Main St. ♿ 🅿 🕐 *Open Apr–Dec daily 9.30am–5pm. Feb & Mar Wed–Sun 9.30am–4pm.* 🚹 *$6. ℘508-888-0251. www.sandwichglassmuseum.org.*
Located across from the village green, the museum was founded in 1907 and owns an extensive collection of the glass made in Sandwich between 1825 and 1888. Moderately priced when it was produced in the 19C, Sandwich glass is today highly valued by collectors.

Exhibits display a variety of patterns in a wide range of Sandwich glass items, such as candlesticks, tableware and vases. Check out fine examples of early pressed lacy glass and the colorful (canary, blue, green, opalescent) mid-period pattern glassware.

The museum also features a gallery of contemporary art glass and daily hot glass demonstrations (*20 min.*) The museum shop sells Sandwich glass reproductions and American art glass.

♟♟ Heritage Museums and Gardens★

67 Grove St. From the Sandwich town hall, turn left onto Grove St. ✖♿🅿
🕐*Open April–Oct daily 10am–5pm, Wed; 10am-8pm, Jul–Aug.* 🎫*$15.*
📞*508-888-3300. www.heritage museumsandgardens.org.*

This impeccably maintained, 76-acre park setting includes three museums as well as an expansive rhododendron garden. The museum's collections of early-American historical artifacts and folk art are arranged in several buildings designed to harmonize with the landscape. Formerly the estate of horticulturist Charles Dexter, who performed extensive research on rhododendrons in the 1920s and 30s, the plantation is especially lovely from mid-May through mid-June, when the plants are in bloom. The **Automobile Museum**, a replica of the Round Stone Barn constructed by the Shakers at Hancock, contains antique automobiles in mint condition dating from 1899 to the 1950s.

The Cape Cod Baseball League Hall of Fame and exhibit, antique toys, and Native American artifacts are among the intriguing items you'll discover at the **American History Museum**—a re-creation of the Publick House (1783) built by the Continental Army in New Windsor, New York.

A superb collection of folk art fills the **Art Museum**, including primitive portraits, wood carvings, metalwork, glass, scrimshaw, and decoys. ♟♟Children will enjoy riding on the vintage 1906-1912 carousel.

▷ As you continue east on Rte. 6A toward the town of Barnstable, cranberry bogs, then sand dunes and salt marshes become visible. Beyond the dunes lies Sandy Neck, a 7mi strip of land that protects Barnstable Harbor. At one time, whalers boiled down whale blubber in cauldrons that lined the shores of Sandy Neck Beach, now a popular swimming area. Continue east through the towns of Yarmouth Port and Dennis.

Yarmouth Port

The beautiful sea captains' homes on Main Street are reminiscent of Yarmouth's era as a busy port. For a close-up look at the home of an 18C trader, tour the c.1780 **Winslow-Crocker House** (*250 Rte. 6A;* ◀▶*visit by 45min guided tour only;* 🕐*Open Jun–mid Oct 2nd and 4th Sat of the month, 11am–5pm;* 🎫*$4;* 📞*617-994-6661; www.spnea.org*).

Dennis

Musicals, dramas and comedies are presented at the **Cape Playhouse**, a well-known summer theater. From **Scargo Hill Tower** (*from Rte. 6A, turn right after the cemetery, then left onto Scargo Hill Rd.*) there is a **view** that extends from Plymouth to Provincetown.

▷ From Dennis, continue east along Rte. 6A to the town of Brewster.

Brewster★

Extending 8mi along Cape Cod Bay, this charming resort town, first settled in the mid 17 C, has preserved many of the stately residences built by prosperous sea captains in the 19C. The town's eight

The General Store

A common roadside sight on the cape is the general store: typically a two-story wood-framed, gable-roofed house painted white, with a US flag mounted on the front. It's hard not to stop at these inviting treasure troves of Americana, past and present, even just for an ice-cream cone. Foodstuffs, souvenirs, clothing, hardware, stationery, pottery, garden tools, pet supplies, beach necessities, beauty and health items—you name it, the general store's got it. Built as a church in 1852, **The Brewster Store** (*1935 Main St.;* 📞*508-896-3744; www. brewsterstore.com*) is just such a place, a purveyor of general merchandise that's open year-round.

Cranberry Bogs

Half of the nation's **cranberries** come from southeastern Massachusetts and Cape Cod, where natural conditions such as marshy areas and sandy bogs lend themselves to the production of this small red berry. Named by Dutch settlers for the likeness of its flower's stamen to a crane's beak, the cranberry is used to make juice, baked goods and jellies. Widespread cultivation of this fruit was begun in the early 19C, when a local resident, Henry Hall, discovered that the berries thrive best when covered with a layer of sand. Each spring sand was spread over the plants, and the berries were harvested in the fall. The process remains basically unchanged, although it is now mechanized. Festivals are held each fall on the Cape to celebrate the harvest of the cranberry crop from the region's bogs.

Cranberry Bog

© Massachusetts Office of Travel & Tourism

public beaches (*accessible from various points along Main St./Rte. 6A*) are note-worthy for the 2mi garnet-tinted flats that are uncovered at low tide.

Sydenstricker Glass Factory (A)

490 Main St. in Brewster. 🅿 🕐 *Open year-round daily 9am–5pm.* 🕐 *Closed 1 Jan, Thanksgiving Day & 25 Dec.* ✆ *508-385-3272. www.sydenstricker.com.*
The late artist Bill Sydenstricker developed an original technique in glass-making. Two sheets of glass are used to make each item; one of the sheets is decorated, then joined to the second according to the principles used in the enameling process. See examples of this at the gallery, where artisans continue the tradition (Sydenstricker glass is also on display at the Museum of Modern Art in New York).

🧍🧍 Cape Cod Museum of Natural History (B)

869 Main St. 🅿 🕐 *Grounds open year-round daily. Museum open daily Jun–Sept 9.30am–4pm, Apr–May, Wed–Sun 11am–3pm, Oct–Dec Wed–Sun 11am–3pm, Feb–Mar, Thu–Sun 11am–3pm. Closed Jan except for special events.*

🕐 *Closed major holidays.* 💳 *$10.* ✆ *508-896-3867. www.ccmnh.org.*
This interactive learning center appeals to visitors of all ages. Two floors of exhibits feature whales, indigenous birds and coastal change, while a series of aquaria hold several species of crustaceans, mollusks, fish, frogs, turtles, and snakes. Three **nature trails** crisscross the museum's 80-acre property, allowing exploration of Cape Cod landscapes such as salt marshes, cranberry bogs, and a pristine beach. Museum naturalists run popular guided Wednesday Walks to different locales around the Cape like the Monomoy River and Lowell Holly Reservation (*trip dates and locations are listed on the website*).

Nickerson State Park

On Rte. 6A. ⛺ ♿ 🅿 🕐 *Open Apr–Sept daily 8am–8pm.Oct–Mar daily dawn–dusk.* ✆ *508-896-3491. www.mass.gov/dcr.*
If you're looking for a great place to camp on Cape Cod, this is it. Nickerson State Park has 420 campsites, including yurts to rent, and enough outdoor fun to keep even the most energetic family occupied. Set on the former estate

of pioneer railroad builder Roland Nickerson, the woodsy park is dotted with freshwater kettle ponds. These are stocked year-round with trout for catch-and-release fishing.Paddling and swimming are permitted in Flax Pond. An eight-mile bike path connects the park to the 22mi Cape Cod Rail Trail; Cape Cod Bay is within walking or biking distance. Park services include bicycle rentals and a small store.

▶ Follow Rte. 6A east to its end at Orleans.

Orleans

Orleans is the first town on the Cape where you will see ocean beaches. **Nauset Beach**, about 10mi long, protects Nauset Harbor, Pleasant Bay, Orleans and Chatham from the violent storms called nor'easters that pound this section of the coast.

CAPE COD NATIONAL SEA SHORE★★★

In 1961 the eastern coast of Cape Cod, with its fragile dunes, cliffs, marshes and woodlands, became a federally protected area: the Cape Cod National Seashore (CCNS). Since that time bicycle trails, nature trails and dune trails for over-sand vehicles (dune buggies, four-wheel-drive vehicles and jeeps) have been created, allowing visitors to enjoy the magnificent landscape. A visitor center is located at each end of the 27,000-acre seashore, and lifeguard services are available at the CCNS beaches: **Coast Guard Beach**, **Nauset Light Beach**, **Marconi Beach**, **Head of the Meadow Beach**, **Race Point Beach**, and **Herring Cove Beach.**
Note: Lifeguards are posted from late June through August. (*$15/day parking fee is charged at all CCNS beaches; seasonal pass is $45; 508-771-2144; www.nps.gov/caco).*

♟♙ Salt Pond Visitor Center★

On US-6 in Eastham. ♿ 🅿 🕐 *Open year-round daily 9am–4.30pm. Extended summer hours.* 🕐 *Closed 25 Dec.* 508-255-3421. www.nps.gov/caco.

Rangers dispense information regarding seashore trails while exhibits showcase Cape Cod's natural history.

Nauset Marsh Trail
🚶 *1mi. Access near the visitor center.* Beautiful views of the pond and marshes can be seen from the trail.

Marconi Station

The area was named after **Guglielmo Marconi**, the Italian physicist who established the transatlantic wireless station that operated here between 1901 and 1917.
The first formal transmission from this station was a communication between President Theodore Roosevelt and King Edward VII on 19 January 1903. Scattered remnants of the station remain; other sections have been destroyed by shore erosion.

Atlantic White Cedar Swamp Trail
🚶 *1.25mi. The trailhead is located at Marconi Station parking lot.*
The trail reveals various aspects of the vegetation on Cape Cod as it leads through the low brush, where beach grasses prevent erosion, then pass into an area of scrub oaks and pitch pines. The trail continues through a white cedar swamp before opening out onto the road that formerly led to the wireless station.

Nauset Beach
© Jerry Callaghan / iStockphoto

Pilgrim Spring Trail

.5mi from the interpretive shelter near the Pilgrim Heights parking lot.

The trail leads through a section of scrub pines and brush to the site of a spring where the Pilgrims are believed to have first found drinking water in 1620.

Province Lands Visitor Center★

Race Point Rd. outside Provincetown.
Open May–Oct daily 9am–5pm.
508-487-1256. www.nps.gov/caco.
Sign up for a guided nature walk here. The observation deck atop the building provides a lovely **panorama★** of the dunes. Follow the road to **Race Point Beach**, where a two-mile walk leads to **Race Point Lighthouse**.

Beech Forest Trail

1.5mi. Access from Beech Forest parking lot.

The trail passes through a beech forest threatened at certain spots by the advancing dunes.

Provincetown★★

See PROVINCETOWN.

ALONG NANTUCKET SOUND

Rte. 28 runs along the South Shore through Hyannis and Dennis Port, the major shopping zones of the Cape. Extremely commercial and tourist-oriented, with its motels, shops and restaurants, this section of the Cape also has a number of pretty villages, including Chatham, Harwich and Falmouth.

Chatham★

Chatham remains an active fishing port and boasts six wide, sandy beaches *(dogs not allowed on the beaches 1 Apr—15 Sept except seeing-eye animals).*

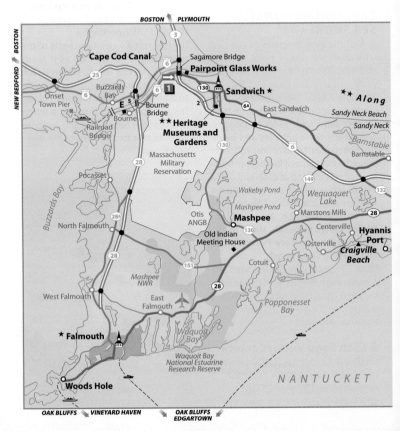

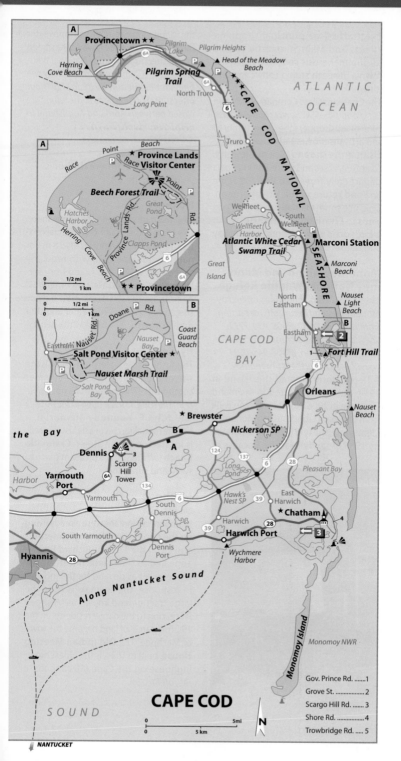

ATLANTIC OCEAN

Provincetown ★★
Pilgrim Lake
Pilgrim Heights
Herring Cove Beach
Pilgrim Spring Trail
Head of the Meadow Beach
Long Point
North Truro

CAPE COD NATIONAL SEASHORE

Truro

A
Beach
Point
Race Point
★ Province Lands Visitor Center
Beech Forest Trail
Hatches Harbor
Great Pond
Province Lands Rd.
Clapps Pond
Herring Cove Beach
★★ Provincetown
0   1/2 mi
0   1 km

Wellfleet
South Wellfleet
Wellfleet Harbor
Atlantic White Cedar Swamp Trail
Marconi Station
Marconi Beach
Great Island
North Eastham
Nauset Light Beach

B
0   1/2 mi
0   1 km
Doane Rd.
Nauset Rd.
Coast Guard Beach
Eastham Nauset Rd.
Nauset Bay
Salt Pond Visitor Center ★
Nauset Marsh Trail
Salt Pond Bay

CAPE COD BAY

Eastham
B
← 2
Fort Hill Trail
1
Orleans
Nauset Beach

★ Brewster
B
A
Nickerson SP
Pleasant Bay
Dennis
Scargo Hill Tower
124 137   6   28
Yarmouth Port
Long Pond
Yarmouth
134
South Dennis
6
Hawk's Nest SP
East Harwich
39
Chatham 4
South Yarmouth
Harwich
28
Harwich Port ← 3
Hyannis
28
Dennis Port
Bass
Wychmere Harbor
the Bay
Harbor

Along Nantucket Sound

SOUND

CAPE COD
0   5mi
0   5 km
N

NANTUCKET

Monomoy Island
Monomoy NWR

Gov. Prince Rd. 1
Grove St. 2
Scargo Hill Rd. 3
Shore Rd. 4
Trowbridge Rd. 5

239

The traffic-free principal shopping streets and Main St. gazebo (venue for summer music concerts) make the town a pleasant stop on any Cape Cod itinerary.

The Chatham Glass Company *(738 Main St.; ℘508-945-5547; www.chathamglass. com)* gives shoppers the opportunity to see artisans blowing glassware before visiting the shop to pick out jewelry, sculpture, vases and more. Fishing boats depart daily from **Fish Pier** *(off Shore Rd.)* and return in the late afternoon. One mile south of Chatham, Shore Road leads to **Chatham Lighthouse**, which affords good **views** of both Pleasant Bay and Nauset Beach.

Monomoy Island and Monomoy National Wildlife Refuge

Seal watching boat tours offered by Monomoy Island Excursions, departing from Harwich Port, ℘508-430-7772; www.monomoysealcruise.com. Wildlife refuge information ℘508-945-0594. www.fws.gov/northeast/monomoy.

A fierce storm created this island in 1958, but it reconnected to mainland Chatham in 2006. Now visitors can walk from Chatham Lighthouse to Monomoy Lighthouse; the two lights are separated by 15mi of sandy beaches. Because of the island's importance as a stopover for birds in the Atlantic Flyway, it has been established as Monomoy National Wildlife Refuge (*open year-round daily one half hour before sunrise to one half hour after sunset*). *Portions of the refuge are closed between April and August due to nesting terns and plovers.*

Harwich Port

Picturesque **Wychmere Harbor** is visible from Rte. 28.

Hyannis

Situated midway along the South Shore, this town is the major commercial center of the Cape. Hyannis is also a major gateway to Cape Cod, with regularly scheduled airline and island ferry services. The **Cape Cod Melody Tent** *(21 W. Main St.; ℘508-775-5630; www.melody tent.com)* features live theater and children's shows.

Hyannis Port

This fashionable waterfront resort is the site of the Kennedy family's summer compound. (*The compound is not visible from the road, nor is it open to the public.*) The **John F. Kennedy Memorial**, a bronze medallion set in a fieldstone wall, is located on Ocean Street. **Craigville Beach** *(off Rte. 28)* is a pleasant place to swim and sunbathe.

Mashpee

On Rte. 130.

Wampanoag Indians were already living on the Cape when the English settlers arrived. In the 17C Rev. Richard Bourne appealed to the Massachusetts legislature to set aside land for the Indians. In response, the lawmakers gave the large tract of land known as Mashpee Plantation to the native residents. In the 19C this parcel of land became the town of Mashpee. The **Old Indian Meeting House**, built in 1684, is the oldest meetinghouse on the Cape (*Meetinghouse Rd., off Rte. 28*).

Hyannis, Cape Cod

© David Noble/Pictures Colour Library

Falmouth★

Despite its development as a tourist town, Falmouth has retained a quaint 19C atmosphere in its village center. Lovely old homes stand near the green.

Woods Hole

Located about 2mi southwest of Falmouth, on the tip of a small peninsula, this former whaling port is a world center for the study of marine life. It's home to the **Woods Hole Oceanographic Institution**, the largest independent marine research laboratory in the US. The institute also maintains the **Ocean Science Exhibit Center** (*15 School St.; ♿☉open May–Oct, Mon–Sat 10am–4.30pm, Nov–Dec, Tues–Fri 10am–4.30pm; ☉closed Easter, 4 July, Thanksgiving and 25 Dec; ☎$2 contribution suggested; ✆508-289-2663; www.whoi.edu*). Tours of the institute are offered in July and August (☞☞1hr; Mon–Fri 10.30am & 1.30pm; reservations required; call ✆508-289-2252*).

The small **Woods Hole Science Aquarium**, used by the National Marine Fisheries Service in its research and open to the public, is home to 140 species of marine life native to the Northeast and Mid-Atlantic waters (*166 Water St., at Albatross St.; ☉open Memorial Day–Labor day daily, 11am–4pm, open rest of year Mon–Fri 11am–4pm; ✆508-495-2001; www.aquarium.nefsc.noaa.gov*).

Cruises – Boats to Martha's Vineyard depart from the Steamship Authority Pier in Woods Hole. ♿*See MARTHA'S VINEYARD.*

CAPE COD CANAL

♿*See Cape Cod map.*
Though the idea of constructing a canal was first considered in 1623 by Miles Standish of the Plymouth Colony, no efforts came to fruition for almost 300 years. Dug between 1909 and 1914, Cape Cod Canal separates Cape Cod from the rest of Massachusetts.

The **Sagamore** and **Bourne bridges** (for vehicles) and a railroad bridge that resembles London's Tower Bridge link the Cape to the mainland. Canalside paths are popular with fishermen, walkers, cyclists and in-line skaters.

ADDRESSES

⌂STAY

BUDGET

The **Outermost Hostel** (*closed in winter*) is located in Provincetown (*28 Winslow St.; ✆508-487-4378*). **American Youth Hostels** are located in Eastham (*75 Goody Hallet Dr., open mid-June–Labor Day; ☎$25-35/dorms; $128-175 / private rooms; ✆508-255-2785; www.capecod.hiusa.org*) and Truro (*111 N. Pamet Rd.; open late-Jun–early Sept; ☎$29-39/dorms; $125-150/private rooms ✆508-349-3889; www.capecod.hiusa.org*). The Truro hostel is set in a former Coast Guard Station on Cape Cod National Seashore, a 5min walk from the beach.

RESERVATION SERVICES

Bed & Breakfast Cape Cod, ✆800-541-6226 www.bedandbreakfastcapecod.com.

CHATHAM

$$$$$ Wequassett Resort – *2173 Orleans Rd. (Rte. 28). ✆508-432-5400 or 800-225-7125. www.wequassett.com. 114 rooms.* Welcoming guests for more than 50 years, this sprawling upscale resort—with several town house- or cottage-style buildings decorated with pale woods, floral chintz and flower-filled wicker baskets—is an inviting place to escape from the Cape's bustle. The main dining room, contained in a 19C house transported here from nearby Brewster, features floor-to-ceiling windows overlooking Pleasant Bay, and the reception building dates back to c.1740. The property includes a beach, golf course and tennis courts.

SANDWICH

$$$ Belfry Inne & Bistro – *8 Jarves St., ✆508-888-8550. www.belfryinn.com. 23 rooms. Restaurant.* Just off Main Street, this 1902 former church and adjacent "painted lady" rectory have been converted into a dramatically different B&B, with a bistro serving contemporary American fare in the former sanctuary. Six sizable guest rooms in the abbey are stylishly appointed with antiques, two-person whirlpool tubs and gas fireplaces, as well as architectural elements retained from the church: vaulted ceilings, arches, stained-glass windows. Rooms in the Drew House next door are attractive, if more conventional, with floral bedding and vintage bathtub.

$$ Spring Garden Inn Motel – *578 Rte. 6A, East Sandwich.* &866-345-5641. *www.springgarden.com. 5 rooms.* The tidy rooms at this gray-shingled motel aren't large, but the flower-patterned comforters and knotty-pine walls give them a cozy feel. Two of the units are efficiency apartments with kitchenettes, and there's also a two-room suite with a sleep sofa in the sitting room. But the best feature is around the back, where the lush green yard, dotted with hammocks, swings and picnic tables, overlooks acres and acres.

♈/EAT

$ Cap'n Frosty's – *219 Main St.* (Rte. 6A), *Dennis. Open Apr–Sept.* &508-385-8548. *www.captainfrosty.com.* **Seafood.** Fried seafood is a Cape specialty, and this Dennis clam shack has been drawing crowds for crispy-battered clams, fish, scallops, and other creatures of the deep since the mid 1970s. Place your order at the counter, then hunt for a seat at one of the Formica-topped tables in the bare-bones dining room. And of course there's ice cream for dessert.

$$$ Cape Sea Grille – *31 Sea St., Harwich Port. Dinner only. Closed mid-Dec–mid-Apr.* &508-432-4745. *www.capeseagrille.com.* **Seafood.** Definitely worth a detour to Harwich Port. Filling an old sea captain's house, the dining rooms—with white tablecloths and captain's chairs—are not particularly spacious. Better to focus on the food: seafood paella with clams, shrimp and chorizo; a crispy seafood piccata with capers and olives; or halibut in an Asian-inspired coconut milk sauce. The warm chocolate truffle cake is a decadent finale.

TAKING A BREAK

Pie in the Sky Bakery – *10 Water St., Woods Hole, MA; next to the post office. Open 5am–10pm most days.* &508-540-5475. www.woodshole.com/pie. Located at the end of the Shining Sea Bike Path and adjacent to the Martha's Vineyard ferry terminal, this is the go-to spot for croissants, pies, cookies, popovers and breads, all made from scratch. There's free Wi-Fi, too.

RECREATION

Saltwater and freshwater **beaches** are located throughout Cape Cod. Waters on the Atlantic Ocean are cooler than waters along the south shore, and unlike the calmer waters of Cape Cod Bay, the ocean has a strong undertow. A parking fee (≈$10–15) is charged at public beaches in the summer. **Bicycle** trails abound on the Cape (🚴*see Cycling the Cape sidebar*). Public **golf** courses are located in Brewster, Falmouth, Dennis and Mashpee. Along the eastern peninsula you'll find excellent opportunities for **bird-watching**. Other outdoor activities include walking the nature trails along the national seashore, sailing, sea-kayaking, deep-sea fishing, and whale-watching. For old-fashioned fun, you can't beat the **Wellfleet Drive-In**, a drive-in movie theater by night, and the Cape's biggest flea market by day.

FACTORY TOUR

For a fun, tasty freebie, tour the **Cape Cod Potato Chip Factory** (*100 Breed's Hill Rd;* 🕐*Open weekdays, 9am–5pm;* &*888-881-2447; www.capecod chips.com*) Cape Cod Potato Chips began as the dream of Steve and Lynn Bernard who in 1980 set up shop in a small store front in Hyannis. The big crunch of the kettle cooked chips soon became a local favorite and the business outgrew the shop. The chips are still cooked the old fashioned way, in small kettles that allow monitoring of flavor, texture and quality.

Concord and Lexington★★

The residential community of Lexington has been linked in the minds of most Americans with the small town of Concord since 19 April 1775, when British and colonial troops clashed at Lexington and at Concord, triggering the events that exploded into the American Revolution. The Revolutionary War sites and monuments preserved here allow visitors to retrace, step by step, the incidents that occurred on that day, over 200 years ago, when the British marched from Boston to Lexington and on to Concord. Named in the 17C for the "concord" of peace established between the Indians and the settlers, the refined colonial town of Concord boasts a distinguished literary past, having been the home, in the 19C, of intellectuals and writers such as Ralph Waldo Emerson, Nathaniel Hawthorne, Henry David Thoreau and Bronson Alcott.

A BIT OF HISTORY

The Revolt Begins – Forewarned of the British soldiers' approach by Paul Revere and his riders, 77 minutemen who had spent the night of 18 April at **Buckman Tavern** in Lexington awaiting the enemy, moved toward the **green** where their leader, Captain Parker, advised them: "Stand your ground and don't fire unless fired upon, but if they mean to have a war, let it begin here!" At about five o'clock in the morning, the British began to arrive, and Parker, realizing that his men were greatly outnumbered, gave the order to disperse. He was too late; a shot rang out, and during the skirmish that followed, eight minutemen were killed and ten others wounded. The British commander ordered his men to regroup and march on to Concord. In Concord, the **minutemen**—untrained, poorly equipped farmers, so-called because of their readiness to take up arms to fight the British at a

- ▶ **Population:** Concord 4,874; Lexington 28,974.
- **Michelin Map:** 581 M 8 .
- **Info:** ✆978-459-6150; www.merrimackvalley.org.
- ▷ **Location:** Concord and Lexington are actually two neighboring towns. Many of the attractions you'll want to visit are located along Rte. 2A.
- **Kids**: The Minuteman Bike Path is a fun way to travel through Lexington (the 10.5mi paved, multi-use trail runs from Cambridge to Bedford).
- **Parking:** Most attractions offer on-site parking. Lexington has a big public parking lot off Mass. Ave.
- **Don't Miss:** The terrific 25min multi media show, "The Road to Revolution" at Minute Man National Historic Park, followed by a walk to the Hartwell Tavern. Drumlin Farm in South Lincoln, is a great place for city folk to explore life on a New England farm; see kitchen gardens, livestock and demonstrations.

minute's notice—arrived from nearby villages and observed the British soldiers from a hilltop.

Aware that fires were burning in the town below, and fearful that the British would raze Concord, the patriots descended to the **Old North Bridge**, where they found themselves confronted by the enemy. There, a battle ensued until the British, weary and reduced in numbers, began their retreat to Boston along Battle Road. Snipers firing from the woods added to the day's British casualties; before nightfall, another skirmish between the two forces took place at **Meriam's Corner**.

Old North Bridge, Concord

© Tim Grafft / Massachusetts Office of Travel & Tourism.

CONCORD★★

978-369-3120.
www.concordchamberofcommerce.org.

▲▲ Minute Man National Historical Park★

*Visitor center located off Rte. 2A in Lexington (see LEXINGTON). *978-369-6993. www.nps.gov/mima.*
This park was established to commemorate events that took place on 19 April 1775 along Battle Road (*Rte. 2A between Lexington and Concord*) and in Lexington, Lincoln and Concord. The 1,000-acre park is essentially a contiguous strip of land 4mi long, stretching over the three townships, with additional sections in Concord. A 5.5mi interpretive trail running alongside Battle Road describes the patriots' guerrilla-style attacks on British troops retreating to Bunker Hill.

A replica of the **Old North Bridge★★** marks the place where colonial farmers advanced on the British and fired the "shot heard 'round the world." Emerson immortalized the old "rude bridge" in his poem *Concord Hymn* (1836). (*Brief interpretive talks are held at the North Bridge Apr–Oct, weather permitting.*) Nearby, **Daniel Chester French**'s famous statue of the **Minute Man (1)** honors the patriots who resisted the British at Concord. The **North Bridge Vistor Center** has exhibits detailing the battle and provides information regarding ranger talks and other special programs (*174 Liberty St., Concord; open Apr–Nov daily 9am–5pm; rest of the year daily 11am–3pm; closed 1 Jan & 25 Dec; *978-369-6993; www.nps.gov/mima*).

As you leave, note on the right the **Old Manse**, where Ralph Waldo Emerson, and later Nathaniel Hawthorne, lived (*269 Monument St.; visit by 45min guided tour only; open late May–Oct Tue–Sun 9am–4pm, mid-Feb–May and Nov–Dec, Sat–Sun noon–4pm, closed Jan–mid-Feb; $8; *978-369-3909; www.thetrustees.org*).

Sally Ann Food Shop

*73 Main St., Concord. *978-369-4558, www.sallyannsbakery.com. Takeout only.*
To revive your flagging spirits while touring Concord's sights, stop into this inviting bakery for a quick pick-me-up. The kids will go for the peanut butter cookies (particularly the ones topped with a chocolate kiss), while Mom and Dad might prefer a pecan-studded sticky bun, a sweetly wholesome muffin, or a chocolate-chip cookie. Drinks and sandwiches are also available.

CONCORD

WHERE TO EAT
Sally Ann Food Shop......①

WALDEN POND STATE RES. ▓ DECORDOVA MUSEUM

👥 Concord Museum★

200 Lexington Rd.
♿🅿🕓*Open Mon–Sat 11am–4pm, Sun 1–4pm.* 🕓*Closed holidays.* ⬟*$10.* ☎*978-369-9609. www. concordmuseum.org.*

This collection of artifacts, documents and period rooms surveys Concord's rich history. The on-going exhibit **Why Concord?** traces the town's history and includes the interior of **Emerson's study** and the renowned **Thoreau gallery**. Also on display is one of the lanterns hung in the steeple of Old North Church to signal Paul Revere on 18 April 1775, as well as objects used by Thoreau at Walden Pond. Upstairs, more than 1,500 objects illustrate trends in **American decorative arts** from the 17C to the 19C. Cummings E. Davis, a Concord merchant, amassed the collection in the mid-19C. The museum also hosts temporary exhibits, story hours for children and special events.

Orchard House

399 Lexington Rd. ☞*Visit by guided tour only (45min) Apr–Oct Mon–Sat 10am–4.30pm, Sun 1–4.30pm. Rest of the year times shorter.* ⬟*$9.* ☎*978-369-4118. www.louisamayalcott.org.*

Orchard House was the home of the Alcott family from 1858 to 1877, the period during which Louisa May Alcott wrote her autobiographical novel *Little Women* (1868).

Walden Pond State Reservation★

1.5mi south of Concord center on Rte. 126 (915 Walden St.). ⬟*$5 parking fee.* ☎*978-369-3254; www.mass.gov/dcr/parks/walden.*

Henry David Thoreau built his cabin on the shore of this lake. To reach the cabin site (marked by a cairn), follow the trail signs to a granite post, where the trail turns right (*15min*). There's a replica of the small cabin near the parking lot. Walden Pond is a busy swimming hole in summertime; in winter, there's ice fishing, cross-country skiing and snow-shoeing on trails that circle the pond.

Sleepy Hollow Cemetery

🅿*Bedford St. at Partridge Lane. From Concord center turn right onto Rte. 62. Enter the cemetery through the second*

Freemasonry

Reputedly the world's largest and oldest global fraternal order, Freemasonry had its origins in the stonemason guilds of the late Middle Ages. Its official founding was in England in 1717. Established in the American colonies in the late 1720s, it was embraced by prominent leaders of the Revolutionary period. George Washington is the best-known member of this society. In fact, 14 US presidents have been Masons. Though Freemasonry is not a secret society, as is often believed, it does maintain secrecy concerning its ritual practices, which include the symbolic use of architectural concepts and implements to recall stonemasonry.

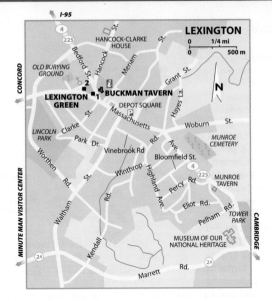

gate on the left and follow signs for *Author's Ridge*.

A short climb from the parking lot leads to **Author's Ridge**, where the Alcotts, Hawthorne, Emerson, Thoreau, Margaret Sydney and others are buried.

EXCURSION
DeCordova Museum and Sculpture Park★★
▶ *51 Sandy Pond Rd., Lincoln.* ✕ ♿ 🅿
🕐*Sculpture park open year-round daily dawn–dusk. Museum open Jul–Sept Tue–Sun 10am–5pm, rest of year Wed–Fri 10am–4pm, Sat–Sun 10am–5pm, and on selected Mon holidays.*
🕐*Closed major holidays.* ✑$14 (museum). ✆781-259-8355. www.decordova.org.

Opened in 1950 on a lush lakeside estate bequeathed by Bostonian Julian de Cordova, this museum is a showcase for contemporary art by Americans, with particular emphasis on New England artists. The permanent collection includes more than 2,000 pieces, augmented by temporary group and individual installations. The 35-acre sculpture park provides a sylvan setting for a rotation of 75 monumental works, made from everything from tree bark to anodized steel by nationally and internationally acclaimed artists. The DeCordova's

annual Art in the Park Festival, held in early June, features the work of more than 100 New England artists.

LEXINGTON★★
▶ *.5mi east of Concord on Rte. 2A.* ✆781-862-2480. www.lexingtonchamber.org.

Minute Man Visitor Center★
Off Rte. 2A in Lexington. ♿ 🅿 🕐*Open Apr–Nov daily 9am–5pm.* ✆978-369-6993. www.nps.gov/mima.

Exhibits and a lively, state-of-the-art multimedia presentation entitled *The Road to Revolution (25min)* introduce visitors to the events of 19 April 1775.

Lexington Green★★
The first confrontation between the British soldiers and the minutemen on 19 April took place in this triangular park. Henry Kitson's statue ***The Minuteman (1)*** represents the leader of the Lexington militia, Captain Parker. Seven of the colonists killed here that day are buried beneath the **Revolutionary Monument (2)**.

Buckman Tavern★
1 Bedford St. 👥*Visit by guided tour only (30min.* 🕐*Open, Apr–Nov daily 10am–4pm.* ✑$7. ✆781-862-5598. www.lexingtonhistory.org.

Transcendentalism

Ralph Waldo Emerson (1803-82), a native of Concord, popularized transcendentalism (a philosophical movement characterized by the belief that God exists in both man and nature) and expressed his philosophical ideas in his *Essays on Nature* (1836), a series of lectures he delivered across the US. Other writers and thinkers, attracted by the liberal ideas and the return-to-nature philosophy inherent in transcendentalism, came to Concord to live near Emerson. Among them was **Henry David Thoreau** (1817-62), who built a cabin in the woods near Walden Pond, where he lived from 1845 to 1847. Thoreau's book *Walden* (1854) recounts the author's experiences during this period.

Nathaniel Hawthorne, Margaret Fuller and others founded Brook Farm, an experimental community near West Roxbury that they envisioned as a retreat from Victorian society and a return to a simple life. **Amos Bronson Alcott**, a proponent of transcendentalism, established his School of Philosophy adjacent to Orchard House, where his daughter **Louisa May Alcott** penned an account of her childhood in *Little Women* (1868 and 1869).

The minutemen gathered here on the evening of 18 April to await the arrival of the British troops. Following the battle between the British and the militia on the green, wounded minutemen were carried to Buckman Tavern for medical care. Restored to its original 18C appearance, the tavern comprises a bar, bedchambers, a ballroom, separate rooms for women, and an attic where, for a few pennies a night, drovers were permitted to sleep.

Deerfield★★

Locally known as "The Street," Deerfield's mile-long main thoroughfare with its limited number of business establishments and many 18C and 19C dwellings, embodies a wealthy early-American farming community. The richness of the surrounding farmlands, threaded by the Deerfield River and nestled below the Pocumtuck Ridge, makes Deerfield's site one of the loveliest in the state. Today the village is known for Historic Deerfield, a collection of restored Colonial and Federal structures open to the public as a museum.

A BIT OF HISTORY

Deerfield was not always the tranquil town it appears to be today. Incorporated in 1673, Deerfield was abandoned two years later after Indians massacred 64 men at Bloody Brook in 1675, and

- ▶ **Population:** 5,125.
- **Michelin Map:** 581 J 8.
- **Info:** ☎413-773-5463; www.franklincc.org.
- **Location:** Check out the day's activity schedule at Hall Tavern Information Center.
- **Kids:** Channing Blake Trail is a child-friendly half-mile meadow walk within the Historic Deerfield property.
- **Timing:** Don't try to see Historic Deerfield in one day; 3–4 houses will likely be more than enough at once. Admission tickets are good for seven consecutive days.
- **Don't Miss:** Historic Deerfield's stunning house museums, and a visit to the Yankee Candle Company (*Rte. 5, S. Deerfield*).

again in 1704 when the village was burned down in a French and Indian attack during Queen Anne's War. A peace treaty signed in 1735 encouraged settlers to return, and during the following century the village grew into one of New England's most prosperous agricultural centers. As a result, many fine houses were built, particularly in the 1740s and 50s. The painstaking renovation of Deerfield's large Colonial and Federal structures began in 1848, the first project of its kind in the US. Of some 55 buildings in Deerfield that pre-date 1825, only two have been moved to the village from other Massachusetts locations. Today the **Brick Church** (1824) and several buildings of **Deerfield Academy**, a prep school founded in 1797, stand on the grassy **common** near the post office, which is a replica of a Puritan meetinghouse. Down the street is the well-appointed 1884 **Deerfield Inn**, a popular lodging and dining spot. Private residences are interwoven with the museum buildings along the Street and side roads.

HISTORIC DEERFIELD★★

Old Main St. ✕♿🅿🕐*Open mid-Apr –Dec daily 9.30am–4.30pm.* 🕐*Closed Thanksgiving Day, 24 & 25 Dec.* 💲*$12.* 📞*413-775-7214. www.historic-deerfield.org.*
Of the more than 60 18C and 19C buildings in Deerfield, a total of 13 structures dating from c.1720 to 1850 are open to the public as house museums. Many of the dwellings, all on their original sites, are topped with gambrel roofs and adorned with richly carved doorways characteristic of the Connecticut Valley style. The interiors are equally luxurious and elegant. More than 25,000 objects dating from 1600 to 1900 are on display. ⓦ*Wear comfortable shoes, since buildings are some distance apart.*
Ashley House – Typical of the dwellings that were built in the Connecticut Valley in the 18C, Ashley House (1730) contains richly carved woodwork and beautiful furnishings. The house was home to Parson Jonathan Ashley, a devoted Tory who, despite threats

from the townspeople, remained loyal to the Crown during the Revolution.
Asa Stebbins House – The Stebbins House (1810), with its distinctive arched doorway, is known for its splendid collection of wall coverings, including 19C French wallpaper illustrating Captain Cook's voyages to the South Seas.
Frary House/Barnard Tavern – This late-18C dwelling was later enlarged to serve as a tavern. Inside is a ballroom with a fiddlers' gallery, and rooms filled with country antiques, pewter and ceramics.
Dwight House – A handsomely carved doorway ornaments the facade of this 1725 dwelling; this feature was typical of Connecticut Valley architecture.
Memorial Hall – This brick building houses the museum of the **Pocumtuck Valley Memorial Association**, a memorial to the Pocumtuck Indians and to the settlers of Deerfield. Exhibits include a large assortment of quilts, household items, furniture, portraits, costumes, military memorabilia, and period rooms.
The **Flynt Center for New England Life** ($7) showcases the decorative arts.

ADDRESSES

🏨 STAY / 🍴EAT

$$$ Deerfield Inn – *81 Old Main St., Deerfield, MA.* 📞*413-774-5587. www.deerfieldinn.com. 24 rooms.*
Built as an inn in 1884 and decorated with period antiques and reproductions, a feeling of comfort and home prevail. Rooms available are king, queen, and twin-sized bed all with private bath with shower. The hotel has a convivial tavern, two pretty living rooms and porch.
For traditional New England fare in a formal setting, the Deerfield Inn will not disappoint.
The spacious **$$$ Champney's** dining room reflects the charm of the Colonial decor found throughout the inn. The seasonal menu may include Vietnamese lettuce wraps, herb-crusted rack of lamb, grilled vegetable lasagna or pan-seared scallops. For dessert, try the Indian pudding served à la mode. Market-driven menu.

Fall River

The site of the famous 1892 trial of Lizzie Borden, who was accused of murdering her parents with an ax (she was ultimately acquitted), Fall River was a major textile center in the 19C and early 20C. During the same period, luxuriant steamships of the Fall River Line linked New York to Boston and carried the wealthy to their summer cottages in Newport. The city was hit hard by the Great Depression, then by the migration of the textile mills to the South and the development of synthetic fibers. Despite these setbacks, the city's textile industry survived. Textiles and clothing are still produced here, and many of the old mill buildings have found new life as factory outlets. In the mid-1960s the state's slain World War II service personnel were commemorated at Fall River's waterfront, initiating what is now a naval museum.

♣♣ BATTLESHIP COVE★

5 Water St. along the waterfront. ✕🕒*Open Apr–Jun 9am–5pm. Jul–Labor Day daily 9am–5.30pm. Rest of Sept–Mar 9am–4.30pm.* 🕒*Closed 1 Jan, Thanksgiving Day & 25 Dec.* 💵*$16.50.* 📞*508-678-1100. www.battleshipcove.com.*
In 1965 the battleship USS *Massachusetts* was moored at Fall River to serve as a permanent memorial to the 13,000 Massachusetts men and women who gave their lives in service to their country during World War II. In recent decades,

▶ **Population:** 88,857.
🚗 **Michelin Map:** 581 M 10.
ℹ **Info:** 📞508-997-1250; www.bristol-county.org.
▶ **Location:** Fall River is 50mi southwest of Boston.
♣♣ **Kids:** The Carousel at Battleship Cove is a delight for small fry (and nostalgic grown-ups).
🕒 **Timing:** A driving tour from New Bedford (👉*see NEW BEFORD*) to Fall River, along I-195, is a good way to see the sights.
👀 **Don't Miss:** Battleship Cove is the top attraction here; if you're interested in the Lizzie Borden story, check out the Lizzie Borden Museum *(92 Second St.; also a B&B)*. Horseneck Beach in Westport is a lovely 3mi stretch of sand, with oceanfront camping.

several other naval ships have joined the *Massachusetts* as exhibits at this outdoor naval museum. Berthed on the waterfront next to State Pier, five vessels are now permanently preserved and open to the public as a means of exploring naval history.

PT Boat 796

The ferocious shark painted on the hull symbolizes the threat these modest-sized boats posed to the enemy. PT boat

Lizzie Borden took an ax ...

No doubt there are people in Fall River who'd rather forget their most infamous resident, **Lizzie Borden**. Lee-Ann Wilber and Donald Wood are not among them! Wilber and Wood are proprietors of the **Lizzie Borden Bed and Breakfast/Museum** *(92 Second St.)*, a Greek Revival house with eight guest rooms, where guests can sleep in the rooms where the murders were committed—the Andrew and Abbey Borden suite, where Lizzie's wealthy father was killed, and the John Morse room, where Lizzie's stepmother met her death. Guests are served a breakfast similar to the one the Bordens might have enjoyed, including jonnycakes *(www.lizzie-borden.com)*.

memorabilia is displayed. Developed in Europe, small, fast PT (Patrol, Torpedo) boats first served the US Navy in World War II. Destroyers, among the fastest ships in the navy, were originally designed to protect the fleet's battleships from enemy torpedo boats. Because of their tactical flexibility, destroyers are now used offensively as well as defensively.

Submarine Lionfish

This World War II submarine carried 20 torpedoes and an 80-member crew. The vessel's sophisticated operating equipment, once considered classified, can be seen in the control room.

USS Joseph P. Kennedy

The ship was named after Joseph, the eldest of the four Kennedy brothers, who was killed on a volunteer mission in World War II. A typical World War II destroyer, the *Kennedy* carried a crew of 275 men.

USS Massachusetts★

Remarkable for its enormous size (longer than two football fields) and the large crew required for its operation (2,300 men), the 46,000ton *Massachusetts* logged 225,000mi in wartime service between 1942 and 1945, and was the first and last US battleship to fire 16-inch shells against the enemy.

Lowell

One of the state's largest cities, Lowell originated as the earliest planned industrial city in the country. The proximity to the Merrimack River was a key factor in its development as a leading 19C producer of textiles. Lowell is also the birthplace of three famous personalities in the arts: painter James Abbott McNeill Whistler *(birthplace/museum at 243 Worthen St., one block from the visitor center),* writer Jack Kerouac and screen star Bette Davis.

A BIT OF HISTORY

First Mill Town – Incorporated as a town in 1826, Lowell quickly rose to prominence as the nation's largest cotton textile producer. Initially the city's labor force consisted of young Yankee women from the farms of New England, but by the mid-19C, the so-called "mill girls" were replaced by Irish and French-Canadian immigrants willing to accept lower wages. Successive waves of newcomers from other European countries followed. The early chapters of America's labor history unfolded in the mills of Lowell, where strikes and social unrest periodically disrupted production.

▶ **Population:** 103,615.
⊙ **Michelin Map:** 581 M 7.
🛈 **Info:** ✆978-459-6150; www.merrimackvalley.org.
▷ **Location:** The city of Lowell is about 30min northwest of Boston.
👫 **Kids:** Children love the colorful spectacle of Butterfly Place.
🕐 **Timing:** Plan your visit around the time of your city canal tour *(must be reserved in advance).* Harold Parker State Forest, in nearby North Andover, is a great, woodsy escape from the city, with swimming holes, hiking and camping.
👁 **Don't Miss:** A ride on a restored vintage trolley around downtown Lowell and the historical park.

A number of factors, including increased competition from Southern mills and the development of steam as an alternative energy source, contributed to the city's decline in the late 19C. The economic crash of 1929 sounded the death knell for Lowell.

Boott Cotton Mills Museum

© Jonathan Parker / National Park Service

Diversification, and an influx of new industry, helped to turn Lowell's economy around. To preserve the city's unique industrial heritage, local and state bodies, in collaboration with the federal government, restored many of Lowell's 19C buildings and its canal system. This successful restoration project has served as a model for similar sights around the US, and has helped Lowell build a base for tourism.

SIGHTS
Lowell National Historical Park★★

246 Market St. Begin your visit at the visitor center at Market Mills to obtain a free map and daily schedule of tours and to reserve a canal tour. ✕ ♿ 🅿
🕐*Visitor center open daily late June–Labor Day, 9am–5.30pm; late Nov–mid-Mar open daily 9am–5pm; rest of year open 9am–5pm daily.* 🕐*Closed 1 Jan, Thanksgiving Day & 25 Dec.* 📞*978-970-5000. www.nps.gov/lowe.*
Established in 1978, the park comprises a group of buildings, canals and walkways scattered throughout Lowell's downtown district. The park **visitor center**, located in a renovated mill complex, offers an introduction to Lowell's history through an award-winning 20min video entitled *Lowell: The Industrial Revolution.* Restored vintage **trolleys** (*free*) run continuously around the downtown area.
Canal tours explore the remarkable man-made water network that channeled the waters of the Pawtucket Falls to the mill turbines (🚢*depart from the visitor center daily late Jun–Labor Day;*

🎟*$8–10; reservations required;* 📞*978-970-5000*).

Boott Cotton Mills Museum★★

♿🕐*Open late Nov–late May daily 9.30am–4.30pm; rest of year, open daily 9.30am–5pm.* 🎟*$6.*
Wedged between the Eastern Canal and the Merrimack River, this imposing industrial complex (1873) houses the park's main exhibit. The first floor **weave room**, equipped with 88 operating power looms (*earplugs provided at entrance*), re-creates the jarring atmos-

---

Urban Adventure: Whitewater-Rafting in Lowell

Whitewater rafting, in the city? Lowell's got it. The same roiling rapids that brought the textile industry to the city are sought out by thrill-seekers (aged 14 and up) in April and May, when dam releases create Class III and IV whitewater. A one-mile stretch of the Concord River goes through the heart of the city; trips include being lifted 17ft through an 1850 lock chamber. The three sets of rapids include "Twisted Sister," "Three Beauties" and "Middlesex Dam[n]." Trips are run on Saturday and Sunday in season, *(April and May)* led by rafting guides from Zoar Outdoors. Call 📞*800-532-7483* or visit *www.zoaroutdoor.com* for more information.

Outdoor Escapes

Whitewater rafting a bit too adventurous for your taste?
Here is a selection of some tamer options:

- **Harold Parker State Forest** in North Andover, offers 3,000-plus acres of wilderness, within a forest dotted with nine ponds. *978-686-3391; www.mass.gov/dcr.*

- **Bradford Ski Area**, near Haverhill, is a favorite small ski area for local families *(night skiing and lessons, too)*. *978-373-0071; www.SkiBradford.com.*

- **Stevens-Coolidge Place** in North Andover, is an historic house museum set on 95 acres. *978-682-3580; www.thetrustees.org.*

- **Weir Hill**, also in North Andover, offers pretty, easy-going hiking, cross-country skiing or snowshoeing along Lake Cochichewick. *978-682-3580; www.thetrustees.org.*

phere of a 1920s textile mill. The second floor features a series of exhibits focused on America's Industrial Revolution, Lowell's history, textile production, and technology and labor relations, including a riveting labor-oriented film *(25min)* entitled *Wheels of Change: The First Century of American Industry*. Recorded oral histories of former mill workers provide poignant testimony to the grim realities of mill life.

ADDITIONAL SIGHTS

Fronting the long facade of the Massachusetts Mills, Eastern Canal Park contains an elegant group of marble monoliths inscribed with quotations from the works of native son and Beat Generation writer **Jack Kerouac** (1922–1969). *A handout locating sights associated with Kerouac is available at the visitor center.*

American Textile History Museum★

491 Dutton St. ✕ & 🅿 🕙*Open year-round Wed–Sun 10am–5pm.* 🕙*Closed 1 Jan, Thanksgiving & 25 Dec.* 🗫$8. *978-441-0400. www.athm.org.*
Housed in a renovated 160,000sq ft brick warehouse, this engaging museum covers 300 years of American textile history. In the main exhibit, "Textile Revolution," visitors try their hand at spinning, weaving and textile design, and discover the role of textiles in firefighters' garb, Olympic athletes' swimsuits, and more.

New England Quilt Museum

18 Shattuck St. & 🕙*Open Tue–Sat 10am–4pm. May–Oct, also open Sun noon–4pm.* 🕙*Closed major holidays.* 🗫$7. *978-452-4207. www.nequilt museum.org.*
This two-level, sunlit gallery showcases traditional and contemporary quilts—some hung like paintings, some thrown over beds—on a rotating basis.

Butterfly Place

120 Tyngsboro Rd., Westford. & 🅿 🕙*Open daily Apr–Aug 10am–5pm; Sept–Oct and mid-Feb–Mar, open daily, 10am–4pm.* 🕙*Closed Dec–mid-Mar, and major holidays.* 🗫$12. *978-392-0955. www.butterflyplace-ma.com.*
This 3,100sq ft glass atrium is filled with up to 500 butterflies, representing as many as 50 species from around the world (and several New England natives). Walk amidst them on a winding pathway, or view the butterflies through the windows of an observation room.

Great Brook Farm State Park

984 Lowell St., Carlisle. 🅿 🕙*Open daylight hours.* 🗫$2. *978-369-6312. www.mass.gov/dcr.*
Holsteins graze on this centuries-old farm. Tour the property *(weekends and Mon holidays, Memorial Day–Columbus Day)*; hike, bike, ski or snowshoe along 20mi of trails.

Marblehead★

Marblehead owes its prosperity as a resort and boating center to its magnificent harbor; this community continues to be one of the East Coast's major yachting capitals. The Old Town historic district, near the harbor, is a charming maze of winding, one-way streets, with antique houses built into the rocky ledges.

A BIT OF HISTORY

Prior to the Revolution, this small fishing port was a flourishing trade center. Marblehead vessels returned home with great wealth, and their owners and captains spent freely in building the Colonial and Georgian houses that line the narrow, winding streets of Old Town. Losses suffered during the war, competition from other ports, and the gale of 1846, which destroyed 10 Marblehead ships and killed 65 men, caused the inhabitants to turn to other industries to earn their living.

The sea became once more the source of prosperity for Marblehead when, in the late 19C and early 20C, the town developed into a resort, with boating as a major attraction. The sailboats and motor yachts that crowd the harbor in season are especially impressive when viewed from **Fort Sewall** (*at the end of Front St.*), **Crocker Park** (*off Front St.*) or the lighthouse on **Marblehead Neck**. Meticulously preserved 18C and 19C structures along **Atlantic Avenue★** and surrounding side streets are crammed with both tony shops and laid-back bars and coffeehouses.

SIGHTS
Jeremiah Lee Mansion★
161 Washington St. 🔍*Visit by guided tour only (50min).* 🕐*Open Jun–Oct Tue –Sat 10am–4pm.* 🎫*$5.* 📞*781-631-1768. www.marbleheadmuseum.org.*

The wood blocks composing the exterior of this dignified 16-room Georgian dwelling, built in 1768 for the successful merchant Col. Jeremiah Lee, have been refinished with a mixture of paint

▸ **Population:** 19,808.
🚗 **Michelin Map:** 581 N 7.
🛈 **Info:** 📞781-639-2863; www.visitmarblehead.com.
▷ **Location:** Geographically, Marblehead is a prominent outcropping of land (the "head") between Boston and Gloucester.
👪 **Kids:** A visit to Devereux Beach *(go early or late)* and a bite to eat at Flynnies at the Beach.
🕐 **Timing:** After popping in to see the massive canvas, *The Spirit of '76* (c.1875), in Abbott Hall (*Washington St., Town Hall*), painted by A.M. Willard, wander along Marblehead's narrow streets, toward the water.
🅿 **Parking:** Most parking is streetside in Marblehead.
🅭 **Don't Miss:** A walk to Fort Sewall, found at the end of Front Street.

and sand to resemble stone. Inside, the immense **entrance hall**, with its grandiose proportions, highly polished mahogany woodwork and English mural wallpapers, makes this house one of the most memorable of the period in New England.

Reproductions of two full-length portraits of the Lees by John Singleton Copley are hung in the hall.

In several rooms, wallpaper hand-painted in the style of the 18C Italian artist Giovanni Pannini depicts classical ruins and fishing scenes. The house contains 18C and 19C furniture, silver, ceramics and textiles.

Across the street, the **Frost Folk Art Gallery** (*no. 170*) displays sculpture and a group of brightly colored primitive seascapes by self-taught Marblehead artist John Frost, formerly a Grand Banks fisherman (🕐*open Jun–Oct Tue–Sat 10am–4pm; Nov–May Tue–Fri 10am–4pm*).

Martha's Vineyard★★

This triangular-shaped island, 6mi south of Cape Cod, is blessed with a stunning landscape. Here, rolling heaths spotted with ponds and lakes give way to forests of oak and pine, seaside cliffs, and broad beaches (both pebble and sand). The towns on the Vineyard are small fishing villages and summer resorts, each with its own history and character.

A BIT OF HISTORY

When Bartholomew Gosnold landed on this island in 1602, he found an abundance of wild grapes growing here. He thus named this land **Martha's Vineyard**, in honor of his daughter Martha. Today, however, wild grapes no longer cover the island. As with the Cape and Nantucket, the population of Martha's Vineyard skyrockets in the summer, bringing a mix of day-trippers and wealthy second-home owners; try to visit off-season if you can.

▶ **Population:** 16,535.
🧭 **Michelin Map:** 581 N, O 10, 11.
🗊 **Info:** ✆508-693-0085; www.mvy.com.
👫 **Kids:** The Flying Horses Carousel (1876).
🕐 **Timing:** Remember this: *up island* means the southwest side while *down island* means the northeast area of the Vineyard.
🅿 **Parking:** Woods Hole has the only car ferry to the island *(reservations are required in high season)*. Tip: skip the car and bring your bike, or rely on the VTA buses to get around (cheap and easy).
👁 **Don't Miss:** A look at the gingerbread cottages of Oak Bluffs; and South Beach (also known as Katama Beach), south of Edgartown.

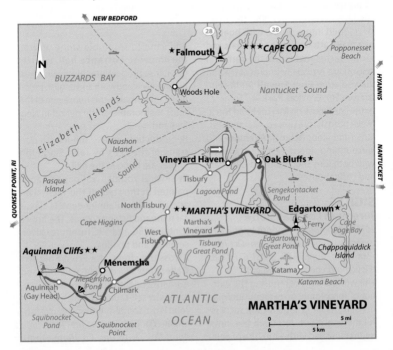

MARTHA'S VINEYARD

VISITOR INFORMATION

Martha's Vineyard Chamber of Commerce, located on Beach Road, provides maps and information (*508-693-0085; www.mvy.com*).

GETTING THERE

Ferries depart from New Bedford, Falmouth, Woods Hole, Hyannis and Nantucket, MA, as well as from New London, CT, and Montauk, Long Island. From **Boston** to **Woods Hole** (*85mi*), take Rte. 3 south to Sagamore Bridge; then take US-6 west to Buzzards Bay, cross the Bourne Bridge and follow Rte. 28 south. From **New York City** to **Woods Hole** (*271mi*), take I-95 north to I-195 east to Rte. 25 east; cross the Bourne Bridge and follow Rte. 28 south. From **Providence** to **Woods Hole** (*83mi*), take I-195 south to Rte. 25 east across the Bourne Bridge, and follow Rte. 28 south. International and domestic flights service **Logan International Airport (BOS)** in Boston (*617-561-1800 or 800-235-6426; www.massport. com*). Service from Boston, Hyannis, Nantucket, New Bedford and Providence is provided by **Cape Air** (*800-352-0714; www.flycapeair.com*). Peter Pan Bus Lines (*800-343-9999; www.peterpanbus.com*); operates **buses** from Boston to the ferries in New Bedford and Woods Hole.

Ferry Service – Several ferry companies service the island. Schedules and fares vary seasonally. In summer reservations are highly recommended. Ferries leaving Woods Hole sail daily year-round and carry both passengers and vehicles. All other ferries carry passengers only and run from spring through fall. The **Steamship Authority** (*508-477-8600; www.islandferry.com*) is the only company offering transportation daily year-round for cars, trucks (*reservations required*), passengers and bikes; departures from Woods Hole to Vineyard Haven and Oak Bluffs (*service to Oak Bluffs mid-May–Sept only*). **Hy-Line Cruises** (*508-778-2600 or 800-492-8082; www.hylinecruises. com*) offers high-speed ferries, and a seasonal traditional ferry (*late May–mid-Oct*) from Hyannis to Oak Bluffs. Hy-Line also runs between Oak Bluffs and Nantucket, mid-June–mid-Sept. **New England FastFerry Co. / Seastreak** connects New Bedford to Vineyard Haven and Oak Bluffs in just one hour (*May–Oct; 800-262-8743; www.nefastferry.com*). The Falmouth to Oak Bluffs route is run by the **Island Queen** (*May–mid-Oct, 25min; 508-548-4800; www.islandqueen.com*).

GETTING AROUND

Streets are often congested and parking may be difficult (*especially in Jul & Aug*). Getting around on foot or by bicycle is easy in the main towns. An island-wide **bus** service links island towns (*limited service off-season; 508-693-9440; www.vineyardtransit. com*). Bicycle rentals in Vineyard Haven, Oak Bluff and Edgartown.

SIGHTS

Vineyard Haven

Ferries arrive at and depart from this upscale community. Shops and eateries border Main Street.

Oak Bluffs★

In the 1830s, the Methodists of Edgartown began to meet regularly in an oak grove at the northern end of town. Each summer the group attracted a larger number of followers who spent three

Mmmmarvelous

Many of the Vineyard's Best Bets begin with the letter "m." There's the **merry-go-round** (Flying Horses Carousel), in Oak Bluffs; the Farmer's **Market** in West Tisbury; and **Menemsha**, a tiny fishing village that's a beloved subject of photographers. Finally, there's **Mad Martha's**, the ice cream emporium.

Aquinnah Cliffs

© Nick Tzolov / iStockphoto

months in a tent camp situated a short distance from the place where religious services were held.

By the 1850s more than 12,000 persons were attending the annual services at Cottage City (as the encampment came to be known), and by the end of the 19C the city had been renamed Oak Bluffs for the oak grove where the first revival meetings were held. At about the same time, small wooden cottages were built to replace the tents that stood near the tabernacle, the center of religious worship.

Trinity Park and Gingerbread Cottages★

Leave the car near the harbor and follow Central Ave. to Cottage City.
Small ornate Victorian "gingerbread" houses, colorfully painted and deco-

rated with lacy wooden trim resembling cake frosting, ring the tabernacle, a beautiful example of ironwork architecture.

Edgartown★

Most of tony Edgartown's large, handsome dwellings were built in the 1820s and 30s when the town was an important whaling center. A number of these houses line North Water Street and face Edgartown Harbor, once dominated by a fleet of whaling vessels and now filled with modern pleasure craft.

Opposite Edgartown, **Chappaquiddick Island** has private houses and unspoiled natural areas sheltered by thick woodlands. The ferry whose name is *On Time*, an ironic reference to its irregular schedule, provides service between Edgartown and Chappaquiddick.

Aquinnah Cliffs★★

Located at the western tip of the Vineyard, these 60ft cliffs are composed of striated layers of clay, appearing as heathery stripes of blue, tan, gray, red, white, and orange. Dating back 100 million years and now designated a National Historic Landmark, the cliffs contain fossils of prehistoric camels, wild horses and ancient whales. Today Aquinnah's Native American residents use the clay to make decorative pottery, for sale at crafts stores lining the short

Casual Bites

Martha's Vineyard is known for fine dining, but sometimes you want hearty, not fancy, cuisine. Try these: The **Newes from America**, the pub at the Kelley House in Edgartown, serves the island's best burger. In Vineyard Haven, the **Waterside Market** on Main St. serves a killer lobster roll, and you can also get breakfast all day.

approach to the overlook, from where you can take in a view of the Elizabeth Islands and Norman's Land Island.

ADDRESSES

🏨 STAY

RESERVATION SERVICES
Nantucket & Martha's Vineyard Reservations, ℘508-693-7200; www.mvreservations.com.

A **youth hostel** is located in Vineyard Haven *(525 Edgartown-West Tisbury Rd.; open mid-May–mid-Oct; ⬛$29–$39/dorm, $150–200/private room; ℘508-693-2665; www.capecod.hiusa.org)*. Set up camp in an oak forest at **Martha's Vineyard Family Campground** *(569 Edgartown Rd., Vineyard Haven; ℘508-693-3772; www.campmvfc.com)* in Vineyard Haven *(season runs from late May–mid-Oct; reservations are essential)*.

EDGARTOWN
$$$$$ Charlotte Inn – *27 S. Summer St. ℘508-627-4751. www.charlotteinn.net. 25 rooms. Restaurant.* The white clapboards and black shutters on the exterior of this Edgartown inn may be traditional New England, but inside each of the five buildings, the luxurious decor is pure English manor house. Gilt-framed paintings of nobles and their regal steeds accent the polished antiques and crystal chandeliers, while the staff promise discreet, polished service. And if that's not appealing enough, the inn's restaurant, **The Terrace**, serves excellent contemporary American fare in a candlelit room facing the gardens.

$$$$-$$$$$ Winnetu Oceanside Resort – *31 Dunes Rd. ℘866-335-1133. www.winnetu.com. 133 rooms.* With a variety of accommodations, from town houses to suites, this property appeals to families who may not want to mingle with antiques at local inns! All rooms are a 5–15 minute walk to South Beach. Resort guests enjoy free use of the children's program and fitness center (including some classes, like yoga on the lawn). All this does come with a price tag, but rates plunge during shoulder seasons.

🍽 EAT

EDGARTOWN
$$$ Alchemy – *71 Main St. ℘508-627-9999.* **French.** White walls and white-cloth-topped tables form the backdrop for the colorful French-inspired cuisine at this smartly casual Edgartown bistro. Dinner entrées run from cornmeal-dusted soft shell crabs and lemon risotto to grilled hanger steak paired with cauliflower gratin. The lighter bar menu offers Cuban sandwiches, and cottage pie with duck confit.

$$ Seafood Shanty – *31 Dock St., Edgartown. ℘508-627-8622. www.theseafoodshanty.com.* **Seafood.** Its Harbor views, tasty seafood (lobster quesadilla is a standout), reasonable prices and festive vibe make this one a reliable choice.

VINEYARD HAVEN
$ Art Cliff Diner – *39 Beach Rd. Closed Wed. ℘508-693-1224.* **American.** Although the open rafters and old-fashioned checkered tablecloths would steer you to order plain old bacon and eggs or a burger and fries here, this diner's fare shows an innovative edge. Eggs might come in a chorizo frittata, waffles might be pumpkin, and lunch options include grilled eggplant sandwiches and an asparagus-prosciutto salad.

RECREATION

Southern **beaches** are known for their heavy surf, while northern and eastern beaches are more protected. Popular **water sports** include sea-kayaking, swimming and sailing. Boats can be rented in the main island towns; windsurfing equipment rentals are available in Vineyard Haven. Paved **biking** trails are located throughout the island. There are two **golf** courses on the island: Farm Neck Golf Club in Oak Bluffs (℘ *508-693-3057*), and Mink Meadows Golf Course in Vineyard Haven (℘*508-693-0600*). **Felix Neck Wildlife Sanctuary** (℘*508-627-4850*) sponsors guided nature hikes and other programs. **Shopping** and art galleries can be found in Edgartown, Vineyard Haven and Oak Bluffs.

Mohawk Trail★★

The scenic 63mi stretch of Rte. 2 through northwestern Massachusetts, running from Millers Falls to the New York border, is known as the Mohawk Trail. Following an old Indian path along the banks of the Deerfield and Cold rivers, through the Connecticut Valley and into the Berkshire Hills, this trail was used by the Mohawks as an invasion route during the French and Indian War. As the road passes through tiny mountaintop hamlets, sheer river gorges and dense forests, views from the highway and off-road overlooks are spectacular—especially in foliage season.

- **Michelin Map:** 581 I, J 7, 8.
- **Info:** ℘866-743-8127; www.mohawktrail.com.
- **Location:** The Mohawk Trail, a segment of Rte. 2, runs east and west.
- **Kids:** The Freight Yard Restaurant, at **Western Gateway Heritage State Park**, has lots to look at, several TVs tuned to sports events, and pub-style food. Also, Kidspace at MASS MoCA is the place for small fry to create cool art.
- **Timing:** Make it a weekend getaway; take in the museums, hike Mt. Greylock, and stay at the happily hip Porches inn.
- **Don't Miss:** MASS MoCA put North Adams on the map.

🚗 DRIVING TOUR

67 mi.

Greenfield

This agricultural town at the eastern end of the Mohawk Trail is named for its fertile green valley. The revitalized Main Street sports a tiny triangular common and handsome brick buildings housing a variety of shops and restaurants.

▷ Follow Rte. 2. After 6 mi the road rises, affording valley views. Continue to the intersection of the road to Shelburne Falls (13.5 mi after Greenfield).

Shelburne Falls★

This quiet mountain village is located beside the falls of the Deerfield River. Glacial potholes, ground out of granite during the last Ice Age, can be seen on the riverbank near Salmon Falls (*Deerfield Ave.*).

Bridge of Flowers

On the south side of the bridge over the Deerfield River.
Originally used by trolleys, this bridge has been transformed into a 400 ft-long path of flower beds above the Deerfield River.

▷ Return to Rte. 2.

Two miles past Charlemont the road enters **Mohawk Trail State Forest**. At the entrance to the forest stands a statue of an Indian brave titled **Hail to the Sunrise**. This bronze sculpture was created as a memorial to the five Indian tribes that once lived along the Mohawk Trail. The road continues through a mountainous and rugged section of Rte. 2. Between Florida and North Adams there are good views to the north of Mt. Monadnock and Mt. Greylock. From **Whitcomb Summit** (the highest peak on the trail at 2,240ft), the Green Mountains stretch into the distance; from **Western Summit** the Hoosac Valley is visible. A **hairpin curve** offers broad **views** across the Hoosac and Berkshire Valley to the Taconic Range.

▷ Just before North Adams turn right onto Rte. 8 North, then turn left after .5mi.

Natural Bridge State Park★

P ⏱Open Memorial Day–Columbus Day daily 9am–5pm. ⚹$2/car. ☎413-663-6392. www.mass.gov/dcr/.

The white marble natural bridge that gives the park its name rises 60ft above the churning waters of a narrow 475ft-long chasm. Glaciers sculpted and polished this marble, which was formed primarily from seashells deposited about 550 million years ago. During summer months, park interpreters are on hand to explain the natural forces that created the park, and its more recent human history. Wander the quarter-mile walkway that runs above and through the chasm, and a half-mile wooded trail.

Massachusetts Museum of Contemporary Art (MASS MoCA)★★

87 Marshall St., North Adams. On Rte. 8, just north of Rte. 2. ✖&P⏱Open July–Aug daily 10am–6pm. Rest of the year Wed–Mon 11–5pm. ⏱Closed 1 Jan, Thanksgiving Day & 25 Dec. ⚹$15. ☎413-664-4481. www.massmoca.org.

Spread out within the spacious, renovated interiors of a former factory, complete with a clock tower, this sprawling modern art campus provides space for large installations of contemporary art. The museum takes advantage of the intimate courtyards and vast wood-floored rooms of the 19C brick buildings to display works that have gone largely unseen because their size and weight made exhibition impossible. The complex occupies a 13-acre site in downtown North Adams, making it the biggest center for contemporary visual and performing arts in the US to date—indeed, one of the 19 galleries measures the length of a football field (Building 5). Works by such artists as Robert Rauschenberg, Jenny Holzer, Sol LeWitt, Don Gummer, and video artist Tony Oursler visit MASS MoCA from studios and museums around the world.

▶ Return to Rte. 2 West, then 1mi after North Adams center turn left onto Notch Rd. Follow the sign for Mt. Greylock.

Mount Greylock★★

9mi ascent by car. ☎413-499-4262. www.mass.gov/dcr.

Located between the Taconic and Hoosac Ranges, Mt. Greylock (3,491ft) is the highest point in Massachusetts. The mountain was named after chief Grey Lock, whose tribe once hunted on these lands. Near the top, the rustic **Bascom Lodge**, a haven for hikers and nature lovers, offers overnight accommodations, meals (reservations required), workshops, snacks, trail guides, and maps. From the War Memorial Tower at the summit there are magnificent **views★★★** of the entire region, including the Berkshire Valley, the Taconic Range, and also nearby Vermont and New York.

▶ Descend to North Adams and continue on Rte. 2 west.

Williamstown★★

&See WILLIAMSTOWN.

Savoy Mountain State Forest★★

260 Central Shaft Rd., Florida. ⏱Open year-round, 8am–dusk. ⚹$5 fee charged mid-May–Columbus Day. ☎413-663-8469. www.mass.gov/dcr.

One of the jewels of the MA state parks system, Savoy Mountain offers pond fishing and swimming, camping (in an old apple orchard), and magnificent hiking (50mi of trails) with waterfalls, valley views and floating bog islands.

ADDRESSES

🏨 STAY

NORTH ADAMS

$$$ The Porches Inn – 231 River St., North Adams. ☎413-664-0400. www.porches.com. 47 rooms. Paint-by-numbers art and claw-foot bath tubs? Somehow it works, with stunning effect, at The Porches. Fashioned from six 1890s row houses, formerly the houses of mill workers in blue-collar North Adams, the inn sits directly across the street from MASS MoCA.

Nantucket★★★

Lying 28mi south of Cape Cod, Nantucket is a triangular patch of land 14mi long and 3.5mi wide that Herman Melville described in Moby Dick as "a mere hillock and elbow of sand." The flat relief, sandy soil, rounded ponds and tree-studded moors are evidence of the island's glacial origins. The island of Nantucket—an Indian word meaning "distant land"—includes the village of the same name, situated on a magnificent harbor protected by a long, narrow barrier of beach.

A BIT OF HISTORY

The Rise and Fall of Whaling – The history of the island is interwoven with that of its famous port, which was the world capital of the whaling industry in the early 19C. In the 17C the Indians taught the settlers how to harpoon whales that passed close to shore. As hunting depleted the whale population in the Atlantic Ocean, Nantucketers sought their prey in the unexploited waters of the Pacific. For almost 100 years, between 1740 and the 1830s, Nantucket reigned as the preeminent whaling port. Merchants and ship owners grew rich by selling as many as 30,000 barrels a year of precious whale oil in London and other major cities. With their wealth, whalers built the magnificent houses that stand on Main Street near the wharves.

▶ **Population:** 10,142.
⏱ **Michelin Map:** 581 O, P 11.
🛈 **Info:** ✆508-228-1700; www.nantucket chamber.org.
◖ **Location:** 30 miles out to sea, Nantucket is reachable by air or ferry.
👪 **Kids:** Jetties Beach has a snack bar, restrooms and a playground. Also, don't miss the chance to visit the tiny Toy Boat store, where a bubblegum machine dispenses marbles!
🕐 **Timing:** The island is at its most crowded in August. Consider coming either in early June or late fall (typically, the weather is pleasant then).
🅿 **Parking:** Avoid bringing a car to the island, especially in season.
👁 **Don't Miss:** Madaket Beach at sunset (bring a picnic of cooked lobsters or some other treats from the supermarket in Nantucket Town).

Then came the decline. A sandbar stretching across the mouth of Nantucket harbor prohibited the entrance of the deep-draft whaling ships that were being constructed in the early 19C, and the island's whaling industry gradually

Nantucket

© Luan Tran / IStockphoto.com

migrated to the deepwater port of New Bedford. A devastating fire in 1846, the California Gold Rush and the discovery of oil in Pennsylvania, all conspired to bring Nantucket's golden era to a close. Nicknamed "the little gray lady in the sea" by early sailors because of its weathered gray cottages covered with pink roses in the summer, Nantucket was spared the industrialization of the 19C. With its comfortable old houses, wharfside structures and cobblestone streets, Nantucket today reigns as one of the most charming, well-preserved destinations on the East Coast.

Nantucketers – The difficult life led by seamen and their wives, and the Quaker religion many of them practised, contributed to the simple, austere and strong character for which Nantucketers are known. **Peter Foulger**, the grand-

Getting off Nantucket ferry

© Kindra Clineff / Massachusetts Office of Travel & Tourism

father of Benjamin Franklin, and **Maria Mitchell**, the first American woman astronomer, were both from the island of Nantucket.

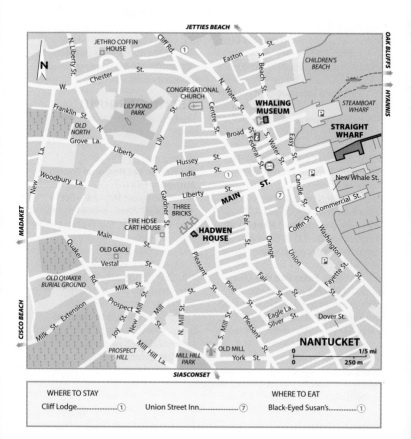

WHERE TO STAY		WHERE TO EAT
Cliff Lodge......................①	Union Street Inn......................⑦	Black-Eyed Susan's................①

VISITOR INFORMATION

Nantucket Island Chamber of Commerce provides maps and information on attractions, accommodations, shopping and recreation (*508-228-1700; www.nantucketchamber.org*). A visitor center is located at 48 Main St.; **Nantucket Visitor Services** office is at 25 Federal St. (*open Mon–Sat 9am–5pm; 508-228-0925*). Two information kiosks operate seasonally on the island.

GETTING THERE

Ferries for Nantucket depart from Hyannis. From **Boston** to **Hyannis** (*76mi*), take Rte. 3 to the Sagamore Bridge and follow US-6 East to Rte. 132 East. From **Providence** to **Hyannis** (*82mi*) take I-195 South to Rte. 25 East to US-6 East; cross the Sagamore Bridge and follow US-6 East to Rte. 132 East. From **New York City** to **Hyannis** (*264mi*) take I-95 North and pick up I-195 South in Providence. International and domestic flights service **Logan International Airport (BOS)** in Boston (*617-561-1800 or 800-235-6426; www.massport.com*). Year-round service from Boston, Hyannis, New Bedford and Providence is provided by **Cape Air** (*800-352-0714; www.flycapeair.com*). Other airlines that offer service from Hyannis (*a 15min flight*) to Nantucket include **Island Airlines** (*800-248-7779; www.islandair.net),* and **Nantucket Airlines** (*800-635-8787; www. nantucketairlines.com*); airfares can vary widely, so check around for the best deal. **Peter Pan Bus Lines** (*800-343-9999; www.peterpanbus. com)* provides service from Boston to the ferry terminals on Cape Cod.
Ferry Service – Three different ferries service the island. Schedules and fares vary seasonally; high-speed boats usually carry passengers only. Reservations are highly recommended in the busy summer season (*Jul–Aug*).

The **Steamship Authority** is the only company offering year-round transportation daily for cars, trucks (*reservations required*), passengers and bikes; departures from Hyannis (*Jan–May*), Woods Hole and Martha's Vineyard (*508-477-8600; www.islandferry.com*). A high-speed ferry operates year-round, making the trip in an hour. The traditional ferry, which is less expensive, operates seasonally (*mid-May–mid-Oct*).
Hy-Line Cruises carry passengers and bikes in season (*May–Oct*); a high-speed ferry runs between Hyannis and Nantucket daily year-round (*no service on 25 Dec; 508-778-2600 or 800-492-8082; www. hylinecruises.com*). Hy-Line also operates inter-island service between Nantucket and Martha's Vineyard.
Freedom Cruise Line offers high-speed ferry service for passengers and bikes, departing from Harwich Port for Nantucket daily (*late May to Oct; 508-432-8999; www.nantucket islandferry.com*).

GETTING AROUND

The best way to get around Nantucket center is on foot or by bicycle, as the streets are often congested and parking may be difficult.
The **Nantucket Regional Transit Authority (NRTA)** operates a shuttle island-wide (*late May–early Oct, daily 7am–11.30pm*), with routes to Madaket, Sconset, the airport, and Surfside and Jetties beaches, and mid-island areas. Order shuttle passes from NRTA (*22 Federal St., Nantucket, MA 02554; 508-228-7025; www. nrtawave.com*). Bicycle and moped rentals are available from Island Bike Co. (*508-228-4070; www.island bike.com*) and Young's Bicycle Shop (*508-228-1151; www.youngs bicycleshop.com*).

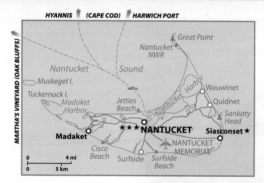

NANTUCKET TOWN★★★

The Nantucket Historical Association sells a combination History Ticket (☞$20), which includes admission to the Whaling Museum and four historic sites: the Hadwen House, Oldest House, Old Mill and the Quaker Meeting House. Purchase tickets at Hadwen House, the Oldest House or at the Whaling Museum (𝒫508-228-1894; www.nha.org).

Hadwen House★

96 Main St. ☞Visit by guided tour only (30min). ⏰Open Memorial Day–Columbus Day daily 10am–5pm.
This impressive dwelling, with its Neoclassical pediment and columns, was built in 1845 for the whale oil merchant William Hadwen. The house and its rich decor bear witness to the life of luxury led by its owner.

Whaling Museum★★

13 Broad St., 508-228-1894.
⏰Open late May–Columbus Day Mon–Sat 10am–5pm, Sun noon–5pm; extended summer hours. Rest of the year, check online calendar for hours at www.nha.org. ☞$20.
Recently renovated, the Whaling Museum is home to a 46ft sperm whale skeleton, hanging from the ceiling. The 1847 factory, where candles were made from whale oil, has been brought back to its authentic glory. Also featured are fine collections of scrimshaw, harpoons, models and paintings. Don't miss a trip to the rooftop observation deck for an overview of Nantucket Harbor.

Lower Main Street
© M. Galvin / Massachusetts Office of Travel & Tourism

Main Street★★★

Shaded by venerable elms, paved with cobblestones and lined with captains' houses and shops, Main Street has preserved its colonial atmosphere despite the upscale boutiques and galleries that fill the storefronts.

Straight Wharf★

This wharf at the eastern end of Main Street and its old fishing sheds have been transformed into modern marinas and shops, art galleries and restaurants. Yachts and other pleasure craft tie up here in the summer.

ADDITIONAL SIGHT
Madaket

A paved bike path leads through the moors to Madaket Beach on the western end of Nantucket Town. Madaket is the perfect place to enjoy a romantic Vineyard sunset.

Nantucket Cottage

© M. Galvin / Nantucket Chamber of Commerce / MOTT

ADDRESSES

🛏 STAY

RESERVATION SERVICES

Nantucket Accommodations, ☎508-228-9559; **Nantucket Concierge**, ☎508-228-8400; www.nantucketconcierge.com.

A **youth hostel** is located 3.5mi from Nantucket ferry wharf (*31 Western Ave.; open late May–mid-Sept; $29–39/dorm, $178/private room;* ☎*508-228-0433 or 888-901-2084; www.capecod.hiusa.org*). Camping is prohibited on the island.

$$$$$ The Wauwinet – *120 Wauwinet Rd. Open late Mar–Oct.* ☎*508-228-0145 or 800-426-8718. www.wauwinet.com. 25 rooms and 5 cottages.* This updated 1850s seaside resort is luxuriously country-chic with Pratesi linens, a private beach and staff who aim to please. The on-site restaurant, **Topper's**, is considered one of the island's best.

$$$$-$$$$$ Union Street Inn – *7 Union St. Closed Jan–Mar.* ☎*508-228-9222 or 800-225-5116. www.unioninn.com. 12 rooms.* This dignified gray-shingled c.1770 house, one block from Main Street, pairs a stately Nantucket ambience with sumptuous appointments. Most rooms have wide-board floors topped with Oriental rugs. Antique four-poster and canopy beds are dressed with Frette linens; six rooms have fireplaces. The full breakfast might include eggs Benedict or apple-cinnamon pancakes; guests can help themselves to coffee, tea and cookies round the clock.

$$$ Cliff Lodge – *9 Cliff Rd.* ☎*508-228-9480. www.clifflodgenantucket.com. 12 rooms.* In this former whaling captain's house, built in the late 1700s, the simple, country-style rooms feature quilt-topped beds, floral wallpapers, and splatter-painted wood floors. The rear-facing bedrooms have glimpses of the harbor, and although some rooms are quite small, the homey space is efficiently designed, with built-in drawers and shelves. Afternoon tea brings cucumber sandwiches and fresh-baked cookies.

🍴 EAT

$$$ Black-Eyed Susan's – *10 India St. Closed Nov–Mar and Sun. Breakfast and dinner only.* ✄ ☎*508-325-0308. www.black-eyedsusans.com.* **American.** It looks like a luncheonette, but this unassuming spot boasts the island's best breakfast; try the sourdough French toast with orange Jack Daniels butter, or the hearty Portuguese scramble with grits.

$$$ Centre Street Bistro – *29 Centre St.* ☎*508-228-8470. www.nantucketbistro.com.* **American.** A casual atmosphere, and moderate prices (at least for Nantucket) make this diminutive bistro worth a stop. The tiny but cheerful dining room is a tight squeeze—try the outdoor patio in good weather. At lunch, there are intriguing salads, perhaps couscous with roasted peppers, olives and feta cheese, as well as updated sandwiches. Dinner follows the same contemporary lines: seared salmon is paired with Asian veggies and wontons, and duck is served with fruited grains.

RECREATION

Swimming is permitted at all island beaches; you can **surf** at South Shore beaches. **Bicycle** paths and **hiking** trails thread the whole island. Specialty **shopping** and supplies can be found in Nantucket Town.

New Bedford★

The whaling capital of the world during the mid-19C, New Bedford is still a working fishing port. Once the anchorage of majestic whaling ships, the wharves are now crowded with modern fishing craft. Cobblestone streets lead to the waterfront, where ships' supplies and antiques are sold. Follow one of these streets up from the waterfront to Johnny Cake Hill to discover memories of New Bedford's illustrious whaling days; well preserved in the Whaling Museum and the Seamen's Bethel, or mariner's chapel. These and other sights are linked together as a national park.

A BIT OF HISTORY

Whaling's Golden Age – New Bedford's 30-year reign as the world capital of the whaling industry began in 1765 when Joseph Rotch, a Nantucketer who had established the whaling industry on his island, came to this fishing village. Rotch's efforts helped launch New Bedford's burgeoning whaling trade. In 1840 Herman Melville described the influence of whaling on New Bedford's economy: "All these brave houses and flowery gardens came from the Atlantic, Pacific and Indian Oceans, one and all they were harpooned and dragged up hither from the bottom of the sea." Factories worked day and night converting sperm-whale oil into candles; whalebone, destined to be transformed into corset stays, umbrellas and walking sticks, was set out along the piers to dry. In the 1850s 80 percent of America's whale ships sailed from this town, and more than 10,000 men—about half of the town's population—participated in whaling.

NEW BEDFORD WHALING NATIONAL HISTORICAL PARK

Created in 1996, the park encompasses a 13-block area adjacent to New Bedford's waterfront and preserves some

- ▶ **Population:** 95,183.
- **Michelin Map:** 581 N 10.
- **Info:** ℘508-997-1250 or 800-288-6263; www.bristol-county.org.
- **Location:** About 60mi south of Boston.
- **Kids:** Climb aboard the replica of the impressive whaleship *Lagoda*.
- **Timing:** Visit the Whaling Museum and the Seamen's Bethel (the c.1832 chapel described in Herman Melville's *Moby Dick)*, and break for lunch at a Portuguese restaurant.
- **Parking:** Elm Street Garage is located one block north of the National Park Visitor Center and two blocks from the Whaling Museum.
- **Don't Miss:** After dark, take in a performance at the Zeiterion Theatre, New Bedford's (c.1923) old-time movie palace (*684 Purchase St.; ℘508-994-2900; www.zeiterion.org*).

70 structures (most of them privately owned) related to the city's whaling heyday. The park visitor center offers maps, guided tours and information (*33 William St.; open year-round daily 9am–5pm; closed 1 Jan, Thanksgiving Day & 25 Dec; ℘508-996-4095; www.nps. gov/nebe*).

New Bedford Whaling Museum★★

18 Johnny Cake Hill. From I-95 Exit 15, follow the signs to downtown New Bedford. Turn right on Elm St., then left on Bethel St. Open May–Sept daily 9am–5pm, Oct–Apr open Tue–Sat 9am–4pm; Sun, 12–4pm (open every 2nd Thu of the month til 8pm, year-round). Closed 1 Jan, Thanksgiving Day & 25 Dec. $14. ℘508-997-0046. www.whalingmuseum.org.

New Bedford Whaling Museum

John Robson/National Park Service

This is the largest museum in America devoted to the history of the American whaling industry. The story of whaling is told through artifacts, paintings, scrimshaw, glassware, textiles, and photography. A highlight is the 89ft half-scale model of the fully rigged whaling bark **Lagoda**. The *Lagoda* made 12 whaling voyages out of New Bedford in the 1800s. Visitors may climb aboard the replica, which is the largest of its kind in the world, to examine the elaborate rigging and the tryworks.

Rotch-Jones-Duff House and Garden Museum★

396 County St. &⟳*Open year-round Mon–Sat 10am–4pm, Sun noon–4pm.* ⟳*Closed Thanksgiving Day & 25 Dec – 1 Jan.* ⊜*$6.* ✆*508-997-1401. www.rjdmuseum.org.*

This Greek Revival mansion (1834) and its sylvan grounds typify the "brave houses and flowery gardens" of New Bedford that Herman Melville immortalized in *Moby Dick*. Sumptuous period rooms and historical exhibits chronicle 150 years of the city's evolution.

ADDRESSES

🛏 STAY

$ Wayfarer Bed and Breakfast – *65 East Clinton St.* ✆*508-994-8881. 3 rooms.* Within walking distance of attractions, this buttercup-yellow, 1907 Colonial is a homey retreat. Amenities include a backyard hot tub and freshly baked breakfast treats.

Newburyport★

This small city at the mouth of the Merrimack River was the home of a large fleet of merchant vessels in the 18C and 19C. The dignified Federal mansions built on High Street by sea captains, and the handsomely-restored Market Square area, evoke Newburyport's heyday as a bustling shipbuilding port and trading center. Newburyport's 19C boatyards produced some of the finest clippers ever to sail the seas. Today, the city's lively waterfront is the setting for many outdoor concerts, and the launching point for whale watching trips and sightseeing cruises.

SIGHTS
High Street★
Ornamented with carved porches and columns, the houses represent the major styles of early American architecture: late Georgian, Federal and Greek

▶ **Population:** 17,552.
⚲ **Michelin Map:** 581 N 7.
🛈 **Info:** ✆978-462-6680; www.newburyportchamber.org.
▷ **Location:** About 40 miles north of Boston, reachable via commuter rail.
🕐 **Timing:** A popular day trip from Boston.
🅿 **Parking:** There is metered parking (*3hr limit*) in the lot off Green St., and all-day parking on the waterfront lot (*Merrimac St.*).
🚫 **Don't Miss:** Exploring downtown on foot, especially during Yankee Homecoming (*late Jul–early Aug*). Plum Island Kayak (✆*978-462-5510; www.plumislandkayak.com*) offers guided sunset paddles journeys.

Revival. **Frog Pond** and **Bartlett Mall**, fronting High Street, provide the setting for the **Court House** (1800) designed by Charles Bulfinch, and later remodeled. At no. 98, the brick **Cushing House** (👁 *visit by guided tour only (1hr);* 🕐 *open Jun–Oct Tue–Fri 10am–4pm, Sat 11am–2pm;* ✆$8; ✆978-462-2681; www. newburyhist.org), built c.1808, was home to three generations of the Cushing family. Caleb Cushing was the first US envoy to China in 1842. Furnishings that Cushing acquired in Asia are exhibited.

Custom House

25 Water St. 🅿🕐*Open May–Dec Tue–Sat 10am–4pm, Sun & Mon holidays noon–4pm, Jan–Apr Sat 10am–4pm, Sun & Mon holidays noon–4pm.* ✆$7. ✆978-462-8681. www.customhouse-maritimemuseum.org.

Designed by Robert Mills, architect of the Washington Monument,, this granite structure once welcomed mariners returning from long sea voyages. Today it contains the **Custom House Maritime Museum**, featuring exhibits on shipbuilding, the Coast Guard and foreign imports.

EXCURSIONS
Plum Island-Parker River National Wildlife Refuge★★

▶ *5 Plum Island Tpk, 3mi south of Newburyport via Water St.* 🅿🕐*Open year-round daily dawn–dusk.* 🕐*Refuge Beach closed Apr–mid-Aug. Refuge closes when parking is at capacity.* ✆$2/pedestrian or cyclist; $5/car. ✆978-465-5753. www.fws.gov/northeast/parkerriver.

This beautiful property is one of the state's premier spots for birding. The southern two-thirds of the island has been designated as a haven for waterfowl in the Atlantic Flyway. Opportunities for bird-watching abound (more than 350 species have been sighted), especially during the spring and fall migrations.

The observation tower at Hellcat Swamp offers **panoramas** of the island's 4,662 acres of dunes, marshlands and beach. Birding hikes are offered frequently.

Crane Beach★

▶ *4.5mi east of Ipswich. From Rte. 1A, take Rte. 133 east toward Essex. Turn left on Northgate Rd. At the end of Northgate Rd., turn right on Argilla Rd. The road ends at Crane Beach.* ✗🕐*Open year-round daily 8am–dusk.* ✆$15–$25/car from Memorial Day–Labor Day; half price after 3pm.* ✆978-356-4354. www.thetrustees.org.

This sandy beach, one of the finest in the state, stretches for more than 4mi along the Atlantic *(avoid it in July, when greenhead flies make their annual appearance).* Beyond the beach, the dunes are covered with a pitch-pine maritime forest and a red-maple swamp. Explore the area by following the **hiking trail** *(access to the right of the parking lot).* 5.5 miles of foot trails skirt the dunes, Ipswich Bay and the Essex River estuary.

ADDRESSES

🛏 STAY

$$$-$$$$ Inn at Castle Hill – *Crane Estate, 280 Argilla Rd., Ipswich, 15mi south of Newburyport.* ✆978-412-2555. www.thetrustees.org/the-inn-at-castle-hill. *10 rooms & suites.* This rambling, shingle-style cottage is the North Shore's most romantic inn. Guest rooms feature views of salt marsh, dunes, Atlantic Ocean or woodlands. Enjoy tea on the veranda and complimentary access to Crane Beach *(see above)*; no TVs or radios intrude on the peace.

TAKING A BREAK

Russell Orchards – *143 Argilla Rd. Ipswich, 15mi south of Newburyport. Open May until the weekend after Thanksgiving Day.* ✆978-356-5366. www.russellorchards.com. En route to Crane Beach, stop by this delightful 125-acre farm. Produce-filled bins and fresh flowers front the large 18C barn. Inside, they sell a variety of farm-grown fruits and vegetables, and other homemade treats. Don't miss a cider donut and a cup of hot or cold apple cider. Pick your own raspberries, strawberries, blackberries and apples in season.

Pioneer Valley★

The fertile Connecticut River Valley was once the haunt of dinosaurs. Today the area is particularly known for its concentration of educational institutions.

A BIT OF GEOGRAPHY

Valley of the Dinosaurs – Of great geological interest are the fine-grained sedimentary rocks containing the tracks of dinosaurs that roamed the Connecticut Valley approximately 200 million years ago. These footprints, pressed into the mud on the valley floor and baked by the sun, were later covered and preserved by additional layers of mud. Eventually, they became layers of sedimentary rocks, primarily sandstone and shale. Today these rocks reveal the fascinating story of the region's prehistoric past. The creatures that once roamed this area were small, about the size of a man, according to the size of their footprints. Dinosaurs did not attain their mammoth size until about 100 million years later. Dinosaur tracks can be seen at the **Pratt Museum** at Amherst College, and in their original formation in Rocky Hill and at various other locations.

A BIT OF HISTORY

Western Boundary – During the 17C the valley was one of the major axes settled by pioneers, who were attracted by its rich soil and plentiful water resources. It remained the western frontier of New England until the 18C, as the colonists did not dare risk crossing the Berkshire Hills and venturing into the Hudson River Valley, the domain of the Dutch.

A Center of Education – More than 60,000 students attend the numerous schools, colleges and the university in the Pioneer Valley. These include the **University of Massachusetts** at Amherst (*www.umass.edu*); **Amherst College** (*www.amherst.edu*), established in 1821; innovative **Hampshire College** (*www.hampshire.edu*); **Smith College** (*www.smith.edu*) at Northamp-

- **Michelin Map:** 581 J, K 7-9.
- **Info:** 800-723-1548; www.valleyvisitor.com.
- **Location:** This region extends from north to south through the center of Massachusetts.
- **Kids:** Visit the Eric Carle Museum of Picture Book Art (*125 West Bay Rd, Amherst; 413-658-1100; www.ericcarlemuseum.org*).
- **Timing:** Beware of spontaneous visits to the five-college area during Parents' Weekends *(fall)* and graduation season, when parents book up local inns and restaurants.
- **Parking:** The towns of Northampton and Amherst have centrally-located parking lots.
- **Don't Miss:** Hiking or driving to the summit of Mt. Holyoke at Skinner State Park. By bicycle, explore the Norwottuck Rail Trail, an 8.5mi bike path on the former Boston and Maine railway bed.
- **Also See:** MOHAWK TRAIL.

ton, one of the most select colleges in the nation for women, founded in 1875; and **Mount Holyoke College** (*www.mtholyoke.edu*), across the river in South Hadley, established in 1837 as the first women's college in the US. The poet **Emily Dickinson** was a student at Mount Holyoke before she settled in Amherst, where she lived the remainder of her reclusive life.

SIGHTS
Deerfield★★
See DEERFIELD.

Quabbin Reservoir★
485 Ware Rd., Belchertown. Access from Rte. 9. 2mi from Belchertown. Drive on Windsor Dam, then follow the signs for

Quabbin Hill ower. ☎413-323-7221.
www.mass.gov/dcr.
Construction of the 28sq mi reservoir
that serves the Boston region was
accomplished by damming the Swift
River and flooding four of the valley
towns. The many islands that stud
Quabbin's vast water reserves (*quabbin*
in the Nipmuck language means "a lot of
water") were created by hilltops jutting
out of the submerged area.
Impressive **views★★** are available
from **Enfield Lookout** and from the
observation tower on Quabbin Hill.
The reservoir offers opportunities for
fishing, hiking, picnicking and scenic
shore drives (⊘*swimming and hunting
prohibited*).

Mount Sugarloaf State Reservation

300 Sugarloaf Rd., S. Deerfield.
☎413-586-8706. www.mass.gov/dcr.
⊘*Open Memorial Day–Labor Day,
dawn to dusk.*
Wind your way to the top of this basalt
ridge for an expansive **view** of the Connecticut River as it meanders through
open farmlands. Small towns fleck the
valley landscape.

Mount Tom State Reservation

125 Reservation Rd., Holyoke. ♿⊘*Open
Memorial Day–Columbus Day Mon–Fri
8am–8pm, weekends 9am–8pm. Rest
of the year daily 8am–4pm.* ⊘*Closed 1
Jan, Thanksgiving Day & 25 Dec.* ☜*$2/
car (summer only).* ☎413-534-1186.
www.mass.gov/dcr.*
Easthampton and Northampton can be
seen in the valley below the access road
to this 2,082-acre recreation area, which
includes some 20mi of hiking trails.
The summit of Mt. Tom commands a
view of the curved arm of the Connecticut River—made famous by Thomas
Cole's painting *The Oxbow* (1836; in
New York City's Metropolitan Museum
of Art)—as well as Northampton and
the Berkshire Hills beyond. The slopes
of Mt. Tom provide a venue for cross-
country skiing in winter.

Northampton★★

Northampton comes as a surprise to
those expecting just another small town.
Like a mini-Cambridge, the town has a
diverse population, a lively vibe, and
a vibrant cultural-and-nightlife scene.
Northampton is known for its enticing
collection of restaurants and for its burgeoning population of gays and lesbians.

Skinner State Park★

*From Rte. 47 follow the signs for the
Summit House.* ⊘*Open Memorial
Day–Labor Day daily, 9am–8pm. Labor
Day–Columbus Day, daily 9am–6pm.
Columbus Day–last Sun in Oct, open
9am–sunset.* ☜*$2/car (weekends &
holidays May–Oct).* ☎413-586-0350.
www.mass.gov/dcr.*
The vantage point from atop Mt.
Holyoke offers panoramic **views** of the
valley. A variety of hiking/snowshoeing
trails lead to the summit and extend on
to Holyoke Range State Park.

ADDRESSES

🛏 STAY

$$$$ Hotel Northampton – *36 King St.*
*☎413-584-3100. www.hotelnorthampton.
com. 106 rooms.* This historic downtown
hotel is a long-time favorite, featuring
up-to-date, spacious rooms, decorated
with period antiques and quality
reproductions. **Wiggins Tavern** on the
ground floor is a cozy hangout.

🍴 EAT

$$ Judie's Restaurant – *51 N. Pleasant St.
Lunch and dinner.* ☎413-253-3491. *www.
judiesrestaurant.com.* A student favorite,
famous for its giant popovers, burgers
and big portions.

$$ Spoleto – *530 Main St. Dinner only.*
*☎413-586-6313. www.spoletorestaurants.
com.* A local institution for upscale Italian
food, served in generous portions. Try
the three-cheese ravioli tossed in vodka-
tomato cream sauce.

$ Atkins Farms Country Market –
1150 West St. ☎413-253-9528. *www.atkins
farms.com.* The go-to place for great takeout. Don't leave without something from
the bakery (say a fresh cider donut?).

Plymouth★★

This attractive town with hilly streets sloping down to the harbor is the site of the first permanent settlement in New England. The long voyage of the *Mayflower*, the hardships the Pilgrims endured and the eventual success of Plymouth Colony form part of the cherished story related in Plymouth's historic monuments and sites.

A BIT OF HISTORY

A Colony off Course – A group of English Puritans known as **Separatists** attempted to reform the Church of England in the 16C. To avoid persecution by the authorities, members of the group emigrated from Scrooby, England, in 1607 to Holland. They remained there until, impressed by favorable accounts of the New World, they decided to emigrate to America. Early in September 1620, 102 passengers, including 35 Separatists, boarded the *Mayflower* at Plymouth, England, and set sail for the Virginia Colony in North America. Diverted north by a storm, the settlers landed two months later on the shores of Cape Cod. They spent five weeks in the region before again setting sail for Virginia.

Detoured a second time by strong winds, the Pilgrims headed for the bay that had been charted six years earlier by Capt. John Smith. It was on the shores of this bay that they established Plymouth Colony.

▶ **Population:** 55,188.
🚴 **Michelin Map:** 581 N 9.
🚩 **Info:** ℘508-747-7533; www.visit-plymouth.com.
◐ **Location:** Plymouth lies about 40mi southeast of Boston off Rte. 3. Plimoth Plantation is located 3mi south of downtown; the *Mayflower II* sits at the Plymouth waterfront.
👥 **Kids:** Lobster Tales offers hands-on lobster excursions (you can pull up traps!) and pirate cruises. (*Town Wharf,* ℘508-746-5342; www.lobster talesinc.com).
🅿 **Parking:** There are several lots in town, including one near the visitor center *(130 Water St.)*.
☺ **Don't Miss:** Plimoth Plantation is the major must-see here.
🚴 **Also See:** CAPE COD.

The First Winter – Harsh weather and a scarcity of food left almost half the colony dead by the end of the first winter. Burials were held at night on **Cole's Hill**, and graves were left unmarked to conceal the settlers' dwindling numbers from the neighboring Wampanoag tribe.

The spring brought hope to the settlement along with a group of Indians who befriended the Pilgrims and taught them how to raise crops, and how to hunt and fish. After the harvest that fall, members of the Plymouth Colony joined with the Indians in a three-day feast, the first American **Thanksgiving celebration**, in gratitude for their blessings. From **Burial Hill**, where an old cemetery contains gravestones dating back to the Plymouth Colony, there are lovely views overlooking the town and out to sea. The **Town Brook**—close to the place where the Pilgrims built their first houses—runs through a lovely public park, **Brewster Gardens**.

Mayflower II

© Massachusetts Office of Travel & Tourism

HISTORIC DISTRICT

Begin at the visitor center (130 Water St; ✕🅿♿🚻🕐*open Jul–Aug daily 8am–8pm; Sept–Nov & Apr–Jun daily 9am–5pm;* 📞*800-872-162; www.visit-plymouth.com).*

Plymouth Rock

© Tim Grafft/Massachusetts Office of Travel & Tourism

👤👤 Mayflower II★★

Berthed at the State Pier, across from 74 Water St. 🕐*Open mid-Mar–Nov daily 9am–5pm.* ✎*$10 (combination ticket with Plimouth Plantation, $29.50).* 📞*508-746-1622. www.plimoth.org.*
The *Mayflower II,* built in England (1957), is a full-scale replica of the ship that carried the Pilgrims to Plymouth in 1620.

👤👤 Plymouth Rock★

On the beach at Water St.
Set at the harbor's edge, this boulder has traditionally been regarded as the stepping stone used by the *Mayflower* passengers when they disembarked. The boulder is sheltered by a multi-columned granite structure. Opposite is **The Pilgrim Mother (1)**, a fountain honoring the women of the *Mayflower*.

Sparrow House (A)

42 Summer St. 🕐*Open daily, Thu–Tue 10am–5pm.* ✎*$2.* 📞*508-747-1240. www.sparrowhouse.com.*
The oldest dwelling (1640) in Plymouth contains 18C furnishings. Locally-made pottery and artwork are on display and available for sale.

Jabez Howland House (B)

33 Sandwich St. 🚶*Visit by guided tour only (1hr).* 🕐*Late May–mid-Oct daily 10am–4.30pm.* ✎*$4.* 📞*508-746-9590.*
This is the only house remaining in Plymouth where Pilgrims are known to have lived.

Pilgrim Hall Museum★

75 Court St. 🅿🕐*Open May–Dec daily 9.30am–4.30pm.* 🕐*Closed 25 Dec.* ✎*$10.* 📞*508-746-1620. www.pilgrimhallmuseum.org.*
Built as a memorial to the Pilgrims and Plymouth Colony, this austere granite structure (1824), designed by Alexander Parris, contains original Pilgrim furnishings and artifacts, including chairs owned by Governors Bradford and Carver; the cradle of Peregrine White, who was born on the *Mayflower*; and Bibles belonging to John Alden and Governor Bradford.

SIGHT
👤👤 Plimoth Plantation★★

137 Warren Ave. ✕♿🅿🕐*Open Apr–late-Nov daily 9am–5pm.* ✎*$25.50 (combination ticket with Mayflower II, $29.50).* 📞*508-746-1622. www.plimoth.org.*
The plantation is a reproduction of the Pilgrims' village as it appeared in 1627. (The spelling "Plimoth" was adopted from **Governor Bradford**'s early journals by the museum curators.) The **Fort/Meetinghouse**, at the entrance to the plantation, offers a good vantage point from which to view the entire village,

Plimoth Plantation

© Tim Grafft / Massachusetts Office of Travel & Tourism

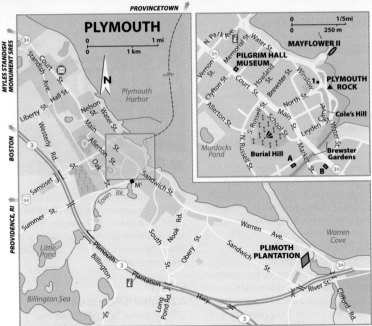

PLYMOUTH

with its neat rows of thatched-roof cottages similar to those inhabited by the Alden, Carver, Bradford and Standish families. Rooms inside the houses are decorated with reproductions of 17C English furnishings. Throughout the village, costumed guides portray specific Pilgrim settlers, chatting with visitors while performing tasks such as gardening, cooking and harvesting crops according to the methods used in the early colony.

There is a path leading to **Hobbamock's Wampanoag Indian Homesite**, where the culture of this Native American group is interpreted by staff members engaged in raising crops, drying food,

weaving, and undertaking other chores traditionally performed by the Wampanoag people. The campsite includes examples of the *wetus*, a domed dwelling once built as shelter by the Wampanoag. Visitors can watch as workers use 17C methods to make handicrafts in the modern **Carriage House Crafts Center**. The walk-through exhibit **Irreconcilable Differences** tells the story of the colony through the perspectives of a *Mayflower* passenger and a Wampanoag sachem.

EXCURSIONS
Myles Standish Monument State Reservation

▶ *In Duxbury, 8mi from Plymouth via Rte. 3A to Crescent St. Turn right and enter through the gate at left.* ⓟ ⓞ*Open mid-Jun–Labor Day daily 8am–8pm.* ☎508-747-5360. *www.mass.gov/dcr.*

Atop a 116ft granite shaft, a 14ft statue of Pilgrim leader Myles Standish overlooks the bay. Visitors can climb the 125 steps up to the observation area to enjoy a **view** of Plymouth, Cape Cod Bay and Provincetown.

Pilgrims' Progress

Every Friday in August and on Thanksgiving Day, Plymouth's modern residents dress up as Pilgrims and take part in a Sabbath procession from up Leyden Street to Burial Hill, where a religious service is held.

Provincetown★★

Extending to the tip of Cape Cod, Provincetown, or "P-town," as it is known to locals, combines elements of a fishing village, artists' colony and resort. During the summer, the arrival of large numbers of tourists, many gay and lesbian, swell the population of the town from 3,000 to 750,000.

A BIT OF HISTORY

Pilgrims and Mooncussers – By the 18C, less than 100 years after the Pilgrims landed on the Cape, Provincetown had grown into the third-largest whaling center after Nantucket and New Bedford. In the mid-19C, 75 wharves could be counted along its shores, and the beaches were covered with fish flakes, or racks for drying fish, and saltworks, wooden structures used to filter salt from seawater. Provincetown vessels recruited seamen in the Azores and Cape Verde Islands, a factor that accounts for the town's large Portuguese population and the traditions they have preserved.

Other Provincetowners found fortune closer to home. Villains known as "mooncussers" erected lights along the shore to lure unwitting ships into dangerous shoals where they ran aground. Mooncussers then boarded the vessels, killed the crew and stole the valuable cargo. The place where these rogues gathered was nicknamed "Helltown" and was cautiously avoided by the village's more respectable citizens.

Provincetown of the Artists – At the beginning of the 20C, Provincetown's wild natural beauty attracted artists and writers to its shores. In 1901 Charles W. Hawthorne founded the **Cape Cod School of Art** in the town, followed 15 years later by the establishment of the **Provincetown Players**, a group of playwrights and actors rebelling against the rigid criteria of the Broadway stage. **Eugene O'Neill**'s career as a playwright was launched at Provincetown in 1916 when his first play, *Bound East for Cardiff*, was produced at the Wharf Theatre.

▶ **Population:** 3,100.
🕹 **Michelin Map:** 581 O 9.
ℹ **Info:** ✆508-362-3225; www.provincetown.com.
◔ **Location:** Provincetown is about 120mi from Boston, at the tip of Cape Cod *(north on Rte. 6).*
👪 **Kids:** With gentler waves than Race Point Beach, Herring Cove Beach is a good pick for families with young children.
🕔 **Timing:** Getting to P-town from Boston can take a long time in traffic *(2.5hrs is a quick trip)*, so stay long enough to make the trip worthwhile.
🅿 **Parking:** The main town lot is located at the western base of MacMillan Pier.
☺ **Don't Miss:** Art's Dune Tours are fun; on a clear day, climb to the top of the Pilgrim Monument and enjoy marvelous views.
🕹 **Also See:** CAPE COD.

At about the same time, the town became a prestigious artists' colony, where writers and dramatists such as O'Neill, John Dos Passos, Sinclair Lewis and Tennessee Williams gathered. Over the ensuing decades, the town has hosted art-world celebrities such as Robert Motherwell and Mark Rothko. Today the numerous galleries along Commercial Street, the **Provincetown Art Association** and the **Provincetown Theater Company** carry out the cultural and artistic traditions so closely associated with the town's character.

ℹ *For a listing of current art shows, consult the free gallery guide available from the visitor center at MacMillan Wharf and from major galleries.*

Tourist Mecca – In the summer, crowds weave in and out of the shops, galleries and eating places that line the narrow streets, especially along **Commercial Street**, the main thoroughfare in

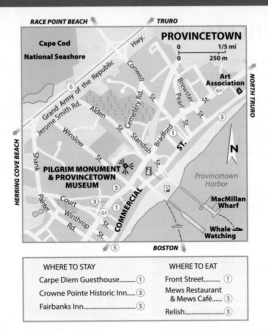

WHERE TO STAY		WHERE TO EAT	
Carpe Diem Guesthouse..........①		Front Street..........①	
Crowne Pointe Historic Inn.....③		Mews Restaurant & Mews Café......③	
Fairbanks Inn...............................⑤		Relish.......................⑤	

town. Visitors and residents alike find the nearby beaches of the **Cape Cod National Seashore** (CCNS)—including **Herring Cove Beach** and **Race Point Beach** (*see Cape Cod map*)—a refreshing contrast to the hustle and bustle. (*In summer, shuttle buses run hourly along Bradford St. and to Herring Cove Beach.*) The **Province Lands Trail** (*7mi*) offers cyclists a challenging, but spectacular ride through forests and dunes with expansive views of the water *for details, contact Cape Cod National Seashore, 508-771-2144; www.nps.gov/caco*).

SIGHTS
MacMillan Wharf
At the end of Standish St.
Public parking lot on the wharf.
Late in the afternoon, fishing boats, announced by the procession of seagulls that greets them, return to the wharf, where their fresh catches are unloaded and shipped to markets in Boston and New York. On the last weekend in June, the **Blessing of the Fleet**, a colorful and impressive Portuguese celebration, takes place in the harbor. This lively pier is also the departure point for ever-popular **whale-watching cruises** (*schedules are available from the visitor center*).

Pilgrim Monument & Provincetown Museum★
High Pole Hill off Winslow St. 🅿 🕐*Open late May–mid-Sept daily 9am–7pm; Apr–late May & mid-Sept–Nov daily 9am–5pm. Last admission 45min before closing.* 💲*$12.* *508-487-1310. www.pilgrim-monument.org.*
Inspired by the 14C bell tower in the Tuscan hill town of Siena, the Pilgrim Monument was completed in 1910 to commemorate the 1620 landing of the Pilgrims at Provincetown. The observation deck atop this 252ft granite structure affords sweeping **views★★** of Provincetown, its harbor, and the lower Cape (*116 steps and 60 ramps*).
Located near the tower, a small history museum serves as the entrance to the facility and houses a permanent collection of historic documents and artifacts, including a model of the *Mayflower*.

Dune Tours★★
Departs from Art's Dune Tours, corner of Standish and Commercial Sts. 🔊*Visit by guided tour (1hr). Commentary.* 🕐*Mid-Apr–mid-Nov daily 10am–dusk.* 💲*$27 and up. Reservations required.* *508-487-1950. www.artsdunetours.com.*

This tour by a four-wheel-drive vehicle is a magnificent way to explore the spectacular Provincetown Dunes of the Cape Cod National Seashore, both of which are constantly being reshaped by the winds. Art's also offers sunrise and sunset tours, and clam bakes on the beach.

Dune Shacks

Dotting the dunes in Provincetown are its famous dune shacks—rustic cottages, which have no electricity, water or indoor plumbing. They may look like weathered wrecks, but they once housed a host of famous American artists and writers like Henry Beston, James Kerouac, Norman Mailer, Eugene O'Neill, and Jackson Pollack. Today, only a few dune shacks remain. Most are still occupied by original squatters, passed down through each family. But 15-year leases on some shacks are sometimes available to the public, and offered to the winners of an open essay contest.

Provincetown Art Association Museum

460 Commercial St. 🕐*Open Memorial Day–Sept Mon–Thu 11am–8pm, Fri 11am–10pm, Sat–Sun 11am–5pm. Rest of year, open Thu–Sun 12–5pm.*🖐*$7.* 📞*508-487-1750. www.paam.org.*
The rarefied ocean light has always drawn artists to Provincetown. You could see some great examples here, including works by Hans Hofman, Edward Hopper and Robert Motherwell.

ADDRESSES

🛏 STAY

$$$-$$$$ Carpe Diem Guesthouse & Spa – *12–14 Johnson St.* 📞*800-487-0132. www.carpediemguesthouse.com. 19 rooms & suites.* What's not to like about an inn where rooms are named after notable literary figures—and you can get chocolate crepes for breakfast? Brandy and port are available all day, and at night guests congregate at the outdoor hot tub.

$$$$-$$$$$ Crowne Pointe Historic Inn & Namaste Spa – *82 Bradford St.* 📞*508-487-6767. www.crownepointe.com.*

40 rooms. This 140-year-old sea captain's estate has rooms spread among six restored buildings done up in soft hues of sand and aqua. All have hardwood floors and many have fireplaces and whirlpool tubs. Complimentary goodies include a daily wine social, home-baked treats at tea time, a hot buffet breakfast, and shuttles to the beach. The property is a short walk from the MacMillan Wharf Dining Room.

$$$ Fairbanks Inn – *90 Bradford St.* 📞*508-487-0386 or 800-324-7265. www.fairbanksinn.com. 15 rooms.* Although this sea captain's house was built in the 18C and its antique furnishings recall that era, the feel is cozy rather than precious. The larger front bedrooms in the main house all sport four-poster beds and fireplaces; yet even the smaller rooms have distinctive touches like a carved-wood headboard or a marble-topped dresser. Fresh-from-the-oven scones or coffee cakes lure you downstairs. There are also two spacious rooms set in a carriage house on the property.

🍽 EAT

$$$ Mews and Café Mews – *429 Commercial St. Open for dinner nightly, Sun brunch offered from Mother's Day–Oct.* 📞*508-487-1500. www.mews.com.* **American.** Set on two floors overlooking the harbor, the Mews is slightly more formal downstairs, with menu items ranging from lobster risotto to lamb chops, with a vodka menu of 281 varieties from 30 countries.

$$ Front Street – *230 Commercial St. Open Jun–Dec, closed Tue in season.* 📞*508-487-9715. www.frontstreetrestaurant.com.* **Mediterranean.** Brick walls, antique wooden booths, and lacquered handmade tables give this dining room a romantic, yet informal, appeal. The menu—updated continental fare with Mediterranean accents—changes every week.

$ Relish – *93 Commercial St. Open May–Oct.* 📞*508-487-8077. www.ptownrelish. com.* **Bakery & Deli.** Your search for the perfect beach picnic ends here. Great fixings include hearty sandwich combos and tasty sides like curried chickpeas. Nobody leaves without a cupcake or two; they're deservedly famous.

Salem★★

Salem—known as a town tormented by its fear of witchcraft in the 17C and as a seaport that launched nearly 1,000 ships in the following centuries—is a bustling and pleasant city where historic districts adjoin industrial sites. While witch-related sites draw lots of tourists, Salem is rightly proud of its restored waterfront, stunning Federalist houses and the first-class Peabody Essex Museum.

A BIT OF HISTORY

A City of Peace – Founded in 1626 by Roger Conant, Salem derives its name from the Hebrew word "Shalom," meaning peace. Ironically, intolerance and violence dominated the early days of this Puritan city. Roger Williams, persecuted by the authorities, fled to Rhode Island in 1636, and thereafter zealous Salemites devoted their energies to driving the "evil ones" out of the colony. Intended to rid the colony once and for all of evildoers, the notorious witch-hunts began in the early 1690s.

The Witchcraft Hysteria – In 1692 several young girls, whose imaginations had been stirred by tales of voodoo told to them by the West Indian slave **Tituba**, began to have visions and convulsive fits. After examining the girls, a doctor declared them to be victims of "the evil hand." Impressionable and frightened, the youngsters accused Tituba and two other women of having bewitched them, and the women were immediately arrested and put into prison. From that point on, fear and panic spread through Salem, leaving no one free of suspicion. More than 200 persons were accused of witchcraft, 150 of whom were imprisoned and 19 found guilty and hanged. The hysteria—credited in retrospect to rivalries between several prominent Salem families—came to an abrupt end about a year later when Governor William Phips' wife was also accused of witchcraft.

An Era of Maritime Glory – Salem's sizable fleet of vessels, important to colonial trade in the 17C, won special recognition during the Revolution. When the ports of Boston and New York were occupied by the British, it was Salem's ships that carried arms and supplies to the colonial troops. Operating as privateers, the town's vessels also weakened the enemy by raiding and capturing about 400 British ships before the war had ended.

After the Revolution, Salem's merchant craft were prominent in worldwide trade. In 1786 the *Grand Turk*, sailing out of Salem to China, returned home to New England laden with luxury goods. To the many ships that followed the *Grand Turk*, the route to the Far East became a familiar one; "To the farthest port of the rich East!" became Salem's motto. The Chinese, who had seen a great number of vessels arriving in their ports bearing Salem's name, imagined Salem was a vast and magnificent country. Two years after the *Grand Turk* set sail for China, trade between Salem and India

> **Population:** 41,340.
>
> **Michelin Map:** 581 N 7.
>
> **Info:** ℘877-725-3662; www.salem.org.
>
> **Location:** Salem lies on the North Shore of Massachusetts, about 20mi north of Boston, off Rte. 128.
>
> **Kids:** Visit local chocolatier Harbor Sweets *(85 Leavitt St.; ℘978-745-7648; www.harborsweets.com)* to watch the chocolate-making process.
>
> **Timing:** Love crowds and crazy costumes? Visit during Haunted Happenings *(Oct)*.
>
> **Parking:** Try the central lots on St. Peter and Derby Streets.
>
> **Don't Miss:** The Peabody Essex Museum's Yin Yu Tang House.
>
> **Also See:** CAPE ANN.

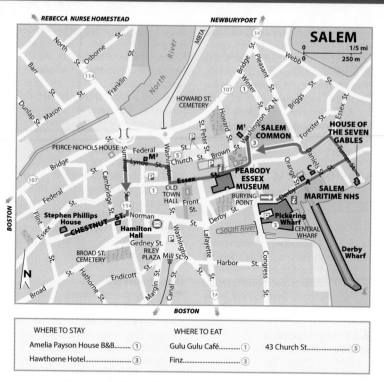

was opened by another Salem ship, the *Peggy*, owned by Elias Hasket Derby. The China trade brought such enormous wealth to Salem that taxes paid in the town on imported goods alone provided 8 percent of the nation's revenues. Salem merchants, including the Derbys, Peabodys and Crowninshields, were among the richest men in America; their mansions were filled with treasures retrieved from the Orient aboard their ships. The decline of the port of Salem, due in part to the embargo on foreign trade enforced by President Jefferson in 1807, was hastened by the development of new, deep-draft clipper ships that could only be outfitted in deepwater ports such as those of Boston and New York.

Salem Today – Renewal programs in the heart of the downtown area, around **Essex Street**, have created the look of the colonial era with brick walkways and a pedestrian mall. A number of shops devoted to the occult offer tarot and psychic readings, and sell witchcraft and New Age items. Operated by

Two Famous Men of Salem

Samuel McIntire (1757–1811), carpenter, wood carver, sculptor, builder, and architect, influenced much of Salem's architecture. His solid, four-square wood and brick mansions, such as the Pierce-Nichols House (1782) on Federal Street (*not open to the public*), ornamented with handsome porches and balustrades, are among the finest examples of American Federal architecture. A leading 19C American literary figure, **Nathaniel Hawthorne** (1804–1864) was born in Salem, where he wrote his earliest stories. Salem provided the inspiration or setting for many of Hawthorne's works, including *The House of the Seven Gables* (1851). Much of the description in his novel *The Scarlet Letter* (1850), especially that of the Custom House, was influenced by the years he spent as surveyor of the port.

the National Park Service, the **visitor center**, housed in the town's renovated turn-of-the-century armory, just off Essex Street, features a 27min film, *Where Past is Present*, which details the history of Essex County (*2 New Liberty St.; 🚻 🕐 open year-round daily 9am–5pm; 🕐 closed 1 Jan, Thanksgiving Day & 25 Dec; 📞 978-740-1650; www.nps.gov/sama*).

SEASIDE SALEM

The historic waterfront district may be visited on foot; begin at the orientation center on Central Wharf.

After more than a century, Salem is once again alive with a vitality reminiscent of its days of maritime supremacy. Salem's **Pickering Wharf** boasts a concentration of restaurants and specialty shops; just beyond it, on Derby Street, is the Salem Maritime National Historic Site.

🚶 Salem Maritime National Historic Site★

193 Derby St. 🕐 Open Nov–Apr Mon–Fri 10am–4pm, Sat–Sun 9am–5pm. Open May–Oct daily 9am–5pm. 🕐 Closed 1 Jan, Thanksgiving Day & 25 Dec. 📞 978-740-1660. www.nps.gov/sama.

The city's historic waterfront site is administered by the National Park Service; guided tours are offered several times daily, including the tall ship

House of the Seven Gables

©PhotoDisc, Inc.

Friendship. The **orientation center** features a film (*17min*) recounting how Salem pioneered trade with the Orient. At one time more than 40 wharves reached out into the harbor from the town's shoreline. **Derby Wharf**, the longest (2,100ft), and for many years a busy mercantile center, still remains.

Custom House★ (A)

👣 Visit by guided tour only.

This Federal-style building with its symbolic eagle was constructed in 1819 to house the customs offices of Salem. Inside, several of the offices, including the one used by Nathaniel Hawthorne when he was an officer of the port, have been restored.

Derby House (C)

👣 Visit by guided tour only.

This brick mansion was built in 1762 for merchant Elias Hasket Derby, whose ships eventually opened trade with India and the Orient, making him very rich. From the waterfront location of this house, Derby could see his ships as they docked near Derby Wharf. Inside, the wave motif ornamenting the stairway and the staircase balusters, carved to resemble twisted rope, is an appropriate feature for the house of a man who earned his living from the sea.

House of the Seven Gables★

115 Derby St. 👣 Visit by guided tour only (45 min). Candlelight tours available. 🅿 🕐 Open Jul–Oct daily 10am–7pm. Rest of the year daily 10am–5pm. 🕐 Closed first 2wks of Jan, Thanksgiving Day & 25 Dec. 💵 $12.50. 📞 978-744-0991. www.7gables.org.

A rambling three-story Colonial with steeply pitched roofs, this house was immortalized by Hawthorne's novel of the same name. Built in 1668, the house was completely restored in 1968. Inside, scenes from Hawthorne's novel come alive as visitors pass from Hepzibah's Cent Shop to the parlor where the judge was found, and into Clifford's room, under the eaves, at the top of a secret staircase. Tours cover six of the sixteen rooms, as well as Hawthorne's birthplace (c.1750, moved from its original location on Union Street). Other buildings in this garden setting include the Retire Becket House (1655, which contains the museum shop), the Hooper-Hathaway House (1682) and a counting house (c.1830).

👤👶 Peabody Essex Museum★★★

East India Square. ⏱*Open Tue–Sun and Mon holidays 10am–5pm).* ⏱*Closed 1 Jan, Thanksgiving Day & 25 Dec.* 🚌*$15 (Admission to Yin Yu Tang, a Chinese House, is $5 plus museum fee).* ☎*978-745-9500 or 866-745-1876. www.pem.org.*

This illustrious museum focuses on America's maritime history from the 17C to the present, and on the historical significance of the city of Salem and Essex County. It pays special tribute to Salem's great 18C and 19C maritime era, during which the town flourished as a major American port. The collections reflect the global range of Salem's ship captains, who returned from their travels with porcelain, carvings and other artifacts from the Far East, India, Africa and the Pacific Islands. Temporary exhibits might feature anything from a collection of Dutch and Flemish masterworks to an anthology of hats curated by British milliner Stephen Jones.

Museum

The collections are spread over three floors, and organized into several categories. Here are some highlights:

Maritime Art and History

The collection of marine paintings includes works by major artists, such as Fitz Henry Lane and Antoine Roux. Portraiture and other paintings by such famed artists as John Singleton Copley and Gilbert Stuart are also featured, as are rare nautical instruments and charts and a dramatic collection of carved ships' figureheads.

Asian Export Art

Considered one of the most complete collections of its kind in the world, the

Peabody Essex Museum

© Timothy Hursley / Peabody Essex Museum

collection features 19C and early-20C decorative and utilitarian porcelain, silver, furniture, textiles, and other precious objects.

Asian, African and Pacific Islands Art

This section encompasses textiles, shields, ritual costumes, masks, and pottery from the tropical Pacific Islands, Indonesia, Japan and Africa. The Edward S. Morse Collection of 19C Meiji costumes and crafts is reputedly the largest of its kind outside Japan.

Native American Arts

The collection includes artifacts from the Indian cultures of the Eastern seaboard, Great Lakes, Great Plains, Northwest Coast, and South America.

Yin Yu Tang: A Chinese House

One of the highlights of a visit to this museum is a tour of a Chinese merchant's house from the Anhui province, more than 200 years old. The house has been reassembled here, on the museum's campus (👣*tours by reservation only;* 🚌*$5 fee applies, which is added to the museum admission*).

ADDITIONAL SIGHTS
Salem Common★

In the 19C a number of Federal mansions were built bordering the common of colonial Salem, called Washington Square.

A notable group of these residences is on Washington Square North.

Chestnut Street★★

This broad street lined with Federal-style mansions illustrates the wealth of 19C Salem. The majority of the dwellings on Chestnut Street were built between 1800 and 1820; their size and richly adorned facades are unrivaled. **Hamilton Hall** (no. 9) was designed by Samuel McIntire. The **Stephen Phillips Memorial Trust House** (no. 34), decorated with furnishings from around the world, is open to the public (*visit by 45min guided tour only;* P Ⓒ *open Jun–Oct Tue–Sun 11am–5pm; Nov–May weekends 11am–5pm. ⊗$5. ℘978-744-0440; www.historicnewengland.org/phillipsmuseum.*

Salem Witch Museum (M1)

19 N. Washington Square. ♿Ⓒ*Open Jul–Aug daily 10am–7pm. Rest of the year daily 10am–5pm (extended hours in Oct).* Ⓒ*Closed 1 Jan, Thanksgiving Day & 25 Dec. ⊗$9. ℘978-744-1692. www.salemwitchmuseum.com.*
The museum presents a multimedia program (*30min*) of 13 life-size scenes that sensationalize the major events of the witchcraft hysteria from 1692 to its final days in 1693. A permanent exhibit titled "Witches: Evolving Perceptions" traces the meaning of the word *witch* up to current times and includes a look at the Wicca movement. Across from the museum stands Henry H. Kitson's statue of Salem's founder, *Roger Conant*.

Witch Dungeon Museum (M2)

16 Lynde St. *Visit by guided tour only (25min).* Ⓒ*Open Apr–Nov daily 10am–5pm. Extended hours weekends in Oct. ⊗$8. ℘978-741-3570. www.witchdungeon.com.*
A live stage presentation, based on historic transcripts of a 1692 witch trial, captures the hysteria that swept Salem in the late 17C. Following the presentation, visitors tour a re-creation of the dank dungeon where local "witches" were jailed in tiny, unlit cells.

Rebecca Nurse Homestead

149 Pine St., in Danvers, 4mi north of Salem. *Visit by guided tour only (1hr).* P Ⓒ*Open mid-Jun–Labor Day Fri–Sun 10am–4pm; Sept–Oct weekends only 10am–4pm. ⊗Adults, $7. ℘978-774-8799. www.rebeccanurse.org.*
Seventy-one-year-old Rebecca Nurse, a victim of the Salem witch-hunts, lived in this saltbox house (c.1678) which includes 25 acres of fields, pasture and woods. Accused of being a witch, Rebecca was tried, convicted and hanged on 19 July 1692, despite a petition in her favor that had been signed by many of the townspeople. A short walk from the house leads to the Nurse Burial Ground, where a monument set up by the Nurse family (1885) marks Rebecca's presumed grave.

ADDRESSES

🛏 STAY

$$$ Hawthorne Hotel – *18 Washington Square West. ℘978-744-4080 or 800-729-7829. www.hawthornehotel.com. 93 rooms. Restaurant and bar.* Sitting opposite the town's Common, this sturdy brick dowager (1925) is a well-situated base for exploring Salem's historic attractions. The feel here is stately and classic, but with modern amenities like flat-screen TVs and Wi-Fi. Guest rooms are furnished with 18C reproductions, brass lamps, and four-poster beds. In the hotel's wood-paneled **Tavern on the Green**, you can get sandwiches, pastas and New England-style seafood; while **Nathaniel's**, the more formal dining room, serves updated continental fare.

$$ Amelia Payson House B&B – *16 Winter St. Open May–mid-Nov. ℘520-744-8304. www.ameliapaysonhouse.com. 4 rooms.* It feels as if you should sit daintily sipping tea in the elegant parlor with its grand piano in this dignified 1845 Greek Revival house, but the warm welcome here reflects more of the present day. This long-established B&B, within a short walk of the historic sights, is furnished with period antiques and plenty of pretty pink. Continental breakfast is served—along with sightseeing tips—in the B&B's formal dining room.

$$ Morning Glory Bed & Breakfast – *22 Hardy St. ☎978-741-1703. www. morningglorybb.com. 5 rooms & suites.* Innkeepers Bob Shea and Marcel Dufour treat guests like family at this 1808 Georgian Colonial, decorated in period style and within walking distance of Salem attractions.

☍EAT

$$$ 43 Church St – *43 Church St. ☎978-745-7665. www.lyceumsalem.com.* **American.** 43 Church St. remains the go-to place to take clients and impress guests. Chef Doug Papows brings an artful hand to a seasonally-changing menu. Fall might bring a root vegetable bisque with toasted pumpkin seeds and pan-seared salmon with Brussels sprouts and maple custard cream, or a pork osso bucco. Lunch features standbys like Caesar salads and burgers.

$$ Finz– *76 Wharf St. ☎978-744-8485. www.hipfinz.com.* **Seafood.** In a seaport like Salem you need at least one go-to spot on the water. In Salem, Finz is the place, with an outdoor deck at Pickering Wharf and a lively bar scene. The food lives up to the setting, especially the fried oysters with spicy remoulade sauce. And you can't go wrong with grilled wild salmon.

$ Gulu Gulu Cafe – *247 Essex St. ☎978-740-8882. www.gulu-gulu.com.* **American.** Open all day and late evening, Gulu Gulu offers good food and then some—music, open mic book and poetry readings, and work by local artists. Menu items (many shareable) include antipasti platters, sweet and savory crepes, wraps and panini. For drinks, try the hot apple cider, the white rasberry latte, or the Andes espresso.

Springfield

A rich industrial past has contributed to making Springfield the hub of business, finance and industry in the Pioneer Valley, and the third-largest city in Massachusetts.

A BIT OF HISTORY

Established on the banks of the Connecticut River in 1636 as a trading post, Springfield grew into an industrial center by the 19C. For over 200 years the city was known for the **Springfield Armory**, the government arsenal that turned out the first American musket (1795) and weapons used by the Union troops in the Civil War.
Every September the Springfield area hosts the **Eastern States Exposition**, "the Big E," which is the largest fair in the Northeast.

SIGHTS
♟♟Basketball Hall of Fame★
1000 W. Columbus Ave. ♿🅿🕑Open year-round Wed–Sun 10am–4pm, Sat 10am–5pm. 🕑Closed Thanksgiving Day & 25 Dec. ☞$19. ☎877-446-6752. www.hoophall.com.

- ▶ **Population:** 153,060.
- ♿ **Michelin Map:** 581 J 9.
- ℹ **Info:** ☎413-787-1548 or 800-723-1548; www.valleyvisitor.com.
- ▷ **Location:** Springfield is located in south-central Massachusetts, about 90mi southwest of Boston.
- ♟♟ **Kids:** The Dr. Seuss National Memorial Sculpture Garden in the Quadrangle is a delight for younger kids.
- 🕑 **Timing:** Visit the basketball hall first (it opens at 10am), and then head over to the Quadrangle for lunch and museum-hopping.
- 🅿 **Parking:** The Dwight St. lot charges $10 for all-day parking.
- 😊 **Don't Miss:** Naismith Basketball Hall of Fame is a must for sports fans, while Six Flags New England, in nearby Agawam, will thrill rollercoaster enthusiasts.
- ♿ **Also See:** WORCESTER.

Basketball was originated by Dr. James Naismith, whose Springfield College team played the first game in 1891. Exhibits trace the development of the sport from amateur to professional and international status. Life-size action photos of such basketball greats as Wilt Chamberlain and Bob Cousy, videotapes of unforgettable coaches in action on the sidelines, film clips of the celebrated Harlem Globetrotters, and a selection of uniforms, equipment and memorabilia constitute the displays.

The Hall is loaded with state-of-the-art interactive exhibits, including a virtual reality area where you can play one-on-one against former stars.

The Quadrangle

220 State St. ✕♿🅿🕐*Science Museum, Museum of Fine Arts, and George Walter Vincent Smith Art Museum open Tue–Sat 10am–5pm, Sun 11am–5pm; Connecticut Valley Historical Museum open Wed–Sat 12–4pm.* ⊗*$15.* ✆*413-263-6800 or 800-625-7738. www.springfieldmuseums.org.*

Four museums are grouped together on the Quadrangle bounded by Chestnut and State Streets. In the center of the action is the ♟♟**Dr. Seuss National Memorial Sculpture Garden**, a series of bronzes of the beloved characters of Dr. Seuss' books.

Museum of Fine Arts

Holdings include European paintings of the 17C Dutch, 18C Italian, and 18C and 19C French schools. The American section contains canvases by eminent 19C painters, such as Winslow Homer and Frederic Edwin Church.

George Walter Vincent Smith Art Museum★

This building, designed to suggest an Italian Renaissance villa, contains a collection of Oriental and American art, and furnishings and casts of ancient Greek and Roman statues. The collection includes 19C American paintings, interesting examples of Japanese armor, screens, lacquers and ceramics, as well as **Chinese cloisonné** (enamel poured into raised compartments).

Connecticut Valley Historical Museum

Changing exhibits of the museum's collection of furniture, pewter, silver and portraits depict the social and cultural development of the Connecticut Valley from the 17C.

♟♟ Springfield Science Museum

The museum contains a planetarium, a hands-on exploration center and the multi-level African Hall, as well as displays devoted to plant and animal life, geology and dinosaurs—including a full-size replica of a *Tyrannosaurus rex*.

♟♟ Forest Park

302 Sumner Ave. ♿🕐*Open Apr–Columbus Day, daily 10am–5pm; Columbus Day–Nov Sat–Sun 10am–5pm.* 🕐*Closed Dec–Mar & Thanksgiving Day.* ⊗*$6.75.* ✆*413-733-2251. www.forestparkzoo.com.*

This pleasant city park features a small zoo, with barnyard animals, a petting zoo, and exotic species such as a South American capybara, emus and wallabies.

EXCURSION
Stanley Park

▶*400 Western Ave. in Westfield. 15mi west of Springfield via US-20, then turn left onto Elm St., left onto Court St., and bear left onto Granville Rd.* ♿🅿🕐*Open first Sat in May–last Sun in Nov daily 7am–dusk.* ✆*413-568-9312. www.stanleypark.org.*

A 61-bell Flemish carillon, an English herb garden and a rose garden are among the many attractions in this expansive 275-acre recreational park. Located in the pond area are a covered bridge, an old mill and a blacksmith's shop. A Westfield curiosity since the late 1940's, black squirrels now populate most areas of the city and have moved into the surrounding communities. They were originally introduced to Westfield Park, as a gift to its founder.

Stockbridge★★

Founded in the early 18C as an Indian mission, this quintessential New England town nestled in the heart of the Berkshires exudes a grace and charm that has traditionally endeared it to well-heeled Bostonians and New Yorkers, as well as to artists and writers.

A BIT OF HISTORY

The town's **Main Street★** is lined with a picturesque row of pedimented buildings bounded to the west by the sprawling white facade of the **Red Lion Inn** (℘413-298-5545; www.redlioninn.com), a cozy country hostelry dating from colonial times. Beyond the inn, Main Street gives way to large clapboard dwellings rimmed by broad landscaped lawns.

Due to its prime location (less than three hours by car from both Boston and New York), Stockbridge welcomes a steady stream of visitors throughout the year. In the summer, performances of classic American drama are presented at the Berkshire Theater Festival.

SIGHTS

See Berkshires map.

▲▲ Norman Rockwell Museum★★

9 Glendale Rd. 2.5mi from Stockbridge center. ⬥🅿🕙Open May–Oct daily 10am–5pm, open Thu 10am–7pm Jul–Aug; Nov–Apr weekdays 10am–4pm, wknds & holidays 10am–5pm.
🕙*Closed 1 Jan, Thanksgiving Day & 25 Dec. ⬙$16. ℘413-298-4100. www.nrm.org.*

Occupying a 36-acre estate overlooking the Housatonic River Valley, this popular museum is the repository of the largest collection of original works by America's premier 20C illustrator.

The core collection comprises Rockwell's personal holdings along with his studio and personal library and archives. In addition, the museum has acquired works through gifts or purchases, bringing the total holdings to more than 500 paintings and drawings, including 172

- **Population:** 2,196.
- **Michelin Map:** 581 I 9.
- **Info:** ℘413-298-5200; www.stockbridge chamber.org.
- **Location:** Stockbridge lies 3hrs west of Boston, off the Mass. Turnpike.
- **Timing:** Stockbridge makes a great base for exploring Berkshires attractions to the north, or Connecticut's Litchfield Hills to the south.
- **Parking:** Street-side parking is available (try the side streets).
- **Don't Miss:** The Norman Rockwell Museum offers a sweet slice of Americana.
- **Also See:** DEERFIELD.

large-scale works. The main building, containing nine galleries, was designed by the eminent Postmodern architect **Robert A.M. Stern** to provide a spacious setting for the collection. The Neoclassical style of the building brings to mind a New England town hall.

On display inside is a sizable sampling of Rockwell's works, including *Stockbridge Main Street at Christmas* (1967), *Triple Self-Portrait* (1960) and *The Problem We All Live With* (1964). Also in the museum's collection is the celebrated ***Four Freedoms Series*** (1943) inspired by President Franklin Delano Roosevelt's 1941 landmark speech rallying the

Norman Rockwell's Stockbridge Studio

© Norman Rockwell Museum

Norman Rockwell: Illustrator of American Life

Norman Rockwell (1894–1978) began his long and prolific career in his teens. At the age of 22 the artist drew his first cover for the *Saturday Evening Post*, thereby beginning a collaboration that would result in a total of 321 covers for the prestigious magazine over the next 47 years.

Rockwell's realistic paintings chronicle the changing times in America, while capturing the timeless essence of humanity—mankind's comic foibles, noble aspirations and wrenching tragedies. His homespun scenes, often depicting the routines of day-to-day living, are seasoned with a sense of humor and wonder. Rockwell often depicted children, and in many cases his subjects were modeled on family, friends or neighbors. When Rockwell embarked upon a 10-year association with *Look* magazine in the 1960s, he focused on contemporary political figures and American social issues, such as the Civil Rights movement and poverty. In 1978 Rockwell died in Stockbridge, his home since 1953.

nation to defend the rights of all people menaced by the Axis powers: freedom of speech, freedom of worship, freedom from want and freedom from fear. During World War II, these poignant images toured the nation on posters that formed the centerpiece of a fundraising drive that yielded over $130 million in government bonds to support the war. Just a short stroll from the museum, on a rise overlooking the valley, stands **Rockwell's studio** (⏰*open May–Oct*), a simple red wooden building relocated from its original site in downtown Stockbridge.

Chesterwood★

3mi from Stockbridge center. Take Rte. 102 west and turn left onto Rte. 183. Continue .8mi and turn right onto Mohawk Lake Rd., then left on Willow St. and continue .5mi to Chesterwood. ♿🅿⏰*Open late-May–mid-Oct daily 10am–5pm.* 👓$15. 📞413-298-3579. www.chesterwood.org.

This large estate, formerly a farm, was acquired in the late 19C by the American sculptor **Daniel Chester French** (1850–1931). Although French achieved his first major success at the age of 25 with his *Minute Man* (1875) statue at Concord, he is probably best remembered for the impressive seated *Abraham Lincoln* (1920) he sculpted for the Lincoln Memorial in the nation's capital. French executed more than 100 public monuments during his lifetime.

Models and casts of French's works, including the Dupont Circle Fountain he sculpted for Washington, DC, occupy the **Barn Gallery**. The large Colonial Revival **house** (designed by Henry Bacon) replaced the farmhouse originally on the property.

The house is furnished as it was when the artist lived here. Also on the grounds is French's spacious, well-lit **studio** (another Henry Bacon design), with its tall double doors and railroad tracks that allowed French to move large works outdoors, where he could work in natural light. A woodland walk (*20min*) affords views of the hilly countryside.

Naumkeag

2mi from Stockbridge center at 5 Prospect Hill Rd. From the intersection of US-7 and Rte. 102 in Stockbridge center, take Pine St. north; bear left on Prospect Hill Rd. and follow it .5mi to entrance. 📞*Visit by guided tour only (45min).* 🅿⏰*Open late May–mid-Oct daily 10am–5pm.* 👓$15. 📞413-298-3239. www.thetrustees.org.

This Norman-style mansion (1886, Stanford White) and its terraced hillside gardens were built for Joseph Choate (1832–1917), US ambassador to England. Naumkeag was the Choate family's summer cottage. The unusual design of the entrance to the Chinese garden was intended to keep the devil out.

Williamstown★★

This beautiful colonial village snuggles in the northwest corner of Massachusetts, at the place where the Mohawk Trail enters the Berkshires. The Berkshires' verdant rolling hills provide a lovely setting for Williams College, as well as for the Sterling and Francine Clark Art Institute and the Williamstown Theater Festival held in summer.

▶ **Population:** 7,754.
   Michelin Map: 581 I 7.
   Info: ℘413-743-4500; www.berkshires.org.
▶ **Location:** Williamstown is located in Berkshire County, in the northwest corner of Massachusetts, just south of the Vermont border.
🕐 **Timing:** Museum-hopping and lunch on Spring Street, then a movie at Images Cinema—now that's a perfect day.
🅿 **Parking:** On-street parking is available; check the side streets.
   Don't Miss: The Clark Art Institute is one of the finest in the region; also, stroll the beautiful grounds of Williams College (1793), with more than 50 buildings from different historical periods.
   Also See: STOCKBRIDGE.

A BIT OF HISTORY

In 1753 the early settlement of West Hoosuck was established here by soldiers from Fort Massachusetts. Later one of the soldiers, Col. Ephraim Williams Jr., bequeathed part of his estate for the founding of a free school in West Hoosuck—provided the town be renamed in his honor. Soon after the colonel's death, West Hoosuck was renamed Williamstown.

Clark Art Institute★★★

225 South St. ✕🅿🕐*Open Jul–Aug daily 10am–5pm. Rest of the year Tue–Sun 10am–5pm.* 🕐*Closed 1 Jan, Thanksgiving Day & 25 Dec.* ⊗*$12.50 (free admission Nov–May).* ℘*413-458-2303. www.clarkart.edu.*

The European and American paintings, sculpture, works on paper and decorative arts of the illustrious **Sterling and Francine Clark Art Institute** were gathered by Robert Sterling Clark and his wife, Francine, during the years between World War I and 1956. The collection, worthy of being compared with those of some of the world's finest museums, reflects the Clarks' early taste for Classical art and, later, 19C paintings. The couple chose Williamstown as the site of their institute for its idyllic natural setting and its location far from urban centers (most likely to be threatened during wartime). The white marble building (1956), designed to house the collection, suggests a private residence and provides a splendid setting for the works. The red granite annex houses additional gallery space as well as the museum's auditorium.

Williamstown Theater Festival

Since 1955, this venerable festival has presented more than 500 plays and musicals, along with outdoor free theater, cabaret performances and readings. Its stage has hosted a cast of Hollywood and Broadway luminaries, including Gwyneth Paltrow, Joanne Woodward, Joel Grey and Calista Flockhart. Held in the Adams Memorial Theatre at Williams College, five Main Stage productions run for two weeks each (*mid-Jun–Aug*). Plays include classic dramas as well as new works from promising young playwrights (*℘413-597-3400 or www.wtfestival.org*).

Spring Street Treats

A college town like Williamstown is bound to have a restaurant on the main shopping drag where the food is good, filling and cheap, and the lines spill out the front door. **Pappa Charlie's Deli** (*28 Spring St.; ℘413-458-5969*) fills the bill, with over-stuffed sandwiches, homemade soups (leek and rice, tomato orzo and *pasta e fagioli*), gargantuan slabs of veggie lasagna and eggplant parmesan—and a mean root beer float to wash it all down. The blackboard reveals dozens of selections, each named in honor of various celebrity patrons, many of which are alumni of the Williamstown Theater Festival.

Afterward walk up the street to **Sweets & Beans** (*61 Spring St.; ℘413-884-1374*), for an ice cream cone (from local SoCo Creamery), or a pastry and latte. Then duck into the intimate **Images Cinema** (*50 Spring St.; ℘413-458-5612; www. imagescinema.org*) to see a foreign film. Housed in a historic brick building, this independent film house also offers film discussions over Sunday brunch, family films, and late-night bites as an alternative to cookie-cutter mall megaplexes.

VISIT

A room off the entrance court is dedicated to the works of Remington, Homer and Sargent. **Frederic Remington** (1861–1909) is known for his paintings of the American West. **Winslow Homer** (1836–1910) chose to depict the rugged New England landscape—the White Mountains of New Hampshire and the rocky Maine coast—in his paintings. In contrast to Remington and Homer, **John Singer Sargent** (1856–1925) was a modern portraitist whose subjects, generally members of high society, were rendered with the artist's flair for sophistication. The museum's earliest works date back to the Renaissance period. Highlighting this section are the Italian paintings, including a seven-part panel altarpiece by Ugolino da Siena and *Virgin and Child Enthroned with Four Angels* (c.1445) by **Piero della Francesca**. However, it is in the realm of 19C French and American art that the collection excels. In the section devoted to the French school, the group of paintings by **Corot** shows the artist's skill in executing landscapes as well as figures. *The Trumpeter of the Hussars* (c.1815) by **Gericault**, the Romantic painter, typifies his masterful style and contrasts with the muted tones used by **Millet**.

The paintings by **Monet** include one from his *Rouen Cathedral* series (1894) and *The Cliffs at Étretat* (1885).

The Postimpressionist **Toulouse-Lautrec** is represented by several works, including his *Dr. Péan Operating* (1892). The Clark collection of American and European silver, one of the finest in the world, includes pieces made by the 18C English silversmith **Paul de Lamerie**.

ADDITIONAL SIGHT
Williams College Museum of Art★

On Main St. between Spring and Water Sts. Look for for Louise Bourgeois's "Eyes" sculptures in the courtyard, ♿🕐Open year-round Tue–Sat 10am–5pm, Sun 1–5pm. Open Labor Day and Columbus Day🕐Closed 1 Jan, Thanksgiving Day & 25 Dec. ℘413-597-2429. www.wcma.williams.edu.

This building, one of the finest on the Williams campus, has gradually evolved over the years from a brick Greek Revival octagon (1846) to its present size, which includes additions by renowned architect Charles Moore. The building's unassuming exterior belies the dramatic atrium and neatly sculpted, well-lit gallery spaces within.

The collection includes 12,000 works that span the history of art, with an emphasis in modern art from the late 18C to the present. It is particularly strong in American art: Copley, Homer, Eakins, Hopper, Inness, O'Keeffe, and Wood are all represented. World art is a growing category here.

Worcester

Worcester, the second largest city in New England, is a commercial and industrial hub. Its central location within the state has promoted the growth of a diverse economy, which includes retail and medical services.

SIGHTS
Worcester Art Museum★★

55 Salisbury St. ✕ P ◷ *Open year-round Wed–Fri and Sun 11am–5pm (3rd Thu of every month til 8pm), Sat 10am–5pm.* ◷ *Closed major holidays.* ◉ *$14 (free first Sat of every month from 10am–noon).* ℘*508-799-4406. www.worcesterart.org.*

The museum owns collections of paintings, sculpture and decorative arts spanning 50 centuries from antiquity to the present. Displayed in a building inspired by Italian Renaissance architecture, the collections are arranged in galleries that surround a central court/arcade. The space includes galleries for prints and drawings, 20C and contemporary art and changing exhibits, and an outdoor garden courtyard.

The **first floor** is devoted to ancient art, the art of the Middle Ages and Asian art, including extensive holdings of Japanese prints from the Edo period. Highlights include the 11-headed Japanese Kannon (9–10C AD); the 12C **Chapter House**, formerly part of a Benedictine priory in France; and *The Last Supper*, one of a group of c.1300 frescoes from Spoleto, Italy.

On the second floor, the European schools of painting from the Middle Ages through the 20C are represented. Highlights include El Greco's intense *Repentant Magdalene* (c.1577); *The Rest on the Flight into Egypt* (c.1627) by Nicolas Poussin; a portrait by Gainsborough of his daughters; Gauguin's *Brooding Woman* (1891); and in the Italian section, the dramatic *Calling of St. Matthew* (c.1620) by Strozzi.

The third-floor **American wing** features the American school of painting with works by John Copley, Worcester native Ralph Earl, James McNeill Whistler, Winslow Homer, John Singer Sargent, Mary Cassatt, Childe Hassam, and the landscapists George Inness, Albert Pinkham Ryder and Samuel Morse.

The museum's distinguished **pre-Columbian collection** (*4th floor*) is also worth viewing.

▶ **Population:** 170,000.
⊙ **Michelin Map:** 581 L 8.
▣ **Info:** ℘508-755-7400; www.centralmass.org.
▷ **Location:** Worcester is located in central Massachusetts, about an hour west of Boston.
👥 **Kids:** The EcoTarium (℘508-929-2700; www.ecotarium.org) is a wonderful nature museum for families.
◷ **Timing:** Plan your visit to the Worcester Art Museum for Saturday morning, when admission is free from 10am to noon.
P **Parking:** There are several surface parking lots in the city.
◉ **Don't Miss:** Good picks include the Worcester Art Museum, Higgins Armory and Purgatory Chasm (*Sutton;* ℘*508-234-3733; www.mass.gov/dcr*). The latter is an 80ft-deep hole, with granite walls that rise 70ft—a cool quirk of nature.
⊙ **Also See:** SPRINGFIELD.

Worcester Art Museum
© Tim Grafft / Massachusetts Office of Travel & Tourism

Old Sturbridge Village

© Old Sturbridge Village

👥 Higgins Armory Museum★

100 Barber Ave. ♿ 🅿 🕐 *Open year-round Tue–Sat 10am–4pm, Sun noon–4pm.* 🕐 *Closed major holidays.* 👓 *$12.* 📞 *508-853-6015. www.higgins.org.*

This museum evolved from the private collection of arms and armor of John Woodman Higgins who was a leading Worcester industrialist. Today, this multi-storied steel and glass building houses a prized collection of armor, as well as early tools and weapons. Presented in multimedia shows, live demonstrations and historical exhibits, these objects provide a unique perspective on knightly culture.

Principal displays are arranged in an enormous exhibit gallery, modeled after the Great Hall of an 11C Austrian castle. Paintings, furnishings, tapestries, banners and stained glass in the gallery add to the illusion of being in a medieval castle. Along the walls stand some 100 suits of parade, combat and jousting armor dating from the 14C to the 16C, including the suit of Maximilian armor named after **Emperor Maximilian**, who preferred fluted armor, and the **Franz von Teuffenbach** armor, with its elaborate decorative etching. Tools and weapons of the Stone and Bronze Ages and a rare gladiator's helmet (1C AD) are included in the other exhibits. On the second floor, children can don medieval dress and a variety of helmets.

EXCURSION
👥 Old Sturbridge Village★★★

▶ *1 Old Sturbridge Village Rd., 22mi southwest of Worchester, in Sturbridge.* 🕐 *Open mid-Apr–mid-Oct daily 9.30am–5pm; rest of the year Wed–Sun 9.30am–4pm.* 🕐 *Closed major holidays.* 👓 *$24. www.osv.org.*

This living history museum re-creates life between 1790 and 1840 in a rural New England community. The museum is the largest outdoor history museum in the Northeast, brought to life by costumed staff. When it opened in 1946, historic houses, farm buildings and shops had been moved to and reconstructed on the Sturbridge site.

En route to the Common, visitors pass the **Friends Meetinghouse** (1796), which typifies the austere piety associated with the Quakers. At the west end of the Common stands the Greek Revival-style **Center Meetinghouse**. The white "saltbox" **Richardson Parsonage** (1748) is the village minister's house. In the **Tin Shop** next door, a smith turns out wares like those used in early-19C households. Near the tiny **Law Office** sits the well-stocked **Knight Store**, typical of country stores of the period. The Federal-style **Towne House** (1796) is similar to dwellings built by prosperous rural families of the period. Beyond the bank lies an early-19C printing officeWith its livestock fields,

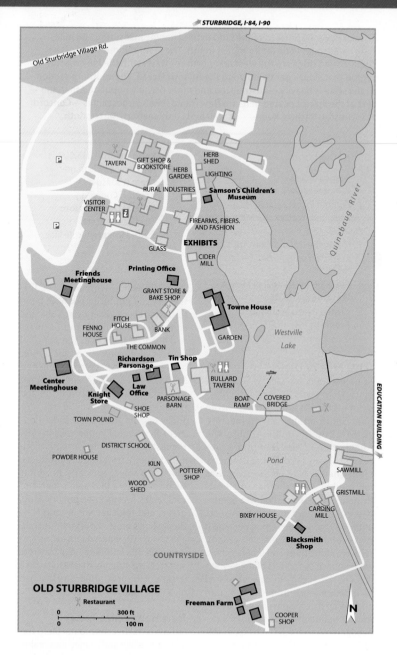

STURBRIDGE, I-84, I-90

Old Sturbridge Village Rd.

Quinebaug River

P

TAVERN

GIFT SHOP & BOOKSTORE

HERB GARDEN

HERB SHED

LIGHTING

RURAL INDUSTRIES

Samson's Children's Museum

VISITOR CENTER

P

FIREARMS, FIBERS, AND FASHION

GLASS

EXHIBITS

CIDER MILL

Friends Meetinghouse

Printing Office

GRANT STORE & BAKE SHOP

FITCH HOUSE

FENNO HOUSE

BANK

THE COMMON

Towne House

GARDEN

Westville Lake

Richardson Parsonage

Tin Shop

Center Meetinghouse

Law Office

Knight Store

PARSONAGE BARN

SHOE SHOP

BULLARD TAVERN

BOAT RAMP

COVERED BRIDGE

EDUCATION BUILDING

TOWN POUND

POWDER HOUSE

DISTRICT SCHOOL

KILN

WOOD SHED

POTTERY SHOP

Pond

SAWMILL

GRISTMILL

CARDING MILL

BIXBY HOUSE

Blacksmith Shop

COUNTRYSIDE

OLD STURBRIDGE VILLAGE

Restaurant

0   300 ft
0   100 m

Freeman Farm

COOPER SHOP

N

Freeman Farm is a lively area. Activities performed here include plowing, harvesting field crops and milking cows. A blacksmith shop, carding mill, gristmill and an 1820 water-powered sawmill are also on the premises. Adjoining the visitor center, the clock gallery contains more than 100 New England clocks. Family activities in the **Samson's Children's Museum** focus on younger children.

Forests cover 80 percent of the land in this triangle measuring 168 miles long by 90 miles wide (at its widest point). The mountainous relief of the Appalachian ridges to the west and north contrasts with the hilly coastal region that slopes gently down to the Atlantic Ocean. The southern section of the state is heavily industrialized and more densely populated than the rest of the state. Located here are New Hampshire's largest cities—Concord, Manchester, Nashua, Keene—as well as its only seaport, Portsmouth.

Highlights

1 Boating on **Lake Winnipesaukee** (p299)
2 Cruising **Piscataqua River** on a tug from Portsmouth Harbor (p312)
3 Hiking the **Appalachian Trail** in White Mountain Nat. Forest (p315)
4 Reaching the summit of **Mount Washington** (p316)
5 Driving the **Kancamagus Scenic Byway** (p321)

▶ **Population:** 1,315,000.
Info: www.visitnh.gov.
Area: 9,304sq mi.
Capital: Concord.
Official Designation: The Granite State.
State Flower: Purple lilac.

"Live Free or Die"

"Here no landlords rack us with high rents. Here every man may be master of his land in a short time," wrote John Smith about New Hampshire in 1614. Despite Smith's tribute, the colonization of New Hampshire proceeded slowly. The first settlement, established in 1623 on the coast, was followed by several other small settlements. New Hampshire was administered as a part of Massachusetts until 1679, when the region became a royal colony. Its people, self-reliant, taciturn, industrious and independent, were staunch supporters of the Revolution. The New Hampshire colony declared its independence from Great Britain and set up its own government seven months before the Declaration of Independence was signed. The heroic words of Revolutionary War colonel John Stark, "live free or die," are immortalized in the state motto.

Economy

In the 19C factory complexes such as the **Amoskeag Mills**, once the world's largest textile manufacturer, were built on the banks of the Merrimack River. Textiles are still produced but have been surpassed by machinery, electronic and computer equipment, and business and financial services as the principal sources of income. Since the 1960s, many companies have established branches in New Hampshire, attracted to the state's favorable tax structure and proximity to Boston.

Today tourism and industrial development share equal importance in New Hampshire's economy. Farming is oriented chiefly toward dairy products, Christmas trees, specialty products such as apples and maple sugar, and vegetables, livestock and poultry. Sand, gravel and feldspar are among New Hampshire's most important minerals, and building granite is quarried on a limited scale. The introduction of concrete and steel construction has resulted in a decline of the granite industry that had given the state its nickname.

New Hampshire Today

From coastal beaches to northern forests, rolling hills and rugged mountains, New Hampshire has a diverse landscape, rich in scenic beauty and historic charm. The southwest region of the state, dominated by Mount Monadnock (one of the most climbed mountains in North America) is New Hampshire's quiet corner. The region is crisscrossed with

Perch Pond in Campton, at the foothill of the White Mountains

scenic backroads leading to woodlands, lakes, small villages, and historic sites. The state has a mere 17 miles of **Atlantic coastline** where you'll find beaches and parks (much of the coastline is public land), and the lovely historic town of Portsmouth. The seaside town, the colonial capital until 1808, is home to the Strawbery Banke Museum, and a thriving arts and culinary scene. Down the road, you'll find the picturesque Odiorne State Park and the rollicking Hampton Beach. New Hampshire's **Lakes Region**, nestled in the center of the state, is dotted with 273 lakes and ponds, including Lake Winnipesaukee, the state's largest. A guided boat tour is the best way to see the 72sq mi lake but you'll also want to take time to visit beaches, explore seaside villages or paddle the shoreline.

The popular and scenic White Mountains region encompasses 780,000-acre **White Mountain** National Forest, the Kancamagus National Scenic Byway, 288-foot Mount Washington (the tallest mountain in the Northeast), more than 100 waterfalls, and thousands of rivers and streams. Busy resort towns are scattered throughout the region, including North Conway, Lincoln and North Woodstock.

North of the White Mountains, undeveloped forest stretches into Canada. Here, the headwaters of the **Connecticut River** flow through the Third, Second and First Connecticut Lakes. Moose, black bear, deer and grouse are plentiful. Don't miss a drive through Dixville Notch, the northernmost of the White Mountain notches, with its jagged cliffs and towering stands of evergreens.

Outdoor Recreation

New Hampshire is an outward bound paradise. **Hiking** is a popular activity with thousands of miles of scenic trails, including 1,200 miles in the White Mountain National Forest. The famed Appalachian Trail traverses the Presidential mountain range, running more than 160 miles through the Granite State; mountain huts and rustic campsites are scattered throughout the White Mountains. For peak-baggers, the state has 48 4,000-footers.

Water sports abound in the Lakes and Northern regions, and along the coastline. Kayaking and canoeing are popular on the Androscoggin River in northern New Hampshire; sailing and powerboating are top activities on Lake Winnipesaukee. Whale watching off the Atlantic coast is popular during the warmer weather months. Outfitters, outdoor centers and guides offer rentals, lessons and guided trips.

The state is home to 19 alpine ski resorts and more than 20 cross-country centers. Skiing, snowboarding, snowshoeing, tubing and dogsledding are popular winter activities. The White Mountains are also known for ice climbing, boasting some of the best conditions for this in the country.

NEW HAMPSHIRE

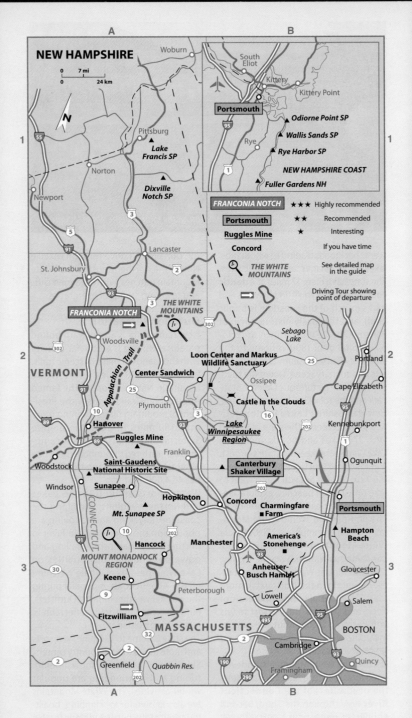

NEW HAMPSHIRE

0   7 mi
0   24 km

N

Woburn

South Eliot

Kittery

Portsmouth

Kittery Point

Pittsburg

▲ Odiorne Point SP

Lake Francis SP

Rye

▲ Wallis Sands SP

Norton

▲ Rye Harbor SP

Newport

Dixville Notch SP

NEW HAMPSHIRE COAST

▲ Fuller Gardens NH

Lancaster

FRANCONIA NOTCH   ★★★ Highly recommended

St. Johnsbury

Portsmouth   ★★ Recommended

Ruggles Mine   ★ Interesting

Concord   If you have time

THE WHITE MOUNTAINS   See detailed map in the guide

FRANCONIA NOTCH

THE WHITE MOUNTAINS   Driving Tour showing point of departure

Woodsville

Appalachian Trail

Sebago Lake

Portland

VERMONT

Loon Center and Markus Wildlife Sanctuary

Center Sandwich

Ossipee

Cape Elizabeth

Plymouth

Castle in the Clouds

Hanover

Lake Winnipesaukee Region

Kennebunkport

Woodstock

Ruggles Mine

Franklin

Ogunquit

Windsor

Saint-Gaudens National Historic Site

Canterbury Shaker Village

Sunapee

Hopkinton

Concord

Portsmouth

Mt. Sunapee SP

Charmingfare Farm

Hampton Beach

Hancock

Manchester

America's Stonehenge

MOUNT MONADNOCK REGION

Keene

Anheuser-Busch Hamlet

Gloucester

Peterborough

Salem

Fitzwilliam

Lowell

MASSACHUSETTS

BOSTON

Greenfield   *Quabbin Res.*

Cambridge

Quincy

Framingham

292

Concord

The capital of New Hampshire since 1808, Concord boasts the largest state legislature in the nation, with 424 representatives. The gilded dome of the State House dominates the cluster of buildings that rise alongside the Merrimack River. A modern center of government and commerce, the city is also the hub for railway and road systems linking all corners of the state. Originally called Rumford, this town was claimed by both the colonies of New Hampshire and Massachusetts. In 1741 a royal declaration settled the dispute by granting Rumford to New Hampshire, and the town was then renamed Concord. The city became known for its granite and for the Concord coaches that were built here from 1813 to 1900.

SIGHTS
State House

107 N. Main St. ✕ ♿ 🕐 *Open year-round Mon–Fri 8am–4.30pm.* 🕐 *Closed major holidays.* ✆*603-271-2154. www.ci. concord.nh.us/tourdest/statehs/*
Completed in 1819, the New Hampshire State House is the oldest state capitol building where the legislature still meets in its original chambers. A visitor center on the ground floor contains exhibits and dioramas of historic events. The House Chamber may also be viewed from a gallery on the third floor.

👥 Museum of New Hampshire History

6 Eagle Sq. ♿ 🅿 🕐 *Open Jul–mid-Oct & Dec Mon–Sat 9.30am–5pm, Sun noon–5pm. Rest of the year closed Mon.* 🕐 *Closed major holidays.* 👓 *$5.50.* ✆*603-228-6688. www.nhhistory.org.*
More than five centuries of the Granite State's history are depicted in the exhibits here. Items include a Concord coach made in the 19C; a sampling of New Hampshire-made furniture (1760–1915); and landscape paintings by such notables as Thomas Hill, Frederic Church and Albert Bierstadt.

▶ **Population:** 45,430.
♿ **Michelin Map:** 581 L 6.
🔲 **Info:** ✆603-224-2508; www.concordnh chamber.com.
▶ **Location:** Concord, in the heart of the state, is located at the intersec-tions of I-89, 93 and 393, and US Highways 3, 4 and 202. The Merrimack River runs through the downtown historic district.
👥 **Kids:** Get up close and personal with more than 200 animals at the nearby Charmingfare Farm.
🕐 **Timing:** Start at the State House, then stroll the Main Street for a look at historic houses, before heading out to the McAuliffe-Shepard Discovery Center.
🅿 **Parking:** All-day parking is available at the Firehouse *(one block west of Main St. between State and Green Sts.)* and Durgin Block *(1/2 block west of Main St. between School and Warren Sts.)* structures. Metered street parking is available throughout downtown *(parking at meters is free after 5pm and on weekends and holidays).*
◉ **Don't Miss:** McAuliffe-Shepard Discovery Center *(be sure to reserve show tickets).*
♿ **Also See:** MANCHESTER.

McAuliffe-Shepard Discovery Center

2 Institution Dr. ♿ 🅿 🕐 *Open year-round daily 10am–5pm.* 🕐 *Closed major holidays.* 👓 *$9.* ✆*603-271-7827. www.starhop.com.*
Named after one of the *Challenger* teacher-astronauts who was a Concord native, the museum is a pleasing mix of small hands-on exhibits and high-tech

Concord Comestibles

The popular and always bustling **Common Man** *(25 Water St.; lunch & dinner daily;* ✆*603-228-3463. www.thecman.com)* mixes rustic charm with well-prepared American cuisine. It's famous for its lobster corn chowder, daily roasted prime rib and country meatloaf.

For a light bite downtown, look for **Bread & Chocolate** *(29 S. Main St.;* ✆*603-228-3330)*, a European bistro/bakery that serves a formidable array of cakes, tarts, breads, cookies and sandwiches. Before or after eating, take time to browse in the adjoining and well-stocked **Gibson's Bookstore** *(27 S. Main St.;* ✆*603-224-0562; www.gibsonsbookstore.com)*.

shows *(reserve show tickets ahead of time as these frequently sell out)*. Special family and teen programs are offered most Friday evenings.

EXCURSIONS
Hopkinton
▶ *8mi west of Concord via Rte. 9.*
Antique hunters often visit this appealing Concord suburb. The town's wide main street is lined with attractive dwellings and shops, the town hall and St. Andrew's Church.

Charmingfare Farm
▶ *20mi southwest of Concord in Candia. Take I-93 south to Exit 9; follow Rte. 27 E. for 4.5mi.* ♿ 🅿 🕐 *Open May–Oct daily 10am–4pm. Special weekends and events throughout rest of year.* ⬤$11. ✆*603-483-5623. www.visitthefarm.com.*
More than 200 animals, including black bear, lynx, cougar, wolf and porcupine,

call this small farm home. There's also a large collection of friendly farm animals, petting areas, wildlife exhibits, as well as a variety of daily demonstrations and exhibits.

Canterbury Shaker Village★★
▶ *20mi north of Concord. From I-93 take Exit 15 E.; follow Rte. 393 E. to Exit 3 and follow signs to Shaker Village. Begin at the visitor center, where a site plan of the village and a schedule of craft demonstrations are available.* 🚶 *Guided tours are offered.* ✕🅿🕐*Open mid-May–Oct daily 10am–5pm.* ⬤$17. ✆*603-783-9511. www.shakers.org.*
Attracted by the serene countryside and the gift of a large tract of land in Canterbury, the **Shakers** established a community near the small village of **Canterbury Center**. Founded in the 1780s, the village was formally organized in 1792, the year the meetinghouse was built,

Canterbury Shaker Village

© NHDTTD / Dave Shafer

and grew to include some 300 residents and 100 buildings on 4,000 acres at the height of the community in the mid-19C. Today 25 original buildings still stand on 694 acres of land.

An idyllic atmosphere pervades the orchards, meadows, vegetable gardens and grassy yards that surround the community's dwellings and farm buildings. Bordered by nature trails, several man-made ponds dot the distant acreage, attracting waterfowl and deer. After your tour of the village, extend your stay in this peaceful area of New Hampshire by picnicking near a pond or strolling along one of the nature trails that run through the grounds, having lunch or dinner at the restaurant or participating in one of the many hands-on craft workshops.

ADDRESSES

🛏 STAY

$$$ Colby Hill Inn – *.5mi west of Henniker Center on Rte. 114, Henniker (17mi west of Concord). ☎603-428-3281. www.colby hillinn.com. 16 rooms. Restaurant.* Just 20 minutes west of Concord, this quintessential New England inn offers elegant accommodations. The inn, originally a 1797 farmhouse, still sports some 18C woodwork and wide pine floorboards. Rooms are individually decorated with floral wall coverings and early-American antiques and reproductions. The inn's **restaurant** is well-known for its seasonal preparations and classic New England dishes.

$$ The Centennial – *96 Pleasant St., Concord. ☎603-227-9000 or 800-360-4839. www.thecentennialhotel.com. 32 rooms.* This elegantly restored brick Victorian Centennial mixes antiques and a classic setting with contemporary flair and modern amenities. It's perfect for travelers who prefer a historical ambience but don't want to give up the creature comforts. If you're ready to splurge, stay in one of the suites located in the inn's towering turrets.

🍴 EAT

$$$ Greenwood's – *288 Shaker Rd. Open mid-May–Oct. Lunch daily 10am–4pm; dinner Thu-Sat. 5pm-9pm; Sun brunch 9am-4pm. ☎603-783-4238. www.shakers.org.* **American.** Built on the site of the historic 1811 Blacksmith Shop at Canterbury Shaker Village, this intimate restaurant, overlooking the Village pastoral grounds, offers a unique dining experience. Entrées, based on Shaker recipes, are served with the freshest of ingredients. Start with the artisan flatbread topped with grilled apple and chicken sausage, or try the smoked butter and garlic mussels. Follow with main dishes like honeyed duck, or bouillabaisse brimming with lobster, scallops, shrimp and mussels, and smoked sausage. Looking for comfort food? Try the Shaker favorite Blond mac-and-cheese, or the slow-cooked Yankee pot roast.

$$ Angelina's Ristorante – *11 Depot St. ☎603-228-3313. www.angelinasrestaurant.com.* **Italian.** The focus at Angelina's is classic Italian fare: daily ravioli, soups, sauces and desserts are all homemade. Bounteous entrées come with soup or salad and a side of pasta.

$ Barley House – *132 North Main S. Open Mon–Sat 11am–1am. Closed Sun. ☎603-228-6363. www.thebarleyhouse.com.* **American.** This casual, local favorite features American classics with international twists, like the Guinness beef stew, and bangers and mash. Other favorites include the curry beer-battered fish and chips, and a selection of gourmet burgers.

$ Hermanos Cocina – *11 Hills Ave. ☎603-224-5669. www.hermanosmexican.com.* **Mexican.** One sip of a Hermanos margarita, made from just-squeezed lemons and limes, and a nibble of the crispy garlic nachos dunked in freshly made salsa, and you'll know why this Mexican restaurant is always hopping. Authentic south-of-the-border fare, with fresh ingredients.

Hanover ★

A regional commercial center for the Upper Connecticut River Valley, Hanover occupies a pretty site on the banks of the Connecticut River. Its claim to fame is Dartmouth College, one of the nation's most prominent Ivy League schools. Despite the town's growth, Hanover's colonial charm and pleasant tree-lined streets remain essentially unspoiled.

DARTMOUTH COLLEGE ★

Main entrance off E. Wheelock St.
603-646-1110. www.dartmouth.edu.
Established in 1769, Dartmouth College today offers its 4,500 students under-graduate programs in the liberal arts and sciences, as well as graduate studies in medicine, engineering, sciences and business administration. Dartmouth's list of illustrious alumni includes lawyer and orator Daniel Webster (1782–1852) and Nelson A. Rockefeller (1908–1979), the former governor of New York and US vice president. The popular Dartmouth **Winter Carnival**, held each February, features skiing, skating, art shows and other special events.

The Green ★

Bounded by Main, Wheelock, Wentworth & College Sts.
This spacious green is bordered by the venerable **Hanover Inn** and a num-ber of college buildings. The corner of Main and Wheelock Streets commands a good view of Dartmouth Row (a group of four Colonial buildings).

▶ **Population:** 11,068
◔ **Michelin Map:** 581 J 4
Info: 603-643-3115; www.hanoverchamber.org.
◗ **Location:** Hanover is the geographic center of the Upper Valley Region, located on the east side of the Connecticut River. It's about an hour's drive north of Concord, easily accessed off I-89.
Kids: Dig for gems at Ruggles Mine.
◷ **Timing:** Start at the Dartmouth College Visitor Center, where you can pick up a campus map.
Parking: All-day parking is available at the Market St. and Water St. parking structures, near the downtown mall. There is metered street parking throughout downtown.
⊛ **Don't Miss:** A tour of Dartmouth College, with its picturesque Colonial buildings, Hood Art Museum and Parker Memorial Library.

Hopkins Center for the Arts

6041 Lower Level Wilson Hall.
P *603-646-2422.*
www.hop.dartmouth.edu.
Recognizable by its multi-storied win-dows, the performing-arts center (1962) houses theaters and two concert halls.

Hanover Hot Spots

A long-standing favorite in the heart of downtown, **Molly's** (*43 S. Main St.; 603-643-2570; www.mollysrestaurant.com*) is a casual restaurant and bar that makes terrific thin crust pizzas (try the Mediterranean pizza with olives, roasted garlic, balsamic-grilled onions, feta and fresh mozzarella cheese), sandwiches, burgers, pasta, and specialties like the wood-fired mac-and-cheese and eggplant rollatini. Another popular spot is the **Dartmouth Co-op** (*21 S. Main St.; 800-634-2667; www.dartmouthcoop.com*), where logo-laden college souvenirs come in all shapes and sizes, from door mats to desk pads, key chains to coffee mugs, as well as sweatshirts, socks and more—all in Dartmouth's school colors.

Hood Museum of Art

On Wheelock St., behind the Hopkins Center facing the south side of Dartmouth Green. &⊙*Open year-round Tue–Sat 10am–5pm (Wed til 9pm), Sun noon–5pm.* ⊙*Closed major holidays.* ✆*603-646-2808. www.hoodmuseum. dartmouth.edu.*

Dartmouth's art museum features Native American, American, European, African and ancient art. On the lower level, a special area displays a group of 9C BC Assyrian reliefs; on the upper level, contemporary art occupies a spacious loft gallery. In addition, the museum oversees the remarkable fresco mural cycle by Jose Clemente Orozco, *The Epic of American Civilization*, which he painted in Baker Library from 1932 to 1934.

Baker-Berry Memorial Library

North end of the Green. &⊙*Open year-round daily, hours vary.* ⊙*Closed major holidays.* ✆*603-646-2704. www.dartmouth.edu.*

The library houses **Epic of American Civilization★**, a series of wall murals painted by the Mexican artist José Clemente Orozco (1883–1949).Powerful and often brutal in their expression of the forces of good and evil, the murals are Orozco's interpretation of the 5,000-year history of the Americas.

Interpretation pamphlet is available at the library information desk.

EXCURSIONS
Saint-Gaudens National Historic Site★

❯*20mi south of Hanover in Cornish. From Hanover, take Rte. 10 south to Rte. 12A. Travel approximately 15mi on Rte. 12A and follow signs to the site.* ✎*Visit of Aspet by guided tour only (30min).* 🅿⊙*Grounds open year-round dawn–dusk. Exhibits open Memorial Day–Oct daily 9am–4.30pm.* ⊙*Closed major holidays.* ⊛*$5.* ✆*603-675-2175. www.nps.gov/saga.*

Nestled in a wooded clearing bordering the Connecticut River, the former house and studio of America's foremost 19C sculptor, **Augustus Saint-Gaudens**, has been open to the public

as a National Historic Site since 1965. Saint-Gaudens is remembered for his monumental Civil War memorials—such as the *Shaw Memorial* on Boston Common—and for his portrait reliefs. During the two decades he lived in Cornish, Saint-Gaudens produced about 150 sculptures. Today five buildings, as well as gardens and an 80-acre woodland, are open to the public.

Ruggles Mine★

❯*28mi southeast of Hanover. Take Rte. 120 south to I-89 south to Exit 17. Follow US-4 east to Grafton Center. Mine is 2mi from the Grafton Center village green; follow signs.* ⊙*Open mid-Jun–mid-Oct daily 9am–5pm. Mid-May–mid-Jun weekends only 9am–5pm. Last admission 1hr before closing.* ⊛*$25.* ✆*603-523-4275. www.rugglesmine.com.*

The mammoth abandoned pegmatite mine on Isinglass Mountain (with its huge arched stone tunnels, winding passageways and large open pits) is a fun place to explore. Amateur rock hounds can rent equipment and dig for mica, feldspar or one of the other 150 minerals that have been found here. Kids love it!

Sunapee★

❯*8mi south of New London on Rte. 11.* This diminutive, colorful lake resort community is dominated by lovely Sunapee Lake. Shops, restaurants and residential houses crowd its shore. The tiny hillside common sports a bandstand and the busy harbor teems with small pleasure craft, cruise boats and fishing vessels. The best way to see the lake is to take a **cruise** aboard the *M.V. Sunapee II (1hr 30min; commentary;* &⊛*$20; for information and schedules, contact Sunapee Cruises,* ✆*603-938-6465 or www.sunapeecruises.com).*

Mount Sunapee State Park

❯*5mi south of Sunapee via Rte. 11 and Rte. 102 east.* &⊙*Open late May–mid-Sept dawn–dusk,* ⊛*$5.* ✆*603-763-5561. www.nhstateparks.org.*

Sunapee Lake and the mountain of the same name form the center of a year-

Fall foliage over Lake Sunapee

round vacation resort. Opposite the entrance to the park is the entrance to the **Sunapee State Beach** on the shores of Lake Sunapee *(off Rte. 103 in Newbury;* ◷*open mid-Jun–Labor Day daily 9am–6pm;* ℘*603-763-5561)*. The **chairlift** to the summit of Mt. Sunapee (2,700ft) operates from North Peak Lodge during the summer and early fall, offering good **views★** of the region *(hours vary; call for information; lift rates vary; Mount Sunapee Resort,* ℘*603-763-3500; www.mountsunapee.com)*.

ADDRESSES

🛏 STAY

$$$$ Hanover Inn– *Wheelock & Main Sts.* ℘*603-643-4300. www.hanoverinn.com. 93 rooms.* This sprawling mainstay on Main Street is a favorite with visiting professors and parents, as well as tourists looking for classic style accommodation and gracious service. Spacious rooms are furnished with fine Colonial reproductions and all have updated marble baths. The **Daniel Webster dining room** is the elegant, special night-out restaurant in the neighborhood and the outdoor terrace is a popular place to nosh during the warmer months.

$$ The Trumbull House Bed & Breakfast – *40 Etna Rd.* 🅿 ℘*603-643-2370 or 800-651-5141. www.trumbullhouse. com. 5 rooms and 1 guest cottage.* You'll feel comfortable the minute you walk into this country home-away-from-home B&B. Set on 16 acres just outside downtown, The Trumbull House offers pastoral surroundings and luxurious accommodations. Take a dip in the swimming pond, or hike nearby paths that hook up with the Appalachian Trail. When you are ready to call it a day, sink into crisp sheets and wrap yourself in a soft down comforter.

🍴 EAT

$$ Murphy's on the Green – *11 N. Main St.* ℘*603-643-4075. www.murphysonthe green.com.* **American.** One of author Bill Bryson's favorite hangouts when he lived in Hanover, this popular neighborhood tavern located in the heart of downtown Hanover attracts a lively and loyal clientele. Menu items range from traditional pub food (Heap 'O Buffalo Wings) to more innovative offerings (pork and bok choy dumplings). There are also lobster pot pies, hefty burgers, fish and chips, black bean cakes, and thick steaks. Check out the back room, which boasts wood wainscoting and c.1898 pews from the Webster Hall at Dartmouth College.

Lake Winnipesaukee Region★

New Hampshire's largest lake covers an area of 72sq mi, has a shoreline of 283mi and is dotted with more than 250 tiny islands. On a clear day, Lake Winnipesaukee, set against the backdrop of the White Mountains, makes a magnificent sight.

LAKESIDE VILLAGES

Each of the villages on the lake possesses its own character. **Laconia** is the industrial and commercial center of the region. The small charming village of **Wolfeboro**, with its large lakeside houses, has attracted summer vacationers for centuries; it's one of the prettiest communities on Lake Winnipesaukee. **Weirs Beach**, with its amusement arcade, souvenir shops and lakefront Victorian dwellings, is a lively family resort. Attractive **Center Harbor** and Meredith, both set on bays at the northern end of the lake, serve as shopping centers for the resort cottages and campgrounds nearby.

Every summer thousands of vacationers enjoy boating on Winnipesaukee's waters. Public docks, marinas and launching ramps abound. Popular beaches include Weirs Beach and **Ellacoya State Beach**. For hikers, walking trails thread the surrounding hills.

○ **Michelin Map:** 581 I, M 4, 5.

⊡ **Info:** ℘603-744-8664; www.lakesregion.org.

▷ **Location:** The largest lake in the state lies south of the White Mountain region, and east of north-south I-93. Rtes. 11, 25, 113 and 109 circle the lake.

♟ **Kids:** The honky-tonk Weirs Beach area is a favorite with families for its rocking arcade, water park and fast-food stands.

○ **Timing:** It's best to base yourself in one of the lakeside towns or villages (see descriptions below) and do day trips from there.

🅿 **Parking:** Free and metered street parking are available in towns and villages surrounding the lake. There is also limited parking at beach areas.

◉ **Don't Miss:** A boat ride on the *M/S Mount Washington* or *M/V Sophie C.*

Sun sets over Lake Winnipesaukee

© NHDTTD / Julia Freeman-Woolpert

During the winter, **Gunstock Ski Area** and **Ragged Mountain Ski Area** teem with activity. Ice fishing, snowmobiling and the dogsled championships held each February in Laconia provide additional winter attractions.

SIGHTS

Sightseeing Cruises★★

The best way to experience the lake is by cruising its waters. Winnipesaukee Flagship Corp. offers scenic cruises on several different excursion vessels, including the *M/S Mount Washington* and the *M/V Sophie C* mailboat. *(For seasonal schedules, rates and information, call 603-366-5531 or 888-843-6686; www.cruisenh.com).*

Castle in the Clouds★

On Rte. 171 east in Moultonborough. ✕&𝗣🕐Open late May–Columbus Day daily 10am–5.30pm. Castle tour $11. Scenic drive, $12 per person. 603-476-5900. www.castleintheclouds.org. This 5,200-acre estate, overlooking Ossipee Mountains was acquired in 1910 by millionaire Thomas Plant. Tour the Lucknow Mansion, the residence Plant commissioned, with its distinctive red slate roof and its eclectic design, incorporating elements from several different countries. From the terrace you can enjoy a **view**★★ of Lake Winnipesaukee with its myriad tree-clad islands. Miles of trails lace the property and a path (*.25mi*) beginning about 1mi from the entrance gate leads to two waterfalls.

Loon Center and Markus Wildlife Sanctuary

In Moultonborough. From Rte. 25 turn onto Blake Rd. (look for the Loon Center sign) and continue 1mi to the end, then turn right onto Lee's Mills Rd. 🕐Trails Center open Jul–Columbus Day daily 9am–5pm; Columbus Day–Dec Mon–Sat 9am–5pm, 2 Jan–Apr Thu–Sat 9am–5pm. 603-476-5666. www.loon.org. Begin your visit inside Loon Center to view the small exhibit area. In the 200-acre wildlife sanctuary, there's a short **Forest Walk** 🚶 through mixed woods

and wildflowers; or opt for the longer **Loon Nest Trail** *(allow 1hr)* through marshland, streams and upland forests bordering Lake Winnipesaukee. Along the way, a lookout permits a view of a loon nesting site, and if your timing is right, an actual loon or two.

ADDRESSES

🛏STAY

$$$$ Wolfeboro Inn – *90 N. Main St., Wolfeboro. 603-569-3016 or 800-451-2389. www.wolfeboroinn.com. 44 rooms. Restaurant.* This elegant hotel, nestled on the eastern shore of Lake Winnipesaukee, has been a mainstay in downtown for nearly two centuries. The original 1812 building has been updated with a soaring three-story addition. There are restored rooms in the historic inn or modern suites in the addition, some with lake-view balconies and private decks. Throughout, you'll find classic country decor, antique furniture, handmade quilts as well as period reproductions.
Be sure to visit **Wolfe's Tavern**; with its old wood beams and brick fireplaces, it's a popular local hangout.

$$$ The Margate on Winnipesaukee *Rte. 3, Laconia. 603-524-5210 or 800-627-4283. www.themargate.com. 141 rooms.* Families looking for a bargain will want to consider this year-round resort on Lake Winnipesaukee. For the sports-minded, activities abound on-site, including indoor and outdoor pools, a health club, tennis courts, a sports bar and lounge, boat rentals and more. Guests wanting to relax can do so on the 400ft private sandy beach. Rooms are motel-style basic, and spread across three separate buildings.

$$ The Inn at Mill Falls – *312 Daniel Webster Hwy., Meredith. 800-622-6455. www.millfalls.com. 101 rooms.* Once a 19C linen mill, this property on the southwest shore of Lake Winnipesaukee is now a replica New England village with four lodging choices. The Inns Spa at Mill Falls features modern guest rooms. Adjacent is the lakefront Inn at Bay Point, surrounded by a formal park, with great views of the lake. Many of the guest rooms at Bay Point feature private balconies and fireplaces. Both the Chase House and the newest property Church Landing have modern lake-view rooms

♀/EAT

$$ The Woodshed – *128 Lee Rd., Moultonborough. Wed–Sat Dinner only.* *603-476-2311. www.thewoodshed nh.com.* **American.** Meander inland from the lake and you'll discover backcountry roads, rolling pastures and rustic farmhouses, like the one that holds this lake region favorite. Most people come here for the homemade soups and breads, as well as for The Woodshed's famous prime rib or thick steaks.

$ Hart's Turkey Farm – *Rte. 3, Meredith.* *603-279-6212. www.hartsturkey farm.com.* **American.** Yes, it's a tourist trap (complete with its own gift store), but Hart's can't be beat for old-fashioned comfort food. Since 1954 the Hart family has been serving up turkey dinners with the works: salad, rolls, veggies, cranberry sauce, stuffing, potatoes, piping hot gravy, and dessert (think Jell-O).

SHOPPING

The **Old Country Store** *(Rtes. 25 & 109, Moultonborough;* *603-476-5750;* *www.nhcountrystore.com)* delights with its bygone-era charm and cluttered array of penny candy, pickle crocks, aged cheddar cheese, New Hampshire maple syrup, and myriad other products. **Keepsake Quilting** *(Rte. 25B, Center Harbor;* *603-253-4026;* *www.keepsakequilting.com)* is known nationwide for its huge selection of fabrics, collections and designs.

Manchester

In the 19C the largest textile factory in the world, the Amoskeag Mills, was built here beside the Merrimack River. The mile-long stretch of brick buildings still standing along the river proves an awesome sight. Financial services have replaced manufacturing as Manchester's main industry.

SIGHTS
Currier Museum of Art★

150 Ash St. ✕ ♿ 🅿 ⏲*Open Sun–Fri (closed Tue) 11am–5pm. Sat 10am–5pm. Closed major holidays.* ✺*$10.* *603-669-6144. www.currier.org.*
A recent, major expansion includes a new winter garden and more gallery space to show off the museum's fine collection of paintings, photographs, sculpture and decorative arts.
Separate galleries contain the **European collection**: early Italian paintings; drawings by **Tiepolo**; and canvases from the French, Spanish, English and Dutch schools; and an American collection of paintings and **decorative art** from the

> ▶ **Population:** 108,580.
> ♿ **Michelin Map:** 581 L 6.
> 🗊 **Info:** *603-666-6600;* www.manchester-chamber.org.
> ⊙ **Location:** Just over the Massachusetts border, this metropolis is bisected by I-93 and I-293. Rte. 101 runs east-west from the seacoast.
> ♟ **Kids:** Little ones love the Clydesdale horses at Anheuser-Busch Hamlet.
> ⊙ **Timing:** Allow 2hrs to tour the Currier Museum of Art and nearly 3hrs for the excursion to Anheuser-Busch Hamlet *(the tour is 90min).*
> ⊛ **Don't Miss:** The Currier Museum of Art, which includes works by Picasso, Monet, Wyeth, LeWitt and O'Keefe.

"The Crest of the Wave" sculpture, Currier Museum of Art

17–19C, with emphasis on New Hampshire pieces. Works by **Andrew Wyeth**, **Edward Hopper**, Georgia O'Keeffe, Louise Nevelson, Alexander Calder, and others represent 20C American painting. Other galleries are devoted to temporary exhibits, and contemporary and 20C art.

Zimmerman House★

Visit by guided tour only (1–2hrs).
Open Apr–mid-Jan, Mon, Thu & Fri 2pm, Sat–Sun10–11.30am & 2pm, Sun 11.30 & 1.30pm. $20. Reservations required. 603-669-6144, ext. 108. www.currier.org.

Designed by Frank Lloyd Wright in 1950, this low-roofed, single-story house made of brick, concrete and cypress typifies the famed architect's "Usonian" style—Wright's own term for the small, utilitarian, yet elegant houses he created late in his career to counter the housing shortage of the Great Depression. The interior contains Wright-designed textiles, as well as his built-in and freestanding furniture.

EXCURSIONS
Anheuser-Busch Hamlet

12mi south of Manchester in Merrimack. Take US-3 (Everett Turnpike) south to Exit 10 and go east on Industrial Dr. to the hamlet, which is located on the grounds of the Anheuser-Busch brewery at 221 Daniel Webster Hwy.
Visit by guided tour only (1hr 30min).
Open Jun–Aug daily 10am–5pm, Jan–May Thu–Mon 10am–4pm, Sept–Dec daily 10am–4pm. Closed major holidays. 603-595-1202. www.budweisertours.com.

Budweiser Clydesdales clip-clop through the picturesque hamlet where they are raised and trained. The "white-stockinged" horses have been the symbol of Anheuser-Busch since 1933, when the company acquired its first team to celebrate the repeal of Prohibition. Today teams of Clydesdales tour the country, appearing in parades and numerous other events.

America's Stonehenge

24mi southeast of Manchester in Salem. Take I-93 south to Exit 3. Follow Rte. 111 east 4.5mi; turn right onto Island Pond Rd. and follow signs to 105 Haverhill Rd. Open daily 9am–5pm. Closed Thanksgiving Day & 25 Dec. $11. 603-893-8300. www.stonehengeusa.com.

The standing granite slabs of this stone complex give the site its name, although these stones are much shorter than their counterparts in England. Many theories exist concerning the site's origin and function; the aligned slabs led scientists to speculate that this may be the remnant of a calendar laid out 4,000 years ago by an advanced civilization with a knowledge of the movement of the stars, moon and sun.

ADDRESSES

⊹/ EAT

$ Chez Vachon – *136 Kelley St.* 603-625-9660. www.chezvachon.com. **French.** The mills of Manchester attracted foreign workers, particularly French Canadians from Quebec. The French influence is still evident today in the city's Franco-American Centre. In this restaurant, try the popular *poutine* dishes (french fries topped with Canadian curd cheese & chicken gravy).

Mount Monadnock Region★

The centerpiece of Monadnock State Park is Mt. Monadnock (3,165ft), looming above pastoral farmlands and tiny villages in southwestern New Hampshire. Hiking to the top of Mt. Monadnock for its spectacular views became popular in the 19C, and today it remains one of the most frequently climbed peaks in the world. Each year some 125,000 persons scale its summit to enjoy the exhilarating views.

KEENE

Keene was first known as Upper Ashuelot, a community granted to soldiers who had fought against Canada. It was founded as a fort town a year later. During King George's War, the village was dismissed by Indians and was abandoned until the early 1750s. Industry established itself here in the mid 19C. Gateway to the Mount Monadnock region, this commercial and manufacturing center has grown rapidly during the past several decades. Tree-lined Main Street sports gift shops, restaurants and retail businesses, as well as several Georgian, Federal, Italianate and Second Empire structures dating from the 1760s *(a walking tour guide is available from the Historical Society of Cheshire County;* ℘*603-352-1895; www.hsccnh. org).* Main Street divides at **Central Square**, which is dominated at the north end by the stately United Church of Christ (1788). Opposite stands the community gazebo on the small common. West of the downtown core lies the Ashuelot River, where 46 acres of riverfront were donated to the city for recreation. The gardens and woods of **Ashuelot River Park** offer opportunities to cycle, walk or jog. Covered-bridge enthusiasts will enjoy a trip on Rte. 10 south to covered bridges **Nos. 2**, **4** and **5** that straddle the river *(roadside markers direct you to the bridges).*

⚲ **Michelin Map:** 581 K 7.
🛈 **Info:** ℘603-352-1303; www.keenechamber.com.
◐ **Location:** Also known as "Currier & Ives" country, the region is tucked in the southwest corner of the state, a 70-minute drive from Manchester and two hours from the seacoast.
👫 **Kids:** Take a hike to the top of Mount Monadnock.
🕐 **Timing:** Allow a day to enjoy Monadnock State Park.
🅿 **Parking:** Street parking is available in Keene and other small towns throughout the area.
☺ **Don't Miss:** A driving tour of the area; it's the best way to see classic New England villages and small towns.
⚲ **Also See:** MANCHESTER.

🚗 DRIVING TOUR

MOUNT MONADNOCK REGION
47mi.

Meander through picturesque historic villages and pretty state parks—including popular Mount Monadnock—on this back-roads journey.

◐ Begin in the town of Fitzwilliam (14mi south of Keene via Rte. 12).

Fitzwilliam

Large clapboard structures, an old meetinghouse, an inn and a Congregational church, which is crowned by a wedding-cake steeple, face the green. To the west *(2.5mi off Rte. 119)*, **Rhododendron State Park** encompasses 16 acres of wild rhododendrons that provide a colorful spectacle when they burst into bloom in July.

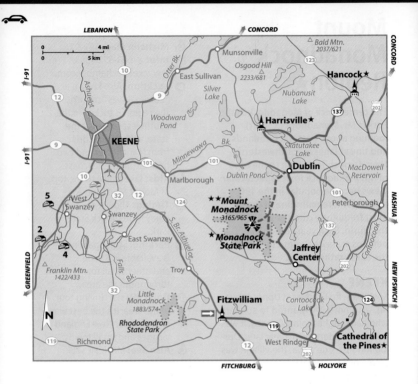

▶ Take Rte. 119 east; after the intersection with Rte. 202, follow the signs for the cathedral located in the town of Rindge.

Cathedral of the Pines★

♿🅿️🕐*Open May–Oct daily 9am–5pm. Contribution requested.* ☎*603-899-3300. www.cathedralofthepines.org.* Situated on the crest of a pine-carpeted hill, this outdoor cathedral is the work of a couple who lost their son in World War II. The Cathedral commemorates all Americans who were killed in battle. The **Memorial Bell Tower**, rising in a clearing, is dedicated to American women who served their country in wartime; Norman Rockwell designed the plaques above the tower arches. The **museum** contains artifacts from around the world, including medals from World War I.

Monadnock Memories

Sometimes it's the little things that make a trip memorable: a stop at a farm, a roadside ice-cream stand, or a trail ride through the woods.

Two miles west of Dublin sits the five-acre 👨‍👧 **Friendly Farm** (*Rte. 101; closed in winter;* 💰*$7.50;* ☎*603-563-8444; www.friendlyfarm.com*) filled with pigs, goats, sheep, ducks, chickens, rabbits and the like. Visitors are encouraged to feed and pet the animals. About a mile east of Jaffrey, along Rte. 124, 👨‍👧 **Kimball Farm Restaurant** (*open mid-Apr–Columbus Day;* ☎*603-532-5765; www.kimballfarm. com*) is a popular stop for ice cream or cold drinks. Across the road from Kimball's is 👨‍👧**Silver Ranch** (*Rte. 124; reservations required;* ☎*603-532-7363*), a livery stable that offers trail, hay and sleigh rides, as well as scenic carriage tours.

▶ Turn left when leaving the Cathedral of the Pines; 1.5mi farther, at the fork, bear right onto Rte. 124.

New Ipswich

The **Barrett House**, a handsome Federal mansion on Main Street, and its sedate rustic surroundings have changed little over the years.

Built in 1800, the house is furnished with family pieces and features two late-19C bathrooms (*visit by 45min guided tour only;* ⓟ *ⓞopen Jun–mid-Oct second & fourth Sat of the month 11am–5pm;* *$5;* *617-994-6675; www.historic-newengland.org*).

▶ Follow Rte. 124 west to Jaffrey. Located at the foot of Mt. Monadnock, Jaffrey provides easy access to Monadnock State Park. Continue on Rte. 124.

Jaffrey Center

Concerts, lectures and meetings are held *throughout the year* at the old meetinghouse on Rte. 124 often in honor of **Amos Fortune**, a former slave who bequeathed a sum of money to the Jaffrey School when he died.

▶ Take Rte. 124 west and .5mi after the meetinghouse turn right.

Monadnock State Park★

△ ⓟ ⓞ*Open year-round daily 8am–dusk.* *$5.* *603-532-8862.* *www.nhstateparks.org.*
Trails to the summit of Mt. Monadnock begin at the end of the tar road beyond the tollbooth.

Mount Monadnock★★

Of the 40 trails leading to this peak, the trail most frequently taken is the **White Dot Trail** 🔼 (*several steep sections; round-trip 3–4hrs*). A similar route, the **White Cross Trail** 🔼 is somewhat more difficult. **Pumpelly Trail** 🔼 is the longest, but easiest, path to the top. The far-reaching **view★★** from the summit on a clear day includes Mt. Washington (*north*) and the Boston skyline (*southeast*). The summit is the only place in

New England from which parts of all six of the region's states can be seen.

▶ As you leave the park, turn left onto Upper Jaffrey Rd.

Mount Monadnock behind Perkins Pond

© NHDTTD / Jeffrey Newcomer

Dublin

Mark Twain summered in this hillside hamlet, today the home of *Yankee Magazine* and *The Old Farmers Almanac*.

◗ Continue north on Upper Jaffrey Rd., turn right on Rte. 101, then left onto New Harrisville Rd.

Harrisville★

This handsome ensemble of modest brick buildings, dwellings, mills and Congregational church reflected in the village pond creates a pleasing tableau of an early rural mill town.

◗ Follow the unmarked road east along the lakes, then turn left onto Rte. 137.

Hancock★

The tranquility of this colonial village is disturbed only once a year, on the 4th of July, when the bells of the meeting-house peal from midnight to one o'clock in the morning to celebrate the anniversary of America's independence. The **John Hancock Inn** sits in the center of the village, opposite the general store.

ADDRESSES

🏠 STAY

$$$ Hancock Inn – *33 Main St., Hancock. ☎800-525-3318 or 603-525-3318. www.hancockinn.com. 14 rooms & suites. Restaurant.* Lovers of historic houses will be enchanted with this inn, which has been in continuous operation since 1789. Although rooms have modern conveniences (beside private baths, air conditioning and cable TV, some also have gas fireplaces and private patios), there is much preserved here, including the original domed ceiling in the Ball Room and hand-painted murals in the Rufus Porter Room. The elegant on-site **restaurant** is popular with both inn guests and locals. Try its signature dish, the Shaker Cranberry Pot Roast, which has been on the menu for more than 25 years and has even featured in *Bon Appétit* magazine.

$$ Woodbound Inn – *247 Woodbound Rd., Rindge. ☎603-532-8341 or 800-688-7770. www.woodbound.com. 45 rooms.* Families looking for down-to-earth accommodations will find plenty to keep them happy at this Monadnock area country estate. Set on 165 acres on the shores of Lake Contoocook, the resort attracts vacationers who enjoy the daily program of sports and outdoor activities—ranging from golf in summer (the inn has its own nine-hole course) to cross-country skiing in winter. Choose from airy, individually decorated rooms in the main inn (14 out of the 19 have private baths); more contemporary rooms in the Edgewood Building; and rustic lakefront cabins.

🍴EAT

$$ Papagallos– *9 Monadnock Hwy., Keene. Dinner only Tue–Fri, Sat–Sun 11am–10pm, closed Mon. ☎603-352-9400. www.papagallos.com.* **Italian.** This popular restaurant specializes in traditional Italian dishes (think: fettucine alfredo, chicken parmigiana and veal picata) in hefty portions and wallet-pleasing prices. The dining room is usually packed, especially on weekend nights, and the atmosphere is casual and fun.

$$ Thorndike's at the Monadnock Inn – *379 Main St., Jaffrey Center. ☎603-532-7800. www.monadnockinn.com.* **American.** This restaurant, set in a rambling 1830s country inn, boasts fresh seasonal dishes, just-baked breads and homemade desserts. Start with an appetizer like sweet potato flan or grilled Caribbean shrimp, and end with a slice of fresh berry pie. In between, you'll have a wide choice of entrées, including meat, poultry, fish and pasta. When a chill is in the air, cozy up to the wood-burning fireplace; in warm weather, dine on the screened porch and enjoy views of the inn's sweeping grounds. The inn pub offers lighter fare.

$ Fritz Belgium Fries– *45 Main St., Keene. ☎603-357-6393. www.fritztheplacetoeat.com.* **European.** Affordable and casual, this Main Street cafe in Keene is known for its hand-cut Belgian fries—which are served with a choice of sauces like curry pineapple, peanut satay, rosemary garlic—and fresh-made paninis.

New Hampshire Coast

Sandy beaches, rocky ledges and state parks line New Hampshire's short 18mi coastline. Skirting the shore, Rte. 1A runs from Seabrook to Portsmouth past resort areas, elegant estates and fine views of the ocean.

SIGHTS
Hampton Beach
On Rte. 1A, 1mi north of Seabrook.
This lively resort center claims a water-front boardwalk, large clusters of ocean-front hotels, motels and eating places, as well as a 3.5mi sandy beach. North of Hampton Beach, the road passes the fashionable waterfront estates of **Little Boars Head**.

Fuller Gardens
10 Willow Ave., North Hampton. P ○*Open mid-May–mid-Oct daily 10am–5.30pm.* ○*$9.* ℰ*603-964-5414. www.fullergardens.org.*
This formal garden occupies the summer estate of Alvan T. Fuller, a former governor of Massachusetts. A stroll through the formal rose beds containing over 2,000 rosebushes, Japanese gardens, greenhouses, and beds of annuals and perennials is punctuated with glimpses of the sea beyond.

Rye Harbor State Park
On Rte. 1A in Rye. ♿○*Open late-May–early-Sep daily 8am–6pm.* ○*$4.* ℰ*603-436-1552. www.nhstateparks.org.*
This rocky headland overlooking the Atlantic Ocean provides good picnic and saltwater fishing grounds. Enjoy ocean breezes and scenic views of the Atlantic, the Isles of Shoals and Rye Harbor (also called Ragged Neck).

Wallis Sands State Park
On Rte. 1A in Rye. ♿○*Open mid-May–early-Sep daily 8am–6pm ○$15/car.* ℰ*603-436-9404. www.nhstateparks.org.*
A gentle surf breaks onto the park's quarter-mile-long beach, which is mobbed in

- ♿ **Michelin Map:** 581 N 6.
- 🗎 **Info:** ℰ603-427-2020; www.seacoastnh.com.
- ◗ **Location:** North-south I-95 and Rtes. 1 and 1A provide access to seacoast towns and beaches.
- 👥 **Kids:** Tide pool at the pretty Odiorne Point State Park and visit the on-site Seacoast Science Center.
- 🕐 **Timing:** Arrive at beaches early to snag parking spots and a place in the sand.
- 🅿 **Parking:** Limited parking at public beaches along Rte. 1A. A large (paid) parking lot is available at Hampton Beach.
- ◉ **Don't Miss:** Rollicking Hampton State Beach with its sugar white sand and plethora of activities.
- ♿ **Also See:** PORTSMOUTH, MAINE COAST.

Isles of Shoals from the New Hampshire coast

© NHDTTD / Tara Lenharth

summer. Amenities include a store that sells a variety of items, food and drinks; a bathhouse with showers and a grassy area with picnic tables.

Odiorne Point State Park

On Rte. 1A near Rye. ♿🕐*Open mid-May–early-Sept daily 8am–6pm.* 🐌*$5.* 📞*603-436-7406. www.nhstate parks.org.*

The ragged promontory of Odiorne Point was the site of the first settlement in New Hampshire. You'll have sweeping ocean views throughout the park's 137 undeveloped acres. Be sure to visit the **Seacoast Science Center** at the park, with exhibits, aquariums and a touch tank (*separate admission fee*). A network of trails criss-cross the park, picking through the thick vegetation.

ADDRESSES

🛏 STAY

$$$$$ Wentworth By-the-Sea – *588 Wentworth Rd., New Castle.* 📞*603-422-7322 or 888-252-6888. www.wentworth.com. 205 rooms.* Arguably the finest place to stay in the seacoast region, this historic grande dame on New Castle island boasts ocean and harbor views. Rooms are bright and airy, with top-notch amenities. Full-service spa, tennis club, two pools, health club, marina and golf course are on-site; the dining room is a favorite among locals and visitors.

$$$ Ashworth by the Sea – *295 Ocean Blvd., Hampton Beach.* 📞*603-926-6762 or 800-345-6736. www.ashworthhotel.com. 105 rooms.* Great views overlooking the popular Hampton Beach and an indoor/outdoor pool make this resort hotel a magnet for vacationing families, who enjoy being in the middle of the action.

$$ The Victoria Inn – *430 High St., Hampton.* 📞*603-929-1437. www. thevictoriainn.com. 6 rooms.* Nestled among oceanfront mansions and stately homes, this small inn offers a quiet oasis from the bustling beach scene. Built in 1875 as a carriage house, the inn's renovated rooms are furnished with Victorian-era antiques.

🍴 EAT

$$ Ron's Landing – *379 Ocean Blvd., Hampton Beach. Closed Mon & Tue. Sunday brunch available Oct–April 11am–3pm. Reservations recommended.* 📞*603-929-2122. www.ronslanding.com.* **American.** Situated in the thick of the beachfront commercial strip, Ron's features two floors of dining, including an enclosed second-story deck over-looking the ocean. A wide selection of seafood, steaks and pastas is offered at this casual, full-service, family-friendly restaurant that's open year-round.

Northern New Hampshire

North of the White Mountains, a dense boreal forest stretches into Canada. Although development of this sparsely settled region has historically been hindered by the challenging terrain of the White Mountains, sports enthusiasts have long been drawn here to hunt, fish, snowmobile, or simply enjoy the area's unspoiled natural beauty. The region is home to scenic Dixville Notch and the Connecticut Lakes, a series of wilderness waterways linked by the Connecticut River.

- ♿ **Michelin Map:** 581 L 1.
- 🗎 **Info:** 📞603-237-8939 or 800-698-8939; www. northcountrychamber.org.
- 📍 **Location:** Rte. 3 snakes through the northern top of the state to the Canadian border. Scenic Rte. 26 travels east-west.
- 👪 **Kids:** Several outfitters offer fishing and boating trips.
- 🕐 **Timing:** Plan a day on the Connecticut Lakes or for a hike in the mountains.
- 👁 **Don't Miss:** A drive through Dixville Notch.

Deer wandering in Colebrook near Dixville Notch

© NHDTTD / Carol Placey

CONNECTICUT LAKES

603-538-7118. www.nhconnlakes.com. Rising in the narrow reaches of New Hampshire, the headwaters of the Connecticut River flow south through the **Third**, **Second** and **First Connecticut Lakes** before turning southwest to form the border between New Hampshire and Vermont. This region is a sports enthusiast's paradise: its woods are home to moose, black bear, whitetail deer, grouse and woodcock, and its lakes teem with trout and landlocked salmon. Along US-3, between the gateway township of Pittsburg and the Canadian border, you can glimpse the lakes through the trees. As you drive north on US-3 through the Connecticut Lakes State Forest, it is not unusual to spot moose browsing along the sides of the road.

LAKE FRANCIS STATE PARK

7mi northeast of Pittsburg via US-3. Turn right onto River Rd.; the park entrance is 2mi past the covered bridge. ⛺ 🅿 🕐*Open mid-May–mid-Oct daily 8am–8pm.* 👟*$4.* *603-538–6965. www.nhstateparks.org.*
Just south of First Connecticut Lake, man-made Lake Francis is southernmost in the chain of lakes connected by the Connecticut River. Surrounded by New Hampshire's northern wilderness, the scenic shores of Lake Francis provide an ideal spot to camp, picnic or fish.

DIXVILLE NOTCH

Rte. 26, between the towns of Colebrook and Errol, passes through Dixville Notch, the northernmost of the White Mountain notches. An area of steep jagged cliffs and thick stands of evergreens, much of the notch falls within the confines of the **Dixville Notch State Park** (*603-323-6707; www.nhstateparks.org*). On the shores of Lake Gloriette, near the highest point (1,871ft) in the notch, stands the grand resort hotel known as **The Balsams**, which among its numerous outdoor sporting facilities, has an 18-hole championship golf course called Panorama, designed by arguably the most influential golf course deisgner in the history of the sport, Donald Ross.

ADDRESSES

RECREATION

The village of **Errol** *(southeast of Dixville Notch on Rte. 26)* is an outdoor center for wilderness camps and river trips, close to the beautiful Androscoggin River. **Saco Bound** (*603-447-2177; www.sacobound. com*) offers a host of cruises, guided paddling and camping trips.

Portsmouth★★

Portsmouth is a small city on the banks of the Piscataqua River, New Hampshire's only seaport and the colonial capital until 1808 (when the seat of government was moved to Concord). In summer tourists flock to its waterfront, historic houses and numerous shops, galleries and restaurants.

A number of Portsmouth's Colonial structures and historic houses are open to the public as museums. One of the most interesting ones is Strawbery Banke, the city's early waterfront community which has been transformed into a living history museum.

A BIT OF HISTORY

In 1630 a group of English settlers arrived on the banks of the Piscataqua River. Noting that the riverbanks were covered with wild strawberries, they named their community "Strawbery Banke." Not until three decades later was the "port at the mouth of the river" renamed Portsmouth.

Vintage Georgian mansions, reminiscent of Portsmouth's past as a lumber and seafaring center, line the streets leading to the waterfront. In the **Old Harbor District—Bow, Market and Ceres Streets**—restored and freshly painted restaurants, art galleries and antique

▶ **Population:** 20,674.

Michelin Map: 581 N 6.

Info: ☎603-436-1118; www.portsmouth chamber.org.

Location: Portsmouth sits on the Piscataqua River, just off N/S I-95.

Kids: Children will enjoy the tugboats in the Old Harbor.

Timing: Start at the Market Square, the hub of downtown activity. Use the map opposite to follow the self-guided walking tour of historic sites. Reserve a half to full day to visit the Strawbery Banke Museum.

Parking: Public car park on Hanover Street near downtown sights and metered parking on streets.

Don't Miss: The Strawbery Banke Museum.

shops, as well as the tugboats tied up at the Ceres Street cove, remind visitors of a time when commerce was the mainstay of Portsmouth's economy. **Harbor cruises** on the Piscataqua River offer a pleasant way to view the city and its environs (*depart from Ceres Street Dock; 1hr 15min; commentary; reservations*

Strawbery Banke Museum

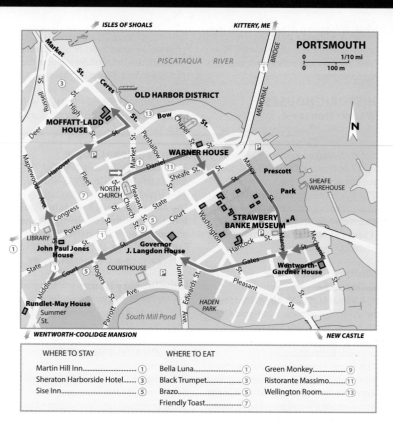

ISLES OF SHOALS   KITTERY, ME

PISCATAQUA RIVER

PORTSMOUTH

0   1/10 mi
0   100 m

N

OLD HARBOR DISTRICT

MOFFATT-LADD
HOUSE

WARNER HOUSE

Prescott
Park

SHEAFE
WAREHOUSE

NORTH
CHURCH

STRAWBERY
BANKE MUSEUM

LIBRARY

John Paul Jones
House

Governor
J. Langdon House

Hancock

Wentworth-
Gardner House

COURTHOUSE

Gates

Pleasant

HADEN
PARK

Rundlet-May House

Summer
St.

South Mill Pond

WENTWORTH-COOLIDGE MANSION

NEW CASTLE

WHERE TO STAY		WHERE TO EAT			
Martin Hill Inn	①	Bella Luna	①	Green Monkey	⑨
Sheraton Harborside Hotel	③	Black Trumpet	③	Ristorante Massimo	⑪
Sise Inn	⑤	Brazo	⑤	Wellington Room	⑬
		Friendly Toast	⑦		

suggested; ✕⏝$17; for seasonal sched-
ules, contact Portsmouth Harbor Cruises:
☏603-436-8084 or 800-776-0915; www.
portsmouthharbor.com).

STRAWBERY BANKE MUSEUM★★

Entrance on Marcy St. ➤Holiday
*house tours offered in Dec 10am–2pm.
Site plan available at the entrance.*
✕🅿🕐*Open May–Oct daily 10am–
5pm.* ⏝$15. ☏603-433-1100.
www.strawberybanke.org.
Overlooking lovely Prescott Park and the
broad Piscataqua River beyond, this vil-
lage-museum is a pleasant assembly of
tree-shaded paths, historic houses and
period gardens that border an expansive
green.

The slower pace of bygone eras enve-
lopes visitors as they enter this remnant
of yesteryear, which traces over 300
years of American architectural styles.

The tour of Strawbery Banke is self-
guided. You may want to follow the
sequence in which the buildings are
numbered on the museum's site plan.
Interpreters in period dress staff several of the structures and are available
to answer questions. Conant House
(c.1791), on the Washington Street side
of the museum, serves lunch and light
refreshments during the day. On the
opposite end, bordering Marcy Street,
the Dunaway Store now houses one
of Portsmouth's finest restaurants. In
addition, some eight period gardens
grace the grounds—a kitchen garden,
Victorian and victory gardens, and a
herb garden among them.

Between Strawbery Banke and the river
lies **Prescott Park**, which is planted with
lush flower gardens during the summer
and filled with weekend picnickers, sun-
bathers, volleyball players and kite fly-
ers. Opposite the entrance to Strawbery

Banke is a **liberty pole** (**A**), similar to those raised by the patriots during Revolutionary days to signify their opposition to the Crown.

HISTORIC HOUSES
Warner House★★

150 Daniel St. ⬤Visit by guided tour only (45 min). 🕐Open mid-Jun–mid-Oct Wed–Mon noon–4pm. 🕐Closed major holidays. ⬤$5. ☎603-436-5909. www.warnerhouse.org.
This brick Georgian mansion was built in 1716 and is decorated with European- and New England-made furnishings. A series of 18C murals adorn the walls of the stairwell.

Moffatt-Ladd House & Garden★

154 Market St. ⬤Visit by guided tour only (1hr). 🕐Open early-Jun–mid-Oct Mon–Sat 11am–5pm, Sun 1pm–5pm. ⬤$6. ☎603-436-8221. www.moffattladd.org.
This elegant three-story Georgian mansion, built in 1763, includes a grand entrance hall with period wallpaper and elaborate wood paneling. A pleasant terraced garden (mid-19C) adjoins the house.

Wentworth-Gardner House

50 Mechanic St. ⬤Visit by guided tour only (1hr). 🕐Open mid-Jun–mid-Oct Wed–Sun noon–4pm. 🕐Closed major holidays. ⬤$5. ☎603-436-4406. www.wentworthgardinerandlear.org.
The facade of this lovely Georgian mansion, built in 1760, casts its reflection on the surface of the Piscataqua River. The pineapple carved above the doorway was the symbol of hospitality in colonial times. Inside, the paneling, balusters and cornices are flawlessly carved.

Governor John Langdon House

143 Pleasant St. ⬤Visit by guided tour only (45min). 🕐Open Jun–mid-Oct Fri–Sun 11am–5pm (on the hour). 🕐Closed major holidays. ⬤$6. ☎603-436-3205. www.historic newengland.org.
This handsome Georgian mansion (1784) is primarily known for its original owner John Langdon, the first president of the US Senate and a former governor of New Hampshire. The interior features wood-carved embellishments, as well as 18C and 19C furniture that was made in Portsmouth.

John Paul Jones House

43 Middle St. 🕐Memorial Day–Oct daily 11am–5pm. ⬤$6. ☎603-436-8420. www.portsmouthhistory.org.
The American naval hero **John Paul Jones** stayed in this Colonial-style house on two occasions during the Revolution. Early furnishings, china, clothing and historical memorabilia are on display.

Rundlet-May House

364 Middle St. ⬤Visit by guided tour only (45min). 🕐Open Jun–mid-Oct first & third Sat of the month 11am–5pm (on the hour). 🕐Closed major holidays. ⬤$6. ☎603-436-3205. www.historic newengland.org.
This elegant three-story Federal residence reflects the taste and lifestyle of the merchant family who owned the property from its construction in 1807 until the 1970s. The interior is appointed with many of the original embellishments and amenities, such as fine pieces of Portsmouth furniture, English wallpaper and innovative early-19C kitchen conveniences. The attached outbuildings and garden further enhance the dwelling's charm.

EXCURSIONS
Cruise to Isles of Shoals★

▶ *Departs from Market St. dock mid-Jun–Labor Day daily. Limited schedule spring & fall. Round-trip 2hrs 30min. Commentary. Reservations recommended. ✕♿🅿Fees & schedules vary; call for information: Isles of Shoals Steamship Co., ☎603-431-5500 or 800-441-4620; www.islesofshoals.com.*
The 10mi boat trip to this group of nine islands follows the banks of the Piscataqua for 5mi before heading out to sea. There are good views of sights along the river, **Fort McClary** (Kittery, Maine), **Fort**

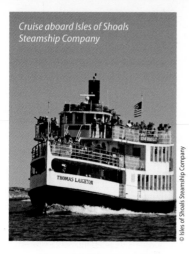
Cruise aboard Isles of Shoals Steamship Company

© Isles of Shoals Steamship Company

Constitution, and the lovely houses in the island town of New Castle.

Wentworth-Coolidge Mansion

▶ *375 Little Harbor Rd. off Rte. 1A, 2mi south of downtown Portsmouth. Cross the Portsmouth city line (.25mi) and turn right just before the cemetery onto Little Harbor Rd. Continue 1mi and follow signs.* ☜*Visit by guided tour only (1hr).* ◷*Open late June–early Sept. Tours at 10am, 11.30am, 12.45pm, 2pm and 3pm.* ☻*$7.* ✆*603-436-6607. www.nhstateparks.org.*

This 40-room 18C mansion on the banks of the Piscataqua River was the home of Benning Wentworth, the son of John Wentworth, New Hampshire's first colonial governor. The house remains an elegant example of the sophisticated early-American architecture of the Portsmouth region. There's a visitor center on the grounds, as well as the well-regarded Coolidge Center for the Arts, displaying works from local, regional and national contemporary artists.

Fort Constitution

▶ *On Rte. 1B at U.S. Coast Guard Station, New Castle. Year-round dawn–dusk.* ✆*603-436-1552. www.nhstateparks.org.*

Originally called Fort William and Mary, this two-acre National Historic Site on the Atlantic Ocean, was built to protect Portsmouth Harbor. On 13 December 1774, Paul Revere sent notice that the British troops were planning to take over the fort. The next day, local residents gathered to collect the gun powder and weapons stored in the fort. There's a short, self-guided walking trail and ocean vistas.

ADDRESSES

🛏STAY

$$$ Martin Hill Inn – *404 Islington St.* ✆*603-436-2287. www.martinhillinn.com. 7 rooms.* A longtime favorite, the Martin Hill Inn is recognizable by its canopied windows and white picket fence. Guest rooms occupy two adjoining historic buildings lined by a short brick pathway through perennial and water gardens. The large master bedroom, with original wide-board pine flooring, Federal-style canopy bed, and antique mahogany English armoire, is a favorite among guests. All rooms have queen-size beds, air conditioning and private baths.

Martin Hill Inn

© Jumping Rocks Inc. / Martin Hill Inn

$$$ Sheraton Portsmouth Harborside – *250 Market St.* ✆*603-431-2300. www.sheratonportsmouth.com. 205 rooms.* This deluxe high-rise hotel is located in the heart of town within easy walking distance to the Market Square and other historic sites. Rooms are contemporary, and there's a fitness center and indoor pool and sauna on the property.

$$$ Sise Inn – *40 Court Street. 603-433-1200 or 877-747-3466. www.siseinn.com. 34 rooms.* Once owned by wealthy Portsmouth merchant John Sise, this centrally located 1881 Queen Anne mansion is decorated in Victorian-era antiques, high-end reproductions and museum prints. Rooms have modern amenities mixed with period furnishings and historic surroundings. The parlor, with its intricate woodwork and paneling, and the sun-filled breakfast room are popular gathering spots.

$$ The Port Inn – *505 US Hwy. 1 Bypass. 603-436-4378. www.theportinn.net. 57 rooms.* If you're looking for a comfortable and surprisingly affordable place to stay in Portsmouth—and don't mind the short, five-minute drive into downtown—consider this property, which is loaded with amenities. Rooms are spacious, with luxury linens, flat, HD TVs, modern baths and free Wi-Fi. There's a seasonal outdoor pool, barbecue area and picnic patio. Rates include a continental breakfast. Studios, with full kitchens, are also available.

⅋/EAT

$$$$ Ristorante Massimo – *59 Penhallow St. Dinner only. Closed Sun. 603-436-4000. www.ristorantemassimo.com.* This upscale restaurant, housed in an historic brick building, is arguably one of Portsmouth's finest eateries. The elegant dining room has stone and brick walls adorned with original oil paintings by renowned artists; tables are decked out with white linen and crystal. The menu features classic Italian dishes made from local, seasonal ingredients, including house-cured meats, homemade breads and pasta.

$$$ Black Trumpet – *29 Ceres St. Dinner only. 603-431-0887. www.blacktrumpetbistro.com.* **American.** Housed in an historic brick and hand-hewn wood beamed building, this elegant, chef-owned restaurant features an ever-changing menu, showcasing fresh, local ingredients and intricate and creative pairings. Start with an appetizer like the braised octopus or fried escargots, followed by entrées like gnocchi sautéed with chard and squash, filet mignon topped with fried oysters, or marinated spring lamb chops. The tiny, upstairs wine bar, overlooking Portsmouth Harbor, is a great place to linger with drinks and small plate appetizers.

$$$ Brazo – *75 Pleasant St. Dinner only. Closed Sun 603-431-0050. www.brazorestaurant.com.* **American.** Order a carafe of freshly-mixed Brazilian sangria or a pomegranate mojito to go with starters like the Yucatan fish tacos, beef empanadas or the papaya glazed shrimp skewers. Entrées at this lively restaurant, located in the heart of downtown, include fire-roasted churrasco, seafood paella and guava BBQ pork.

$$$ Green Monkey – *86 Pleasant St. Dinner only. Closed Sun. 603-427-1010. www.thegreenmonkey.net.* **American.** A snazzy standout in Portsmouth's thriving restaurant scene, this casually elegant eatery serves up tasty American cuisine with flourish and flair. Start with the Fuji apple and pork wontons, or the lemongrass steamed mussels, followed by Thai BBQ short ribs, pan-seared scallops or roasted local cod served with butter poached lobster mashed potatoes.

$$$ Wellington Room – *67 Bow St. Dinner only. Closed Mon & Tue. 603-431-2989. www.thewellingtonroom.com.* **American.** This intimate dining room, with only a handful of tables overlooking Portsmouth Harbor, has won rave reviews from local diners and critics alike. Owner-chef Matthew Sharlot prepares a small menu of seasonal choices which includes selections like local cod simmered in coconut green curry broth, shellfish bouillabaisse and pan-roasted duck with dried cherries.

TAKING A BREAK

Bordering North Church, the popular square at the intersection of Market, Pleasant, Daniel and Congress Streets, is a great place for people-watching, relaxing and eating.

$ The Friendly Toast *(121 Congress St.; 603-430-2154, www.thefriendlytoast.net)* is popular for its funky garage-sale interior and creative menu. Start the day with the popular Almond Joy cakes (buttermilk pancakes, chocolate chips, coconut and almonds) or one of the stuffed omelets. The lunch menu includes a variety of salads, burgers and club sandwiches, like the grilled anadama bread with black beans, salsa, cream cheese, cheddar and avocado.

The White Mountains★★★

Spreading across northern New Hampshire and into Maine, the White Mountains make this region the most mountainous in the whole of New England. Included in this area, the federally managed White Mountain National Forest is renowned for its 772,000 acres of spectacular natural attractions, picnic areas, campgrounds and more than 1,200mi of hiking trails. The region's long winter offers numerous opportunities for skiing, both in the National Forest and in the valleys close by. Throughout the summer, hikers and motorists enjoy the cool woods and waterfalls, as well as the views from the mountain summits; in the fall, nature transforms the White Mountains into a leaf-peeper's paradise.

GEOLOGICAL NOTES

Named for the snow that blankets the area during most of the year, these mountains, dominated by Mt. Washington (6,288ft), are characterized by their rounded summits and deep, broad, U-shaped valleys known as **notches**. The mountains are remnants of ancient, primarily granite, mountain ranges. During the last Ice Age, they were covered by an immense ice sheet, which ground and carved the summits until they were rounded. As the ice sheet retreated, glaciers created steep-walled valleys, polishing them to smooth U-shaped notches, while the swirling action of melting glacial water sculpted giant potholes, such as the basin found in Franconia Notch.

A BIT OF HISTORY

Giovanni da Verrazzano sighted the White Mountains from the coast in 1524, and as early as 1642 a settler scaled the peak we now call Mt. Washington. The artists and writers who visited the region in the early 19C depicted the rugged beauty of the White Mountains

- **Michelin Map:** 581 K-M 2-4.
- **Info:** ✆603-745-8720; www.visitwhite mountains.com.
- **Location:** The popular White Mountain region dominates the central part of the state. Rte. 16 travels north-south on the eastern border; I-93 runs north-south on the west side of the region. Rte. 302 travels west and northwest; the scenic Kancamagus Highway *(Rte. 112)* runs east-west.
- **Kids:** Family friendly activities are everywhere! Young children love the characters and rides at Story Land. Take a ride on the historic Cog Railway to the top of Mount Washington, and squirm through the narrow passageways at Polar Caves Park.
- **Timing:** Plan a day or two for scenic drives, and at least another day for outdoor activities like hiking, biking or boating. Join a guided hike with the **Appalachian Mountain Club**; free daily trips are offered from the AMC Highland House in Crawford Notch.
- **Parking:** You'll pay *($5 a day)* to park at some of the popular trailheads.
- **Don't Miss:** Flume Gorge, with towering waterfalls and cascades.

in their paintings, novels, short stories and poetry. During the same period, New Hampshire residents named Mt. Washington and the other peaks in the Presidential Range after former US

Early winter snow atop Mount Washington behind Mount Washington Resort

© NHDTTD / Ann Colotti

Dining with a View

The **1785 Inn** (*603-356-9025; www.the1785inn.com*) is known for its award-winning cuisine and fine views of Mt. Washington. Soak up sweeping mountain vistas and feast on creative dishes, like the venison carpaccio, lobster flan and herb crepe, raspberry-glazed duckling or the melt-in-your-mouth apple wood smoked rabbit.

presidents. By the end of the century, with the construction of the railroad and the abundance of Victorian hotels that had sprung up in the valley, tourism had established itself on a grand scale in the White Mountains. Many of the fine old hotels have since been destroyed by fire and replaced by clusters of country inns, motels and cottages.

MOUNT WASHINGTON★★★

Mount Washington is the highest point in New England (6,288ft) and the principal peak in the Presidential Range.

A subarctic climate—characterized by bitter cold, wind and ice—predominates in the higher altitudes of this peak. Some of the strongest winds ever recorded (231mph) swept across Mt. Washington's summit on 12 April 1934.

Snow falls on this peak during every month of the year. Fog-bound at least 300 days each year, the summit of Mt. Washington, with its group of mountaintop buildings, has been dubbed the "City Among the Clouds."

GETTING AROUND

Many scenic routes traverse White Mountain National Forest, including I-93 from **Plymouth** to Exit 35 *(30mi)*; Rte. 112 from **Lincoln** to **Conway** *(37mi)*; and Rte. 15 from **Milton Mills** (south of the National Forest) to **Gorham** *(86mi)*.

The **Mount Washington Valley Chamber of Commerce** offers maps and information on attractions, accommodations, dining and recreation in the area (*603-356-3171; www.mtwashingtonvalley.org*). The **Appalachian Mountain Club (AMC)** runs a visitor center at the base of Mt. Washington in Pinkham Notch and at the Highland House in Crawford Notch (*603-466-2727; www.outdoors.org*). Trail maps and guide books are available at the visitor center. For information on campgrounds, hiking trails and scenic drives in the **White Mountain National Forest**, check with the forest headquarters (*603-536-6100; www.fs.fed.us/r9/white*).

Tax-Free Shopping and Miniature Golfing

North Conway is a shopper's paradise, with top designer outlet shops and local specialty stores —and shopping is tax free! Stop by the historic **North Conway 5¢ and 10¢** for penny candy, homemade fudge and cheesy souvenirs. **Zeb's General Store** is a handsome emporium filled with maple syrup, jams, candy, books, puzzles and other New England-made products. **The Penguin Gallery** stocks wind chimes, banners, rocking chairs, hammocks, books and other merchandise. After your shopping spree, head for a round of miniature golf at **Banana Village** (*603-356-2899*) or **Pirate's Cove** (*603-356-8807*), both on Rte. 16.

The Summit

The Mount Washington Cog Railway and the Auto Road (closed during severe weather) are the quickest means of reaching the summit. Hikers in good condition can try one of the four strenuous trails that lead to the summit.

Among the half-dozen structures that cap Mt. Washington are the stone-walled Tip Top House (1853), radio and TV broadcasting facilities, and the Summit Building. The **Sherman Adams Summit Building** is the home to the Mt. Washington Weather Observatory (✕ ♿ 🅿 ⏰ *open May–mid-Oct daily 8am–8pm; 603-356-2137; www.mountwashington.org*). On a clear day, the rooftop deck of the building offers an impressive **panorama★★★**.

Mount Washington Cog Railway★★

6mi east of Fabyan. See description.

🚗 DRIVING TOUR

On this scenic driving tour you'll have sweeping views of the Presidential Mountains, waterfalls and lakes, and you'll travel through three of its dramatic notches. The tour includes stops at some of New Hampshire's favorite attractions, like Flume Gorge, Arethusa Falls and the Mount Washington Cog Railway.

1 PINKHAM NOTCH★★

North Conway to Mount Washington via Glen House – 45km.

> Starting at North Conway head North on Rte. 302.

North Conway★

Situated on the edge of the White Mountain National Forest, this bustling resort town is chockfull of restaurants, inns, outfitters and shops.

The Roman-style railroad station (1874) has been transformed into a museum and ticket office (*on Rte. 16*) for the **Conway Scenic Railroad**, which operates several different tours through the Saco Valley and Crawford Notch (*departs from North Conway depot mid-Apr–late Oct daily; ✕ 🅿 call for information: Conway Scenic Railroad, 603-356-5251 or 800-232-5251; www.conwayscenic.com*).

> At Glen turn right onto Rte. 16.

Story Land

✕ ♿ 🅿 ⏰ *Open mid-Jun–Labor Day daily 9am–6pm. Memorial Day–mid-Jun & Sept–mid-Oct weekends 9am–5pm. $29.99. 603-383-4186. www.storylandnh.com.*

This popular theme park features life-size characters and settings from children's stories and nursery rhymes, along with rides and a picnic grove.

Glen Ellis Falls★

Off Rte. 16. Parking left side of the road. The falls and its pools, located on the east side of the road (*take the underpass*), are formed by the Ellis River.

Wildcat Mountain

Parking area off Rte. 16.
Ski trails that look across Pinkham Notch to Mt. Washington have been cut on the slopes of Wildcat Mountain (4,422ft). An aerial gondola provides access to the summit, which offers **views★★** of Mt. Washington and the northern peaks of the Presidential Range (✗&🕐*gondola operates mid-Jun–mid-Oct daily 10am–5pm; mid-May–mid-Jun weekends only;* ⊚*$15.* 🕾*603-466-3326 or 888-754-9453; www.skiwildcat.com).*

Auto Road

✗&🕐*The road is open to private vehicles mid-May–mid-Oct daily 8am–4pm (weather permitting); extended hours in summer.* ⊚*$26/car & driver; guided van tours (1hr 30min) depart from Great Glen Lodge; $35.* 🕾*603-466-3988. www.mount washingtonautoroad.com.*
The 8mi trek to the summit of Mt. Washington begins at **Glen House**, from where you can drive your car or take a guided tour to the top. From the summit and scenic outlooks there are spectacular views of the Great Gulf Wilderness Area and the Presidential Range.

2 CRAWFORD NOTCH★★

Glen to Mount Washington via Fabyan – 24mi.

▷ Via Rte. 302 from Glen.

Rte. 302 follows the Saco River through Crawford Notch, a broad valley in the heart of the White Mountains. The road passes the **Attitash/Bear Peak**, a popular ski resort, and continues to Bartlett. In **Bartlett** a road located just past the library leads south through Bear Notch.

Bear Notch★

An additional 8mi between Bartlett and the Kancamagus Hwy.
This drive is especially scenic during the foliage season. At the point where the road leaves Crawford Notch *(3.5mi after Bartlett),* there is a beautiful **view** of the valley.

Crawford Notch★★

(1,773ft) This pass was named after the Crawford family, White Mountain pioneers who cut the first trail to the summit of Mt. Washington in the 19C, and whose house in the notch served as a shelter for hikers.

Arethusa Falls★

🅿*Parking lot on the left side of the road. Cross the railroad tracks, then follow the path (right) into the woods.*
The trail *(round-trip 2hrs)* follows a brook, then crosses it just before reaching the falls, situated in a refreshing forest setting. Continue N. on Rte. 302, passing in front of the rustic **Willey House** and **Mount Webster**, its slopes covered in places with the rocky debris of recent landslides. Farther on you will pass the **Silver Cascade**, a roadside waterfall tumbling from a high ledge.

Bretton Woods

The slopes of the Presidential Range form the backdrop for the **Mount Washington Resort**, a sprawling complex that is one of the few 19C grand hotels still in existence. In 1944 the hotel was the site of the United Nations Monetary and Financial Conference (Bretton Woods Conference), which established the American dollar as the medium of international exchange and developed plans to establish the World Bank.

▷ Continue north on Rte. 302.
At Fabyan, turn right onto the road leading to the Cog Railway.

👥 Mount Washington Cog Railway★★

🅿🕐*Departs from Marshfield Base Station 6mi east of Rte. 302 mid-Jun–Jul daily 9am–4pm. Aug–Labor Day daily 9am–5pm (hourly). Rest of the season departure times vary; call for hours. Three hours round-trip (includes 20min stop at summit). Commentary.* ⊚*$62. Reservations suggested.* 🕾*603-278-5404. www.thecog.com.*
This small steam train is almost as famous as the mountain itself. Built in 1869, the 3.5mi railway represents an

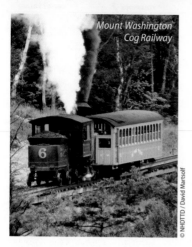

Mount Washington
Cog Railway

© NHDTTD / David Martsolf

outstanding technological achievement for its day, and still offers passengers a thrilling ride to the summit of the mountain, especially as the train ascends **Jacob's Ladder**, the steepest grade (37 percent) on the trestle. During the leisurely ride to the top, note how the vegetation and landscape change with the increasing altitude.

③ FRANCONIA NOTCH TO KINSMAN NOTCH★★★
Via Lincoln – 19mi. Drive south on US-3.

Running along the floor of this scenic notch cradled between the Franconia and Kinsman ranges, US-3 offers easy access to **Echo Lake** *(Rte. 18)* and to many of the area's natural attractions.

Cannon Mountain
An **aerial tramway** travels to the summit (4,060ft) of this ski mountain, which overlooks Echo Lake and affords a **view★★** of the notch (&⊙*tramway operates Memorial Day–mid-Oct daily 9am–5pm; round-trip 15min; commentary;*⊚*adult, $15;* ℘*603-823-8800; www.cannonmt.com*).
Located next to the Cannon Mountain tramway station, the **New England Ski Museum** illustrates skiing history with audiovisual presentations, photographs, equipment and memorabilia (ℙ⊙*open Memorial Day–Mar daily 10am–5pm;* ℘*603-823-7177; www.skimuseum.org*).

Lonesome Lake★
🧗 *Trail (3hrs) leaves from the parking lot at Lafayette Campground. Follow the yellow markers.*
This lake occupies a clearing 1,000ft above Franconia Notch. A trail around the lake leads to the **Appalachian Mountain Club** Hut, which accommodates hikers in the summer.

The Basin★
The action of churning waters rushing down from the falls above has formed this 30ft granite pothole.

Flume Gorge★★
On US-3/Franconia Notch Parkway in Franconia Notch State Park. ✕ℙ
⊙*Open early-May–late-Oct daily 9am–5pm.* ⊚*$15.* ℘*603-745-8391. www.nhstateparks.org.*
Discovered in 1808, this natural gorge runs for 800ft along the base of Mt. Liberty. Its narrow walls of Conway granite rise to 90ft. Beginning at the visitor center, a series of connecting paths, boardwalks and stairways lead to falls and cascades.

Lincoln
Located at the southern entrance to Franconia Notch, Lincoln is a center for neighboring resorts, boasting a plentiful assortment of motels, restaurants, shops and commercial attractions.

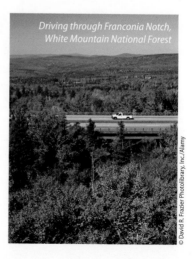

Driving through Franconia Notch, White Mountain National Forest

© David R. Frazier Photolibrary, Inc./Alamy

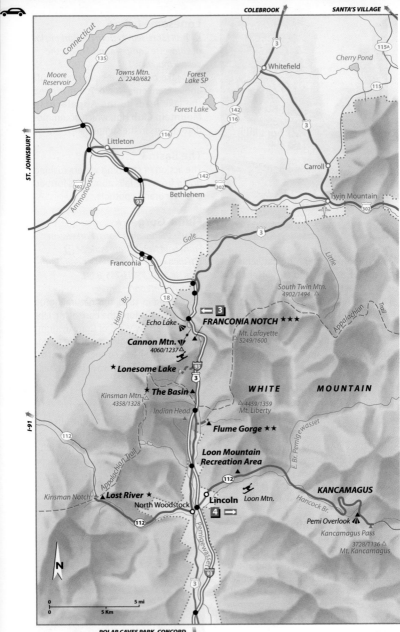

En-route to Lost River, travelers pass the colorful mountain community of **North Woodstock**, whose main street brims with shops and eateries.

▶ Drive west on Rte. 112 for 7mi.

Lost River★

✕🅿🕒*Open Jul & Aug daily 9am–5pm, mid-May–Jun & Sept–mid-Oct daily 9am–4pm. Last ticket sold 1hr before closing.* ⊜*$17.* ✆*603-745-8031. www.findlostriver.com.*

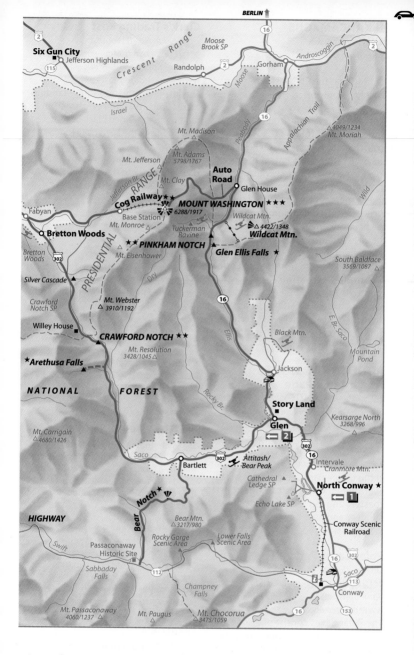

Six Gun City

Jefferson Highlands

Moose Brook SP

Crescent Range

Randolph

Androscoggin

Gorham

Jefferson Br.

Israel

Mt. Moriah
4049/1234

Appalachian Trail

Mt. Madison

Mt. Jefferson

Mt. Adams
5798/1767

Mt. Clay

Auto Road

Glen House

Fabyan

RANGE

Cog Railway ★★

MOUNT WASHINGTON ★★★
6288/1917

Base Station

Mt. Monroe

Wildcat Mtn.

4422/1348

Wildcat Mtn.

Tuckerman Ravine

Bretton Woods

Bretton Woods

PRESIDENTIAL

★★ PINKHAM NOTCH

Mt. Eisenhower

Glen Ellis Falls ★

South Baldface
3569/1087

Silver Cascade

Crawford Notch SP

Dry

Mt. Webster
3910/1192

Willey House

CRAWFORD NOTCH ★★

Mt. Resolution
3428/1045

★ Arethusa Falls

NATIONAL   FOREST

Ellis

Black Mtn.

Jackson

Mountain Pond

E. Br. Saco

Rocky Br.

Mt. Carrigain
4680/1426

Saco

Story Land

Glen   2

Kearsarge North
3268/996

Bartlett

302

Attitash/ Bear Peak

Intervale

Cranmore Mtn.

North Conway ★   1

Notch

Bear

Cathedral Ledge SP

Echo Lake SP

HIGHWAY

Bear Mtn.
3217/980

Rocky Gorge Scenic Area

Lower Falls Scenic Area

Conway Scenic Railway

Swift

Passaconaway Historic Site

Sabbaday Falls

112

Champney Falls

Saco

Conway

Mt. Passaconaway
4060/1237

Mt. Paugus

Mt. Chocorua
3475/1059

153

Located in Kinsman Notch, between the Connecticut and Pemigewasset valleys, the Lost River Gorge is a steep-walled glacial ravine filled with enormous boulders that have been sculpted into potholes by the river. A system of board-walks and staircases allows visitors to tour the caves, potholes and waterfalls in the gorge.

4 KANCAMAGUS HIGHWAY★★★

Lincoln to Conway – 35mi.

▶ Northeast on Rte. 112 from Lincoln. About 1hr.

This road through the White Mountain National Forest follows the **Hancock Branch** of the Pemigewasset River and the **Swift River**. It is one of the most spectacular drives in New England during the foliage season, when the maples and birch trees take on their fall colors. Picnic areas and campgrounds along the highways invite visitors to relax by the clear mountain streams, waterfalls and scenic rapids.

The road passes in front of the **Loon Mountain Recreation Area**, a year-round resort, then begins to climb to Kancamagus Pass. During the ascent, there is an exceptionally scenic **view★** from the **Pemi Overlook**. The road then dips into the Saco Valley.

ADDITIONAL SIGHTS
🧍🧍 Santa's Village

Rte. 2 in Jefferson. 🅿🕐*Open daily mid-Jun–Labor Day. Weekends only May–mid-Jun & Sept–Dec. Call for special Nov & Dec holiday hours.* 👓*$27.* 📞*603-586-4445. www.santasvillage.com.*
You'll find Christmas 12 months a year at this theme park, set in a grove of tall evergreens. Children can ride roller coasters and log flumes, feed Santa's reindeer and help the "elves" working in Santa's workshop.

Polar Caves Park

On Rte. 25, 5mi west of Plymouth. ✗🅿🕐*Open May–early Oct daily 9am–5pm.* 👓*$16.* 📞*603-536-1888. www.polarcaves.com.*
The Polar Caves consist of a series of caves and stone passageways. Five conveniently placed stations with taped commentaries allow visitors to tour the different chambers at their own pace along wooden walkways.

Clark's Trading Post

On Rte. 3 in North Woodstock. ✗🅿🕐*Open mid-May–early Oct daily 9.30am–6pm.* 👓*$19.* 📞*603-745-8913. www.clarkstradingpost.com.*
One of New England's long-standing attractions, this quirky attraction is famous for its trained black bear shows. Also popular is the Seyranyan Family Circus show and the 30min steam-powered train ride through the woods. On hot days, kids flock to the Old Mill Pond to ride the water blaster boats.

ADDRESSES

🛏 STAY

Most lodgings are located in towns near the southeastern edge of the National Forest. The **Appalachian Mountain Club** *(p316)* administers a system of huts and shelters along the Appalachian Trail, a lodge at the base of Mt. Washington and in Crawford Notch. **Camping** is permitted year-round *(advance reservations available for many campsites through New Hampshire state parks;* 📞*603-271-3628; www.nhstateparks.org).* 🔥Camping on Mt. Washington is **not** permitted. Permits are not required for **backcountry camping**.

BRETTON WOODS

$$$$$ Mount Washington Resort – *Rte. 302 in Bretton Woods.* 📞*603-278-1000; www.omnihotels.com.* It is hard to miss this grand resort, resting at the bottom of the Presidential Mountain range, in the shadow of mighty Mount Washington. The historic 1902 hotel, with its 900-foot veranda, opulent lobby and expansive grounds, retains much of its stately glamour. The resort features indoor and outdoor pools, a formal dining room, golf, tennis and other daily activities; cross country/ downhill skiing and sleigh rides are offered in winter. Children are welcome.

FRANCONIA

$$$ The Franconia Inn – *1300 Easton Rd., Franconia.* 📞*603-823-5542 or 800-473-5299. www.franconiainn.com. 32 rooms. Restaurant.* You'll think you've stepped into a Currier and Ives painting when you enter this pristine, three-story white clapboard Colonial, surrounded by the Franconia and Kinsman mountain ranges. In all seasons, the 100-acre property offers recreational activities galore— nature walks, horseback riding, tennis, hiking, cross-country skiing, gliding, sleigh rides, and snowshoeing. All this, and fine cuisine, too—the inn's chef prepares gourmet fare using locally-produced ingredients.

JACKSON

$$$ Dana Place Inn – *Rte. 16 in Pinkham Notch. ✆603-383-6822 or 800-537-9276. www.danaplace.com. 34 rooms.* This sprawling 1890s resort sits on 300 acres, flanked by the meandering Ellis River and surrounded by the White Mountain National Forest. In summer, you can hike, bike, play tennis and fish; when the mercury drops, try cross-country skiing, snowshoeing or sleigh riding—then warm up with a brandy next to the fireplace in the wood-paneled library.

$$$ The Inn at Thorn Hill – *Thorn Hill Rd., Jackson Village. ✆603-383-4242 or 800-289-8990. www.innatthornhill.com. 36 rooms and 3 private cottages.* Arguably the poshest—and most romantic— inn in the valley. This top-notch, upscale property offers luxurious accommodations (think: fine linens, fireplaces, jacuzzis, steam showers). Located in postcard-pretty Jackson Village, the inn boasts breathtaking mountain views. Added bonus: reserve a table in one of the three elegant dining rooms for award-winning, creative cuisine.

⏐/EAT

$$ Red Parka Steakhouse & Pub – *Rte. 302, Glen. ✆603-383-4344. Open daily for dinner. www.redparkapub.com.* **American.** Popular with both locals and the après-ski crowd, this casual restaurant is named after the red parkas with yellow crosses once worn by members of the local ski patrol. Here you'll find traditional pub fare, from nachos and potato skins to ribs, chicken, pasta, salads, and the restaurant's signature massive burgers and steaks. Live music is featured downstairs on weekends.

JACKSON

$$$ Wentworth Inn – *Corner of Rte. 16A and Carter Notch Rd. in Jackson Village. ✆603-383-9700 or 800-637-0013. Open daily for dinner; reservations suggested. www.thewentworth.com.* **American.** For country dining in a grand manner, stop in at this well-appointed resort hotel, established in 1869. In the formal dining room, appetizers such as the boneless wild boar ribs prove a fitting precedent to entrées like mustard crusted rack of lamb, pan-roasted native cod or the slow braised veal cheeks. After dessert and coffee, linger beside the lobby fireplace or stroll the extensive grounds, which contain various cottages and condominiums, a swimming pool, a tennis court and an 18-hole golf course.

NORTH CONWAY

$$ Horsefeathers – *Main St., across from Schouler Park and the train station. North Conway. Sun–Thu 11am–11pm Sat–Sun 11am–12pm. ✆603-356-2687. www.horsefeathers.com.* **American.** This perennially popular eatery has been a North Conway mainstay for 30-plus years. The casual, friendly restaurant boasts an impressive menu. Munch on appetizers like spicy Maine lobster and crab cakes, salads (try the calamari caesar or the seared beef and snow pea), homemade soups, sandwiches (grilled crab and havarti or the best reuben in town), signature burgers, grilled fish, ribs, steaks and much more.

WOODSTOCK

$$$ Woodstock Inn – *135 Main St., N. Woodstock. ✆ 603-745-3951. Daily 11.30am–10pm. www.woodstock innnh.com.* **American.** Stop for lunch or dinner at this popular restaurant and brewpub. There's indoor dining in the Clement Room and in the glass-enclosed "petticoat porch;" or dine outdoors on the umbrella-covered patio during warmer weather. Sandwiches and dinner are also served evenings in the informal **Woodstock Station**, along with a selection of beers made on the premises at the micro-brewery that uses the traditional seven-barrel system.

RHODE ISLAND

The smallest state in the nation, Rhode Island measures only 48 miles long by 37 miles wide. In 1524 Italian navigator Giovanni da Verrazzano sailed into Narragansett Bay and along the coast of the island known to the Indians as Aquidneck. Impressed by the brilliance of the natural light here, Verrazzano noted the similarity in appearance between Aquidneck and the Greek isle of Rhodes. More than a century later, Aquidneck was renamed Rhode Island. Its official name, the State of Rhode Island and Providence Plantations, reflects its origin as a series of independent settlements. The Royal Charter of 1644 united "Providence Plantations" at the head of the Narragansett Bay with settlements at Newport and Portsmouth on Aquidneck Island. Today the state is the third most densely populated in the United States.

Highlights

1 Biking the rolling farmlands on **Block Island** (p327)
2 Listening to jazz artists play at **Fort Adams State Park** (p331)
3 **Sailing Narragansett Bay** on a 12m America's Cup winner (p343)
4 Attending the mesmerizing **Waterfire** show (p345)
5 Dining in Providence's historic **Federal Hill** (p351)

▶ **Population:** 1,050,292.
ℹ **Info:** www.visitrhode island.com.
Area: 1,214sq mi.
Capital: Providence.
Nickname:
The Ocean State.
State Flower: Violet.

A Land of Tolerance

Early colonists came to Rhode Island in search of religious freedom denied them in Massachusetts. The first to arrive, in 1630, was the **Rev. William Blackstone**, fleeing the Puritans' invasion of his privacy on the Shawmut Peninsula. He was followed by the minister **Roger Williams**, who founded Providence in 1636. Exiled from Massachusetts for his "new and dangerous opinions," Williams established Providence Plantations, a farming community, on lands that he purchased from the Narragansett Indians. Two years later a group of disgruntled Bostonians bought the island of Aquidneck and started the colony of Portsmouth (north of present-day Newport). The religious leader **Anne Hutch-**

The Breakers

© Patrick O'Conner / The Preservation Society of Newport County

Mohegan Bluffs, Block Island

inson joined them in 1638, with her own adherents in tow. Newport was founded in 1639 by 11 former Portsmouth colonists who left after a factional dispute. Relations between the colonists and the Indians remained friendly until 1675 when Philip, chief of the Wampanoags, led his tribe, along with the Narragansetts and Nipmucks, in raids against the settlers in **King Philip's War** (1675–76). During the Great Swamp Fight (in Mount Hope, RI) on 19 December 1675, colonists launched a surprise attack on the Narragansetts, Rhode Island's most powerful tribe. The war dissipated the tribe's strength and greatly reduced the local Indian population.

Rhode Island's economy was at first based on the sea, with Newport and Providence vying for positions as the nation's leading seaports. By the 1650s Rhode Island had gained a portion of the trade between New England and the West Indies. The great fortunes made from trade provided capital for the textile industry, which had its beginnings at Pawtucket in 1793.

One of the country's leading textile producers throughout the 19C, Rhode Island soon became the most heavily industrialized state in the US. The exodus of the textile factories to the South after World War II led to an emphasis on diversified manufacturing, which today ranks as the state's leading source of income and its largest employer.

Rhode Island's early manufacture of machine tools gave rise in 1796 to the production of jewelry and silverware, now a major industry. Tourism generates over a billion dollars a year in revenues for the state.

Most visitors know that Rhode Island is home to the fabulous **Newport mansions**, but the this small state's other charms are less well-known. The city of **Providence** is, in fact, the third largest in New England, and it has come into its own as a sophisticated urban area, with stellar restaurants, gracious hotels, a thriving arts scene, and the beautifully preserved architectural district of **College Hill**, home to both the Rhode Island School of Design and Brown University.

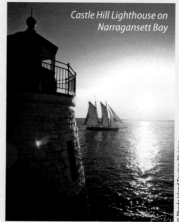

Castle Hill Lighthouse on Narragansett Bay

RHODE ISLAND

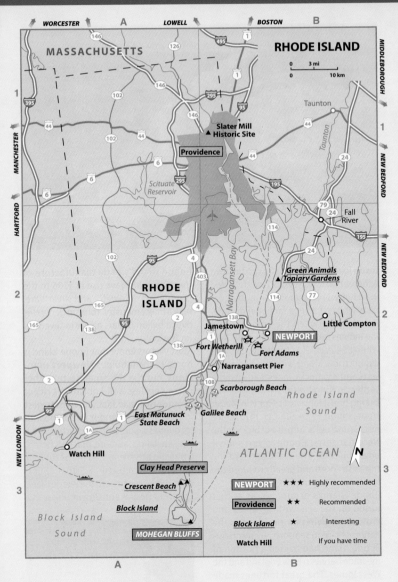

WORCESTER   A   LOWELL   BOSTON   B

RHODE ISLAND

0   3 mi
0   10 km

MASSACHUSETTS

MIDDLEBOROUGH

Slater Mill
▲ Historic Site

Providence

Taunton

Scituate
Reservoir

Fall
River

NEW BEDFORD

**RHODE
ISLAND**

Narragansett Bay

Green Animals
▲ Topiary Gardens

Jamestown

Little Compton

Fort Wetherill

NEWPORT

Fort Adams

Narragansett Pier

Scarborough Beach

Rhode Island
Sound

East Matunuck
State Beach

Galilee Beach

NEW LONDON

Watch Hill

ATLANTIC OCEAN

N

Clay Head Preserve

NEWPORT	★★★	Highly recommended
Providence	★★	Recommended
Block Island	★	Interesting
Watch Hill		If you have time

Crescent Beach

Block Island

MOHEGAN BLUFFS

Block Island
Sound

HARTFORD   MANCHESTER

Urban revitalization projects like Waterplace Park have added new life to the city's downtown area. Outdoor concerts, shows at the acclaimed Trinity Repertory Company, and Waterfire, a summer-long event featuring bonfires accompanied by music, make Providence a pleasant surprise for visitors.

Among Rhode Island's true gems is **Block Island,** set 12 miles off the mainland and reachable by ferry. Some compare it to Nantucket or Martha's Vineyard, 20 years ago. With a lovely rural vibe, few cars, and old Victorian-style hotels, Block Island is an enchanting place to relax on the beach, take a bike ride to the bluffs, and forget modern cares.

Other places around the region that offer an escape to simpler times include the **villages** of Wickford, Little Compton and Watch Hill.

Block Island★

This unspoiled island, 7mi long and 3mi wide at its widest point, is a delightful low-key getaway off the coast of mainland Rhode Island. Quaint Victorian hotels and storefronts hug the shore of Old Harbor, where the ferry comes in to port. Quickly, civilization gives way to a pastoral landscape of rolling hills and inland moors. The preferred mode of transport is a bicycle—you'll pedal past grazing sheep, kids with lemonade stands, and beautiful natural areas.

A BIT OF HISTORY

Block Island was named for Adriaen Block, the Dutch navigator who explored the region in 1614. The first permanent colonists arrived at the beginning of the late 17C to farm and fish. Following the advent of steamboat travel some 200 years later, the island developed into a summer resort, and Victorian-style hotels sprang up along Water Street in **Old Harbor**.

Today, shops, inns and restaurants line the quaint streets of Old Harbor. **New Harbor**, the other hub of activity on the island, is home to a large marina for visiting pleasure boats. Great Salt Pond is a haven for paddlers. The island is ringed by 17mi of beaches.

SIGHTS
Mohegan Bluffs★★★

Along the island's southernmost tip is a series of spectacular multi-colored cliffs known as Mohegan Bluffs. Climb up a path (about 200ft elevation) and gaze out over the Atlantic. Wooden stairs descend to the Mohegan Bluffs beach, secluded but pebbly. Large, flat-topped boulders make a great place for a picnic.

Clay Head Preserve★★

Much of Block Island is protected space, including this lovely property maintained by the Nature Conservancy. After you pass Clay Head Swamp, bear right to get to the beach. Or, bear left to climb up above the clay cliffs to "the maze," a

▶ **Population:** 1,033.
Ġ **Michelin Map:** 581 L 11.
Info: ✆800-383-BIRI; www.blockislandinfo.com.
▶ **Location:** Block Island is located 12mi off the coast, reachable by ferry from Pt. Judith and Newport, RI (2hr from Boston) (866-783-7996 or 401-783-7996; www.block islandferry.com), or New London, CT (✆860-444-4624 or 401-466-2212; www.goblockisland.com).
Kids: Stop by Justin's Farm to meet resident llamas, camels, emus and kangaroos.
Timing: Many inns have minimum-stay requirements in summertime; plan to stay for a week if you really want to unwind.
P **Parking:** Unless you're spending the summer here, there's no reason to bring a car. Rent a bicycle to get around on-island (rentals are available in Old Harbor and New Harbor, including kid-sized bikes and tagalong systems) or hire a taxi.
Don't Miss: Bicycling around the island, with stops at Mohegan Bluffs and Clay Head Preserve; visit Block Island Farmers' Market for local treats like cinnamon honey from Littlefield Bee Farm.

series of interwoven nature trails lined with shrubs and filled with songbirds.

Crescent Beach★

Just north of Old Harbor, the eastern shore of Block Island is lined with a sandy stretch of beaches. Crescent Beach (entrance off Corn Neck Rd.) has dressing rooms, a snack bar, showers and a lifeguard.

Newport★★★

Set on an island in Narragansett Bay, Newport has evolved from a bustling colonial port to a 20C resort for the fabulously rich and famous to its present incarnation as a modern tourist mecca. Now, as in bygone days, Newport's allure hails from the sea: Sailboats crowd the harbor in summer and visitors cruise the offshore waters in a variety of vessels. And, of course, the best of Newport's renowned mansions enjoy ocean views.

A BIT OF HISTORY

A Harbor of Refuge – In the wake of a political dispute with Anne Hutchinson in Portsmouth, **William Coddington**, another Boston exile, led a group of settlers to the southern part of Aquidneck Island in 1639. There, on the shore of a large harbor, they founded Newport. Other religious minorities—Quakers, Baptists and Jews—soon followed, seeking the religious tolerance for which the Rhode Island settlements were known. These settlers were talented entrepreneurs, and with their help the colony rapidly developed.

Newport's fortunes were abruptly reversed with the outbreak of the American Revolution. Marked by the British for destruction, Newport was occupied from 1776 to 1779. Inhabitants were forced to house English soldiers, and looting and burning were widespread. Following the British defeat, French troops, allies of the Americans, occupied Newport. It was here that meetings between General Washington and Count Rochambeau took place. By the end of the war Newport lay in ruins. Most of its merchants had fled to Providence, and the colony would never again regain its commercial splendor.

Playground of the Wealthy – During the years before the Revolution, planters from Georgia and the Carolinas escaped the heat of the southern summer by vacationing in Newport. In the mid 19C, with the introduction of steamboat travel between New York

▶ **Population:** 24,661.

🚻 **Michelin Map:** 581 M 10.

🛈 **Info:** ✆800-976-5122; www.gonewport.com.

◖ **Location:** Newport is an island, linked by bridges to mainland Rhode Island (there is also a ferry service between Newport and Providence and Newport and Jamestown).

👫 **Kids:** Check out the fanciful animal-shaped tree sculptures at Green Animals Topiary Gardens in Portsmouth.

🕐 **Timing:** Make your first stop the Gateway Visitors Center at 23 America's Cup Ave, a great source for tours, tickets and advice on what to do.

🅿 **Parking:** Parking lots are located on Church St. (off Thames St.), on America's Cup Ave. near Commercial Wharf and at the Gateway Visitor Center.

🚹 **Don't Miss:** A walk along Cliff Walk, Newport's 3.5mi oceanfront path, and a peek at a couple of the mansions. If you feel like looking a little further, try Sachuest Point National Wildlife Refuge, in Middletown, or go surf fishing from the shore line.

and Newport, an increasing number of visitors arrived each year. Following the Civil War, America's wealthiest families—including the Astors, Belmonts and Vanderbilts—began to summer here. Impressed by the magnificence of the palaces and châteaux they had seen while touring Europe, they commissioned America's finest architects to design the enormous "cottages" (as they whimsically called them) that grace Ocean Drive and Bellevue Avenue.

© Rhode Island Tourism Division

Newport and Sports

Several sports owe their development and popularity to Newport society, whose favorite pastimes included tennis, golf and boating. In 1881 the first US tennis championships were held on the courts of the Newport Casino; annual tennis tournaments, including the **International Tennis Hall of Fame Grass Court Championships** (*held in early July*), are still played here. The first US amateur and open golf championships took place on a nine-hole course laid out on Brenton Point in 1894 by members of society's elite "400," as compiled by Mrs. William Astor, wife of real estate heir William Backhouse Astor Jr.

It was, however, in the realm of sailing—especially yachting—that Newport became internationally famous. By the late 19C several yachting clubs had been established in Newport, and from 1930 to 1983 the city hosted the celebrated **America's Cup** races. These races, an international competition among the most sophisticated sailing yachts in the world, date from 1851. It was in that year that the New York Yacht Club sent the schooner *America* across the Atlantic to compete against the British for the prestigious Hundred Guinea Cup. The *America* won the race and returned home with the cup— actually an ornate silver pitcher thereafter known as the America's Cup. Newport is the starting point of the biennial 685mi **Newport-Bermuda Race** and the destination of the **Original Single-Handed Transatlantic Race** that begins in Plymouth, England.

In summer Newport's rich, part-time residents held fabulous picnics, dinner parties and balls, famed for their extravagance. Presiding over these events were Mrs. William Astor, Mrs. O.H. Belmont, Mrs. Hermann Oelrichs and other high-society matriarchs. During a single summer season, each social maven might spend as much as $300,000 just on entertaining. The search for unusual diversions led to such eccentricities as the champagne and caviar dinner given by Harry Lehr for his friends and their pets, during which masters and pets ate and drank at the same table; and the fleet of full-size model ships made for Mrs. Oelrichs and placed on the ocean to convey the impression of a harbor. Attracted by the latest fads and inventions, the affluent residents of Newport drove the first motor cars, built the first roads, filled the harbor with princely mahogany and brass-trimmed yachts, and introduced sailboat racing to the town.

Newport Today - Newport provides an architectural sampler of the nation's most aesthetically pleasing building

GETTING THERE

BY CAR - From the north, take I-95 south to US-1 south; follow US-1 to Rte. 138 east, cross the Claiborne Pell Bridge (*$4 one-way for passenger vehicles*) and follow signs (*Boston to Newport, 74mi; Providence to Newport, 37mi*). From the south or west, take I-95 north to Rte. 138 east across the bridge (*New York City to Newport, 181mi*).

BY PLANE - Domestic and international flights service **T.F. Green Airport** (PVD) in Warwick (*℘401-691-2471 or 888-268-7222; www.pvdairport. com*), located 27mi northwest of Newport (*Exit 13 off I-95*). Taxis and van shuttles are available from the airport to downtown Newport.

BY TRAIN - The nearest Amtrak **train** stations are in Providence (*34mi; ℘800-872-7245; www.amtrak.com*) and Kingston (*18mi; in South Kingstown, near the University of Rhode Island and Narragansett beaches*). The Acela train from Providence takes just under 3 hours to Penn Station in New York. If you are coming from Boston, the MBTA commuter trains are a cheaper option.

BY BUS - Peter Pan Bus Lines provides **bus** service from New York City and Boston to Gateway Visitor Center at 23 America's Cup Ave. in Newport (*℘800-343-9999; www.peterpan bus.com*).

GETTING AROUND

Walking is the best way to get around in the downtown and historic areas. Metered street parking and public lots are available, but in the summer season, spaces are at a premium. Rhode Island Public Transit Authority (RIPTA) buses offer service on the island. RIPTA provides year-round trolley service to Newport attractions, including the mansions and Cliff Walk (*trolleys depart from Gateway Center; $6/all-day pass; ℘401-781-9400 or www.ripta.com*). They also offer trolley bus service from Newport to Providence (*$2 per ride or $6 one-day pass*).

VISITOR INFORMATION

The **Gateway Visitor Information Center**, run by the Newport County Convention and Visitors Bureau, provides maps and information about area attractions, accommodations, and activities (*23 America's Cup Ave., Newport, RI 02840; ℘800-326-6030; www.gonewport.com*).

Newport Bridge at sunset

©Photo Disc, Inc.

Cliff Walk

© Rhode Island Tourism Division

styles dating from the 17C to the 19C. The city's large group of colonial structures range from the simple and austere Quaker meetinghouse to Trinity Church, inspired by the work of renowned 17C British architect Christopher Wren. More than 100 restored dwellings stand in the **Historic Hill** (*in the vicinity of Trinity Church*) and **Easton's Point** (*the area along the harbor north of Bridge St. and west of Farewell St.*) neighborhoods. Most of the restored homes in The Point—as it's known to locals—date from the 18C, when the neighborhood prospered as a colonial mercantile community.

The city sponsors several notable music festivals, including the **Newport Music Festival**, a series of musical programs presented in the mansions (including Rosecliff, Marble House, Beechwood, The Elms and The Breakers) during the month of July. The **Newport Jazz Festival** draws thousands of fans to hear some of the music industry's top jazz musicians in a spectacular outdoor setting—Fort Adams State Park— in August. Attracting a totally different crowd to Fort Adams in early August is the **Newport Folk Festival**.

THE MANSIONS★★★

The nine mansions operated by the Preservation Society of Newport County (The Breakers, Marble House, Château-sur-Mer, Rosecliff, The Elms, Hunter House, Isaac Bell House, Kingscote and Chepstow) can be visited by guided tour only (1hr for each mansion).

Houses are generally open mid Mar–Oct daily 10am–6pm (last tour at 5pm). Schedules vary the rest of the year. Call for information about opening times & schedule: ℘401-847-1000; www.newportmansions.org.

Tickets are available at the mansions, at the Newport County Convention and Visitor Bureau (23 America's Cup Ave.), and online (website above). Combination tickets are available at a saving and include Green Animals Topiary Garden in nearby Portsmouth, another Preservation Society property.

Newport's other mansions are The Astor's Beechwood, Belcourt Castle and Rough Point. See entries for details.

World-famous for their mammoth size, decor and ostentation, Newport's "cottages" were built in the late 1800s and early 1900s by some of America's richest families. The evolution in the style of these estates begins with the eclecticism of the mid-19C Victorian period, as illustrated by Kingscote (1839) and Château-sur-Mer (1852). Displaying a splendor and magnificence never before expressed in American architecture, Marble House (1892), The Breakers (1895), The Elms (1901) and Rosecliff (1902) represent elaborate imitations of the châteaux of France and the palaces of Italy. Taken together they provide a fascinating picture of the excesses of the gilded age.

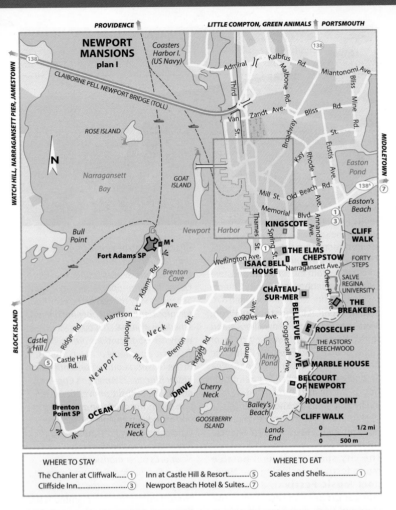

NEWPORT MANSIONS
plan I

WHERE TO STAY

The Chanler at Cliffwalk......①	Inn at Castle Hill & Resort............⑤
Cliffside Inn............................③	Newport Beach Hotel & Suites...⑦

WHERE TO EAT

Scales and Shells....................①

Marble House

© John Corbett / The Preservation Society of Newport County

The majority of the mansions may be seen by driving along **Bellevue Avenue★★★**, which runs south from Memorial Boulevard to Land's End where it intersects with **Ocean Drive★★**. From that point, Ocean Drive follows the coast for 10mi to the southern end of the island. Be sure to catch the breathtaking sunset **views** along Ocean Drive, especially from **Brenton Point State Park**. Straddling the rocky shoreline that separates The Breakers, Rosecliff, Marble House and Salve Regina University (*Ochre Point Ave.*) from the sea, **Cliff Walk★★** winds for 3.5mi along the bluffs overlooking the sea. In the 19C, when fishermen protested against estate owners who attempted to close off the path, the state ruled in favor of the "toilers of the sea," and the walk has remained a public way ever since. Cliff Walk extends from Memorial Boulevard (*near Easton's Beach*) to Bailey's Beach (*private*), with an additional access point at the Forty Steps (*at the end of Narragansett Ave.*).

The Breakers★★★

44 Ochre Point Ave. ♿🅿🕐*Open year-round daily 9am–5pm.* 👓*$19.50.*
In 1885 **Cornelius Vanderbilt II**, the grandson of the "Commodore," who had made his fortune in steamships and railroads, purchased the Ochre Point property with its modest wood and brick summer house. After the original structure burned down in 1892, Vanderbilt hired architect **Richard Morris Hunt** to design another summer residence on the site. Selecting a High Renaissance Italian palace as his model, Hunt created this opulent 70-room mansion, which was completed in 1895. The exterior, heavily ornamented with arcades, columns and cornices, reveals the Italian influence. Within, The Breakers blends rich marbles and wooden trim with 22-carat gilded plaster, mosaics and ceiling painting.

Interior

The **Great Hall**, more than two stories high, showcases a spectacular array of columns and pilasters, marble plaques and ornate cornices. In the Music Room, the coffered ceiling bears a painting with figures representing Music, Harmony, Song and Melody. The **Morning Room** contains corner panels painted in oil on silver leaf representing the Muses; the room looks out onto the loggia, where a beautiful hand-laid Italian mosaic decorates the ceiling. Most richly embellished of all the rooms is the 2,400sq ft **Dining Room** where the Vanderbilts entertained their guests amid a setting of warm rose alabaster columns, a vaulted carved ceiling, oil paintings and gilt. Two 12ft-high Baccarat chandeliers light this room.

Marble House★★★

596 Bellevue Ave. 🅿🕐*Open mid Mar–Dec daily 10am–5pm. Rest of the year, call for schedule.* 👓*$14.50.*
Built for millionaire yachtsman **William K. Vanderbilt** and his wife Alva in 1892, Marble House, with its classical portico supported by four marble Corinthian columns, recalls the Petit Trianon at Versailles. Among the most lavish dinner parties and balls held at Marble House was the debut of Consuelo Vanderbilt, who, after the celebration, locked herself in her room to protest her upcoming marriage to the ninth Duke of Marlborough. The marriage nevertheless took place a short time later, in 1895.

Interior

Containing some 500,000 cubic feet of American, African and Italian marble, the interior is as elegant as the exterior suggests. Tapestries decorate the huge entrance hall, which is faced with yellow Siena marble. In the **Gold Ballroom**, the most ornate ballroom in Newport, gilt panels, pilasters, arches and doorways are reflected in the glittering crystal chandeliers and mirrors that capture every ray of light. In striking contrast to the ballroom is the subdued mood of the **Gothic Room**, where the Vanderbilt collection of medieval art objects was displayed. The elaborate use of pink Numidian marble creates the luxuriant atmosphere of the **Dining Room**. The bronze Louis XIV chairs, weighing about 70 pounds each, made it necessary for the host to provide each guest with a footman, who would move the chair when the guest wished to sit or leave the table. The tour includes a visit to the spacious basement **kitchen**, boasting an elegance all its own with its 25ft-long stove, built-in iceboxes and shiny monogrammed cookware.

The Elms★★

367 Bellevue Ave. **P** ⏱*Open mid-Mar–Dec daily 10am–5pm. Rest of the year, call for schedule.* 🎫*$14.50.*

Inspired by the 18C Château d'Asnières near Paris, architect Horace Trumbauer designed this dignified country estate for **Edward Julius Berwind**. The son of German immigrants, Berwind rose to prominence in the second half of the 19C as the "king" of America's coal industry. In 1899, he commissioned Trumbauer to build a residence to rival the cottages of Newport's established millionaires, who regarded him as a nouveau-riche outsider.

The housewarming given by the Berwinds in August 1901 was the social highlight of the season; countless varieties of exotic plants were used to adorn the house, and monkeys scampered about the grounds.

Interior

The large-scale proportions of the rooms, especially of the entrance hall and **ballroom**, are impressive. In the ballroom, smoothly curved corners, restrained decoration, and an abundance of natural light create an inviting and pleasant atmosphere, despite the size of the room. The French Classical style predominates: the **Conservatory** was intended to house tropical flora, the **Drawing Room** reflects the Louis XVI style, the stucco reliefs and fine woodwork of the ballroom suggest the earlier style of Louis XV. Three of the four black and gold lacquer panels ornamenting the **Breakfast Room** date from China's K'ang-hsi period (17C); the fourth is a reproduction.

Rosecliff★★

548 Bellevue Ave. ♿**P** ⏱*Open mid-Mar–Nov daily 10am–5pm. Rest of the year, call for schedule.* 🎫*$14.50.*

In 1891 **Theresa Oelrichs**, the daughter of a wealthy Irish immigrant who had discovered the Comstock Silver Lode in Nevada, purchased the Rosecliff estate—named for its many rose beds. Finding the house on the property too modest for her taste, she engaged **Stanford White** to design a more elaborate residence. The result was a graceful imitation of the Grand Trianon at Versailles.

Rosecliff Ballroom

© Rhode Island Tourism Division

Mrs. Oelrichs was one of Newport's most celebrated hostesses.

At one of her noteworthy galas, the "Mother Goose" Ball, guests dressed as fairy-tale characters.

Designed primarily for entertaining, Rosecliff boasts the largest **ballroom** (80ft by 40ft) in Newport. Windows open onto the terraces, allowing the outdoors to become an extension of the ballroom. Scenes from *The Great Gatsby* (1974) were filmed here.

Château-sur-Mer★

474 Bellevue Ave. P ⏰*Open mid-Mar–mid Nov daily 10am–5pm. Rest of the year, call for schedule.* 👓*$14.50.*
Constructed in the Second Empire style, this "Castle by the Sea," with its massive asymmetrical silhouette, was built in 1852 for **William S. Wetmore**, who earned his wealth in the China trade. Extremely spacious and luxurious for its day, Château-sur-Mer was enlarged in 1872 by Richard Morris Hunt. After Hunt's substantial alterations were completed, Château-sur-Mer was considered the most "substantial and expensive residence in Newport."
Inside, light streams into the three-story entrance hall through a colored-glass ceiling panel 45ft above its floor; the hall, the Morning Room and the grand staircase are all paneled with white oak wainscoting hand-carved in the Eastlake style. Illuminated by stained-glass windows, the stairwell is lined with canvas painted to resemble tapestries.

Kingscote★

253 Bellevue Ave. P ⏰*Open mid-May–mid Oct daily 10am–5pm.* 👓*$14.50.*
Designed in 1839, this house is an early example of the Gothic Revival motif. Kingscote's irregular shape—expressed in wood rather than stone, and emphasized by gables, arches, eaves and varied rooflines—forms a striking contrast to the symmetrical, solid shape of other earlier dwellings.
This mansion was built for southern planter **George Noble Jones**, then sold in the 1860s to **William H. King** after whom it (King's Cottage) was named.

The Victorian interior contains Tiffany windows, heavy furniture and somber rooms. Among the furnishings is a prized collection of Oriental paintings, rugs and porcelain.

Isaac Bell House★

Corner of Bellevue Ave. and Perry St. ⏰*Open late Jun–mid-Oct daily 10am–5pm.* 👓*$14.50.*
When wealthy New York cotton trader Isaac Bell retired to Newport at age 31, he chose the newly formed firm of McKim, Mead and White to design his retreat on Bellevue Avenue. The shingle and brick house, completed in 1883, is a superb example of the American Shingle style with its gabled roof and rounded, tower-shaped, two-story porch. Arranged in an open floor plan, the interior features handsome oak paneling in the living room, rattan wall coverings in the dining room, and large sash windows in the drawing room that allow guests to walk out onto the porch.

Chepstow★

Narragansett Ave. at Clay St. ⏰*Late Jun–mid-Oct daily 10am–5pm.* 👓*$14.*
Built for Dutch bachelor W.C. Schermerhorn by Newport architect George C. Mason, Chepstow was completed in 1860. The white Italianate villa-style mansion later came to be owned by the Gallatin family, who named the house after a Welsh castle. Today the rooms reflect the "Victorian clutter" favored by Chepstow's most recent owner, along with a fine collection of 17C and 18C antiques and paintings by Fitz Henry Lane and members of the Hudson River school.

Hunter House★★

54 Washington St., in Newport's historic Point section. 🔆*See Additional Sights.*

OTHER MANSIONS

The mansions listed below are privately owned and do not operate under the auspices of the Preservation Society of Newport County.

Belcourt of Newport★

657 Bellevue Ave. 🚶*Visit by guided tour (1hr).* 🅿 ⏱*This property was recently purchased by a new owner and is currently undergoing restoration. Please check website for details and current status of public tours. www.belcourt.com.*

A hunting lodge owned by Louis XIII was the model for this castle (1896) designed for the 35-year-old bachelor **Oliver Hazard Perry Belmont**.

In 1898 Belmont married Alva Smith Vanderbilt, after her divorce from William K. Vanderbilt. After she moved in, Alva had the house redecorated. The castle, owned from 1959 to 2012 by the Tinney family, contains an outstanding **collection** of European furnishings and decorative arts. In 2012, the Tinneys sold the property to jewelry designer Carolyn Rafaelian of the Rhode Island-based company Alex and Ani.

The interior is inspired by different periods of French, Italian and English design. Adorned with plush red upholstery and stained-glass windows, the vast **Banquet Hall** can comfortably accommodate 250 dinner guests. A huge, tiered crystal chandelier, which formerly graced a palace in St. Petersburg, Russia, dominates the room.

From the oval Family Dining Room on the second floor there is a view out to the ocean. The spacious **French Gothic Ballroom** contains 13C French stained-glass windows, Oriental carpets, tapestries, distended vaults and an enormous fireplace surmounted by a 32ft-high plaster castle. The ballroom's 70ft-high ceiling creates excellent acoustics; in

the castle's heyday, a 60-piece orchestra played from the upper-level gallery.

Rough Point★★

At the south end of Bellevue Ave. ♿⏱*Open mid Apr–mid May Thu–Sat 10am–2pm; mid May–early Nov Tue–Sat 9.45am–3.45pm. Advance reservations recommended.* 💰*$25.* 📞*401-847-8344. www.newportrestoration.org.*

Named for the rocky spit of land on which it sits, Rough Point was built in 1891 for Frederick W. Vanderbilt (grandson of the Commodore) on a ten-acre oceanfront site landscaped by Frederick Law Olmsted. The Gothic-style manse was purchased in 1922 by James B. Duke, North Carolina tobacco magnate and founder of energy company Duke Power. James Duke died in 1925, and his only child, Doris, inherited the house and its collection of art and antiques. In the 68 years that Doris owned Rough Point, she added significantly to that collection, purchasing a wealth of fine European furnishings and portraits dating from the 16C to the 18C.

Interior

Today the 40,000sq ft "cottage" is a monument to Duke's discerning taste, left virtually unchanged since her death in 1993 when she bequeathed it to the Newport Restoration Foundation—an organization she founded. The monumental **Great Hall** remains a gallery for art and tapestries, including a set of c.1510 Brussels tapestries, 17C portraits by Anthony Van Dyck and Ferdinand Bol (a student of Rembrandt), and a group of Ming Dynasty garden seats and

Rough Point

© Discover Newport

wine jars. Used as a drawing room, the graceful **Yellow Room** is outfitted with Louis XVI furniture, some boasting its original embroidered fabric. The **Music Room**, with its rock-crystal chandeliers and hand-painted 18C Chinese wallpaper, was a favorite of Duke, who spent several hours a day here playing the Steinway piano. Upstairs, Duke's **bedroom** contains striking French mother-of-pearl pieces: an oval side table, two delicate chairs and a settee.

●●WALKING TOUR

COLONIAL NEWPORT ★★

Newport's extraordinarily large group of colonial structures constitutes one of the nation's great architectural treasures. The itinerary below represents a selection of these dwellings and public buildings.

◉ From the Gateway Information Center, head south on America's Cup Ave. and turn left on Marlborough St. Turn right on Thames St. and walk one block south to the Brick Market.

Brick Market★
127 Thames St.
This handsome three-story building with its arcaded base and massive pilasters above provides a fine example of the Palladian style's influence on Georgian architecture. The market was the commercial center of Newport; open market stalls were located on the ground floor, while the upper floors were reserved for offices and storage. Today two floors are occupied by the **Museum of Newport History** (**M1**), which includes displays on Newport's early colonial life, maritime commerce and naval history (🅿 🕒 *open daily 10am–5pm; ⊚$4; ℘401-841-8770; www.newporthistorical.org*).

Old Colony House★
Washington Square. ℘401-846-2980.
This building, designed by **Richard Munday**, was the seat of Rhode Island's government from the colonial period

Old Colony House
© Newport Historical Society

through the early 19C. In 1781 General Washington and Count Rochambeau, the leader of the French troops, met here to discuss plans for the battle of Yorktown.

Furniture made by local craftsmen Goddard and Townsend, and one of Gilbert Stuart's full-length portraits of George Washington decorate the interior.

◉ Turn left on Farewell St. and continue to Marlborough St.

Great Friends Meeting House
Marlborough St. ●●Visit by guided tour only (45min). ♿🕒Open Jun–Nov, 11am–3pm. ⊚$8. ℘401-846-0813. www.newporthistorical.org.
By the end of the 17C, Newport supported a large population of Quakers. This meetinghouse, constructed by the Society of Friends in 1699 and enlarged as the society grew, served as the regional center for New England's Quakers.

The building is architecturally interesting for its pulley-operated walls, its large stone supports—which prevent the lower floor from resting directly on the ground—and its remarkable vault.

◉ Walk back to Broadway and turn left.

Wanton-Lyman-Hazard House
17 Broadway. ●●Visit by guided tour only (45min). ♿🕒Open Jun–Nov, 11am–3pm ⊚$8. ℘401-846-0813. www.newporthistorical.org.

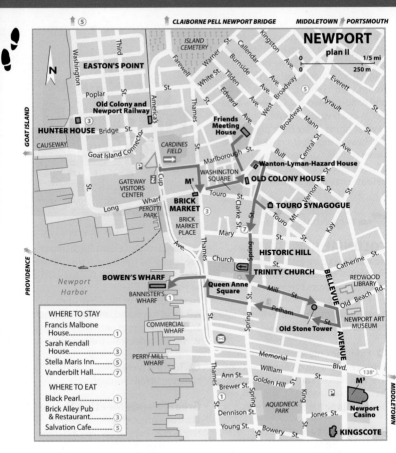

Prior to the Revolution, this house (c.1675) was the residence of Martin Howard, a Loyalist and lawyer widely criticized by opponents of the Crown. During the Stamp Act riots, while the patriots ransacked his house, Howard fled Newport. Considering himself fortunate to have escaped, he eventually settled in England, never to return.

In 1765 Quaker merchant John Wanton purchased the house, which was owned by his relatives until 1911. Rooms in the house, which were recently restored, are furnished with period pieces reflecting the late 17C to the early 18C.

▶ Walk around the house to Spring St. Turn right and follow Spring St. to Touro St. Turn left onto Touro St.

Touro Synagogue★★

85 Touro St. 🚶 *Visit by guided tour only (20min).* ♿🕐*Open mid Mar–Apr Sun 12pm–2pm May–Jun Sun–Fri 12pm–2pm.* 🕐*Closed Sat & Jewish holidays.* 💰*Donations accepted.* 📞*401-847-4794. www.tourosynagogue.org.*

Touro Synagogue

© Discover Newport

Bowen's Wharf

© Newport Harbor Corporation

The earliest members of Newport's Jewish community arrived from the Caribbean in 1658. However, it was not until a century later, under the guidance of their leader, Isaac de Touro, that a synagogue was dedicated in 1763.

One of the earliest synagogues constructed in the US, the building was designed by architect **Peter Harrison** and successfully adapts the Georgian style to Sephardic Jewish tradition. Situated on a quiet street and set on a diagonal with the east wall facing the direction of Jerusalem, the exterior of the synagogue is almost stark in appearance. The interior is richly adorned with hand-carved paneling, balustrades and 12 Ionic columns

▶ Return to Spring St. and turn left.

Trinity Church★
Queen Anne Sq. ♿🕐*Open Jul–Aug daily 10am–4pm. May–mid Jun & last two weeks of Oct Mon–Fri 10am–1pm. Mid Jun–mid Jul & Sept–mid-Oct Mon–Fri 10am–4pm.* 🎫*$2 contribution suggested.* 📞*401-846-0660. www.trinitynewport.org.*
This white clapboard church (1726) rising above **Queen Anne Square**, features an arcaded belfry with a tall Colonial spire. Inside, the original three-tiered pulpit is the only one of its kind in the country. The left wall of the nave features two Tiffany stained-glass windows, one

of which commemorates Cornelius Vanderbilt (the face is said to be that of the Commodore himself).

▶ Continue south on Spring St. and turn left on Mill St.

Old Stone Tower
Nicknamed the Mystery Tower because of the various legends surrounding its origin, this stone structure has been attributed to the Vikings, the Portuguese, the Indians and the Irish. Less romantic is the theory that the tower is the remnant of a 17C windmill.

▶ Continue on Bellevue Ave. Turn right on Pelham St., which is lined with colonial dwellings. Turn right on Thames St., then left on Mill St. to the waterfront.

Bowen's Wharf★
Salty old dockside structures have been transformed into indoor and outdoor eateries. Along with neighboring craft shops and boutiques, they form the focal point of this waterfront square.

ADDITIONAL SIGHTS
Hunter House★★
54 Washington St. 🚶*Visit by guided tour by appointment only (45min).* 🕐*Open late Jun–mid-Oct daily 10am–5pm. Early May–late Jun, weekends & holidays only.*

Newport Festivals

Newport hosts numerous special events throughout the year (visit www.gonewport.com for details).

April:	Newport Restaurant Week
June:	Great Chowder Cook-Off
July:	Newport Music Festival
	Black Ships Festival
	Newport Kite Festival
	Newport Folk Festival
Aug:	Newport Jazz Festival
	Classic Yacht Regatta
	Waterfront Reggae Festival
Sept:	Newport Mansions Wine & Food Festival
Oct:	Bowen's Wharf Seafood Festival
Nov/Dec:	Christmas at the Newport Mansions

Chartered in the 19C, the railway experienced its busiest year in 1913 when 24 trains, including the Boston "Dandy Express," arrived and departed from Newport daily. Today the railway offers scenic excursions via a 10mi round-trip along the eastern shore of Narragansett Bay. Travel through the Navy base, between two large naval aircraft carriers, and get a look at the pleasure boats in Newport Harbor.

International Tennis Hall of Fame (M3)

194 Bellevue Ave. ◐Open year-round daily 9.30am–5pm. ◐Closed Thanksgiving Day & 25 Dec. ◉$12. ✆401-849-3990. www.tennisfame.com. Located in the historic **Newport Casino**, the 2,000sq ft Tennis Hall of Fame is home to one of the largest collections of tennis memorabilia in the US. An interactive museum offers the only lawn courts available for public use in the US.

Fort Adams State Park

Fort Adams Rd., off Harrison Ave. Park Fort open by guided tour only (45min), mid-May–Columbus Day 10am–4pm. Winter tours available by request. ◐Open year-round daily dawn–dusk. ◉$12. ✆401-841-0707. www.fortadams.org.

The largest coastal fortification in the US is a short drive or water taxi from Newport Harbor. You can visit the soldiers' quarters, enter the casemates, explore the tunnel system and climb the bastions to enjoy the views.

With walls made of granite hauled from Maine by schooner, Fort Adams was built to guard the entrance to Narragansett Bay. The fort ultimately developed into the command post for the coastal batteries in the Northeast; until 1945 it was the center of a system of defenses used to protect the bay and Long Island Sound. Today it is a state park and site of the annual **Newport Jazz Festival**, as well as the **Newport Folk Festival** (both in Aug). From the park's roadway there is a sweeping **view★★** of the harbor, Newport Bridge and downtown Newport.

◉$28. ✆401-847-1000. www.newportmansions.org. This elegant dwelling—built in 1748 by a prosperous merchant—was purchased by ambassador William Hunter and subsequently served as the home of two governors, as well as the headquarters of Admiral Charles de Ternay, commander of the French fleet during the Revolution.

The house is a beautiful example of the 18C Colonial style. The carved pineapple ornamenting the doorway is a symbol of hospitality that originated during the colonial period when a sea captain, returning home from a voyage, placed a pineapple outside his house to announce his safe arrival and to invite everyone to share the refreshments that were waiting inside.

Old Colony and Newport Railway

Departs from depot at 19 America's Cup Ave. ◐Open year-round. Trips Sun 11.45am and 2pm. ◉$10. ✆401-624-6951. www.ocnrr.com.

Museum of Yachting

🅿 🕒 *Open Jun 1–Oct 1 Wed–Mon 10am–5pm at Fort Adams State Park. Closed Tue.* 🎫*$5.* ✆*401-847-1018. www.moy.org.*

This small museum houses exhibits on the history of the America's Cup in Newport and other highlights in Newport yachting history. Also featured is the story of the ongoing restoration of the historic 133-ft schooner Coronet, first launched in 1885 and moored in Newport Harbor.

EXCURSIONS

Jamestown

▷ *3mi west of Newport via the Claiborne Pell Newport Bridge (toll), on Conanicut Island in Narragansett Bay.*

At this residential island's center stands the 1787 **Jamestown Windmill** (*380 N. Main Rd.;* 🅿 🕒 *open Jul–Sept wknds 10am–4pm;* 🎫 *donation requested;* ✆*401-423-0784*). Several of the island's sites offer great **views**: from **Beaver Tail Lighthouse** (*end of Beaver Tail Rd.*) you can see along the south shore; an expansive vista across the bay to Newport stretches from **Fort Wetherill** (*off Rte. 138 & Walcott Ave.*), whose ramparts are built on 100ft granite cliffs. The shores of picturesque **Mackerel Cove** are flecked with summer houses.

Green Animals Topiary Gardens★

👥👤 ▷ *9mi north of Newport via Rte. 114 in Portsmouth. Turn left off Rte. 114 onto Cory's Lane.* 🅿 🕒*Open early May–mid Oct daily 10am–5pm.* 🎫*$14.* ✆*401-847-1000. www.newportmansions.org.*

Textile executive Thomas Brayton began creating this garden when he bought the seven-acre estate in 1872.

Today flower beds, arbors and fruit trees punctuate the 80 boxwood and tree sculptures (these include fanciful representations of a giraffe, a unicorn and an elephant, some of them now 80 years old). The modest country house contains a toy museum, a doll collection and dollhouses.

Little Compton

▷ *23mi east of Newport via Rte. 138 East and Rte. 77 South.* ✆*401-849-8048. www.gonewport.com.*

Located in the southeastern portion of the state and known for its production of "Rhode Island Red" chickens, Little Compton is one of Rhode Island's prettiest villages. Fittingly, it is the only place in the country with a monument dedicated to a chicken. Marshes fringe the narrow tree-lined roads (such as Route 77) that wind through the rural countryside down to the coast.

Narragansett Pier

▷ *11mi southwest of Newport. Cross the Jamestown Bridge and take Rte. 1A south. From Narragansett Pier, drive south on Ocean Rd. (Rte. 1A) along the coast to Galilee.*

In the 19C heyday of this fashionable seaside resort, activity centered on the pier (now only the name survives), which extended from the southern end of Town Beach into the ocean. Today, the **Towers**, two stone structures joined by an arch extending across Ocean Road, are all that remain of the lavish Narragansett Casino (1884, McKim, Mead and White). The casino's main section along with many of Narragansett's grand hotels were destroyed by fire in 1900. Narragansett Pier, the coastal region extending south to the rocky headland of Point Judith, and the fishing villages of Galilee and Jerusalem possess some of New England's finest beaches.

Scarborough Beach's lively atmosphere draws a young crowd, while surfers prefer **East Matunuck State Beach**. Families with young kids are drawn to **Galilee Beach**'s calm waters.

Watch Hill

▷ *45mi southwest of Newport via Rte. 138 west to US-1 south. At Haversham, pick up Rte. 1A & follow it south to Watch Hill.*

Located at the southwestern-most point on Rhode Island's mainland, Watch Hill was named during King George's War (1740s) when a watchtower was built to survey Block Island Sound for signs of naval attack. Today this fashionable seaside area boasts elegant summer houses and a host of recreational activities (such as golf, boating and shopping along Bay St.). Kids will enjoy taking a spin on the c.1883 **Flying Horse Carousel** 👥👤 (*Bay St. and Larkin Rd.;* 🕐 *open Memorial Day– Columbus Day;* 💰 *$2; kids only*), whose 20 hand-carved wooden horses feature leather saddles, agate eyes, and manes and tails made of real horsehair. And "fly" they do, as they hang from a central unit, swinging outward as the carousel turns. The kid who can grab the traditional brass ring wins a second ride for free.

ADDRESSES

🛏 STAY

Reservation Services: Bed & Breakfast Newport, Ltd. (☎ *401-846-1828 or 800-800-8765; www.bbnewport.com*); Historic Inns of Newport (☎ *800-427-9444; www.historicinnsofnewport.com*).

$$$$$ Inn at Castle Hill & Resort – *590 Ocean Dr.* ☎ *401-849-3800 or 888-466-1355. www.castlehillinn.com. 25 rooms.* Originally the home of marine biologist Alexander Agassiz, this Victorian seaside inn, set on a 40-acre peninsula with sweeping ocean views, has moved up a notch after a restoration by new owners. Rooms in the Victorian mansion are the grandest, with sumptuous paneling, fireplaces and whirlpool tubs; though the harbor houses and the beach houses possess charms of their own—and porches. Guests enjoy complimentary breakfast and afternoon tea. Dining in the sunset room (*open to the public*), whose curved window walls create the illusion of a ship's bridge, captures the magic of the site.

$$$$$ Vanderbilt Hall – *41 Mary St.* ☎ *401-846-6200 or 888-826-4255. www.vanderbiltgrace.com. 33 rooms.* The YMCA is not your usual first choice for an overnight, especially one built in 1909, but when it's one with the Vanderbilt imprimatur that has been transformed into a four-star mansion-hotel, well, that's a YMCA of a different color. Thanks to a major renovation, the property has gone from fusty and funky to modern and luxurious. Each of the 33 guest rooms

(mostly suites) is outfitted with flat-screen TVs and DVD players. Many rooms also enjoy harbor views. The property also features indoor and outdoor pools, a spa and fitness center, and a fine dining restaurant, Muse. Rates include a Cornish cream tea with scones. Even if you stay elsewhere, it's worth coming by to see a YMCA in a class by itself.

$$$$ Chanler at Cliff Walk– *117 Memorial Blvd.* ☎ *401-847-1300 or 866-793-5664. www.thechanler.com. 20 rooms.* This elegant small hotel, housed in an opulent Newport seaside mansion, features 20 uniquely-styled rooms reflecting a different historical time period or theme. All rooms have modern amenities and lush furnishings, including flat screen TVs, DVD players, marble or granite baths, luxury linens, fireplaces, original art and fine antiques. Most have ocean views. Footsteps away is Newport's popular Cliff Walk.

$$$$ Francis Malbone House – *392 Thames St.* ☎ *401-846-0392. www.malbone.com. 20 rooms.* Designed by Peter Harrison (architect of Touro Synagogue), the Georgian-style inn was built in 1760 for shipping merchant Francis Malbone. Today this historic hostelry wraps guests in comfort in large rooms decorated with period reproductions, gas fireplaces, down comforters and eyelet-trimmed sheets. If it's chilly, warm yourself by a crackling fire in one of the front parlors. Rates include a lavish afternoon tea and a hearty breakfast, served in the elegant dining room. For those desiring complete privacy, the refurbished c.1750 Benjamin Mason House next door features two luxury suites.

$$$ Cliffside Inn – *2 Seaview Ave. Open year-round.* ☎ *401-847-1811 or 800-845-1811. www.cliffsideinn.com. 16 rooms. No children under age 13.* Located a few steps from Cliff Walk (near First Beach), this antique-filled Victorian inn has one of America's top 50 tea rooms, thanks to its decadent afternoon tea service (try the swoon-worthy macaroons). Breakfast is delightful as well. Guest rooms—oozing romance— have fireplaces and four-poster beds; some have big, share-able tubs. The most intriguing feature, though, are the more than 100 self-portraits painted by mysterious beauty Beatrice Turner, who lived here for several years.

$$$ Newport Beach Hotel & Suites–
*1 Wave Ave., corner of Memorial Blvd &
Wave Ave. ☎401-846-0310. www.newport
beachhotelandsuites.com. 68 rooms &
suites.* You can't beat the location—right
on the beach—and the water views at
this newly renovated hotel. Rooms in the
original, historic hotel have been updated
to include imported marble and granite
baths, plush linens and featherbeds
and custom-made wood furniture. All
have sweeping water views. An all-suite
addition sits next to the original historic
hotel with rooms ranging from 550 to
1,300sq ft. All have master baths with
whirlpool tubs, waterfront balconies,
separate living and dining areas and full
kitchens. The property also includes an
indoor pool area, with a rooftop deck
with hot tub and firepit, overlooking
Newport Pond.

♈ EAT

$$$ Black Pearl – *Bannister's Wharf.
Closed early Jan –mid Feb. ☎401-846-5264.
www.blackpearlnewport.com* **Seafood.**
A classic New England seafood house
perched on Bannister's Wharf, the Black
Pearl serves surf—and turf—specialties
in its dark-paneled tavern or in the more
formal (and pricier) Commodore Room
(*jacket required*) overlooking the marina.
The seafood menu changes daily to
feature such fresh catches as lobster,
sweet Nantucket Cape scallops and
grey sole. Local clams fill the restaurant's
creamy, ward-winning chowder.

$$$ Scales and Shells – *527 Thames St.
Dinner only. No credit cards. ☎401-846-
3474. www.scalesandshells.com.* **Seafood.**
The atmosphere is boisterous and casual
at this popular restaurant, located on
bustling Thames Street. Diners can watch
their meal being prepared in the open
kitchen, where a vast, ever-changing
menu of fish and shellfish specials—red
snapper, halibut, coho salmon, striped
bass, lobster, to name a few—are grilled
over fragrant wood. Start your meal
with a selection of oysters, cherrystones
(half-grown quahog clams) or littlenecks
(small, young quahog clams) from
the raw bar. Devoted carnivores go
elsewhere as this restaurant serves only
seafood.

$$ Brick Alley Pub & Restaurant –
*140 Thames St. ☎401-849-6334.
www.brickalley.com.* **American.** Visitors
and savvy locals alike give a thumbs-up
to the Brick Alley. With its lively decor—a
fire truck on the roof, a 1937 truck as a
room divider, sports paraphernalia—
as well as an affordable menu, this
pub/restaurant offers the proverbial
"something for everyone." Start with
portobello fries, jumbo crab cakes or ahi
tuna sliders, followed by entrées like the
gourmet mac-and-cheese with chouriço,
chicken enchilada lasagna, lobster ravioli
and roast prime rib. Hefty dinners come
with soup, salad and bread buffet and
a choice of one side (the garlic mashed
potatoes and tangled onions are popular
choices). Choose a table on the tree-
shaded patio in summertime.

$$ Salvation Cafe – *140 Broadway.
☎401-847-2620. www.salvationcafe.com.*
American. Grab a spot in the open-air
tiki bar at this fanciful, come-as-you-are
cafe where locals love to gather. The
menu is as eclectic as the decor; dishes
range from truffled mac-and-cheese to
pad Thai to grass fed beef filet wrapped
in gorgonzola. The bamboo basket with
steamed vegetable dumplings and the
duck tacos are popular starters. Save
room for desserts like the pumpkin
brandy cheesecake.

RECREATION

Newport is dubbed the sailing capital of
the world for good reason. Predictable
winds, a bustling, picturesque harbor
on deep and protected Narragansett
Bay and a short sail to the open waters
of the Atlantic Ocean make it one of the
best sailing spots on the East coast. A
variety of sightseeing cruises, from 2hr
sails aboard a 72ft schooner to three-
night excursions to Martha's Vineyard
or Nantucket on a 160ft yacht, are
available from Classic Cruises of Newport
(*☎401-847-0398 or 800-395-1343; www.
cruisenewport.com*). Sailing enthusiasts
can also charter one of the 12m America's
Cup winners for a sunset sail or a
cruise of **Narragansett Bay** (*America's
Cup Charters; ☎401-846-9886. www.
americascupcharters.com*).

Providence★★

The capital of Rhode Island, and the third-largest city in New England (after Boston and Worcester, Massachusetts), Providence is the hub of a metropolitan region. The city's location on a natural harbor at the head of Narragansett Bay offered special advantages for the shipping and commercial activity that allowed Providence to prosper and expand. One result of this expansion was the development of the College Hill district with its lovely 18C and 19C structures. Today this tree-shaded residential neighborhood is the home of Brown University and the Rhode Island School of Design. Across the city from College Hill, the majestic capitol building rises above the growing business area below.

A BIT OF HISTORY

After **Roger Williams** was banished from his pastorate in Salem, Massachusetts, he traveled south with a group of his followers until they arrived on the banks of the Moshassuck (later the Providence) River in June 1636. Settling here, they bought land from the Narragansett Indians and named it Providence, in honor of the divine Providence they believed had led them to this place. Williams declared that the new colony would be a safe refuge for all people seeking freedom of worship.

Originally a farming settlement, Providence rapidly developed into a commercial center as its inhabitants turned to shipping and trade. Strongly defended as the "backdoor to Boston" during the Revolution, Providence prospered as a privateering and supply depot. Following the war, the city emerged as Rhode Island's leading port. In 1787 Providence resident John Brown sent his first ship to China. Other merchants followed his lead and amassed great fortunes in the China trade.

Providence Today – The city has been recognized for its urban revitalization projects in recent years, notably **Water-**

▶ **Population:** 178,053.
🖰 **Michelin Map:** 581 M 10.
ℹ **Info:** ℘800-233-1636; www.goprovidence.com.
◗ **Location:** Providence is located off I-95, about 90 miles from Boston.
👪 **Kids:** Roger Williams Park Zoo is a fun excursion for kids.
🕓 **Timing:** A perfect day in Providence: join a historic walking tour; take in a performance at the renowned Trinity Repertory Company, and have dinner at one of the city's best restaurants.
🅿 **Parking:** The city has several public parking lots, including a multi-level garage at Providence Place Mall.
🜊 **Don't Miss:** WaterFire, a public art event, held on some Sat. nights May–Oct. In winter, don't miss a spin around the Bank of America Skating Center. If you are looking for an excursion out of town, Slater Mill Historic Site, in Pawtucket (7mi north of Providence) is a five-acre site built around the first water-powered textile mill in the US.

place Park (*near Exchange St.*) site of summer concerts and other events. Downtown buildings include the landmark Art Deco **Fleet Building** (*Fulton St.)* and the 1828 Arcade. Located near the State House, block-long **Providence Place Mall** dominates downtown, housing major retailers like Nordstrom and local specialty stores as well as myriad eateries and entertainment venues, including an IMAX theater. The famed **Trinity Repertory Company** holds performances in Lederer Theater Sept–Jun (*201 Washington St.; ℘401-351-4242; www.trinityrep.com*). **WaterFire** has

WaterFire

Photo Courtesy of Providence Warwick CVB / Photo by Nicholas Millard

become a popular rite of summertime. During these public art events, bonfires, accompanied by music, are lit after dark in 100 iron braziers placed in and along the rivers fronting Waterplace Park and the Riverwalk (*for schedule, call ℘401-273-1155 or access www.waterfire.org*).

COLLEGE HILL★★

This area's charming, tree-shaded streets, lined with architecture ranging from Colonial to Italianate, represents one of the most beautifully preserved historic districts in the nation. High on the hill sits **Thayer Street**—the shopping center of the university community—which brims with bookstores, coffeehouses, shops and restaurants. Former warehouses below the hill on South Main Street have been converted into boutiques and restaurants, adding to the aura of the past that pervades this section of the city. This district is home to **Brown University**.

⚓ WALKING TOUR

Located downtown, the Providence/ Warwick Convention and Visitors Bureau (144 Westminster St.; ℘800-233-1636; www.goprovidence.com) provides maps and information about the city.

▶ Begin at the intersection of College and Main St., and walk north on Main.

First Baptist Church in America★

75 N. Main St. ⟐⟐Open for self-guided and guided tours Memorial Day–Labor Day Mon–Fri 10am–noon & 1–3pm. Self-guided tours only rest of year, Mon–Fri 10am–noon & 1–3pm. ⟐Closed major holidays. ⟐$2. ℘401-454-3418. www.fbcia.org.

Founded by Roger Williams, the Baptist Church dates back to 1638. The first house of worship built by the Baptists in America stood on North Main Street, a short distance from the present site of this wooden clapboard church (1775) designed by Joseph Brown. The handsome steeple rises 185ft. Inside, the

First Baptist Church in America

Photo Courtesy of Providence Warwick CVB / Photo by Robert Wesley Rolland

345

Culinary Museum

Foodies will love a visit to the **Johnson & Wales Culinary Arts Museum**, showcasing the history of culinary arts in America. The museum includes exhibits on American diners (including a real diner that was donated to the museum), vintage equipment and antique stoves, New England taverns, and kitchen gadgets and appliances. The impressive collection of White House china and sample menus from state dinners is a popular display. The museum also includes an exhibit on well-known chefs who have attended Johnson & Wales University. *315 Harborside Blvd. Open year-round Tue–Sun 10am–5pm. Closed academic and major holidays. ☜$7. ✆401-598-2805. www.culinary.org.*

paneling, scrolled pediments, lighted urns and arches are painted in soft tones of green and white. Enormous columns support the galleries and roof, leading the eye upward to the carved ceiling.

▷ Return to Waterman St. and turn left. After one block, turn right on Benefit St.

Benefit Street

Spend some time strolling Benefit Street so that you can admire the more than 100 houses—ranging from Colonial to Victorian in style—that line the narrow streets and brick walks leading to the Rhode Island School of Design and to Brown University.

Rhode Island School of Design

Bounded by Waterman, Prospect, Benefit and Thomas Sts. ✆401-454-6100. www.risd.edu.
Established in the 19C to train artisans for industry, RISD (RIZ-dee) is renowned as a teaching institution for design, architecture and the visual arts. Facilities available to the school's 2,200 students include sculpture, wood and metal labs; apparel design studios; and textile workshops.

Museum of Art, Rhode Island School of Design★★

224 Benefit St. ♿🕐Open year-round Tue–Sun 10am–5pm. Third Thu of month until 9pm. 🕐Closed major holidays. ☜$12. ✆401-454-6500. www.risdmuseum.org.
The museum presents, in an engaging manner, collections of art from vari-

RISD Museum's Grand Gallery

© Erik Gould / RISD Museum

ous periods and civilizations: Egyptian, Greek, Roman, Asian, European, African and American. Many exhibits are arranged in chronological order, but they often cross period boundaries to illustrate common trends in contemporary sculpture, painting and textiles. The fourth level (*entrance level*) is devoted to special exhibitions; third-floor galleries contain 20C art.
Medieval carvings, 19C American and French paintings, and Greek bronzes fill the fifth level. On the sixth floor you'll find Oriental, Eastern and Egyptian art. Standing nearly 10ft tall, the **Dainichi Buddha** (10C Japan), a wooden temple figure discovered in 1933 in the attic of a farmhouse, claims a gallery to itself. Adjoining the museum is the elegant **Pendleton House**, built in 1906 to dis-

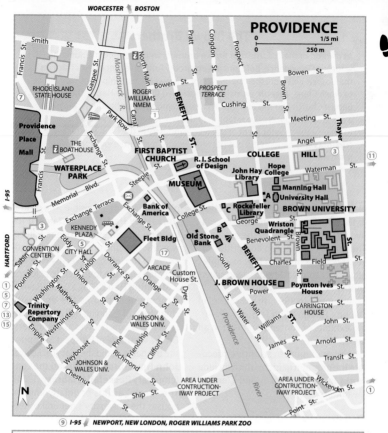

WORCESTER BOSTON

PROVIDENCE

| 0 | | 1/5 mi |
| 0 | 250 m | |

Smith St.
Francis St.
Gaspee St.
Moshassuck R.
Park Row
RHODE ISLAND STATE HOUSE

North Main
ROGER WILLIAMS NMEM
Pratt
Congdon
Prospect

Bowen St.
Bowen St.
BENEFIT
PROSPECT TERRACE
Cushing
Brown St.
Meeting St.
Thayer
Angel St.

Providence Place Mall
THE BOATHOUSE
Exchange St.
Francis St.
WATERPLACE PARK

FIRST BAPTIST CHURCH
R.I. School of Design
MUSEUM
Steeple
College St.

COLLEGE HILL
Hope College
John Hay Library
Waterman
Manning Hall
University Hall
BROWN UNIVERSITY
Rockefeller Library
George
Wriston Quadrangle

I-95
HARTFORD

Memorial Blvd.
Exchange Terrace
Exchange St.
Bank of America

KENNEDY PLAZA
Eddy
Fleet Bldg
Old Stone Bank
C
B
A

Benevolent St.
Brown St.
Field St.

1
5
7
13
15

Sabin
CONVENTION CENTER
CITY HALL
Dorance St.
Fulton
Union
Fountain St.
Washington St.
Mathewson St.
Empire St.
Westminster St.

ARCADE
Orange
Custom House St.
Dyer St.

BENEFIT
Charles St.

J. BROWN HOUSE
Power
Poynton Ives House
CARRINGTON HOUSE
John St.

Trinity Repertory Company
Weybosset
Pine
Richmond
Friendship
Clifford St.
JOHNSON & WALES UNIV.
JOHNSON & WALES UNIV.
Chestnut
Ship St.

South St.
Water St.
Williams St.
James St.
Arnold St.
Transit St.

Providence River

AREA UNDER CONTRUCTION-IWAY PROJECT
AREA UNDER CONTRUCTION-IWAY PROJECT
Wickenden St.
Point St.

N

9 I-95 NEWPORT, NEW LONDON, ROGER WILLIAMS PARK ZOO

WHERE TO STAY		WHERE TO EAT			
Jacob Hill Inn	1	Blue Grotto	1	La Laiterie Bistro	11
Omni Providence	3	Café Paragon	3	Mediterraneo Caffe	13
Providence Biltmore	5	Caffe Dolce Vita	5	Nick's on Broadway	15
Renaissance Providence Hotel	7	Caffe Dolce Vita	7	Pot au Feu	17
		CAV	9		

Historic Benefit Street

The Brown Brothers

At the end of the 18C, the four Brown brothers were prominent among the leaders of Providence. Bold and adventurous, **John**, a leader of the attack on the *Gaspee*, was a prosperous merchant. His was the first ship from Providence to reach China. **Joseph**, an architect, designed the Market House, the First Baptist Church and the John Brown House, among other buildings. **Moses**, a prosperous Quaker who established the Providence Bank, was the first to finance the development of the textile industry in the US at Pawtucket. **Nicholas** was a successful businessman whose mercantile enterprise was internationally known.

play the **Charles Pendleton collection** of 18C American furnishings and decorative arts, the highlight of the museum. The group of American and British silver (17C–20C) includes fine examples of work by colonial Rhode Island silversmiths.

Constructed in 1993, the three-level Daphne Farago Wing features changing exhibits of contemporary art in all media.

A number of modern sculptures decorate the museum garden, which include works by George Rickey and Clement Meadmore.

▶ Turn left on College St.

Brown University★
Bounded by George, Prospect, Waterman and Thayer Sts. ✆*401-863-1000. www.brown.edu.*
The seventh college established in the US (1764), this Ivy League school was founded at Warren as the Rhode Island College and renamed in 1804 for its principal benefactor, Nicholas Brown II. The university is known for its liberal education philosophy, implemented in 1969. Approximately 5,800 undergraduate and 1,800 graduate students are enrolled at Brown's 140-acre College Hill campus, which consists of some 245 buildings.

At the main entrance to the university, on Prospect Street, are the **Van Wickle Gates (A)**, which are opened twice a year: inward on the first day of classes for freshmen, and outward on commencement day. From within the gates Brown's

oldest buildings are visible. The central **University Hall** (1771), a stately brick building known as the College Edifice, was the sole university structure until 1822. To the left of University Hall, the building with the four granite columns is **Manning Hall** (1835), a Greek Revival structure that houses the University chapel; left of Manning Hall is **Hope College** (1822), which serves as a dormitory. On the west side of Prospect St., opposite the gates, stand the Classical Revival **John Hay Library** (1910) and the contemporary **Rockefeller Library** (1964). The "Rock," as it is popularly known, houses the university's general collection in humanities and social sciences.

▶ Continue south one block on Prospect St. and turn left on George St. After one block, turn right on Brown St.

On Brown Street you will pass **Wriston Quadrangle** (1952), the campus residence of approximately 1,000 students. Continue south on Brown St. to Power St. At the corner of Brown and Power Streets stands **Poynton Ives House** (*no. 66*), a classic example of Federal architecture.

John Brown House★★
52 Power St. 👣*Visit by guided tour only (45min).* 🕐*Open Apr–Nov, Tue–Fri 1.30pm–3pm, Sat 10.30am–3pm, Dec–Mar, Fri–Sat, 10.30am–3pm.* 💰*$10* ✆*401-273-7507. www.rihs.org.*
The three-story brick mansion (1788), designed for John Brown by his brother

Joseph, impressed many who came to see it. John Quincy Adams, who visited the house, proclaimed it to be "the most magnificent and elegant private mansion that I have ever seen on this continent."

Inside, the carved doorways, columns, cornices and lavish plaster-ornamented ceilings provide an appropriate setting for the treasured collection of Rhode Island furnishings, most of which are Brown family pieces. The unique **blockfront secretary** boasts nine shells carved into its front (shell secretaries normally have only six shells). Attributed to Rhode Island cabinetmaker John Goddard, this piece is one of the finest existing examples of American Colonial furniture.

▶ Continue west on Power St. and turn left on Benefit St. Continue south on Benefit St. and then turn left on Williams St. At no. 66 stands another Federal-style mansion, the Carrington House. Return to Benefit St. and continue north.

Just beyond Benevolent Street, there is a good **view** of the gilded ribbed dome of the **Old Stone Bank** on South Main Street. A little farther, on the left, is an 18C red clapboard dwelling, the **Stephen Hopkins House** (no. 43) (**B**), formerly the home of Quaker governor Stephen Hopkins, signer of the Declaration of Independence and also ten-time governor of Rhode Island. The Greek Revival style is represented by the **Providence Athenaeum** (**C**) (1838, William Strickland) where, after the death of his wife in 1847, Edgar Allen Poe unsuccessfully courted poet Sarah Whitman, a resident of Benefit Street.

ADDITIONAL SIGHTS
Trinity Repertory Company★
201 Washington St. ✆*401-351-4242. www.trinityrep.com.*
This Tony Award-winning regional theater offers a variety of new works and classic plays, year-round. The annual production of "A Christmas Carol" is a highlight of the holiday season.

Bank of America City Center Skating Rink

Photo Courtesy of Providence Warwick CVB / Photo by Nicholas Millard

Bank of America City Center Skating Rink
2 Kennedy Plaza. ⏱*Open daily mid Nov–mid March Mon–Fri 10am–10pm Sat–Sun 11am–10pm.* ∞*$6.* ✆*401-331-5544.*
Ice-skate surrounded by skyscrapers at this 14,000sq-ft outdoor rink—twice the size of the rink in New York City's Rockefeller Center.

Gallery Night
⏱*Mar–Nov; www.gallerynight.info/.*
On the third Thursday of each month, 21 galleries, museums and art shops open their doors after hours, with live music, refreshment and local celebrities. Free bus transportation is available.

Roger Williams Park Zoo
1000 Elmwood Ave. ⏱*Open year-round daily 9am–4pm.* ∞*$14.95.* ✆*401-785-3510. www.rwpzoo.org.*
This accredited zoo has more than 100 different animal species, including African giraffes, zebras, wildebeessts and elephants. Monkeys, bats and two-toed sloths roam the tropical rainforest house.

ADDRESSES

STAY

$$$$ Jacob Hill Inn – *120 Jacob St., Seekonk, MA.* 📞*401-527-3629 or 888-336-9165. www.inn-providence-ri.com. 10 rooms and suites.* This elegant and well-appointed country inn, housed in a former 1722 country estate, is located just over the border in Massachusetts, about a 10 minute drive from downtown Providence. Luxury is the name of the game here; rooms are spacious and plush with small sitting areas, whirlpool baths, fireplaces and deluxe linens. The property, overlooking 50 acres of rolling farmland, also has an indoor pool, tennis court and billiard room. It's a perfect oasis for those wanting a more intimate and romantic setting than the typical high-rise chain hotel in the heart of downtown Providence.

$$$ Omni Providence – *1 W. Exchange St.* 📞*401-598-8000. www.omnihotels.com. 564 rooms.* Among the chain hotels, the Omni is the most stylish choice. Hard to find, it's not: the red brick, turreted towers of this 25-story hotel rise over downtown. Sleekly spare, Euro-style guest rooms are done up in crisp white linens; many have views of the city. The best reason to stay here is the convenience factor: the hotel is connected by skywalks to the convention center and Providence Place Mall. There's also an indoor swimming pool, fitness center and an on-site restaurant and lounge.

$$ Providence Biltmore – *11 Dorrance St.* 📞*401-421-0700 or 800-294-7709. www. providencebiltmore.com. 292 rooms.* The Biltmore, a local institution since 1922, is the unquestioned grand dame of Providence hotels. Lavishly refurbished, it boasts spacious contemporary guest rooms (the state's largest, with the majority of rooms measuring 600sq ft) and modern amenities, including a 24hr fitness center and a full-service spa. But the property's claim to fame continues to be the hotel's original soaring gold-leafed lobby with its centerpiece glass elevator and marble staircase. Between the lavish lobby and the restored rooftop ballroom, you feel you have stepped back into a more gracious era. Even so, most of the revitalized downtown, including the Rhode Island Convention Center and Providence Place Mall, is within easy walking distance.

$$ Renaissance Providence Hotel – *5 Avenue of the Arts.* 📞*401-919-5000 or 800-468-3571. www.marriott.com. 272 rooms.* Built in 1929 as a Masonic temple, this Neoclassical building has been transformed into a stylish hotel that celebrates the artistic side of Providence. Its bold colors, vivid artwork and a check-in desk that's curtained like a stage set provide a sense that exciting things happen here. Amenities like a 24hr fitness center, a Mediterranean-themed restaurant (**$$ R Restaurant + Lounge**) and Wi-Fi, all add to the appeal of one of the city's hottest properties.

EAT

$$$ Nick's on Broadway – *500 Broadway.* 📞*401-421-0286, www.nicksonbroadway.com.* **American.** This casual, contemporary restaurant is a popular place for breakfast (expect a wait), lunch and dinner. The grilled shrimp frittata, brioche French toast and black beans and eggs are popular early morning dishes. For dinner, start with the gnocchi with pork belly and blue cheese or the cheese plate of local cheeses and fruits. Signature entrées include the herb-grilled boneless duck with wild mushrooms, crispy-skinned salmon with cauliflower risotto and the grilled sirloin with smoked bacon. The grilled house-made rustic bread is a popular side. The restaurant also offers a tasting menu with a choice of three or six courses. Wine pairings are also available.

$$$ Pot au Feu – *44 Custom House St. Closed Sun.* 📞*401-273-8953. www.pot aufeuri.com.* **French**. The late Julia Child declared Pot au Feu the kind of place she wished she had access to in Cambridge. Whether she was referring to the upstairs salon's classically inspired Parisian cuisine (*carré d'agneau bordelais, entrecôte de veau Robert, tournedos Diane*) or the downstairs bistro's provincial fare (bouillabaisse, crepes steak frites and the eponymous beef stew), one can only guess. But legions of others share her enthusiasm. Owner Robert Burke, a fourth-generation Rhode Islander, prides himself on his fresh seafood (*coquilles St. Jacques Nantucket, homard en croûte*) and prix-fixe option. The bistro is one of the best values in Providence.

$ Café Paragon/Viva – *234 Thayer St.*   *401-331-6200. www.paragonand viva.com.* **American.** College students know the best places to dine well on the cheap, and in Providence, they favor this two-for-one cafe (Paragon is the light, bright, quieter side, Viva the darker, louder, more clubby side). The food is hip American, with sandwiches (try the Thai chicken wrap or lobster club), gourmet pizzas, pastas, the cafe's renowned namesake salads and half-pound gourmet burgers available at lunch and dinner. The dinner menu adds trendy tapas (white mussels, saku sushi tuna, crab and lobster cakes) and value-packed entrées (grilled flat iron steaks, peppercorn tuna, slow-roasted chicken). Tables spill onto the sidewalk during warmer months.

$$ La Laiterie – *188 Wayland Ave. Dinner only.*   *401-274-7177. www.farmstead inc.com.* **American**. This award-winning restaurant specializes in local, seasonal food, dubbing itself the destination for "haute farmhouse cuisine." The intimate and understated dining room features rust-colored paper lights, vintage barn wood, hand wrought iron accents, Vermont soapstone and copper pots. The menu changes frequently to reflect seasonal ingredients. Small plates and starters may include dishes like marinated beets, grilled sardines, seared Vermont chicken livers and marinated prawns. Signature entrées include ham with melted brie, grilled pheasant breast and pan roasted pork chops with crispy sweetbreads.

$$ CAV – *14 Imperial Place.* *401-751-9164. www.cavrestaurant.com.* **Mediterranean.** Like its eclectic decor—a mix of Tabriz tapestries, ships' models, antiques and art objects from around the world—the global menu at this unique restaurant (CAV stands for Coffee, Antiques, Vittles) reflects the owner's desire to bring world cultures together. This is fusion fare at its finest. Try the pistachio-crusted crab cake, *poulet aux poires* (a pan-seared chicken breast with pears poached in red wine and ginger pear sauce), braised lamb shanks and pan seared scallops with lobster butter. Other delights include house-made pasta dishes like the ravioli filled with carmelized onions and topped with

arugula pistachio pesto, and the herb and garlic fettucine served with chunks of lobster and asparagus in a sage and white truffle sauce. For dessert, Milanese *frutti di bosco* is *magnifico*.

FINE DINING IN FEDERAL HILL
You're in the area known as Federal Hill when you pass under the huge *pigna* (pine cone), the Italian symbol for abundance that graces the arch spanning the eastern end of **Atwells Avenue**, located west of Empire Street. Never mind that some locals claim it's a pineapple or even an artichoke. Atwells is *the* street for Italian food, no matter what your budget.

$$ Mediterraneo Caffé (*no. 134;* *401-331-7760; www.mediterraneocaffe.com*) draws youngish crowds with its artsy decor, alfresco seating and nouvelle cuisine, while the formal **$$$ Blue Grotto** (*no. 210;* *401-272-9030; www. bluegrottorestaurant.com*) is a go-to destination for exquisitely prepared upscale Italian food and impeccable service. (The landmark **$$$$ L'Epicureo Ristorante** has moved to the Hotel Providence at 311 Westminster St).

A nice middle ground is **$$$ Camille's Roman Garden** (*71 Bradford St.;* *401-751-4812; www.camillesonthehill.com*), where the food is always superb, enhanced by the friendly service. Have your after-dinner espresso and dessert at **$$ Caffé Dolce Vita** (*59 DePasquale Square;* *401-331-8240; www.caffedolcevita.com*).

In 1609, when French explorer **Samuel de Champlain** first set eyes on the forested mountains extending southward from the lake that now bears his name, he reportedly exclaimed, *"Les verts monts!"* (**"The green mountains!"**). More than a century later, Champlain's description of these peaks was adopted as the state's official name. Rural and uncluttered, Vermont has miles of back roads that skirt rocky streams and cross wooden covered bridges scattered throughout the open countryside. Dormant under a heavy cover of glistening white snow in winter, the region becomes a palette of rich greens in summer and blazes with color in autumn.

Highlights

▶ **Population:** 621,270.
Info: ✆802-828-3237 or 800-VERMONT; www.travel-vermont.com.
Area: 9,609sq mi.
Capital: Montpelier.
Nickname: The Green Mountain State.
State Flower: Red clover.

An Independent State

In 1777 Vermont declared itself independent, and a constitution was drawn up outlawing slavery and eliminating property ownership. Denied admission to the Union due to land claims by New York, Vermont was independent for 14 years, coining its own money and negotiating with foreign powers. The dispute with New York settled, Vermont joined the Union in 1791 as the 14th state.

Economy

Agriculture, primarily dairy farming, fuels the state's economy. Vermont's farms supply milk and dairy products, including the famous **cheddar cheese**, to the Boston region and southern New England. **Maple syrup** is the state's other important agricultural product. **Granite** quarried near Barre and **marble** from the Green Mountains near Danby are leading state exports. Year-round tourism is the second-largest industry. Outdoor advertising is prohibited by law; a uniform state-wide sign system indicates lodging and services.

Vermont Today

Vermont offers a delightful blend of historic charm, quiet villages, pastoral and mountainous landscapes, smart resorts and thriving arts and culinary hot spots. In the south, **Manchester** is a popular summer and winter resort and cultural center, with a cluster of shops, restaurants, well-regarded country inns, and an historic town center. **Burlington**, nestled on the shores of Lake Champlain and home to the University of Vermont, is the state's most modern and populous city. **Stowe**, in the shadows of Mount Mansfield (Vermont's tallest peak), is a year-round resort town, with elegant lodgings and dining. **Woodstock,** in central Vermont, is a not-to-be-missed historic village, with gracious 18C and 19C architecture, now housing modern eateries, shops, and luxury lodgings. Quiet **St Johnsbury,** home to the Fairbanks Museum and Planetarium, is the gateway to Vermont's vast, rural Northeast Kingdom.

Sports and Recreation

Vermonters love the outdoors, and no wonder; the largely undeveloped landscape of rolling hills and rugged mountains, dense forests and pictur-

Lake Willoughby

esque farmlands, make a perfect playground. You'll have no trouble finding something to do year-round (with the exception of spring, which Vermonters aptly call "mud season").

There are more than 700 miles of **hiking** trails across the state, several recreational paths and hundreds of back roads and country lanes to explore. Two major hiking trails run along the spine of the Green Mountains. The Appalachian Trail and the Long Trail follow the same route from the state's southern border to Sherburne Pass, where the Appalachian Trail turns east and the Long Trail continues north to the Canadian border; there are several access points along the way.

Cycling is popular across the state, with more than 9,000 miles of backroads and old logging trails weaving through villages suspended in time, and rolling farmlands. Outfitters offering rentals, guided pedaling and multi-day biking trips (including inn-to-inn excursions) are easy to find. Ask the local tourist office staff or your friendly innkeeper for suggestions on biking routes. The recreational paths in Stowe and Burlington are popular with families and provide easy-to-manage outings.

Vermont is known for its top-notch **mountain biking** terrain. Mount Snow in southern Vermont is home to the nation's first mountain biking school.

Other mountain biking hot spots include Mad River Glen and East Burke in northern Vermont. Most ski resorts also have trails and lift-serviced biking.

If you are interested in **fishing**, there are more than 5,000 miles of fishable streams in the valleys of Vermont—where anglers cast for brook, brown and rainbow trout—including the famed Battenkill River in southern Vermont. The American Museum of Fly Fishing in Manchester is devoted to the history of the sport and showcases equipment once belonging to Daniel Webster and Ernest Hemingway, among others. There are a host of fly-fishing guides and services throughout the state. Vermont also has more than 400 lakes and ponds – including the 125-mile long Lake Champlain.

When the mercury drops, Vermonters head outdoors! **Winter** activities abound in the Green Mountain State. There are more than 20 alpine ski resorts and almost 50 cross country centers. You can learn more about the history of skiing at the Vermont Ski Museum in Stowe. The Trapp Family Lodge, also in Stowe, is known worldwide for its cross country skiing terrain, and is credited with reviving the sport in the East. Snowshoeing, sledding, and ice fishing are also popular wintertime pursuits.

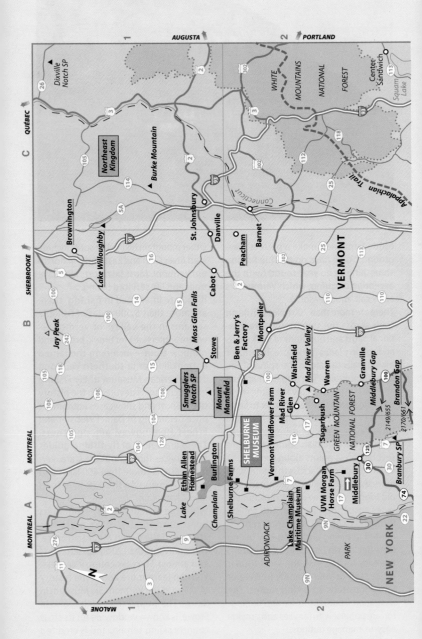

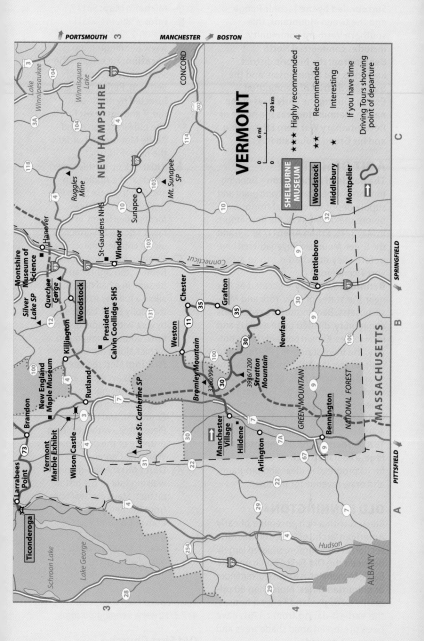

Bennington★

Surrounded by the Taconic Range and the Green Mountains, this southern Vermont community includes commercial North Bennington; the historic district known as Old Bennington; and the business district of Bennington Center. During the early days of the nation, Bennington was the home of Revolutionary War hero Ethan Allen and his Green Mountain Boys.

A BIT OF HISTORY

The Battle of Bennington – Bennington was an important rallying point and supply depot for colonial troops even before the outbreak of the Revolution. In May 1775, **Ethan Allen** (1738-89) and the Green Mountain Boys gathered here before they marched north to attack Fort Ticonderoga.

Bennington Today – Located as it is near the states of New York and Massachusetts, Bennington is a crossroads community, divided by several US and local routes. Known primarily for its pottery, the town supports gift shops and craft centers that sell a variety of ceramics and glassware made by local artisans. Chief among these is the **Potters Yard**, where Bennington Potters was founded in 1948 (the craft of pottery had its actual beginnings in Bennington in the 1820s). Tourism and **Bennington College**, a liberal-arts school distinguished for its progressive ideas and programs, also draw revenue for the town.

OLD BENNINGTON★

Blessed with a rich ensemble of early American architecture, this historic section of Bennington, situated largely between the Old First Church and the Battle Monument, is a peaceful reminder of unhurried times. More than 80 primarily Georgian and Federal houses, the earliest dating from c.1761, have been preserved amid shade trees and expansive grounds.

A walking-tour brochure is available from the Chamber of Commerce on Rte. 7, one mile north of downtown or can be

▶ **Population:** 15,737.

Michelin Map: 581 I 7.

Info: ℰ802-447-3311 or 800-229-0252; www.bennington.org.

▶ **Location:** Tucked into the southwestern corner of Vermont, Bennington is bisected by north-south Rte. 7 and east-west Rte. 9. The old First Church and Battle Monument border the historic district.

Kids: Pick up freshly baked goods at the Apple Barn and Country Bake Shop (*Rte. 7, ℰ888-827-7537; www.theapplebarn.com*). In the fall, it's home to Vermont's oldest cornfield maze.

Timing: Most downtown Bennington sights can be seen in a half day, but allow a full day to drive the Molly Stark Trail scenic byway, with ample time for browsing, swimming and picnics along the way.

Parking: Metered street parking is available, and there are several downtown lots, including one on County St. and two on Pleasant St., within walking distance of the downtown Welcome Center.

Don't Miss: A self-guided walking tour of the historic district. Maps are available from the Bennington Convention and Visitors Center (*ℰ802-447-3311 or 800-229-0252; www.bennington.com*).

downloaded from their website (ℰ802-447-3311; www.bennington.com).

Old First Church★

Monument Ave. at Church Lane. From the junction of Rtes. 9 and US-7, take Rte. 9 West and turn left onto Monu-

ment Ave. ◷Open weekends Memorial Day–Jun daily Jul–mid-Oct Mon–Sat 10am–noon & 1pm–4pm, Sun 1pm–4pm. ☎802-447-1223. www.oldfirst churchbenn.com.

This white clapboard church (1805) was built on the site of the 1763 meeting-house that served as the first Protestant church in Vermont. The old cemetery behind the church is the resting place of Revolutionary War soldiers and early founders of Vermont. One tombstone marks the grave of poet **Robert Frost** (1874-1963).

Bennington Battle Monument

15 Monument Ave. ♿🅿◷*Open mid-Apr–Oct daily 9 am–5pm.* ✆*$2.* ☎*802-447-0550. www.benningtonbattle monument.com.*

This 306ft obelisk, erected in 1891, commemorates the Battle of Bennington. The **view★★** from the observation deck includes the Berkshires, Green Mountains and New York State.

Bennington Museum★

1mi west of Bennington center at 75 W. Main St. (Rte. 9). ♿🅿◷*Open Thu–Tue 10am–5pm, daily Sept–Oct. Closed Wed Nov–Jun.* ◷*Closed the month of Jan & major holidays.* ✆*$10.* ☎*802-447-1571. www.benningtonmuseum.org.*

The museum's collections showcase Vermont and New England history. Highlights include fine 19C and 20C American glassware, 18C and 19C American furniture, 19C **Bennington pottery** and the Bennington Flag, one of the oldest Stars and Stripes in existence. Here you'll also find the largest public collection of paintings by **Grandma Moses**.

EXCURSIONS
Molly Stark Trail

This scenic 40mi stretch of Rte. 9 between Bennington and Brattleboro winds through forested mountains and small towns. About 10mi east of Bennington, you'll come to 400-acre **Woodford State Park** (♿⛺🅿◷*open Memorial Day–Columbus Day daily 10am–9pm;* ✆*$3/day;* ☎*802-447-7169; www.vtstate-*

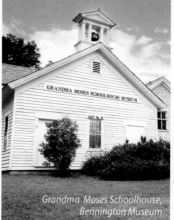

Grandma Moses Schoolhouse, Bennington Museum

© Stephen Goodhue / VermontVacation.com

parks.com). Midway along Rte. 9, stop at the roadside village of **Wilmington** to browse shops and eateries. From the turnout on **Hogback Mountain** (2,410ft), there are views east to Mt. Monadnock (3,165ft) in New Hampshire and south to the Berkshire Hills and the Holyoke Range in Massachusetts.

At the end of the trail, the commercial center of **Brattleboro** lies beside the Connecticut River. Check out the work of international and local artists at the **Brattleboro Museum and Art Center** (*10 Vernon St.* ◷*open Sun–Thu 11am–5pm Fri 11am–7pm Sat 10am–5pm;* ◷*closed Tue & major holidays* ✆*$8;* ☎*802-257-0124; www.brattleboro museum.org*).

Grandma Moses

The story of **Anna Mary Robertson Moses**' career as a painter is as memorable as her paintings. Grandma Moses (1860-1961), as she became known, lacked formal training in art. After years of life as a farm wife, she began to paint at the age of 70. Her simple scenes of the countryside and farm life appealed to the public, and her first show, in 1940, won her immediate fame. Grandma Moses continued to paint until her death at the age of 101.

ADDRESSES

♈/EAT

BENNINGTON

$$ Rattlesnake Cafe - *230 North St. ℘802-447-7018. www.rattlesnakecafe.com.* Awash in eye-catching colors, this small house in Bennington Center is home to fine and festive south-of-the-border cuisine, popular with the local dinner crowd. The menu offers a large selection of dishes. For appetizers, try the rattlesnake nachos or the super spicy El Loco chicken wings. Favorite entrées include the shrimp quesadillas, the hefty fajita bowl, the pan sautéed shrimp smothered with garlic, onions, capers and olives, and the steak roja, a hand-cut grilled ribeye topped with cheese and ranchero sauce. Also popular is the build-your-own Mexican pizza.

BRATTLEBORO

$$ Top of the Hill - *632 Putney Rd. ℘802-258-9178. www.topofthehillgrill.com.* This popular roadside BBQ grill serves authentic pit barbecue meats, in addition to Mexican and Cajun specialties. Grab a seat at a picnic table in the screened, heated outdoor deck where you'll have mountain-to-valley views. Meats, including hickory smoked pulled pork, beef brisket, chicken and ribs, are smoked on the premises. The apple-smoked turkey is a favorite, too. A selection of fajitas, burritos and enchiladas is offered, along with Cajun dishes, like the grilled catfish, chicken and sausage gumbo and jambalaya.

Burlington★

Located on Lake Champlain, Burlington, the most populous city in the state, reigns as the urban and industrial heart of Vermont; its success as a 19C industrial center and commercial port is evidenced in the lovely residences that remain from the period.

A BIT OF HISTORY

The colorful, four-block downtown pedestrian mall, **Church Street Marketplace★**, forms the retail heart of the city with its bustling cafes, boutiques and lively student atmosphere. Enjoy the lake views from **Battery Park** and **Ethan Allen Park** (*North Ave. to Ethan Allen Pkwy.*) or experience Lake Champlain firsthand by taking one of the several cruises offered (*&see Lake Champlain*).

SIGHTS
University of Vermont

Main campus bordered by Prospect St., East Ave., Main St. and Colchester Ave. ℘802-656-3131. www.uvm.edu. As old as the state itself, the university was chartered in 1791 as the fifth

▶ **Population:** 38,889.
  Michelin Map: 581 H 2.
▪ **Info:** ℘802-863-3489; www.vermont.org.
▶ **Location:** The city is easily accessed via north-south I-89.
♣ **Kids:** ECHO Lake Aquarium and Science Center (*on the waterfront; ℘802-864-1848; www.echovermont.org*) has an array of kid-friendly exhibits.
🕐 **Timing:** Start at Church Street Marketplace, to browse shops, then visit one of the waterfront beaches. Allow a full day for scenic drives and another to tour Shelburne Museum.
🅿 **Parking:** The Waterfront Lot (*on the right just before the Boathouse Circle*) offers all-day parking.
😊 **Don't Miss:** A guided boat excursion on Lake Champlain; nearby Shelburne Museum is a must-stop.

© VermontVacation.com

college in New England. From the campus green (*between S. Prospect St. and University Pl.*), the grounds rise to a line of buildings that includes the landmark **Ira Allen Chapel** (1925), and the adjacent **Billings Center** (1885).

Robert Hull Fleming Museum

61 Colchester Ave. on university campus. ♿️🅿️🕐*Open Labor Day–Apr Tue Thu–Fri 9am–4pm, Wed 9am–8pm weekends 1pm–5pm. Rest of the year Tue–Fri noon–4pm, weekends 1pm–5pm.* 🕐*Closed academic & major holidays.* 👓*$5.* 📞*802-656-0750. www.uvm.edu.*
The museum's collection includes Egyptian, Asian and Native American artifacts and contemporary Vermont art, as well as **American paintings** and **European works** from the 17C to the 19C. On the grounds, note the abstract, five-figure sculpture entitled *Lamentations Group* (1989) by Vermont resident Judith Brown.

LAKE CHAMPLAIN

📞*802-863-3489. www.vermont.org.*
Cradled in a broad valley between the Adirondacks and the Green Mountains, this 125mi-long lake straddles the Vermont–New York border. Lake Champlain (which locals like to refer to as the sixth Great Lake) and its surroundings have become a popular recreation and vacation area. Several kayaking, canoeing, and boating excursions are offered by local outfitters. At the northern end of the lake, bridges provide access to Isle la Motte, North Hero and Grand Isle.

Cruises★

Departs from Burlington Boathouse (College St.). 🍴♿️🅿️ ⛴*Round-trip 1hr 30min. Commentary.* 👓*$16.21.* 📞*802-862-8300. www.soea.com.*
The stern-wheeler *Spirit of Ethan Allen* offers narrated scenic cruises on Lake Champlain with views of the islands and the Adirondacks.

Ferries

Ferry services operating on Lake Champlain provide lake crossings between Grand Isle, Burlington and Charlotte, Vermont and New York State.
Contact Lake Champlain Ferries (📞*802-864-9804 or www.ferries.com*) for fares and schedules. Fort Triconderoga Ferry (📞*802-897-7999; www.forttiferry.com*) offers service from Larrabees Point to Fort Ticonderoga in New York. Ferries operate in winter.

Burlington Boathouse

Situated at the foot of College Street, the community's sizable boathouse (🕐*open May–Oct;* 📞*802-865-3377*) contains public phones and restrooms, a cafe, a visitor information booth and sailboat rentals (*in season;* 📞*802-863-5090*). It's also the departure point for some of the scenic cruises on Lake Champlain. Order a morning coffee or afternoon lemonade and take in the lake views, the cool breezes and waterfront activities from the vantage point of this lovable landmark.

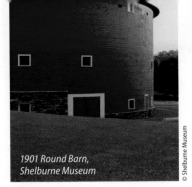
1901 Round Barn,
Shelburne Museum

© Shelburne Museum

some of the many highlights.

Shelburne Farms
▶ 1611 Harbor Rd., 1.5mi northeast of Shelburne Village. ✕🅿🕐Open mid-May–Oct daily 9am–5.30pm. 🐾 Walking trails open year-round weather permitting. ⊚$8 general admission, $11 guided property tour. ☏802-985-8686. www.shelburnefarms.org.

This grand 19C agricultural estate and National Historic Landmark on the shore of Lake Champlain was the country home of railroad tycoon **William Seward Webb** and his wife **Lila Vanderbilt Webb**, granddaughter of Cornelius Vanderbilt, who founded the Vanderbilt dynasty.

The 1,400-acre farm now operates as an nonprofit environmental education center, with a working dairy on the premises. Visitors can view cheesemaking in process, visit the dairy farm and market gardens, and take a wagon ride to the Children's Farmyard. There are a variety of hands-on activities and demonstrations held daily. Save time to walk the network of footpaths that meander the estate, offering scenic views along the way. **Shelburne House★**, a 110-room 1899 country manor house boasting **views★★** of Lake Champlain and the Adirondacks, operates as the 24-room **Inn at Shelburne Farms** (🕐open mid-May–mid-Oct; ☏802-985-8498; www.shelburnefarms.org). Tours of the inn are also available by reservation only.

EXCURSIONS
👥 Shelburne Museum★★★
▶ 12mi south on Rte. 7. in Shelburne Village. ♿✕🅿🕐Open mid-May–Oct daily 10am–5pm Nov–Dec Tue–Sun 10am–5pm.⊚$20. ☏802-985-3346. www.shelburnemuseum.org.

Established by New Yorker **Electra Havemeyer Webb**, this endearing museum preserves many of the home crafts, folk art, fine arts, trade tools, modes of transportation and furnishings that she began collecting in 1907. Now encompassing some 80,000 pieces, the preeminent collection represents 300 years of American life, history and art, and is housed in 37 buildings spread across 45 acres on a magnificent site overlooking the Lake Champlain Valley. Shelburne's collection of 18C and 19C American folk art is one of the finest in the nation. Weathervanes, whirligigs, cigar store figures, trade signs, ship's carvings, scrimshaw, and sculptures are displayed. The museum also boasts an impressive collection of 19C and 20C American paintings.

The museum's internationally recognized quilt collection features over 400 18C and 19C American quilts, making it the largest and one of the finest museum collections of its kind in the country.

Vermont Wildflower Farm
▶ 5mi south of Shelburne on US-7 in Charlotte. 🅿🕐Open Apr–Oct daily 10am–5pm. ☏802-425-3641. www.vermontwildflowerfarm.com.

Meadows abloom with Jack-in-the-pulpit, black-eyed Susans, asters and Devil's paintbrush color the farm's six acres from spring through fall. Paths are lined with more than 1,000 species of wildflowers. Also on the premises are a seed store and a gift shop, offering a variety of garden-based gifts and Vermont-made products.

Ethan Allen Homestead★

▶ *2mi north on Rte. 127. From Burlington, take US-7 north, turn left on Pearl St., then right on N. Champlain St. to road's end. Turn left, then immediate right onto Rte. 127 north and exit at North Ave. Beaches. Take the first right at the sign for the homestead.* ♿ ⏰ *Open mid-May–mid-Oct Thu–Mon 10am-4pm*💬📷*Visit of house by guided tour (30min) only, on the half hour.* 💲*$7.* ☏ *802-865-4556. www.ethanallenhomestead.org.*

Dedicated to the legendary folk hero, this 5-acre site threaded by the Winooski River includes a reconstructed frame house (c.1785) believed to have been the final home of **Ethan Allen**.

The modern visitor center houses exhibits on regional history and the escapades of Allen and his Green Mountain Boys. A re-created tavern in the center serves as the setting for a multimedia presentation (*15min*) in which Allen is remembered by friends and associates. Trails lead along the river.

Ben and Jerry's Ice Cream Factory

▶ *Located in Waterbury. Take exit 10 off I-80, go north on Rte. 100 for 1mi.* ⏰*Open Jul–mid-Aug daily 9am–9pm. Mid-Aug–late-Oct daily 9am–7pm. Late-Oct–Jun daily 10am–6pm.* 📷*$4.* ☏ *802-846-1500. www.benjerry.com.*

The bucolic setting, overlooking the Worcester Range of the rolling Green Mountains, is the perfect place for a picnic. Bring your picnic basket goodies, grab a table outside under the colorful

Ben and Jerry's Ice Cream Factory

© Ben and Jerry's Ice Cream Factory

Royal Lipizzan Stallions

North Hero, Vermont, serves as the summer residence of these famed horses, who are presented to the public there yearly in July and August under the direction of Col. Ottomar Herrmann. The stallions take their name from the little village of **Lipizza** (now Lipica), Slovenia (formerly part of Yugoslavia), near Trieste, Italy, where the Archduke Karl of Austria founded a stud farm in 1580. The farm was established to breed and rear stallions for the **Spanish Riding School of Vienna**, one of the few places in the world where *haute école* dressage, a rigorous equestrian ballet dating from the 16C, can still be seen. Horses are taught a repertoire of exacting movements based on Renaissance battle maneuvers, including trots, jumps, and pirouettes (the horse turns on its haunches at the canter). But the show-stopper is the demanding **capriole**, in which the horse jumps up and kicks his hind legs out parallel to the ground.

The present Lipizzaners descend from several great sires, all stemming from an old Spanish strain, famous at the time of Caesar. These magnificent white horses are born grey, bay or chestnut and get their brilliant white coats between 4 and 10 years of age. Characterized by their intelligence, agility and vigor, they are considered the best saddle and parade horses in the world.

umbrellas and relax. Young kids can romp in the playground. For dessert, head inside the store. But first, take the fun-filled tour of the factory.

ADDRESSES

🛏 STAY

$$$$ Basin Harbor Club – *On Lake Champlain, Vergennes.* ☎802-475-2311 or 800-622-4000. www.basinharbor.com. *115 rooms.* This longstanding beachside resort on Lake Champlain has been family owned and operated for more than a century. There are 38 rooms in the original historic lodge and 77 more housed in individual one-, two- and three-bedroom cottages. Each room is unique; many overlook the lake and feature fireplaces. On-site are a golf course, tennis center and a wealth of water-sports options from kayaking to fishing. Four restaurants serve award-winning cuisine. Accommodation costs vary with the season and selected meal plan: a Modified American Plan is offered in spring and fall; the Full American Plan is the only choice in summer.

$$$ The Essex – *70 Essex Way, Essex Junction.* ☎802-878-1100 or 800-727-4295. *120 rooms.* www.vtculinaryresort.com. Located just a few miles away from Burlington and the airport, this Colonial-style inn offers all the comforts of home with gourmet dining to boot. Accommodations range from standard "Country Inn" rooms, individually appointed in tones of forest green, cranberry and indigo, to mini-suites with kitchenettes and spacious deluxe suites. Many rooms boast gas fireplaces and some have whirlpool tubs.
Diners at **Amuse Restaurant** or at the casual **Tavern** feast on American cuisine created by students of the New England Culinary Institute, which is located on-site.

$$$ Willard Street Inn – *349 S. Willard St.* ☎802-651-8710 or 800-577-8712. *www.willardstreetinn.com. 14 rooms.* Built by Vermont State Senator Charles Woodhouse in the 1880s, this brick Georgian Revival-style home is immaculately preserved today, with intricate moldings, cherry-paneled foyer and original wooden floors. The inn's convenient location lies within walking-distance of Church Street Marketplace and the waterfront. All rooms have private baths and are furnished with a mix of antiques and period reproductions to recall the turn of the 19C. Breakfast and afternoon tea, served in a solarium overlooking Lake Champlain, are included in the rates.

🍽 EAT

$$$ Trattoria Delia – *1152 Saint Paul St.* ☎802-864-5253. www.trattoriadelia.com. **Italian.** Housed in an historic, former hotel, this intimate eatery features wooden posts and beams, a giant stone fireplace, dim lights and linen-topped tables. The menu offers a wide selection of authentically-prepared Italian dishes, including fried calamari, wood-grilled smoked mozzarella and beef carpaccio. Follow with signature entrées like the osso buco, veal scallopine and fish stew.

$$ Penny Cluse – *169 Cherry St.* ☎802-651-8834. www.pennycluse.com. **American.** Bring your appetites to this casual restaurant, open for breakfast and lunch. Locals claim it to have the best breakfast in town. You'll find the usual eggs and bacon fare, along with huevos rancheros, black bean and andouille sausage and egg platters, and sides of biscuits with homemade herb cream gravy.

$ Al's – *1251 Williston Rd.* ☎802-862-9203. www.alsfrenchfrys.com. **American.** This busy hole-in-the-wall is practically a landmark in Burlington. The family-owned place has been around since the late 1940s. There are burgers, hot dogs, steak rolls and grilled chicken. But the real claim to fame are the piping hot, crispy on the outside, soft in the middle, house-made, hand-cut french fries. Get them plain or with cheese, gravy or chili.

$ Red Onion Café – *140 ½ Church St.* ☎802-865-2563. www.redonioncafe. webs.com. **American.** Simplicity has never gone out of style at this small bakery/cafe where the locals go for Burlington's best sandwiches. Six types of bread, from honey-oat to baguettes, baked fresh on the premises each morning, are used to make an array of overflowing sandwiches in creative combinations.

Manchester★

Favored as a summer resort and cultural center for more than a century, Manchester has more recently become popular during the winter, with the development of Bromley and Stratton ski areas.

A BIT OF HISTORY

Manchester Center is a busy place year-round, with its restaurants and shops, while farther south off Rte. 7A, countrified estates nestle among the foothills of the Taconic Range. In **Manchester Village★**, the 19C Equinox Hotel has catered for years to an elite clientele, including presidents Grant, Theodore Roosevelt and Taft.

Manchester is home to the Orvis Company, one of the oldest surviving (1856) fishing tackle manufacturers in the US. Today it is joined by numerous designer and upscale outlet stores along Rtes. 7A and 11.

SIGHTS
Hildene★

On Rte. 7A, 2mi south of the junction with Rte. 11/30. P ○*Open daily 9.30am–4.30pm.* ⊚*$16 general admission house tours, $21.* ✆*802-362-1788. www.hildene.org.*

This 412-acre estate was the home of **Robert Todd Lincoln** (1843-1926), the eldest of the four children of Abraham and Mary Lincoln. The furnishings are family pieces, and the tour includes a demonstration of the 1,000-pipe Aeolian organ (1908). From the gardens there are sweeping **views★★** of mountains and valleys below.

American Museum of Fly-Fishing

Seminary Ave., north of the Equinox Hotel at Rte. 7A. ♿○*Open year-round Tue–Sat 10am–4pm, Jun–Oct Tue–Sun 10am–4pm.* ○*Closed major holidays.* ⊚*$5.* ✆*802-362-3300. www.amff.com.* Anglers will be interested in this museum devoted to the history and lore of fly-fishing. Early books on the subject, an array of artificial flies, and fly-fishing

▶ **Population:** 3,622.
⏱ **Michelin Map:** 581 I 6.
🛈 **Info:** ✆802-362-6313 or 800-362-4144; www.manchestervermont.net.
▶ **Location:** Tucked into the southwestern corner of the state, the city is easily accessed off north-south Rte. 7. Rte. 7A runs through historic Manchester Village.
👫 **Kids:** The alpine slide at Bromley Mountain is a thrill.
○ **Timing:** Allow a day for a scenic drive, another day for an outdoor activity like fly-fishing or hiking.
🅿 **Parking:** Street parking is available; most shops and restaurants in Manchester Center have free lots.
✋ **Don't Miss:** A driving tour of the nearby villages of southern Vermont.

tackle belonging to Daniel Webster, Andrew Carnegie, Ernest Hemingway and other well-known Americans are among the artifacts in the collection.

Southern Vermont Arts Center★

West Rd. From the village green, take West Rd. 1mi north. Follow the winding drive to the mansion. ♿○*Open daily Tue–Sat 10am–5pm. Sun noon–5pm* ⊚*$6.* ✆*802-362-1405. www.svac.org.* Founded in the 1930s to support Vermont artists, the permanent collection of more than 800 paintings, sculptures and works on paper is now housed in the highly praised **Elizabeth de C. Wilson Museum**, designed by noted architect Hugh Newell Jacobsen.

Equinox Skyline Drive

5mi south of Manchester by Rte. 7A. ○*Open May–Oct daily 9am–dusk.* ⊚*$15/car & driver $5 per passenger.* ✆*802-362-1114. www.equinoxmountain.com*

Appalachian Trail

The longest continuous marked footpath in the US, the 2,167mi **Appalachian National Scenic Trail** begins at Springer Mountain in north Georgia and traverses 14 states, 2 national parks, and 8 national forests before ending on the rocky summit of Mt. Katahdin in Maine. Tracing part of an ancient Native American route, the well-maintained but often rugged path crosses some 250,000 acres of mostly mountainous terrain along the Appalachian chain. The nation's first official scenic trail is protected by the National Trails System Act of 1968, which includes the preservation of natural habitats bordering the trail and the hundreds of species inhabiting them.

The trail's 3 million annual users, on average, are mostly weekend hikers, but the number of "through hikers," who begin in Georgia in early spring and walk northward for three to five months, is growing. Those not inclined to walk the entire "A.T." can start on any of 500 access points located at roughly 5–10mi intervals along the trail's length. Permits are not required for hiking, but they are mandatory for overnight camping in Shenandoah National Park, the Great Smoky Mountains National Park and Baxter State Park. More than 250 shelters are situated roughly a day's hike apart and campsites are numerous; lodges are located in New Hampshire's White Mountains. No bicycles, motorized vehicles or even pack animals are allowed on the trail; dogs must be kept on a leash.

The 5.5mi drive leads to the crest of Mt. Equinox (3,816ft), the highest point in the Taconic Range. The **view★** reaches from the Hudson River Valley deep into the Green Mountains.

Arlington
8mi south of Manchester by Rte. 7A.
This tranquil village and its residents served as models for illustrator **Norman Rockwell**, who lived here at one time. The **Batten Kill River** provides Arlington with some of the best trout fishing in New England.

🚗 DRIVING TOUR

VILLAGES OF SOUTHERN VERMONT★★

Take this backroads journey through classic Vermont villages.

▶ Leave Manchester Village by Rte. 7A. At Manchester Center take Rte. 30 East and continue on Rte.11.

🚶🚶 Bromley Mountain
The Bromley ski area has become popular during the summer season because of its **alpine slide, zipline, giant trampoline, mini-golf**, and more (✆802-824-5522; www.bromley.com). Bromley's summit (3,260ft) can be reached by hiking trails or a scenic chairlift ride and offers **views** of the Green Mountains.

Long Trail to Bromley Summit
From the Bromley ski area, follow Rte. 11 approximately 2mi east. A small sign indicates the Long Trail. Parking is on the right.
The trail (🥾5.6mi round-trip) is a segment of both the Long Trail and the **Appalachian Trail**. After gently ascending through forest for 2mi, the trail climbs steeply, then crosses open meadowland. A **panorama★★** of the surrounding Green Mountains can be seen from an observation tower.

▶ Two miles after Bromley, take the road on the left through Peru. At the fork bear left and continue through North Landgrove, turning left in front of the town hall. After the Village Inn, bear right at the fork and continue to Weston.

Weston★

With its attractive village green and shops, Weston is a popular stop on Rte. 100. The **Farrar-Mansur House**, a late-18C tavern serves as the local history museum (🅿 🕐*open Memorial Day–Jun Sat–Sun 1pm–4pm Jul–Labor Day daily 1–4pm; $2; 802-824-8190; www.vmga.org*).

▷ Follow Rte. 100 past the green, then bear right at the sign for Chester. Continue through Andover, then east on Rte. 11.

Chester

The wide main street of this community is lined with lodgings and shops, several of which are housed in historic buildings (*a walking-tour brochure is available from the information booth on the village green Jun–Oct*).

▷ Take Rte. 35 to Grafton.

Grafton★

Check out the **Grafton Village Cheese Company** (*800-472-3866; www.graftonvillagecheese.com*) and the 1801 **Old Tavern**, once frequented by Ulysses S. Grant, Oliver Wendell Holmes and Rudyard Kipling,

▷ In Grafton turn right, cross the bridge and turn left before the tavern. Follow this road to Rte. 35, into Townshend, then take Rte. 30 south.

Newfane

Situated deep in the Green Mountains, this town has grown little since the 18C, when it was selected as the Windham county seat. Newfane's village **green★**, with its white Congregational church, **Windham County Courthouse** and two old inns, is pretty at any time of year, but it becomes a spectacular sight in the fall.

▷ Take Rte. 30 back through Townshend. Continue through Jamaica into Bondville; turn left on Stratton Mountain Rd.

Stratton Mountain

With 92 trails accessible by a gondola and 14 chairlifts, this mountain (3,936ft) is one of the major ski areas in Vermont (*800-787-2886; www.stratton.com*).

▷ Return to Manchester via Rte. 30.

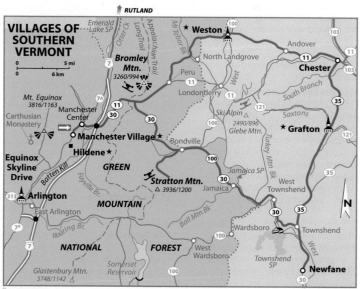

VILLAGES OF SOUTHERN VERMONT

Maple Sugaring

Vermont is the leading producer of **maple syrup** in the US. From early-March to mid-April, when night temperatures drop below freezing but the days get steadily warmer, more than 1,000,000 hard rock or sugar maple trees are tapped with small metal spouts. Under these spouts buckets are hung to collect the 10 to 15 gallons of sap each tree is liable to produce. The sap is then taken to a ventilated sugarhouse to be boiled down, filtered through layers of cloth, and jarred. Each gallon of syrup is the product of about 40 gallons of sap. Some 60 sugaring enterprises throughout the state invite visitors to witness the process during the season, or sample their wares off-season at roadside gift shops. Syrup comes in three grades: delicate light amber, all-purpose medium amber and robust dark amber. Try all three, and be sure to sample the sweet maple-sugar candy, too.

ADDRESSES

🏠 STAY

$$$$$ Inn at Sawmill Farm – *Crosstown Rd. & Rte 100, West Dover. Closed Apr & May. ☎802-464-8131. www.theinnatsawmillfarm.com. 20 rooms.* Set on a pastoral hillside in a quiet corner of southern Vermont, the Inn at Sawmill Farm is operated by chef/owner Brill Williams, whose architect father restored the farmhouse to create this Relais & Châteaux property—incorporating the barn's hand-hewn beams and weathered boards. Rooms, whether in the main building or cottage suites, are individually decorated in English chintzes with antiques; many feature fireplaces. The inn's acclaimed **restaurant** (*open to the public; dinner only*) has won numerous industry awards—for its continental fare, as well as for its 30,000-bottle wine cellar. Rates include breakfast and a gourmet dinner.

$$$$ The Equinox – *Rte. 7A, Manchester Center. ☎802-362-4700 or 800-362-4747. www.equinoxresort.com. 183 rooms.* The largest full-service resort in Vermont, the Equinox was renovated by its previous owner, Guinness Brewing Co., as the sister resort to Scotland's fabled Gleneagles. As such, the resort claims some unusual activities—a falconry program, the Land Rover off-road driving school, shooting and fly-fishing instruction. Rooms in the white-columned main building are all differently shaped and laid out along labyrinthine corridors. The resort also offers rooms in a variety of nearby historic inns, including the 1811 Inn (below.)

The Equinox

© The Equinox

$$$ 1811 House – *3654 Main St., Manchester Center. ☎877-854-7625 or 800-362-4747. www.equinoxresort.com. 13 rooms.* This elegant inn, once the home of Abraham Lincoln's granddaughter, is surrounded by gardens, and within walking distance to Manchester Village. Updated rooms are individually decorated with period antiques, canopied beds, fireplaces, original art and private porches. Each has a modern private bath and air conditioning; some have mountain views. In your leisure time, you can play chess in front of the fireplace in one of the common rooms, enjoy a game of pool in the basement, or sample the adjoining pub's extensive list of single-malt whiskies.

🍷 EAT

$$ The Perfect Wife – *2594 Depot St. (Rte. 11/30), Manchester. Dinner only. ☎802-362-2817. www.perfectwife.com.* **New American.** Chef-owner Amy Chamberlain has become a minor culinary celebrity in Vermont, and her intriguing restaurant explains why. She utilizes fresh local produce and offers a menu emphasizing mainstream entrées (jumbo shrimp scampi, grilled filet mignon, sesame-crusted yellowfin tuna), but she also features pure vegan selections. Don't pass up the acclaimed crab cake appetizer. The farmhouse setting offers diners the choice of a unique cobblestone-walled dining room with piano accompaniment, or a greenhouse garden room.

$ Curtis' Barbecue – *Rte. 5 at Exit 4 off I-91, Putney. Open Thu–Sun Apr-Oct. 11am-6.30pm.* 802-387-5474. *www. curtisbbqvt.com.* **Barbecue.** More of a roadside stand than a restaurant, Curtis' occupies a compound consisting of two old school buses—one converted into a large smoker—and several picnic tables. For more than 25 years, Curtis has been serving up some of the finest BBQ in Vermont.

SHOPPING

Vermont Country Store - *Main St./ Rte. 100, Weston Village.* 802-824-3184. *www.vermontcountrystore.com.* Founded in 1946, this popular general merchandiser has expanded over the years from its original home to four buildings (and there's a second store in Rockingham, VT). The growth has resulted largely from the firm's mail-order catalog business and its penchant for selling what "must work, be useful, and make sense." The store itself (open daily year-round 8.30am–6pm) enjoys a statewide reputation for its varied merchandise, from local cheeses to long underwear.

Middlebury★

Set amid gently sloping hills and rolling countryside, Middlebury is a typical Vermont village with its central green, pristine Congregational church, and Victorian-style buildings converted into stores and restaurants. The town was founded in 1761 and is known today as the site of Middlebury College.

A BIT OF HISTORY

Overlooking the village green, the stately **Middlebury Inn** still welcomes visitors as it has since 1827 (*see Addresses*). The inn serves afternoon tea and a nightly candlelight buffet dinner. Middlebury is also the starting point for scenic excursions through Brandon and Middlebury gaps, which cut through the hills and dales of Green Mountain National Forest southeast of town.

SIGHTS
Middlebury College
Campus bounded by S. Main St. and College St. (Rte. 125). 802-443-5000. *www.middlebury.edu.*

▶ **Population:** 8,183.
Michelin Map: 581 H 4
Info: 802-388-7951; www.addisoncounty.com.
◗ **Location:** Just south of Burlington on the western side of the state, Middlebury is easily accessed by north-south Rts.30 and 7.
Kids: The tiny Lake Champlain Maritime Museum is a delight.
🕐 **Timing:** Allow a day to explore the Brandon and Middlebury gaps and poke around the nearby villages.
P **Parking:** Limited street parking is available spring, summer and fall (no street parking allowed during winter months). There are a few municipal lots, such as on Bakery Lane.
Don't Miss: A hike to the Falls of Llana at Branbury State Park.

The main campus covers some 500 acres and features impressive stone and marble buildings of eclectic architectural styles. Highlights are **Painter Hall** (1815), the oldest surviving college building in the state, and **Le Château** (1925), modeled after a pavilion of the French Château de Fontainebleau.

Mahaney Center for the Arts
On Rte. 30, .5mi from US-7.
This center houses a dance and studio theater, a concert hall and the **Middlebury College Museum of Art** (✕🚻♿🅿 🕐*open year-round Tue–Fri 10am–5pm, weekends noon–5pm;* 🕐*closed holidays and during college breaks;* 📞*802-443-5007; www.middlebury.edu/arts/mcfa.*
The museum's permanent collection includes works by such notables as Vermont native Hiram Powers, Gilbert Stuart, Alexander Calder and John Frederick Kensett. The museum also includes works ranging from ancient European, Near Eastern, and Asian art to contemporary paintings, prints, sculpture, and photography.
Among the 1,500 examples are works by Rembrandt, Honore Daumier, Pablo Picasso, Salvador Dalí, Joan Miró, Willem de Kooning, Man Ray, Southworth and Hawes, Andy Warhol, Robert Rauschenberg, and many others.
European and American paintings from the 17C through 19C are another strength of the collection.

EXCURSIONS
👥 UVM Morgan Horse Farm
▶*2.5mi northwest of Middlebury, in Weybridge. From the center of Middlebury bear right onto College St. (Rte. 125), then turn right onto Rte. 23 (Weybridge St.). Follow the signs to the farm, bearing left at the fork with the covered bridge.* ♿🅿🕐*Open May–Oct daily 9am–4pm.* 💲*$5.* 📞*802-388-2011. www.uvm.edu/morgan.*
Owned by the University of Vermont, the farm operates as a breeding, training and instructional facility. Visitors may tour the 19C barn, where descendants of the original Morgan are housed (*20min slide presentation shown hourly*).

Branbury State Park★
▶*10mi southeast of Middlebury. Take US-7 south, then Rte. 53. 3570 Lake Dunmore Rd.* ♿⛺🅿🕐*Open mid-May–mid-Oct daily 10am–dusk.* 💲*$3/day.* 📞*802-247-5925 (in season); 800-837-6668 (off season). www.vtstateparks.com.*
This popular warm-weather destination has a large sandy beach on Lake Dunmore (*boat rentals available*) and hiking trails to the **Falls of Lana** (*1.1mi round-trip*) and to **Silver Lake** (*3mi round-trip*).

Falls of Lana, Branbury State Park

© Ben Hudson / Vermont State Parks

👥 Lake Champlain Maritime Museum★
▶*21mi northwest of Middlebury in Basin Harbor. Take US-7 north to Vergennes, then southwest along Main St. to Panton Rd. Turn right onto Basin Harbor Rd.* ✕🅿🕐*Open mid-May–mid-Oct daily 10am–5pm.* 💲*$10* 📞*802-475-2022. www.lcmm.org.*
Ten exhibit buildings, including a stone schoolhouse (c.1818), trace the history of the lake and its maritime traditions. The grounds showcase a variety of full-sized working replicas of historic vessels that have plied the waters of Lake Champlain.

BRANDON AND MIDDLEBURY GAPS
📞*802-247-6401. www.brandon.org.*
This itinerary leads through the Green Mountain National Forest and into the Lake Champlain Valley. Along the way you'll traverse wooded mountain gaps

and cross open farmlands. Outdoor enthusiasts will find many reasons to linger in this area.

🚗 DRIVING TOUR

81mi. This tour begins and ends in Middlebury. Take Rte. 125 east, named Robert Frost Memorial Dr. for the well-known New England poet.

On Rte. 125, 2mi beyond Ripton, the **Robert Frost Interpretive Trail** offers a 1mi loop through scenic marshland and forest, punctuated by markers inscribed with poems by the renowned poet.

▷ Continue east on Rte. 125 through Middlebury Gap (2,149ft).

Texas Falls Recreation Area
Left from Rte. 125.
A short trail leads to a series of falls that tumble over rocks and giant holes formed by glaciers.

▷ Continue east to the tiny crossroads community of Hancock. From Hancock, take Rte. 100 South to Rochester and follow Rte. 73 west through Brandon Gap.

Rte. 73 passes tidy houses and tranquil meadows along the White River

Valley as it enters the Green Mountain National Forest and skirts the base of rocky **Mt. Horrid** (3,216ft) before reaching **Brandon Gap★** (2,170ft). From this point there is a **view★** of the Lake Champlain Valley, with the Adirondacks as a backdrop.

Descending west through the gap, the road continues to the village of **Brandon**, chartered in 1761 and now anchored by its historic inn. Begun as a one-room tavern in 1786, the current stone and wood hostelry features a late-19C Dutch Colonial interior. After Brandon Rte. 73 continues west to Lake Champlain, yielding vistas of rock-stud-

Lake Champlain Maritime Museum's lakeside facility

Fort Ticonderoga

© Carl Heilman

ded pasturelands, dairy farms and the Adirondack Mountains to the west.

At **Larrabees Point** the ferry (*for schedules, see Lake Champlain, under BURLINGTON*) crosses Lake Champlain, and provides access to Fort Ticonderoga in New York.

♟♙ Fort Ticonderoga★★

Rte. 74 in Ticonderoga, New York.
✕🅿🕐*Open early-May–late-Oct daily 9.30am–5pm.* ☜*$17.50. Fife & drum corps performances & artillery drills Jul & Aug daily.* ✆*518-585-2821. www.fort-ticonderoga.org.*

Built in 1755 by the French, Fort Ticonderoga was captured by the British in 1759. The fort is famous for the surprise attack launched here against the British on 10 May 1775 by **Ethan Allen** and the **Green Mountain Boys** along with **Benedict Arnold** and his men. The supplies captured here were used the following spring by General Washington to drive the British out of Boston.

▷ Take the ferry back to Vermont and follow Rte. 74 East through Shoreham and West Cornwall to Cornwall. Then take Rte. 30 North back to Middlebury.

ADDRESSES

🛏 STAY

$$$ Whitford House Inn - *912 Grandey Rd., Vergennes (13mi northwest of Middlebury via US-7).* ✆*802-758-2704 or 800-746-2704. www.whitfordhouseinn.com. 3 rooms & 1 guesthouse.* Set on 37 acres surrounded by the verdant farmlands of peaceful Champlain Valley, this

inviting inn boasts exquisite views of the Adirondacks. Three rooms house guests in the late-18C country house and a guest cottage nearby features its own brick patio for taking in the views. Complimentary perks include fresh flowers in every room, Wi-Fi, use of bicycles and a bottomless cookie jar.

$$$ The Middlebury Inn – *On the Green in Middlebury.* ✕🕐🅿 ✆*802-388-4961 or 800-842-4666. www.middleburyinn.com. 70 rooms.* Location is everything, and the inn sits in the center of town, within walking distance of both downtown and the college. The inn has been operating for more than 150 years, and still specializes in New England hospitality and fare, with both a fine-dining restaurant and a casual tavern. Lodging choices in one of four buildings run the gamut from contemporary motel rooms to a deluxe suite in the Porter House Mansion, which is decorated in traditional Victorian style.

🍷 EAT

$ Mister Up's – *25 Bakery Lane, Middlebury.* ✆*802-388-6724. www.misterupsvt.com.* **American.** This burger-and-beer, pub-style restaurant is great in the summer when you can sit outside on the deck, overlooking Otter Creek. You'll find decently-prepared tavern fare (steaks, sandwiches, burgers and hot-fired wings), a salad bar, and strong drinks (try the spicy Bloody Mary, a top seller during Sunday brunch), all at fair prices. Food served until midnight on Friday and Saturday.

$$ Storm Cafe (*3 Mill St., Middlebury.* ✆*802-388-1063. www.thestormcafe.com*). This great little place, on the bottom floor of Frog Hollow Mill, is open for lunch and dinner. An outdoor patio overlooking Otter Creek invites alfresco dining and there's indoor seating in the small, attractive dining room. A variety of soups and salads, sandwiches, burgers and light-lunch combos are presented at lunch. For dinner, start with an appetizer, like the seared sea scallops or spicy steamed mussels. Entrées include signature dishes like the apple-stuffed pork Wellington, mushroom and risotto cakes, and the daily fresh fish selection. There are also a selection of house-made pasta dishes.

Montpelier

This small city, the capital of Vermont since 1805, sits among the wooded hillsides that rise above the Winooski River. The golden dome of the State House, ablaze in the afternoon sun, dominates the city and makes a magnificent sight when the trees change color in autumn. The granite industry, which enabled the city to develop and prosper, has been supplanted in importance by state government and the insurance industry.

SIGHTS
State House
State St. ✕♿🕐*Open year-round Mon–Sat 8am–4pm.* 📷*Free 30min guided tours Jul–mid-Oct Mon–Fri 10am–3.30pm, Sat 11am–2.30pm.* 🕐*Closed major holidays.* 📞*802-828-0386. www.leg.state.vt.us/sthouse/sthouse.htm.*
This elegant Classical Revival edifice, built in 1859, is the third state house erected on this site. The first state house (demolished) dated from 1808. The second (1838) was destroyed by fire. The present structure incorporates the Doric columns and portico of the second state house, which was modeled after the Temple of Theseus in Greece. A 14ft statue of Ceres, the Roman goddess of agriculture, rises from the pinnacle of the golden dome.

Vermont Museum★
109 State St., in the Pavilion Office Building. ♿🕐*Open year-round Tue–Sat 10am–4pm* 💲*$5 ($12 family rate)* 📞*802-828-2291. www.vermont history.org.*
The Victorian facade of this building was modeled after the Pavilion Hotel,

▶ **Population:** 8,035.
♿ **Michelin Map:** 581 J 3
🗊 **Info:** 📞802-229-4619; www.central-vt.com.
▶ **Location:** North-south I-89 provides easy access to the city. The Winooski River runs parallel to State St., while North Branch River bisects downtown near Capitol Plaza.
👫 **Kids:** North Branch Nature Center (*2mi from downtown;* 📞*802-229-6206; www.north branchnaturecenter.org*) is a hit with young and old alike, with riverside trails, butterfly garden, critter room and special events and activities.
🕐 **Timing:** Pick up maps and brochures for three self-guided walking tours (State St. tour, Main St. tour and College St. tour) at the information booth on State Street or in City Hall. The tours, about an hour each, will give you a good feel for the city.
🅿 **Parking:** There are several parking lots in the downtown area including two on State St. near Capitol Plaza. The city is compact and pedestrian friendly; you can walk to major sights, parks and attractions.
☺ **Don't Miss:** A tour of the historic State House.

which stood on the site between 1876 and 1965. Inside, the 19C lobby has been reconstructed. Beyond it are the rooms occupied by the Vermont Historical

Society. Photographs, documents and artifacts relate the history, economy and traditions of Vermont.

MAD RIVER VALLEY★

Remote, rural, and set in the midst of broad expanses of rolling, mountainous terrain, the Mad River Valley is a premier four-season resort famed for its ski areas, **Sugarbush** and **Mad River Glen**. The lovely setting, abundant accommodations and superb downhill and crosscountry skiing facilities have contributed to its appeal.

🚗 DRIVING TOUR

8mi from Waitsfield to Warren.
Covered bridges, a round barn, and town squares await you on this scenic drive.

Warren
23mi southwest of Montpelier via I-89 west to Rte. 100 South.
This small village contains craft shops and a country store frequented for its freshly baked goods and salads. The Warren covered bridge is reflected in the Mad River, which flows underneath it. If time permits, continue south from Warren on Rte. 100 to **Granville** and enjoy spectacular **views★★** of the Green Mountains.

▶ Take E. Warren Rd./Rte. 100 north to Waitsfield.

The drive along East Warren Road parallels the Mad River and the Green Mountains. After 5mi, you will pass the **Round Barn** (1909), one of several built in the valley, now part of an inn.

▶ Continue straight ahead over the Waitsfield covered bridge (1833) and cross the Mad River to Waitsfield.

Waitsfield
This town has been a commercial center since the 19C, when the daily stagecoach from Waitsfield linked the valley with the railroad in nearby Middlesex. Two shopping centers today provide the

inhabitants and visitors in the area with a variety of stores and services. Farming continues to be a principal activity in Waitsfield, despite the influx of professionals and artists in recent years.
At Waitsfield, consider a detour west along Rte. 17 through the **Appalachian Gap** (2,356ft), where **views★★** of the region's unspoiled beauty unfold.

ADDRESSES

🛏 STAY

$$$$$ The Pitcher Inn – *275 Main St., Warren. ☎802-496-6350. www.pitcherinn.com. 11 rooms.* This tiny gem (the second of Vermont's two Relais & Châteaux properties) is one of the top inns in the country. Each of its 11 exquisite guest rooms is decorated with original art and antiques representing some facet of Vermont: The Trout Room turns the interior into an actual log cabin, while in the School Room, a huge slate blackboard serves as a mantelpiece. One room celebrates the life of Calvin Coolidge, the only Vermont-born president. More than half the rooms are outfitted with fireplaces and Jacuzzi tubs; others boast wet bars and steam rooms.

🍽 EAT

$$$ The Common Man – *At Sugarbush Ski Resort, Warren. Dinner only. ☎802-583-2800. www.commonmanrestaurant.com.* **Continental.** For nearly four decades, this restaurant has been the standout among the many dining choices along the access road to the Sugarbush ski area. Set in a dramatic 19C barn, with exposed wood and rafters in every direction, and anchored by a huge fireplace at one end, The Common Man fully captures the feel of a country ski town, while serving up fine European cuisine. Appetizers include pan crisped sweetbreads and Arborio rice crusted shrimp, while an ever-changing menu might offer duck, steak and shellfish entrées.

$$ American Flatbread – *At The Lareau Farm Inn, 46 Lareau Rd., Waitsfield. Open Thur–Sun 5pm–9.30pm. ☎802-496-8856. www.americanflatbread.com.* **Pizza.** Considered by connoisseurs to be the best frozen pizzas available, these Vermont-made flatbreads are sold at gourmet shops and supermarkets in 20 states. Every weekend, the actual factory itself becomes a restaurant, allowing patrons to sample the wares straight from the wood-fired ovens. This is as rustic an experience as can be found, with a handful of tables arranged amidst the ovens in one building of the working farm that yields many of the organic ingredients. Flatbreads themselves are made from organic wheat custom-milled for the purpose, unfiltered well water and fresh yeast.

$$ NECI on Main – *118 Main St., Montpelier. Mon lunch only.* ✆802-223-3188. www.neci.edu. **New American.** This casual venue is run by the New England Culinary Institute, and is open for lunch and dinner (brunch also on Sun). Choose among the floor-level main room and a pub or wine room downstairs. An observation window allows diners to watch their food being prepared upstairs. The innovative menu includes farm-to-dinner dishes like New England oyster chowder, Vermont cheese platter and grille farm-raised venison.

Rutland

Situated at the junction of Otter and East creeks, Rutland is Vermont's second-largest city. The surrounding mountains and lakes make the region a year-round playground for those who love outdoor activities such as hiking, sailing and mountain biking. Killington, one of the largest ski resorts in the East, lies nearby to the east.

A BIT OF HISTORY

Settled in the 1770s, the town developed into a railroad center in the 19C and marble quarrying flourished, giving Rutland the nickname "the marble city."

SIGHTS
Norman Rockwell Museum

2mi east of Rutland near the corners of Rte. 4 and Rte. 7. ♿🅿🕒*Open year-round daily 9am–3.30pm.* 🕒*Closed major holidays.* 💲$6.50 ✆802-773-6095 or 877-773-6095. www.normanrockwellvt.com.

The museum contains over 2,500 examples of the work of **Norman Rockwell** (1894-1978), illustrator, humorist and chronicler of more than half a century of American life.

The series of more than 300 magazine covers that Rockwell created for the *Saturday Evening Post,* and for which he is best remembered, is displayed here

- ▶ **Population:** 16,742.
- 🚗 **Michelin Map:** 581 I 5
- ℹ **Info:** ✆802-773-2747. or 800-756-8880; www.rutlandvermont.com.
- ▶ **Location:** East-west Rte. 4 and north-south Rte. 7 provide access to the city. Rte. 7 has sprawled with fast food outlets, gas stations, chain stores and more. Head a couple of blocks west for the historic center of town, and a fine collection of historic houses and mansions.
- 👪 **Kids:** The Killington Ski area has year-round outdoor activities.
- 🕐 **Timing:** Allow a few hours each for your visits to the Vermont Marble Exhibit and Norman Rockwell Museum. Plan a half day or more (depending on activities) at the Killington mountain resort.
- 🅿 **Parking:** Street parking is available, as well as store and mall lots.
- 👁 **Don't Miss:** Vermont Marble Exhibit.

together with other magazine covers, movie and war posters, advertising work, calendars and greeting cards— which also brought him fame.

Artifacts inside New England Maple Museum

EXCURSIONS
Vermont Marble Museum★

▶ *52 Main St., Proctor. 6mi north of Rutland via West St. and Rte. 3 North.* ♿🅿🕐*Open mid-May–mid-Oct daily 9am–5pm.* 💲*$7.* ✆*802-459-2300. www.vermont-marble.com.*

Visitors explore the origin, quarrying and finishing of marble. Polished marble slabs from Vermont and around the world illustrate the rich diversity of colors and graining characteristic of this stone. Visitors can view a video about marble (*13min*) and observe a sculptor at work.

Wilson Castle

▶ *W. Proctor Rd., 4mi south of Proctor.* 🅿 ☛*Visit by guided tour only (45min). Open late-May–mid-Oct daily 9am–5pm. $10.* ✆*802-773-3284. www.wilsoncastle.com.*

This massive brick mansion (1867), built by a Vermont doctor, offers a glimpse of the opulence that characterized the private homes of 19C America's upper classes. Luxurious furnishings and art pieces are complemented by the surrounding heavily carved woodwork, stained-glass windows and hand-painted and polychromed ceilings. Note the Louis XVI crown-jewel case.

New England Maple Museum

▶ *On Rte. 7, in Pittsford. 9mi north of Rutland via Rte. 7.* ♿🕐*Open mid-May–Oct daily 8.30am–5.30pm; Nov–mid-Dec & mid-Mar–mid-May daily 10am–4pm.* 💲*$2.50.* ✆*802-483-9414. www.maplemuseum.com.*

Located in the rear of a large retail store, this small museum features homespun exhibits on the history of maple sugaring. The self-guided tour ends with a 10min slide show illustrating the entire process, plus a display relating to syrup grades.

Killington✻

▶ *10mi east of Rutland on Rte. 4.*

⛷With over 200 trails cut on six interconnecting mountains and on Pico Mountain, Killington is one of New England's largest and most popular ski resorts. The **Killington gondola** is reputedly the longest (*2.5mi*) ski lift of its kind in the US (*station located 15mi east of Rutland on Rte. 4;* ♿🅿 ✆*802-422-6200 or 877-458-4637; www.killington.com*). A ride on the gondola affords great **views★★** of the Green Mountains. Summer activities include mountain biking, golf, guided nature walks and hiking.

Lake St. Catherine State Park

▶ *20mi southwest of Rutland on Rte. 30; 3mi south of Poultney. Take Rte. 4 to Exit 4, then Rte. 30 south.* ⛺🅿🕐*Open mid-May–early-Sept daily 10am–dusk.* 💲*$3/day.* ✆*802-287-9158 (in season) or 802-483-2001 (off season). www.vtstateparks.com.*

Cool breezes sweep the calm surface of Lake St. Catherine, making this a popular spot for windsurfing, sailing and fishing for trout and northern pike. The park sits on 117 acres and has a popular picnic and swimming area, as well as a snack bar. There are rowboat and paddle boat rentals, too.

ADDRESSES

🏠 STAY

$$$ Cortina Inn – *103 Rte. 4, Killington.* 📞*802-772-7118. www.cortinainn.com. 96 rooms.* Just outside downtown Rutland, halfway between the city and the nearby ski resorts of Killington and Pico, sits one of the area's best hotels. Although modern, the inn features distinctive New England architecture, with dormers and peaked roofs, and the common areas are log-cabin cozy. On-site facilities include both a full-service restaurant and tavern, a fly-fishing school, tennis courts and snowmobiling equipment. For romantic winter getaways, larger rooms feature fireplaces and whirlpool baths or hot tubs, and the inn offers horse-drawn sleigh rides around the grounds.

$$ Inn At Long Trail – *Sherburne Pass, Rte. 4, Killington.* 📞*802-775-7181 or 800-325-2540. www.innatlongtrail.com. 19 rooms.* Living up to its name, the inn sits at the intersection of the state's longest hiking trail and the even longer Appalachian Trail. The availability of limited and reasonably priced lodging in the summer (note: rates can go up considerably during ski season) mail and package handling, and Guinness stout on tap have made the inn an extremely popular way station for through-hikers on both routes. A trailhead in the inn's parking lot leads day hikers to the summit of Pico Mountain, burning calories to justify the shepherd's pie, corn beef and red-cabbage reuben, or the house specialty—Guinness stew— that is served in the popular Irish pub. Rooms are no-frills basic but the log-beamed common room is cozy and the tavern is tops. A crowd of hikers or skiers can be found here anytime of year.

$$$$ The Inn at Weathersfield (*1342 Rte. 106 in Perkinsville,* 📞*802-263-9217; www.weathersfieldinn.com*) is a hidden gem, tucked away in south central Vermont, a few minutes from Ludlow and the Okemo Ski Resort. Rooms in the historic inn have been elegantly updated; the tavern is cozy, the innkeepers friendly, and the dining room, emphasizing fresh, local ingredients is one of the top in the state.

🍽 EAT

$$ Little Harry's – *121 West St., Rutland. Dinner only.* 📞*802-747-4848. www. litteharrys.com.* **International.** One of Vermont's most eclectic restaurants, Harry's successfully dispenses both New England regional specialties and Pacific Rim cuisine, with a touch of Italian thrown in. The decor is local tavern, and the dishes range from tasty peanut-infused pad Thai noodles to rack of local lamb. Appetizers are equally thought-provoking, and choices may include grilled jerk scallops, steamed ginger chicken wontons with peanut sauce, and red-chili shrimp.

$ Gill's Deli – *68 Strongs Ave., Rutland.* 📞*802-773-7414. www.gillsdeli.com. Closed Sun.* **American.** This landmark deli in downtown Rutland has been family-owned – and loved by locals and visitors alike – since 1964. Grinders are their specialty; they come in four sizes, all freshly made and generous. Try the hot Italian meats, like hot peppered ham and salami or the foot-long hot sausage with peppers and onions. They also have a decent Maine crabmeat sub and all the traditional meats and cheeses. Sides include standard baked beans and coleslaw, along with mac and tuna, and deviled and pickled eggs.

$$ Three Tomatoes Trattoria – *88 Merchants Row, Rutland. Dinner only.* 📞*802-747-7747. www.threetomatoes trattoria.com.* **Italian.** The prominent wood-fired oven is the major feature of this casual, airy trattoria. Crispy thin-crust pizzas topped with choices such as soprasetta, artichoke hearts and smoked salmon, are just a small part of the extensive menu. Main courses put the hardwood-charcoal-burning oven to good use as well, producing meat with a smoky, roasted flavor. Traditionally prepared pasta dishes emphasizing garlic and olive oil are also available, along with an impressive selection of Italian wines.

St. Johnsbury

Manufacturing and maple syrup production are major occupations in this small, quiet town, gateway to the vast, rural Northeast Kingdom. St. Johnsbury began to prosper in the 1830s when a grocer named Thaddeus Fairbanks invented and began to manufacture the platform scale here; Fairbanks scales have been produced and shipped around the world ever since. The St. Johnsbury Athenaeum and the Fairbanks Museum and Planetarium, both in the downtown area, were established by members of the wealthy Fairbanks family, devoted patrons of their hometown.

SIGHTS
St. Johnsbury Athenaeum★

1171 Main St. ♿ 🅿 🕐*Open year-round Mon–Fri 10am–5.30pm Sat 10am–4pm.* 🕐*Closed Sun and major holidays. $8* 🖉*802-748-8291. www.stjathenaeum.org.* Horace Fairbanks built this brick Second Empire building as a public library in 1871, adding an **art gallery** in 1873. With paintings still hung in the style of a Victorian salon, the gallery is dominated by Albert Bierstadt's monumental painting *Domes of Yosemite* (1867). Also represented are Asher B. Durand and other painters of the Hudson River school as well as Vermont natives Hiram Powers and Thomas Waterman Wood. The handsome building, with its ornate woodwork and spiral staircases, is a National Historic Landmark.

👥 Fairbanks Museum and Planetarium★

1302 Main St. ♿ 🕐*Open Apr-Oct Mon-Sat 9am-5pm Sun 1pm-5pm, Nov-Mar Tue-Sat 9am-5pm Sun 1pm–5pm.* 🕐*Closed major holidays.* 👛*$8 museum, $5 planetarium.* 🖉*802-748-2372. www.fairbanksmuseum.org.* This institution was founded in 1891 by industrialist Franklin Fairbanks, who donated his collection of taxidermied wildlife to the museum. Today the museum houses 4,500

- ▶ **Population:** 6,492.
- 🕐 **Michelin Map:** 581 K 2
- 🗒 **Info:** 🖉802-748-3678, 800-639-6379; www.nekchamber.com.
- 🔘 **Location:** St. Johnsbury hugs the New Hampshire border, tucked up into Vermont's northeast corner. It's easily accessed from major highways I-91 and I-89.
- 👥 **Kids:** They'll love the stuffed animals and the bizarre bee art at the Fairbanks Museum.
- 🕐 **Timing:** Allow a half day to explore Fairbanks Museum and a day to tour the Northeast Kingdom.
- 🅿 **Parking:** Street parking is available throughout the small town.
- 😊 **Don't Miss:** Fairbanks Museum.

mounted birds and mammals and a large collection of antique dolls. The ornate Romanesque Revival **building★**, designed by Vermont architect Lambert Packard, is carved of red sandstone, and the interior features a magnificent barrel-vaulted ceiling.

👥 Maple Grove Farms

On Rte. 2 east of the city center. 🕐*Open Jun–late-Dec Mon–Fri 8am–5pm Sat–Sun 9am–5pm Apr–May closed Sat–Sun.* 🕐*Closed major holidays.* 👛*$1.* 🖉*802-748-5141 or 800-525-2540. www.maplegrove.com.* Exhibits and brief films illustrate how maple syrup is harvested and produced. The factory tour (🕐*20min;* 👛*$1)* introduces visitors to the step-by-step procedures involved in transforming maple syrup into Maple Grove candies.

NORTHEAST KINGDOM★★

🖉*802-626-8511 or 800-884-8001. www.travelthekingdom.com.* This region of forests, lakes, wide-open valleys and back roads that girdle tiny villages includes the three northeastern counties (Caledonia, Essex and Orleans) that surround St. Johnsbury and extend to the Canadian and New Hampshire borders. The region is busiest in the fall, when the countryside is a symphony of color: copper, gold, and the blazing reds of the maple trees.

Seven villages in the region—Barnet, Cabot, Groton, Marshfield, Peacham, Plainfield and Walden—participate in the week-long **Northeast Kingdom Foliage Festival** (*late-Sept–early-Oct; 802-748-3678*) during which a different village, each day, hosts activities ranging from church breakfasts to house tours and craft shows.

Two other interesting towns in the area are **Craftsbury Common**, with its immense hilltop village green that appears to meet the sky at the horizon; and Danville, home of the American Society of Dowsers.

🚗 DRIVING TOUR

LAKE WILLOUGHBY AND BROWNINGTON★
Circle tour north of St. Johnsbury. 87mi.

Historic villages, pretty parks and scenic views can be found on this circle tour of the Northeast Kingdom.

▷ From St. Johnsbury, take Rte. 5 north through Lyndonville to Rte. 114. Continue north on Rte. 114 to East Burke. From there, follow an unmarked road north to Burke Hollow and West Burke.

The Burkes
East Burke, Burke Hollow and West Burke are tiny hamlets at the base of the Burke Mountain ski area. The gentle mountain landscape is especially scenic when viewed from the road that leads to the summit of **Burke Mountain** (3,262ft). In the distance, you can see Lake Willoughby to the northwest through the gap. *Access to the Burke Mountain Auto Road (toll) is from Rte. 114 in East Burke.*

▷ From West Burke take Rte. 5A north to Lake Willoughby.

Lake Willoughby★
Two mountains rising abruptly opposite each other in a formation resembling the entrance to a mountain pass signal the location of Lake Willoughby (*swimming in season*). The taller mountain, towering above the southeastern end of the lake, is **Mt. Pisgah** (2,751ft).

▷ Follow Rte. 5A north along the lake shoreline to Rte. 58 west. Continue approximately 4mi on Rte. 58 to Evansville. Turn right on the road marked Brownington Center, which becomes a dirt road. Take the second left and continue to Brownington Center. There, bear right up the hill 1.5mi to Brownington Village Historic District.

Brownington Village Historic District★
This charming hamlet has changed little since the early 19C. A four-story granite dormitory building called the **Old Stone House** (1836) now functions as a museum, with period rooms and exhibits about the school; five additional historic buildings are also on the 55-acre grounds. (🅿️🕐*open mid-May–mid-Oct Wed–Sun 11am–5pm; $8; 802-754-2022; www.oldstonehousemuseum. org*). At the north edge of the village, an observatory platform on Prospect Hill affords a **panorama**★★ of Willoughby Gap (*southeast*), Mt. Mansfield (*southwest*), Jay Peak (*west*) and Lake Memphremagog (*north*).

▷ From Prospect Hill, turn right, continue past the Congregational Church and follow the unmarked road 2mi west to the junction with Rte. 58. Turn right and continue through the town of Orleans (1mi). Take Rte. 5 south for 5mi to Rte. 16 south. Take Rte. 16 through the town of Glover, then turn left onto Rte. 122 south and continue for about 1mi.

Jay Peak

Located only 8mi from the border crossing into southern Quebec at North Troy, **Jay Peak** (3,861ft) attracts both Americans and Canadians during the winter. An **aerial tram** lifts passengers to the peak's summit (⊙*open Jul–Labor Day & mid-Sep–Columbus Day, daily 10am–4pm; commentary;* ⊘*$10;* ♿ 𝒫*802-988-2611 or 800-451-4449; www.jaypeakresort.com*). From the top, there are sweeping **views★★** of Lake Champlain, the Adirondacks, the White Mountains and, to the north, Canada.

Several drives in the area are especially picturesque during Indian summer; in particular, **Rte. 242** from Montgomery Center to Rte. 101, and **Rte. 58** from Lowell to Irasburg, offer views of northern Vermont against the backdrop of the surrounding mountain ranges.

Bread and Puppet Museum

Rte. 122. ⊙*Open Jun–Oct daily 10am–6pm.* 𝒫*802-525-3031. www.breadandpuppet.org.*

In a cavernous barn built in 1863, the socially committed Bread and Puppet Theater Company dramatically displays its larger-than-life puppets. These head masks and mannequin-like creations have been used in pageants and shows in Europe, Latin America and the US.

▶ Return to St. Johnsbury via Rte. 5 south. From St. Johnsbury take Rte. 2 west to Danville.

🚗 DRIVING TOUR

PEACHAM AND BARNET CENTER

Circle tour south of St. Johnsbury 65mi.

Stop at a creamery and enjoy rolling farmland views on this Northeast Kingdom tour.

▶ From St. Johnsbury, take Rte. 2 to Danville.

Danville

Because of its high elevation, this rural agricultural community enjoys refreshing breezes and clear air even on hot summer days.

▶ Continue south on Rte. 2 to Marshfield. Turn right onto Rte. 215 to Cabot.

Cabot

This small community is home to **Cabot Creamery**. In business since 1919, it's perhaps the best-known purveyor of Vermont dairy products. A tour (🕐30min; ⊘$2) of the plant operation explains in detail how cheese, yogurt and butter are made (*on Main St.;* ♿ 🅿 ⊙*open Jun–Oct daily 9am–5pm; rest of the year Mon–Sat 10am–4pm;* ⊙*closed major holidays;* 𝒫*800-837-4261; www.cabotcheese.com*).

▶ Return to Danville via Rtes. 215 and 2. Take the unmarked road south through Harvey and Ewell Mills to Peacham.

Peacham★

Surrounded by a breathtaking hill-and-dale setting, Peacham may be the most photographed of all Vermont's villages during the fall.

▶ Continue to Barnet Center through South Peacham, turning left to West Barnet. At Barnet Center, turn left before the church and continue up the hill.

Barnet Center

From a vantage point past the church near the top of the hill, you can look down on a beautiful pastoral scene of a large barn with its silo. Beyond the barn stretches a spectacular **view★★**.

▶ Return to the foot of the hill and turn left toward Barnet. From there, take Rte. 5 North to St. Johnsbury.

ADDRESSES

🍽 STAY

$$$$ Rabbit Hill Inn – *48 Lower Waterford Rd., Lower Waterford.* ☎*802-748-5168 or 800-762-8669. www.rabbithillinn. com. 21 rooms.* Decorated in lace, this romantic getaway caters to couples. More than half the rooms have oversized tubs or two-person Jacuzzi baths, and many have fireplaces, dressing areas and other special touches. In summer, wander the paths along the banks of the Connecticut River; in winter, hone your cross-country skiing or snowshoeing skills. The friendly innkeepers are the best you'll find and the gourmet dining is top-notch.

Stowe★

As Rte. 108 winds through this small village, situated at the foot of Stowe's distinctive landmark, Mt. Mansfield, the slender white spire of Christ Community Church comes into view. The valley's exceptionally long snow season and abundance of Swiss-style chalets, lodgings and restaurants account for Stowe's sobriquet, "the ski capital of the east."

A BIT OF HISTORY

During the winter up to 8,000 skiers use the trail systems on the slopes of Stowe's two interconnected mountains, **Mt. Mansfield** (4,393ft), Vermont's highest peak, and **Spruce Peak** (3,320ft). Colorful shops, galleries and restaurants line Stowe's Main Street. Serving the townspeople since 1895, **Shaw's General Store** is a local institution, offering a wide variety of outdoor clothing, sporting goods, footwear and household supplies. Ski buffs will enjoy a visit to the **Vermont Ski and Snowboard Museum** located in the Old Town Hall, where displays of skiing memorabilia chronicle the 100-year history of skiing in Vermont (*1 S. Main St.;* ♿ 🅿 🕐 *open year round Wed–Mon noon–5pm. $3.* ☎*802-253-9911; www. vtssm.com*).

SIGHTS
Mount Mansfield★★

From the summit there is a sweeping **view★★** of the entire region, including Jay Peak to the northeast, Lake

- ▶ **Population:** 4,339.
- 🚇 **Michelin Map:** 581 I 2
- ℹ **Info:** ☎802-253-7321 or 877-GO-STOWE; www.gostowe.com.
- ▶ **Location:** The mountain village of Stowe sits in north-central Vermont at the junction of Rtes. 108 and 100 (10 miles north on Rte. 100 from I-89). Most of the activities are centered on the historic village and along Mountain Road leading from the village to the ski area.
- 👥 **Kids:** The fast-moving alpine slide and the summit-climbing gondola ride at Stowe Mountain Resort are sure to be hits.
- 🕐 **Timing:** Start with a meander through the historic village and allow a half-day or more for a hike (try the Pinnacle Trail, a 1.4mi hike to the summit of 2,740-foot Pinnacle peak).
- 🅿 **Parking:** There's free parking in the village, on the street and in small lots off Main St.
- ⊙ **Don't Miss:** A bike ride along the award-winning Recreation Path. Several shops on or near the 5.3mi paved trail offer bike rentals.
- 🚇 **Also See:** MONTPELIER.

Mountain biking at Trapp Family Lodge, Stowe

© Stephen Goodhue / VermontVacation.com

Champlain and the Adirondacks of New York to the west and the White Mountains of New Hampshire to the east. On a clear day, you can see Montreal to the north.

There are several ways to access the summit: via the 4.5mi **Mt. Mansfield Auto Road** (*Rte. 108, 7mi north of Stowe;* ♿🕐*open mid-May–mid-Oct daily 9am–4pm;* 💳*$27/car;* 📞*802-253-3000 or 800-253-4754; www.gostowe.com*); or aboard the eight-passenger **Mt. Mansfield Gondola** (*Rte. 108, 8mi north of Stowe; operates Jul–mid-Oct daily 10am–4.30pm;* 💳*$25; www.stowe.com*), which lifts visitors to the Cliff House and back.

Driving through Smuggler's Notch

© Stephen Goodhue / VermontVacation.com

Smugglers Notch★★

Rte. 108, 7mi north of Stowe; 🕐*Closed in winter.* ⚠*Exercise caution when proceeding between the large roadside boulders that have split from the walls of the notch.*

The road linking Stowe and Jeffersonville to the northwest is extremely narrow and climbs rapidly as it twists through the rugged scenic notch (2,162ft) between Mt. Mansfield and Spruce Peak. The forest admits little light, even on a bright day. Smugglers Notch earned its name because of the slaves and contraband items that were smuggled from the US into Canada through this pass during the War of 1812.

Moss Glen Falls

Rte. 100, 3mi north of Stowe. From Rte. 100, take Randolph Rd., then the first right to the small parking area.
A short trail leads to the falls and continues somewhat steeply (*not well marked*) upstream to a brook where you can take a dip in the cool water.

👤👤 Alpine Slide

Spruce Peak. Rte. 108, 8.5mi north of Stowe. 🕐*Open mid-Jun–mid-Oct. daily 10.30am–4.30pm.* 💳*$17 single ride $44 4-ride pass.* 📞*802-253-3000 or 800-253-4754. www.stowe.com.*
Stowe is one of several ski areas in New England where an alpine slide operates on the mountain slopes during the mild seasons.

Stowe Spas

Stowe is home to two of the top, full-service, destination spas in New England. **The Spa at Topnotch** (*Topnotch Resort, 4000 Mountain Rd., 888-460-5567; www.topnotchresort.com*) is surrounded by views of the Green Mountains and minutes from Stowe Mountain Resort (home to Vermont's highest peak.) The 35,000 sq ft facility offers more than 120 treatments, including exotic, Eastern-inspired sessions. Try the Vermont herbal fusion body wrap or the aroma mountain massage, both featuring local herbs and flowers. There's also a large fitness center, a tennis center and three swimming pools.

The **Stoweflake Spa** (*Stoweflake Mountain Resort, 1746 Mountain Rd., 800-253-2232; www.stoweflake.com*) features a water therapy solarium with hydrotherapy waterfalls, and a mineral soaking pool. There are more than 120 treatments, including the signature Vermont maple sugar body polish, and the après-ski massage. There's a fully-equipped sports and wellness center, indoor and outdoor swimming pools, and sauna and steam rooms.

ADDRESSES

🛏 STAY

$$$$$ Trapp Family Lodge – *700 Trapp Hill Rd., off Rte. 108. ℘802-253-8511 or 800-826-7000. www.trappfamily.com. 96 rooms.* After the famous singing Von Trapp family fled the Nazis and inspired the movie *The Sound of Music*, they ended up here in Stowe, where they opened this rustic Tyrolean chalet-style lodge. Expanded repeatedly over the years, the lodge now sits on 2,700 acres and comprises a main building, numerous outlying chalets, an Austrian tea house and a wide range of sporting facilities including clay tennis courts and over 70mi of cross-country skiing trails. And yes, the descendants of the Von Trapps still don their costumes and perform regularly for guests.

$$$ Green Mountain Inn – *18 Main St. ℘802-253-7301 or 800-253-7302. www. greenmountaininn.com. 100 rooms.* The

Stowe Recreation Path

Traversing farmlands, wildflower meadows and wooden bridges on the West Branch River, this 5mi paved trail through the Green Mountains is a delight for cyclists and walkers. The path begins behind the village's Community Church and ends on Brook Road. Views from the trail are particularly beautiful in spring and fall. (*For details, contact the Stowe Area Association: ℘800-24-STOWE or 802-253-7321; www.gostowe.com.*)

largest hotel in the pedestrian-friendly Main Street area, this inn has been in continuous operation since 1833. Guest rooms are spread between the main inn and adjacent town houses, and all feature handmade quilts and period furnishings. The modern Mansfield House offers 22 deluxe rooms with Jacuzzi tubs and other modern amenities. The inn maintains 120 private acres of hiking, cross-country skiing and snowshoeing trails for guests. A freestanding three-bedroom carriage house is available at the ski center.

🍽/EAT

$$ Gracie's – *1652 Mountain Rd. ℘802-253-8741. www.gracies.com* **American.** A canine theme pervades this casual all-day eatery. Pictures of dogs adorn the walls, and menu items are all named for different breeds. Enjoy chicken wings from mild to Dalmatian, followed by a choice of more than a dozen specialty burgers (the Chihuahua, for example, comes with lettuce, tomato and guacamole). Salads and Mexican specialties are also available.

$$ Harrison's – *25 Main St. ℘802-253-7773. www.harrisonsstowe.com* **International.** The dining room, with barn board paneling, historical black and white photos of Stowe, comfy booths and a roaring fireplace is an inviting place to dine. Locals and visitors alike rave about the food, too, which includes an extensive array of dishes. Start with appetizers like the lobster bisque, asiago cheese fries or coconut shrimp. Favorite entrées include grilled rib-eye steak, Italian-style meatloaf and fish and chips.

The bar, with micro-brews on tap and signature martinis, is usually bustling.

$$ Pie in the Sky – *492 Mountain Rd. ℘802-253-5100. www.pieintheskyvt.com.* **Pizza.** Locals deem this funky eatery the best place in town for pasta and pizza. Home-made thin crust and more than 43 fresh toppings are the draw. Go ahead and create your own pie or pick from a selection of gourmet pizzas, like the Vermonter with cheddar, apples and ham or the mogul run with pepperoni, sausage, beef and bacon. Pasta and sauces are all house-made and there's also a selection of specialty entrées like the chicken marsala, lasagna and three cheese ravioli.

Woodstock★★

A touch of urban elegance has characterized this pretty village since the 18C, when it was selected as the Windsor County seat. Businessmen, lawyers, doctors and teachers settled here during the next 200 years, building frame, brick and stone dwellings and shops that reflected the wealth of the community. A lack of industrial development in the 19C and the devotion of the town's residents to Woodstock's architectural heritage have ensured the preservation of the gracious 18C and 19C structures bordering the village green and lining Elm, Pleasant and Central Streets.

A BIT OF HISTORY

Established in 1761 by settlers from Massachusetts, Woodstock developed quickly after it was selected as the county seat. During the 19C, the prosperous, self-sufficient village became a fashionable vacation spot.

The lovely Woodstock Inn, facing the village green, was opened in 1969. The hotel's lodging and conference facilities attract business travelers as well as tourists. **F.H. Gillingham & Sons** has been the town's general store since 1886 and stocks handmade Vermont products as well as hardware, housewares, gourmet foods, pet supplies and fresh produce.

SIGHTS

To enjoy Woodstock, stroll along **Elm** and **Pleasant Streets**, browse in the emporiums and galleries on **Central**

▶ **Population:** 3,232.
🚴 **Michelin Map:** 581 J 5
ℹ **Info:** ℘802-457-3555 or 888-496-6378; www.woodstockvt.com.
▶ **Location:** Accessed off north-south I-89 and bisected by east-west Rte. 4.
👫 **Kids:** The nearby Vermont Institute of Natural Science (*0.25mi west of Quechee Gorge on Rte. 4; ℘802-359-5000; www.vinsweb.org*) has a cool raptor center and hands-on exhibits.
🕐 **Timing:** Plan two hours at the Billings Farm and Museum and reserve a day to enjoy outdoor activities.
🅿 **Parking:** Street parking is available around the village green.
🐾 **Don't Miss:** Billings Farm and Museum; also cross-country skiing or hiking on area trails.

Street and walk across the covered bridge (*in the middle of town*) that spans the Ottauquechee River. The oval **village green** is fringed with buildings of different styles: Federal mansions, the Greek Revival **Windsor County Courthouse** and the Romanesque-style **Norman Williams Library**. Located near the corner of Elm and Central Streets, the Town Crier bulletin board

© Billings Farm & Museum

Billings Farm

posts notices of auctions, flea markets and other community events.

🚶🚶 Billings Farm and Museum★★

River Rd. at Rte. 12 North. Follow Elm St., cross the bridge, turn right, then .2mi on River Rd. ♿ P ⏱*Open May–Oct daily 10am–5pm, Nov–Feb weekends 10am–3.30pm.* ⏱*Closed Thanksgiving Day & 25 Dec.* ✆*$12.* ✆*802-457-2355. www.billingsfarm.org.*

The Billings complex is both an operating modern-day dairy farm and an interpretive museum depicting life on a Vermont farm in 1890. The restored 1890 **farmhouse**, appointed with period furniture and tiled fireplaces, features a basement creamery with daily demonstrations of butter making. Life-size displays in several restored barns illustrate the daily activities performed by a 19C Vermont farm family. Visitors can view the Academy Award-nominated film (1999), *A Place in the Land* (30min), which examines the property's role in the history of conservation in the US.

Marsh-Billings-Rockefeller National Historical Park★★

Across the street from the Billings Farm and Museum. ♿ P ⏱*Open late-May–Oct daily 10am–5pm. $8 mansion tours,* ✆*$17 (park, Billings Farm and*

Museum). ✆*802-457-3368. www.nps.gov/mabi.*

Opened in June 1998, Vermont's first national historic site centers on a meticulously preserved, art-filled Queen Anne mansion and the conservation efforts of three of its residents: prescient environmentalist George Perkins Marsh, author of *Man and Nature* (1865); Frederick Billings, founder of the Billings Farm; and Billings' granddaughter Mary French Rockefeller, who, with her husband, Laurance, sustained the farm and property from the mid- to late 20C. American landscape paintings by such renowned artists as Thomas Cole, Albert Bierstadt and Asher B. Durand deck the house's sumptuous interior.

EXCURSIONS
Quechee Gorge★

▷ *6mi east of Woodstock via US-4.*

The focal point of Quechee State Park is Vermont's deepest gorge, formed by glacial activity approximately 13,000 years ago. Formed over thousands of years by the erosive action of the Ottauquechee River, Quechee Gorge is spanned by the Rte. 4 highway bridge—which provides the best view. Sheer walls of the gorge rise approximately 165ft from the river below. A trail, steep in sections (*round-trip 1.5mi*), leads to the bottom of the gorge, a popular swimming area in season. Hikers can park at the gift shop on the east side of the bridge.

Water from falls and the mill pond just above the gorge were used to power the A. G. Dewey Company wool mill in the 19C. The mill closed in 1952. Remains of the mill and dam can still be seen at the head of the gorge.

Silver Lake State Park

◐ *10mi north of Woodstock via Rte. 12 in Barnard.* ⛺ 🅿 🕐*Open mid-May–early-Sept daily 10am–9pm.* 🕶*$3.* 🖉*802-234-9451. www.vtstateparks.com.*
Located within walking distance of Barnard village, the park contains a small lakefront beach, picnic area, country store and campsites set in a fragrant pine grove. Boat and canoe rentals are also available.

Windsor

◐ *25mi southeast of Woodstock via US-4 East and I-91 South.*
The State of Vermont was born in this historic town on the banks of the Connecticut River in 1777 when representatives met in an old tavern here. That tavern is now the Old **Constitution House** (*16 N. Main St.;* 🅿 🐾*visit by 1hr-guided tour only, late-May–mid-Oct, Sat–Sun 11am–5pm;* 🕶*$2.50;* 🖉*802-672-3773; www.historicsites.vermont.gov*), where exhibits describe the development of the state's constitution and include examples of early Vermont crafts.
Spanning the Connecticut River between New Hampshire and Vermont, the **Windsor-Cornish Covered Bridge** (*south of Constitution House; after two sets of lights, turn left*) ranks as the longest covered bridge (460ft) in New England.

President Calvin Coolidge State Historic Site

◐ *15mi southwest of Woodstock via Rte. 4 west to Rte. 100A south in Plymouth Notch.* ⛺ 🅿 🕐*Open late-May–mid-Oct daily 9.30am–5pm.* 🕶*$7.50.* 🖉 *802-672-3773. www.historicsites.vermont.gov.*
A visit to the tiny town of Plymouth Notch, and boyhood home of President Calvin Coolidge is like stepping back in time. The homestead remains exactly as it was the night Coolidge took office, sworn in by his father, the local notary public. Coolidge, vice president at the time, was visiting his home when he received news of President Warren Harding's death. The Calvin Coolidge State Historic Site is considered one of the best preserved Presidential sites in the nation.
In addition to the homestead, visitors may tour the Plymouth Cheese Factory, (established by the President's father) the Cilley General Store, the Post Office, the Wilder Restaurant (serving lunch), the church, several barns displaying farming tools of the era, the dance hall that served as the Summer White House, and the home where the future President was born.

Montshire Museum of Science

◐ *11mi northeast of Woodstock via US-4 east and I-91 north (exit 13), Norwich.* 🅿 🕐*Open year-round daily 10am–5pm.* 🕶*$12.* 🖉*802-649-2200. www.montshire.org.*
Set on 110 acres along the Connecticut River, this nature-focused, hands-on museum features more than 60 exhibits, including live animals and aquariums. Outdoor interpretive trails meander the woods, with exhibits weather, ecology, native wildlife and more. The gentle walks —perfect for young families— also offer scenic river views.

ADDRESSES

🛏 STAY

$$$$ Woodstock Inn – *14 The Green, Woodstock.* ☎*802-457-1100 or 888-338-2745. www.woodstockinn.com. 144 rooms.* Laurence S. Rockefeller purchased, renovated and expanded the inn in 1969, and kept it as a prized family possession when he later sold the rest of his acclaimed Rockresorts chain. Today the property still overlooks one of New England's most beautiful village greens, a short walk to shops, galleries and restaurants. Woodstock Inn is a full-service resort with a spa facility, indoor and outdoor tennis courts, golf course and cross-country centers. Rooms vary in size and shape, but all accommodate guests lavishly with such amenities as handmade quilts, glassed-in sun porches and wood-burning fireplaces.

$$ Juniper Hill Inn – *153 Pembroke Rd., Windsor.* ☎*802-674-5273 or 800-359-2541. www.juniperhillinn.com. 16 rooms.* This lovely country inn successfully blends historic charm with modern amenities. All 16 rooms have private baths, many with antique claw-foot tubs. More than half have fireplaces, and all are individually decorated with four-poster beds and period antiques. Bedside chocolates and sherry decanters in each room add a homey touch. If you're a history buff, book the grand suite with private balcony, which once hosted President Teddy Roosevelt.

🍽 EAT

$$ Mountain Creamery Restaurant – *33 Central St. Breakfast & lunch only.* ☎*802-457-1715. www.mountaincreameryvt.com.* **American.** This farm-to-table restaurant is well-known and beloved for its fresh, hearty country breakfasts, homemade soups, sandwiches, ice cream and pies. Start your day with made-from-scratch buttermilk pancakes, locally smoked bacon and ham, the signature corned beef hash, and just-baked muffins, scones and coffee cake. Homemade soups are favorites for lunch, along with the hand-carved, roasted turkey reuben sandwich served with a side of organic apple sauce. Don't leave without a slice of pie topped with a scoop of famous Mountain Creamery ice cream.

$$ Osteria Pane e Salute – *61 Central St., second floor. Closed Mon–Wed and Nov & Apr.* ☎*802-457-4882. www.osteria paneesalute.com.* The delights of Italy land in Woodstock at this tiny osteria. In its 22-seat green-walled dining room, diners will be treated to a taste of *la dolce vita*. Seasonal fare spotlights local produce, cheeses and meats raised in Vermont, as well as traditional products imported from Italy. If you're not up for a multi-course meal, try one of the thin-crust Tuscan pizzas, or take a seat in the cozy wine bar to sample hard-to-find Italian wines and nosh on tasting plates.

$$ The Skunk Hollow Tavern – *12 Brownsville Rd., Hartland Four Corners. Dinner only. Closed Mon & Tue.* ☎*802-436-2139.* **American.** Locals flock from throughout the region to enjoy this quintessential New England tavern. The two-part menu includes tavern favorites such as burgers, enchiladas and the house specialty, Chicken Carlos—a spicy half-fried, half-baked chicken with hand-cut fries. The other section features fine-dining entrées (filet mignon, chicken, fish and lamb, each with a different preparation weekly) along with exquisite homemade soups. A full-time baker turns out fresh popovers and an extensive slate of desserts, including the signature Heathbar cake.

$$ The Prince & the Pauper – *24 Elm St. Dinner only;* ☎*802-457-1818; www. princeandpauper.com.* **French.** Tucked away off a charming alley, The Prince & the Pauper serves formal food in an informal atmosphere. In the simply decorated main dining room, choose from French-inspired reasonably-priced three-course prix fixe or the bistro menu. Starters such as lobster ravioli or goat cheese souffle, are followed by entrées, like the boneless rack of lamb in puff pastry or crispy five spice duckling. Good, if short, wine list.

INDEX

INDEX

INDEX

INDEX

INDEX

INDEX

🏨 STAY

♀/EAT

MAPS AND PLANS

THEMATIC MAPS

MAPS

Connecticut

Maine

Massachusetts

New Hampshire

Rhode Island

Vermont

COMPANION PUBLICATIONS

MAP 583 NORTHEASTERN USA/ EASTERN CANADA
MAP 584 SOUTHEASTERN USA

Large-format map providing detailed road systems; includes driving distances, interstate rest stops, border crossings and interchanges.

♦ Comprehensive city and town index
♦ Scale 1 : 2,400,000 (1 inch = approx. 38 miles)

MAP 761 USA ROAD MAP

Covers principal US road networks while also presenting shaded relief detail of overall physiography of the land.

♦ State flags with statistical data and state tourism office telephone numbers
♦ Scale: 1 : 3,450,000
(1 inch = approx. 55 miles)

NORTH AMERICA ROAD ATLAS

A geographically organized atlas with extensive detailed coverage of the US, Canada and Mexico. Includes 246 city maps, a distance chart, state and provincial driving requirements, and a climate chart.

♦ Comprehensive city and town index
♦ Easy to follow "Go-to" pointers

MAP LEGEND

★★★ **Highly recommended**
★★ **Recommended**
★ **Interesting**

Sight symbols

Recommended itineraries with departure point

⛪ ⸸	Church, chapel		Building described
○	Town described		Other building
B	Letter locating a sight	▪	Small building, statue
▪ ▲	Other points of interest	○ ⁂	Fountain – Ruins
⚒ ⌒	Mine – Cave	🛈	Visitor information
🌾 ⚲	Windmill – Lighthouse	⊂ ⚓	Ship – Shipwreck
☆ ⛪	Fort – Mission	⁑ ⇞	Panorama – View

Other symbols

🛡	Interstate highway	🛡	US highway	⑱⑧⓪ Other route
	Highway, bridge		Major city thoroughfare	
	Toll highway, interchange		City street with median	
	Divided highway		One-way street	
	Major, minor route		Tunnel – Pedestrian street	
18	Distance in miles		Steps – Gate	
2149	Pass (elevation in feet)	🅿 ✉	Parking – Main post office	
△ 6288	Mtn. peak (elevation in feet)	🚂 🚌	Train station – Bus station	
✈ ✈	Airport – Airfield		Cemetery	
⚓	Ferry: Cars and passengers		Swamp	
⚓	Ferry: Passengers only		International boundary	
⟵⟵⬭	Waterfall – Lock – Dam		State boundary	
🍷	Winery	●	Subway station	

Recreation

•–○–○–○–•	Gondola, chairlift		Park, garden
⚓ ◗	Harbor, lake cruise – Marina	🦌	Wildlife reserve
⛷ ⚑	Ski area – Golf Course	🐾	Zoo
⌖	Stadium	– – – –	Walking path, trail

Abbreviations

NP	National Park	NMem	National Memorial	SF	State Forest
NM	National Monument	NHS	National Historic Site	SP	State Park
NWR	National Wildlife Refuge	NHP	National Historical Park	SR	State Reserve

Symbols specific to this guide

⛪	Picturesque village	⚓	Seasonal ferry: Cars and passengers
🏛	Covered bridge	⚓	Seasonal ferry: Passengers only

FZ Map grid reference

All maps are oriented north, unless otherwise indicated by a directional arrow.

The Michelin Adventure

It all started with rubber balls! This was the product made by a small company based in Clermont-Ferrand that André and Edouard Michelin inherited, back in 1880. The brothers quickly saw the potential for a new means of transport and their first success was the invention of detachable pneumatic tires for bicycles. However, the automobile was to provide the greatest scope for their creative talents.

Throughout the 20th century, Michelin never ceased developing and creating ever more reliable and high-performance tires, not only for vehicles ranging from trucks to F1 but also for underground transit systems and airplanes.

From early on, Michelin provided its customers with tools and services to facilitate mobility and make traveling a more pleasurable and more frequent experience. As early as 1900, the Michelin Guide supplied motorists with a host of useful information related to vehicle maintenance, accommodation and restaurants, and was to become a benchmark for good food. At the same time, the Travel Information Bureau offered travelers personalised tips and itineraries.

The publication of the first collection of roadmaps, in 1910, was an instant hit! In 1926, the first regional guide to France was published, devoted to the principal sites of Brittany, and before long each region of France had its own Green Guide. The collection was later extended to more far-flung destinations, including New York in 1968 and Taiwan in 2011.

In the 21st century, with the growth of digital technology, the challenge for Michelin maps and guides is to continue to develop alongside the company's tire activities. Now, as before, Michelin is committed to improving the mobility of travelers.

MICHELIN TODAY

WORLD NUMBER ONE TIRE MANUFACTURER

- 70 production sites in 18 countries
- 111,000 employees from all cultures and on every continent
- 6,000 people employed in research and development

Moving
for a world

Moving forward means developing tires with better road grip and shorter braking distances, whatever the state of the road.

CORRECT TIRE PRESSURE

RIGHT PRESSURE

- Safety
- Longevity
- Optimum fuel consumption

-0,5 bar

- Durability reduced by 20% (- 8,000 km)

-1 bar

- Risk of blowouts
- Increased fuel consumption
- Longer braking distances on wet surfaces

forward together
where mobility is safer

It also involves helping motorists take care of their safety and their tires. To do so, Michelin organises "Fill Up With Air" campaigns all over the world to remind us that correct tire pressure is vital.

WEAR

DETECTING TIRE WEAR

The legal minimum depth of tire tread is 1.6mm. Tire manufacturers equip their tires with tread wear indicators, which are small blocks of rubber moulded into the base of the main grooves at a depth of 1.6mm.

Tires are the only point of contact between the vehicle and road.

The photo below shows the actual contact zone.

NEW TIRE

WORN TIRE
(1,6 mm tread)

If the tread depth is less than 1.6mm, tires are considered to be worn and dangerous on wet surfaces.

Moving forward
means sustainable mobility

INNOVATION AND THE ENVIRONMENT

By 2050, Michelin aims to cut the quantity of raw materials used in its tire manufacturing process by half and to have developed renewable energy in its facilities. The design of MICHELIN tires has already saved billions of litres of fuel and, by extension, billions of tons of CO2.

Similarly, Michelin prints its maps and guides on paper produced from sustainably managed forests and is diversifying its publishing media by offering digital solutions to make traveling easier, more fuel efficient and more enjoyable!

The group's whole-hearted commitment to eco-design on a daily basis is demonstrated by ISO 14001 certification.

Like you, Michelin is committed to preserving our planet.

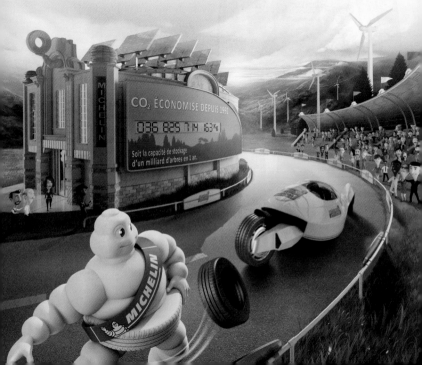

Chat with Bibendum

Go to
www.michelin.com/corporate/en
Find out more about
Michelin's history and the
latest news.

QUIZ

Michelin develops tires for all types of vehicles.
See if you can match the right tire with the right vehicle...

Michelin Travel Partner

Société par actions simplifiées au capital de 11 629 590 EUR
27 cours de l'Île Seguin - 92100 Boulogne Billancourt (France)
R.C.S. Nanterre 433 677 721

No part of this publication may be reproduced in any form
without the prior permission of the publisher.

© Michelin Travel Partner
ISBN 978-2-067186-52-1
Printed: July 2013
Printed and bound in France : Imprimerie CHIRAT, 42540 Saint-Just-la-Pendue - N° 201307.0202

Solution : A-6 / B-4 / C-2 / D-1 / E-3 / F-7 / G-5